Lecture Notes in Computer Science 11591

Commenced Publication in 1973
Founding and Former Series Editors:
Gerhard Goos, Juris Hartmanis, and Jan van Leeuwen

Editorial Board Members

David Hutchison
　Lancaster University, Lancaster, UK
Takeo Kanade
　Carnegie Mellon University, Pittsburgh, PA, USA
Josef Kittler
　University of Surrey, Guildford, UK
Jon M. Kleinberg
　Cornell University, Ithaca, NY, USA
Friedemann Mattern
　ETH Zurich, Zurich, Switzerland
John C. Mitchell
　Stanford University, Stanford, CA, USA
Moni Naor
　Weizmann Institute of Science, Rehovot, Israel
C. Pandu Rangan
　Indian Institute of Technology Madras, Chennai, India
Bernhard Steffen
　TU Dortmund University, Dortmund, Germany
Demetri Terzopoulos
　University of California, Los Angeles, CA, USA
Doug Tygar
　University of California, Berkeley, CA, USA

More information about this series at http://www.springer.com/series/7409

Panayiotis Zaphiris · Andri Ioannou (Eds.)

Learning and Collaboration Technologies

Ubiquitous and Virtual Environments for Learning and Collaboration

6th International Conference, LCT 2019
Held as Part of the 21st HCI International Conference, HCII 2019
Orlando, FL, USA, July 26–31, 2019
Proceedings, Part II

Editors
Panayiotis Zaphiris
Cyprus University of Technology
Limassol, Cyprus

Andri Ioannou
Cyprus University of Technology
Limassol, Cyprus

ISSN 0302-9743 ISSN 1611-3349 (electronic)
Lecture Notes in Computer Science
ISBN 978-3-030-21816-4 ISBN 978-3-030-21817-1 (eBook)
https://doi.org/10.1007/978-3-030-21817-1

LNCS Sublibrary: SL3 – Information Systems and Applications, incl. Internet/Web, and HCI

© Springer Nature Switzerland AG 2019
This work is subject to copyright. All rights are reserved by the Publisher, whether the whole or part of the material is concerned, specifically the rights of translation, reprinting, reuse of illustrations, recitation, broadcasting, reproduction on microfilms or in any other physical way, and transmission or information storage and retrieval, electronic adaptation, computer software, or by similar or dissimilar methodology now known or hereafter developed.
The use of general descriptive names, registered names, trademarks, service marks, etc. in this publication does not imply, even in the absence of a specific statement, that such names are exempt from the relevant protective laws and regulations and therefore free for general use.
The publisher, the authors and the editors are safe to assume that the advice and information in this book are believed to be true and accurate at the date of publication. Neither the publisher nor the authors or the editors give a warranty, expressed or implied, with respect to the material contained herein or for any errors or omissions that may have been made. The publisher remains neutral with regard to jurisdictional claims in published maps and institutional affiliations.

This Springer imprint is published by the registered company Springer Nature Switzerland AG
The registered company address is: Gewerbestrasse 11, 6330 Cham, Switzerland

Foreword

The 21st International Conference on Human-Computer Interaction, HCI International 2019, was held in Orlando, FL, USA, during July 26–31, 2019. The event incorporated the 18 thematic areas and affiliated conferences listed on the following page.

A total of 5,029 individuals from academia, research institutes, industry, and governmental agencies from 73 countries submitted contributions, and 1,274 papers and 209 posters were included in the pre-conference proceedings. These contributions address the latest research and development efforts and highlight the human aspects of design and use of computing systems. The contributions thoroughly cover the entire field of human-computer interaction, addressing major advances in knowledge and effective use of computers in a variety of application areas. The volumes constituting the full set of the pre-conference proceedings are listed in the following pages.

This year the HCI International (HCII) conference introduced the new option of "late-breaking work." This applies both for papers and posters and the corresponding volume(s) of the proceedings will be published just after the conference. Full papers will be included in the *HCII 2019 Late-Breaking Work Papers Proceedings* volume of the proceedings to be published in the Springer LNCS series, while poster extended abstracts will be included as short papers in the HCII 2019 *Late-Breaking Work Poster Extended Abstracts* volume to be published in the Springer CCIS series.

I would like to thank the program board chairs and the members of the program boards of all thematic areas and affiliated conferences for their contribution to the highest scientific quality and the overall success of the HCI International 2019 conference.

This conference would not have been possible without the continuous and unwavering support and advice of the founder, Conference General Chair Emeritus and Conference Scientific Advisor Prof. Gavriel Salvendy. For his outstanding efforts, I would like to express my appreciation to the communications chair and editor of *HCI International News,* Dr. Abbas Moallem.

July 2019 Constantine Stephanidis

HCI International 2019 Thematic Areas and Affiliated Conferences

Thematic areas:

- HCI 2019: Human-Computer Interaction
- HIMI 2019: Human Interface and the Management of Information

Affiliated conferences:

- EPCE 2019: 16th International Conference on Engineering Psychology and Cognitive Ergonomics
- UAHCI 2019: 13th International Conference on Universal Access in Human-Computer Interaction
- VAMR 2019: 11th International Conference on Virtual, Augmented and Mixed Reality
- CCD 2019: 11th International Conference on Cross-Cultural Design
- SCSM 2019: 11th International Conference on Social Computing and Social Media
- AC 2019: 13th International Conference on Augmented Cognition
- DHM 2019: 10th International Conference on Digital Human Modeling and Applications in Health, Safety, Ergonomics and Risk Management
- DUXU 2019: 8th International Conference on Design, User Experience, and Usability
- DAPI 2019: 7th International Conference on Distributed, Ambient and Pervasive Interactions
- HCIBGO 2019: 6th International Conference on HCI in Business, Government and Organizations
- LCT 2019: 6th International Conference on Learning and Collaboration Technologies
- ITAP 2019: 5th International Conference on Human Aspects of IT for the Aged Population
- HCI-CPT 2019: First International Conference on HCI for Cybersecurity, Privacy and Trust
- HCI-Games 2019: First International Conference on HCI in Games
- MobiTAS 2019: First International Conference on HCI in Mobility, Transport, and Automotive Systems
- AIS 2019: First International Conference on Adaptive Instructional Systems

Pre-conference Proceedings Volumes Full List

1. LNCS 11566, Human-Computer Interaction: Perspectives on Design (Part I), edited by Masaaki Kurosu
2. LNCS 11567, Human-Computer Interaction: Recognition and Interaction Technologies (Part II), edited by Masaaki Kurosu
3. LNCS 11568, Human-Computer Interaction: Design Practice in Contemporary Societies (Part III), edited by Masaaki Kurosu
4. LNCS 11569, Human Interface and the Management of Information: Visual Information and Knowledge Management (Part I), edited by Sakae Yamamoto and Hirohiko Mori
5. LNCS 11570, Human Interface and the Management of Information: Information in Intelligent Systems (Part II), edited by Sakae Yamamoto and Hirohiko Mori
6. LNAI 11571, Engineering Psychology and Cognitive Ergonomics, edited by Don Harris
7. LNCS 11572, Universal Access in Human-Computer Interaction: Theory, Methods and Tools (Part I), edited by Margherita Antona and Constantine Stephanidis
8. LNCS 11573, Universal Access in Human-Computer Interaction: Multimodality and Assistive Environments (Part II), edited by Margherita Antona and Constantine Stephanidis
9. LNCS 11574, Virtual, Augmented and Mixed Reality: Multimodal Interaction (Part I), edited by Jessie Y. C. Chen and Gino Fragomeni
10. LNCS 11575, Virtual, Augmented and Mixed Reality: Applications and Case Studies (Part II), edited by Jessie Y. C. Chen and Gino Fragomeni
11. LNCS 11576, Cross-Cultural Design: Methods, Tools and User Experience (Part I), edited by P. L. Patrick Rau
12. LNCS 11577, Cross-Cultural Design: Culture and Society (Part II), edited by P. L. Patrick Rau
13. LNCS 11578, Social Computing and Social Media: Design, Human Behavior and Analytics (Part I), edited by Gabriele Meiselwitz
14. LNCS 11579, Social Computing and Social Media: Communication and Social Communities (Part II), edited by Gabriele Meiselwitz
15. LNAI 11580, Augmented Cognition, edited by Dylan D. Schmorrow and Cali M. Fidopiastis
16. LNCS 11581, Digital Human Modeling and Applications in Health, Safety, Ergonomics and Risk Management: Human Body and Motion (Part I), edited by Vincent G. Duffy

17. LNCS 11582, Digital Human Modeling and Applications in Health, Safety, Ergonomics and Risk Management: Healthcare Applications (Part II), edited by Vincent G. Duffy
18. LNCS 11583, Design, User Experience, and Usability: Design Philosophy and Theory (Part I), edited by Aaron Marcus and Wentao Wang
19. LNCS 11584, Design, User Experience, and Usability: User Experience in Advanced Technological Environments (Part II), edited by Aaron Marcus and Wentao Wang
20. LNCS 11585, Design, User Experience, and Usability: Application Domains (Part III), edited by Aaron Marcus and Wentao Wang
21. LNCS 11586, Design, User Experience, and Usability: Practice and Case Studies (Part IV), edited by Aaron Marcus and Wentao Wang
22. LNCS 11587, Distributed, Ambient and Pervasive Interactions, edited by Norbert Streitz and Shin'ichi Konomi
23. LNCS 11588, HCI in Business, Government and Organizations: eCommerce and Consumer Behavior (Part I), edited by Fiona Fui-Hoon Nah and Keng Siau
24. LNCS 11589, HCI in Business, Government and Organizations: Information Systems and Analytics (Part II), edited by Fiona Fui-Hoon Nah and Keng Siau
25. LNCS 11590, Learning and Collaboration Technologies: Designing Learning Experiences (Part I), edited by Panayiotis Zaphiris and Andri Ioannou
26. LNCS 11591, Learning and Collaboration Technologies: Ubiquitous and Virtual Environments for Learning and Collaboration (Part II), edited by Panayiotis Zaphiris and Andri Ioannou
27. LNCS 11592, Human Aspects of IT for the Aged Population: Design for the Elderly and Technology Acceptance (Part I), edited by Jia Zhou and Gavriel Salvendy
28. LNCS 11593, Human Aspects of IT for the Aged Population: Social Media, Games and Assistive Environments (Part II), edited by Jia Zhou and Gavriel Salvendy
29. LNCS 11594, HCI for Cybersecurity, Privacy and Trust, edited by Abbas Moallem
30. LNCS 11595, HCI in Games, edited by Xiaowen Fang
31. LNCS 11596, HCI in Mobility, Transport, and Automotive Systems, edited by Heidi Krömker
32. LNCS 11597, Adaptive Instructional Systems, edited by Robert Sottilare and Jessica Schwarz
33. CCIS 1032, HCI International 2019 - Posters (Part I), edited by Constantine Stephanidis

34. CCIS 1033, HCI International 2019 - Posters (Part II), edited by Constantine Stephanidis
35. CCIS 1034, HCI International 2019 - Posters (Part III), edited by Constantine Stephanidis

http://2019.hci.international/proceedings

6th International Conference on Learning and Collaboration Technologies (LCT 2019)

Program Board Chair(s): **Panayiotis Zaphiris and Andri Ioannou,** *Cyprus*

- Ruthi Aladjem, Israel
- Carmelo Ardito, Italy
- Mike Brayshaw, UK
- Scott Brown, USA
- Fisnik Dalipi, Norway
- Paloma Díaz, Spain
- Camille Dickson-Deane, Australia
- Anastasios A. Economides, Greece
- Maka Eradze, Estonia
- Mikhail Fominykh, Norway
- David Fonseca, Spain
- Francisco José García-Peñalvo, Spain
- Preben Hansen, Sweden
- Tomaž Klobučar, Slovenia
- Zona Kostic, USA
- Birgy Lorenz, Estonia
- Ana Loureiro, Portugal
- Antigoni Parmaxi, Cyprus
- Marcos Román González, Spain
- Yevgeniya S. Sulema, Ukraine

The full list with the Program Board Chairs and the members of the Program Boards of all thematic areas and affiliated conferences is available online at:

http://www.hci.international/board-members-2019.php

HCI International 2020

The 22nd International Conference on Human-Computer Interaction, HCI International 2020, will be held jointly with the affiliated conferences in Copenhagen, Denmark, at the Bella Center Copenhagen, July 19–24, 2020. It will cover a broad spectrum of themes related to HCI, including theoretical issues, methods, tools, processes, and case studies in HCI design, as well as novel interaction techniques, interfaces, and applications. The proceedings will be published by Springer. More information will be available on the conference website: http://2020.hci.international/.

General Chair
Prof. Constantine Stephanidis
University of Crete and ICS-FORTH
Heraklion, Crete, Greece
E-mail: general_chair@hcii2020.org

http://2020.hci.international/

Contents – Part II

Mobile and Ubiquitous Learning

Design of a Novel Web Utility that Provides Multi-lingual Word
Definitions for Child E-Book Applications 3
   Deeksha Adiani, Daniel Lewis, Vanessa Serao, Kevin Barrett,
   Amelia Bennett, Derick Hambly, Martina Shenoda, Samuel West,
   Garrett Coulter, Sultan Shagal, Toheeb Biala, Medha Sarkar,
   Joshua Wade, and Nilanjan Sarkar

Design Principles for Wearable Enhanced Embodied
Learning of Movement 13
   Ilona Buchem

Analyzing Students' WhatsApp Messages to Evaluate the Individual
Acquisition of Teamwork Competence 26
   Miguel Á. Conde, Francisco J. Rodríguez-Sedano,
   Francisco J. Rodríguez-Lera, Alexis Gutiérrez-Fernández,
   and Ángel M. Guerrero-Higueras

An Analysis of *ProjectEdu*: A Mobile Learning Application
for Software Project Management Education 37
   Maria Lydia Fioravanti, Raul Donaire Gonçalves Oliveira,
   Gustavo Martins Nunes Avellar, Camila Dias de Oliveira,
   and Ellen Francine Barbosa

Wearable Technologies in Education: A Design Space 55
   Vivian Genaro Motti

Ready, Steady, Move! Coding Toys, Preschoolers, and Mobile
Playful Learning 68
   Katriina Heljakka and Pirita Ihamäki

Evaluating the Usability of Pervasive Conversational User Interfaces
for Virtual Mentoring 80
   Earl W. Huff Jr., Naja A. Mack, Robert Cummings, Kevin Womack,
   Kinnis Gosha, and Juan E. Gilbert

Learn Chinese in Sindhi: App Development and Evaluation 99
   Zahid Hussain, Meiyu Lu, Xiangang Qin, and Muhammad Faheem

Measuring Hedonic and Content Quality of Social Networking Sites
Used in Interactive Learning Ecosystems 110
   Tihomir Orehovački and Snježana Babić

A Simple Web Utility for Automatic Speech Quantification
in Dyadic Reading Interactions 122
   *Michael Schmidt, Robert Walters, Bryce Ault, Khem Poudel,
   Adam Mischke, Stone Jones, Austin Sockhecke, Marcus Spears,
   Patrick Clarke, Rober Makram, Sam Meagher, Medha Sarkar,
   Joshua Wade, and Nilanjan Sarkar*

Virtual Reality and Augmented Reality Systems for Learning

UX Aspects of Kinect-Based Movement Schemes Inside Virtual
Environments for Museum Installations 133
   Viviana Barneche-Naya and Luis A. Hernández-Ibáñez

An Immersive Virtual Reality Experience for Learning Spanish 151
   *Sarah Garcia, Denis Laesker, Derek Caprio, Ronald Kauer,
   Jason Nguyen, and Marvin Andujar*

Immersive Community Analytics for Wearable Enhanced Learning 162
   Ralf Klamma, Rizwan Ali, and István Koren

Virtual Companions and 3D Virtual Worlds: Investigating the Sense
of Presence in Distance Education 175
   *Aliane Loureiro Krassmann, Felipe Becker Nunes, Maximino Bessa,
   Liane Margarida Rockenbach Tarouco, and Magda Bercht*

Pedagogical-Agent Learning Companions in a Virtual Reality
Educational Experience 193
   *David Novick, Mahdokht Afravi, Adriana Camacho, Aaron Rodriguez,
   and Laura Hinojos*

A VRLE Design Scheme for the Learning of Film Making 204
   Xi Qiao, Zhejun Liu, and Yunshui Jin

Application of Virtual Reality and Gamification in the Teaching
of Art History 220
   *Evelyn Marilyn Riveros Huaman, Roni Guillermo Apaza Aceituno,
   and Olha Sharhorodska*

Indoor Navigation Through Storytelling in Virtual Reality 230
   Philipp Ulsamer, Kevin Pfeffel, and Nicholas H. Müller

Collaboration Technology

Accessibility in Mobile Applications of Portuguese
Public Administration 243
   *Marcos Carneiro, Frederico Branco, Ramiro Gonçalves,
Manuel Au-Yong-Oliveira, Fernando Moreira, and José Martins*

Toward Improving Situation Awareness and Team Coordination
in Emergency Response with Sensor and Video Data Streams 257
   Samantha Dubrow and Brenda Bannan

Parent and Child Voice Activity Detection in Pivotal Response
Treatment Video Probes. 270
   *Corey D. C. Heath, Troy McDaniel, Hemanth Venkateswara,
and Sethuraman Panchanathan*

Geolocation Search with SharePoint Fast Search Feature
and A (star) Search Algorithm 287
   H. Chathushka Dilhan Hettipathirana and Thameera Viraj Ariyapala

A Study of Internship Satisfaction and Future Job Intention of Taiwanese
Young Generation Z Students with Different Levels of Technology. 296
   Yi-an Hou

Requirements for Wearable Technologies to Promote Adherence
to Physical Activity Programs for Older Adults. 312
   *Robert Klebbe, Anika Steinert, Ilona Buchem,
and Ursula Müller-Werdan*

Facilitating Access to Cross-Border Learning Services
and Environments with eIDAS 329
   Tomaž Klobučar

Barriers to Success in a Collaborative Technological Ecosystem:
A Study on the Perception of the Interoperability Problem
in Civil Engineering Education 343
   *Jeffrey Otey, Jorge D. Camba, José Ángel Aranda Domingo,
and Manuel Contero*

Towards Supportive Mechanisms for Crowd Collaboration – Design
Guidelines for Platform Developers. 353
   Navid Tavanapour and Eva A. C. Bittner

Interactive System for Collaborative Historical Analogy. 373
   Ryo Yoshikawa, Ryohei Ikejiri, and Yasunobu Sumikawa

Author Index 387

Contents – Part I

Designing and Evaluating Learning Experiences

Personal Data Broker: A Solution to Assure Data Privacy in EdTech. 3
  Daniel Amo, David Fonseca, Marc Alier,
  Francisco José García-Peñalvo, María José Casañ, and María Alsina

Measuring Students' Acceptance to AI-Driven Assessment in eLearning:
Proposing a First TAM-Based Research Model. 15
  Juan Cruz-Benito, José Carlos Sánchez-Prieto, Roberto Therón,
  and Francisco J. García-Peñalvo

Measuring the Impact of E-Learning Platforms on Information
Security Awareness. 26
  Tobias Fertig, Andreas E. Schütz, Kristin Weber,
  and Nicholas H. Müller

An App to Support Yoga Teachers to Implement a Yoga-Based Approach
to Promote Wellbeing Among Young People: Usability Study 38
  Alicia García-Holgado, Iñaki Tajes Reiris, Nick Kearney,
  Charlotta Martinus, and Francisco J. García-Peñalvo

Study of the Usability of the WYRED Ecosystem Using
Heuristic Evaluation 50
  Francisco J. García-Peñalvo, Andrea Vázquez-Ingelmo,
  and Alicia García-Holgado

An Experience Making Use of Learning Analytics Techniques
in Discussion Forums to Improve the Interaction in Learning Ecosystems . . . 64
  Luis Magdiel Oliva Córdova, Héctor R. Amado-Salvatierra,
  and Klinge Orlando Villalba Condori

User-Centered Research and Design of a K-5 Digital Literacy Curriculum . . . 77
  Jennifer Palilonis

Designing a Multimodal Analytics System to Improve Emergency
Response Training. 89
  Hemant Purohit, Samantha Dubrow, and Brenda Bannan

SHAUN—A Companion Robot for Children Based
on Artificial Intelligence 101
  Tianjia Shen and Ting Han

Design Thinking and Gamification: User Centered Methodologies......... 115
    Eva Villegas, Emiliano Labrador, David Fonseca,
    Sara Fernández-Guinea, and Fernando Moreira

**Theoretical and Pedagogical Approaches
in Technology-Enhanced Learning**

The Neuro-Subject: A Living Entity with Learnability................. 127
    Ángel Fidalgo-Blanco, María Luisa Sein-Echaluce,
    and Francisco José García-Peñalvo

Information and Communication Science Challenges for Modeling
Multifaceted Online Courses.. 142
    Karim Elia Fraoua, Jean-Marc Leblanc, Sarah Charraire,
    and Olivier Champalle

Let's Talk About Tools and Approaches for Teaching HCI 155
    Adriano Luiz de Souza Lima and Fabiane Barreto Vavassori Benitti

Four-Dimensional Learning, a Response to Social Responsibility
in Learning 171
    Rafael Molina-Carmona, Pilar Arques-Corrales,
    and Faraón Llorens-Largo

Learning Translation in Geometric Transformations Through Digital
and Manipulative Artefacts in Synergy 191
    Antonella Montone, Michele Giuliano Fiorentino,
    and Maria Alessandra Mariotti

Fables for Teachers and Pupils: Incrementally Defined Scenario-Based,
Interactive and Spatial Stories.................................... 206
    Andrea Valente and Emanuela Marchetti

Cognitive and Psychological Issues in Learning

Proposing an Estimation Method of Mental Fatigue by Measuring Learner's
Leg Movement 227
    Daigo Aikawa, Yasutaka Asai, and Hironori Egi

Collaborative Meaning Construction in Socioenactive Systems:
Study with the *mBot* 237
    Ricardo Caceffo, Eliana Alves Moreira, Rodrigo Bonacin,
    Julio Cesar dos Reis, Marleny Luque Carbajal,
    João Vilhete V. D'Abreu, Camilla V. L. T. Brennand, Luma Lombello,
    José Armando Valente, and Maria Cecília Calani Baranauskas

Gender Difference in Language Learning with Technology 256
  Yen-ju Hou

Cognitive Load Levels While Learning with or Without
a Pedagogical Agent 266
  Madlen Müller-Wuttke and Nicholas H. Müller

Where the User Does Look When Reading Phishing
Mails – An Eye-Tracking Study 277
  Kevin Pfeffel, Philipp Ulsamer, and Nicholas H. Müller

Automated Behavioral Modeling and Pattern Analysis of Children with
Autism in a Joint Attention Training Application: A Preliminary Study 288
  Tiffany Y. Tang and Pinata Winoto

Student Emotion Recognition in Computer Science Education:
A Blessing or Curse?. 301
  Dustin Terence van der Haar

Technology in STEM Education

Creative Learning and Artefacts Making: Promises and Challenges
in Practice 315
  *Eliana Alves Moreira, Marleny Luque Carbajal,
  and Maria Cecília Calani Baranauskas*

Effects of Teaching Methodology on the Students' Academic Performance
in an Introductory Course of Programming. 332
  *Patricia Compañ-Rosique, Rafael Molina-Carmona,
  and Rosana Satorre-Cuerda*

Adaptive Learning Case Studies Implementation at Architectural BIM
Construction Courses. 346
  Jose Ferrándiz and David Fonseca

Case Studies of Applications to Encourage Students
in Cyber-Physical Environment. 357
  *Yuko Hiramatsu, Atsushi Ito, Miki Kakui, Yasuo Kakui, Kazutaka Ueda,
  and Rina Hayashi*

Supporting the Teaching and Learning for Subject of Computer Sciences. . . . 370
  *Ana Ktona, Anila Paparisto, Alda Kika, Verina Çuka,
  Denada Çollaku (Xhaja), and Jezuina Koroveshi*

Programming Teaching Tools Feature Assessment Associated with
Brazilian Curriculum Base Obtained Through BPL Platforms Analysis 380
  *Aléssio Miranda Júnior, Deisymar Botega Tavares,
  and Jordana Caires Carvalho*

How E-Learning Can Facilitate Information Security Awareness 390
   Andreas E. Schütz, Tobias Fertig, Kristin Weber,
   and Nicholas H. Müller

Learning with Trees: A Non-linear E-Textbook Format
for Deep Learning. 402
   Eric Spero, Milica Stojmenović, Ali Arya, and Robert Biddle

Technology-Enhanced Learning: Correlates of Acceptance of Assistive
Technology in Collaborative Working Setting. 423
   Wiktoria Wilkowska, Thiemo Leonhardt, Matthias Ehlenz,
   and Martina Ziefle

Author Index 441

Mobile and Ubiquitous Learning

Design of a Novel Web Utility that Provides Multi-lingual Word Definitions for Child E-Book Applications

Deeksha Adiani[1], Daniel Lewis[1], Vanessa Serao[1], Kevin Barrett[1], Amelia Bennett[1], Derick Hambly[1], Martina Shenoda[1], Samuel West[1], Garrett Coulter[1], Sultan Shagal[1], Toheeb Biala[1], Medha Sarkar[1], Joshua Wade[2(✉)], and Nilanjan Sarkar[2]

[1] Computer Science, Middle Tennessee State University, Murfreesboro, TN 37132, USA
[2] Adaptive Technology Consulting, LLC, Murfreesboro, TN 37127, USA
josh@innovateatc.com

Abstract. The use of mobile computing devices to gain access to the Internet and to interact with a range of applications has become ubiquitous, impacting on education, entertainment, healthcare, and many other domains. Engaging applications such as e-books used by children and their parents or educators have also become increasingly common, especially in the context of childhood education. An e-book that presents the reader with challenging words has the potential to improve and expand vocabulary. However, the seamless combination of methods for definition-retrieval, word sense disambiguation, and multi-lingual support are not currently available in a simple tool for the specific application of children's e-book reading. In this work, we present WordWeaver, an open-source tool for use in child reading scenarios where context-sensitive, multi-lingual definitions of unfamiliar words are determined and provided to the user via a simple web API. Our proof-of-concept design includes support for English, Spanish, and French language definitions. Preliminary results support the feasibility of WordWeaver including excellent levels of usability based on the System Usability Scale (i.e., mean SUS = 87.17). Future work will include extending support to include additional languages, definition selection tailored to individual reading skill level, and the ability to address more complicated cases of word and part-of-speech disambiguation.

Keywords: Vocabulary acquisition · Dictionary · E-book · Multi-lingual · Context-sensitive

1 Introduction

For children, an essential component of literacy development is vocabulary acquisition. Evidence shows that the clarification of word meanings during reading training produces greater gains in vocabulary than training that does not provide this information

[1, 2]. E-book use by children and their parents and/or educators has become increasingly common [3, 4] and may offer a unique opportunity to present readers with challenging words that have the capacity to improve and expand vocabulary. A tool that provides context-sensitive definitions for unfamiliar words would therefore be a valuable component of an e-book application. Furthermore, support for a wide variety of languages would facilitate broader adoption and impact.

In this work, we present WordWeaver, an open-source tool for use in child reading scenarios where context-sensitive, multi-lingual definitions of unfamiliar words are provided via a simple web protocol [5]. Our proof-of-concept design currently includes support for English, Spanish, and French language definitions, but support for other languages, including Arabic, is part of ongoing work. The proposed multi-lingual dictionary utility is a web-based resource for an e-book application that provides definitions for words according to both language and context. Unlike existing single-language dictionary APIs, WordWeaver returns definitions tailored to the individual's preferred language, resulting in a more individualized e-book reading experience. While resources like Webster's Dictionary API are robust, they do not offer a one-stop solution for word definition-retrieval, language translation, word sense disambiguation, and other natural language processing functions. By unifying such functionality in a single application, we believe that WordWeaver can serve to fill this gap and offer a useful means by which to perform such functions, and, ultimately, to facilitate learning.

2 System Design

Given a specified word and surrounding text from which contextual information can be inferred, WordWeaver, the novel utility, provides context-sensitive definitions to users in a variety of languages. For proof-of-concept demonstration, the frontend consisted of a simple application supporting word selection via double-click or -tap and was implemented using the Unity game engine (www.unity3d.com). Client queries (i.e., requests for definition) are sent to a server application via HTTP POST requests consisting of JavaScript Object Notation (JSON)-serialized objects, and the server responds with a structured JSON object containing query results. The backend consists of a Python application and utilizes a range of powerful resources including Natural Language Toolkit (NLTK, version 3.3) [6], spaCy version 2.0 [7], Glosbe API [8], and Pywsd [9] for context interpretation and translation functionalities.

2.1 Front End

The user interface was created using built-in User Interface (UI) tools and data structures in the Unity game engine (version 2018.2) as well as TextMesh Pro [10], a text-manipulation package supported by the game engine. All frontend scripting was implemented in C#. The proof-of-concept tool is composed of a simple story and supports features such as text-selection, text-highlighting, requests for definitions, and definition display (Fig. 1). While reading a story in the e-book, the reader may encounter an unfamiliar word. The text-highlighting feature implemented using TextMesh Pro allows the user to select the unfamiliar word by double-clicking on it—or

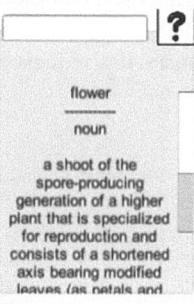

Fig. 1. Simple UI developed in unity to test communication with WordWeaver.

tapping in the case of mobile device use—thus initiating a new definition request. The selected word, the context in which the word is found, and the active story language are transmitted to the server via Transmission Control Protocol (TCP) as a JSON-serialized object, such as that shown in the following example:

```
{
    "word":"quick",
    "context":"The quick brown fox jumped over the lazy dog.",
    "language":"English"
}
```

The server, after processing this information, returns the most appropriate definition of the word, which can finally be presented to the user by the client in the manner appropriate to the particular client application.

2.2 Backend

The backend of the tool is written entirely in Python (version 3.6) and consists of a simple Flask server [11]. A word sense disambiguation module returns a context-appropriate definition based on information contained in each JSON object. The JSON object includes a language tag, a word to be defined, and a context in which the word appears. The word is defined with respect to the context. In WordWeaver, this is accomplished by performing word sense disambiguation based on the Lesk algorithm [12]. This is accomplished through utilization of information from Wordnet [13] which is a large lexical database of English words. Before this step occurs, WordWeaver first checks whether the word is a stop word (high-frequency words like *the*, *to* and *also*; [14]). Because our domain is specific to children's literature, it is likely that stop words will be used in the most common sense, and are, moreover, largely ignored by Wordnet (i.e., they are not defined). We simply return the most common definition found in a separate dictionary if a request is for a stop word.

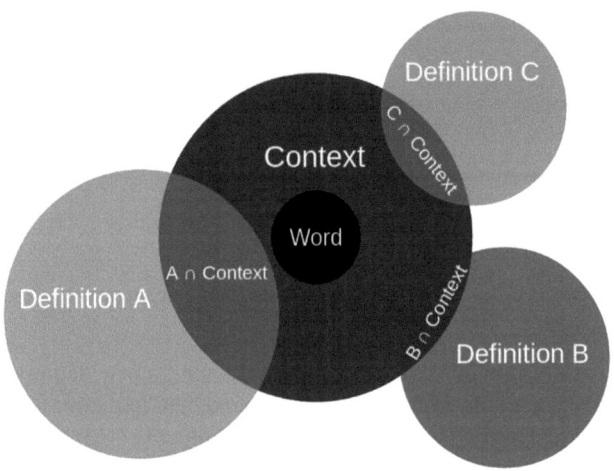

Fig. 2. A visualization of a simple lesk algorithm. In this instance definition A would be chosen.

Currently, if a request is not in English, then a translation to English must be performed before the disambiguation step can be executed. This translation is performed through a call to the Glosbe API [8]. Next, word sense disambiguation happens in two main steps. First, two versions of the lesk algorithm from the Pywsd module are used [9]; Pywsd shares an implementation and author with the built in Wordnet version of the Lesk algorithms. A simple Lesk (shown in Fig. 2) and a cosine Lesk are performed with the given context (i.e., the surrounding text), the word, and the part of speech. The results from these two algorithms are compared by checking which definition has the highest percentage of overlap with the context. Overlap is defined as the set of words in common with the context. After this step is done, some checks are made to ensure that the result is reasonable before returning result to the client. For instance, given the domain of children's literature, we can disregard rare and archaic uses of a word as uses of these words imply a higher reading level. A simple check is made to ensure that the definition returned is in the top four most common definitions for the given word. If an error occurs at any point during this process, an error message is returned and displayed to the user. WordWeaver's step-by-step process is detailed in Appendix A.

3 Results and Discussion

The preliminary usability of WordWeaver was gauged using the System Usability Scale (SUS), which is a widely used measure of the perceived ease of use of digital systems [15]. N = 15 volunteers in an undergraduate program in the lead author's university interacted with the frontend application. Subjects were asked to progress through an example story and to select words of their choosing for definition by the novel tool. The mean cumulative SUS reported by participants was 87.17 (SD = 13.46), which is interpreted as "excellent" usability based on benchmarks reported in the literature [16]. Detailed participant responses on the SUS are given in Table 1. In addition, Fig. 3 shows the results of WordWeaver for an example input word ("quick") and context ("the quick brown fox jumped over the lazy dog") in English, Spanish, and French. Cumulatively, our preliminary results indicate that WordWeaver is capable of reliably reporting user-requested definitions and that client-server interactions perform as expected.

Table 1. Interpretation of SUS cumulative scores.

Adjective	SUS cutoff	% Respondents above cutoff
Worst Imaginable	12.5	0%
Awful	20.3	0%
Poor	35.7	0%
OK	50.9	13%
Good	71.4	20%
Excellent	85.5	20%
Best Imaginable	90	47%

SUS = System Usability Scale [15]. See [16] for interpretation of scores.

English	{ "definition":"accomplished rapidly and without delay" }
Spanish	{ "definition":"Que se mueve con velocidad o rapidez, o que es capaz de hacerlo" }
French	{ "definition":"Se déplaçant avec vitesse ou rapidité, ou capable de le faire" }

Fig. 3. WordWeaver output for the word "quick" and context ("the quick brown fox jumped over the lazy dog") in English, Spanish, and French.

4 Conclusion

There are several opportunities for future development and improvement of WordWeaver. First, the use of the Glosbe API to translate non-English requests into English has some key limitations. The most important is that many words simply do not translate directly into another single word, and machine translation is often incorrect—the reader has likely experienced this when interacting with commercial tools such as Siri, Amazon Alexa, or Google Assistant. The versions of the Lesk algorithm we used rely on Wordnet, and not every language's version of Wordnet currently provides this functionality. In the future, we hope to rectify this and fully realize the design equally across languages rather than relying on an English translation, or perhaps by using other methods such as cross referencing among the translated languages to disambiguate word meaning. In the future, we hope to additionally provide definitions at the optimal reading level of the child, but because the Lesk algorithm requires a definition and example sentences in which the word is used, a simple children's dictionary alone may not provide the algorithm with enough information to permit such fine-tuning at this time. Also, the availability of children's dictionaries and example sentences is quite limited. Another area of future work involves distinguishing proper nouns such as character names from their literal meanings. For instance, if a character is named "Mrs. Red" and the user taps on the word "Red", then a definition should not necessarily be returned by WordWeaver. One way to address cases such as these may be to have the client application maintain a list of keywords that are unique to a particular story. Then, when the user attempts to request a definition for an identified keyword from WordWeaver, the client-side application could preempt the request and returns the appropriate definition locally. Such changes as those described are in fact part of ongoing development with WordWeaver.

Appendix

Appendix A. Detailed Procedures for Returning a Definition in WordWeaver

See Fig. 4.

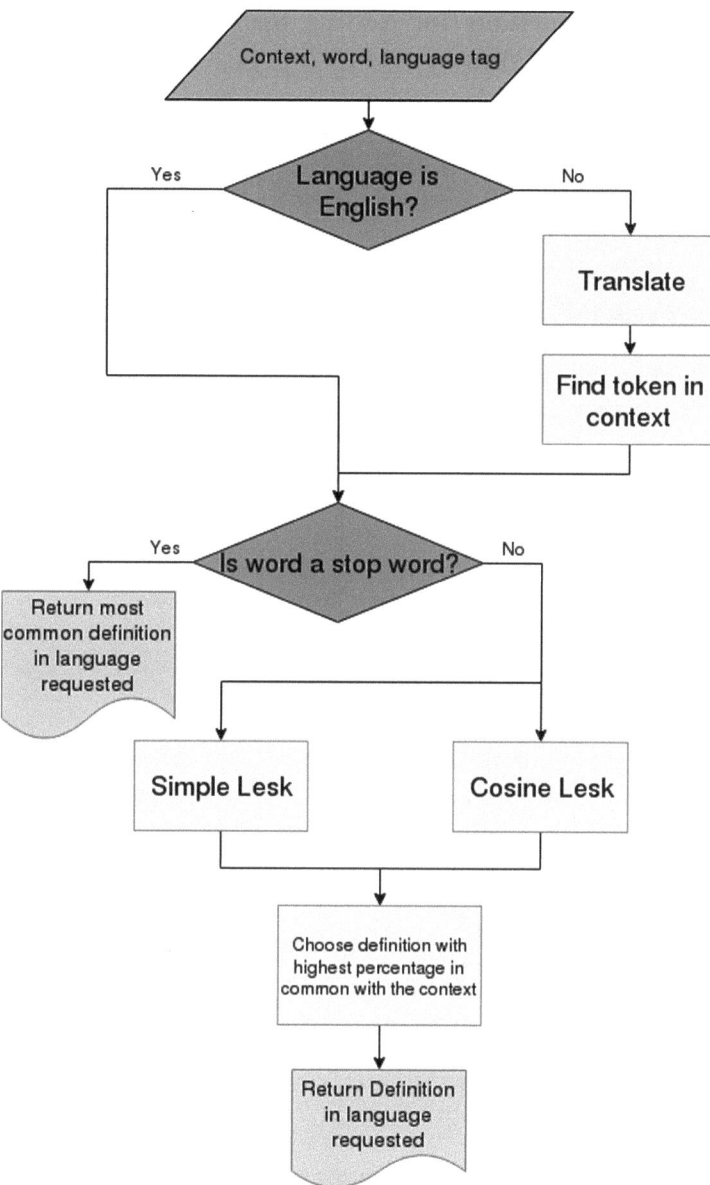

Fig. 4. WordWeaver's procedures for returning a context-sensitive and multi-lingual definition.

Appendix B. Instructions for Setting up and Utilizing the Open-Source Project WordWeaver

In order to communicate with WordWeaver's server-side application, clients must submit queries via HTTP POST requests. A complete example is given in the code listing below (C# console application), which utilizes the Json.NET implementation of JSON (i.e., Newtonsoft.Json.dll) (Fig. 4).

```
using System;
using System.Net;
using System.Collections.Generic;
using System.Text;
using Newtonsoft.Json;

public static class TCP
{
  public static void Main() {
    string serverName = "https://0.0.0.0/"; //server name
    WebClient webClient = new WebClient();
    byte[] resByte;
    byte[] reqByte;

    var data = new Dictionary<string, string> {
      {"word", "quick"},
          {"context", "The quick brown fox jumped over
             the lazy dog."},
      {"language", "English"}
    };

    webClient.Headers["content-type"]="application/json";
       reqByte = Encoding.Default.GetBytes(
         JsonConvert.SerializeObject(
         data,Formatting.Indented);
       resByte = webClient.UploadData(serverName +
         "get_def","post",reqByte);

       Console.WriteLine(Encoding.Default.GetString(
         resByte));
    webClient.Dispose();
  }
}
```

WordWeaver was designed to be easily deployed as a lightweight server application. WordWeaver can be setup on either a dedicated hosting service or locally using a service such as ngrok (www.ngrok.com). In order to launch the server, users must execute the file Server.py (see code listing below; source code available at [5]):

```python
from flask import Flask, request, jsonify
import json
from wsd import wsddef
app = Flask(__name__)


@app.route('/get_def', methods=['POST'])
def get_definition():
    definition = wsddef.get_def(request.json)
    return jsonify(definition)


if __name__ == '__main__':
    app.run(host='0.0.0.0', port=4321, debug=True)
```

References

1. Elley, W.B.: Vocabulary acquisition from listening to stories. Read. Res. Q. **24**, 174–187 (1989). https://doi.org/10.2307/747863
2. Biemiller, A., Boote, C.: An effective method for building meaning vocabulary in primary grades. J. Educ. Psychol. **98**(1), 44 (2006). https://doi.org/10.1037/0022-0663.98.1.44
3. Yuill, N., Martin, A.F.: Curling up with a good e-book: mother-child shared story reading on screen or paper affects embodied interaction and warmth. Front. Psychol. **7**, 1951 (2016). https://doi.org/10.3389/fpsyg.2016.01951
4. Baron, N.S.: Words Onscreen: The Fate of Reading in a Digital World. Oxford University Press, Oxford (2015)
5. WordWeaver (2018). https://github.com/danielyoureelewis/dictionary_group. Accessed 30 Jan 2019
6. Bird, S., Loper, E.: NLTK: the natural language toolkit. In: Proceedings of the ACL 2004 on Interactive Poster and Demonstration Sessions, p. 31 (2004). https://doi.org/10.3115/1219044.1219075
7. spaCy. https://spacy.io/usage/v2. Accessed 21 Jan 2019
8. Glosbe - the multilingual online dictionary. https://glosbe.com/. Accessed 30 Jan 2019
9. Tan, L.: Pywsd: python implementations of word sense disambiguation (WSD) technologies (2014)
10. TextMesh Pro 1.2.2 (2018). https://assetstore.unity.com/packages/essentials/beta-projects/textmesh-pro-84126. Accessed 30 Jan 2019
11. Ronacher, A.: Welcome—flask (a python microframework) (2010). https://flask.pocoo.org/. Accessed 30 Jan 2019
12. Banerjee, S., Pedersen, T.: An adapted lesk algorithm for word sense disambiguation using wordnet. In: Gelbukh, A. (ed.) CICLing 2002. LNCS, vol. 2276, pp. 136–145. Springer, Heidelberg (2002). https://doi.org/10.1007/3-540-45715-1_11

13. Miller, G.: WordNet: An Electronic Lexical Database. MIT Press, Cambridge (1998). https://doi.org/10.1002/9781405198431.wbeal1285
14. Bird, S., Klein, E., Loper, E.: Natural language processing with python (2014). https://www.nltk.org/book/ch02.html#stopwords_index_term. Accessed 30 Jan 2019
15. Brooke, J.: SUS-a quick and dirty usability scale. Usability Eval. Ind. **189**(194), 4–7 (1996). https://doi.org/10.1.1.232.5526
16. Bangor, A., Kortum, P.T., Miller, J.T.: An empirical evaluation of the system usability scale. Intl. J. Hum.-Comput. Interact. **24**(6), 574–594 (2008). https://doi.org/10.1080/10447310802205776

Design Principles for Wearable Enhanced Embodied Learning of Movement

Ilona Buchem[(✉)]

Beuth University of Applied Sciences, 13353 Berlin, Germany
buchem@beuth-hochschule.de

Abstract. Human Computer Interaction (HCI) has seen increased interest in designing embodied experiences and interactions. This also includes the field of Wearable Enhanced Learning which marks the transition from the desktop age through the mobile age to the age of wearable, ubiquitous computing. Wearable enhanced learning relates to learning in a state of physical mobility supported by body-worn devices and sensors. While computer-mediated communication has been observed to enhance conscious experiences without self-reference leading to the sense of disembodiment, wearable technologies have the potential to enhance embodied experience with a strong self-reference. In fact, the affordances of wearable technologies to support embodied learning make wearable enhanced learning unique compared to other technology enhanced learning approaches. The concept of embodiment is based on the assumption that thoughts, feelings, and behaviours are grounded in movement and bodily interactions. Wearable Enhanced Embodied Learning is enabled by transmitting bodily information gathered by wearable sensors onto dynamic displays and making bodily information accessible to learners, in this way extending the learning experience. This paper draws on literature review in HCI and Embodiment research and collates a set of principles to inform the design of wearable enhanced embodied learning of movement.

Keywords: Wearable Enhanced Learning · Embodied learning · Learning design · Technology enhanced learning · Learning experience · Wearables

1 Introduction

"An overview of 20th century commercial products will show how design increasingly neglected our perceptual motor skills while burdening our cognitive abilities" [1: 8].

Embodiment establishes the body as the foundation of a human experience and calls for a higher appreciation of embodied experience. Embodiment can be defined as "an integrity of mind, body, and action accompanied by some awareness in the broader social context" [2: 27]. Wearable technologies has brought new possibilities to enhance embodied experience with a strong self-reference including (but not limited to) learning of movement (motor learning domain). This paper draws on literature review in HCI and Embodiment focused on the design of embodied (learning) experiences and collates a set of principles to inform the design of wearable enhanced embodied learning of movement, i.e. motor domain, beyond cognitive domain.

1.1 Wearable Enhanced Learning

Wearable Enhanced Learning (WELL) has emerged as one of the earmarks of the transition from the desktop age through the mobile age to the age of wearable, ubiquitous computing [3]. Wearable devices and sensors are body-worn and can be seamlessly integrated into daily activities and support learning while the learner is moving, e.g. running, exercising, interacting or engaging in everyday tasks [3]. With wearables allowing for the convergence of mobile technologies, body-worn and environmental sensors, augmented, virtual and mixed reality, internet of things and big data, wearable enhanced learning can be designed to provide rich contextual learning experiences. A number of research and development projects and publications have demonstrated how wearable computing can support learning of diverse groups, e.g. students, disabled and senior learners, and how different technologies, e.g. fitness trackers, smart clothing, smart glasses, can support individual learning processes, e.g. knowledge construction, inquiry-based learning, teamwork, worked-based learning and healthy ageing [4].

Wearable technologies have specific affordances which allow for new pedagogical approaches and new forms of learning, including embodied learning, and teaching, including embodied teaching [4, 31]. Some of the key affordances of wearable technologies include capturing data directly from the body of the learner, using the information from the context to support hands-free access to contextually relevant knowledge, provide in-situ contextual information and guidance, recording of information, communication streams integrated into daily routines, engaging immersive educational experience, unobtrusive and contextualised feedback, and allowing for greater efficiencies in learning [4, 5]. Embodied affordances of wearable technologies include the capability to enable the user to see through the eyes of a virtual body (first-person view) and the virtual body to react based on user actions, the capability to allow the user to act upon represented entities such as artefacts in augmented, virtual and mixed reality environments, which can be picked up, examined, manipulated, and rearranged by the user [6], and the capability to enhance embodied learning experience embedded or immersed in virtual environments [7]. In fact, the affordances of wearable technologies which support embodied learning make wearable enhanced learning unique compared to other technology enhanced learning approaches.

1.2 Embodied Learning

Human Computer Interaction (HCI) has only recently seen an increased interest in the design embodied user experiences. The complexity of human movement may have been one of the reasons accounting for the previous lack of focus on embodied experience in HCI [8]. A number of authors have pointed out the contemporary shift from technology-based to anthropological perspective in design in general as well as a shift away from technology-driven approach in embodied learning. Technology-driven approach has determined the design of embodied experiences by technological abilities, while human-centred, anthropological approaches have focused on human factors in designing computing systems in general and strived towards designing intuitive and engaging wearable applications in particular [1, 8]. For example, [10] have described a conceptual framework and architecture for wearable enhanced embodied learning in context of supporting healthy ageing through physical exercises embedded in a Massive Open Online Learning (MOOC) settings with integrated fitness trackers to ensure sustained physical activity through gamified and social learning in a community of senior learners. [11] described a technology-based framework to support embodied mathematics educational scavenger hunt games using wearable devices such as smart garments with Arduino-lilypads devices sewn on sweatshirts, smart watches and smart phones strapped to the forearms of the learners allowing learners to move freely and search for objects hidden in a physical space. [12] proposed a framework for creating embodied learning environments for STEAM (Science, Technology, Engineering, Math, Art and Design) domains. [13] examined the potential of smart textiles as part of an Internet of Things (IoT) ecosystem, to support embodied learning experiences. Publications on wearable enhanced embodied learning have built on a diversity of concepts of embodiment. Embodiment can be defined as the recognition of movement as part of the self [27]. The different perspectives on embodiment in designing learning experiences are outlined below.

Disembodiment. A number of authors have addressed the phenomenon of disembodiment in traditional pedagogies including technology-enhanced learning. For example, [13] views learning with wearable technologies as a welcome challenge to traditional pedagogies which presume learning as a "disembodied" activity. [14] point out that traditional computer-mediated communication may lead to disembodiment through enhancement of experiences without self-reference. Disembodiment can be experienced as a disconnection of thought and body in a virtual environment [15]. Wearable technologies, on the contrary, may enhance embodied experience, e.g. through gathering, transmitting and utilising bodily information for learning. The distinction between disembodied and embodied learning is considered by some authors as imposed by traditional curriculum designs and teaching methods which presuppose the learner as a passive recipient of knowledge [13].

Embodied Cognition. A number of authors build on the concept of embodied cognition by Merleau-Ponty and a perspective on thinking as an embodied event [16]. Human cognition is embodied in the sense of being interwoven with the body, i.e. perception, emotion and experiences are always embodied [13, 16] view embodied cognition as a natural view on learning and point out that traditional learning technologies, compared to wearable technologies, have not been able to support embodied cognition. Authors building on the concept of embodied cognition perceive thoughts, feelings and behaviours as grounded in bodily interaction with the environment and focus on designing for bodily interaction with the environment [17, 18].

Embodied Interaction. Embodied interaction is a perspective on the relationship between people and systems and asks the questions of how a system should be developed, explored and instantiated [20]. Embodied interaction can be defined as an inter-subjective and bodily activity [20]. Embodied interaction is implicitly embedded in wearable systems, as any system is designed to support some interactions and inhibit others [20]. Embodied interaction is applied as an approach by [1] to design a smart, proprioceptive wearable in context of healthcare. Authors building on the concept of embodied technologies emphasise that meaning is created during physical interactions and these interactions can be supported by wearable technologies [1].

Embodied Learning. Embodied learning can be defined as learning which uses physicality and tangible interactions of learners and with physical objects rather than with abstract concepts [19]. An embodied pedagogy therefore encompasses embodied learning and embodied teaching, with physical interactions between teachers and students playing the key role in the learning process [19]. Embodied learning involves the creation, manipulation, and sharing of meaning through engaged interaction with artefacts [20]. Activity Theory has been used as a theoretical framework for embodied learning, e.g. by [11, 21]. Embodied learning has been considered as an alternative to prevailing technological and cyber learning models which focus on the acquisition of information and neglect the diverse modes of learning including physical interactions with the real world [22]. Interactions with the real world require learners to acknowledge the complexity and ambiguity of human experience. [22] argues that an embodied learning approach re-introduces learners to the joy and depth of personal learning experience through physical presence and engagement.

Embodied Training. Embodied trainings aim at developing bodily memory aids to positively influence the learning process through body experiences [29]. Embodied trainings have been successfully applied in learning therapies for persons with reading and spelling problems. For example, the "syllable swinging" method, which requires learners to swing or dance the speech rhythm of words with their bodies, has shown improvements in reading and spelling through embodied syllable analysis. To support embodied training by wearable technologies, accelerometers can be used to recognise body interactions such as movements or gestures. The aim of wearable enhanced, embodied learning design described by [29] is to maintain the learners' learning curve, motivation and an enjoyable learning experience over a longer period of time.

Embodied Knowledge. Building on Bourdieu's theory of practice, embodied knowledge has been viewed as part of the habitus [9]. The development of embodied knowledge requires a transformation in strength, flexibility, mobility, and is expressed in transformations of kinaesthetic styles, daily habits, social interactions, personal practices and perceptions of the world [9]. These elements constitute the habitus, which has been defined as a constellation of cognitive structures implemented as practical knowledge to act in the social world through everyday movements of the body [9]. Habitus serves as an "internal compass" to guide the practices of a person and is expressed in the way a person stands, walks, talks or moves [9]. Embodied learning can be also viewed as a mode of non-discursive knowledge acquisition, wich results in the shifts the sensory experience and habits of everyday life [9]. It has been argued that the body registers fundamental categories of a world view acquired through education and socialisation, and expresses them in the form of reactions, gestures or postures [23]. Since embodied knowledge is obtained on an intuitive level, the vocabulary to express embodied experiences and the verbalisation of bodily experiences is necessary to bring embodied knowledge to a conscious level [8]. Designing for the development of embodied knowledge, e.g. through new movements, focus on technological mediation of the learning process [27].

2 Research Methods

The research approach of this paper follows the systemic design approach [24], applied to the domain of designing for wearable enhanced embodied learning. This type of design may be considered as a design of higher order systems encompassing multiple (technical and non-technical) subsystems [24]. Systemic design approach is used to describe, recommend and reconfigure complex systems, such wearable enhanced learning. The variety of concepts, perspectives and frameworks applied to designing embodied learning may be challenging for teams and projects working on prototypes and solutions in the area of wearable enhanced learning. The view on systems as networks of interconnected functions designed to achieve intended outcomes [24], calls for multi-/interdisciplinary approach to design learning experiences. Therefore, systemic design can give an orientation for advancing design practices for complex, multi-system and multi-stakeholder services [24].

The research method applied in this paper is a literature review based on secondary data from scientific and research publications [25] and aims at eliciting a set of design principles for wearable enhanced embodied learning through an iterative analysis process. The aim of the literature review presented in this paper is to enhance the understanding of design principles applied to designing embodied learning of and through movement in order to inform the design practice. The following research question has guided the literature review: *What are the key design principles applied for designing wearable enhanced embodied learning of movement?*

Literature sources were drawn from the relevant fields, including HCI, Embodiment, Technology Enhanced Learning, and included a wide range of publications published in scientific journals, conference and workshop proceedings and project reports. The search for relevant sources for literature review was based on a search string related to research studies and designs of embodied, wearable enhanced learning and included such key words as "wearable learning", "embodied learning" and "wearable embodied learning". Google Scholar, ResearchGate and ScienceDirect were the primary search engines and databases used to find and select relevant literature. The selection of sources focused on academic publications including empirical studies and conceptual papers describing designs of wearable enhanced and/or embodied learning, in order to allow for a broad coverage of the design practices in various applications fields. The selection of publications for the review was based on the thematic relevance and quality criteria for appraisal of academic publications [25]. Table 1 lists publications selected for the synthesis of design principles for wearable enhanced embodied learning of movement.

Table 1. Literature selected for the synthesis of design principles

Author (Year)	Context of analysis
Moen (2007)	Modern dance
Wilde (2008)	Performance
Downey (2010)	Capoeira
Hallam et al. (2014)	Ballet
Overhage (2015)	Parkinson's Disease
Mencarini et al. (2016)	Learning to climb
Hassib et al. (2016)	Biosensing
Smyrnaiou et al. (2016)	Learning Science through Theatre
Holz et al. (2017)	Reading and speaking

3 Design Principles

The findings from the literature review have been extracted as principles for designing wearable enhanced embodied learning of movement, focusing on the motor domain as opposed to the cognitive and affective domains. Extracted design practices and extracted design principles are summarised below.

Human-Centred, Kinaesthetic Perspective. A number of authors emphasise that embodied interaction should be designed not from a technological but from a human-centred and kinaesthetic point of view. For example [8], leaning on the methods and theories of modern dance described five aspects of human movement which can serve as orientation and aims for the design of embodied learning experiences: (a) *kinaesthetic awareness,* i.e. developing awareness of differences in movements and of own limitations and possibilities, aims at developing sensibility for knowledge within the body and trust in the bodily memory; (b) *phrasing* as a way of grouping movements, aims at recognising rhythms and phrases within the movements; (c) *forming* in the sense of creating forms or patterns to create meaning, aims at organising movements so that they make sense to the mover and others; (d) *relating,* i.e. relating to others' movement, aims at learning to know own movement patterns and expressions and at developing kinaesthetic empathy, e.g. when working in groups; (e) *abstracting,* i.e. abstracting the essence of a movement aims to explore and manipulate movements to find out what a given movement is about.

Whole-Body Interaction Design. Numerous authors emphasise the importance of the whole-body interaction design. For example, the Kinaesthetic Movement Interaction (KMI) approach, which focuses on whole body interaction design and the development of a kinaesthetic ability to sense and experience own movements, has been applied in the design of a wearable enhanced learning system by [8]. KMI calls for the design of free and expressive movement aimed at individual communication and/or interaction with the system [8]. It can be differentiated from partial body movement such as hand movement and the design of haptic interfaces and from full-body applications depending on screen-based output, such as video games, which tends to lock the user to a certain interaction direction, possibly limiting the variety of movements [8].

The interaction design principles for whole-body interaction design include: (a) *personal interaction space*: design of a three dimensional, user-defined interaction space with tangible interactions near the body and independency of visual or audio output; (b) *natural movements*: design of support free, explorative movements based on individual preferences; (c) *movement impulses*: design of movement-triggers to generate and stimulate movement, without defining "correct" or "incorrect" uses and abstaining from any "punishments"; (e) *movement as impression and expression*: design for a wide range of spontaneous movements, recognition of all kinds of movements and enhancement of the movement dialogue; (f) *movement as fun*: design for movement for the sake of movement [8]. These design principles can be used to create engaging, intuitive and enjoyable embodied interaction experiences. An example design is provided by [8], who designed a movement-based interaction prototype, called *BodyBug*, an electronic box on a wire which can be worn and used in personalised ways, e.g. as a piece of jewellery, dance partner, moving pet, computer game, electronic yo-yo or hula-hoop. Another examples is provided by [26] who described the design of a wearable musical interface for self-expression and body-centric experience called *hipDisk* and explored how the wearers of the *hipDisk* learned to use the wearable interface through own bodies. One of the insights from related research is that wearable interfaces enable to move beyond the reliance on linguistic support towards more open, dynamic and fluid forms of expression [26]. Example of embodied training by [29] and [30] show how physical exercises can support learners with reading and spelling difficulties through the use of whole-body movements and gestures as part of the learning therapy. [29] have developed a set of embodied training games called *Prosodiya* enhanced by wearable technologies such as fitness trackers to support learners with reading and spelling problems in developing the awareness of rhythmic structures of speech such as syllable emphasis. The swing movements of learners are recorded with accelerometers and gesture recognition, extracted and classified as patterns to enable automatic evaluation of learner movements. An integrated learner model models the knowledge level of the learners and individually adapts the type of exercise and the difficulty level during the course of the embodied training. [29] indicate a number of design principles for embodied training, e.g. systems must be adapted to the needs and behaviour of individual learners, the correct execution of gestures must be trained in detail, e.g. via a learning game.

Social Context of Movement. A number of authors emphasise the importance of including the social context of movement in design of embodied experiences. For example, the motivation to move may be closely linked to social settings which define which movements are appropriate in a given context [8]. Designs should therefore consider appropriate movement-triggers which include not only visual (e.g. other people's movements and actions) and audio cues (e.g. music and sound), but also social aspects (e.g. social acceptance of movements in a specific context) [8]. An aspect related to the social context of movement is self-confidence, which can be described in relation to the fears and experiences of clumsiness and embarrassment resulting from own (lack of) movement, the level of movement skills and perceived or visible differences between skilled and less skilled movers [8]. On the design level, the negative experiences related to movement (e.g. fears) can be addressed by enhancing learning about own and others' movement patterns and understanding intentions to move in a specific way [8]. Designs should also focus on creating new socially accepted movements and encouraging user to perform these new movements [8]. A relevant design principle in this context is a sustained focus on how a movement should feel, rather than which (ideal) movement should be performed [8]. The social context of movement can be also included by the application of the apprenticeship approach, which allows learners to develop a specific lifestyle which is expressed as an attitude used to confront everyday challenges [9].

Meaningful Learning. The social context of movement is related to the perceived meaningfulness of a bodily activity and in consequence of the meaningfulness of learning. One of the design methods to enhance the perception of actions as meaningful is to convert these actions into first-person simulations [9]. Another design method is to enhance apprenticeship learning, which allows practitioners to develop a "sense of the game" for any system of bodily movements [9]. The apprenticeship approach to embodied learning through observing and imitating an expert enhances the acquisition of experiential knowledge and a specific lifestyle which is expressed in an attitude used to confront everyday challenges [9]. Meaningful learning can be also enhanced by means of a collaborative learning design. Based on constructivist principles and embedded in the approach to learning through theatrical plays, [34] consider embodied learning from the perspective of the development of skills such as creativity and critical thinking, active engagement with scientific topics and interdisciplinary connection of science with art. [34] recommend to design for learner cooperation, e.g. in context of meaning making of scientific concepts.

Learning Through Mimesis and Imitation. Drawing the concept of habitus by Bourdieu, the acquisition of embodied practice through bodily training can be seen as learning through mimesis, which (contrary to imitation) is related to identification and is acquired without intention or awareness, resulting in implicit knowledge (as opposed to explicit, declarative knowledge) [9]. Practical mimesis allows a set of corporeal schemes to be passed directly from practice to practice in the process of embodied socialisation [9]. Referring to Tomasello's perspective on imitation ("children are imitation machines"), [9] explores how imitation can be included in the embodied learning and teaching practice. For example, the correspondence problem, which emerges with matching a visual image of someone moving in a particular way with own motor control, can be addressed in design by a number of techniques such as scaffolding imitation, slowing down the movement, parsing the technique into smaller units, offering verbal help, physically adjusting student bodies, abstracting parts of a technique, creating movement drills to teach basic components [9].

Reducing Complexity. A number of authors argue for the simplification in the design of embodied experience. For example, [27] describe the design of a wearable garment in context of a ballet technique taught to adult beginners embedded in a phenomenological framework. A wearable, smart garment worn by an instructor and incorporating visual feedback is proposed as a supplement to the teacher-student relationship [27]. Embodied experience is enhanced through mirrored synchronous movements and management of chunking aimed at decreasing the complexity of the visual-motor sequencing of movement [27]. The system proposed by [27] lights up instructor's limbs, breaks basic movements down into starting and stopping positions and allows the student to focus on the key frames to see a movement as a chunk. Key design principles included visual simplification, using key frames to chunk movement, highlight important points and to establish dominant positions of movement, allowing learners to start and stop in correct moments and to measure learners performance against the ability to follow the instructor [27].

Augmented Communication. Design for wearable enhanced embodied learning should provide the involved actors (e.g. learners, teachers, peers) with augmented communication [31]. In their design of wearable enhanced learning in context of climbing, [31] consider augmented communication as a means to address both motor and emotional aspects of learning, for example designing for support of wearable devices when negative emotions appear during the learning process. Especially beginners may experience negative emotions, such as discomfort, clumsiness, stress, fear, panic. Negative emotions are often caused by the lack of motors skills, the novelty of the movement and the abandonment of the usual motor schemes [31]. With communication playing an important role in teaching, including the provision of coping strategies in case of negative emotions, an augmented communicative support is of particular relevance. Designing for augmented communication has to be based on clear understanding of the different forms of communication used in a given learning/teaching setting. For example, [31] observed the interpersonal communication in context of learning how to climb and arranged the different forms of communication along two dimensions ranging from functionality to emotionality, and from abstraction to concreteness, to define the design space for wearables as communication tools.

Design for Wellbeing. Design for wellbeing aims at empowering users, especially enabling people with disabilities to "influence their living conditions through active participation in the design of the assistive devices they use daily" [1, 28]. Embedded in the context of wearable rehabilitation technologies, [1] describes a prototype for proprioceptive wearable technology developed following the principles of design for wellbeing. The prototype which can assist in improving the quality of life for patients of Parkinson's Disease, which includes postural instability and equilibrium problems. The proposed prototype is a system monitoring the upper body posture and providing bodily feedback to guide the patient towards the desired posture [1]. The design of wearable systems for well-being focuses on improving the quality of life by helping users to make a transformation from an actual state to a desired state, without making users feel weak, incapable or invalid, e.g. by attracting attention to the disabilities [1]. Further design principles include comfort in wearing during every day activities (wearability) and the focus on look and feel (aesthetics) as important factors for the perception of quality of life [1]. The approach taken by [1] is a design inspired by gemstones and jewellery, which aims to achieve an unobtrusive yet aesthetic appeal to communicate a healthy lifestyle. This design approach allows to shift the focus from designing a medical device to designing an appealing high-tech, fashion accessory.

Acquiring, Sharing and Receiving Data. Design for wearable enhanced embodied learning should also consider user needs for acquiring, sharing and receiving data including bio-data [33]. A number of design have focused on exploiting wearables to extract bodily information to provide value for users [33]. [33] have conducted research to identify user needs related to the utility, connectivity, and feedback of the biometric and affective wearables. The results show that data most interesting for the users include learning about own *cognitive state,* especially in stressful situations such as conflicts and knowing about own high mental concentration peaks; *physiological data* such as heart rate, blood pressure, body temperature, breathing rate; and *emotional information*, including for happiness and anger [33]. Designs should account for these different types of information and provide diverse modalities of feedback, e.g. subtle, tactile, haptic, olfactory, air-based feedback [33]. Designs for embodied learning should be based on a deeper understanding of the context of sharing data, e.g. sharing of data with negative valence for relief and support from others, as well as consider ways of encouraging mutual sharing of information [33].

4 Limitations and Future Work

The literature review presented in this paper has a number of limitations. The selection of relevant literature is preliminary and limited in scope. The review has been conducted with focus on learning of and though movement and the selected literature is limited to motor learning or learning of skills in the motor domain. Thus, this literature review is not exhaustive and provides only a few examples of design practices and principles in context of wearable enhanced embodied learning. Future work should include a more comprehensive analysis, possibly a meta-study, with a broader focus and encompassing learning in psychomotor, cognitive and affective domains. Design principles for wearable enhanced embodied learning are expected to inspire and support designers in focusing on relevant aspects of embodiment in learning.

5 Conclusion

Designing for wearable enhanced embodied learning raises a number of design challenges, e.g. how to design for learning of and though movement, what kind of support the technology could provide, and how to balance individual user needs with constraints of available technologies. The literature review presented in this paper shows that the systemic design of wearable enhanced embodied learning draws on a number of approaches including interaction design, service design, experience design, learning design, information and visual design. The analysis of the current literature revealed that a substantial body of work already exists in the area of motor and cognitive learning, while the affective domain tends to be underrepresented in the current research and design practice. Based on the design principles described in this paper, further design considerations related to the design of wearable enhanced embodied learning can combine these design principles with taxonomies of learning objectives in the motor domain, such as the taxonomy by [32], which can be used to scaffold learning experiences at different levels of complexity. To conclude, designs for wearable enhanced embodied learning should consider a number of design principles including a human-centred and kinaesthetic perspective, consider whole body interaction design (as opposed to the focus on selected parts of the body), analyse and consider the social context of movement (e.g. which movements are socially acceptable and/or how to make new movements socially acceptable), enhancing meaningful learning (e.g. through the apprenticeship approach), enhance learning through mimesis and imitation, strive for reducing complexity (e.g. through chunking of movement and application of key frames), design for augmented communication (e.g. to support learners in coping with negative emotions), design for wellbeing (e.g. focusing on improving the quality of life not only though functional features but also on the level of aesthetic design).

References

1. Overhage, D.: Wearable proprioception: designing wearable technology to improve postural instability in Parkinsons disease. Mater thesis, Malmö University, Sweden (2015)
2. Crowdes, M.S.: Embodying sociological imagination: pedagogical support for linking bodies to minds. Teach. Sociol. **28**(1), 24–40 (2000)
3. Buchem, I., Merceron, A., Kreutel, J., Haesner M., Steinert, A.: Gamification designs in wearable enhanced learning for healthy ageing. In: International Conference on Interactive Mobile Communication Technologies and Learning (IMCL), pp. 9–15. IMCL, Thessaloniki (2015)
4. Buchem, I., Klamma, R., Wild, F. (eds.): Perspectives on Wearable Enhanced Learning. Current Trends, Research and Practice. Springer, New York (2019). https://doi.org/10.1007/978-3-319-64301-4
5. Bower, M., Sturman, D.: What are the educational affordances of wearable technologies? Comput. Educ. **88**, 343–353 (2015)
6. Cordeil, M., Cunningham, A., Dwyer, T., Thomas B.H., Marriott, K.: ImAxes: immersive axes as embodied affordances for interactive multivariate data visualisation. In: Proceedings of the 30th Annual ACM Symposium on User Interface Software and Technology (UIST 2017), pp. 71–83. ACM, New York (2017)
7. Shin, D.D.H.: Empathy and embodied experience in virtual environment: to what extent can virtual reality stimulate empathy and embodied experience? Comput. Hum. Behav. **78**, 64–73 (2017)
8. Moen, J.: From hand-held to body-worn: embodied experiences of the design and use of a wearable movement-based interaction concept. In: Proceedings of the 1st International Conference on Tangible and Embedded Interaction, TEI 2007, Chapter 6 - BODY MOVEMENTS, Baton Rouge, Louisiana, pp. 251–258 (2007)
9. Downey, G.: Practice without theory: a neuroanthropological perspective on embodied learning. In: Marchand, T.H.J. (ed.) Making Knowledge: Explorations of the Indissoluble Relation Between Mind, Body and Environment. Journal of the Royal Anthropological Institute Special Issue Book Series, vol. 4, pp. 21–38. Wiley, Chichester (2010)
10. Buchem, I., Merceron, A., Kreutel, J., Haesner, M., Steinert, A.: Wearable enhanced learning for healthy ageing: conceptual framework and architecture of the "fitness MOOC". J. Interact. Des. Architect. Focus Sect. Innovative Des. Soc. Mob. Wearable Technol. Creative Teach. Learn. **24**, 111–124 (2015)
11. Arroyo, I., Micciolo, M., Casano, J., Ottmar, E., Hulse, T., Rodrigo, M.M.: Wearable learning: multiplayer embodied games for math. In: CHI PLAY (2017)

12. Karakostas, A., Palaigeorgiou, G., Kompatsiaris, Y.: WeMake: a framework for letting students create tangible, embedded and embodied environments for their own STEAM learning. In: Kompatsiaris, I., et al. (eds.) INSCI 2017. LNCS, vol. 10673, pp. 3–18. Springer, Cham (2017). https://doi.org/10.1007/978-3-319-70284-1_1
13. Ojuroye, O., Wilde, A.: On the feasibility of using electronic textiles to support embodied learning. In: Buchem, I., Klamma, R., Wild, F. (eds.) Current Trends Research and Practice. Springer, New York (2019). https://doi.org/10.1007/978-3-319-64301-4
14. Ugur, S.: A design practice on emotional embodiment through wearable technology. Wearing Embodied Emotions. SpringerBriefs in Applied Sciences and Technology, pp. 61–74. Springer, Milano (2013). https://doi.org/10.1007/978-88-470-5247-5_4
15. Akter, T., Kocak, S., Fuat, N.: Looking glass self and disembodiment in virtual environment: exploratory study of the Turkish cypriot facebook users and isolation from bodies. In: International Conference on Communication, Media, Technology and Design (ICCMTD), Istanbul, Turkey (2012)
16. Bahler, B.: Merleau-Ponty on embodied cognition: a phenomenological interpretation of spinal cord epidural stimulation and paralysis. Essays Philos. **2**(4), 17 (2016)
17. Wilson, M.: Six views of embodied cognition. Psychon. Bull. Rev. **9**, 625–636 (2002)
18. Meier, B.P., Schnall, S., Schwarz, N., Bargh, J.A.: Embodiment in social psychology. Top. Cogn. Sci. **4**(4), 705–716 (2012)
19. Dixon, M., Senior, K.: Appearing pedagogy: from embodied learning and teaching to embodied pedagogy. Pedagogy, Cult. Soc. **19**(3), 473–484 (2011)
20. Dourish, P.: Where the Action Is: The Foundations of Embodied Interaction. MIT Press, Cambridge (2001)
21. Clegg, T., et al.: Live physiological sensing and visualization ecosystems: an activity theory analysis. In: Computer Human Interaction Conference (CHI 2017) (2017)
22. Emig, J.: Embodied learning. Engl. Educ. **33**(4), 271–280 (2001)
23. Asimaki, A., Koustourakis, G.: Habitus: an attempt at a thorough analysis of a controversial concept in Pierre Bourdieu's theory of practice. Soc. Sci. **3**, 121–131 (2014)
24. Jones, P.H.: Systemic design principles for complex social systems. In: Metcalf, G.S. (ed.) Social Systems and Design. TSS, vol. 1, pp. 91–128. Springer, Tokyo (2014). https://doi.org/10.1007/978-4-431-54478-4_4
25. Bolderston, A.: Writing an effective literature review. J. Med. Imaging Radiat. Sci. **39**, 86–92 (2008). Elsevier Inc.
26. Wilde, D.: The hipdiskettes: learning (through) wearables. In: OZCHI 2008, Cairns, QLD, Australia, pp. 259–262, 8–12 December 2008
27. Hallam, J., Keen, E., Lee, C., McKenna, A., Gupta, M.: Ballet hero: building a garment for memetic embodiment in dance learning. In: Proceedings of the 2014 ACM International Symposium on Wearable Computers: Adjunct Program, pp. 49–54. ACM, New York (2014)
28. Larsson, A., Larsson, T., Leifer, L., Van der Loos, M., Feland, J.: Design for wellbeing: innovations for people. In: Proceedings of ICED 2005, 15th International Conference on Engineering Design, Melbourne, Australia (2005)
29. Holz, H., Beuttler, B., Kirsch, A.: Bewegungserkennung mit wearables für embodied trainings in serious games. In: Burghardt, M., Wimmer, R., Wolff, C., Womser-Hacker, C. (eds.) Mensch und Computer 2017 - Tagungsband, pp. 259–262. Gesellschaft für Informatik e.V, Regensburg (2017)
30. Holz, H., Beuttler, B., Brandelik, K., Brandelik, J.: Prosodiya - ein Lernspiel zur Förderung des Sprachrhythmus bei Kindern mit LRS. Mensch und Computer 2017 Tagungsband, pp. 395–398. Gesellschaft für Informatik e.V, Regensburg (2017)

31. Mencarini, E., Leonardi, C., De Angeli, A., Zancanaro, M.: Design opportunities for wearable devices in learning to climb. In: Proceedings of the 9th Nordic Conference on Human-Computer Interaction, p. 48 (2016)
32. Harrow, A.: A Taxonomy of Psychomotor Domain: A Guide for Developing Behavioral Objectives. David McKay, New York (1972)
33. Hassib, M., Khamis, M., Schneegass, S., Shirazi, A.S., Alt, F.: Investigating user needs for bio-sensing and affective wearables. In: CHI EA 2016: 34th Annual ACM Conference Extended Abstracts on Human Factors in Computing Systems, San Jose, CA, USA, pp. 1415–1422, 07–12 May 2016
34. Smyrnaiou Z., Sotiriou M., Georgakopoulou E., Papadopoulou E.: Connecting embodied learning in educational practice to the realisation of science educational scenarios through performing arts. In: Inspiring Science Education International Conference (2016)

Analyzing Students' WhatsApp Messages to Evaluate the Individual Acquisition of Teamwork Competence

Miguel Á. Conde[1(✉)], Francisco J. Rodríguez-Sedano[2], Francisco J. Rodríguez-Lera[1], Alexis Gutiérrez-Fernández[1], and Ángel M. Guerrero-Higueras[1]

[1] Department of Mechanics, Computer Science and Aerospace Engineering, Robotics Group, Universidad de León, Campus de Vegazana S/N, 24071 León, Spain
{mcong,fjrodl,alexis.gutierrez, am.guerrero}@unileon.es

[2] Department of Electric, Systems and Automatics Engineering, Robotics Group, Universidad de León, Campus de Vegazana S/N, 24071 León, Spain
francisco.sedano@unileon.es

Abstract. In our present professional and educational contexts one of the key competences to assess is the teamwork competence. However, this require not only to explore the development of the competence by a group but how it is acquired by each of its members. In order to do so it is necessary to analyze several issues and one of the most relevant is students' interaction. The problem is that the tools that students employ to interact in their learning context are not those that they use in their daily life. That's why it is necessary to explore the students' interaction that happens through instant messaging tools, and the most popular is WhatsApp. This paper explores the problem of analyzing WhatsApp messages and how to compile these evidences in such a way that they can be explored through a learning analytics tool. The implementation shows that the use of WhatsApp messages is possible but requires to take into account other issues such as how to manage interoperability and how to deal with user sensitive information.

Keywords: Teamwork competence · Interaction · WhatsApp · Instant messaging

1 Introduction

Our current society, that may be considered as the Information society, the Knowledge society or the Technological society; requires better prepared professionals in order to address the problems and requirements of a continuously changing world. These professionals should acquire several competences while they are learning in order to succeed in a very competitive environment. One of the key competences to acquire is teamwork competence (TWC) which is promoted by the educational institutions and very demanded by industry [1]. The acquisition of this competence is especially relevant because: (1) TWC development contribute to improve students' learning as they need to share information and discuss among them, which facilitates building mental models in a cooperative way [2, 3]; (2) in institutions and organizations is common to work in teams, so it is desirable that all the professionals know how to develop their work in this way [4]; (3) Bologna process understands TWC as one of the key competences to acquire by the students in Higher Education [5].

Although institutions are devoting many effort and investing great quantities of resources to promote and foster TWC, it is necessary to assess if the competence has been acquired or not. This is a difficult task that requires of the evaluation of multiple evidences. Most of the time the assessment of TWC is determined by the final result or work that teams deliver, ignoring what happens during the different stages of the process or variability between the amount and relevance of individual contributions [6].

It is necessary to apply a methodology that allows not only assessing the final result of a group but the individual acquisition of teamwork assessment. In this sense there are three possible categories of instruments that can be used [7]:

- Observational rating scales. These are standardized measurement protocols, which train observers to record and rate observable team behavior. Some examples could be Behaviorally Anchored Rating Scales BARS [8] or Communication and Teamwork Skills (CATS) [9]. The problem of this type of methodology is that is very hard to apply them when the number of groups to evaluate is high and because is difficult to assess part of the teamwork, especially when it is not carried out in a controlled environment.
- Team self-assessment. These methodologies could be also applied to try to assess teamwork. With them the students rate their own work in the group and also their peers work. Examples of this kind of instruments could be the Hackbert questionnaire for peer and self-assessment [10], the instrument defined by Ríos-Carmenado et al. [11] or the Team Work Behaviour Questionnaire (TWBQ) [12]. In this case the problem is that peer evaluation can be biased by the context of the student and the relationship with her peers.
- Event-based approach. These techniques were defined to deal with performance evaluation in complex simulation scenarios [13, 14]. In this approach critical events which provide opportunities to perform key teamwork competencies are in the simulated scenarios. The problem of this methodology is that it cannot easily be applied all kind of educational approaches.

Most of these methodologies present different problems to evaluate the individual acquisition of TWC. Given this situation the authors of this work decide to apply Comprehensive Training Model of the Teamwork Competence (CTMTC) [15, 16] in several academic contexts. This is a methodology that analyses the learning evidences recorded by the IT-based learning tools that the teams use when developing a project or a learning activity [16]. CTMTC is based on a set of stages adapted from the International Project Management Association (IPMA) [17]. The students are going to complete these stages in order to develop their project. CTMTC is a methodology focused on the evaluation of issues of group-based learning: teamwork phases (mission and goals, responsibility maps, planning, implementation and organization of documentation), collaborative creation of knowledge, and cloud computing technologies (wikis, forums, social networks and cloud storage systems) [16]. The people in charge of the application of this methodology can track continuously what students are doing and how they are collaborating to develop the project, and can analyze how an individual is contributing to the group work. In addition it facilitate teachers to do partial summative assessments of TWC [18]. The method has been tested in very different contexts with high rate of success and acceptance [6, 18–23], and it was possible to adapt it easily which show how flexible it is.

But not all that happens in those experiments was good. One of the main problems found with these experiences were the tools employed to show the communication between team members. The most common tool to use was the forum provided by a Learning Management System, more specifically Moodle forum. Moodle forum is a very powerful tool that can be used to carry out several type of learning activities [24]. However, students were used to employ synchronous tools more than the asynchronous ones, since their messages in in forums look artificial, it does not reflect the real interaction that they could have in other applications such could be an instant messaging client as is WhatsApp. This was suggested in the qualitative assessment carried out in the above cited experiments and fits with other research conclusions [25].

Given this context, the present work aims to make possible importing the WhatsApp messages of the members of a team that is applying CTMTC methodology. This is a complex task because of three main reasons: (1) WhatsApp is a commercial tool that is not included in the Learning Management System but in the personal devices of each student; (2) The information recorded in WhatsApp links a person with a telephone number which is sensitive information that should not be stored; and (3) it is necessary to study if it is possible to apply the same learning analytics techniques and tools with the data source obtained from WhatsApp than from the information recorded into the LMS.

This paper is going to deal with these three issues. It is structured as follows: Sect. 2 analyses other existing works that employs instant massaging such as WhatsApp in learning activities; Sect. 3 describes how facilitate the connection between the LMS and WhatsApp; and Sect. 4 how the tool is implemented and the information is parsed. Finally, some conclusions are posed.

2 Research Context

Nowadays one of the technological tools most used are Instant Messaging (IM) apps. These are online tools that facilitate a synchronous communication among users that has become very popular with their inclusion in the smartphones and the popularization of this kind of devices. In the educational field, IM apps allow students to exchange text, chat in group, share images, videos, voice and even talk.

In 2018 the most popular apps for IM were: WhatsApp with 1,5 billion users, Facebook messenger with 1,3 billions, WeChat with around 1 billion, QQ mobile with 803 millions, Skype with 300, Snapchat with 291, Viber with 260, Line with 203 and Telegram with 200 (stats provided by stadista.com based on We are Social, Kepios and other sources [26]).

These stats show how significant is IM in individuals daily live something especially relevant when focusing in students, that prefer to use these apps instead of email or phone calls to stay in touch with their friends [27, 28]. Students do not understand IM as technology, a term associated in many people's minds with objects that are complicated and difficult to understand or operate, but as common communication way [29].

IM apps have been applied in learning contexts in different ways, but one of the most common is helping to improve students communication with peers and faculty [30–35]. From this experiments it is possible to say that IM facilitates interactivity between peers and knowledge sharing, increases participants sense of presence, fosters collaboration and makes possible ubiquity [35, 36]. However, if the learners use these tools when studying, and not necessarily with educational proposes, they may have a negative effect, because IM apps can be a distraction in the learning process [37, 38]. This means that IM apps could be interesting tools in educational activities but they should be used in a controlled way and with educational proposes.

One of the main potential contributions of IM apps is that it can enhance communication between students which is in one of the key issues for the acquisition of TWC. In this sense, there are several cases where instant messaging is applied as a communication channel for students groups [36] and in some the contents of the interaction is analyzed [39]. However, in those works the learning evidences are not used to assess TWC acquisition as the author of this paper aims to do.

Given this context it is clear that IM can be used to communicate groups of students, but, What IM app should be used? In this sense the present work explores th e use of WhatsApp as one the most popular IM tools. There are several studies about the possibilities that WhatsApp provides in educational contexts [40–42], samples of the application of WhatsApp for communication [32, 36] and other related with the development of specific competences [43, 44].

This work goes beyond the existing research on this field, because it aims to employ WhatsApp to facilitate cooperation among the members of students' groups, that work together to develop a project, and later allow analyzing the interaction of the team members in order to assess the individual acquisition of the TWC.

3 The Interconnection Between WhatsApp and the LMS

In order to design the possible implementation of the connection between the learning analytics tool and WhatsApp it is necessary to consider the main components of this interaction:

- Learning Analytics Tool (LA Tool). It is an ad-hoc defined tool that gathers, analyze and represent information about the students' interaction in groups when they are applying CTMTC to address their projects. The system allows choosing a forum within the course and then display the data for the student–student interactions, with three different view modes [19]:
  - Forum view. With general stats about the interaction in the forums by each group and by students.

- Team view. That provides information for a specific team in all the threads of a forum
- Thread view. Which shows specific information for a group and a thread

The information is gathered by using an ad-hoc defined Moodle webservice and a client. The client will request the information to Moodle by using the webservice layer, compile this information and preprocess it. Figure 1 shows the information represented by the client for a specific team.

- Moodle. It is one of the most popular LMS and is used in lot of institutions all around the world [45–47]. Moodle, as other LMS, provides tools to support the teaching and learning processes. Between these tools one of the most common are forums. In CTMTC the forum is used as a way to gather the interactions that the team members have among them. This information is accessed by the LA tool. For this project the idea is to store WhatsApp evidences also into Moodle database so they can be easily accessed by the LA client without the necessity of dealing with a different database.

Porcentaje de mensajes largos de la disusión: 45%

Número de mensajes cortos por usuario: 43.75

Número de mensajes largos por usuario: 35.25

Nombre de la discusión	Fecha de creación	Mensajes	Mensajes cortos	Mensajes largos	Vistas
BUSQUEDA MIEMBRO RESTANTE	2018/12/05 19:27:05	5 (1.58%)	5 (1.58%)	0 (0%)	34
CREACCION Y REPARTO DE TAREAS	2018/12/17 11:20:35	24 (7.59%)	17 (5.38%)	7 (2.22%)	108
ELECCIÓN COORDINADOR DEL GRUPO	2018/12/05 19:16:11	8 (2.53%)	8 (2.53%)	0 (0%)	61
EVOLUCIÓN PRÁCTICA	2018/12/18 13:26:50	83 (26.27%)	34 (10.76%)	49 (15.51%)	317
MISIÓN Y OBJETIVOS	2018/12/11 14:27:42	18 (5.7%)	11 (3.48%)	7 (2.22%)	105
NOMBRE DEL GRUPO	2018/12/11 14:14:56	8 (2.53%)	7 (2.22%)	1 (0.32%)	44
REPARTO DE TRABAJO Y CREACIÓN WIKI	2018/12/11 13:59:14	20 (6.33%)	15 (4.75%)	5 (1.58%)	92
TAREA 1: MAIN	2018/12/19 23:27:29	19 (6.01%)	14 (4.43%)	5 (1.58%)	66
TAREA 3: ACCIONES USUARIO	2018/12/19 23:30:15	47 (14.87%)	24 (7.59%)	23 (7.28%)	185
TAREA 4: ACCIONES FACTURADOR	2018/12/19 23:30:54	45 (14.24%)	20 (6.33%)	25 (7.91%)	164

Resultados evaluación sumativa

Nombre	Apellidos	Mensajes	Mensajes cortos	Mensajes largos
		64 (20.25%)	44 (13.92%)	20 (6.33%)
		77 (24.37%)	41 (12.97%)	36 (11.39%)
		68 (21.52%)	31 (9.81%)	37 (11.71%)
		107 (33.86%)	59 (18.67%)	48 (15.19%)

Fig. 1. Learning analytics client tool. It shows the information for a specific group and forum. The information about students has been blurred

- WhatsApp. It is the tool where the interaction of students could happen. It is necessary to find a way to send the interactions to Moodle database. There are three possible options:
  - Modify WhatsApp to include interoperability specifications. This is not possible because it is a proprietary software tool, so modifications are not allowed.

- Define a middleware that gathers information from WhatsApp and implements interoperability specifications as the proposed by Conde et al. in other works [48, 49]. The problem of this solution is that there is not an official WhatsApp Open API and only WhatsApp Business API that can be employed to define commercial solutions. In this case the mediator could not be the best option because it is necessary to pay to access to the API.
- Define a component into Moodle that gathers the WhatsApp evidences and store them in Moodle database, so later could be represented in the LA tool client.

Given these options the best and more affordable solution is the last one. The idea is to define a widget with a form that can be installed in Moodle. In such component students should upload a text file with the WhatsApp conversation (a WhatsApp default functionality) and the information will be processed and stored into Moodle.

4 The Implementation and Information Process

Once made the decision to define a Moodle widget, authors should decide what type of widget develop. They considered that the best option could be a module, that would be instanced in the course. In this module the teacher should decide the forum to which the conversations will be associated. Through the module, students could upload a text file with the conversation and the information will be stored in the database. However, an important issue was detected related with WhatsApp messages structure. Figure 2 shows the structure of a WhatsApp message. The first part of the message is the date, after a "-" it is possible to see the phone number of the person that is speaking or her contact name.

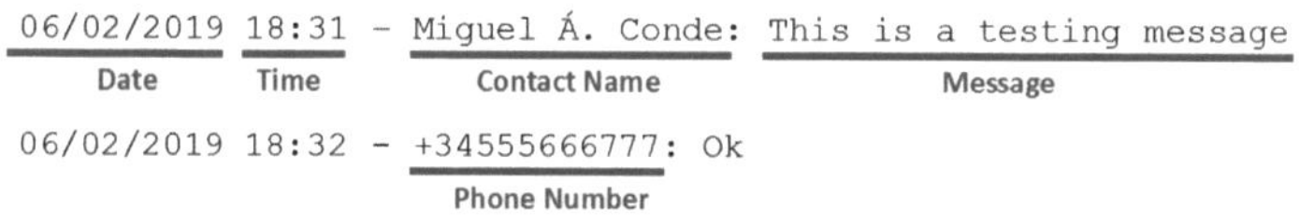

```
06/02/2019  18:31  -  Miguel Á. Conde:  This is a testing message
   Date      Time        Contact Name              Message
06/02/2019  18:32  -  +34555666777: Ok
                        Phone Number
```

Fig. 2. WhatsApp message structure

This means that the WhatsApp conversation does not include students' IDs, which could be a problem to link the messages with the specific students in the LMS database. In addition, storing sensitive information, such as a phone-numbers with students' IDs, can break the EU General Data Protection Regulation (GDPR). Given this situation the text file should be parsed. The students are going to associate, when uploading the file, the ID to a specific phone number or contact name. With this information the parser will extract messages and associate them to the students' IDs. Figure 3 shows an example of the form included in the module.

Figure 4 shows a Business Process Model Notation (BPMN) diagram that shows the process of uploading and storing the information. In such diagram it is possible to see that the student export and upload a file and fulfill a form to link user ids with contact names or phone numbers. If the form is properly fulfilled the information is parsed and stored in the data base. If there were errors these will be shown to the user that must fulfill again the form.

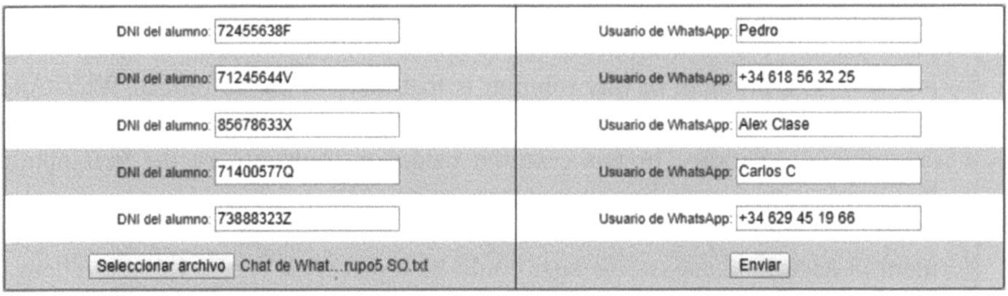

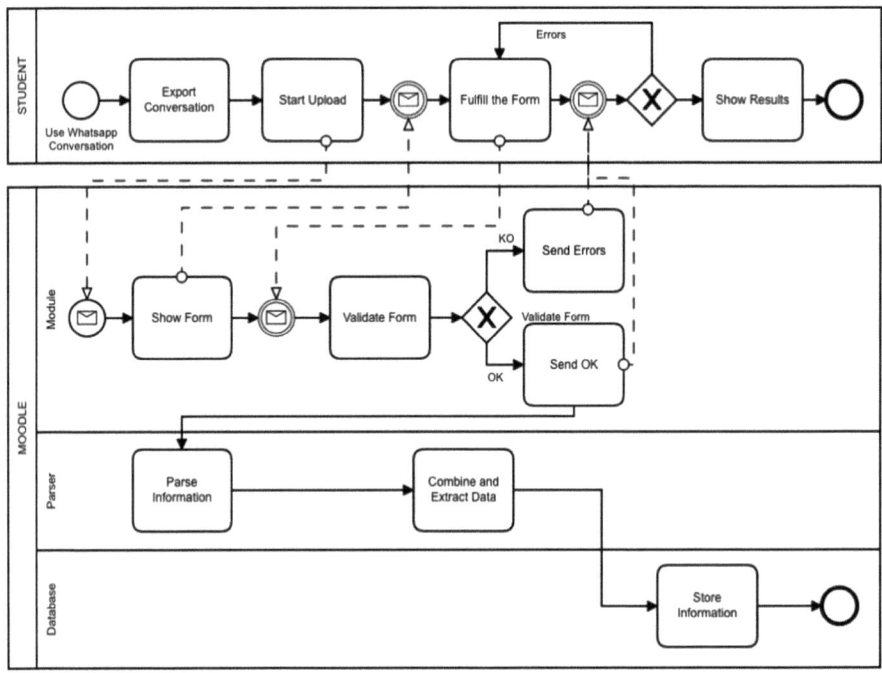

Fig. 3. Module form to upload the file and associate student ID with a contact name or a number. Information shown in the image is not real

Fig. 4. BPMN Diagram to describe the process of uploading a conversation and storing it. Click the following link for zoom: http://doi.org/10.5281/zenodo.2559595

The last part of the development consists of the integration of new methods into Moodle Web Services that allow retrieving WhatsApp messages for a specific group and to modify the LA tool client to facilitate data representation. Authors are currently working on this part.

5 Conclusions

TWC acquisition by an individual is closely related to her interaction with her peers. This kind of interaction could be carried out in forum posts, blogs or with other tools linked to an educational environment. However, students do not interact usually by using these tools. It is much more common that they employ IM tools and the most popular tool nowadays is WhatsApp.

In this paper we have explored how WhatsApp is employed in learning activities and we have provided a way to store WhatsApp conversations in the LMS database so later it can be explored through a LA tool in order to evaluate real students' interactions. This required to define a tool to upload conversations, parse sensitive information and store it in a coherent way with Moodle database structure.

From the experience it has been possible to say that the interoperability between tools that belong to the student informal learning context can be combined with those from the formal one, but it is necessary an intervention by the student in order this can be done in the proper way. This fits with some previous works [48, 50].

The next step is to validate the integration of the tool through some experiments where we will compare the results about individual TWC acquisition distinguishing between groups that upload WhatsApp conversation and those which prefer using the forum. Moreover, students that employ WhatsApp will be surveyed in order to know their perception about the integration carried out and what other tools they would use.

References

1. Colomo-Palacios, R., Casado-Lumbreras, C., Soto-Acosta, P., García-Peñalvo, F.J., Tovar-Caro, E.: Competence gaps in software personnel: a multi-organizational study. Comput. Hum. Behav. **29**, 456–461 (2013)
2. Leidner, D.E., Jarvenpaa, S.L.: The use of information technology to enhance management school education: a theoretical view. MIS quarterly **19**, 265–291 (1995)
3. Vogel, D.R., Davison, R.M., Shroff, R.H.: Sociocultural learning: a perspective on GSS-enabled global education. Commun. Assoc. Inf. Syst. **7**, 1–41 (2001)
4. Iglesias-Pradas, S., Ruiz-de-Azcárate, C., Agudo-Peregrina, Á.F.: Assessing the suitability of student interactions from moodle data logs as predictors of cross-curricular competencies. Comput. Hum. Behav. **47**, 81–89 (2015)
5. European Ministers Responsible for Higher Education: The Bologna Process 2020 - The European Higher Education Area in the new decade. Communiqué of the Conference of European Ministers Responsible for Higher Education, Leuven and Louvain-la-Neuve, 28–29 April 2009. https://goo.gl/ABJX7x
6. Conde, M.Á., Rodríguez-Sedano, F.J., Sánchez-González, L., Fernández-Llamas, C., Rodríguez-Lera, F.J., Matellán-Olivera, V.: Evaluation of teamwork competence acquisition by using CTMTC methodology and learning analytics techniques. In: Proceedings of the Fourth International Conference on Technological Ecosystems for Enhancing Multiculturality, pp. 787–794. ACM, Salamanca (2016)
7. Rosen, M.A., et al.: Tools for evaluating team performance in simulation-based training. J. Emerg. Trauma Shock **3**, 353–359 (2010)

8. Schwab, D., Heneman III, H.G., DeCotiis, T.A.: Behaviorally anchored rating scales: a review of the literature. Person. Psychol. **28**(4), 549–562 (2006)
9. Frankel, A., Gardner, R., Maynard, L., Kelly, A.: Using the communication and teamwork skills (CATS) assessment to measure health care team performance. Jt. Comm. J. Qual. Patient Saf. **33**, 549–558 (2007)
10. Hackbert, P.H.: Building entrepreneurial teamwork competencies in collaborative learning via peer assessments. J. Coll. Teach. Learn. **1**, 39–52 (2004)
11. Ríos-Carmenado, I., Figueroa-Rodríguez, B., Gómez-Gajardo, F.: Methodological proposal for teamwork evaluation in the field of project management training. Procedia Soc. Behav. Sci. **46**, 1664–1672 (2012)
12. Tasa, K., Taggar, S., Seijts, G.H.: The development of collective efficacy in teams: a multilevel and longitudinal perspective. J. Appl. Psychol. **92**, 17–27 (2007)
13. Dwyer, D.J., Oser, R.L., Salas, E.: Event-based approach to training (EBAT). Int. J. Aviat. Psychol. **8**, 209–221 (1998)
14. Lane, N.E., Salas, E., Franz, T., Oser, R.: Improving the measurement of team performance: the TARGETs methodology. Mil. Psychol. **6**, 47–61 (1994)
15. Fidalgo-Blanco, Á., Lerís, D., Sein-Echaluce, M.L.: Monitoring indicators for CTMTC: comprehensive training model of the teamwork competence in engineering domain. Int. J. Eng. Educ. (IJEE) **31**, 829–838 (2015)
16. Lerís, D., Fidalgo, Á., Sein-Echaluce, M.L.: A comprehensive training model of the teamwork competence. Int. J. Learn. Intellect. Cap. **11**, 1–19 (2014)
17. NCB.- Bases para la competencia en dirección de proyectos. http://www.lpzconsulting.com/images/CP-_Trabajo_en_Equipo.pdf. Accessed 28 Feb 2014
18. Séin-Echaluce, M.L., Fidalgo Blanco, Á., García-Peñalvo, F.J., Conde, M.Á.: A knowledge management system to classify social educational resources within a subject using teamwork techniques. In: Zaphiris, P., Ioannou, A. (eds.) LCT 2015. LNCS, vol. 9192, pp. 510–519. Springer, Cham (2015). https://doi.org/10.1007/978-3-319-20609-7_48
19. Fidalgo-Blanco, Á., Sein-Echaluce, M.L., García-Peñalvo, F.J., Conde, M.Á.: Using learning analytics to improve teamwork assessment. Comput. Hum. Behav. **47**, 149–156 (2015)
20. Fidalgo, A., Leris, D., Sein-Echaluce, M.L., García-Peñalvo, F.J.: Indicadores para el seguimiento de evaluación de la competencia de trabajo en equipo a través del método CTMT. Congreso Internacional sobre Aprendizaje Innovación y Competitividad - CINAIC 2013, Madrid (2013)
21. Sein-Echaluce, M.L., Fidalgo-Blanco, Á., García-Peñalvo, F.J.: Students' knowledge sharing to improve learning in engineering academic courses. Int. J. Eng. Educ. **32**, 1024–1035 (2016)
22. Conde, M.A., Colomo-Palacios, R., García-Peñalvo, F.J., Larrucea, X.: Teamwork assessment in the educational web of data: a learning analytics approach towards ISO 10018. Telematics Inform. **35**(3), 551–563 (2018)
23. Conde, Miguel Á., Hernández-García, Á., García-Peñalvo, F.J., Fidalgo-Blanco, Á., Sein-Echaluce, M.: Evaluation of the CTMTC methodology for assessment of teamwork competence development and acquisition in higher education. In: Zaphiris, P., Ioannou, A. (eds.) LCT 2016. LNCS, vol. 9753, pp. 201–212. Springer, Cham (2016). https://doi.org/10.1007/978-3-319-39483-1_19

24. González, I., Martín, R.M., García, F.J., Seoane, A.M., Conde, M.Á.: Interacción, aprendicaje y enseñanza basada en foros. Un caso de estudio sobre la plataforma ClayNet. In: Redondo-Duque, M.Á., Bravo-Santos, C., Ortega-Cantero, M. (eds.) Diseño de la Interacción Persona-Ordenador: Tendencias y Desafíos. Actas del VII Congreso Internacional de Interacción Persona-Ordenador, Interacción 2006, pp. 303–313, Puertollano, Ciudad Real, Spain (2006)
25. Alghamdi, E.A., Rajab, H.: Unmonitored students self-created WhatsApp groups in distance learning environments: a collaborative learning tool or cheating technique. Int. J. Eng. Educ. **5**, 71–82 (2016)
26. Most popular global mobile messenger apps as of October 2018 Statista (2019). https://www.statista.com/statistics/258749/most-popular-global-mobile-messenger-apps/. Accessed 5 Feb 2019
27. Carnevale, D.: Email is for old people. Chron. High. Educ. **53**, A57 (2006)
28. Junco, R., Mastrodicasa, J.: Connecting to the net.generation: what higher education professionals need to know about today's students. NASPA, National Association of Student Personnel Administrators, Student Affairs Administrators in Higher Education, US (2007)
29. Lewis, C., Fabos, B.: Instant messaging, literacies, and social identities. Read. Res. Q. **40**, 470–501 (2005)
30. Hrastinski, S., Edman, A., Andersson, F., Kawnine, T., Soames, C.-A.: Informal math coaching by instant messaging: two case studies of how university students coach K-12 students. Interact. Learn. Environ. **22**, 84–96 (2014)
31. Cifuentes, O.E., Lents, N.H.: Increasing student-teacher interactions at an urban commuter campus through instant messaging and online office hours. Electron. J. Sci. Educ. **14**, 1–13 (2010)
32. Smit, I., Goede, R.: WhatsApp with BlackBerry; can messengers be MXit? A philosophical approach to evaluate social networking sites. Cape Peninsula University of Technology (2012). https://repository.nwu.ac.za/handle/10394/13628
33. Sweeny, S.M.: Writing for the instant messaging and text messaging generation: using new literacies to support writing instruction. J. Adolesc. Adult Lit. **54**, 121–130 (2010)
34. Lauricella, S., Kay, R.: Exploring the use of text and instant messaging in higher education classrooms. Res. Learn. Tech. **21**, 1 (2013)
35. Klein, A.Z., da Silva Freitas, C.J., da Silva, J.V.V.M.M., Barbosa, J.L.V., Baldasso, L.: The educational affordances of mobile instant messaging MIM: results of WhatsApp used in higher education. Int. J. Dist. Educ. Tech. **16**, 51–64 (2018)
36. Bouhnik, D., Deshen, M.: WhatsApp goes to school: mobile instant messaging between teachers and students. J. Inf. Technol. Educ. Res. **13**, 217–231 (2014)
37. Fox, A.B., Rosen, J., Crawford, M.: Distractions, distractions: does instant messaging affect college students' performance on a concurrent reading comprehension task? Cyberpsychol. Behav. **12**, 51–53 (2009)
38. Junco, R., Cotten, S.R.: Perceived academic effects of instant messaging use. Comput. Educ. **56**, 370–378 (2011)
39. Gronseth, S., Hebert, W.: GroupMe: investigating use of mobile instant messaging in higher education courses. TechTrends **63**, 15–22 (2019)
40. Willemse, J.J.: Undergraduate nurses reflections on WhatsApp use in improving primary health care education. Curationis **38**, 1–7 (2015)
41. Barhoumi, C.: The effectiveness of WhatsApp mobile learning activities guided by activity theory on students' knowledge management. Contem. Educ. Technol. **6**, 221–238 (2015)
42. Aljaad, M., Hamad, N.J.E.: Whatsapp for Educational Purposes for Female Students at College of Education-King Saud University. Education **137**, 344–366 (2017)

43. Awada, G.: Effect of WhatsApp on critique writing proficiency and perceptions toward learning AU - Awada. Ghada. Cogent Education **3**, 1–25 (2016)
44. Andújar-Vaca, A., Cruz-Martínez, M.-S.: Mobile instant messaging: WhatsApp and its potential to develop oral skills. Comunicar **25**, 43–52 (2017)
45. Cole, J., Foster, H.: Using Moodle. O'Really, Sebastopol (2007)
46. Al-Ajlan, A., Zedan, H.: Why Moodle. In: 12th IEEE International Workshop on Future Trends of Distributed Computing Systems, pp. 58–64. Kunming (2008)
47. Molist, M.: Moodle llena la geografía educativa española de campus virtuales. Diario el Pais (2008). http://www.elpais.com/articulo/portada/Moodle/llena/geografia/educativa/espanola/campus/virtuales/elpeputec/20081204elpcibpor_1/Tes
48. Conde, M.Á., García-Peñalvo, F.J., Rodríguez-Conde, M.J., Alier, M., García-Holgado, A.: Perceived openness of learning management systems by students and teachers in education and technology courses. Comput. Hum. Behav. **31**, 517–526 (2014)
49. Conde, M.Á., García-Peñalvo, F.J., Alier, M., Mayol, E., Fernández-Llamas, C.: Implementation and design of a service-based framework to integrate personal and institutional learning environments. Sci. Comput. Program. **88**, 41–53 (2014)
50. García-Peñalvo, F.J., et al.: TRAILER project (Tagging, recognition, acknowledgment of informal learning experiences) a methodology to make visible learners' informal learning activities to the institutions. J. Univers. Comput. Sci. **19**, 1661 (2013)

An Analysis of *ProjectEdu*: A Mobile Learning Application for Software Project Management Education

Maria Lydia Fioravanti[(✉)], Raul Donaire Gonçalves Oliveira,
Gustavo Martins Nunes Avellar, Camila Dias de Oliveira,
and Ellen Francine Barbosa

Institute of Mathematics and Computer Science (ICMC),
University of São Paulo (USP), São Carlos, SP, Brazil
{mlfioravanti,raul.oliveira,gustavo.avellar,camila_oliveira}@usp.br,
francine@icmc.usp.br

Abstract. Learning applications play a key role in educational activities, both in academia and in industry. In this scenario, mobile learning has emerged as a new and promising learning modality, providing more attractiveness, agility, interactivity and flexibility to learners, tutors and teachers in carrying out educational activities and practices. In a different but related perspective, according to ACM/IEEE curricula, Software Project Management is an important topic to be taught in Computing degree programs. Despite its relevance, frequently, there is no specific course to teach Project Management, so its concepts are taught along with the other concepts of Software Engineering. However, even when there is a course dedicated to the subject, in its traditional format, the subject of Project Management is approached in a theoretical way. In this context, it is important to seek strategies that motivate the teaching-learning process, such as, for instance, mobile learning. In order to provide a more interesting approach to learn Software Project Management, we designed, prototyped and evaluated a tool entitled *ProjectEdu*. In general, users were enthusiastic and positive about the use of the mobile learning application, but they also pointed out some improvement points to make the tool more attractive.

Keywords: Mobile learning · Project management education · Usability Test

1 Introduction

Learning applications play a key role in educational activities, both in academia and in industry [10,26]. The miniaturization of electronic components and their cheapening have allowed the development of devices with processing capacity and functionalities equivalent or superior to those of many computers [30]. These changes associated with ubiquitous computing have leveraged a new modality of learning called mobile learning (m-learning) [11,15,27,29]. In this scenario, mobile learning has emerged as a new and promising learning modality, providing more interactivity and flexibility to learners, tutors and teachers in carrying out educational activities and practices [14].

As with many emerging paradigms, there are several attempts to define m-learning. However, it is noteworthy that, regardless of the various definitions over the years [11,12,15,16,20,21], there is a convergence in definitions regarding the use of mobile devices to promote learning anytime, anywhere. Based on such definitions, we have adopted the following definition for this work:

> "Mobile learning is a learning modality characterized by the ability to provide an effective interaction among users (learner, teachers and tutors), allowing them to contribute, participate and access the educational environment through mobile devices (cell phones, PDAs, smartphones, tablets, laptops, and so forth) anytime, anywhere."

Portable technologies, together with computational networks as well as the dissemination and easy access to the Internet, are becoming more and more present in the daily life, promoting access to information in an easy and fast way [6]. This scenario has favored the emergence of new learning modalities, providing new means to address the deficiencies of traditional teaching, making it more agile, flexible and attractive [17].

When such technologies are used for educational purposes, they can promote an improvement in student learning and become pedagogical support for the teacher [28]. New technologies and teaching techniques, as well as current studies on learning processes, can provide more effective resources to meet and motivate those involved in the teaching and learning processes.

The challenges associated with mobile learning have been investigated and several supporting mechanisms have been proposed to assist in the design and evaluation of mobile learning applications. For instance, a pedagogical pattern language, namely *MLearning-PL* [13], and a requirements catalog, namely *ReqML-Catalog* [23].

In a different but related perspective, *Association for Computing Machinery* (ACM) and *Computer Society of the Institute for Electrical and Electronic Engineers* (IEEE-CS) have been involved in initiatives to develop curricular guidelines for typical Computing degree programs (such as Computer Engineering, Computer Science, Information Systems and Software Engineering). Among the guidelines, a body of knowledge was identified, organized hierarchically in areas, units and topics of knowledge to each program.

Following the structure of areas, units and topics proposed by ACM/IEEE to the Computer Science Curricula (version CS2013 [2]), Software Project Management unit is part of the Software Engineering area and must be addressed. Similarly, curriculum recommendations of other Computing undergraduate degree programs also include Project Management topics, such as Information Systems [3], Computer Engineering [1], Information Technology [4], and Software Engineering [5].

Despite its relevance, frequently, Software Project Management is approached in a theoretical way. In this context, it is important to seek strategies that motivate the teaching-learning process, for instance, mobile learning.

In order to provide a more attractive approach to learn Software Project Management, we designed a tool entitled *ProjectEdu*. The idea was to use the aforementioned artifacts and investigate whether the learners remained more motivated and committed to using the mobile learning app.

Considering this scenario, in this paper we evaluated *ProjectEdu*, a mobile learning application for Software Project Management education. The research question we aimed to answer is: *"What do users of mobile learning applications expect in order to keep themselves motivated and committed to using such applications, considering their different learning styles and needs?"*. In general, users were enthusiastic and positive about the use of the mobile learning application, but they also pointed out some improvement points to make the tool more attractive.

The remainder of the paper is organized as follows. In Sect. 2, we briefly present some studies about the supporting mechanisms used to design *ProjectEdu*. In Sect. 3, we discuss *ProjectEdu* and its design process. In Sect. 4, we present the evaluation methods used and discuss the results. Finally, we draw conclusions and provide directions of future work in Sect. 5.

2 Background

When dealing with domain-specific software, such as learning applications, we must be concerned about domain requirements, which are derived from the application domain of the system [24]. On the other hand, we must be concerned with specific needs and opinions of the end users.

We designed *ProjectEdu* aiming at a more attractive and motivating application. To achieve this goal, we used two main artifacts: *ReqML-Catalog* and *MLearning-PL*.

ReqML-Catalog is a requirements catalog for mobile learning applications. The proposition of *ReqML-Catalog* was motivated by a scenario where there was no complete and well-defined set of requirements for mobile learning applications. Aiming to bridge this gap, the work of Soad et al. [23] intended to be a step forward in this direction.

The categories defined in the catalog are divided into 12 requirements subcategories. Three subcategories are defined for the *Pedagogical* category. The first is *Learning*, which is defined by the application's ability to provide features that contribute to student learning. Additionally, *Content* is defined by the ability to deliver manageable and quality content and *Interactivity* is defined as the ability of the application to provide features that help users interact with each other and with the application.

The *Social* category comprises *Socioeconomic* and *Sociocultural* subcategories. Finally, the *Technical* category is subdivided into *Functional Suitability*, *Performance Efficiency*, *Compatibility*, *Usability*, *Reliability*, *Security* and *Portability*.

In a related perspective, *MLearning-PL* [13] is a pedagogical pattern language for mobile learning applications, comprised of 14 patterns. The main audience of *MLearning-PL* is novice educators who occasionally must play a requirements analyst role in a mobile learning application project. Those educators can be benefited from *MLearning-PL*, once they can reuse pedagogical knowledge from senior educators.

It aims to assist in the definition of mobile applications for keeping learners motivated and committed to using such applications, according to their different learning styles and an effective knowledge acquisition. *Let's Play* [13], for instance, is a pattern which suggests to add games elements to the learning process to make learning fun.

Such artifacts are complementary and can be applied together in the process of defining a mobile learning application.

3 Overview of *ProjectEdu*

ProjectEdu is a mobile learning application prototype focused on users who want to learn Software Project Management. Several mobile applications can be found in order to carry out the management activities throughout the project, but *ProjectEdu* stands out since it focuses on teaching Project Management theory as well as its practice.

ProjectEdu is in its prototype version, being developed using Justinmind[1] tool. Figure 1(a) and (b) show some of the first screens the user will be in touch with: the main screen and login screen.

In its current version, *ProjectEdu* has the following main features:

Activities: In this area of the app, the learner has access to all the theoretical content of Software Project Management and also to some related activities and practices.
Statistics: This feature allows the learner to check his/her progress since the user may access his/her score and see how much he/she has learned from the application through statistical data.
Ranking: This feature allows the learner to compare his/her progress with others learners by participating in competitions and seeing their ranking among other users of the application.
Settings: This feature allows the user to set the app preferences concerning notifications, sounds and some system options.

Concerning the *Activities* feature, *ProjectEdu* provides theoretical content of Software Project Management and also activities and practices. As Fig. 2 shows, the main topics are:

- Introductory concepts of Project Management;
- Project Management Foundations;
- Project Management Knowledge Areas; and
- Business Environments in Projects.

 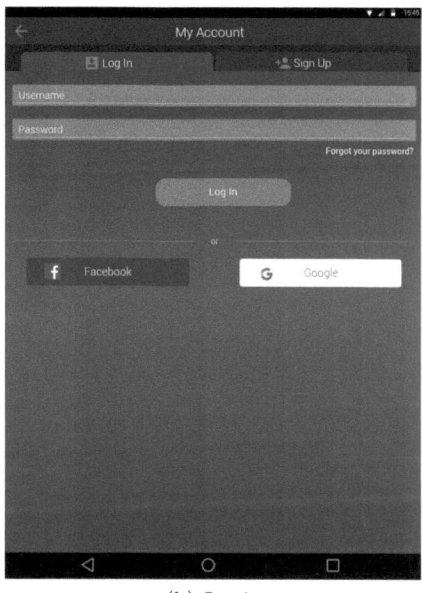

(a) Main (b) Login

Fig. 1. *ProjectEdu* first screens

Figure 3(a) shows in detail a screen in which the learner is provided with some theoretical content and Fig. 3(b) shows an exercise related to that content.

Regarding *Statistics*, Fig. 4 shows the learner can access some important information about his/her use of the app. For instance, the learner can see how many points were earned, how many days he/she is engaged using the app and the percentage of the content that he/she has already completed. The learner can also follow the daily progress and see how many points he/she earned in each day of the week. The *Ranking*, shown in Fig. 5, shows a global vision of the learners' performance. He/she can see his/her position among all the users.

Although some of these features are usual in mobile learning apps, *ProjectEdu* has been designed considering two artifacts aimed at systematizing the designing of m-learning apps, discussed in Sect. 2. We opted for an iterative and incremental development process, with short phases and proximity to the final target audience, so that the application is well accepted by them. In this sense, the features are inserted and tested gradually.

In the current version of *ProjectEdu*, *ReqML-Catalog* guided the definition of *learning* and *usability* requirements. Since we want to provide a more attractive approach, it is important to consider user interface and usability aspects to achieve this goal.

---

[1] https://www.justinmind.com/.

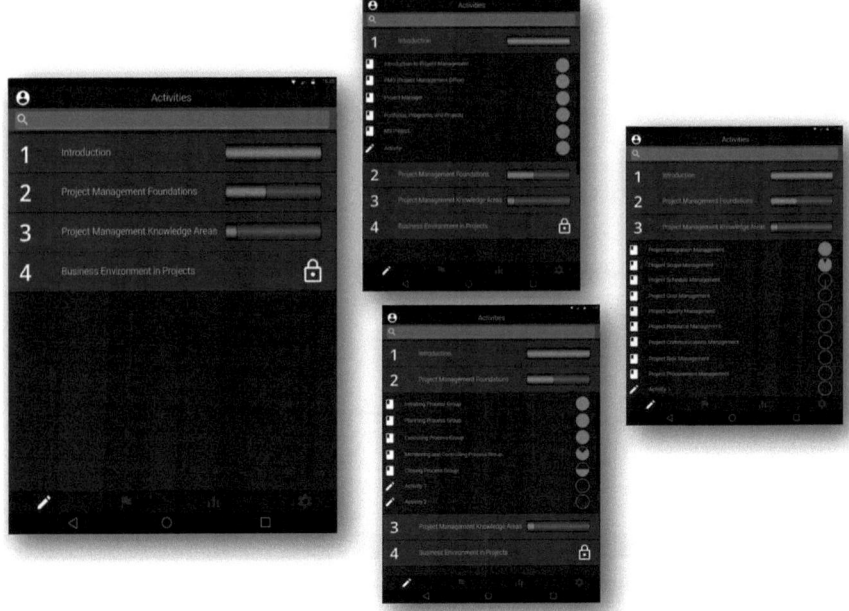

Fig. 2. Topics of project management

ProjectEdu has the following usability requirements suggested by *ReqML-Catalog*: attractiveness, continuity, information presentation, homogeneity of layout and components and concise messages.

Furthermore, we considered the learning requirements suggested by *ReqML-Catalog*, such as: learning style, knowledge at the right time, educational activities, motivation, engagement and progress tracking.

Progress tracking can be seen applied in the *Activities* feature, which shows a progress bar for each topic, and also in the *Statistics* screen, in which the learner can see his/her progress.

Dealing with motivation, engagement, learning styles and so forth is not an easy task. *MLearning-PL* guided this process of the design by applying pedagogical patterns. Following, we present in Table 1 how each pattern was applied in *ProjectEdu*.

4 Evaluation

Aiming to answer our research question, we chose to carry out the evaluation of *ProjectEdu* conducting a usability test. Usability is most often defined as the ease of use and acceptability of a system for a particular class of users carrying out specific tasks in a specific environment. Ease of use affects the users' performance and their satisfaction, while acceptability affects whether the product is used [8].

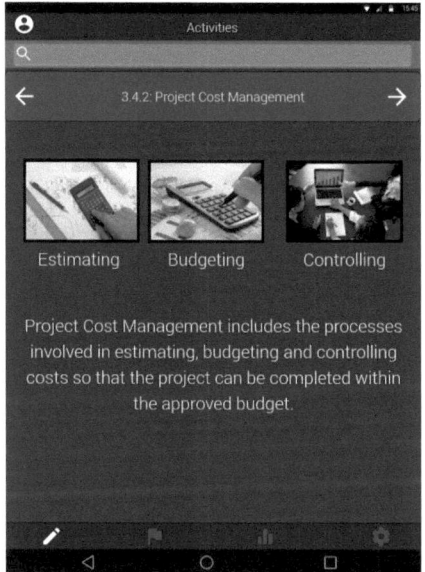 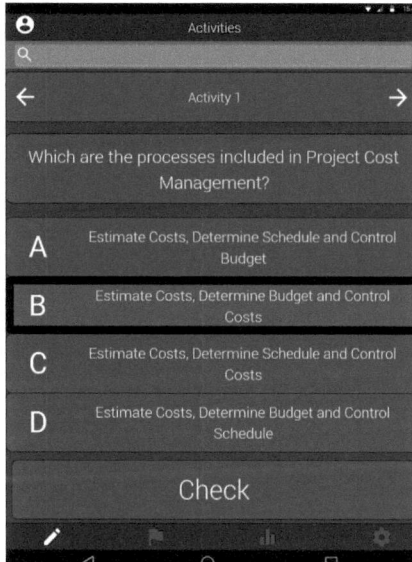

(a) Theoretical (b) Exercise

Fig. 3. *ProjectEdu* activities

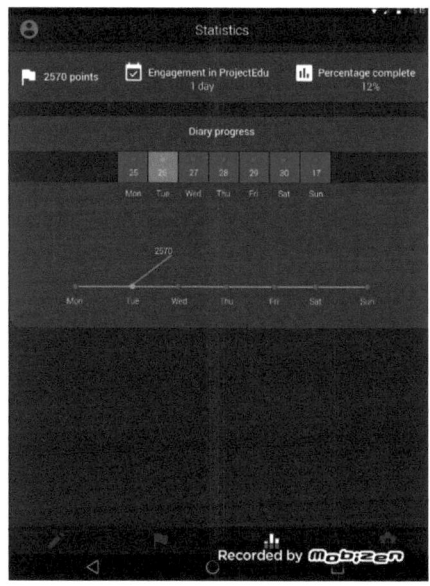 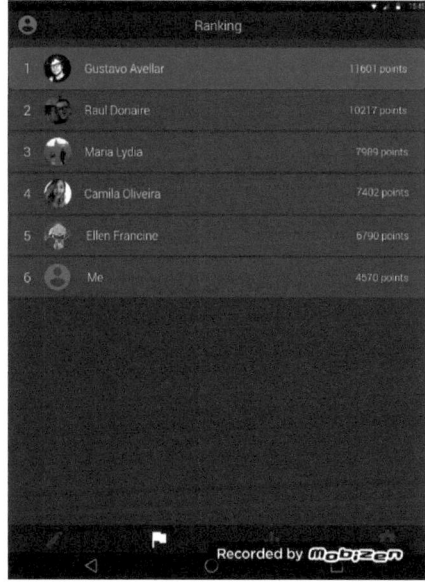

Fig. 4. Statistics **Fig. 5.** Ranking

Table 1. Application of each pattern of *MLearning-PL* in *ProjectEdu*

Pattern	Application in *ProjectEdu*
Be Active	Providing theoretical and hands-on activities
Give Them a Treat	Giving the learners a score when a topic is finished
Gold, Silver and Bronze Medal	Showing publicly the results in the Ranking
Little by Little	Organizing the topics in the smallest unit possible
As Soon As Possible	Providing most important knowledge first
Suitable for You	Providing different types of media, such as images, videos and texts

To ensure a software project has these essential usability characteristics, we used methods we divide into test methods (with end users) and inspection methods (without end users).

4.1 User Tests

Testing with end users is the most fundamental usability method and is in some sense indispensable. It provides direct information about how people use our systems and their exact problems with a specific interface.

We conducted the test with 14 participants throughout an afternoon and early evening in a prepared room from one of our research labs building in the Institute of Mathematics and Computer Science (ICMC), University of São Paulo (USP). During the tests, there were only the researchers and the participant inside the room, moreover we video recorded the user's hands and the tablet screen for further analysis. The participants were undergraduate and graduate students of the Computer Science area from ICMC/USP.

Aiming to characterize the 14 participants of our user tests, we asked them some questions. Participants were firstly asked which type of mobile devices they had: smartphone and/or tablet. As Fig. 6 shows, all of them have smartphones and only three have tablets.

Next, we wanted to know if they have ever used a mobile learning application and as shown in Fig. 7, 79% (11) of the participants have previously used a mobile learning application.

From this participants with previous experience with m-learning apps, we wanted to know how their experience was. Figure 8 shows that 27% had an excellent experience; 55%, i.e, more than half of the experienced participants, had an average experience; 9% had a good experience; and the remainder 9% had a fair experience.

After answering these characterization questions, the user test was divided in three parts: (i) Thinking Aloud; (ii) System Usability Scale; (iii) Open Questions.

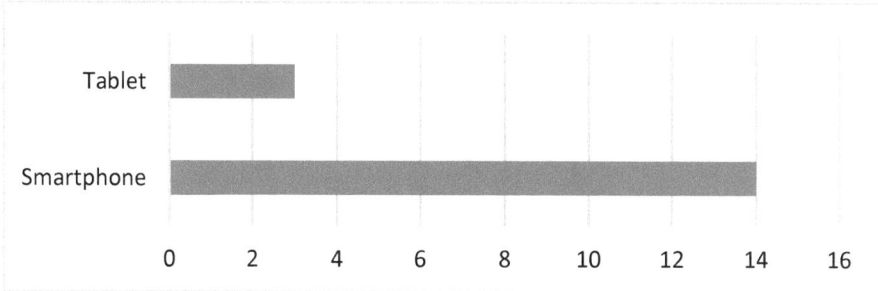

Fig. 6. Which of these mobile devices do you have?

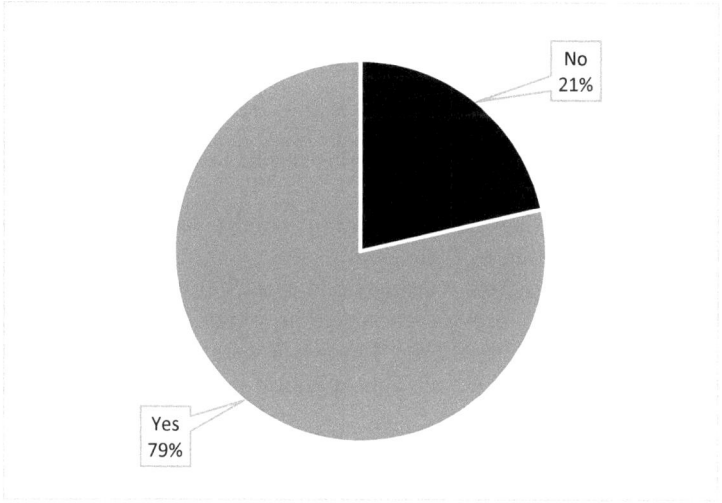

Fig. 7. Have you ever used mobile learning applications?

Thinking Aloud. Thinking aloud (TA) [18] may be the single most valuable usability engineering method. It involves having an end user continuously thinking out loud while using the system. By verbalizing their thoughts, the test users enable us to understand how they view the system, which makes it easier to identify the end users' major misconceptions. By showing how users interpret each individual interface item, TA facilitates a direct understanding of which parts of the dialogue cause the most problems. In TA the time is very important, since the contents of the users' working memory contents are desired.

During this part of the test, the participants followed a set of steps to guide their interaction, available at https://goo.gl/WJcmJq.

We based the analysis of our acquired results on some procedures of Grounded Theory [25] to analyze users' comments based on the concept of coding, such as: *open coding* makes possible identification of concepts that are separated into

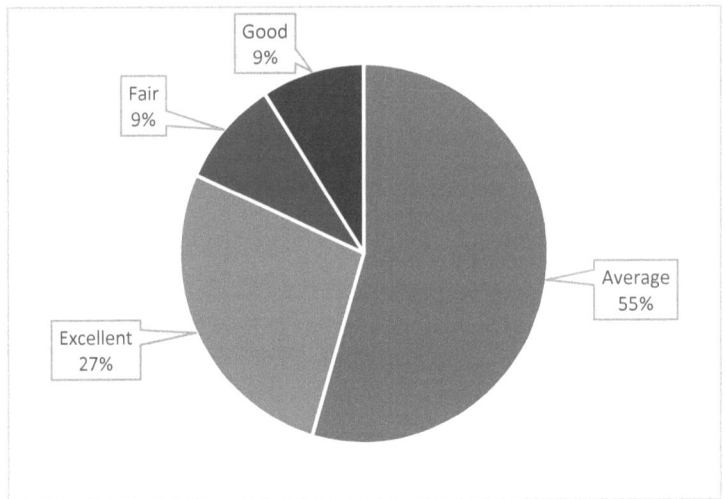

Fig. 8. How was your experience using mobile learning applications?

discrete parts for analysis; and *axial coding* handles connections among codes and groups them according to their similarities.

Our data sample consisted of transcribed recordings from users' TA session. In general, the idea is to provide the users an experience with an m-learning application, in this case *ProjectEdu*. The users were encouraged to constantly verbalize their thoughts and share their opinions on the app functionalities.

All reports were organized on a single file and each sentence was analyzed to derive the codes by using open coding procedures.

Learners controlling the study was one of the main extracted codes. It reinforces the idea that the students using m-learning applications have a need of constant controlling their learning process, task that were previously assigned to instructors in the traditional learning [22]. It is exemplified in the sentences below: *"I think it needs to be very clear when the questions are about to appear. The app should have the option of skipping it if the user is not willing to answer the questions in that moment. Sometimes he/she just want to refresh his/her mind and avoid answering stuff"* and *"I don't know how it would work in a video, but it would be interesting to mark what I have already seen, where I stopped, also that I could comment, in private or public, do notes. I would help my learning process"*

In addition, users described their experience with the feedback of the system: *"I'm not so sure if I finished the last topic. I need to move forward until I get to the end? Now I'm not sure, I was at the question screen, now I don't know if this new screen belongs to the new content"* and *"It would also be nice if I had a sense of how long it takes to finish this, keep clicking 'Next' without knowing when it will stop it's demotivating"*. According to Nielsen [18], this topic is critical to a systems usability, hence such sentences were coded in **System feedback needs to be improved.**

Users also reported their experience with the navigability of the application: *"An exit icon is missing"*, *"I didn't see if there is a button to return into the activities. It's not cool to click again all this way through to come back to where I was"*, *"The navigability of the content is the most misleading part"* and *"It's odd that you have to click in the icon again to return. I can get used to that, I guess."*. These information was clustered into `Navigability did not please`.

Another code retrieved was `Red/Yellow/Green have special meaning`. Through the test, users were often expecting that items with red/yellow/green elements had an extra meaning, the concepts of right (green) and wrong (red) were attached to that. This code can be exemplified by the following quotes: *"Probably green means that I got right"*, *"This diagram is presented with borders on different colors, I can't understand the relation between the border and the content. It's some kind of priority scheme? A traffic light?"* and *"Hmm ok! I've gotten something here and the statistics and the ranking turned to yellow. Why is it yellow?"*.

In summary, we identified eight codes and using axial coding procedures, we aggregated each code into categories based on their similarity. We performed open and axial coding several times aiming to refine the emerging codes and categories. Furthermore, we mitigated an eventual bias in the coding process by discussing the codes and categories among the researchers until they came to an agreement for all the concepts found. The categories are presented next, followed by the assigned codes.

Usability: System feedback needs to be improved, Navigability did not please, Non-Intuitive icons, Red/Yellow/Green have special meaning.

Requirements: Statistics needs clarity and dynamism, Application to be practical/fast/safe, Content must be attractive, Learners controlling study.

The categories and codes emerged through Grounded Theory procedures allowed us to suggest some assumptions from our findings. For example, there is an overall agreement of the users that they enjoy to control how to handle their learning process. They also reported this need of deciding what to study (which topic or content), how to study (reading, videos, exercises) and when to study. And in order to proper establish their routine, they reported a need of two major requirements from the system: feedback and navigability. Feedback provides the real time information that will assist their decisions: *How many topics have I already completed? How many exercises does this activity have? Which questions have I answered correctly?* And navigability is the final piece of this structure, the user needs a fast paced, dynamic and intuitive system in order to fully apply their routine. A clunky and uninformative application can demotivate the student, as could be seen in the quotes.

System Usability Scale. Questionnaires are useful for studying how end users use the system and their preferred features, but need some experience to design. They are an indirect method, since this technique does not study the actual user interface: it only collects the opinions of the users about the interface.

There are numerous surveys available to usability practitioners to aid them in assessing the usability of a product or service. Many of these surveys are used to evaluate specific types of interfaces, while others can be used to evaluate a wider range of interface types. The System Usability Scale (SUS) [9] is one of the surveys that can be used to assess the usability of a variety of products or services. There are several characteristics of the SUS that makes its use attractive. First, it is composed of only ten statements, so it is relatively quick and easy for study participants to complete and for administrators to score. Second, it is nonproprietary, so it is cost effective to use and can be scored very quickly, immediately after completion. Third, the SUS is technology agnostic, which means that it can be used by a broad group of usability practitioners to evaluate almost any type of user interface, including Web sites, cell phones, interactive voice response (IVR) systems (both touch-tone and speech), TV applications, and more. Lastly, the result of the survey is a single score, ranging from 0 to 100, and is relatively easy to understand by a wide range of people from other disciplines who work on project teams.

According to Bangor et al. [7] the average study mean is about 70. Considering that the result for *ProjectEdu* was 75, it was above average. However, we wanted to understand what were the points that brought this score down. Aiming to verify the specific objectives proposed for this research, we used the relation between the quality components indicated by Nielsen and the SUS questions. The results are shown in Fig. 9 and discussed next.

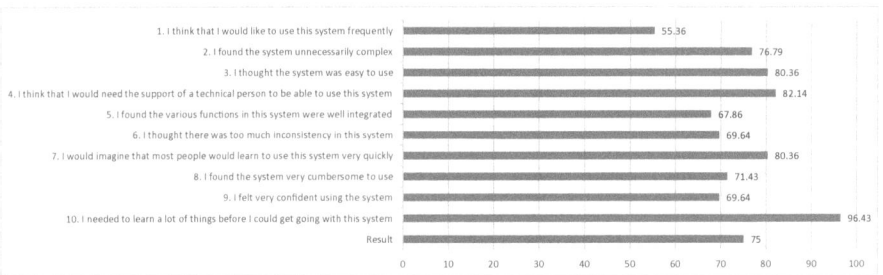

Fig. 9. SUS results

Learnability: learnability is represented in the questions 3, 4, 7 and 10 of SUS. The average of the result of these questions is 84.82, so we can conclude that the users had an easy time learning to use the system.
Efficiency: the items 5, 6 and 8 are related to system efficiency. Analyzing the average of these questions, we obtained 69.64, which means the users consider the system efficient, although the result is slightly inferior to 70.
Memorability: the ease of memorization is assessed by question 2, the score of 76.79 shows satisfaction concerning this item.
Errors: inconsistencies or minimization of errors are measured through question 6. In this item, the SUS score was 69.64, again slightly inferior to 70, but still a relevant result.

Satisfaction: user satisfaction is represented by items 1, 4 and 9. The average of these questions was 69.05, also slightly inferior to 70, but expected since the participants raised some points of improvement.

Overall, the *ProjectEdu* SUS Score of 75 demonstrates that the system meets usability requirements and the quality component analysis gives us indications of the improvement points that should be prioritized, such as system feedback and content navigation.

Personal Opinions. The last questions of the user test took participants' personal opinions about the experience with *ProjectEdu* and also about their mobile learning applications, in general.

First, we asked them to describe if they have faced any difficulties during the use of *ProjectEdu*. Most of them mentioned not facing major difficulties, but some minor difficulties were raised, such as: (i) Statistics screen; (ii) Next button; and (iii) Content navigation.

Next, we asked if they could change *ProjectEdu*, what kind of changes they would make. In addition to the improvements to the items that caused difficulties in the user experience, other interesting improvements were suggested. We can highlight: (i) social network integration; and (ii) a space for adding personal notes.

Proceeding to their experiences with mobile learning applications, in general, we aked, if they would use a mobile learning application to learn a new content in a daily basis. Figure 10 shows that 93% (13) would use and only 7% (1) would not.

When asked the reason why using or not a mobile learning applications, the participants who answered positively mentioned that (i) they already use another m-learning app; (ii) it is easy to use anytime and anywhere; (iii) it is practical and flexible way of learning a new content; and so forth. Regarding the participant who would not engage in a mobile learning app, the reason is not being able to commit to a long-term course.

The last question of the survey took free-text answers about respondents experiences. In general, they reported a pleasant and interactive experience and mentioned *ProjectEdu* is an interesting app that they would definitely use.

4.2 Heuristic Evaluation

Heuristic evaluation (HE) is the most common informal method. It involves having usability specialists judge whether each dialogue or other interactive element follows established usability principles [19].

The original and adopted approach is for each individual evaluator to inspect the interface alone. Only after all the evaluations have been completed are the evaluators allowed to communicate and aggregate their findings. This restriction is important in order to ensure independent and unbiased evaluations. During a single evaluation session, the evaluator goes through the interface several times,

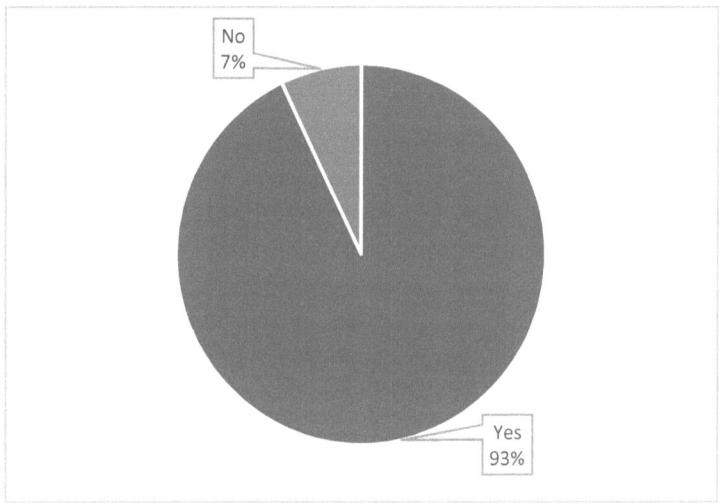

Fig. 10. In your day-to-day life, would you use a mobile learning application to learn a new content?

inspects the various interactive elements, and compares them with a list of recognized usability principles (in this case, Nielsen's Usability Heuristics [18]).

Our heuristic evaluation was performed by four usability specialists who followed the instructions available at https://goo.gl/B5FoN9 and fill in a table with the following information:

- ID: Sequential numbering that identifies the problem pointed out by the expert.
- Heuristic: Represents the numbering of each of Nielsen's heuristics.
    1. Visibility of system status
    2. Match between system and the real world
    3. User control and freedom
    4. Consistency and standards
    5. Error prevention
    6. Recognition rather than recall
    7. Flexibility and efficiency of use
    8. Aesthetic and minimalist design
    9. Help users recognize, diagnose, and recover from errors
    10. Help and documentation
- Description of the problem: Description presented by the expert for the problem found.
- Task: Represents the tasks previously presented.
- Screen: Name that best represents the system screen where the problem was identified.
- Degree of severity:

- 0 = I don't agree that this is a usability problem at all
- 1 = Cosmetic problem only: need not be fixed unless extra time is available on project
- 2 = Minor usability problem: fixing this should be given low priority
- 3 = Major usability problem: important to fix, so should be given high priority
- 4 = Usability catastrophe: imperative to fix this before product can be released

After they completed the individual evaluations and then their findings were aggregated, 42 issues were identified. In Table 2, we highlight the issues which also were mentioned by the users during the user tests and identified using Grounded Theory.

We grouped the average and maximum severities by heuristic (Fig. 11) to analyze the strengths and weaknesses identified.

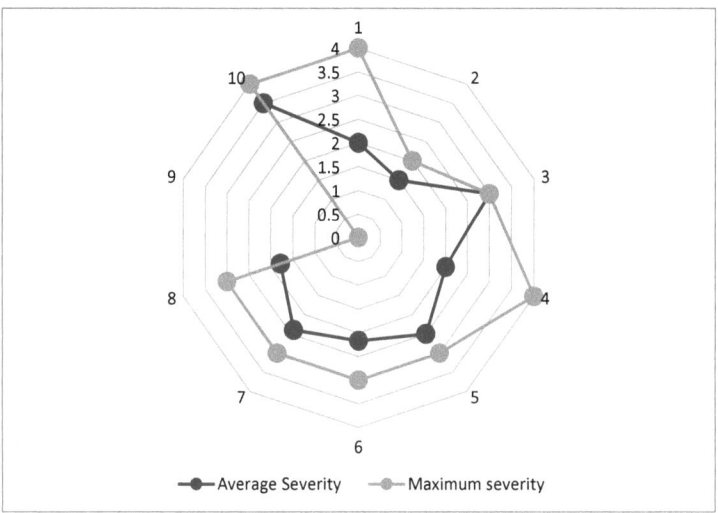

Fig. 11. Nielsen's heuristics vs. severities

As we can see, heuristic #9 regarding *aesthetic and minimalist design* was not a raised concern. On the other hand, three heuristics were violated with maximum severity, which were #1, #4 and #10, regarding, respectively, *visibility of system status*, *consistency and standards*, and *help and documentation*.

Analyzing the comments of the evaluators, we agreed that some improvements must be made in order to evolve *ProjectEdu* and we will definitely take their observations into consideration. On the other hand, most of their suggestions will be solved when *ProjectEdu* will no longer be a prototype, since the issues mentioned are due the prototyping tool.

Table 2. Issues identified in the heuristic evaluation

Heuristic	Description of the problem	Degree of severity
1	Missing sign up confirmation feedback (`System feedback needs to be improved`)	2
4	The forward arrow does not work (`Navigability did not please`)	4
2	The icon used to represent the ranking functionality is not intuitive, usually the systems use the icon of a "medal" or award (`Non-intuitive icons`)	2
4	The "Ranking" and "Statistics" elements of the lower toolbar are in highlighted yellow placement indicating that there have been changes. Badges are usually used above the icon when there are updates or notifications (`Red/Yellow/Green have special meaning`)	1
6	The first place in the ranking is highlighted by color, if there are many people participating in the ranking it will be difficult to find the classification (`Statistics needs clarity and dynamism`)	3
6	Explanations of the initial tutorial are displayed one at a time, and if the user clicks in one of the icons in the middle of the tutorial, he/she can not see the explanations again (`Application to be practical/fast/safe`)	1
6	When there are lots of "Lessons and Activities" in the expansions it is difficult to know which of them is the marker of progress (`Content must be attractive`)	1
1, 7	Information about the system status is missing. I suggest putting a breadcrumb, since there are sub-activities (`Learners controlling study`)	3

5 Conclusions and Future Work

This paper has presented an evaluation of a mobile learning application prototype, entitled *ProjectEdu*. In general, users were enthusiastic and positive about the use of mobile learning applications. Although *ProjectEdu* is still a prototype and requires improvements, the evaluated version has fulfilled the requirements of usability.

On the other hand, in order to be as attractive as the users expect and they really feel motivated to use, several improvements still must be made: more attractive content, more dynamic statistics, more intuitive icons, better navigability, feedback, and self-learning mechanisms.

As future work, we aim at considering all the improvement points raised during the evaluations conducted to develop the first version of *ProjectEdu*. Moreover, we intend to conduct other types of evaluations concerning learning aspects while using the mobile app. Shortly, we intend to include other relevant requirements of an m-learning app, using *ReqML-Catalog* as a basis.

Acknowledgements. This study was financed by the University of São Paulo (USP) and the Brazilian funding agencies: Coordenação de Aperfeiçoamento de Pessoal de Nível Superior - Brasil (CAPES) - Finance Code 001, CNPq and FAPESP. The authors are also grateful to the HCI experts for their valuable contributions to this work and also to all those who helped by participating in the studies.

References

1. ACM/IEEE-CE: Computer Engineering Curricula (2016). https://www.acm.org/binaries/content/assets/education/ce2016-final-report.pdf
2. ACM/IEEE-CS: Curriculum Guidelines for Undergraduate Programs in Computer Science (2013). https://www.acm.org/binaries/content/assets/education/cs2013_web_final.pdf
3. ACM/IEEE-IS: Curriculum Guidelines for Undergraduate Degree Programs in Information Systems (2010). https://www.acm.org/binaries/content/assets/education/curricula-recommendations/is-2010-acm-final.pdf
4. ACM/IEEE-IT: Curriculum Guidelines for Baccalaureate Degree Programs in Information Technology (2017). https://www.acm.org/binaries/content/assets/education/curricula-recommendations/it2017.pdf
5. ACM/IEEE-SE: Curriculum Guidelines for Undergraduate Degree Programs in Software Engineering (2014). https://www.acm.org/binaries/content/assets/education/se2014.pdf
6. Alexander, B.: Going nomadic: mobile learning in higher education. Educause Rev. **39**(5), 28–35 (2004)
7. Bangor, A., Kortum, P., Miller, J.: Determining what individual SUS scores mean: adding an adjective rating scale. J. Usability Stud. **4**(3), 114–123 (2009). http://dl.acm.org/citation.cfm?id=2835587.2835589
8. Bevan, N.: Measuring usability as quality of use. Software Qual. J. **4**(2), 115–130 (1995)
9. Brooke, J., et al.: SUS-A quick and dirty usability scale. Usability evaluation in industry **189**(194), 4–7 (1996)
10. Craig, A., Coldwell-Neilson, J., Goold, A., Beekhuyzen, J.: A review of e-learning technologies-opportunities for teaching and learning. In: CSEDU 2012–4th International Conference on Computer Supported Education, pp. 29–41. [INSTICC] (2012)
11. Crompton, C.: A historical overview of mobile learning: toward learner-centered education. In: Berge, Z.L., Muilenburg, L.Y. (eds.) Handbook of Mobile Learning, pp. 3–14. Routledge, Florence (2013)
12. Farooq, U., Schafer, W., Rosson, M.B., Carroll, J.M.: M-education: bridging the gap of mobile and desktop computing. In: Proceeding of the IEEE International Workshop on Wireless and Mobile Technologies in Education, pp. 91–94. IEEE (2002)

13. Fioravanti, M.L., Barbosa, E.F.: A Pedagogical Pattern Language for Mobile Learning Applications. In: Proceedings of 24th Conference on Pattern Languages of Programs (PLoP 2017), October 2017, Vancouver, BC, Canada (2017)
14. Kearney, M., Schuck, S., Burden, K., Aubusson, P.: Viewing mobile learning from a pedagogical perspective. Res. Learn. Tech. **20**, 14406 (2012)
15. Keegan, D.: The incorporation of mobile learning into mainstream education and training. In: World Conference on Mobile Learning, p. 11, Cape Town (2005)
16. Kinshuk, S.J., Sutinen, E., Goh, T.: Mobile technologies in support of distance learning. Asian J. Dist. Educ. **1**(1), 60–68 (2003)
17. Naismith, L., Lonsdale, P., Vavoula, G.N., Sharples, M.: Mobile technologies and learning (2004)
18. Nielsen, J.: Usability Engineering. Elsevier, New York (1994)
19. Nielsen, J.: Usability inspection methods. In: Conference Companion on Human Factors in Computing Systems, pp. 413–414. ACM, New York (1994)
20. O'Malley, C. et al.: Guidelines for learning/teaching/tutoring in a mobile environment (2005), public deliverable from the MOBILearn project (D.4.1)
21. Quinn, C.: mLearning: Mobile, wireless, in-your-pocket learning. LiNE Zine **2006**, 1–2 (2000)
22. Sarrab, M., Alzahrani, A., Alwan, N.A., Alfarraj, O.: From traditional learning into mobile learning in education at the university level: undergraduate students perspective. Int. J. Mob. Learn. Organ. **8**(3–4), 167–186 (2014). https://doi.org/10.1504/IJMLO.2014.067014
23. Soad, G.W., Fioravanti, M.L., Falvo Júnior, V., Marcolino, A.S., Duarte Filho, N.F., Barbosa, E.F.: ReqML-catalog: the road to a requirements catalog for mobile learning applications. In: Proceedings of the 47th Annual Frontiers in Education Conference (FIE 2017), Indianapolis, Indiana, USA, October 2017
24. Sommerville, I.: Software Engineering, 9th edn. Addison-Wesley Publishing Company, Boston (2010)
25. Strauss, A., Corbin, J.: Basics of Qualitative Research: Techniques and Procedures for Developing Grounded Theory. SAGE Publications, Thousand Oaks (1998). https://books.google.com.br/books?id=wTwYUnHYsmMC
26. Svetlana, K., et al.: Adaptation e-learning contents in mobile environment. In: Proceedings of the 2nd International Conference on Interaction Sciences: Information Technology, Culture and Human, pp. 474–479. ACM (2009)
27. Traxler, J., Leach, J.: Innovative and sustainable mobile learning in Africa. In: Proceedings of the 4th IEEE International Workshop on Wireless, Mobile and Ubiquitous Technology in Education (WMUTE 2006), pp. 98–102. IEEE (2006)
28. UNESCO: Information and communication technology in education: A curriculum for schools and programme of teacher development. UNESCO (2002)
29. Wu, W.H., Wu, Y.C.J., Chen, C.Y., Kao, H.Y., Lin, C.H., Huang, S.H.: Review of trends from mobile learning studies: a meta-analysis. Comput. Educ. **59**(2), 817–827 (2012)
30. Zamfirache, V., Olteanu, A., Tapus, N.: Collaborative learning assistant for android. In: 11th Roedunet International Conference (RoEduNet 2013), pp. 1–6. IEEE, Sinaia (2013). https://doi.org/10.1109/RoEduNet.2013.6511757

Wearable Technologies in Education: A Design Space

Vivian Genaro Motti[✉]

George Mason University, Fairfax, VA 22030, USA
vmotti@gmu.edu

Abstract. Wearable Technologies have a tremendous potential to improve education, empowering students as well as instructors in their teaching and learning experiences. Beyond the affordances of head-mounted displays to present information and of smartwatches to passively monitor students, the variety of form factors and sensors available enable a large number of applications to be developed. Their features range from data collection and monitoring of students' behaviors and affective states, to timely delivery of personalized notifications, alerts and reminders. This paper provides an overview of how wearable technologies have been applied in educational settings in recent years. Drawing on insights from students' feedback and analysis of the literature, we discuss opportunities and challenges involved when enhancing teaching and learning using wearable applications. Based on findings from a user study, we report what students would like to have available from wearable applications. Lastly, we identify actual concerns related to wearable technologies and point out the major challenges and design implications for next-generation devices.

Keywords: Wearable · Learning · Design space

1 Wearable Technologies

Research and development in wearable computing gained increasing attention in past decades thanks to numerous advances in hardware as well as software. Such advances include miniaturized electronic components, more efficient energy sources, improved network connections and data storage solutions, altogether they are responsible to boost the sales of wearable computers in the market and also the number of applications available. In addition to that, development toolkits (such as Lilypad Arduino [23] and Teknikio [43]) and dedicated operating systems (such as Android Wear OS [2] and Samsung Tizen [45]) further incentivized the research and development in the domain, enabling developers and designers to build on off-the-shelf technologies and create customized solutions of hardware and software applications. The increased popularity of wearable technologies not only ensured that users became more familiar and adapted to them, but also made wearables more affordable and accessible to a large range of users [1].

Wearable technologies are versatile thanks to diverse form factors, sensors and actuators that exist. When combined such components extend the opportunities for interactive applications to be built. Regardless of their placement on the human body, wearable technologies are promising to support and to improve the education of students [6] at various levels, in a global scale [38], across disciplines [16], and with long-term benefits [22]. Beyond serving as a performance tool to support stakeholders, wearables hold a tremendous potential to be transformative, adding value to the learning experiences, and serving as incentive to increase students' motivation and engagement levels [16]. By exploring the hands-free as well as the heads-up solutions [37], wearables are able to re-design the relationship between teaching and learning [10]. In the classroom specifically, wearable technologies can serve as a valuable asset [7].

1.1 Affordances Per Form Factor

Although diverse form factors of wearables exist [26], head-mounted and wrist-worn devices stand out in the research and development of wearable applications. Existing applications are described as follows.

Using head-mounted displays, students can immerse themselves virtually in real-world scenarios and have a full-body experience to learn diverse concepts [29] through a hands-free experience [3]. For instructors, head-mounted displays enable real-time access to feedback information about their teaching performance [48]. Virtual as well as Augmented Reality [3] are useful resources in teaching and learning, being explored to support a number of subjects [48], including surgical education [34]. Diverse types of devices can be used to implement augmented reality solutions in the classroom, including glasses and headgear that enable students to see computer-generated images imprinted on their reality [3]. Examples of immersive scenarios that can help to teach complex concepts range from surgery training [27, 44] to social and communication skills [48]. Headsets can also help with audio contents, passively delivering podcasts and audio books on demand. Head-mounted displays can offer prompt access to information, opportunities for seamless collaboration, training, and a potential for sharing and learning [15].

Wrist-worn devices offer unique opportunities for students, for instance when learning new vocabulary for a course, science [12–14, 18], physical education, mathematics [16] or even a new language. Despite smartwatches not supporting advanced renderings of graphic user interfaces when compared to head-mounted displays, these devices are lightweight and blend themselves seamlessly with students' outfits. They are also continuously available for users to access, enabling students and instructors to receive notifications and access information promptly, unobtrusively, whenever and wherever they go. Fitness trackers specifically can be valuable for users when trying to learn physical activities that require: continuous monitoring of body posture, repetitions counting, prompt feedback about physiological responses and motor skills, and brief instructions. By collecting users' data these devices help students to connect theoretical concepts to real world activities [16]. Examples of wrist-worn applications include their assessments to support dance classes, swimming, climbing [25], golf and piano lessons [19, 41].

Wearable technologies represent the next frontier in technology integration [7], but despite the growing number of research projects in the domain [39], little is known about how wearables can effectively support students' learning [18], especially in the long run, when novelty effects are less likely to interfere with the users' motivations and enthusiasm [16].

1.2 Wearable Applications in Educational Settings

The research and development of wearables in educational settings across disciplines followed the growth of the wearable market in the past years [9], with applications that aim at facilitating teaching for instructors, learning for students or monitoring tasks for practitioners. For Popat and Sharma (2013), wearable computers often perform background tasks, including: providing reminders, collecting data, and retrieving time-sensitive information in support of the user [35].

In teaching activities, smartwatches have been explored for children [13, 18], for instance using gloves to teach piano lessons [19], and glasses to enhance communication [48]. In medical education, wearables have become a widespread trend [21, 36], for instance through the usage of real-time augmented reality to improve surgical education [34].

For monitoring activities [33], attendance [22], behavior, classroom involvement [17] and engagement [7], wearable sensors have been explored to understand and analyze physiological signals and emotional responses from learners in real-time [18], to assess sleep quality, stress levels and mental health, in college students [40] and children [12]. Monitoring has also been investigated as a means to prevent academic cheating using wrist-worn devices [46].

To improve students' productivity in learning scenarios [7], smartwatch applications notify students about the time they have left for exams and in-class activities [22]. Existing projects also include the evaluation of a reading glove [42] and embodied games for math [4]. For climbing activities, a design space has been defined through user-centric design [25].

Wearable technologies have a promising potential to improve educational experiences [1] and their penetration in the market has been increasing, but in educational settings existing solutions are still limited and remain exploratory. There exists a large room for further development in the domain, and future research should unveil the opportunities and affordances of wearables to improve education [39] and fully exploit the potential of on-body interfaces in teaching and learning contexts.

1.3 Key Benefits

One of the major benefits of wearable technology is its ability to add a new engaging element to the teaching curriculum. For Labes et al. (2015), besides providing access to useful information in a timely, ubiquitous fashion [7], wearable devices can also present information in a context-sensitive and personalized manner [22]. In addition to that, wearables can serve as assistive technologies in classroom settings, for instance to support students with visual impairments [22] or intellectual disabilities [32]. For Zarraonandia et al. (2013), augmented reality systems for feedback can help to support the communication between students and instructors [48]. For Antonioli et al. (2014), despite rare, the existing tools are becoming more user-friendly and accessible. By requiring less programming and technical skills such solutions can become also more attractive to the common educator [3]. According to consumer surveys, the key advantages of wearables include: helping users to exercise (82%), helping parents to keep their children safe (73%), improving personal accountability (69%), and increasing efficiency at home (65%) and at work (63%) [28].

1.4 Major Challenges

Despite the growth in wearable market in general, and in education enhanced by wearable specifically, few examples of wearable applications in actual courses exist [1]. For Bower et al. (2016), the main reason for that is that educators do not identify sufficient pedagogical value to justify the usage of wearables in the classrooms. Besides this, it is also complex for instructors to deploy wearable technologies in their classes [9]. For Antonioli et al. (2014), most instructors do not have the ability to program their own wearable solution and have to rely on pre-made creation tools, which are not so common [3]. For students, the technologies may be too heavy, uncomfortable, embarrassing to wear [3] or difficult to learn [11]. For Alvarez et al. (2016), the wide variety of wearable devices available makes it challenging for educators to decide which technology to introduce into education contexts. They also claim that the potential of wearables in education is not yet well understood, most likely because the technology is relatively new thus research in the domain is still limited [1]. In addition to that, wearables stand on a moving ground, and rapid development of novel technologies challenge educators in properly understanding which technologies can be used in educational settings and how to maximize its benefits for students.

2 Methods

To better understand how wearable technologies have been applied in educational scenarios, in this paper we report the results of a user-centered design mixed-method approach, in which we combine a review of the literature on state-of-the-art solutions of wearables for teaching and learning with a discussion session with undergraduate students. The literature review provides a retrospective analysis of existing work in the domain and the findings from the discussion session with 40 undergraduate students provides prospective opportunities for further implementations. In the literature review we analyzed publications written in English, extracted for two digital libraries: ACM DL and Google Scholar. In the search, we primarily included 'wearable' and 'education' as keywords. No constraints regarding venue or time of publication were set for selecting the articles for analysis. Mendeley was used to assist the data collection and annotation process.

The results of the study led to a design space for wearable education, encompassing alternative form factors, key beneficiaries, use case scenarios for teaching and learning, and infrastructural solutions. We elicit and discuss system requirements, preferred features and major challenges from the end users' perspectives. By focusing on a high-level, top-down approach, the design space proposed covers subjects from multiple disciplines matching those to form factors and learning strategies.

In addition to the literature review, to identify the most convenient format to deliver content for students, we inquiry potential end users (undergraduate students) about their expectations in what regards features and form factors for educational wearables. The discussion of the data collected focuses on eliciting requirements for formats, delivery strategy and customization choices. Drawing on prior research on microinteractions [30], wrist-worn wearables are compelling to teach mainly simple concepts, such as new vocabulary, or to guide the positioning of users when trying to execute physical movements as required to play a new instrument [41]. Head-mounted displays on the other hand afford more complex scenarios that require multisensory input and output, as well as exposure to multimedia scenes, including but not limited to medical examinations and troubleshooting engines.

To gather feedback from end users, we collected data in a 1-hour long discussion session in class, retrieving information about students' experiences with wearable devices, as well as their interest and concerns about novel wearable applications in education. Through an empirical approach, drawing on the expertise of the research team, and the analysis of the findings from the literature review and students' discussion session, we assess the potential benefits and drawbacks of specific modalities and form factors, and analyze the users' responses quantitatively and qualitatively to define a set of dimensions, their granularity levels, and guidelines of the design space. Inspired by [31], our design space will inform stakeholders in the decision-making process to apply wearable technologies in their daily practices and to assess novel solutions. Unlike prior work on wearables in education from the perspective of instructors [9], which may be restricted in terms of feasibility constraints and hesitance in technology acceptance, we assessed wearable solution in the light of existing literature and the students' perspectives.

3 Results

Educational applications leveraging on wearable platforms should empower users to experience multimodal contents across different platforms seamlessly, transitioning from one device to another to access contents as needed (in the wild and on the go). We expect wearable applications in education scenarios to also allow users to customize their learning experiences according to their individual's needs and preferred modalities, through personalized learning technologies [7]. For Billinghurst and Starner (1999) a wearable computer must satisfy three major goals: (1) be mobile, (2) augment the users' reality, and (3) be context sensitive [6]. Driven by such principles, we define our design space for wearables in educational settings (Fig. 1) in terms of beneficiaries, infrastructural needs, features, and form factors.

3.1 Key Beneficiaries

Three main stakeholders benefit from wearables in education:
- **Students:** through enhanced learning experiences students are exposed to interactive materials which can improve their education, also by using wearables as

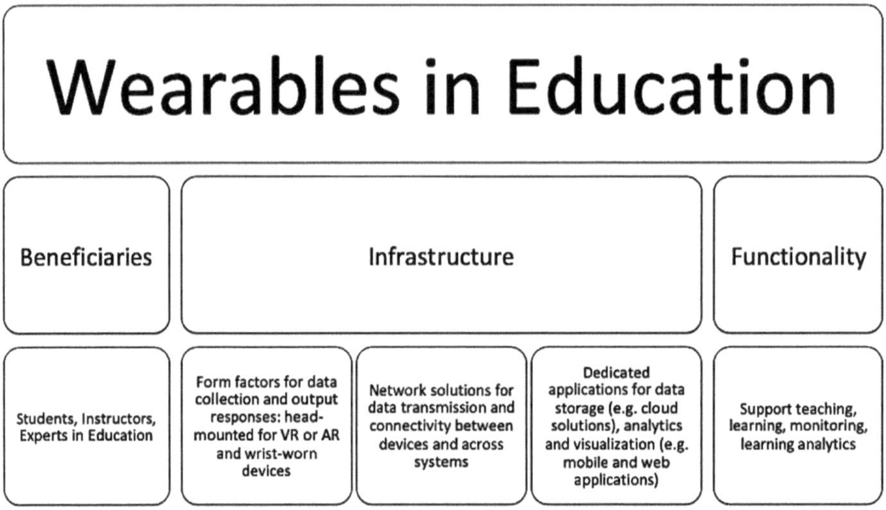

Wearables in Education

Beneficiaries	Infrastructure				Functionality
Students, Instructors, Experts in Education	Form factors for data collection and output responses: head-mounted for VR or AR and wrist-worn devices	Network solutions for data transmission and connectivity between devices and across systems	Dedicated applications for data storage (e.g. cloud solutions), analytics and visualization (e.g. mobile and web applications)		Support teaching, learning, monitoring, learning analytics

Fig. 1. Wearable technologies in educational settings – a design space.

support tools, students are more likely to succeed in their executive functions, new technologies also afford personalized and engaging strategies to deliver educational materials, such solutions are expected to enhance knowledge acquisition, retention and application. Students with diverse needs can also benefit from wearables that provide them assistance, augmenting their individual abilities.

- **Instructors:** they can become more aware about the students' performances and engagement levels in real-time in class activities, be it at the individual or collective level; through augmented solutions, instructors are able to enhance their teaching strategies on-the-fly; wearables can also facilitate content delivery, through immersive experiences for training purposes.
- **Experts in education:** the continuous data collection from wearables used to instrument students, classrooms, or instructors can help education experts in taking more informed decisions, at an individual or collective level; with the analysis of the data collected experts are empowered to identify patterns and also to draw correlations between students' performances and specific teaching styles; in addition to that, the evaluation of effectiveness of wearable teaching can assist experts in adopting strategies that can more successfully improve the education system.

3.2 Infrastructural Needs

In what regards technical infrastructure, there are four major components for wearables to support education. They are defined as follows:

- **Form factors:** the wearable devices used continuously and in direct contact with end users, with capabilities to sense data from the environment or from each individual, and to provide notifications, reminders and content delivery.

- **Network:** most wearables are not stand alone, and still rely on external devices for power, improved storage, and additional capabilities, smartwatches and fitness trackers usually depend on mobile applications to work. Similarly, head-mounted devices when not wired to desktop computers to access applications and retrieve content, also depend on wireless connections (such as Bluetooth or Wi-Fi) to run. While the connectivity extends the potential of wearable devices, it also drains their battery more quickly and may result in data loss or unstable connections depending on external factors (Bluetooth connections for instance are limited to a 100-meter range).
- **Storage:** given their limited dimensions and computational capabilities, wearables per se have reduced memory and thus frequently depend on cloud services (or external devices) to maintain the data that is collected continuously and in long term and to enable information retrieval.
- **Analytics and Visualization:** the potential to identify patterns, correlations and trends in the data collected through wearables adds value to the educational experiences, therefore to fully exploit it, wearable applications should have available tools that are dedicated to the exploration of the data collected, facilitating its interpretation and sense-making by stakeholders, be it end users at the individual level, or instructors collectively.

Wearable experiences should be interactive and adaptive allowing students to express themselves freely, to assess their understanding of the subject through the application and to receive contents and feedback that are tailored to their specific needs and profiles. For future avenues, we expect the data collection with wearable sensors to facilitate the identification of individual profiles, improving teaching strategies and enhancing learning outcomes with more personalized solutions.

3.3 Wearable Features

Depending on the functionality implemented in the wearable, the target users, use case scenarios, as well as the sensors available, the wearable applications envisaged in an educational context can serve multiple purposes. From a high-level perspective, werarables serve to collect data from users (be it behavioral data or environmental data), to process and interpreted the data collected, and to deliver reminders, notifications, alerts and feedback for end users. When analyzing prior work in the domain, we note a wide range of applications that have been explored. These applications are detailed in Table 1, including the form factor used, the activity supported, the study population, and subject.

Instructors' Perspectives
The literature reports benefits for instructors to receive feedback in real time when teaching [8], including information about how engaged or confused the students are at a given time [48]. For Bower and Sturman (2015), wearables help instructors to record data, to simulate scenarios, to support communication, to increase engagement, to guide users, and to gamify users' experiences [8]. In terms of non-functional requirements, they highlight the efficiency of the solutions ("faster access to

Table 1. An overview of wearable technologies (wrist-worn and head-mounted devices) in educational settings: 8 case studies.

Form factor	Task	Population & time	Subject	
Wrist-worn Fitbit	Collect, analyze and visualize data	K-12 students (teenagers), 2 weeks	Math, science, physical education	[16]
Smartwatch ASUS Zenwatch 2	Reflected learning (self-efficacy)	Children (n = 18), 5 weeks	Science	[18]
Head-mounted Glass for AR	Communication system for instructors (feedback)	Instructors (n = 20) and students (n = 70), during 7 weeks, 2-h lectures	Programming classes	[48]
Glass for mixed reality Epson Emotiv EPOC Oculus Rift	Wild-life preservation (serious games), brain science research, role-playing for training	Higher education, undergraduate students paired in small groups (n = 5), 2-h sessions	Environmental education Cognitive and brain sciences Teacher training	[1]
Glass (AR)	Transmit medical procedures (broadcasting)	Medical students (n = 1)	Surgery	[21]
Glass (AR)	Support experiments	High school (n = 36)	Physics (acoustics)	[24]
e-Textiles Lilypad Arduino	Makers workshop for training	Teenaged students (n = 10), 1 week	Science discovery	[11]
e-Textiles Teeboard	Learn how to prototype and program wearable electronics	Teenaged students (n = 25), 5-day workshop	Computing and engineering	[31]

information"), unobtrusive feedback, and context-sensitive information (e.g. depending on the users' location).

Students' Perspectives

To complement the analysis from previous literature and gather students' insights on wearable solutions that would be helpful for them in postsecondary education, we asked 40 undergraduate students about their preferred features. The students who participated in the study follow an Information Technology major. As main features for wearables in educational settings, they mentioned: (1) check-in (attendance taking), (2) monitoring and tracking, (3) access control, (4) notifications and (5) information delivery as the top features of their preference (Table 2). Ten students (out of 40) already owned a wearable device (fitness tracker or smartwatch). All students, except one, proposed features for wrist-worn wearables, likely because of the easier access and popularity of this specific form factor. A glass application was proposed to help with record keeping of the lectures.

Table 2. Preferred features for wearable computers in assisting students' education.

Check-in	take attendance	12
Monitoring	attention, health, stress levels, heart rate, behavior	9
Tracking	miles, classes, parking, movement	8
Access Control	biometrics	6
Notifications	reminders, timer, alarm, alert, question, parking, delay, next class	6
Class Information	record, notes, aids, personalized	6
Intervention	wellbeing, health, focus	5
Q+A	clicker	5
Organization	schedule	4
Navigation	maps, on campus, classrooms	3
Communication	connection	3
Emergency contact	urgent events, crisis	2
Reservation	room	1

3.4 Implementation Challenges

There are several obstacles that challenge the acceptance, adoption and sustained engagement of wearable computers in educational settings in a large scale. Among those, we can highlight that the widespread adoption of wearables raises privacy and security concerns in what regards the students' data [16]. Also, wearable solutions may rely and depend on outside vendors for storage, retrieval and analysis. Lastly, the costs associated to wearable can limit their access to students depending on socioeconomic status [7], which could contribute to further increase inequality and digital exclusion as well.

From the analysis of the students' perspectives, we learned that the major concerns they have are: fear of distraction, issues with connectivity and compatibility, problems to learn how to efficiently use the device and application (need for high usability levels in order to ensure acceptance and sustain adoption), fear of high costs to afford the technology, battery issues and privacy concerns.

From the analysis of the literature, we note that there are common concerns when comparing students' responses and investigators' perspectives, including the challenges related to affordability [7, 22, 35], technical infrastructure [5, 8, 26], distraction [3, 8, 9], security [10], inequalities, dependence [8], ethics [16] and privacy [7, 9]. For Labus et al. (2015), if wearable devices are used in the process of learning, their interaction must be simple and intuitive, to minimize the cognitive load on learners and allow them to fully focus on main tasks [22]. For Zarraonandia et al. (2017) students fear the constant recording of their actions and may also hesitate to adopt the technology;

therefore brief trainings are recommended to reduce students' anxiety [48]. For Antonioli et al. (2014) hardware as well as software malfunctions can impair the learning experiences of students [3].

Concerns that were exclusively remarked in the scientific literature include: the volatility of the wearable market [48], which can challenge sustained adoption of wearable solutions; need to calibrate the devices for each individual student [3, 16]; data ownership and the access to the data collected, when conducting research studies in scale, since some wearable devices (such as Fitbit) restrict data access in their proprietary software [16]. In addition to that, the continuous data collection also results in large data sets, which can be overwhelming for posterior analysis [16]. Lastly, the process of synchronizing, accessing and converting each individual's data is not only complicated but also time-consuming [16].

Although privacy concerns have been reported by students and in prior work in the literature, they are more frequent in an adult population, especially among investigators and instructors. Egen et al. (2018) report that the teenaged students who participated in their study were not overly concerned about privacy issues, mostly because of a limited understanding about the privacy risks associated with tracking technologies [16]. Privacy challenges can be exacerbated if the students belong to a vulnerable population –including minors [16] or students with intellectual disabilities [32]– and also when the data collected by wearables is stored in cloud services, which may not comply with laws and governmental policies that protect students' privacy (e.g. FERPA in the U.S. [47]). Connections from unauthorized parties can also pose additional risks in what regards access to the student's data and tampered notifications.

4 Final Remarks

Advances in wearable technologies have facilitated access to the devices and enabled more research and development to be conducted in the domain. Despite the growth in the use of wearable devices in recent years [20] and the consensus of promising opportunities across domains, most of the research is still exploratory in an attempt to unveil the hidden opportunities for wearables to improve education. The uptake of wearable technologies in higher education has not yet been fully realized [9], but preliminary findings demonstrate that there is a large potential for wearables to enhance students experience when learning new concepts across disciplines.

A number of questions remain open [10], leading to a research roadmap in wearable learning. These questions involve: (1) the design for a multi-device learning environment; (2) the assessment of the added value of wearable learning in what regards the cost of devices and implementation; and (3) the enhancements in teaching and learning experiences in a sustained manner. The effect of time on students' motivations and enthusiasm to use wearables in the long run is unclear, since most studies were conducted in short durations. Even though there is a consensus in the community that privacy concerns are important, there are no consolidated solutions available to ensure that students' have their right to privacy assured, mostly because existing technological solutions are in their infancy, and the privacy risks, threats and implications are still unclear.

References

1. Alvarez, V., Bower, M., de Freitas, S., Gregory, S., de Wit, B.: The use of wearable technologies in Australian universities: examples from environmental science, cognitive and brain sciences and teacher training. In: Dyson, L.E., Ng, W., Fergusson, J. (eds.) Mobile Learning Futures–Sustaining Quality Research and Practice in Mobile Learning, pp. 25–32 (2016). University of Technology, Sydney
2. Android Wear OS (Operating System). https://wearos.google.com/. Accessed 24 Jan 2019
3. Antonioli, M., Blake, C., Sparks, K.: Augmented reality applications in education. J. Technol. Stud. **40**(1/2), 96–107 (2014). http://www.jstor.org/stable/43604312
4. Arroyo, I., Micciollo, M., Casano, J., Ottmar, E., Hulse, T., Rodrigo, M.M.: Wearable learning: multiplayer embodied games for math. In: Proceedings of the Annual Symposium on Computer-Human Interaction in Play (CHI PLAY 2017), pp. 205–216. ACM, New York (2017). https://doi.org/10.1145/3116595.3116637
5. Attallah, B., Ilagure, Z.: Wearable technology: facilitating or complexing education? Int. J. Inform. Educ. Technol. **8**(6), 433–436 (2018). https://doi.org/10.1504/IJGUC.2019.097227
6. Billinghurst, M., Starner, T.: Wearable devices: new ways to manage information. Computer **32**(1), 57–64 (1999)
7. Borthwick, A.C., Anderson, C.L., Finsness, E.S., Foulger, T.S.: Special article personal wearable technologies in education: value or villain? J. Digit. Learn. Teacher Educ. **31**(3), 85–92 (2015)
8. Bower, M., Sturman, D.: What are the educational affordances of wearable technologies? Comput. Educ. **88**, 343–353 (2015)
9. Bower, M., Sturman, D., Alvarez, V.: Perceived utility and feasibility of wearable technologies in higher education. In: Mobile Learning Futures–Sustaining Quality Research and Practice in Mobile Learning, p. 49 (2016)
10. Bartlett-Bragg, A.: Wearable technologies: shaping the future of learning. Training Dev. **41**(3), 13 (2014)
11. Buechley, L., Eisenberg, M., Catchen, J., Crockett, A.: The LilyPad Arduino: using computational textiles to investigate engagement, aesthetics, and diversity in computer science education. In: Proceedings of the SIGCHI conference on Human Factors in Computing Systems (CHI 2008), pp. 423–432. ACM, New York, USA, April 2008. https://doi.org/10.1145/1357054.1357123
12. Byrne, V.L., Kang, S., Norooz, L., Velez, R., Katzen, M., Clegg, T.: Scaffolding authentic wearable-based scientific inquiry for early elementary learners. In: ICLS 2018 Proceedings (2018)
13. Chu, S.L., Garcia, B.M.: Toward wearable app design for children's in-the-world science inquiry. In: Proceedings of the Eleventh International Conference on Tangible, Embedded, and Embodied Interaction (TEI 2017), pp. 121–130. ACM, New York (2017). https://doi.org/10.1145/3024969.3025008
14. Clegg, T., et al.: Live physiological sensing and visualization ecosystems: an activity theory analysis. In: Proceedings of the 2017 CHI Conference on Human Factors in Computing Systems (CHI 2017), pp. 2029–2041. ACM, New York (2017). https://doi.org/10.1145/3025453.3025987
15. Coffman, T., Klinger, M.B.: Google Glass: using wearable technologies to enhance teaching and learning. In: Society for Information Technology & Teacher Education International Conference, pp. 1777–1780. Association for the Advancement of Computing in Education (AACE), March 2015

16. Engen, B.K., Giæver, T.H., Mifsud, L.: Wearable technologies in the K-12 classroom—cross-disciplinary possibilities and privacy pitfalls. J. Interact. Learn. Res. **29**(3), 323–341 (2018). Waynesville: Association for the Advancement of Computing in Education (AACE). https://www.learntechlib.org/primary/p/184757/. Accessed 24 Jan 2019
17. Ezenwoke, A., Ezenwoke, O., Adewumi, A., Omoregbe, N.: Wearable technology: opportunities and challenges for teaching and learning in higher education in developing countries. In: Proceedings of INTED 2016 Conference, pp. 1872–1979, Valencia, Spain, 7–9 March 2016
18. Garcia, B., Chu, S.L., Nam, B., Banigan, C.: Wearables for learning: examining the smartwatch as a tool for situated science reflection. In: Proceedings of the 2018 CHI Conference on Human Factors in Computing Systems (CHI 2018), p. 256, 13 pages. ACM, New York, USA, April 2018. https://doi.org/10.1145/3173574.3173830
19. Hsiao, C., Li, R., Yan, X., Yi-Luen Do, E.: Tactile teacher: sensing finger tapping in piano playing. In: Proceedings of the Ninth International Conference on Tangible, Embedded, and Embodied Interaction (TEI 2015), pp. 257–260. ACM, New York (2015). https://doi.org/10.1145/2677199.2680554
20. Hitlin, P.: Internet, social media use and device ownership in U.S. have plateaued after years of growth. Pew Research Center (2018). Accessed 31 Jan 2019
21. Knight, H.M., Gajendragadkar, P.R., Bokhari, A.: Wearable technology: using Google Glass as a teaching tool. BMJ case reports, bcr2014208768 (2015). https://doi.org/10.1136/bcr-2014-208768
22. Labus, A., Milutinovic, M., Stepanic, Ð., Stevanovic, M., Milinovic, S.: Wearable computing in e-education. J. Univ. Excellence **4**(1), A39–A51 (2015), Appendix March 2015, ISSN: 2232-5204
23. LilyPad Arduino. https://www.arduino.cc/en/Main/ArduinoBoardLilyPad/. Accessed 24 Jan 2019
24. Lukowicz, P., et al.: Glass-physics: using Google Glass to support high school physics experiments. In: Proceedings of the 2015 ACM International Symposium on Wearable Computers (ISWC 2015), pp. 151–154. ACM, New York, USA (2015). https://doi.org/10.1145/2802083.2808407
25. Mencarini, E., Leonardi, C., Angeli, A., Zancanaro, M.: Design opportunities for wearable devices in learning to climb. In: Proceedings of the 9th Nordic Conference on Human-Computer Interaction (NordiCHI 2016). ACM, New York (2016). Article 48, 10 p. https://doi.org/10.1145/2971485.2971509
26. Motti, V.G., Caine, K.: Human factors considerations in the design of wearable devices. In: Proceedings of the Human Factors and Ergonomics Society Annual Meeting, vol. 58, no. 1, pp. 1820–1824. SAGE Publications, Los Angeles, September 2014
27. Guze, P.A.: Using technology to meet the challenges of medical education. Trans. Am. Clin. Climatol. Assoc. **126**, 260 (2015)
28. PwC: The wearable life 2.0: Connected living in a wearable world (2017). https://www.pwc.se/sv/pdf-reports/the-wearable-life-2-0.pdf. Accessed 31 Jan 2019
29. Makransky, G., Wismer, P., Mayer, R.E.: A gender matching effect in learning with pedagogical agents in an immersive virtual reality science simulation. J. Comput. Assist. Learn. **35**(3), 349–358 (2018)
30. Motti, V.G., Caine, K.: Micro interactions and multi dimensional graphical user interfaces in the design of wrist worn wearables. In: Proceedings of the Human Factors and Ergonomics Society Annual Meeting, vol. 59, no. 1, pp. 1712–1716. SAGE Publications, Los Angeles, September 2015
31. Ngai, G., Chan, S.C., Cheung, J.C., Lau, W.W.: Deploying a wearable computing platform for computing education. IEEE Trans. Learn. Technol. **3**(1), 45–55 (2010)

32. Zheng, H., Motti, V.G.: Assisting students with intellectual and developmental disabilities in inclusive education with smartwatches. In: Proceedings of the 2018 CHI Conference on Human Factors in Computing Systems (CHI 2018), p. 350, 12 pages. ACM, New York, USA, April 2018. https://doi.org/10.1145/3173574.3173924
33. Müller, L.: Pervasive monitoring to support reflective learning. In: Proceedings of the 2013 ACM conference on Pervasive and Ubiquitous Computing Adjunct Publication (UbiComp 2013 Adjunct), pp. 349–354. ACM, New York, USA, September 2013. https://doi.org/10.1145/2494091.2501088
34. Ponce, B.A., Menendez, M.E., Oladeji, L.O., Fryberger, C.T., Dantuluri, P.K.: Emerging technology in surgical education: combining real-time augmented reality and wearable computing devices. Orthopedics **37**(11), 751–757 (2014)
35. Popat, K.A., Sharma, P.: Wearable computer applications a future perspective. Int. J. Eng. Innovative Technol. **3**(1), 213–217 (2013)
36. Regal, G., Wais-Zechmann, B., Gattol, V., Garschall, M., Tscheligi, M.: Smart pocket watch: exploring the design space for wearable technology in healthcare. In: Proceedings of the 11th PErvasive Technologies Related to Assistive Environments Conference (PETRA 2018), pp. 269–272. ACM, New York, USA, June 2018. https://doi.org/10.1145/3197768.3201524
37. Sapargaliyev, D.: Learning with wearable technologies: a case of Google glass. In: Brown, T.H., van der Merwe, H.J. (eds.) mLearn 2015. CCIS, vol. 560, pp. 343–350. Springer, Cham (2015). https://doi.org/10.1007/978-3-319-25684-9_25
38. Samdanis, M., Kim, Y., Lee, S.H.: The emergence of wearable space: a review and research implications. In: CHI Extended Abstracts on Human Factors in Computing Systems (2013)
39. Sandall, B.K.: Wearable technology and schools: where are we and where do we go from here? J. Curriculum Teach. Learn. Leadersh. Educ. **1**(1), 9 (2016)
40. Sano, A., et al.: Recognizing academic performance, sleep quality, stress level, and mental health using personality traits, wearable sensors and mobile phones. In: 2015 IEEE 12th International Conference on Wearable and Implantable Body Sensor Networks (BSN), pp. 1–6. IEEE, June 2015. https://doi.org/10.1109/BSN.2015.7299420
41. Seim, C., Estes, T., Starner, T.: Towards passive haptic learning of piano songs. In: World Haptics Conference (WHC), 2015 IEEE, pp. 445–450. IEEE, June 2015. https://doi.org/10.1109/WHC.2015.7177752
42. Tanenbaum, K., Tanenbaum, J., Antle, A.N., Bizzocchi, J., Seif el-Nasr, M., Hatala, M.: Experiencing the reading glove. In: Proceedings of the Fifth International Conference on Tangible, Embedded, and Embodied Interaction (TEI 2011), pp. 137–144. ACM, New York, USA, January 2011. https://doi.org/10.1145/1935701.1935728
43. Teknikio. https://www.teknikio.com/. Accessed 12 Feb 2019
44. Thomsen, A.S.S., et al.: Operating room performance improves after proficiency-based virtual reality cataract surgery training. Ophthalmology **124**(4), 524–531 (2017)
45. Tizen OS, Samsung. https://www.tizen.org/. Accessed 12 Feb 2019
46. Wong, S., Yang, L., Riecke, B., Cramer, E., Neustaedter, C.: Assessing the usability of smartwatches for academic cheating during exams. In: Proceedings of the 19th International Conference on Human-Computer Interaction with Mobile Devices and Services (MobileHCI 2017). ACM, New York (2017). Article 31, 11 p. https://doi.org/10.1145/3098279.3098568
47. US Department of Education. Family educational rights and privacy act (FERPA) (2015)
48. Zarraonandia, T., Díaz, P., Montero, Á., Aedo, I., Onorati, T.: Using a Google Glass-based classroom feedback system to improve students to teacher communication. IEEE Access, **7**, 16837–16846 (2019). https://doi.org/10.1109/ACCESS.2019.2893971

Ready, Steady, Move! Coding Toys, Preschoolers, and Mobile Playful Learning

Katriina Heljakka[1] and Pirita Ihamäki[2(✉)]

[1] University of Turku, Pori, Finland
[2] Prizztech Ltd., Pori, Finland
`pirita.ihamaki@prizz.fi`

Abstract. This paper introduces a study focusing on preschool children's employment of coding toys as a part of their daily play activities. Twenty preschoolers, aged 5–6 years, and their preschool teachers participated in a three-month study of playful learning and the STEM topic of coding. The main interest was to explore how preschoolers explore, utilize, and challenge the hybrid play affordances of the Dash robot, in relation to coding exercises, and how their teachers concurrently expanded their own knowledge of how a contemporary smart toy can support the learning of 21st-century skills. We approached this two-part research question through a multimethod approach, including diary methods, thematic teacher interviews, and an analysis of preschoolers' own videos of their play sessions. The findings of our study highlight the mobility aspect of the playful learning of coding with Dash. Our study also shows how preschoolers quickly learned to build obstacle courses for Dash by coding them with an app on an iPad, and how the movement of the toy inspired the preschoolers to come up with new play ideas, incorporating themselves as players. In light of these findings, the authors suggest that coding toys, such as Dash, can be evaluated from the perspective of mobile playful learning, which centers around the use of interactive, smart, and mobile toys. Our study also shows that these toys playfully invite and encourage young learners to physical activity while they learn the logic and skills related to coding.

Keywords: Internet of Play · Mobile playful learning · Coding toys · Internet of Toys · Physical activity

1 Introduction

The *Internet of Play* refers to a future in which smart playthings not only relate one-on-one to children, but also represent screenless toys and other interactive experiences that are wirelessly connected to the Internet. Key affordances of the so-called Internet of Toys (IoToys) include linked interaction that is guided by sound, light, and movement. Many of these contemporary, connected toys are, thanks to their technological enhancements, suitable for use in the early learning of STEM subjects, including coding. Furthermore, most of the IoToys, which both enable movement and function as a tool for teaching coding, are composed of playthings that are mobilized by the players through commands simulating coding language. Some of the toys, such as the Dash robot, are coded by the players to move through obstacle paths using an app. Earlier studies have demonstrated how elements of the IoToys, such as the coding toy that Wonder Workshop's Dash robot represents, facilitate skill-building related to 21st-century skills such as multiliteracy and transmedia play [1]. In our understanding, coding, as a part of current STEM education, develops capabilities in problem-solving and ludic literacy—playful communication skills essential for understanding how technologies work in the current landscape of playful interactive media.

Play itself, often recognized as the "work" of children, is a "primary affective motivational" activity that facilitates the development of different skills [2]. During the past few years, playful learning, gamified education, and digital learning materials have gained growing interest among Finnish educators [3, 4]. Besides the activity of playing, there is an interest in integrating physical activity into different school subjects. Play supported by gamification, physical activity, and experimental approaches in early education have been highlighted as important means to facilitate playful learning and to strengthen the possibilities of thinking creatively. Physical activity has also been categorized into physical, social, and mental performance, guided by play, the playing of games, or both [5]. In this way, play and games function as tools in the learning of various subjects. For example, according to Downess, the playing of games on the streets steers learning styles toward active exploration. A major part of this playful learning is guided by the use of technologies [6]. Preschoolers—in the context of our research, Finnish kindergarten students between the ages of 5 and 6 years—are very familiar with mobile technology. For example, in some kindergartens, preschool-aged children are being introduced to the use of tablets on a daily basis as part of early education.

This study focuses on the mobility aspect of coding toys, which are an emerging sub-category of the IoToys. Our aim is two-fold: first, in addition to investigating the evolution of play in the digitalized world, our goal is to understand the universal educational value of coding toys as tools for playful learning. Second, we are interested in the toys' particular value for the Finnish early education curriculum. This paper presents a case study in the use of coding toys as a part of playful learning in Finnish kindergartens. In our study, 20 preschool-aged children, each of whom had their own tablets in kindergarten, engaged with the Dash robot over a three-month period. The preschool teachers used this coding toy with small groups of children by first introducing the toy, and then giving the preschoolers an assignment to code with Dash. The preschool-aged children coded the toy using iPads through a coding app, and made the toy move along trails.

The article is organized as follows: we first explain the concept of *playful learning* and describe how current elements of the IoToys, such as coding toys, may be viewed as edutainment that belongs to the ecosystem of connected play, or what we call here the Internet of Play. This is followed by a discussion of the Internet of Play, with a special focus on the learning context and the role of the IoToys in early education. We then present our case study of coding toys, as a sub-category of the IoToys, used in a preschool context. We describe how teachers have used Wonder Workshop's Dash robot toy in early education, and how preschool children have responded by using Dash in their play. In the subsequent section, we discuss the results and limitations of our study and propose further ideas for what should be considered when using coding toys in future preschool education. Finally, we suggest how the phenomenon under scrutiny could be studied in the next phases of research.

2 The Internet of Play as a Context for Playful Learning

The Internet may be viewed as a worldwide playground that presents plentiful opportunities for learning. Play is considered an important part of learning processes, and teachers' responsibilities to facilitate play in preschool learning was elucidated in Scandinavian curricula as early as 1998 by, for example, the Department of Education in Sweden and the Stockholm Ministry of Education and Science. The Department of Education has also pointed out that play and joyful learning stimulate several abilities, including fantasy, empathy, communication, symbolic thinking, collaboration, and problem-solving [7]. The Internet of Play as a learning setting refers to (1) learning that allows, stimulates, and promotes learner creativity and knowledge-collaboration working skills; (2) learning exercises using tools, such as the IoToys, for "edutainment" purposes; and (3) promotion of learning through a variety of playful and physical activities.

Kangas described playfulness, creativity, narration, collaboration, insight, emotions, embodiment, and activity as central to creativity and playful learning. Playfulness refers to an attitude toward learning and a way of learning through play and games within the playful learning environment (PLE) [8]. Creativity refers to creative knowledge that may be developed by learning how to use new technology, such as connected or "smart" toys and games [9]. Narration refers to a storytelling mode of thinking and understanding as a key aspect of meaning-making [10–12]. One way to make sense of experience and the world while learning is through narratives; by using the possibilities of the Internet of Play, we can become involved with global narratives.

Collaboration emphasizes co-design, knowledge co-creation, and play processes. Collaboration helps and motivates children to learn and engage cognitively [13]. Insight refers to the opportunity to explore and solve problems [14]. Emotions are involved in all human activity, which give them a key role in thinking and learning [15, 16]. Embodiment and activity refer to physical activities in which children use the whole body in the learning processes through which embodied knowledge can be achieved [17].

There are many opportunities for social play, whether competing against each other or collaborating to achieve a common goal through physical activities. This can involve having fun with technology, whether it be in peer-to-peer play or collaborative play on tablets with smart toys, or in how children play together and become involved in physical activities. Today, the IoToys have extended children's desire to play with smart toys and coding toys, which makes it possible for children to create their own culture through the Internet of Play, with the help of some guidance from teachers and parents.

2.1 The Internet of Toys and Coding Toys

This paper discusses the IoToys, with a particular emphasis on coding toys, within wider theoretical debates about the affordances of new digital materialities and their employment in toy-based learning. To understand recent transformations of children's digitalizing play practices, following Berriman and Mascheroni, we suggest that it is necessary to consider physical toys' capabilities for connecting to wider digital ecosystems.

The IoToys "has brought talking dolls, interactive pets, and programmable robots into western children's play worlds" [18]. Producers of these contemporary smart toys enhance physical toys with features such as sensors, speech-recognition, and network connectivity and, in this way, offer new interactive and personalized play experiences [ibid.].

Smart toys have also become the subject of increasing research interest. Previous research has focused largely on the suitability of the IoToys in education (see e.g., [1, 19–26]). This paper contributes to this growing research field by proposing new ways of theorizing coding toys in early education as a sub-category of the IoToys. Researchers claim that the IoToys have significantly transformed how children and toys interact, giving rise to new forms of play that challenge boundaries between the material and digital. Moreover, the IoToys increasingly share characteristics with domestic media and computing devices [18], such as the Dash robot. The robot has multiple apps, one of which is the Blockly App, which is in standard use in elementary schools and recommended for children by Code.org. With Blockly, "your child or student can take on coding challenges and make their own programs for Dash. […] you can create your own dance, record your voice, and have Dash play it back, play tag, or even program Dash to follow you around. With the new tutorial section, it is possible to program with no previous experience". [27] While this programmable robot is sold directly to families, Dash and its counterpart, Dot, have become part of schools' curricula and coding clubs. According to Kolodny, some 8,500 schools are now using Dash and Dot around the world for such purposes [ibid.].

In recent years, new learning standards and best practices for integrating technology into early childhood education have gained more interest [28]. To teach technology and engineering to young children in a developmentally appropriate way, robotics and computer programming initiatives have grown in popularity among early education researchers and educators [29]. Earlier research has shown, for example, how the field of robotics holds special potential for early education by facilitating both cognitive and social development [30]. Recent research suggests that children as young as 4 years old can successfully build and program simple robotics projects, while learning a range of engineering and robotics concepts in the process [31, 32]. Using coding toys and computer programming in early education has been claimed to support cognitive and social development; studies with the text-based language *Logo* have, for example, shown that computer programming can help young children with a variety of cognitive skills, including number sense, language skills, and visual memory [33]. It is notable how many robotics activities do not involve sitting alone in front of a computer; rather, they encourage play: robotic manipulatives allow children to develop fine motor skills and hand-eye coordination while also engaging in collaboration and teamwork [34]—a finding that the current case study with Dash also supports. For instance, Dash encourages children to move physically, such as running after the toy. Furthermore, when children learn a programming language, they are not "just learning code, they are coding to learn" [35].

 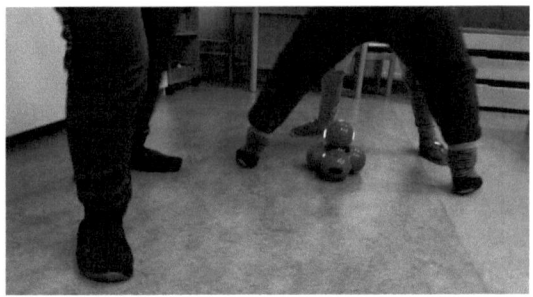

Fig. 1. (On the left). The coding toy Dash by Wonder Workshop moves fast.

Fig. 2. (On the right). Dash is coded to move along paths created by the players.

2.2 Playful Learning

Playfulness, as a part of the learning process, is a broad and complex phenomenon; it involves the learner's attitude, orientation, engagements, and capability for collaboration. "Playfulness as an orientation to activity also has a misbehaving stance, a disposition toward joking, breaking rules, pushing the cover of normal modes of activity, an alternation between serious intent and non-serious probing of possibilities" [36]. In learning, playfulness refers to the learning actions and their qualities [37]. Related literature suggests that playfulness is assumed to have positive effects on learning in different playgrounds; at various school levels, as well as learning in working life [38]. Kangas defined a PLE as a pedagogically validated learning environment that combines information and communication technologies both in the classroom and in the outdoor playground. A PLE is the basis for a variety of learning experiences in local schools, as well as in Internet games, which offer opportunities for learning in globally created learning environments [8]. The point of departure for our study was to evaluate preschool children's play practices and coding exercises with the Dash robot (see Fig. 1). What guided our interest was an investigation of the creative and playful learning processes for which the use of the toy provides. In this study, we extended the PLE to the context of mobility and investigated how preschool children explore, utilize, and challenge the affordances of the coding toy. We were also interested in how preschool teachers build their knowledge of how contemporary smart toys support the learning of 21st-century skills, such as coding.

3 Methods

3.1 Goal of the Study and Research Questions

The goal of the study was to investigate preschool children's play and learning, and their teachers' experiences with a coding toy in an early education setting in Finland. We sought to examine how children approach playful learning with a coding toy, and to contrast the use of the coding toy Dash in learning processes that are based on edutainment, collaborative education, and playing, with a typical coding classroom in which children are usually sitting on chairs.

In our study, we asked the following research questions:

1. How do preschool-aged children play and learn with a coding toy in the context of early education, given opportunities to use the toy in playful learning both (a) solitarily and (b) socially?
2. To what kinds of new knowledge does a coding toy like Dash contribute for preschool teachers, when used as a tool for toy-based learning?

3.2 Research Design, Data Collection, and Data Analysis

In this study, we have used a multimethod approach to understand the complexity of coding toys' play and educational value for children. We used the diary method by creating a Google Drive diary for the preschool teachers, which we followed and analyzed over a three-month period. In the diary document, the teachers wrote about their experiences of the coding toy itself, how they used the toy as a part of their early education processes, how the preschool children played with the toy, and what they learned from playing with the toy.

The study also employed research material collected by the two teachers, who photographed and videotaped the children playing with the Dash robot. The preschool children also made videos of each other playing with the coding toy.

The multimethod approach allowed us to conduct both a narrative and visual analysis of the data. We also analyzed the material using content analysis. The rich data set gave us a comprehensive overview of how the coding toy was used in the Finnish early education environment and a firsthand understanding of what kinds of values the coding toy communicated while being used in playful learning. We analyzed the data using content analysis to form a holistic perspective of the value of coding toys for playful learning. We also compared the children's testimonials of their memorable experiences with the coding toy, which gave a holistic overview of their perspective, especially in terms of how they explained their encounters with Dash the robot, such as the play scenario in which they ran around following it.

3.3 Participants

The study was conducted between November 2018 and February 2019 with two preschool groups at a Finnish kindergarten. The participants (N = 20) were 5–6 years old. All children had their own iPads during their year in preschool, which they used daily for both entertainment and edutainment. We gave the preschool two smart toys—Wonder Workshop's Dash robot and Fisher-Price's Smart Toy Bear—to use in preschool education. In this part of the study, we focus on the programmable Dash robot, which is considered a coding toy. First, the participants were introduced to the coding toy and guided by the researchers to use the *Path* app on their tablets. Smaller groups of children (3–5 participants) then started to play with the robot and practice the coding, which they continued over the three-month research period.

4 Results: Play in the Mobile Playful Learning Environment

Collaborative problem-solving, in combination with play, encourages children to learn. The flipped classroom is a recently emerged and popular technology-infused learning model. Hamdan et al. offered the following definition: "In the Flipped Learning model, teachers shift direct learning out of the large group learning space and move it into the individual learning space, with the help of one of several technologies" [39]. In other words, this is a learning model in which content attainment shifts out of the normal classroom into the mobile context, such as in our case study, which used a coding toy with mobile app-enabled activities.

To analyze the content attainment and application stages of playful learning, we used Bybee's 5-E learning cycle. The 5-E cycle consists of five instructional phases, which we applied to the insights collected from our research materials related to the *mobile playful learning environment* (MPLE), which we also refer to as the Internet of Play [40]. The first three phases (engagement, exploration, and explanation) facilitate content attainment. The elaboration phase is when preschoolers apply the concepts they constructed in the content attainment stage, and represents the concept application stage [41]. We use these phases to elaborate on the results of our study:

- *Engagement*: The preschool children used the Path app to program the robot using a single line of code on an obstacle course of their own. The preschoolers engaged with Dash by coding the toy, and in so doing made other children run after the toy, and to create obstacles for it (see Fig. 2). In this way, the children discovered "fun learning" experiences by familiarizing themselves with coding.
- *Exploration*: The Path app allowed the preschool children to explore the educational content of the toy and to construct their own understanding, before introducing what they had learned to the other children. In this case study, the preschoolers actively engaged with the coding toy to explore educational patterns (coding exercises), and they also employed the flipped classroom approach by teaching other children what they had previously learned.
- *Explanation*: By playing with the Dash robot through coding exercises on the Path app, the preschoolers learned new ways to code and collaborated by teaching their peers how they had played with the robot. This showed how the preschoolers could link their own constructions to facilitate collaborative knowledge-building.
- *Elaboration*: The coding with Dash also gave the preschoolers the option to learn more about coding if they wanted to create more elaborate obstacle paths for the robot. The preschoolers also wanted to film their own play with Dash and to make short videos of their coding exercises. One of the observations we made was that when a preschooler learned something new, he or she wanted to share this with others, who then wanted to do the same. Creating videos with Dash also demonstrated the children's willingness to participate in the creation and sharing of documentation of play and, in this way, to participate socially in contemporary play culture.

- *Evaluation*: Coding with the Dash robot serves as an example of the engagement with the Internet of Play, which can take the form of both formative and summative assessments that test preschoolers' understanding of the concepts they have just learned. In this case study, the evaluation took the form of children videotaping their own memorable experiences of the coding exercises and free-form play with the Dash robot. In the research materials collected, the participants described learning coding, teaching others, and creating new games with and for Dash, and for the other children.

4.1 Modes of Mobile Playful Learning: Solitary and Social Play

This study shows that the participating preschoolers experienced *mobile playful learning* when engaging with the coding toy Dash. The engagement happened in three ways: (1) the preschoolers interacted with the Dash robot solitarily through bodily motion (they made eye contact with Dash, which has sensors and voice recognition); (2) the preschoolers coded their own trails and made Dash move; and (3) the preschoolers became socially mobile by running after Dash and trying to catch it, or by coding obstacle paths for it together with other children. Through these forms of engagement, the children not only learned themselves, but also started to teach their peers and, in this way, used what they knew in the flipped classroom approach.

The findings of the study show that by far the most engaging aspects of play were connected to social interaction with Dash, when one child controlled the tablet to move the Dash robot, and the other children in the group ran after Dash. The preschoolers also made their own rules of play for coding the Dash robot's path. For example, they decided that one child would code for about 10 or 15 min, after which it would be someone else's turn, and the first child would get to run after the toy. This example shows how the preschoolers innovated their own play patterns for coding in the mobile playful environment. The children also started to use the flipped classroom idea by teaching others coding, thereby engaging in social playful learning and learning in a collaborative way. The findings of our study also show how the preschool children who participated in the coding exercises became physically active and learned social communication skills while playing with the Dash toy. It is therefore possible to claim that the preschoolers not only became physically mobile, but also became socially engaged by making their own rules for play. This activity, which the preschoolers created themselves, resembles gameplay. Taking turns by changing the person coding, so that everybody gets to run after the toy, is reminiscent of many games in which players alternate. This example illustrates how the preschoolers, while playing with Dash, came up with a gamified exercise by coding the Dash robot to become part of mobile playful learning.

The main contribution of this study is the finding that Dash, as a coding toy, enabled children to become physically mobile in group exercises in which one child was coding and the others were following the Dash robot by running after it and discovering where the toy was heading next. It is therefore possible to claim that the coding robot improved the wellbeing of the preschool children by activating them in various cognitive, social, and physical ways.

This study has also shown that coding toys, such as Dash, increase collaborative physical activity because they mobilize young learners not only through solitary, but also social forms of play. At the same time, it is important to understand that, by coding the toy while playing, the participating children were involved in physical, educational, and technological activities while participating in a learning process. In summary, mobile playful learning that happens with the help of the children enables them to actively take part in learning within a framework of creation, exploration, collaboration, and play.

5 Conclusion and Future Studies

In our study, the researchers allowed two preschool groups to interact with the Dash robot for a three-month period. Our aim was both to create possibilities for free-form, or open-ended, play, and to prompt playful learning by guiding the preschoolers to use the Path app to code different tracks for the Dash robot. In this way, free play, supported by early education professionals, merged the playful learning context with the curricular goals of learning 21st-century skills, such as coding. The results of our study show that, when given a coding toy and allowed to freely interact with it, preschoolers start to learn by themselves by exploring, utilizing, and challenging its hybrid (digital–material) affordances for play. In terms of Bybee's 5E learning model, they are able to engage, explore, explain, elaborate, and evaluate their mobile playful learning experiences.

These findings illustrate how a coding toy, like Dash, suits the goals of the Finnish early education curriculum, which states that exercise should happen at all stages of primary school in a playful way [5]. This paper presents a novel approach to the understanding of the use of coding toys in mobile, playful learning, in which the preschoolers themselves innovated gamified and physically activating approaches. The preschoolers who participated in the study could, in this way, take control of the learning situation by using creativity to employ the coding toy in engaging, mobilizing, and social ways.

As the results of our study have demonstrated, the use of an MPLE, such as the Internet of Play in combination with a smart coding toy like Dash, may be an excellent way to combine situated and active learning with fun in the context of early education. Thus, the learning potential of using coding toys lies in the possibility of embedding educational goals (like the ones related to learning the logic of coding, collaborating, and being physically active in group play in a mobile learning environment), enhancing engagement (using a coding robot to mobilize the children), and fostering learning (by taking on new challenges, such as coding more difficult obstacle paths for the toy) outside traditional and formal educational settings (such as the flipped classroom approach).

Mobile playful learning constitutes an expanding research domain. The main scholarly contribution of this case study is in the use of a coding toy as part of a mobile playful learning process enhanced with toy-based approaches, which had a positive effect on young learners' physical activity. Our study shows that coding toys, such as Dash, can be useful tools in engaging children as young as 5–6 years of age to simultaneously learn about coding and be socially mobile. In future research, we aim to introduce preschoolers to another coding robot, Botley, to determine if this alternative toy invites and encourages preschoolers to code and move, as Dash did, and further, to deepen our analysis about how these coding toys, as part of the IoToys, can enhance children's wellbeing, physical activities, and coding skills on a more general level.

According to recommendations given for physical exercise by the Finnish authorities, children and youth aged 7–15 years should be physically active for more than an hour each day. A recent study has shown how only around a third (38%) of Finnish 7–15 year-olds reach this goal [42]. Consequently, the authors would like to start a dialogue about the usefulness of toy-based learning with smart coding toys, combined with mobile playful learning, for age groups beyond preschool.

References

1. Heljakka, K., Ihamäki, P.: Preschoolers learning with the internet of toys: from toy-based edutainment to transmedia literacy. Seminar.net – Int. J. Media Tech. Lifelong Learn. **14**(1), 85–102 (2018)
2. LaFraniere, P.: Children's play as a context for managing physiological arousal and learning emotion regulation. Psihologijske Teme **22**(2), 183–204 (2013)
3. Järvilehto, L.: Hauskan oppimisen vallankumous (A revolution of fun learning). PS-kustannus, Juva (2014)
4. Kiili, K., Perttula, A., Lindstedt, A., Arnab, S., Suominen, M.: Flow experience as a quality measure in evaluating physically activating collaborative serious games. Int. J. Serious Games **1**(3), 35–49 (2014)
5. POPS, Perusopetuksen opetussuunnitelman perusteet 2014 (Basic Education National Core Curriculum), Regulations and Instructions 2014:96, Finnish National Board of Education (2014). https://www.oph.fi/download/163777_perusopetuksen_opetussuunnitelman_perusteet_2014.pdf. Accessed 08 Feb 2019
6. Downes, T.: Playing with computing technologies in the home. Educ. Inf. Technol. **4**(1), 65–79 (1999)
7. Department of Education: Curriculum for Preschool (Stockholm, Ministry of Education and Science in Sweden) (1998)
8. Kangas, M.: Creative and playful learning: Learning through game co-creation and games in a playful learning environment. Thinking Skills Creativity **5**, 1–15 (2010)
9. Craft, A.: Creativity in Schools: Tensions and Dilemmas. Routledge, Abingdon (2005)
10. Bruner, J.: The Culture of Education. Harvard University Press, Cambridge (1996)
11. Bruner, J.: Making Stories: Law, Literature, Life. Farrar, Strauss & Giroux, New York (2002)
12. Bruner, J.: The narrative construction of reality. In: Mateas, M., Sengers, P. (eds.) Narrative Intelligence, pp. 41–62. John Benjamins Publishing Co, Amsterdam (2003)
13. Blumfield, P.C., Kempler, T.M., Krajcrik, J.S.: Motivation and cognitive engagement in learning environments. In: Sawyer, R.K. (ed.) The Cambridge Handbook of the Learning Sciences, pp. 475–488. Cambridge University Press, New York (2006)
14. Joubert, M.M.: The art of creative teaching: NACCCE and beyond. In: Craft, A., Jeffery, B., Liebling, M. (eds.) Creativity in Education, pp. 17–34. Continuum, London (2001)
15. Mahn, H., John-Steiner, V.: The gift of confidence: a Vygotskian view of emotions. In: Wells, G., Claxton, G. (eds.) Learning for Life in 21st Century. Sociocultural Perspectives on the Future of Education, pp. 46–58. Blackwell, Cambridge, MA (2002)
16. Vygotsky, L.S.: Mind in Society. Harvard University Press, Cambridge (1978)

17. Hyvönen, P.: Affordances of playful learning environment for tutoring playing and learning. Doctoral Dissertation. Acta Universitatis Lappoensis 152, University of Lapland, Faculty of Education, University of Lapland Printing Centre, Rovaniemi (2008)
18. Berriman, L., Mascheroni, G.: Exploring the affordances of smart toys and connected play in practice. New Media & Society, SAGE Journals (2018). https://doi.org/10.1177/1461444818807119
19. Holloway, D., Green, L.: The Internet of toys. Commun. Res. ad Prac. **2**(4), 506–519 (2016)
20. Mascheroni, G., Holloway, D. (eds.): The Internet of Toys: A report on media and social discourses around young children and IoToys. In: DigiLitEY (2017). http://digilitey.eu/wpcontent/uploads/2017/01/IoToys-June-2017-reduced.pdf. Accessed 08 Feb 2019
21. Marsh, J.: The internet of toys: a posthuman and multimodal analysis of connected play. Teach. Coll. Rec. **119**(15), 120305 (2017)
22. Ihamäki, P., Heljakka, K.: Smart, skilled and connected in the 21st century: educational promises of the of Internet of Toys (IoToys). In: 2018 Hawaii University International Conference, Art, Humanities, Social, Science & Education, 3–6 January 2018, Honolulu (2018)
23. Ihamäki, P., Heljakka, K.: Smart toys for game-based and toy-based learning: study of toys marketers', preschool teachers' and parents' perspectives on play. In: The Eleventh International Conference on Advances in Human-Oriented and Personalized Mechanisms, Technologies and Services, CENTRIC 2018, 14–18 October 2018, Nice, France
24. Ihamäki, P., Heljakka, K.: The Internet of Toys, connectedness and character-based play in early education. In: Arai, K. Bhatia, R., Kapoor, S. (eds.) Proceedings of the Future Technologies Conference (FTC) 2018. FTC 2+18. Advances in Intelligent Systems and Computing, vol. 880, pp. 1079–1096. Springer, Cham (2018)
25. Heljakka, K., Ihamäki, P.: Verkottunut esineleikki osana esiopetusta: Lelujen Internet Leikillisen oppimisen välineenä. Lähikuva **31**(2), 29–49 (2018)
26. Heljakka, K., Ihamäki, P.: Persuasive toy friends and preschoolers playtesting IoToys. In: Mascheroni, G., Holloway, D. (eds.) Internet of Toys – Practices, Affordances and the Political Economy of Children's Smart Play, pp. 159–178. Palgrave Macmillan, Cham (2019). https://doi.org/10.1007/978-3-30-10898-4
27. Kolodny, L.: Kids can now program dash and dot robot through swift playgrounds. In: TechCrunch.com. https://techcrunch.com/2016/10/18/kids-can-now-program-dash-and-dot-robots-through-swift-playgrounds (2016). Accessed 12 Feb 2019
28. NAEYC & Fred Rogers Center for Early Learning and Children's Media: Technology and interactive media as tools in early childhood pragmas serving children from birth through age 8. "joint position statement. NAEYC, Washington DC, Fred Rogers Center for Early Learning at Saint Vincent College, Latrobe, PA. http://www.naeyc.org/files/naeyc/file/positions/PS_technology_WEB2.pdf. Accessed 08 Feb 2019
29. Bers, M.: Blocks to Robots: Learning with Technology in the Early Childhood Classroom. Teachers College Press, New York (2008)
30. Bers, M.U., Seddighin, S., Sullivan, A.: Ready for robotics: bringing together the T and E of STEM in early childhood teacher education. J. Technol. Teach. Edu. **21**(3), 355–377 (2013)
31. Cejka, E., Rogers, C., Portsmore, M.: Kindergarten robotics: using robotics to motivate math, science, and engineering literacy in elementary school. Int. J. Eng. Educ. **22**(4), 711–722 (2006)
32. Sullivan, A., Kazakoff, E.R., Bers, M.U.: The wheels on the bot go round and round: Robotics curriculum in pre-kindergarten. J. Inf. Tech. Edu.: Innovations Pract. **12**, 203–219 (2013)

33. Clements, D.H., Sarama, J.: Young children and technology: what's appropriate? In: Masalski, W.J. (ed.) Technology-Supported Mathematics Learning Environments Sixty-Seventh Yearbook, pp. 51–73. NCTM, Reston (2005)
34. Wing, J.: Computational thinking. Commun. ACM **49**(3), 33–35 (2006)
35. Resnick, M.: Learn to code, code to learn. how programming prepares kids for more than math. EdSurge 8 (2013). https://www.edsurge.com/news/2013-05-08-learn-to-code-code-to-learn. Accessed 25 Feb 2019
36. Lempke, J.: Games and Learning: Diversifying Opportunity or Standardizing Advantage?. In: AERA-conference (American Education Research Association) 27 April 2013–1 May 2013, San Francisco, USA (2013)
37. Bodrovka, E., Leong, D.J.: The importance of being playful. Educ. Leadersh. **60**(7), 50–53 (2003)
38. Sawyer, R.K.: Educating for innovation. Thinking Skills and Creativity **1**, 41–48 (2006)
39. Hamdam, N., McKnight, P., McKnight, K., Arfstrom, K.M.: A Review of Flipped Learning, Flipped Learning Network, Person and George Mason University. (2013) https://flippedlearning.org/wp-content/uploads/2016/07/LitReview_FlippedLearning.pdf. Accessed 12 Feb 2019
40. Bybee, R.: An Instructional Model for Science Education: Developing Biological Literacy. Biological Sciences Curriculum Studies, Colorado Springs (1993)
41. Jensen, J.L, Kummer, T.A., Godoy, P.D. d. M.: Improvements from a flipped classroom may simply be the fruits active learning. CBE – Life Sciences Education **14**(1), 1–12 (2015). https://doi.org/10.1187/cbe.14-08-0129
42. Kokko, S., Martin, L. (eds.): Lasten ja nuorten liikuntakäyttäytyminen Suomessa. Exercising behavior of children and youth in Finland. In: LIITU-tutkimuksen tuloksia, Results of the LIITU study, Valtion Liikuntaneuvoston julkaisuja (2018). http://www.liikuntaneuvosto.fi/files/634/VLN_LIITU-raportti_web_final_30.1.2019.pdf. Accessed 25 Feb 2019

Evaluating the Usability of Pervasive Conversational User Interfaces for Virtual Mentoring

Earl W. Huff Jr.[1(✉)], Naja A. Mack[2], Robert Cummings[3], Kevin Womack[3], Kinnis Gosha[3], and Juan E. Gilbert[2]

[1] Clemson University, Clemson, SC 29630, USA
earlh@clemson.edu
[2] University of Florida, Gainesville, FL 32611, USA
[3] Morehouse College, Atlanta, GA 30314, USA

Abstract. To improve the academic and professional achievement of underrepresented minorities in computing, a newfound interest in innovative mentoring practices has captivated STEM education researchers. Studies suggest that virtual mentoring conversational agents can be leveraged across multiple platforms to provide supplemental mentorship, offsetting the lack of access to in-person mentorship in disadvantaged communities. A within-subjects mixed-method experiment was carried out to assess the usability of a mentoring conversational agent. Mobile interfaces (Twitter and SMS) were compared to each other and against a web-based embodied conversational agent (ECA). Results suggest that mobile interfaces are more usable than the web-based ECA. The findings from this study help to identify areas for improvement in virtual learning alternatives and other potential applications for pervasive conversational interfaces.

Keywords: Virtual mentoring · Underrepresented minorities · Short message service · Twitter · Embodied conversational agents · Conversational agents

1 Background

1.1 The Need for Underrepresented Minorities in Computing

The substantial demand for projected computing careers [17] reinforces the importance of better preparing underrepresented minorities to qualify for and persevere within computing careers. There is a glaring lack of Black and Latinx representation in graduate and doctoral computing programs [14]. This deficit can be attributed to an array of socioeconomic and psychosocial circumstances [39]. One of the significant perpetuations of the deficit is the lack of faculty, staff, and administrators in computing at the graduate-level to encourage and support underrepresented minorities. Such a presence would, in turn, develop students' sense of belonging and self-efficacy [4,35,38,47]. Consequently, the underperformance of underrepresented minorities in computing positively correlates with future underemployment [15].

1.2 Conversational Agents

Many initiatives have been implemented to address the achievement gap. One method of interest is the use of virtual learning alternatives such as conversational agents (also referred to as chatbots or virtual agents), which are computer programs that engage human users in natural language conversations. Conversational agents have been used for decades to facilitate effective communication with and disseminate crucial information to users in various applications and settings [6,10,51]. From a usability perspective, the varying content and intended user population impact the conversational agent's visual design and its effectiveness.

An embodied conversational agent (ECA) is a Web browser interface featuring an anthropomorphic interface agent that can engage with a user in real-time dialogue by employing different channels of communication such as speech and gesture, thereby emulating face-to-face human interaction [7]. ECAs have been implemented as a virtual learning alternative in various disciplines, such as psychosocial support therapy [34,49] and academic advice [3]. Another area where ECAs have been used involves preparing African American students for graduate school in computer science [21,22]. However, findings from a study measuring the effectiveness of an ECA that was designed to serve as a supplemental mentor for undergraduate computer science students at a Historically Black College suggested that the ECA was not an ideal channel when there is a demand for maximizing and simplifying access [32].

In the United States, 91% of the population owns a smartphone [46]. Mobile learning has been popularized as a field, focusing on the mobility of the learner, digitalizing existing analog signals and information, and personalizing instruction [44,52]. According to Penfold [46], Mobile learning can be more advantageous than traditional practices due to convenience, flexibility, lack of travel, lack of space, personalized engagement and interaction, and the instruction distribution [46].

1.3 The SMS Platform

Short message service (SMS), otherwise known as text messaging, is the most widely used telecommunications service and an integral part of daily communication [11,44]. There are many advantages (typically medical or health-related) to SMS being implemented into virtual learning alternatives including: reminder and appointment capability, common use, remote access, and cost-effectiveness (as compared to traditional person-to-person advisement) [1,2,30,33,36,43,50]. Studies, predominantly medical or health-related, also suggest SMS to be feasible and appropriate in learning and advisement interventions targeting African

Americans [9,31,32,40,48]. SMS is particularly active with teenagers and young adults, producing lingo, abbreviations, and terminology commonly used around their focal social circles [41].

1.4 The Twitter Platform

Social media platforms can also be leveraged for virtual learning alternatives. Twitter is a microblogging social networking platform that is suggested to be effective at establishing connections between students and their desired audience in a succinct form [16,20]. The highly accessible and interactive platform contains a timeline of information covering varying topics, self-regulated content creation, content sharing, and has been suggested to be a viable source for learning [12]. Additionally, social media allows for private communications via direct messaging addressivity between users to conduct discussions similar to face-to-face conversations [28]. Twitter has been suggested to be productive in teaching and managing research for higher education students with typical same-day responses. Content searched on Twitter as opposed to other social media platforms, tends to focus more on activities and captioned photos; many of the activities are work-related such as conferences, and many of the captioned photos are inspirational quotes and advisement [42]. Very few studies that have successfully leveraged Twitter to implement virtual learning have an African American targeted population [25,53]; however, the Twitter's notable sociopolitical activity performed by African Americans known as Black Twitter suggests underrepresented minorities are high activity and resourcefulness on the social media platform [19,23,24].

2 Method

Research on virtual learning alternatives for academic and career advisement, particularly for African Americans in the computer and information sciences is minimal. An expert conversational agent was developed to provide underrepresented minority undergraduate and graduate computing students with advice on how to prepare and be successful in graduate school. The conversational agent ran on three interfaces: a web-based ECA, Twitter, and SMS. The study intended to answer the following research questions:

RQ1: How do underrepresented minorities use the graduate school conversational agent?

The foundational research question was to determine the behaviors and opinions of using the conversational agent for a short term. The research team will be able to use the user experience and usability data for future tool development and improvement. Each interface should have similar responses for the base virtual mentoring system as well as interface-specific behaviors and opinions.

RQ2: How usable are the mobile conversational agent interfaces compared to the web-based ECA interface?

It is hypothesized that mobile conversational agent interfaces will have better-perceived usability than the web-based ECA. Users should feel more at ease to engage with the conversational agent through mobile interfaces than through a Web browser. As Twitter direct messaging and SMS operate similarly, it was hypothesized that users would have similar subjective usability for Twitter and SMS.

2.1 Participants

The study was conducted in two settings: (1) a computing conference where the majority of attendees were African American students, faculty, and professionals in computing; (2) a historically black college in the southeastern United States. The target population was African American students who are pursuing either an undergraduate or graduate degree in computing. Thirty-five African American students participated in the study in some capacity. All participants used at least one interface and completed a qualitative user experience assessment about the conversational agent. Twenty participants completed the assessments for user experience and usability for all three interfaces. Random sampling was used to select from interested volunteers at the computing conference. Convenience sampling was used at the historically Black college from a computer science course.

2.2 Conversational Agent Development

Virtual Mentor. The virtual mentoring system (VMS) is a computer software application developed to engage in natural language conversation with the user. The VMS is comprised of several components: (1) the content knowledgebase, (2) a natural language understanding engine, and (3) the user interface. The content knowledgebase provides the information that the VMS provides to the user based on the questions. Obtaining the content involved developing questions that users would want to ask a mentor and formulating answers that mentors would give based on the questions. The process required identifying "experts" with knowledge of applying to graduate school, funding opportunities for graduate school, and employment options for post-graduation. The experts identified work as administrators, faculty, and professionals in industry. This process is similar to the one performed in Gosha's study for developing the first virtual mentoring system [21]. The experts' responses were transcribed and developed into a final answer for each question added to the VMS.

At the core of the VMS, a natural language understanding (NLU) engine is necessary for the system to engage in natural language conversation with the user. For the VMS developed, Google's Dialogflow was chosen as the NLU engine. Dialogflow, formerly Api.ai, is a natural language platform built using Google's machine learning suite and runs on the Google Cloud Platform. Dialogflow can be used to build text-based and voice-based applications for many platforms and devices including, but not limited to, websites, smartphones, Google Assistant,

Facebook Messenger, and other devices and platforms. Dialogflow's applicability to a vast number of platforms and devices made it an ideal choice for our engine. Integrating the expert content into Dialogflow's engine involve mapping intended questions from the user utterances/intents to the answers provided by the experts. When a user asks the VMS a question, Dialogflow will use machine learning and natural language processing to determine which question best fit what the user is asking if it is not the same question that is stored in the system. After a match is found, the answer is returned to the VMS and displayed through the user interface (see Fig. 1 for visual representation).

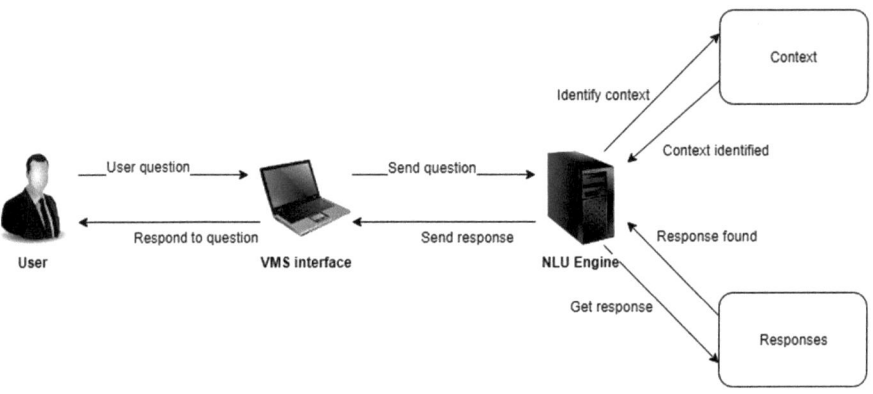

Fig. 1. VMS dialogue flow

Interfaces. The first virtual mentoring system used a graphical avatar as its interface; this is called an embodied conversational agent (ECA) [21]. The VMS designed for the present study also developed a web-based ECA to serve as the baseline. The ECA was developed using SitePal, a website the enables users to create Flash-based graphical avatars with the ability to engage in conversations with users. Once an avatar is created, it can be inserted into any website using the provided embed code. Using JavaScript code, the Dialogflow engine can be connected to the ECA. Besides the web-based ECA interface, two additional interfaces were developed: one for Twitter and one using short message service (SMS).

The Twitter-based interface uses Twitter's direct messaging feature to engage users. Integrating Dialogflow into Twitter involves (1) creating a twitter account to serve as the virtual agent "interface" and (2) connecting it to Dialogflow through the Twitter Developer Platform. We created a Twitter account to serve as the user interface. Then we created a Twitter app on the Twitter Developer Platform. Connecting Dialogflow to the interface involves connecting the engine to the Twitter app and then connecting the Twitter app to our Twitter account. For users to engage the VMS via Twitter, the user must send a direct message to the VMS Twitter account and ask their questions.

The SMS-based interface was developed using Twilio, a cloud-based communications platform that offers APIs for building SMS, voice and messaging applications. Twilio enables users to obtain a phone number and attach a service (messaging, SMS, or voice) to that number. Setting up the SMS interface involves obtaining a phone number from Twilio, adding the Programmable SMS Messaging Service to the number, and adding the phone number, account token, and service ID to Dialogflow. To interact with the SMS interface, users merely send their question as a text message to the phone number connected to the VMS.

2.3 Study Procedure

A mixed method approach was used in this repeated measures study to explain the usability and user experience of a graduate school expert conversational agent to be used to prepare underrepresented minorities for graduate school in computing. Selected participants were provided information on how to contact the graduate school expert conversational agent: the SMS phone number, Twitter username handle, and URL to the ECA interface in a Web browser. Participants were also provided with the URL link to complete an online survey. The online survey instrument included a qualitative user experience assessment and a quantitative usability assessment. To increase participant confidentiality, each participant was provided with an identification number to use on all three assessments. The user experience questionnaire asked participants about their short-term experience using the conversational agent. Six open-ended user experience questions were assessing prominent user experience themes. These themes were determined by supporting the user experience themes established by the Interactive Design Foundation [29] (usefulness, usability, credibility, desirability, accessibility, value) and by reviewing user experience literature to further validate those themes [13,26,27,37]. Alternatively, the accessibility theme was assessed in a dichotomous yes-no question, along with if participants would recommend the tool (see Table 1). The final open-ended question was if there were more appropriate audiences for the tool to be used. The assessment also asked participants if their reaction changed their reaction from before using the conversational agent. The System Usability Scale (SUS) was another part of the online survey assessment [8]. The SUS is a 10-item questionnaire that utilizes 5-point Likert scales from strongly disagree to strongly agree. Participants were not given a time restriction nor a question limit for interacting with the system. Participants were instructed to use all three interfaces one at a time, completing the online survey immediately after they were finished using an interface. Study participants were given compensation through online gift card after completing the study.

2.4 Data Analysis

Qualitative open-ended responses were analyzed through a hybrid deductive-inductive content analysis approach [18]. The research team developed a coding guide following the user experience themes [29] including expectation/reaction change and recommended audience (see Table 2). Four researchers coded the responses based on user experience literature; results were compared and modified excluding the theme of findability for the nature of this investigation. Data from the assessment was summarized, and themes were determined, contextualized, and synthesized. Quantitative user experience data was observed with simple descriptives (see Table 3).

A repeated-measure multilevel linear model was used to compare mobile (Twitter and SMS) interface usability to the usability of the web-based ECA. A multilevel linear model provides a number of affordances over a repeated-measures ANOVA including (1) avoiding any assumption of independence, homogeneity, and sphericity, (2) being able to use more than a two-level hierarchy and (3) able to work with missing data.

Table 1. Descriptive user experience responses

Code	Twitter		SMS		ECA	
	Yes	No	Yes	No	Yes	No
Recommend tool?	70% (14)	30%(6)	70%(14)	30%(6)	40%(8)	60%(12)
Accessible tool?	80%(16)	20%(4)	95%(19)	5%(1)	85%(17)	15%(3)

Note. Two user experience questions were dichotomous (yes or no). This table shows the percent of participants (number of participants) who selected yes and no per interface.

3 Results

3.1 User Experience and Usability

Demographics. There were a total of 20 participants that used all three interfaces. From the pool of participants, 50% (10) identified as Ph.D. students, 20% as Ph.D. candidates, 15% as other (postdoctoral or faculty), 10% as undergraduate seniors, and 5% as undergraduate juniors. When asked if they have ever used or interacted with a conversational agent prior to the study, 95% (19) of the participants answered 'Yes'. Prior to the study, they were asked about the likelihood of using a system for learning about applying to graduate computing programs and careers in computing. Forty-five (45) percent indicated either likely or very likely while 35% indicated somewhat likely. After interacting with the conversational agent, 14 (70%) participants for SMS, 14 (70%) participants for Twitter, and 8 (40%) participants for the web-based ECA agreed that they would recommend the conversational agent to someone. For SMS, 19 (95%) participants agreed that they felt the conversational agent is easily accessible to everyone, compared to 17 (85%) for ECA and 16 (80%) for Twitter.

Table 2. User experience descriptions

Code	Definition
Useful	The conversational agent has a purpose and meaning allowing one to accomplish a task using the tool
Usable	The conversational agent is effective and efficient at achieving its objective
Credible	The content provided by conversational agent is trustworthy, accurate, well-intentioned, and will remain so for a reasonable amount of time
Desirable	The conversational agent has an attractive aesthetic and its content reflects a positive brand identity
Valuable	The conversational agent and its content is worth a great deal and could provide solutions to challenging and expensive problems
Expectation	After using the conversational agent, I had a satisfying reaction different than what i had expected prior to using the agent
Recommended audience	The conversational agent and its content would benefit a population

Usability. The SUS has 10 usability items. The evaluation yielded a composite measure of the overall usability of each conversational agent. The maximum score for conversational agent usability is 100. Twitter conversational agent usability scores ranged from 47.5 to 100 with the median being 68.75. SMS conversational agent usability scores ranged from 17.5 to 100 with the median being 73.75. ECA usability scores ranged from 27.5 to 97.5 with the median being 60.

User Experience. Short responses were collected from six open-ended user experience questions from six user experience codes. The results of the hybrid thematic analysis are listed in Table 3 with themes for each code. In each interface, participants indicated that the conversational agent is useful for helping to make decisions about pursuing graduate studies and applying to graduate school. Participants reported that they could use the conversational agent *"to get another perspective and/or idea about what [they] should do to approach a task or objective"*. The conversational agent serves particularly useful *"as a starting point to begin searching for more answers. If you didn't know anything, this at least gives you a place to start. It mentions various resources to find specific information"*. There were a few variations in usefulness per interface. Participants specifically found *"linking to URLs via the SMS"* useful as well as *"[liking] SMS because I can go back and review at a later date"*. One participant expressed that they believed the Twitter conversational agent *"would help students use social media as a way to not only stay connected but to obtain advice"*.

All participants found each interface to be easy to understand and use. There were few errors. One participant reported that *"there was a little bit of an issue for me to start using the chatbot as I was not clear on the type of questions I should be asking, but once I got the hang of it, it got much easier to use"*. One participant *"found [Twitter] more usable compared to the other two (SMS and text). I believe the platform flowed better because I was used to seeing such responses via twitter"*. Another participant noted that *"the advice was spotty, the bot would sometimes answer the question completely wrong"*. One participant said that *"the voice of the [ECA] was creepy"*. In all three interfaces, the vast majority of the participants indicated that they found the conversational agent to be an accessible tool.

For credibility, participants believed the systems' *"answers seemed legit"*. *"The mentor seemed authentic because there were detailed explanations of the words I typed into the messaging system."* The feedback also included *"no spelling errors, [and] professional dialogue"*. Twitter users believed the advice to be even more credible because the account profile picture: *"photo of an actual person made the advice seem more credible. Not having an artificial voice or visage made it seem like I was chatting with a real person"*. SMS did not feature a profile photo, leaving participants to express that *"the missing face/embodiment in the other two interfaces makes me trust this one a little less"*; *"I don't know who was texting me, so that left me questioning the information."* ECA credibility responses varied. One participant explained *"the mentor was an older woman who appeared very professional, giving a credible presentation. She also seemed relatable to me, being a woman of color"*. Another believed *"the mentor did seem credible [however] the page itself may need a little more embellishment to make me feel stronger about this"*.

Although believing the ECA was valuable was the most frequent response, there was no clear saturation of value for ECAs. Themes ranged from very valuable to not valuable. The conversational agent ranged in value from *"Eh"*, *"Not much"* to *"very valuable"* with the majority believing the conversational agent to be valuable. Some of the poorer rationales included that the system was *"personally not for me perhaps for someone who is inquiring about what to do...I wanted immediate answers and the virtual mentors didn't provide me with such. After receiving the response, I was kinda unsatisfied because it was a chunk of text, it wasn't too personal which I needed"*. There were a decent amount of participants who believed the content was too generic for a mentoring system: *"It was good generic advice. It'd be great if it were personalized but I realize this was our first encounter. It was almost like a Google search"*. Another participant commented on the conversational flow: *"The advice seemed genuine but the conversation didn't flow"*. Most would agree that *"it was good for the initial steps"*.

All three interfaces met the expectations of the participants during their interaction. When asked about how their reaction to the tool changed after interacting with each interface. One participant admitted that *"my reaction slightly softened, but I still prefer human interaction"*. Another participant said *"my initial reaction was of confusion but afterwards once the interface became more clear, it was easier to get"*. Participants' experiences ranged from no change to positive for the Twitter interface. A Twitter user expressed that *"I was apprehensive, especially, to the twitter platform. but a LOT of students use twitter and this very quick interaction might just hit the mark"*. *"I like the DM interaction. It feels a little more private and personal."* Very few participants' reactions changed for the SMS interface. One participant believed that *"I was hesitant about this one, but it was okay. I think i may prefer the other two over this one as the pictures helped to feel like i was 'talking' to a 'person"'* and *"It takes time to type on the phone, but useful for mobile and travel"* while others claim to have *"liked the SMS best"*, *"I would consider it. It was the simplest version to use"*, and *"Stayed the same, this was probably the one I felt most comfortable with"*. ECA reactions ranged most greatly, being either no change, a generally positive change, or being rather surprised. One participant mentioned how *"it was faster for me to read what she was saying than wait to hear from her, which in my mind makes [the ECA] unnecessary."* Whereas another participant said *"At first, I was apprehensive to the thought of a virtual mentor, but after interacting with it, I think it was pretty cool"*.

For the all interfaces, the conversational agent was recommended for novices in the field such as high school students, school counselors, undergraduates, family members of computer scientists, and anyone looking to get into computing. The Twitter platform is recommended for active Twitter users and SMS interfaces, Most of the participants indicated that they would recommend the conversational agent to others in the Twitter and SMS interface. Most participants indicated that they would not recommend the ECA. Some recommendations for the ECA included fixing the slow-pace and freezing face glitch, considering a voice change option, making the speak button have an indicator to show it is working, ensuring the speak option does not cut off mid-sentence and to allow the ECA on a mobile platform.

3.2 Multilevel Linear Model for Interface Usability

We hypothesized that using either mobile interfaces (SMS or Twitter) would result in higher perceived usability than using the web-based ECA. It was also hypothesized that the SMS interface would result in similar usability scores as the Twitter interface. Figure 2 shows a bar chart of the means and 95% confidence interval of the SUS scores for each interface. From the chart, the SMS and Twitter interfaces have a significantly higher mean score than the ECA interface. This may indicate that participants favor using both of the mobile interfaces as compared to the ECA.

Figure 3 shows boxplots for the SUS scores of each interface. The median for SMS is the highest of the three; however, both SMS and Twitter have fairly extended boxes, suggesting the middle 50% of scores are variable. Additionally, the median score for the ECA is closer to the lower quartile (Q1), leading us to believe that the lower half of participant scores have less variation than the upper half. The long lower whiskers of both ECA and SMS interfaces indicate

Table 3. Qualitative user experience responses

UX Codes	Twitter Themes	SMS Themes	ECA Themes
Useful	To deal with specific questions To make grad school decisions To ask beginner questions	Tool saved advice when needed Useful in applying to grad school To obtain helpful resources Get quick answers To ask about funding opportunities	To make grad school decisions To ask beginner questions To create a schedule/plan To asked questions a user feels ashamed of
Usable	Tool was easily understandable Tool features were limited Tool did not understand question	Tool was understandable Tool was simple to use Needed instructions Tool did not converse well Tool did not understand question	Tool was easily understandable Tool was simple to use Tool had errors
Credible	Profile picture felt real Tool not credible Tool gave predictable, yet credible answers Ethnicity of profile felt authentic	Tool used professional language (punctuation, grammar) Tool gave predictable, yet credible answers Tool not credible Information felt believable Tool felt authentic Tool did not feel authentic Tool provided supporting resources	Tool gave predictable, yet credible answers Tool felt authentic Tool not credible
Desirable	Tool met expectations Tool desirable Tool was not personable enough	Tool met expectations Tool was not personable enough Information was desirable Tool not desirable Tool was repetitive Tool was ok	Tool met expectations Tool was repetitive Tool was not personable enough Tool not desirable
Valuable	Tool was valuable Tool somewhat valuable Tool not valuable	Tool was valuable Tool somewhat valuable Tool not valuable	Tool was valuable Tool not valuable Tool somewhat valuable
Expectation	Positive change Little to no change Negative change	Little to no change Faster than anticipated More comfortable than anticipated Negative change	Positive change Little to no change Positively surprised by virtual human Negatively surprised by virtual human
Recommended Audience	Prospective graduate students High school students Twitter users Undergraduate student Computing novices School counselors Family members of computer scientists	High school students Prospective graduate students Computing novices Undergraduate students School counselors Family members of computer scientists	High school students Undergraduate students Computing novices Prospective graduate students School counselors Family members of computer scientists

views in the lower 25% quartile range are variable while the short upper and lower whiskers for Twitter show that scores among participants at both ends of the quartile range are less variable.

We tested our hypotheses using a repeated-measures multilevel linear model. The usability scores were dependent of the interfaces. To execute the multilevel linear model, we created two linear models: one as the baseline with perceived usability as the outcome variable and a random intercept denoting the absence of the interface variable; another one with the interface variable added to the model. This is to show if adding the interface variable has a significant overall effect. To assess if the interface-added model was a significant improvement of fit over the baseline, we observe the likelihood ratio and its corresponding p-value. The different interfaces were the independent variable and dependent variable is the perceived usability. From our tests, we can conclude that the type of interface had a significant effect on the perceived usability of the virtual mentor, $\chi^2(2) = 8.46$, p = .015. While our test proved that the type of interface used affects usability, it did not tell us which interfaces had an effect.

Hence, we additionally ran planned orthogonal contrasts to ascertain the direction of the effect on usability. Two contrasts were created in order to test our hypotheses: web vs. mobile and SMS vs. Twitter. Planned contrasts revealed that percieved usability was significantly higher for mobile interfaces than for web-based ECA (b = 6.19, t(38) = 2.74, $p_{one-tailed}$ = .005) and there was no significant difference between SMS and Twitter (b = 3.13, t(38) = 1.2, $p_{one-tailed}$ = .238). Therefore, we accept our hypothesis that using mobile interfaces will result in higher perceived usability than using a web-based ECA and that there is no significant difference between SMS and Twitter-based interfaces.

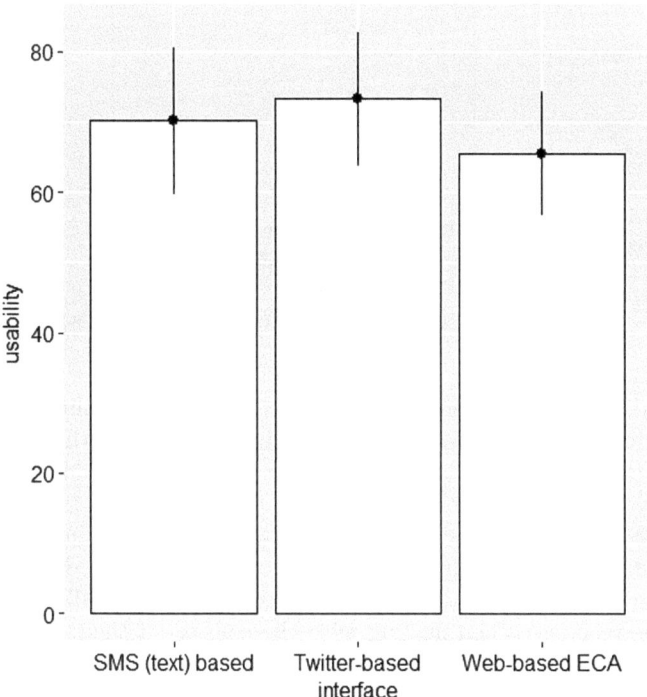

Fig. 2. Bar chart of means of usability scores by each interface

4 Discussion

4.1 Usability

It is important to note that the short-form System Usability Scale only measures the individual experience of users as an entirety. Thus individual item results of the usability scale will not be implied. According to Bangor, Kortum and Miller [5],

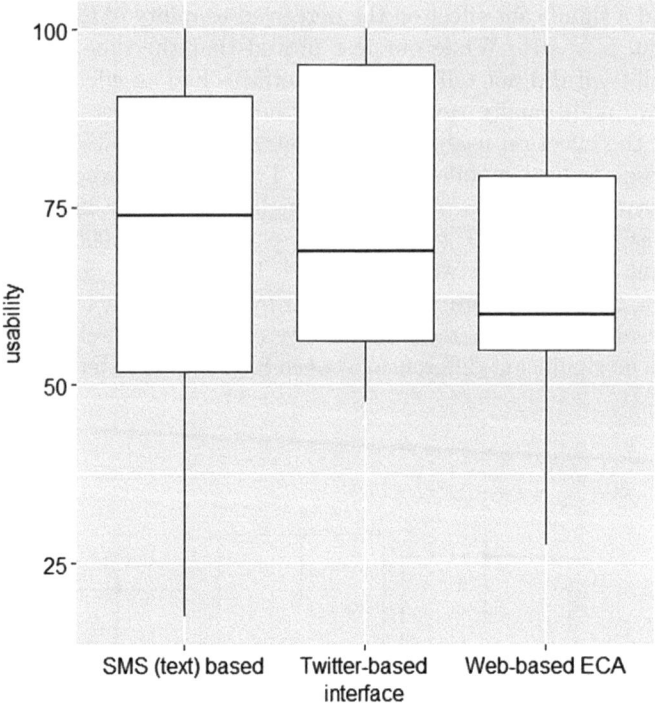

Fig. 3. Boxplots of usability scores for each interface

the SMS median usability score of 73.75, Twitter median usability score of 68.75, and ECA median usability score of 60 were all good scores, with SMS being low-range excellent. Good scores identify the conversational agent is a usable virtual mentoring system with minor defects.

The conversational agents also presented the information in a simple, easily understandable manner, with responses that can remain saved in the dialogue flow between the user and the conversational agent. This allows the user to return to the response when dealing with the context of their questions rather than having to ask an advisor every time the context of their questions arises.

The results suggest mobile (SMS and Twitter) interfaces are more usable than the web-based ECA [1,30,32]. After analyzing user experience data, some additional features that may have contributed to the lower results include the ECA's face freezing or having a delay, the voice recognition cutting off at the tail end of a user's voice input, and formatting preferences of the website. The ECA also needed an indicator to show that the ECA is listening when the users hit the speak button, whereas SMS provides clear delivery and speech notification [30]. The web-based product also has less accessibility than mobile sources due to its lack of mobile compatibility. SMS had higher usability scores than Twitter. This may be attributed to Twitter requiring users to have a Twitter account and internet access. These data support the participants' preferences in recommending the conversational agent on mobile interfaces.

4.2 User Experience

Usefulness and Usability. The graduate school preparatory conversational agent could be used to make graduate school decisions. The conversational agent for Twitter direct messages was useful at work/school-related activities and advisement [42]. The feature of having advisement saved in SMS dialogue for remote access was also suggested be useful [1,30]. There were common themes for recommendations to improve the usefulness and usability of the tool. There is a need to clarify the instructions of usage. There were participants that were confused at what questions to ask. The tool should be better integrated with mentoring interventions and scenarios to better assist a user's understanding of the types of questions to ask the conversational agent. On Twitter, the conversational agent currently only runs through direct message, however a user reported *"I initially tried tweeting the @"*. Therefore, interface-specific instructions need to be provided to users. Conversational theory can be applied to better improve the flow of conversations. For instance " being able to follow up on responses the bot just provided without rewriting the entire question." is essential for a healthy conversation. Furthermore, greeting, ebonics, and abbreviations are necessary for the conversational agent to understand, particularly with mobile interfaces. Participants reported *"allow for abbreviations. People tend to abbreviate when texting"* and *"because it's through text messaging I would want to greet the mentor before engaging in a conversation. Would the system understand ebonics?"*. The ability to link resources on all interfaces can be very useful in communicating information that is length or very detailed.

Expectation. Prospective participation in virtual graduate school mentorship for minorities in computing is broad, as most everyone used conversational agents previously and 80% were at least somewhat likely to use an underrepresented minority-computing graduate school preparation conversational agent. The conversational agents were what many of the participants expected as active users of Twitter and SMS [11,24]. Users of all interfaces generally had a low-level positive change of their feelings towards the tool from before using the tool and after using the tool: *"I wouldn't mind interacting with a mentor via twitter since I already use the platform"*. There was a significant number of participants who were surprised by the ECA. Though the tool met their expectations, they still were not used to interacting with an ECA. Some participants had a positive reaction and found the moving ECA to be memorable or notable, while one participant found it to be "freaky". These responses have many implications on how the ECA can be tweaked, particularly in ensuring the ECA is as personable. Personability should compliment users' comfort of seeing a character rather than just text. The image of the ECA may need to be reworked to eliminate some uncanniness.

Credibility. Credibility also varied between the interfaces. Twitter users felt the profile of an African American computer science professor made it feel like they were speaking to someone rather than a conversational agent, supporting the value of personability [44,52] and the importance of having an advisor for underrepresented minorities be of their same ethnicity [14,39]. While using SMS, participants believed the professional language the conversational agent used made the conversational agent seem more credible, supporting the informal use of texting [41].

Value. The conversational agents were generally valuable to users. As many of the participants were Ph.D. students or candidates, the valuability may have been limited, as many participants agreed the conversational agents at its current potential is more valuable to high school students, undergraduate students, or prospective graduate students. Participants pointed out that they were already familiar with the responses to many of their questions making the system credible, notably for SMS and ECA, and applicable for all interfaces. This is another supportive finding that the content needs to be more relevant to graduate students and is currently more support. It is necessary to make the content more in-depth, less generic, and more personalized in order to reflect a mentoring relationship.

Other Implications. Other themes varied. A few participants wished the conversational agents would be more personable, an implication that would support the notion that graduate school preparation needs both expert knowledge and responsive mentoring [21,44,52]. This is especially apparent due to the underrepresented minority target demographic [9,21]. Other participants mentioned how terminology and abbreviations should be better utilized within the system's knowledgebase. Other comments include usability issues and suggestions for improvement such as the conversational agent's response if it doesn't understand the user and allowing for the user to greet the conversational agent. Though many factors show SMS and Twitter to be more usable and have preferred user experiences, it is unclear why there is such a significant variance in the prospective recommendation in mobile tools and the web-based ECA.

4.3 Limitations

The research study featured a small sample size. For a simple usability assessment, the sample size is sufficient [45]. However, the comparative statistical analysis requires more population normality for validity. As the SUS and the qualitative user experience data are sound, caution should be used in observing the statistical analysis data. Data were collected from 35 participants and was used in the usability and user experience results. All 35 participants identified as Black/African American. Only 20 participants were used in the comparative analysis, including the demographic questions. This participant disparity was due to the lack of interacting and completing the assessment for all three interfaces.

User experience questions were developed from the Interactive Design Foundation's [29] seven factors that influence user experience: valuability, accessibility, desirability, usefulness, usability, findability, and credibility. As participants were not required to find the conversational agents on their own, the findability factor was omitted from the assessment. Survey items rating the accessibility of the tool and there recommended audience were asked explicitly asked and not a part of a validated scale. No analysis for these two factors was performed.

5 Conclusion

Mobile interfaces are a viable direction in improving the quality of mentoring conversational agents. The conversational agent has many areas where improvement could be realized, yet showed promising results for future implementation. In the near future, more in-depth conversational theory will be applied to the conversational agent to improve conversational flow. Mentoring attributes, particularly those in psychosocial areas that are critical to African Americans who are pursuing computing, will be included to the virtual mentoring system to provide a more thorough and reliable supplement for traditional mentorship. There will be additional scrutiny in the content development process to ensure potential users have the best insightful responses to their questions and concerns with pursuing graduate studies in computing. Other fields can use these findings to aid their virtual learning alternatives in their respective disciplines.

References

1. Abu Ziden, A., Rosli, M., Gunasegaran, T., Azizan, S.: Perceptions and experience in mobile learning via SMS: a case study of distance education students in a Malaysian public university. Int. J. Interact. Mobile Technol. (iJIM) **11**, 116 (2017)
2. Aguilera, A., Muñoz, R.: Text messaging as an adjunct to CBT in low-income populations: a usability and feasibility pilot study. Prof. Psychol.: Res. Pract. **42**, 472–478 (2011)
3. Andre, E., Pelachuad, C.: Interacting with embodied conversational agents. In: Chen, F., Huggins, R.M. (eds.) Speech Technology, pp. 123–149. Springer, Heidelberg (2010)
4. Aronson, J., Fried, C., Good, C.: Reducing the effects of stereotype threat on african american college students by shaping theories of intelligence. J. Exp. Soc. Psychol. **38**, 113–125 (2002)
5. Bangor, A., Kortum, P., Miller, J.: Determining what individual SUS scores mean: adding an adjective rating scale. J. Usability Stud. **4**, 114–123 (2009)
6. Benotti, L., Martinez, M., Schapachnik, F.: Engaging high school students using chatbots. In: Proceedings of the 2014 Conference on Innovation & Technology in Computer Science Education. pp. 63–68. ACM, New York (2014)
7. Bickmore, T., Cassell, J.: Relational agents: a model and implementation of building user trust. In: Proceedings of the SIGCHI Conference on Human Factors in Computing Systems, pp. 396–403. ACM, New York (2001)
8. Brooke, J.: SUS: a retrospective. J. Usability stud. **8**, 29–40 (2013)

9. Carter, L., Corneille, M., Hall-Byers, N., Clark, T., Younge, S.: Exploring user acceptance of a text-message base health intervention among young African Americans. AIS Trans. Hum.-Comput. Interact. **7**, 110–124 (2015)
10. Coniam, D.: Evaluating the language resources of chatbots for their potential in English as a second language. ReCALL **20**(01), 98–116 (2008)
11. Corrocher, N.: The Development of Short Message Services. https://www.cairn.info/revue-economique-2013-1-page-149.htm
12. Dabbagh, N., Kitsantas, A.: Personal learning environments, social media, and self-regulated learning: a natural formula for connecting formal and informal learning. Internet and High. Educ. **15**, 3–8 (2012)
13. Deaton, M.: The elements of user experience. Interactions **10**, 49 (2003)
14. Dillon, E.C., Gilbert, J.E., Jackson, J.F.L., Charleston, L.: Expanding the pipeline, the state of African-Americans in computer science: the need to increase representation. Comput. Res. News **27**(8), 2–6 (2015)
15. DiSalvo, B., Guzdial, M., Meadows, C., Perry, K., McKlin, T., Bruckman, A.: Workifying games: successfully engaging African American gamers with computer science. In: Proceeding of the 44th ACM Technical Symposium on Computer Science Education, pp. 317–322. ACM, New York (2013)
16. Evans, C.: Twitter for teaching: can social media be used to enhance the process of learning? Brit. J. Educ. Technol. **45**, 902–915 (2013)
17. Fastest Growing Occupations: Occupational Outlook Handbook: U.S. Bureau of Labor Statistics. https://www.bls.gov/ooh/fastest-growing.htm
18. Fereday, J., Muir-Cochrane, E.: Demonstrating rigor using thematic analysis: a hybrid approach of inductive and deductive coding and theme development. Int. J. Qual. Methods **5**, 80–92 (2006)
19. Freelon, D., Lopez, L., Clark, M., Jackson, S.: How Black Twitter and other social media communities interact with mainstream news (2018)
20. Gikas, J., Grant, M.: Mobile computing devices in higher education: student perspectives on learning with cellphones, smartphones & social media. Internet High. Educ. **19**, 18–26 (2013)
21. Gosha, K.: The application of embodied conversational agents for mentoring African American STEM doctoral students (2013)
22. Gosha, K., Gilbert, J., Middlebrook, K.: Virtual graduate school mentoring using embodied conversational agents. J. Comput. Sci. Inf. Technol. **3**(2), 15–38 (2015)
23. Graham, R., Smith, S.: The content of our characters. Sociol. Race Ethn. **2**, 433–449 (2016)
24. Graham, R.: Digital Sociology in Action: A Case Study of Research on Black Twitter. SAGE Research Methods (2018)
25. Hampton, L., Gosha, K.: Development of a Twitter graduate school virtual mentor for HBCU computer science students. In: Proceedings of the ACMSE 2018 Conference, p. 42. ACM, New York (2018)
26. Hassenzahl, Marc: The thing and I: understanding the relationship between user and product. In: Blythe, M., Monk, A. (eds.) Funology 2. HIS, pp. 301–313. Springer, Cham (2018). https://doi.org/10.1007/978-3-319-68213-6_19
27. Hassenzahl, M., Tractinsky, N.: User experience - a research agenda. Behav. Inf. Technol. **25**, 91–97 (2006)
28. Honeycutt, C., Herring, S.: Beyond microblogging: conversation and collaboration via twitter. In: Proceedings of the 42nd Hawaii International Conference on System Sciences, pp. 1–10. IEEE (2009)

29. Interaction Design Foundation: The 7 Factors that Influence User Experience. https://www.interaction-design.org/literature/article/the-7-factors-that-influence-user-experience
30. Iribarren, S., et al.: Scoping review and evaluation of SMS/text messaging platforms for mHealth projects or clinical interventions. Int. J. Med. Inf. **101**, 28–40 (2017)
31. James, D., Harville, C., Sears, C., Efunbumi, O., Bondoc, I.: Participation of african americans in e-Health and m-Health studies: a systematic review. Telemed. e-Health **23**, 351–364 (2017)
32. Julian, L., Gosha, K., Huff Jr., E.: The development of a conversational agent mentor interface using short message service (SMS). In: Proceedings of the 2018 ACM SIGMIS Conference on Computers and People Research, pp. 123–126. ACM, New York (2018)
33. Kaphle, S., Chaturvedi, S., Chaudhuri, I., Krishnan, R., Lesh, N.: Adoption and usage of mHealth technology on quality and experience of care provided by frontline workers: observations from rural india. JMIR mHealth and uHealth **3**, 61 (2015)
34. Kenny, P., Parsons, T.D., Gratch, J., Rizzo, A.A.: Evaluation of justina: a virtual patient with PTSD. In: Prendinger, H., Lester, J., Ishizuka, M. (eds.) IVA 2008. LNCS (LNAI), vol. 5208, pp. 394–408. Springer, Heidelberg (2008). https://doi.org/10.1007/978-3-540-85483-8_40
35. Khalifa, M.A., Gooden, M.A., Davis, J.E.: Culturally responsive school leadership: a synthesis of the literature. Rev. Educ. Res. **86**(4), 1272–1311 (2016)
36. king, C., et al.: Electronic data capture in a rural african setting: evaluating experiences with different systems in Malawi. Global Health Act. **7**, 25878 (2014)
37. Kuniavsky, M.: Smart Things. Morgan Kaufmann, Burlington (2010)
38. Kyoung Ro, H., Lattuca, L., Alcott, B.: Who goes to graduate school? Engineers' math proficiency, college experience, and self-assessment of skills. J. Eng. Educ. **106**, 98–122 (2017)
39. Lewis, S., Simon, C., Uzzell, R., Horwitz, A., Casserly, M.: A Call for Change: The Social and Educational Factors Contributing to the Outcomes of Black Males in Urban Schools. https://eric.ed.gov/?id=ED512669
40. Le, D., et al.: Feasibility and acceptability of SMS text messaging in a prostate cancer educational intervention for african american men. Health Inf. J. **22**, 932–947 (2016)
41. Ling, R., Bertel, T., Sundsøy, P.: The socio-demographics of texting: an analysis of traffic data. New Media Soc. **14**, 281–298 (2011)
42. Manikonda, L., Meduri, V., Kambhampati, S.: Tweeting the mind and instagramming the heart: exploring differentiated content sharing on social media. In: ICWSM, pp. 639–642. AAAI (2016)
43. McNabb, M., et al.: Assessment of the quality of antenatal care services provided by health workers using a mobile phone decision support application in northern nigeria: a prepost-intervention study. PLOS One **10**, e0123940 (2015)
44. Moura, A., Carvalho, A.A.: Mobile learning: using SMS in educational contexts. In: Reynolds, N., Turcsányi-Szabó, M. (eds.) KCKS 2010. IAICT, vol. 324, pp. 281–291. Springer, Heidelberg (2010). https://doi.org/10.1007/978-3-642-15378-5_27
45. Nielsen, J.: Why You Only Need to Test with 5 Users. https://www.nngroup.com/articles/why-you-only-need-to-test-with-5-users/
46. Penfold, S.: Why mobile learning is important for elearning. https://www.elucidat.com/blog/why-mobile-learning-is-important/

47. Sadler, J., Brown, M.: Focus on teacher education: culturally relevant instruction by student teachers: a case study approach. Childhood Educ. **91**(2), 150–154 (2015)
48. Sheats, J., Petrin, C., Darensbourg, R., Wheeler, C.: A theoretically-grounded investigation of perceptions about healthy eating and mhealth support among african american men and women in new orleans. Louisiana. Family Commun. Health **41**, S15–S24 (2018)
49. Tartaro, A., Cassell, J.: Using virtual peer technology as an intervention for children with autism. In: Lazar, J. (ed.) Universal Usability: Designing Computer Interfaces for Diverse User Populations, pp. 231–262. Wiley, New Jersey (2007)
50. Van Dam, J., et al.: An open-access mobile compatible electronic patient register for rheumatic heart disease ('eRegister') based on the world heart federation's framework for patient registers. Cardiovasc. J. Afr. **26**, 227–233 (2015)
51. Weizenbaum, J.: ELIZA–a computer program for the study of natural language communication between man and machine. Commun. ACM **9**(1), 36–45 (1966)
52. West, D.: Mobile Learning: Transforming Education, Engaging Students, and Improving Outcomes. The Brookings Institute, Washington (2013)
53. Xu, S., Markson, C., Costello, K., Xing, C., Demissie, K., Llanos, A.: Leveraging social media to promote public health knowledge: example of cancer awareness via Twitter. JMIR Public Health and Surveill. **2**, 17 (2016)

Learn Chinese in Sindhi: App Development and Evaluation

Zahid Hussain[1(✉)], Meiyu Lu[2], Xiangang Qin[2], and Muhammad Faheem[1]

[1] Quaid-e-Awam University of Engineering,
Science and Technology, Nawabshah, Pakistan
{zhussain,13itl3}@quest.edu.pk
[2] School of Digital Media and Design Arts,
Beijing University of Posts and Telecommunications, Beijing, China
meiyulv@163.com, qinxiangang@bupt.edu.cn

Abstract. This paper describes the results of the usability study that was conducted to evaluate the newly developed app for learning Chinese language. The app is developed for the people who speak and read Sindhi language which is mostly spoken in Sindh province of Pakistan. The app is designed for such people who want to visit China or want to speak basic Chinese language for daily conversational purposes. For this study, the target audience was the students of grade X aged between 16 to 17 years. The app has been evaluated through cognitive walkthrough, usability testing and a questionnaire. The results show that the app was easy to use and effective and the students were satisfied. This app can help the learners, particularly the students, for learning basic Chinese language. By using this app anywhere and at any time, the learners can gain better learning experiences as well.

Keywords: Human-computer interaction · Usability evaluation · Chinese learning mobile app

1 Introduction

Smartphones are being increasingly utilized for mobile learning (m-learning) now-a-days [1]. Many m-learning apps do exist for learning, e.g., m-learning app for higher education studies [2], learn English-Sindhi app [3], English vocabulary learning app [4, 5], learn English language [6], learn English tenses [7], app for English language and literature [8], Bengali language learning app [9], app for learning idioms and collocations [10], app for learning Chinese characters [11], and learn Chinese language courses [12].

Learning a new language is both fun and beneficial for a learner. Chinese language is one of the most spoken languages of the world. China shares borders with Pakistan; many Pakistani businessmen are doing business with their Chinese counterparts. Recently, a multi-billion-dollar project called China-Pakistan Economic Corridor has been initiated in Pakistan with the help of China. This is one of the important projects linking China to Arabian Sea via Gwadar port in Pakistan. Many Chinese engineers are working on this project as well as on other projects in Pakistan. With regard to this, the education department of provincial government of Sindh has signed the memorandum of understanding (MOU) with the Chinese officials for teaching the Chinese language in the secondary schools of Sindh province in Pakistan. Therefore, learning Chinese for Pakistani people, particularly the students would be beneficial. Although few apps do exist for learning Chinese in English [12] or learning Chinese in other languages do exist on the Google play store and other app stores. To the best of our knowledge, an app for learning Chinese in Sindhi for the people who speak and read Sindhi language does not exist yet. Moreover, usability is one of the crucial aspects for the acceptance of software applications, specifically the mobile apps, among the masses [3]. So, there was a need to develop such type of app having good usability. Due to this reason, we developed the *Learn Chinese in Sindhi* app. We also evaluated its usability through cognitive walkthrough, usability testing and a questionnaire. The details are given in the subsequent sections.

2 Related Work

Wuttikamonchai developed a mobile application for Android operating system to learn English tenses. Learning outcomes of the students were assessed and users' satisfaction was also evaluated. Sample of population was the students of information technology department. The results revealed that the students were satisfied with the English tenses learning mobile app [7]. Rockahr et al. have discussed the e-learning app economy. They conducted interviews both from teachers and pupils; both of them regard m-learning apps to be a worthwhile supplement in learning [13]. Ng et al. developed an Android based mobile app for beginners to learn fundamental Japanese language. The app provides basic knowledge about Japanese language so as the beginners may gain self-learning proficiency in Japanese. The results of the evaluation reveal that the app was effective. More than 60% learners were agreed or strongly agreed that the app was useful in reading, writing, listening, and speaking simple Japanese [14]. Hussain et al. evaluated the usability of Urdu learning mobile apps for children. Fun Toolkit was also used in this study [15]. In another research study, an Android based app was developed for the Sindhi speaking students to learn English. Its usability testing was conducted. The results show that the app was effective and equally efficient for all the participating children [3]. Arain et al. developed a mobile learning app for the students of higher education institutes. The usability of the app was evaluated through a test and system usability scale (SUS). The results show that the app was effective and efficient; most of the students were satisfied in this regard [2]. García-Peñalvo et al. conducted the usability test of WYRED Platform: a project for children and young people regarding digital society. SUS was used to evaluate the usability and learnability of the system. Two groups were formed for usability test: group 1 (users who tested the platform for earlier version) and group 2 (users who tested the improved version). According to the results, the SUS score of group 1 was 64.67 and the SUS score of group 2 was 66.54. Both SUS scores were under the threshold (which is 68) but can be considered as decent score. The general perception of the participants about the system was positive [16]. Kortum and Sorber evaluated the usability of 10 mobile apps based on iOS and

Android operating systems for mobile phone and tablet PC. They conducted two experiments with 3575 users using SUS. The results revealed that the apps on mobile phones were more usable than tablet platforms [17]. Many researchers have extensively explored other aspects of m-learning, e.g., Sánchez-Prieto et al. worked on m-learning [18], more specifically on extending technology acceptance models [19, 20]. As the effective, efficient and user-friendly app for learning Chinese in Sindhi was not available, so we developed the app and evaluated its usability.

3 Learn Chinese in Sindhi App

The *Learn Chinese in Sindhi* app has been developed at Quaid-e-Awam University of Engineering, Science and Technology, Nawabshah, Pakistan. The app is developed for the people who speak and read Sindhi language which is mostly spoken in Sindh province. The app is designed for such people who want to visit China or want to speak a little bit Chinese language. Owing to the MOU signed by the two governments, the target audience also includes the students of grade VI to grade X in the age group of 11–17 years. The app provides three translation opportunities to the users: from Sindhi to Chinese language, Urdu to Chinese language and English to Chinese language. However, Internet connection is required for this translation feature (چيني ترجمو ڪريو).. Additionally, the app contains various sentences and features of daily use, e.g., Conversation (حال احوال), Tour (سياحت), Emergency (هنگامي حالت) and Business (ڪاروبار). Moreover, the app has also useful basic information regarding the names of colors, fruits, animals, days, months and numbers from Sindhi to Chinese language. Figure 1 shows few screenshots of the app.

Fig. 1. Screenshots of the app: (a) Main menu (b) Name of fruits (c) Business sentences

4 Methodology

The app was evaluated through a *variant of cognitive walkthrough* [21], usability tests and the SUS questionnaire. For the initial version, the cognitive walkthrough was conducted and the usability testing along with the questionnaire was also conducted. The problems found during these evaluations were fixed. After few weeks, another usability test along with the questionnaire was conducted for the improved version of the app. Twenty students of grade X in the age group of 16–17 years of a local secondary school participated in the usability tests. All the students had their own smartphones. 75% students were male and 25% were female. All the participants were native speakers of Sindhi language. During the second usability evaluation conducted on the improved version of the app, the same three tasks were performed by the same students. However, the order of the tasks was counterbalanced.

5 Results

The subsections present the results of the cognitive walkthrough and the usability tests along with the questionnaires.

5.1 Cognitive Walkthrough

The *variant of cognitive walkthrough* [21], a usability inspection method, was performed by two of the authors on the initial version of the app. According to the results, the prototype of the app was relatively simple. The amount of interfaces was appropriate; the information structure was clear; and the interactive mode was simply tapping. Hence the app was relatively easy to understand and easy to use. Above all, in terms of structure, the content category was used as navigation in the home page, and at the secondary page users could view the specific words under the category. However, the secondary page title was the same as the first page, and there were no back buttons. Users could only return using the Android system return key, which may cause a trek. Moreover, visual style of the icons was inconsistent.

The information on the first interface consisted of two parts: The Sindhi text on the left and the icons on the right (as shown in Fig. 2(a)). Overall it was clear and without any visual noise. However, few problems were found. The icons for "name of days" and " name of months" were not accurate enough to express their meanings. Without reading the text, users cannot fully understand what these two icons mean and cannot tell the difference between them.

There was no dividing line between two rows; and the distance between texts and icons was too far (as shown in Fig. 2(a)). It may visually cause a misunderstanding for the middle column to be a whole, and the right column to be a whole. This can create difficulty for users to correspond the text to the icon.

Usually on mobile devices, users focus on what the center of screen displays. In this version of the app, the current center of the screen contained the Sindhi texts while the right side was the icons. However, the texts were smaller than the icons. While the icons are supposed to assist the texts, thus they should have been smaller to highlight the texts.

Moreover, the left margin was much broader than the right margin (as shown in Fig. 2 (b)), which causes visual imbalance. Overall, visual style of the icons was inconsistent.

The icons of Arabic numerals were more like podium icons; moreover, the icons for fruits needed to be redesigned. Regarding the content layout, although the vocabulary was quite basic and common, there was no content of social aspects in the current version. Moreover, the current version lacked information of airports and tourism.

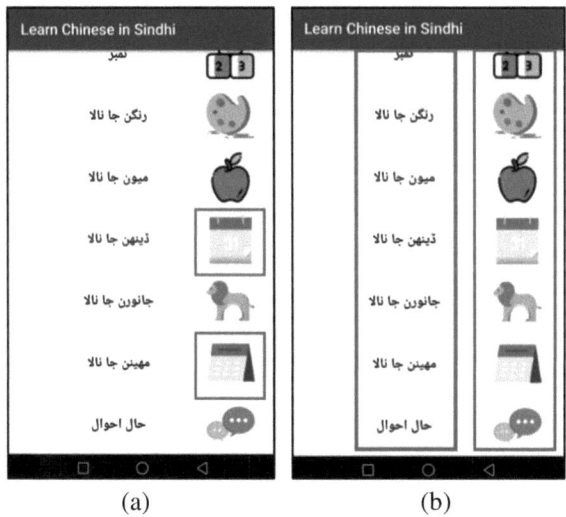

Fig. 2. Screenshots of the initial version of the app (a) and (b)

The second interface was a words learning page which covered four main contents: Chinese and Pinyin, icons, Sindhi, and pronunciation buttons. The overall layout and information were not complicated. However, the layout of the page needed to be rearranged. The visual focus of a mobile device should be the center of screen, and on this screen the icons were at the center. Moreover, since this is an app for learning Chinese, so it would have been better to place the Chinese text at the most conspicuous position. Apart from this, placing the pronunciation button next to the Sindhi text could cause a misunderstanding as the pronunciation was in Sindhi; thus the button should have been placed next to the Chinese text. Therefore, the order should have been: icon → Sindhi text → Chinese text → pronunciation button as shown in Fig. 3.

Fig. 3. Screenshots of numbers

The first letter of Chinese Pinyin did not need to be capitalized. Pronunciation is a very important and frequently used function for language learning apps; hence the icon should be intuitionistic. The pronunciation icon in this interface was too ambiguous as a pronunciation button. Moreover, the buttons were small and did not have any feedback when being tapped which may get users confused. There was also a small flaw: the icon depicted a male, while the voice was of female which could lead to inconsistency. Furthermore, what makes Chinese text differ from Western languages is that it consists of single block characters, thus adding a pronunciation button for each single Chinese character may be more in line with Chinese learning habits. There was no obvious distinction between the title bar and the content as shown in Fig. 4.

Fig. 4. Screenshot of numbers

The title bar of the Arabic numerals page showed "Counting", while the other pages only had Sindhi written on them. According to the Chinese language habits, the Pinyin labels of each character should be separated with spaces, otherwise it is easy to be understood as just for one character, especially for westerners. Some pages were in accord with this habit, some were not (as shown in Fig. 5). Besides, it was better to have a one-to-one correspondence between the text and the Pinyin.

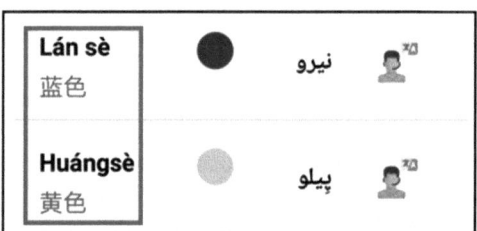

Fig. 5. Screenshot of the name of colors

The label of the word "ڳاڙهو (Red)" lacked "色" after "红" (as shown in Fig. 6), which was inconsistent with other labels, such as "蓝色", "黄色". Also, the label of "نارنگي (Orange)" ("橙色") was wrong (as shown in Fig. 6). The label of the word "سومر (Monday)" lacked "一" after "星期". The labels of "ڍڳي (Cattle)" ("牛") and "شينهن (Lion)" ("狮子") (as shown in Fig. 6) were incorrect; the word "ٻلي (Cat)" ("猫") was labeled in traditional Chinese, which was inconsistent with other words. Pinyin of the word "نومبر (November)" ("十一月") (as shown in Fig. 6) was wrong too.

Fig. 6. Four sub-screens of the app (Color figure online)

5.2 Usability Testing

Besides cognitive walkthrough, the usability testing along with the questionnaire was also conducted for the initial version of the app. The problems found through the cognitive walkthrough and the usability testing methods were fixed in the newer version of the app. After few weeks, another usability testing along with the questionnaire was conducted for this improved version of the app. The compared results are discussed here. Table 1 shows the tasks that were performed during both of the usability tests. The order of the tasks was counterbalanced.

Table 1. Usability tasks

Task #	Usability tasks
1.	Find out and listen to the name of color "پيلو" (Yellow)
2.	Find out and listen to the name of month "اپريل" (April)
3.	Find out and listen to the name of animal "ٻلي" (Cat)

According to the results of the usability tests, all the students completed all the tasks successfully on both versions of the app. So, the total task completion rate was 100% for both versions of the app which shows that the app was effective and easy to use.

Table 2 shows descriptive statistics of the tasks completion time (in seconds) of three usability tasks conducted on the initial version and the improved version of the app, clearly indicating that the students took lesser time on the improved version.

Table 2. Descriptive statistics of the tasks completion time

Usability tasks	Initial version of the app		Improved version of the app	
	Mean	SD	Mean	SD
Task-1	10.60	2.62	7.45	1.10
Task-2	8.25	1.74	6.2	0.95
Task-3	8.55	3.36	5.6	1.14

The students took on average 27.40 s to perform all the tasks on the initial version of the app. While for the improved version of the app, the students took on average 19.25 s only to complete all the tasks. Table 3 shows statistical results for the initial version and improved version of the app, regarding the total tasks completion time.

Table 3. Paired samples t-test regarding the tasks completion time

Test	Groups	t-value	p-value
Paired samples t-test	Initial version of the app - Improved version of the app	$t(2) = 8.03$	$p = 0.015$

The results show that there was statistically significant difference ($p < 0.05$) across the groups on the total tasks completion time. The participants took lesser time to perform the usability tasks on the improved version of the app; this shows that the improved version of the app was more efficient than the initial version.

5.3 System Usability Scale

After performing the tasks, SUS questionnaire [22] was immediately administered in both of the usability tests. A paired-samples t-test was conducted to compare the SUS scores for the initial version and the improved version of the app. The result shows that there was a statistically significant difference in the SUS scores for the initial version of the app (mean = 71.87, SD = 5.248) and for the improved version of the app (mean = 78, SD = 5.104); $t(19) = -4.307$, $p < 0.001$. The result clearly indicates that the students were more satisfied with the improved version of the app. Although for the initial version of the app, the SUS score is also above the threshold value. This shows that the students were satisfied with the both versions; however, they were more satisfied with the improved version of the app. For the improved version of the app, besides SUS, the adjective rating scale was also filled by the students. The range of the adjective rating scale is from 1 (Worst Imaginable) to 7 (Best Imaginable). According to their responses, 75% participants rated the app as *Excellent*, 15% rated the app as *Good* and 10% participants rated the app as *OK*. After the second usability test, the students were also asked to give their preference for both versions of the apps. Their results show that all the students preferred the newer version of the app. In addition, three more questions adapted from [23] were also included for getting the general perception of the students regarding the improved version of the app. The results in Fig. 7 show that all the students responded as either *strongly agree* or *agree* for the statement that they are satisfied with the app. Most of the students (94.10%) perceived that it was fun to use the app. Moreover, 96.30% students responded that they would recommend the app to their friends.

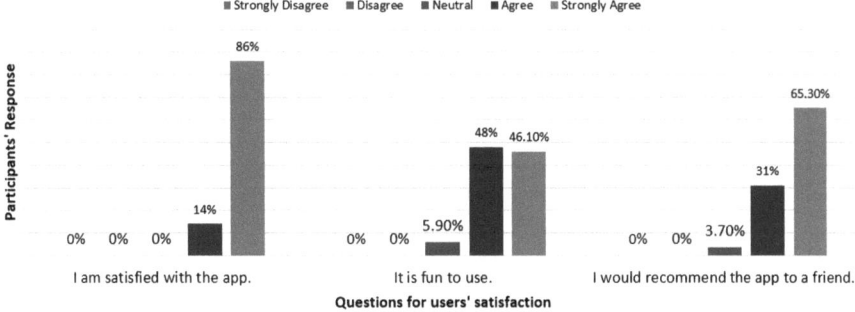

Fig. 7. General perception of the students regarding the improved version of the app

6 Conclusions

The usability study regarding the evaluation of the newly developed app for learning Chinese in Sindhi language was conducted. For the initial version, the usability was assessed using two methods: cognitive walkthrough and the usability testing along with the questionnaire. The cognitive walkthrough revealed many significant problems. Moreover, few problems were also found during the usability testing. These problems were fixed. Later for the improved version of the app, another usability testing along with the questionnaire was conducted. The results show that the total task completion rate was 100% for both versions of the app which shows that both versions of the app were effective and easy to use. Regarding the efficiency of the app, the results show that there was statistically significant difference across the groups on the total tasks completion time. The participants took lesser time to perform the usability tasks on the improved version of the app; this shows that the improved version of the app was more efficient than the initial version. Regarding the assessment of the perceived usability, the SUS score for the improved version of the app was greater than the initial version. The results show that there was statistically significant difference across the groups on the SUS scores, clearly indicating that the students were more satisfied with the improved version of the app. Moreover, all the students preferred the newer version of the app. It is recommended that the usability of the apps, specifically the m-learning apps, may be assessed with various usability methods, whenever possible; as good usability leads to more satisfied users. The combination of these methods helps in finding more usability problems that need to be fixed. Moreover, as the education department of provincial government of Sindh has already signed the MOU for teaching the Chinese language in the secondary schools of Sindh province so it is recommended that the app may be introduced in the schools where Chinese would be taught in the traditional classroom setting for better learning outcomes of the students. As this app can be used anywhere and at any time so by complementing this mobile learning app with the traditional classroom learning, the students can gain better learning experiences.

References

1. Arain, A.A., Hussain, Z., Rizvi, W.H., Vighio, M.S.: An analysis of the influence of a mobile learning application on the learning outcomes of higher education students. Univ. Access Inf. Soc. **17**(2), 325–334 (2018)
2. Arain, A.A., Hussain, Z., Rizvi, W.H., Vighio, M.S.: Evaluating usability of m-learning application in the context of higher education institute. In: Zaphiris, P., Ioannou, A. (eds.) LCT 2016. LNCS, vol. 9753, pp. 259–268. Springer, Cham (2016). https://doi.org/10.1007/978-3-319-39483-1_24
3. Hussain, Z., Slany, W., Rizvi, W.H., Riaz, A., Ramzan, U.: Measuring usability of the mobile learning app for the children. In: Zaphiris, P., Ioannou, A. (eds.) LCT 2017. LNCS, vol. 10295, pp. 353–363. Springer, Cham (2017). https://doi.org/10.1007/978-3-319-58509-3_28
4. Wu, Q.: Designing a smartphone app to teach English (L2) vocabulary. Comput. Educ. **85**, 170–179 (2015)
5. Ahmad, K.S., Sudweeks, F., Armarego, J.: Learning english vocabulary in a Mobile Assisted Language Learning (MALL) environment: a sociocultural study of migrant women. Interdis. J. e-Skills Life Long Learn. **11**, 25–45 (2015)
6. Siu, W.L., Lim, T.S., Chen, Y.R., Chen, Y.L., Jou, Y.A., Chen, Y.C.: Using an English language education app to understand the english level of students. In: Wireless and Optical Communication Conference (WOCC), pp. 1–3. IEEE (2018)
7. Wuttikamonchai, O.: The development of mobile application in English tenses. In: The 8th International Conference on Science, Technology and Innovation for Sustainable Well-Being (STISWB VIII), Yangon, Myanmar, pp. 15–17 (2016)
8. Ivić, V., Jakopec, T.: Using mobile application in foreign language learning: a case study. Libellarium J. Res. Writ. Books Cult. Herit. Inst. **9**(2), 217–230 (2017)
9. Ahmed, R.U., Mahmudul, A.S.M., Sultana, M.A., Iqbal, M.I., Johora, U.F.T.: Jonaki-an mlearning tool to reduce illiteracy in Bangladesh. Int. J. Comput. Appl. **128**(17), 21–25 (2015)
10. Amer, M.: Language learners' usage of a mobile learning application for learning idioms and collocations. CALICO J. **31**(3), 285–302 (2014)
11. Lu, J., Meng, S., Tam, V.: Learning Chinese characters via mobile technology in a primary school classroom. Educ. Media Int. **51**(3), 166–184 (2014)
12. Ohkawa, Y., Kodama, M., Konno, Y., Zhao, X., Mitsuishi, T.: A study on UI design of smartphone app for continuous blended language learning. In: 5th International Conference on Business and Industrial Research (ICBIR), pp. 584–589. IEEE (2018)
13. Rockahr, P., Griesbaum, J., Mandl, T.: Mobile e-learning app economy. Int. J. Inf. Educ. Technol. **8**(4), 267–272 (2018)
14. Ng, S.C., Lui, A.K., Wong, Y.K.: An adaptive mobile learning application for beginners to learn fundamental Japanese language. In: Li, K.C., Wong, T.L., Cheung, S.K.S., Lam, J., Ng, K.K. (eds.) Technology in Education. Transforming Educational Practices with Technology. CCIS, vol. 494, pp. 20–32. Springer, Heidelberg (2015). https://doi.org/10.1007/978-3-662-46158-7_3
15. Hussain, N., Hussain, Z., Ali, B.: Assessing the usability of urdu learning mobile apps for children. In: Zaphiris, P., Ioannou, A. (eds.) LCT 2018. LNCS, vol. 10924, pp. 117–126. Springer, Cham (2018). https://doi.org/10.1007/978-3-319-91743-6_8
16. García-Peñalvo, F.J., García-Holgado, A., Vázquez-Ingelmo, A., Seoane-Pardo, A.M.: Usability test of WYRED platform. In: Zaphiris, P., Ioannou, A. (eds.) LCT 2018. LNCS, vol. 10924, pp. 73–84. Springer, Cham (2018). https://doi.org/10.1007/978-3-319-91743-6_5

17. Kortum, P., Sorber, M.: Measuring the usability of mobile applications for phones and tablets. Int. J. Hum. Comput. Interact. **31**(8), 518–529 (2015)
18. Sánchez-Prieto, J.C., Olmos Migueláñez, S., García-Peñalvo, F.J.: Understanding mobile learning: devices, pedagogical implications and research lines. Teoría de la Educación. Educación y Cultura en la Sociedad de la. Información **15**(1), 20–42 (2014)
19. Sánchez-Prieto, J.C., Olmos-Migueláñez, S., García-Peñalvo, F.J.: MLearning and pre-service teachers: an assessment of the behavioral intention using an expanded TAM model. Comput. Hum. Behav. **72**, 644–654 (2017)
20. Sánchez-Prieto, J.C., Olmos-Migueláñez, S., García-Peñalvo, F.J.: Informal tools in formal contexts: development of a model to assess the acceptance of mobile technologies among teachers. Comput. Hum. Behav. **55**, 519–528 (2016)
21. Mahatody, T., Sagar, M., Kolski, C.: State of the art on the cognitive walkthrough method, its variants and evolutions. Intl. J. Hum. Comput. Interact. **26**(8), 741–785 (2010)
22. Brooke, J.: SUS: a "quick and dirty" usability scale. In: Jordan, P.W., Thomas, B., Weerdmeester, B.A., McClelland, I.L. (eds.) Usability evaluation in industry, pp. 189–194. Taylor & Francis, London (1996)
23. Lund, A.M.: Measuring usability with the USE questionnaire. Usability Interface **8**(2), 3–6 (2001)

Measuring Hedonic and Content Quality of Social Networking Sites Used in Interactive Learning Ecosystems

Tihomir Orehovački[1(✉)] and Snježana Babić[2]

[1] Faculty of Informatics, Juraj Dobrila University of Pula,
Zagrebačka 30, 52100 Pula, Croatia
tihomir.orehovacki@unipu.hr
[2] Polytechnic of Rijeka, Trpimirova 2/V, 51000 Rijeka, Croatia
snjezana.babic@veleri.hr

Abstract. The aim of the work presented in this paper was to examine the psychometric features of the measuring instrument designed for evaluating hedonic- and content-related dimensions of quality in the context of social networking sites. Therefore, an empirical study was carried out in which students from two Croatian higher education institutions constituted a representative sample of users. Considering that introduced questionnaire has met requirements related to both reliability and validity, it can be employed as a benchmark for improving quality of existing social networking sites as well as an evaluation asset when developing the new ones.

Keywords: Social networking sites · Hedonic quality · Content quality · Questionnaire · Empirical study

1 Introduction

Social network sites (SNS, e.g. Facebook, Twitter, Instagram, Pinterest, Snapchat, YouTube, etc.) are specific kind of Web 2.0 applications that are transforming how people connect and communicate with each other and have become a significant phenomenon in human interaction [5]. This is because SNS enable users to become visible and facilitate building connections between individuals [5]. Today, SNS are being used in many areas of human activity. To begin with, social media and SNS offer different advantages to various organizations including increased sale, facilitated word-of-mouth communication, sharing business information and providing social support to consumers [10]. Many companies are therefore investing heavily in electronic word-of-mouth (eWOM) with respect to SNS. Tien et al. [28] found that perceived persuasiveness, perceived informativeness and source expertise have an impact on the usefulness of eWOM in the context of SNS. Furthermore, SNS have become important platforms for governments and have influenced how they communicate with citizens [27]. In educational ecosystem, instructors are employing SNS as a mean for connecting with students thus creating digital classroom [9] which stimulates and encourages informal learning [3]. According to study carried out by Lovari and

Giglietto [16] in 2012, nearly half of the universities in Italy had an official presence on at least one social media. Kumar and Nanda [12] proposed the framework for integrating specific channels of social media into different processes at higher education institutions. They argue that social media are improving communication between students and other relevant stakeholders being involved in educational process and in the same time are assisting in promotional and developmental activities of higher education institutions such as attracting new students, facilitating their life at campus and maintaining communication with them after they leave the campus.

The quality of SNS is one of main component which significantly affects their adoption by different stakeholders of interactive learning ecosystem and thus their success. Chan et al. [5] emphasize that early studies were mostly focused on the adoption and initial use of SNS but nowadays they are concentrated on identifying motivational factors (e.g. meeting new people, entertainment, maintaining relationships, learning about social events, sharing media, status updating, etc.) that encourage the aforementioned stakeholders to use them. Success of SNS can be generalized into two aspects: (i) the user experience (UX) that the platform offers and (ii) the quality of the content [26]. According to Orehovački et al. [21], there are two major facets of quality in use when Web 2.0 applications are taken into account: (i) usability which refers to the product centered evaluation of pragmatic attributes by means of objective measuring instruments and (ii) user experience (UX) which denotes the use of subjective measuring instruments for the assessment of hedonic attributes.

Objective of the work presented in this paper is to examine hedonic quality of four SNS and quality of content published on them. The remainder of the paper is structured as follows. Theoretical background to our study is provided in the next section. Research methodology is discussed in the third section. Study findings are reported in the fourth section. Conclusions are drawn in the last section.

2 Related Work

The large number of people in the world are using SNS to meet and help each other, to exchange opinions, or to have fun [6]. It is therefore of great importance that facets of user experience are examined before and after development of SNS [6]. In their study, Ou et al. [23] confirmed the significant role of information quality, system quality and networking quality in determining success of SNS (e.g. Facebook and Twitter). Kim and Kim [11] found that respondents who are more gratified with entertainment and need for recognition aspects are those who are using Facebook while respondents who are gratified with the browsing aspect of gratifications and those who have positive attitudes toward levels of openness are those who are using Instagram. According to Sawalha et al. [27], performance expectancy, social influence, effort expectancy, personal innovativeness and enjoyment significantly affect the continuous use of e-government pages on Facebook. Leong et al. [14] discovered that perceived task-technology fit is the great predictor of perceived usefulness and users' intention to adopt mobile SNS for pedagogical purposes. Results of the study conducted by Chan et al. [5] indicate that perceived critical mass, social presence, and social norms are influential and major factors that determine continuance intention of SNS. Makkonen and Siakas [17] identified understanding of content sharing as a prerequisite for planning the learning/teaching activities based on social media. Pöyry et al. [24] discovered that there is a difference between consumers' hedonic (to participate in the community) and utilitarian (to browse the community page) motivations for using SNS (e.g. travel agency's Facebook page). Based on the results of their study, Orehovački and Babić [19] concluded that recoverability, loyalty, reliability, attitude towards use, response time, customizability, adaptability, pleasure, understandability, navigability, aesthetics, error prevention, recoverability, reliability, interactivity and memorability are the most relevant determinants of perceived mobile quality in the context of social Web applications designed for collaborative writing. Aladwani [1] found that content quality in the context of using social media affects customers' continued interest, active confidence, and feedback openness. Ali et al. [2] discovered that information quality motivates usage intention but does not affects students' academic use of social media. Rodríguez-Ardura and Meseguer-Artola [25] uncovered perceived playfulness as the essential driver of Facebookers' experience and perceived usefulness as the major predictor of adopting social media for learning and academic purposes. The results of the study conducted by Nedra et al. [18] have shown that perceived pleasure, social identity (cognitive, affective and evaluative) and perceived ease of use have the positive impact on the intention to use Instagram whereas perceived usefulness have not shown significant influence in that respect. The outcomes of the study conducted by Lee and Kim [13] revealed that system quality, service quality, and hedonic value have an impact on flow experience, information and service quality, and hedonic value influence the relationship quality of SNS whereas the flow experience and relationship quality while using SNS affect the continuance usage intention of SNS. Wu and Chen [29] found that social influence and information quality contribute to users' continuance intentions to use Facebook in educational context. Finally, the results of the systematic literature review on research related to SNS in the field of information systems carried out by Cao et al. [4] uncovered lack of studies concerning human-computer interaction context.

All the aforementioned indicates that current studies are predominantly focused on exploring pragmatic aspects of quality and adoption of SNS while studies related to both hedonic and content quality are rather scarce. Therefore, we initiated a study focused on exploring hedonic and content dimensions of quality with respect to SNS. Details on the proposed methodology are provided in the following section.

3 Methodology

Research Framework. The quality model designed for the purpose of this study is composed of two distinctive dimensions: hedonic quality and content quality. Hedonic quality (HDQ) refers to six attributes meant for measuring facets of user experience with respect to interaction with SNS [19, 21]. Aesthetics (AES) denotes the degree to which the SNS has visually appealing user interface. Uniqueness (UNQ) signifies the extent to which the SNS is distinctive among applications with the same purpose. Playfulness (PLY) represents the degree to which the interaction with the SNS is focused and stimulates their curiosity. Pleasure (PLS) indicates the extent to which the employment of SNS arouses users' emotional responses. Satisfaction (STF) denotes the degree to which users are content with using the SNS. Loyalty (LOY) signifies the extent to which users have the intention to continue to use the SNS and recommend it to others. Content quality (CNQ) refers to five attributes designed for measuring the degree to which the content that the SNS provides is suitable for a specific goal in a defined context [20, 22]. Accuracy (ACU) indicates the extent to which content offered by SNS is correct, valid and free of errors. Credibility (CDB) denotes the degree to which content provided by SNS is unbiased, trustworthy and verifiable. Coverage (CVG) implicates the extent to which content published on SNS is appropriate, complete and compactly represented. Timeliness (TLS) represent the degree to which content offered by SNS can be supplemented, modified, and updated. Added value (ADV) signifies the extent to which content published on SNS is advantageous for users.

Procedure. The study was conducted in a controlled lab conditions and was composed of evaluating hedonic quality and content quality of four social networks (Facebook, Instagram, Twitter, and YouTube). Upon arriving to the lab, the participants were welcomed and briefly informed about the quality evaluation study. After completing the questionnaire, study subjects were debriefed and thanked for their participation. The duration of the study was twenty minutes.

Apparatus. The study adopted a within-subjects design comparing four SNS. Data was collected by means of the questionnaire which was administrated online by means of the Google Forms questionnaire builder. The questionnaire was composed of 7 items related to participants' demography, 30 items meant for exploring hedonic quality and 16 items designed for examining content quality in the context of SNS. Responses to the questionnaire items were modulated on a five point Likert scale (1- strongly disagree, 5 – strongly agree). Each attribute was measured with between three and six items. For the purpose of data analysis, quality attributes and categories were operationalized as composite subjective measures. Values for quality attributes were estimated as a sum of responses to items that are assigned to them. The same holds for perceived quality (PCQ) whose value was estimated as sum of all items meant for measuring facets of hedonic quality (HDQ) and content quality (CNQ). Overall quality (OVQ) was assessed directly by a six-point item (0 - cannot evaluate, 1 - insufficient, 5 - excellent). The internal consistency of quality attributes was tested with Cronbach's Alpha [8] coefficient values. After the reliability of questionnaire was determined, it was necessary to examine its validity. However, since there were no previously validated measuring instruments for evaluating perceived hedonic quality and content quality of SNS, it was not possible to conduct predicted or concurrent evaluation to obtain a quantitative measure of validity. As an alternative to measuring the validity of a measuring instrument, Lewis [15] suggested the inspection of variables that systematically influence the questionnaire. In this study those variables were four SNS. The sensitivity of measuring instrument, in terms of examining differences between evaluated SNS, was explored by means of the Friedman's ANOVA. The rationale behind the choice to employ this nonparametric equivalent to the one-way ANOVA with repeated measures draws on the outcomes of Shapiro-Wilk Tests which revealed that at least one of the variables in a pairwise comparison violates the assumption of normality in data (p < .05). In that respect, all the reported results are expressed as the median values. To identify where the differences actually occur, we ran separate Wilcoxon Signed-Rank Tests on the different combinations of SNS being assessed. With an aim to declare a result significant and avoid a Type I error, we applied a Bonferroni correction on the results obtained from the Wilcoxon Signed-Rank Tests. The Bonferroni correction was calculated by dividing significance level of .05 by number of comparisons. The effect size (r) is an objective measure of the importance of effect. It was estimated by dividing Z-value by square root of number of observations. According to Cohen [7], the values of .10, .30, and .50 denote small, medium, and large effect size, respectively.

4 Results

Participants. A total of 322 respondents took part in the study. They ranged in age from 18 to 49 years (M = 21.23, SD = 4.318). The sample was composed of 66.15% male and 33.85% female students. At the time when the study was conducted, 59.32% of study subjects were enrolled to one of the undergraduate study programs at Polytechnic of Rijeka (POLYRI) whereas remaining 40.68% were students at the Faculty of Informatics, Juraj Dobrila University of Pula (FIPU). Majority of respondents (85.09%) were full-time students whereas 63.98% of them were in their first year of study. They had been using regularly almost all SNS that were the subject of an evaluation. More specifically, 57.77% and 62.73% of study participants had used Facebook and Instagram, respectively, at least 4 h a week, 9.93% of them had used Twitter at least up to one hour a week while 59.32% of respondents had used YouTube at least 11 h a week. When the ofteness of employing those SNS was considered, it appeared that 52.17%, 57.45%, and 64.97% of students had used Facebook, Instagram, and YouTube, respectively, at least three times a day while 10.85% of them had used Twitter at least once a week. The aforementioned findings indicate that the most popular social networking site among students is YouTube followed by Instagram, Facebook, and Twitter.

Measuring Instrument Reliability. The Cronbach's alpha values presented in Table 1 ranged from .639 (for attribute added value in the case of YouTube) to .955 (for attribute loyalty with respect to Instagram), thus indicating a high reliability of the scale in the context of exploratory study for all four evaluated SNS.

Table 1. Internal reliability of the scale for social networking sites (SNS)

Attributes	Number of items	Cronbach's α			
		Facebook	Instagram	Twitter	YouTube
Content quality					
Accuracy	3	.873	.886	.909	.880
Credibility	3	.901	.889	.921	.887
Coverage	4	.755	.783	.860	.764
Timeliness	3	.767	.789	.856	.755
Added value	3	.713	.750	.780	.639
Hedonic quality					
Aesthetics	5	.842	.903	.882	.786
Uniqueness	4	.827	.839	.820	.801
Playfulness	6	.837	.845	.906	.746
Pleasure	4	.913	.948	.951	.907
Satisfaction	6	.912	.929	.943	.800
Loyalty	5	.906	.955	.928	.830

Findings. The outcomes of data analysis indicate that evaluated SNS differ significantly ($\chi^2(3) = 199.863$, $p < .001$) with respect to the accuracy of content they are providing. Post hoc analysis with Wilcoxon Signed-Rank Tests was conducted with a Bonferroni correction applied, resulting in a significance level set at $p < .008$. Medium in size differences were discovered between YouTube and Twitter ($Z = -10.654$, $p = .000$, $r = -.42$) as well as between YouTube and Facebook ($Z = -8.005$, $p = .000$, $r = -.32$) while differences between Instagram and Twitter ($Z = -7.167$, $p = .000$, $r = -.28$), YouTube and Instagram ($Z = -6.911$, $p = .000$, $r = -.27$), Facebook and Twitter ($Z = -5.615$, $p = .000$, $r = -.22$), and Instagram and Facebook ($Z = -3.166$, $p = .002$, $r = -.13$) appeared to be small in size. Friedman's ANOVA revealed a significant difference ($\chi^2(3) = 177.775$, $p < .001$) among four SNS in the context of content credibility. As a follow up for this finding, a post hoc analysis with the significance level set at $p < .008$ was applied. The difference in terms of the extent to which particular social networking site contains unbiased content was found between YouTube and Twitter ($Z = -10.047$, $p = .000$, $r = -.40$), YouTube and Facebook ($Z = -8.437$, $p = .000$, $r = -.33$), and between YouTube and Instagram ($Z = -7.798$, $p = .000$, $r = -.31$) was medium in size. In addition, post hoc analysis uncovered small in size difference between Instagram and Twitter ($Z = -5.695$, $p = .000$, $r = -.22$), Facebook and Twitter ($Z = -4.005$, $p = .000$, $r = -.16$), and between Instagram and Facebook ($Z = -2.679$, $p = .007$, $r = -.11$). The degree to which content is perceived by study participants as complete is significantly ($\chi^2(3) = 279.407$, $p < .001$) affected by the social networking site they are using. Wilcoxon tests were used to follow-up this finding. A Bonferroni correction was applied and all effects are reported at a .01 level of significance. There was no significant difference between Instagram and Facebook ($Z = -.870$, $p = .380$). However, medium in size difference was found between YouTube and Twitter ($Z = -12.443$, $p = .000$, $r = -.49$), Instagram and Twitter

($Z = -9.442$, $p = .000$, $r = -.37$), Facebook and Twitter ($Z = -8.733$, $p = .000$, $r = -.34$), and between YouTube and Facebook ($Z = -7.776$, $p = .000$, $r = -.31$) while difference between YouTube and Instagram ($Z = -7.228$, $p = .000$, $r = -.29$) was small in size. A statistically significant difference ($\chi^2(3) = 136.430$, $p < .001$) regarding content timeliness was found among four SNS that were involved in the study. The follow-up tests with significance level set at .01 revealed medium in size differences between Facebook and Twitter ($Z = -10.206$, $p = .000$, $r = -.40$) and between YouTube and Facebook ($Z = -7.861$, $p = .000$, $r = -.31$) as well as small in size differences between Instagram and Facebook ($Z = -7.179$, $p = .000$, $r = -.28$), Instagram and Twitter ($Z = -5.558$, $p = .000$, $r = -.22$), and between YouTube and Twitter ($Z = -4.739$, $p = .000$, $r = -.19$). However, it appeared that YouTube and Instagram do not differ significantly ($Z = -1.415$, $p = .157$) when the degree to which content they provide can be modified is concerned. Data analysis also uncovered a significant difference ($\chi^2(3) = 363.350$, $p < .001$) among evaluated SNS with respect to the extent to which users believe that content SNS are offering is beneficial for them. To follow-up this finding, Wilcoxon tests with Bonferroni correction were applied. The large in size difference was found between YouTube and Twitter ($Z = -13.378$, $p = .000$, $r = -.53$), medium in size differences were identified between YouTube and Instagram ($Z = -11.062$, $p = .000$, $r = -.44$), Facebook and Twitter ($Z = -9.864$, $p = .000$, $r = -.39$), YouTube and Facebook ($Z = -9.699$, $p = .000$, $r = -.38$), and between Instagram and Twitter ($Z = -7.884$, $p = .000$, $r = -.31$) while difference between Instagram and Facebook ($Z = -4.543$, $p = .000$, $r = -.18$) appeared to be small in size. The reported results were at $p < .008$ significance level. All the aforementioned contributed to significant difference ($\chi^2(3) = 292.334$, $p < .001$) among evaluated SNS when their content quality is taken into account. More specifically, the large in size difference was determined between YouTube and Twitter ($Z = -13.855$, $p = .000$, $r = -.55$), differences between Facebook and Twitter ($Z = -10.094$, $p = .000$, $r = -.40$), YouTube and Instagram ($Z = -9.619$, $p = .000$, $r = -.38$), Instagram and Twitter ($Z = -9.241$, $p = .000$, $r = -.36$), and between YouTube and Facebook ($Z = -8.564$, $p = .000$, $r = -34$) appeared to be medium in size whereas difference between Instagram and Facebook ($Z = -1.881$, $p = .060$) in the context of content quality was not significant. All reported findings were at $p < .01$ level of significance.

There was a significant difference among all SNS that took part in the study with respect to the level to which users perceive their interface as visually attractive ($\chi^2(3) = 343.151$, $p < .001$). With a significance level set at $p < .008$, post hoc analysis with Bonferroni correction yielded large in size difference between YouTube and Twitter ($Z = -12.804$, $p = .000$, $r = -.51$), medium in size differences between Instagram and Twitter ($Z = -11.352$, $p = .000$, $r = -.45$), Facebook and Twitter ($Z = -9.411$, $p = .000$, $r = -.37$), and between YouTube and Facebook ($Z = -7.675$, $p = .000$, $r = -.30$), and small in size difference between Instagram and Facebook ($Z = -4.693$, $p = .000$, $r = -.19$) and between YouTube and Instagram ($Z = -3.215$, $p = .001$, $r = -.13$). When the degree to which particular social networking site is perceived as exceptional was considered, Friedman's ANOVA revealed significant difference ($\chi^2(3) = 308.551$, $p < .001$) among all four SNS that were examined in the study. Results of post hoc analysis are divided in three different groups. Large in size difference was determined between YouTube and Twitter (Z = −13.073, p = .000, r = −.52). Medium in size differences were discovered between Instagram and Twitter (Z = −9.821, p = .000, r = −.39), YouTube and Facebook (Z = −9.349, p = .000, r = −.37), Facebook and Twitter (Z = −9.146, p = .000, r = −.36), and between YouTube and Instagram (Z = −8.550, p = .000, r = −.34). Difference between Instagram and Facebook (Z = −2.031, p = .042) was not significant. All reported results were at p < .01 significance level. The results of data analysis are also implying significant difference ($\chi^2(3) = 472.711$, p < .001) among examined SNS with regard to the extent to which users are immersed when interacting with them. To follow up on this finding, Wilcoxon Signed-Rank Tests with a Bonferroni correction were conducted. With a significance level set at p < .008, large in size differences were identified between YouTube and Twitter (Z = −14.921, p = .000, r = −.59) and between Instagram and Twitter (Z = −12.677, p = .000, r = −.50), medium in size differences were found between YouTube and Facebook (Z = −12.315, p = .000, r = −.49), Facebook and Twitter (Z = −10.897, p = .000, r = −.43), and between YouTube and Instagram (Z = −9.600, p = .000, r = −.38), while small in size difference was determined between Instagram and Facebook (Z = −5.625, p = .000, r = −.22). Friedman's ANOVA revealed a significant difference ($\chi^2(3) = 472.711$, p < .001) among four SNS in terms of the degree to which study participants are enjoying when employing them. As a follow up to this finding, a post hoc analysis with the significance level set at p < .008 was applied. Identified difference between YouTube and Twitter (Z = −14.453, p = .000, r = −.57) was large in size, differences between Instagram and Twitter (Z = −12.428, p = .000, r = −.49), Facebook and Twitter (Z = −11.845, p = .000, r = −.47), YouTube and Facebook (Z = −10.547, p = .000, r = −.42), and between YouTube and Instagram (Z = −8.069, p = .000, r = −.32) were medium in size whereas difference between Instagram and Facebook (Z = −3.543, p = .000, r = −.14) was small in size. A significant difference ($\chi^2(3) = 476.800$, p < .001) among examined SNS with respect to the degree to which they have met users' expectations was also discovered. Bonferroni pairwise comparisons with a significance level set at p < .008 uncovered large in size difference between YouTube and Twitter (Z = −14.800, p = .000, r = −.58), medium in size differences between Instagram and Twitter (Z = −12.203, p = .000, r = −.48), Facebook and Twitter (Z = −11.749, p = .000, r = −.46), YouTube and Facebook (Z = −11.547, p = .000, r = −.46), and between YouTube and Instagram (Z = −8.908, p = .000, r = −.35), and small in size difference between Instagram and Facebook (Z = −3.847, p = .000, r = −.15). A significant value of chi square ($\chi^2(3) = 526.792$, p < .001) indicates the existence of differences among examined SNS with regard to the degree to which study participants are their loyal consumers. A post hoc procedure with the significance level set at p < .01 revealed large in size difference between YouTube and Twitter (Z = −15.002, p = .000, r = −.59) as well as medium in size differences between Facebook and Twitter (Z = −12.477, p = .000, r = −.49), Instagram and Twitter (Z = −12.350, p = .000, r = −.49), YouTube and Facebook (Z = −11.080, p = .000, r = −.44), and between YouTube and Instagram (Z = −9.651, p = .000, r = −.38). However, no significant difference was found in that respect between Instagram and Facebook (Z = −.762, p = .446). The reported findings resulted in significant difference ($\chi^2(3) = 519.561$, p < .001) among evaluated SNS with respect to their hedonic quality. Wilcoxon tests were used to follow-up this finding. A Bonferroni correction was applied and all effects are reported at a $p < .008$ level of significance. Five large in size (between YouTube and Twitter ($Z = -15.322$, $p = .000$, $r = -.60$), Instagram and Twitter ($Z = -13.215$, $p = .000$, $r = -.52$), YouTube and Facebook ($Z = -13.152$, $p = .000$, $r = -.52$), Facebook and Twitter ($Z = -12.649$, $p = .000$, $r = -.50$) and between YouTube and Instagram ($Z = -10.261$, $p = .000$, $r = -.40$)) and one small in size (between Instagram and Facebook ($Z = -4.773$, $p = .000$, $r = -.19$)) difference were determined in that respect.

A significant difference ($\chi^2(3) = 543.219$, $p < .001$) among examined SNS was found with respect to single-item subjective measure designed for evaluating overall quality. Large in size differences were discovered between YouTube and Twitter ($Z = -15.021$, $p = .000$, $r = -.59$), YouTube and Facebook ($Z = -13.371$, $p = .000$, $r = -.53$), Facebook and Twitter ($Z = -13.038$, $p = .000$, $r = -.51$), and between Instagram and Twitter ($Z = -12.759$, $p = .000$, $r = -.50$), difference between YouTube and Instagram ($Z = -9.636$, $p = .000$, $r = -.38$) was medium in size, while difference between Instagram and Facebook ($Z = -4.202$, $p = .000$, $r = -.17$) appeared to be small in size.

Drawing on findings related to hedonic quality and content quality, significant difference ($\chi^2(3) = 512.102$, $p < .001$) among SNS that were involved in the study in terms of their perceived quality was determined. More specifically, large in size difference was identified between YouTube and Twitter ($Z = -15.383$, $p = .000$, $r = -.61$), Instagram and Twitter ($Z = -12.980$, $p = .000$, $r = -.51$), YouTube and Facebook ($Z = -12.909$, $p = .000$, $r = -.51$), and between Facebook and Twitter

Table 2. Outcomes of data analysis (note that a higher score means a better result)

Attributes	χ^2*	Facebook		Instagram		Twitter		YouTube	
		Mdn	σ	Mdn	σ	Mdn	σ	Mdn	σ
CNQ	292.334	56.00	11.943	56.00	12.744	48.00	13.773	62.50	11.250
ACU	199.863	9.00	3.242	9.00	3.319	9.00	3.090	11.00	3.350
CDB	177.775	9.00	3.322	9.00	3.257	9.00	2.987	9.00	3.474
CVG	279.407	14.00	3.861	15.00	4.015	12.00	4.166	16.00	3.760
TLS	136.430	15.00	3.098	13.00	3.488	9.00	3.608	12.00	3.564
ADV	363.350	13.00	2.923	11.00	3.103	9.00	3.228	15.00	1.971
HDQ	519.561	120.00	26.891	130.00	28.981	82.00	27.967	140.00	14.288
AES	343.151	23.00	4.598	25.00	4.343	17.00	5.570	25.00	3.153
UNQ	308.551	16.00	4.396	16.00	4.385	12.00	4.380	20.00	3.408
PLY	472.711	18.00	6.596	21.00	6.833	12.00	6.259	25.00	5.214
PLS	476.800	18.00	4.936	20.00	4.852	11.00	5.185	20.00	2.404
STF	478.711	24.00	7.012	27.00	6.905	16.00	6.977	30.00	3.776
LOY	526.792	22.00	6.060	23.00	6.812	10.00	6.018	25.00	2.699
OVQ	**543.219**	3.00	.995	4.00	1.559	1.00	1.571	5.00	.571
PCQ	**512.102**	175.00	34.499	186.00	38.048	129.50	37.722	201.50	21.449

* $df = 3$, $p = .000$

($Z = -12.647$, $p = .000$, $r = -.50$), medium in size difference was uncovered between YouTube and Instagram ($Z = -10.774$, $p = .000$, $r = -.43$), while difference between Instagram and Facebook ($Z = -3.736$, $p = .000$, $r = -.15$) was small in size. All reported findings are summarized in Table 2.

5 Conclusion

The aim of the work presented of this paper was to examine the validity of the measuring instrument designed for evaluating hedonic and content related dimensions of quality in the context of social networking sites (SNS). For that purpose, an empirical study was conducted during which psychometric features of introduced questionnaire were confirmed. More specifically, the Cronbach's Alpha exceeded the .70 cut-off value for all quality attributes in the case of all four SNS involved in the study (with an exception of added value attribute in the case of YouTube) thus indicating the high level of inter-item consistency reliability. When the validity of the questionnaire was tackled, study findings suggested that all proposed quality attributes can be employed for determining significant differences among SNS. Taking into account attributes aimed for examining hedonic quality and content quality separately, they managed to discover 12.12% large in size, 56.06% medium in size, and 26.76% small in size differences among four SNS included in the study. The highest deal (33.33%) of large in size differences was discovered by means of the attribute designed for measuring perceived playfulness. Majority of medium in size differences was determined with two attributes associated with content quality (coverage and added value) and four attributes assigned to hedonic quality (uniqueness, pleasure, satisfaction, and loyalty). The highest amount of small in size differences was discovered with an attribute meant for measuring content accuracy. At least one non-significant difference among examined SNS was found with two attributes designed for measuring content quality (coverage and timeliness) and two attributes aimed for evaluating hedonic facets of quality (uniqueness and loyalty). While differences yielded by content quality as a composite measure were mainly medium in size, differences identified by hedonic quality in the same respect were mostly large in size. Both overall quality and perceived quality determined the same amount of large (66.66%), medium (16.67%), and small (16.67%) in size differences. All the aforementioned indicates that practitioners can use proposed questionnaire as an instrument for measuring quality of existing SNS as well as set of guidelines when designing new SNS. Considering that the study carried out for the purpose of this paper is empirical one, it has several limitations. The first one is related to homogeneity of participants. Although students can be perceived as representative users of SNS since they can be used in educational ecosystem, heterogeneous group of study respondents could have provided different answers to questionnaire items related to particular attributes of content quality and hedonic quality. The second limitation deals with the interpretation of reported findings because they are generalizable only to SNS included in our study. Taking the above into account, in order to draw generalizable sound conclusions and to examine the robustness of reported findings, further studies should be conducted.

References

1. Aladwani, A.M.: Compatible quality of social media content: conceptualization, measurement, and affordances. Int. J. Inf. Manag. **37**(6), 576–582 (2017). https://doi.org/10.1016/j.ijinfomgt.2017.05.014
2. Ali, M., Yaacob, R., Iskandar, R.A., Al-Amin Endut, M.N., Sulam, M.: The influence of contents utility on students' use of social media. Pertanika J. Soc. Sci. Hum. **26**(S), 93–110 (2018)
3. Callaghan, G., Fribbance, I.: Facebook and informal learning. In: Creativity and Critique in Online Learning, pp. 81–102. Palgrave Macmillan, Cham (2018). https://doi.org/10.1007/978-3-319-78298-0_5
4. Cao, J., Basoglu, K.A., Sheng, H., Lowry, P.B.: A systematic review of social networks research in information systems: building a foundation for exciting future research. Commun. Assoc. Inf. Syst. **36**(1), 727–758 (2015). https://doi.org/10.17705/1CAIS.03637
5. Chan, T., Cheung, C., Shi, N., Lee, M., Lee, Z.: An empirical examination of continuance intention of social network sites. Pac. Asia J. Assoc. Inf. Syst. **8**(4), 69–90 (2016)
6. Chen, H.G., Zhu, Y.Q.: User experience as service at social networking. In: AHFE conference on Advances in the Human Side of Service Engineering, pp. 53–59 (2014). https://doi.org/10.1007/978-3-319-60486-2
7. Cohen, J.: Statistical Power Analysis for the Behavioral Sciences. Lawrence Erlbaum Associates, Hillsdale (1988)
8. Cronbach, L.J.: Coefficient alpha and the internal structure of tests. Psychometrika **16**(3), 297–334 (1951)
9. Denker, K.J., Manning, J., Heuett, K.B., Summers, M.E.: Twitter in the classroom: modeling online communication attitudes and student motivations to connect. Comput. Hum. Behav. **79**, 1–8 (2018). https://doi.org/10.1016/j.chb.2017.09.037
10. Hajli, M.N.: A study of the impact of social media on consumers. Int. J. Mark. Res. **56**(3), 387–404 (2014). https://doi.org/10.2501/IJMR-2014-025
11. Kim, B., Kim, Y.: Facebook versus instagram: how perceived gratifications and technological attributes are related to the change in social media usage. Soc. Sci. J. (2018, in press). https://doi.org/10.1016/j.soscij.2018.10.002
12. Kumar, V., Nanda, P.: Social media in higher education: a framework for continuous engagement. Int. J. Inf. Commun. Technol. Educat. **15**(1), 109–120 (2019). https://doi.org/10.4018/IJICTE.2019010108
13. Lee, S., Kim, B.G.: The impact of qualities of social network service on the continuance usage intention. Manag. Decis. **55**(4), 701–729 (2017). https://doi.org/10.1108/MD-10-2016-0731
14. Leong, L.W., Ibrahim, O., Dalvi-Esfahani, M., Shahbazi, H., Nilashi, M.: The moderating effect of experience on the intention to adopt mobile social network sites for pedagogical purposes: An extension of the technology acceptance model. Educat. Inf. Technol. **23**(6), 2477–2498 (2018). https://doi.org/10.1007/s10639-018-9726-2
15. Lewis, J.R.: IBM computer usability satisfaction questionnaires: psychometric evaluation and instructions for use. Int. J. Hum.-Comput. Inter. **7**(1), 57–78 (1995). https://doi.org/10.1080/10447319509526110
16. Lovari, A., Giglietto, F.: Social media and Italian universities: an empirical study on the adoption and use of Facebook, Twitter and Youtube (2012). https://doi.org/10.2139/ssrn.1978393
17. Makkonen, P., Siakas, K.: Social media usability in higher education: a cross-cultural analysis with IS/ICT students. In: Society for Information Technology & Teacher Education International Conference, pp. 2292–2300, Association for the Advancement of Computing in Education (2018)

18. Nedra, B.A., Hadhri, W., Mezrani, M.: Determinants of customers' intentions to use hedonic networks: the case of Instagram. J. Retail. Consum. Serv. **46**(C), 21–32 (2019). https://doi.org/10.1016/j.jretconser.2018.09.001
19. Orehovački, T., Babić, S.: Identifying the relevance of quality dimensions contributing to universal access of social web applications for collaborative writing on mobile devices: an empirical study. Univ. Access Inf. Soc. **17**(3), 453–473 (2018). https://doi.org/10.1007/s10209-017-0555-7
20. Orehovački, T., Cappiello, C., Matera, M.: Identifying relevant dimensions for the quality of web mashups: an empirical study. In: Kurosu, M. (ed.) HCI 2016. LNCS, vol. 9731, pp. 396–407. Springer, Cham (2016). https://doi.org/10.1007/978-3-319-39510-4_37
21. Orehovački, T., Granić, A., Kermek, D.: Evaluating the perceived and estimated quality in use of web 2.0 applications. J. Syst. Soft. **86**(12), 3039–3059 (2013). https://doi.org/10.1016/j.jss.2013.05.071
22. Orehovački, T.: Proposal for a set of quality attributes relevant for web 2.0 application success. In: Proceedings of the 32nd International Conference on Information Technology Interfaces, pp. 319–326. IEEE Press, Cavtat (2010)
23. Ou, C.X., Davison, R.M., Huang, V.Q.: The social networking application success model: an empirical study of Facebook and Twitter. Int. J. Knowl. Content Dev. Technol. **6**(1), 5–39 (2016). https://doi.org/10.5865/IJKCT.2016.6.1.005
24. Pöyry, E., Parvinen, P., Malmivaara, T.: Can we get from liking to buying? Behavioral differences in hedonic and utilitarian facebook usage. Electron. Commer. Res. Appl. **12**(4), 224–235 (2013)
25. Rodríguez-Ardura, I., Meseguer-Artola, A.: The playfulness of facebook-shaped by underlying psychological drivers and gender differences. Telematics Inform. **35**(8), 2254–2269 (2018). https://doi.org/10.1016/j.tele.2018.09.004
26. Sánchez-Adame, L.M., Mendoza, S., González-Beltrán, B.A., Rodríguez, J., Viveros, A.M.: UX evaluation over time: user tools in social networks. In: 2018 15th International Conference on Electrical Engineering, Computing Science and Automatic Control (CCE), pp. 1–6. IEEE Press, Mexico City (2018). https://doi.org/10.1109/iceee.2018.8533950
27. Sawalha, S., Al-Jamal, M., Abu-Shanab, E.: The influence of utilising Facebook on e-government adoption. Electron. Gov. Int. J. **15**(1), 1–20 (2019). https://doi.org/10.1504/EG.2019.096573
28. Tien, D.H., Rivas, A.A.A., Liao, Y.K.: Examining the influence of customer-to-customer electronic word-of-mouth on purchase intention in social networking sites. Asia Pac. Manag. Rev. (2018, in press). https://doi.org/10.1016/j.apmrv.2018.06.003
29. Wu, C.H., Chen, S.C.: Understanding the relationships of critical factors to facebook educational usage intention. Internet Res. **25**(2), 262–278 (2015). https://doi.org/10.1108/IntR-11-2013-0232

A Simple Web Utility for Automatic Speech Quantification in Dyadic Reading Interactions

Michael Schmidt[1], Robert Walters[1], Bryce Ault[1], Khem Poudel[1], Adam Mischke[1], Stone Jones[1], Austin Sockhecke[1], Marcus Spears[1], Patrick Clarke[1], Rober Makram[1], Sam Meagher[1], Medha Sarkar[1], Joshua Wade[2(✉)], and Nilanjan Sarkar[2]

[1] Computer Science, Middle Tennessee State University, Murfreesboro, TN 37132, USA
[2] Adaptive Technology Consulting, LLC, Murfreesboro, TN 37127, USA
josh@innovateatc.com

Abstract. Adult-child reading interactions can produce efficient childhood learning outcomes when formal methods of adult-initiated prompting and dialog are employed. In order to quantify instances of such prompting, child development researchers often manually code speech recordings or transcripts taken from adult-child readings, which can be a laborious process. For researchers, it would therefore be valuable to have the capacity to automatically capture quantitative measures of communication from adult-child reading interactions. This paper introduces SoundCount, a new open-source utility for extracting descriptive features from recordings of speech during communication between an adult and child reading an eBook together. In a simple web-based framework, SoundCount consolidates functionalities for speech analysis and quantification in the context of dyadic reading interactions, specifically providing measures related to word count and speaker differentiation. Our preliminary results demonstrate the functional feasibility of SoundCount, and our technical discussion will enable readers to use SoundCount in their own research. Given the technical viability of SoundCount, future work will include the implementation of additional measures for the system, new features such as automated audio segmentation based on speaker, and a test of the efficacy of real-time feedback systems based on speech measures

Keywords: eBook · Dialogic reading · Childhood education · Speech quantification · Speech recognition

1 Introduction

Evidence suggests that children learn more efficiently from story reading when an adult such as a parent or teacher actively engages the child in dialogue about the story [1, 2]. The formalized technique of dialogic reading involves adult-child reading scenarios in which a child practices vocabulary while receiving real-time feedback from the adult [3]. Researchers have typically employed manual human coding methods to quantify instances of such "dialogic questioning", which can be a laborious activity [4]. For researchers, it would therefore be valuable to have the capacity to automatically capture quantitative measures of communication during adult-child reading interactions. Specifically, a measure of the proportion of speech by the adult, as well as by the child, could provide valuable information regarding reciprocal communication even without analysis of the semantic content [5]. In addition, information such as the number of vocalizations or the number of words that occur during a reading—both from the adult and child—as well as the change in the number of vocalizations or words over time would allow researchers to design protocols aimed at optimizing adult-child communication during reading in order to improve learning outcomes for young children.

Mobile computing devices such as tablets, smartphones, and e-readers are now commonly used for reading and education and have shown increased acceptance over time. Teaching through the use of electronic books (eBooks) has shown evidence of significantly enhanced learning among children [6], although researchers do recommend limiting screen time exposure especially before bedtime [7]. Some of the strengths of eBooks over traditional books include the ability of eBooks to (a) define unfamiliar words directly within the application, (b) display story text in other languages, (c) dynamically adapt the story text the reader, such as according to reading ability, (d) prompt interaction and communication, such as between a child and an educator or parent, to optimize learning outcomes, and (e) automatically capture process and performance measures to track performance and learning.

In the current work, we designed a tool for child development researchers who wish to automatically capture quantitative measures of speech from adult-child communication during eBook readings. *SoundCount*, the proposed speech recognition system, is an open-source utility for extracting descriptive features from recordings of speech during communication between an adult and child reading an eBook together [8]. While commercial speech-to-text services, such as those available by Google Cloud and Microsoft Azure, offer a vast range of functionality, SoundCount was designed to produce a simple set of measures in the specific context of dyadic reading, thus helping researchers to better understand and track learning outcomes in children.

2 System Design

2.1 System Overview

SoundCount used Python (version 3.6.6) as the principal programming language and was built using several established support frameworks. SoundCount uses Flask [9] as a simple Hypertext Transfer Protocol (HTTP) server to receive audio files via HTTP POST requests. For speech recognition, Python's SpeechRecognition library was selected for its support of multiple recognition engines. Using this library, transcripts of users' speech is produced from an audio file, from which a word count approximation is easily computed. Additionally, SoundCount also leverages Python's Natural Language Toolkit (NLTK) [10] part-of-speech tagger, specifically the Averaged Perceptron Tagger, to identify and label part-of-speech meta-information from the transcript. The overall software architecture of SoundCount is given in Fig. 1. Using a persistent model—trained previously on data from [11]—an analysis of the speech is conducted which attempts to identify gender, age, and the language dialect of the speaker. Finally, SoundCount reports the duration of the speech in the audio recording. All results are returned in a single JavaScript Object Notation (JSON)-encoded object.

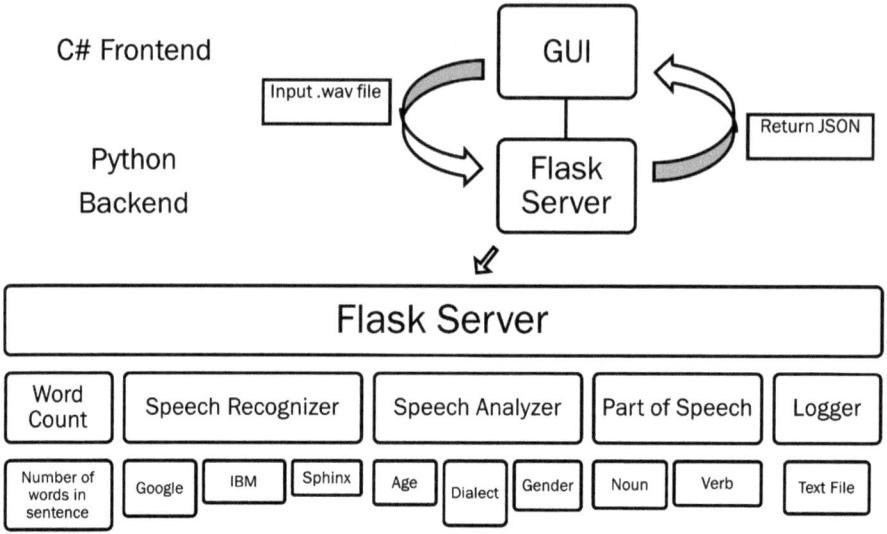

Fig. 1. SoundCount software architecture overview

2.2 System Architecture

From a high-level perspective, SoundCount was designed as a web service operating as a daemon process. By interfacing with client applications via standard HTTP methods, client applications would remain modular and non-dependent on various frameworks, such as packages for recording/analyzing audio, user interface toolkits, and/or operating systems. This design pattern gave SoundCount deployment flexibility as well, where the daemon application receiving each HTTP request over a network interface might reside on the localhost machine via a loopback address, a computer on a small wireless network such as a home or office, or as a process accessible via an Internet client. In this way the application's scope is not be limited to a single user/machine, and the daemon can easily scale on demand; each client interface needs only to specify a host and port number. The daemon could run on dedicated hardware. For example, a website might act as an interface to the daemon process for its users, or multiple instances of the daemon could spawn on different ports with a load balancing mechanism. For test cases described in the current work, a standalone C♯ GUI application was created to interface with SoundCount on a standard PC running Microsoft Windows 7 (see Fig. 2). The daemon process was developed on machines running Ubuntu 16.04 and macOS High Sierra.

Because most speech recognizers support the Waveform Audio (.*wav*) format, we used this format exclusively in the current work. Planned future development will add support for additional formats. For example, Python's PyDub library can be used to

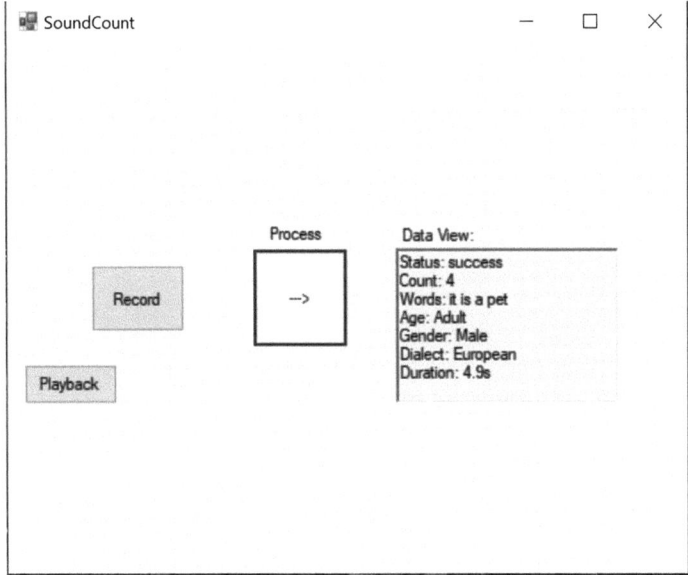

Fig. 2. Frontend GUI developed for testing SoundCount.

convert MPEG Layer 3 (*.mp3*), and other proprietary formats on demand to *.wav* files, and most recognizers support popular formats. Received audio files are not preprocessed upon receipt; the data is temporarily stored to disk and renamed using a randomly generated Universally Unique Identifier (UUID) to avoid filename collisions. The Flask server checks that the HTTP POST requests does contain a "file" field which corresponds to the audio file and responds with an error if the field is absent.

The abbreviated code listing below presents the behavior of the server-side *post()* method used by SoundCount to process client requests. Lines 11–19 receive and parse the client request and save the audio data as a file identified by the "tempfile" variable. Lines 22 and 23 perform speech recognition and run the audio through the voice analyzer, respectively. Both of these functions return *dict()* types so the payload's meta information is updated in place. Line 27 uses Python's built-in *len()* function to estimate word count, and line 28 uses NTLK's Averaged Perceptron Tagger to tag the list of words. The duration of the file is calculated using the audio's frame count divided by the frame-rate; this is done on line 29. Finally, the temp file is removed, and the complete payload is returned. Flask coverts Python's *dict()* type into a serialized JSON string for convenient parsing on the client-side.

```
 1 def post(self):
 2 """
 3 Handles HTTP POST request given a form with a 'file.'
 4 'file' represents the user's audio submission.
 5 :file: (WAV) waveform audio Via HTTP POST form-data.
 6 :returns: dict() Meta-information of the audio.
 7 """
 8
 9 ...
10
11 parse = reqparse.RequestParser()
12 parse.add_argument('file',
       type=werkzeug.datastructures.FileStorage,   loca-
       tion='files')
13 args = parse.parse_args()
14
15 try:
16     audio_file = args['file']
17     audio_file.save(tempfile)
18 except AttributeError:
19     ...
20
21 try:
22     payload['meta'].update(speech_rec(tempfile))
23     payload['meta'].update(voice_analyzer(tempfile))
24 except:
25     ...
26
27 payload['count'] = len(payload['meta']['text'])
28 payload['meta']['text'] =
       pos_tagger([payload['meta']['text']])
29 payload['meta']['duration'] = duration(tempfile)
30
31 ...
32
33 return payload
```

The aptly named SpeechRecognition library was selected for its ability to query application program interfaces (APIs) such as Google Cloud, Bing, Houndify, and an offline recognizer called Sphinx. To simplify SoundCount's configuration, an *environment.py* file provides a Python dictionary of user-configured credentials for paid services. The environment file also specifies a host/port combination on which the daemon shall listen for requests. In the current work, we opted for the offline recognizer, Sphinx, which has strong runtime performance and a word error rate of about 14% [12]. Note that word error rate is impacted by word identification in addition to word count. While a word error rate of this size would be too large for reliable speech content analysis (i.e., understanding the exact phrase spoken), it is adequate in the current work given the priority placed on measuring speech duration and frequency. The SpeechRecognition library recognizer outputs a string of text that is tokenized into a list of string natural lexemes. NLTK's Perceptron tagger receives the lexemes as input to tag a part-of-speech field. The role of NTLK in SoundCount was to resolve ambiguity surrounding certain language complexities. For example, the word *can't* may appear in a transcript as one word but is actually a contraction of two words and could be counted as such. Similarly, *right-handed* may appear as one word, but could be regarded as a combination of two instead. SoundCount's policy for handling such edge cases is to base its word count on the number of parts-of-speech recognized, rather than on the possible decomposition of words containing hyphens and apostrophes.

In addition to identifying the parts of speech, SoundCount attempts to label the gender, dialect, and age of the speaker. This exploratory component of SoundCount leverages an existing open-source (MIT license) project called Voice-Analyzer to capture preliminary metrics. Voice-Analyzer uses SciPy's DecisionTreeClassifier to classify audio samples, and reports reasonable accuracy (e.g., nearly 90% in the prediction of both age and gender), albeit from a relatively homogeneous training set (88% of the training data were male, 85% were adult, and 49% had an American dialect) [11]. Also, because many speech-to-text machine learning models employ artificial neural network models for temporal data processing through convolution, a decision tree approach may result in a less robust predictor for these labels. Nonetheless, SoundCount supports serialized objects (sometimes referred to as *pickled* objects) should models improve in the future.

Finally, all of the metadata associated with a client-provided audio recording are packaged into a Python dictionary. The dictionary structure is serialized into a JSON object and returned via Flask, completing the HTTP POST request. Each JSON object includes (a) a "status" field with a value of either *success* or *failure*, (b) a "count" field containing the part-of-speech count, and (c) a nested object "meta" containing a list of words with part-of-speech, gender, age, dialect, and the duration of the audio, such as that shown in the following example:

```
{
  "status": "success",
  "count": 9,
  "meta": {
      "text": [
          ["the", "DT"],
          ["quick", "JJ"],
          ["brown", "NN"],
          ["fox", "NN"],
          ["jumps", "VBZ"],
          ["over", "IN"],
          ["the", "DT"],
          ["lazy", "JJ"],
          ["dog", "NN"]],
        "gender": "Male",
        "age": "Adult",
        "dialect": "European",
        "duration": 5.120816326530612
  }
}
```

3 Results and Discussion

Although the primary contribution of this work is the development of a novel utility that brings together disparate functionalities and resources for speech quantification, we tested a key element of SoundCount's data output. Using the novel GUI (Fig. 2) to capture speech, data were collected from four adult volunteers (two males and two females; mean age = 38.25) to gauge the word-count estimation error of SoundCount. Subjects were asked to read from randomly selected sections of an online article while their speech was recorded by a laptop microphone. All phrases were read in English and ranged in length from 1–34 words. This was repeated 10 times for each subject, producing 40 data points for error analysis. Audio recordings were sent to SoundCount via the post method detailed in Table 1, and a JSON object containing speech analysis results was returned to the client. Using the actual number of words spoken by the subject and the number of words reported by SoundCount, we computed the Mean squared error (MSE), Root-mean-square error (RMSE), and Pearson correlation coefficient for each subject. Using the comparatively simple Sphinx model [13], RMSE were quite low and the Pearson correlation values were large (i.e., >.50; [14]). Moreover, SoundCount correctly predicted the speaker's gender and language in each test case. While this small sample cannot be used to make inferences about system performance within naturalistic settings, it does provide evidence of the feasibility of SoundCount and demonstrate that the system operates well within relatively constrained settings.

Table 1. Error of word count prediction.

Subject	MSE	RMSE	r
Female 1	4.2	2.05	0.985
Female 2	17.9	4.23	0.966
Male 1	3.0	1.73	0.842
Male 2	0.9	0.95	0.922

MSE = Mean squared error
RMSE = Root-mean-squared error
r = Pearson correlation coefficient

4 Conclusion

SoundCount is a new open-source utility for extracting descriptive features from recordings of speech during communication between an adult and child reading interaction. By automatically quantifying speech measures spoken during dyadic interactions, SoundCount will help researchers who have typically hand-coded such information and will facilitate the development of sophisticated systems that utilize speech data in an adaptive manner.

While our current work demonstrates the feasibility of SoundCount for its intended function, planned future work will address some of the current limitations of the tool. First, SoundCount currently functions under the assumption that audio segmentation is performed on the client-side and that audio files contain the voice of only one speaker at a time; because a major aim of SoundCount is to seamlessly quantify the proportion of speech by speaker, future work will investigate automatic segmentation of audio recordings based on speaker profile. Indeed, work is currently under way to develop an automatic segmentation component of the SoundCount speech processing algorithm. This segmentation step will produce an array of audio segments that will be iteratively processed using the current capabilities. Second, SoundCount performs reliably when the speaker's voice is captured clearly by the microphone and is not currently enabled to handle cases in which two or more speakers may be speaking at the same time or if there is significant background noise. Third, the current work's frontend testbed did not implement a buffer to read and seek audio data from despite our frameworks supported this input method. Finally, the data is not explicitly validated as an audio file type. Future development will implement these checks in order to produce a more robust system.

Our preliminary results demonstrate the functional feasibility of SoundCount, and our technical discussion will enable readers to use SoundCount in their own research. Given the technical viability of SoundCount, future work will include the implementation of additional measures for the system as well as a test of the efficacy of real-time feedback systems based on speech measures. Upcoming future work with SoundCount will test the validity of data acquisition in the context of adult-child reading interactions, and our team is actively working to add new metrics to SoundCount based on the requirements of child development researchers. For instance, we intend to use vocal intonation to interpret the sentiment of users' speech, which could provide a useful indication of user engagement within the reading interaction.

References

1. Hargrave, A.C., Sénéchal, M.: A book reading intervention with preschool children who have limited vocabularies: the benefits of regular reading and dialogic reading. Early Child. Res. Q. **15**(1), 75–90 (2000). https://doi.org/10.1016/S0885-2006(99)00038-1
2. Fleury, V.P., Schwartz, I.S.: A modified dialogic reading intervention for preschool children with autism spectrum disorder. Top. Early Child. Spec. Educ. **37**(1), 16–28 (2017). https://doi.org/10.1177/0271121416637597
3. Zevenbergen, A.A., Whitehurst, G.J.: Dialogic reading: a shared picture book reading intervention for preschoolers. Read. Books Child. Parents Teach. 177–200 (2003). https://doi.org/10.4324/9781410607355
4. Whitehurst, G.J., et al.: Accelerating language development through picture book reading. Dev. Psychol. **24**(4), 552 (1988). https://doi.org/10.1037/0012-1649.24.4.552
5. Harbison, A.L., Woynaroski, T.G., Tapp, J., Wade, J.W., Warlaumont, A.S., Yoder, P.J.: A new measure of child vocal reciprocity in children with autism spectrum disorder. Autism Res. **11**(6), 903–915 (2018). https://doi.org/10.1002/aur.1942
6. Union, C.D., Union, L.W., Green, T.D.: The use of eReaders in the classroom and at home to help third-grade students improve their reading and English/language arts standardized test scores. TechTrends **59**(5), 71–84 (2015). https://doi.org/10.1007/s11528-015-0893-3
7. Dube, N., Khan, K., Loehr, S., Chu, Y., Veugelers, P.: The use of entertainment and communication technologies before sleep could affect sleep and weight status: a population-based study among children. Int. J. Behav. Nutr. Phys. Act. **14**(1), 97 (2017). https://doi.org/10.1186/s12966-017-0547-2
8. SoundCount (2018). https://github.com/vanities/SoundCount. Accessed 20 Jan 2019
9. Ronacher, A.: Welcome—flask (a Python microframework), p. 38 (2010). http://flask.pocoo.org/. Accessed 02 Feb 2015
10. Bird, S., Loper, E.: NLTK: the natural language toolkit. In: Proceedings of the ACL 2004 on Interactive poster and demonstration sessions, p. 31 (2004). https://doi.org/10.3115/1219044.1219075
11. Voice-Analyzer (2018). https://github.com/lreynolds18/Voice-Analyzer. Accessed 20 Jan 2019
12. Huggins-Daines, D., et al.: A free, real-time continuous speech recognition system for hand-held devices. In: IEEE International Conference on Acoustics, Speech and Signal Processing Proceedings, ICASSP 2006, vol. 1, p. I (2006). https://doi.org/10.1109/icassp.2006.1659988
13. PocketSphinx (2018). https://github.com/cmusphinx/pocketsphinx. Accessed 20 Jan 2019
14. Ellis, P.D.: The Essential Guide to Effect Sizes: Statistical Power, Meta-analysis, and the Interpretation of Research Results. Cambridge University Press, Cambridge (2010)

Virtual Reality and Augmented Reality Systems for Learning

UX Aspects of Kinect-Based Movement Schemes Inside Virtual Environments for Museum Installations

Viviana Barneche-Naya and Luis A. Hernández-Ibáñez[✉]

videaLAB, Universidade da Coruña, A Coruña, Spain
{viviana.barneche,luis.hernandez}@udc.es

Abstract. Museum installations, especially those related to the display of virtual archaeology, often make use of natural user interaction (NUI). Those sets require methods of interaction that are intuitive and easy to all users, independent of their previous skills and experience with similar or related technologies. The use of depth cameras such as the Kinect system is a common way to allow visitors to move and interact within the digital replicas of buildings and spaces. This paper presents a study of User Experience (UX) applied to four movement schemes implemented on one such installation. For this research, a mixed method approach is used, using a sample of users segmented into three groups based on their previous skills and experience with video games. The four movement schemes studied combine a user gesture to move forward with another gesture for turning. The quantitative and qualitative data obtained for each movement scheme and user group were analyzed, and several usability metrics were combined to obtain a single UX score, which were then used to compare their performance and suitability for their use in the context of a museum.

Keywords: User experience · Natural interaction · Kinect · Museum installation · Virtual environments

1 Introduction

Nowadays, gestural systems stand out among the most popular forms of natural interaction. One can find many examples of the use of gestures to interact with devices such as smartphones, videogames and virtual reality applications. At the present time, all 3D videogame platforms support some kind of gesture-based interaction schemes by means of spatial scanning.

Among those devices, the Microsoft Kinect system depth camera facilitates obtaining a very comprehensive description of user's poses and gestures. The application of these devices is not limited to videogames; indeed, this device is being used profusely in multifarious fields, where virtual environments have to be explored by means of natural interaction [1]. Among those fields, virtual museums demand good walk-through paradigms for exploring the space and contemplating the environment and the objects on display, prior to enabling further interactions [2].

From the early nineties, the evolution of real time technologies entailed a great deal of interest in research on the topic of navigation in virtual environments and its application in different disciplines i.e. [3–7]. Bowman, Koller & Hodges wrote a remarkable work on the analysis and evaluation of travel techniques for use in immersive virtual environments, and defined a set of quality factors to measure and characterize the performance of a given travel technique [8].

In a previous work, the authors of this paper analyzed six walk-through paradigms for virtual environments using Kinect-based natural interaction [9]. Those movement schemes were implemented in a virtual environment depicting a reconstruction of a 4th century Roman villa, which was developed using the popular game engine Unreal Engine 4. The Kinect-based interaction was coded inside this system using the K4U libraries [10]. Within this virtual recreation, users can walk freely around the historical complex, enjoying the architectural spaces, mosaics, wall paintings, furniture, and other examples of material culture.

The analysis of the results of the aforementioned experiment did not consider a segmentation of the sample of users based on their previous experience with real-time environments (i.e. video games). It is important to note that one of the main goals in a NUI-based installation for museums is to find the most effective ways to interact and navigate inside a virtual environment. The movement and interaction paradigms chosen may be intuitive, easy to learn and useful for both novice and experienced users.

The work continues the previously mentioned research in movement paradigms, now focused on finding the most effective movement scheme for all users of a virtual museum, independent of their skills and experience on video games. Some studies suggest a positive correlation with previous experience with 3D video games, and navigation and interaction within the virtual world e.g. [11, 12]. Nevertheless, such consideration may result in a clear disadvantage for inclusive design of this kind of installation.

This paper describes a study on user experience (UX) for three user groups based on the user's previous skills as video game players—*no experience*, *casual player* and *frequent player*—as they tried four different movement schemes that combined different gestures to advance and turn as the user navigated in the virtual world: *Point forward/Twist upper body, Lean forward/Twist upper body; Step forward/Point sideways, Step forward/Twist upper body*.

This study uses an approach based on mixed methods [13]. Dependent variables in this experiment were task time, time in collision state (objective and measurable) and users' perception of ease, accuracy, need of attention, physical fatigue, and comfort and enjoyment with the experience. As qualitative data, the authors collected the "think aloud feedback" given by the participants during their performance for each movement scheme.

2 Methodology

2.1 Participants

Authors contacted and recruited participants from the university's students, faculty and other staff. A total of 27 participants (13 male, 14 female) were involved in a usability test. Ages ranged from 17 to 25 (66.7%), 26 to 35 (18.5%), and 36 to 55 (14.8%).

The criteria used to select the participants were based on their representation of the larger population who will use the application. Namely, we created three subgroups segmented for self-reported expertise. To ensure statistically significant evidence in the sample size [14], 9 people were used in each subgroup: *no experience* user (3 male, 6 female), *casual player* (5 male, 4 female), and *frequent play*er (5 male, 4 female).

2.2 Session Procedures

The individuals participated in the study separately in order to avoid any kind of contamination. All users performed all tasks using all movement schemes. Each session lasted approximately 45 mins for each individual.

Before the beginning of the test, the moderator explained the mechanics of the session to the participant and required the user to fill out a brief demographic questionnaire (age, gender, self-reported expertise). Then, the user took a two-minute free walk to contemplate the house and the elements exhibited inside it. At this point, the participant utilized the *Point forward/Point sideways* movement scheme as a training for the subsequent tasks.

Next, the subject tried different movement schemes in random order to accomplish two predefined tasks. During the course of the test, the system monitored and recorded the user moves in order to extract relevant data about time to complete the task, number of collisions and time spent in a collision condition. A post-task questionnaire was filled out immediately after completion of every task.

Users also completed a post-test questionnaire at the end of the session. Post-task and post-test questionnaires, together with the record of the comments made freely by the participants, provided a good source for subjective data.

2.3 UX Measuring

To measure the user experience in this test, we used the approach described by Tullis and Albert [15], where UX is the combination of all behaviors and attitudes people have while interacting with an interface. These include and go beyond traditional usability [16] and broader metrics dealing with users' attitudes and perceptions. In order to follow this approach, it is necessary to combine both objective and subjective measures to enable satisfaction analysis as a *"subjective sum of the interactive experience"* [17].

Since this study deals with a 3D interactive installation, it is important to include certain measurable characteristics of the quality of navigation as a mean to solve certain tasks [8] such as accuracy, attention and user comfort. The degree of motivation and pleasure is also evaluated, since hedonic, emotional, and experiential perspectives have an influence on the perception of product quality [18]. Furthermore, the emotional factor influences the potential of learning new skills and acquiring new knowledge, which are keypoints of this kind of installation.

To begin with, there are many definitions of the concept of "usability" [19–21]. There is a common understanding that the scope of usability includes the evaluation of effectiveness, efficiency, satisfaction, or the absence of usability problems [22]. The international standard ISO 9241-11:2018 [23] describes usability as the *"extent to which a system, product or service can be used by specified users to achieve specified goals with effectiveness, efficiency and satisfaction in a specified context of use".*

Measurement of quality in use is defined in ISO/IEC 25010 [24], which includes measures for the components of usability that are defined in ISO 9241-11. Within the satisfaction criteria, a series of sub-characteristics are defined, namely usefulness, trust, pleasure and comfort. Those last two concepts are included in this study.

1. Effectiveness is defined as accuracy, completeness and lack of negative consequences with which users achieved specified goals [23]. In this dimension, we measure the completion rate, the number of collisions and the number of frames that the system registered where the user collided with walls and objects, which can be expressed as time in collision state.
2. Efficiency is defined as resources expended in relation to the accuracy and completeness with which users achieve goals [23]. In this study, two aspects were measured: task time, and time spent in collision state, thus analyzing the influence of this data in the user's efficiency to perform the task.
3. Satisfaction relates to positive attitudes, emotions and/or comfort resulting from the use of a system, product or service [23]. Within this dimension, six criteria were evaluated. The first two are related to the satisfaction with task performance and the last four to the degree of satisfaction with the experience:

   – Ease of learning: how fast a user who has never seen the user interface before can accomplish basic tasks
   – Accuracy: proximity to the desired target [8]
   – Fatigue: subjective perception of physical effort during the completion of the tasks
   – Attention: this parameter measures the ratio of attention devoted by the user to control the navigation vs attention devoted to enjoyment of the experience itself. This evaluation is very important for a NUI system, since one of the main goals of a natural user interface is to remain as non-intrusive and invisible to the user as possible, so he or she can focus completely on the experience
   – Comfort: the extent to which the user is satisfied with physical comfort [24]
   – User pleasure: degree to which a user obtains pleasure from fulfilling their personal needs [24].

2.4 Gestures

In the proposed study, participants used gestural movement schemes to perform two tasks with different objectives. The user gestures implemented in the system [10] can be divided into two groups. The first group, which we may call "march gestures related to start, maintain and stop the walk", with constant or varying speed, and the second group, which we may call "turn gestures related to changing the walking direction". Both sets of gestures were combined to configure four different schemes involved in the study. Table 1 summarizes the combinations and displays the naming convention used in the graphs in this paper.

Table 1. Movement schemes.

	G01_PT	G02_LT	G03_SP	G04_ST
March	Point	Lean	Step	Step
Turn	Twist	Twist	Point	Twist
MOVEMENT SCHEMES				

3 Experiment Design

The experiment set consisted of a low-lit room with a projection screen having a Kinect sensor underneath, and some marks on the floor, one of them indicating the starting point of the experience, located 3.80 m in front of the screen. In this range the depth and skeleton views from the sensing device cover the entire user's body.

A digital reconstruction of a 4th century Roman *Domus* (Fig. 1) was used as test environment. It provided a good and comprehensive set of scenarios, which were used for obtaining all the measurements required for the usability tests, while at the same time serving as an entertaining and educational experience for the users involved in the experiment.

Fig. 1. Roman villa "El Alcaparral" Casariche Museum of Roman Mosaic, Spain

The usability data was collected in several sessions. During those sessions, two moderators observed and interacted with the users as they were completing the tasks using the different movement paradigms. Participants had to complete two different tasks:

- Navigation between two points: The first test began in front of the main door of the *Domus*. The user had to cross the vestibule to the main atrium, surround it and exit the atrium through a doorway located in the side opposite the entrance until they reached another exit leading to the garden. The purpose of this first stroll was to facilitate evaluating the ease of use of the system by measuring the task completion time, the number of collisions detected and the number of frames in collision state (Fig. 2).

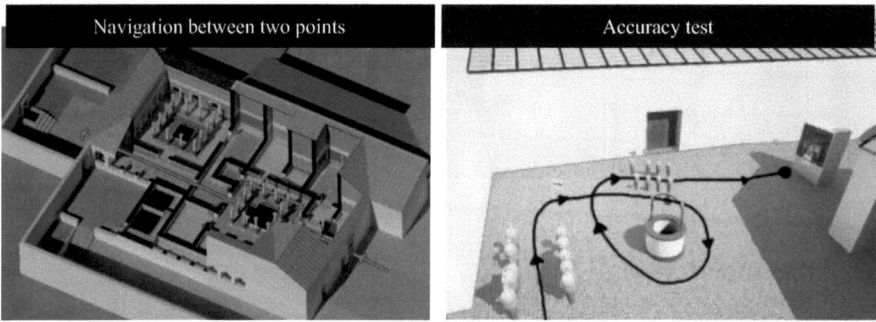

Fig. 2. Pathways for tasks 1 and 2

- Accuracy test: In the second test, the user performed another walkthrough, different from the first, to help measure the accuracy of every paradigm. This one required more precise maneuvering, since the user was asked to pass between two rows of objects and circle another object to finish, stopping in a given place. Again, we measured the task completion time, the number of collisions detected and the number of frames in collision state.

While the users performed the different tasks, they made spontaneous comments about their impressions related to the experience that were recorded. After each task, the participants were asked to rate the movement paradigms on a 7-point rating scale:

- Post-task 1 question: Single Ease Question (SEQ) [25] was used to ask the user to rate the difficulty of the activity they just completed, from Very Difficult to Very Easy.
- Post-task 2 question: a questionnaire was used to ask the user to rate the accuracy of the system for the activity they just completed, from Very Inaccurate to Very Accurate.

At the end of the session, users answered a short 7-point rating scale questionnaire about their impressions and perception of the experience as a whole. This questionnaire included four subjective measures:

- Attention focus: asks the user to rate the level of attention they put into the experience instead of on controlling the system, from Most Attention Devoted to System to Most Attention Devoted to Experience.
- Physical fatigue: asks the user to rate the level of fatigue, from Very Tired to Very Relaxed.
- User comfort: asks the user to rate the level of comfort, from Very Comfortless to Very Comfortable.

- User pleasure: asks the user to rate how exciting and enjoyable the experience was, from Very Unlikable and Boring to Very Pleasing and Exciting.

In addition, the authors asked users for general comments and recommendations for improvement.

4 Analysis and Interpretation of Data

4.1 Effectiveness

All the tasks were completed successfully. Data collected by the system during the execution of the tasks indicate that sometimes as the user advanced, he or she stuck to the walls instead of returning to the center of the path, or the user stuck against obstacles for a while. The analysis of the number of collisions and time in collision state helped to figure out how quickly the user learned to drive the system properly.

Collisions are a kind of unintended action a user makes while trying to do something on an interface even though the goal is correct. Norman used the term "slips" for these kinds of actions [26].

Figure 3 shows the percentage of users who collide very little to very much for every movement paradigm. Task #1 GP03_SP stands out as less prone to colliding (77.8% of the users collided less than 4 times). In the accuracy task, the best value goes to G04_ST (44.4%).

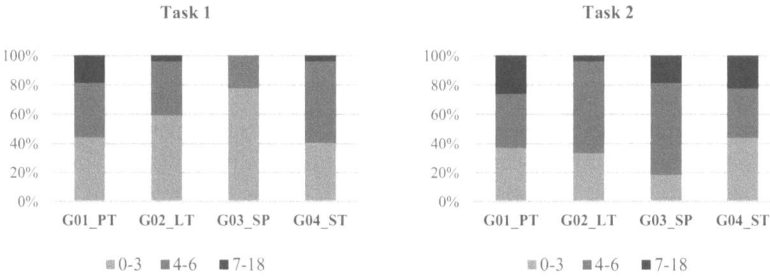

Fig. 3. Number of collisions per user for each task

Number of collisions is a datum of special interest related to time in collision state. The system counted the number of frames of the simulation that every user spent colliding (even tangentially) to walls or objects. Considering a frame rate of 30 fps, we can obtain the time in collision state and the percentage of the task performed in collision state in relation to the total task time. Analyzing this data, considering every movement paradigm and type of user (Fig. 4), the data shows that for task #1, G01_PT obtained the worst results, with a higher percentage of collision time related to task time for users of all groups, while G04_ST got the best results, with less time in collision state.

Unlike task #1, results for time in collision state for task #2 (accuracy) vary depending on the user group. G03_SP presents the highest (worse) values for *no experience* users, G01_PT for *casual players*, and G02_LT for *frequent players* and *all users*.

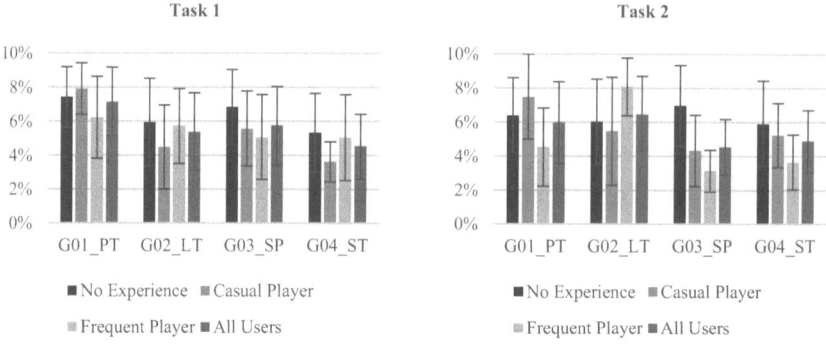

Fig. 4. Percentage of time in collision state according to each task and user group

The movement paradigms with the lowest time in collision state were G04_ST for *no experience users* and G03_SP for the rest of the groups. In any case, none of the movements exceed 8.1% (±1.7%) of time in collision state, so it has a relatively small effect on task performance [27].

4.2 Efficiency

Task #1 Time

The best time to completion for task #1 was 53 s. This value establishes an ideal time for this task in order to obtain the average task time estimate for a small sample. In order to set up a benchmark, we considered efficient times to be all times smaller than the ideal time multiplied by 1.5 [14]. Hence, any time smaller than 79.5 s. should be considered efficient.

Figure 5 summarizes the average task #1 time by movement scheme and user group. The confidence interval is based on the t-distribution, which works on small sample sizes [14]. Upon analysis of the data, G02_LT is the movement scheme with smaller times for all user groups, while G01_PT is the movement scheme that needs longer times for all user groups to complete tasks.

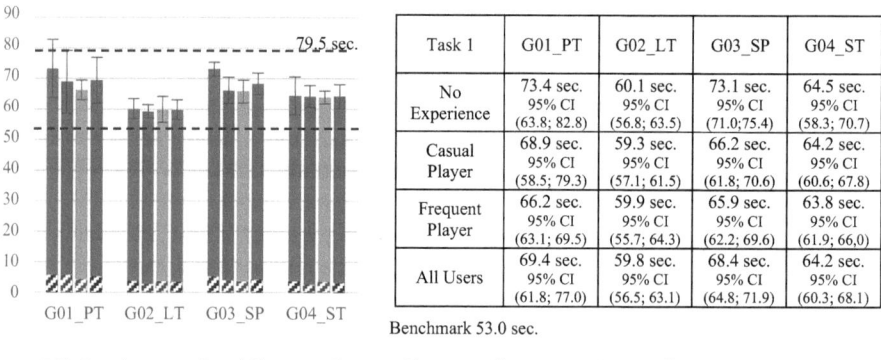

Fig. 5. Average task #1 time by movement scheme and user group

Regarding the benchmark, all the averages for task #1 fall inside the range of efficient time.

Task #2 Time

Regarding the average task time for task #2, G02_LT is the movement scheme with lower times for all groups. G01_PT has higher times for all user groups. The best time in this task was 34 s, giving an efficient task #2 time of < 51 s.

Figure 6 summarizes the average task #2 time by movement scheme and user group. Analysis of the data shows that most average task 2 time results fall inside the range of efficient time, with the exception of the *no experience* user group for G01_PT.

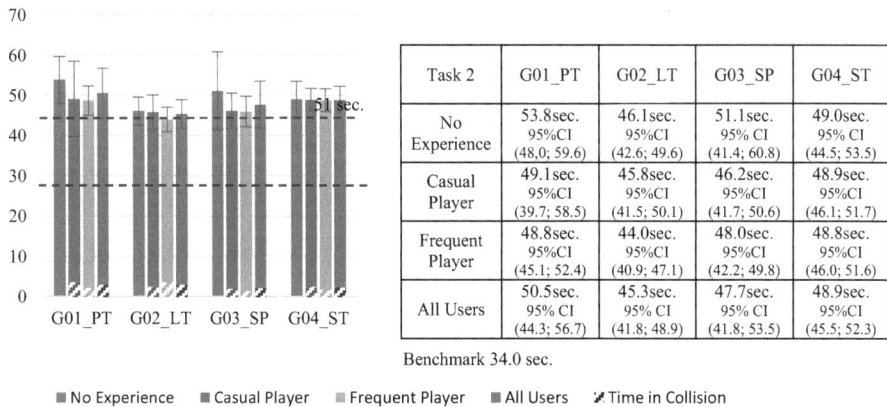

Fig. 6. Average task #2 time by movement scheme and user group

Task Performance Satisfaction

1- Post-Task 1 question: ease

After task 1, Single Ease Question (SEQ) was used to measure the degree of difficulty perceived by users during task performance. Analyzing the results, at a general level, the percentage of positive answers (describing the task as easy) reach values between 77.8% and 88.9%, achieving 100% for G04_ST (Fig. 7, Table 1). These results reflect that, generally speaking, all movement schemes are considered to be easy by users of all groups. All users, regardless of their group, perceived G02_LT as the easiest movement scheme for task #1 (≥ 6.0), followed by G04_ST. All groups perceived G03_PT as somewhat more difficult.

Linking the results of task #1 time and SEQ, task times between 59.9 s to 63.7 s correspond to SEQ values of 5.89 to 6.1, while task times between 63.8 s to 73.4 s correspond to SEQ values from 5.44 to 5.89.

2- Post-Task 2 question: accuracy.

After task 2, users were asked to fill out a questionnaire to rate the accuracy of the system in the activity they just completed. Generally, the percentage of positive answers, defining the movement scheme as accurate, reaches values ranging from 77.8% to 88.9% (Fig. 8, Table 1). A higher percentage of negative answers (describing

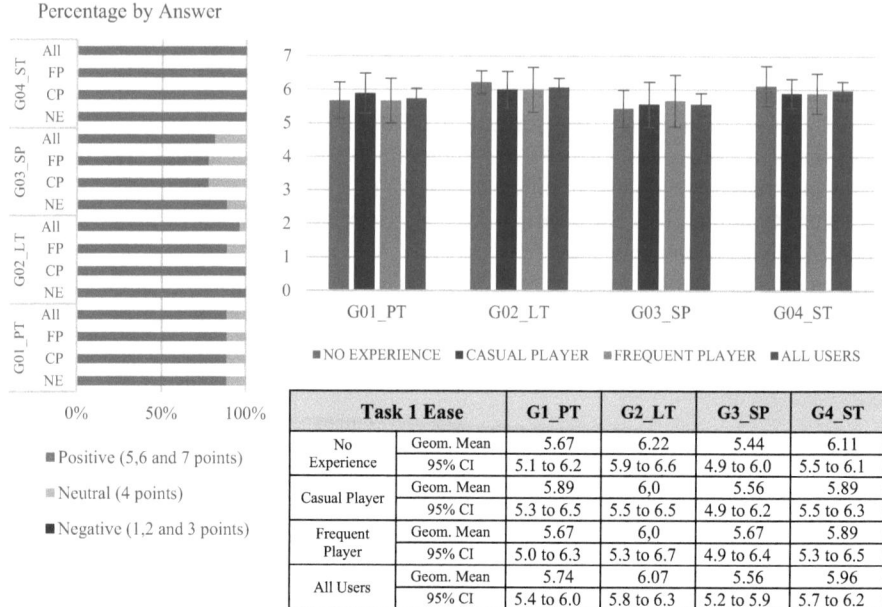

Fig. 7. Post-task 1 Single Ease Question by movement scheme and user group

the system as less accurate) corresponds to G02_LT for casual player (22.2%) and all users (11.1%). All movement schemes are considered relatively accurate (≥ 5.1). If we consider every single movement scheme, G01_PT is the scheme considered more accurate for the *no experience* user and all users for task #2, while *casual player* chooses G04_ST and *frequent player* chooses G03_SP.

It is worth noting that for task #2 the results regarding time and the questionnaire of accuracy do not match as expected. In some cases, the user perception does not coincide with the efficiency in time to complete. For instance, G01_PT results give the highest completion time for the *no experience* user group (53.8 s), but it is perceived as the most accurate (6.2). Inversely, G02_LT gives the best time for the *frequent player* group (44 s), but it is perceived as less accurate (5.1).

Overall Satisfaction

Upon finishing the test, users answered a questionnaire related to their physical fatigue, attention, comfort and pleasure with the usage and performance of the corresponding movement scheme.

1- Physical fatigue

The question intended to rate the level of fatigue after using the system provided the results depicted in Fig. 9. The G04-ST movement scheme obtained the highest percentage of positive answers (being less tiring); it reached values between 77.8% and 88.9%, while G01-PT obtained the highest percentage of negative answers (7.4% to 11%).

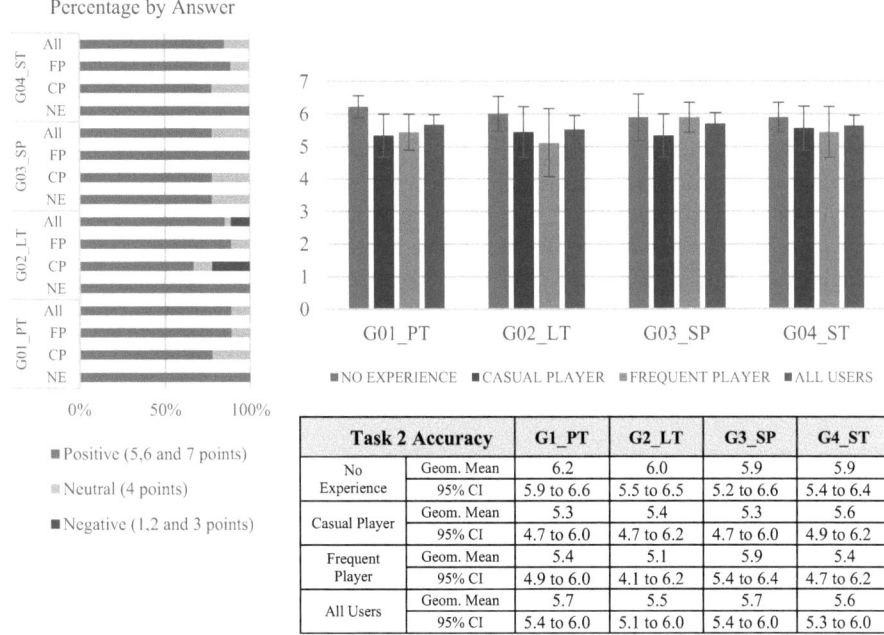

Fig. 8. Post-task 2 Accuracy Question by movement scheme and user group

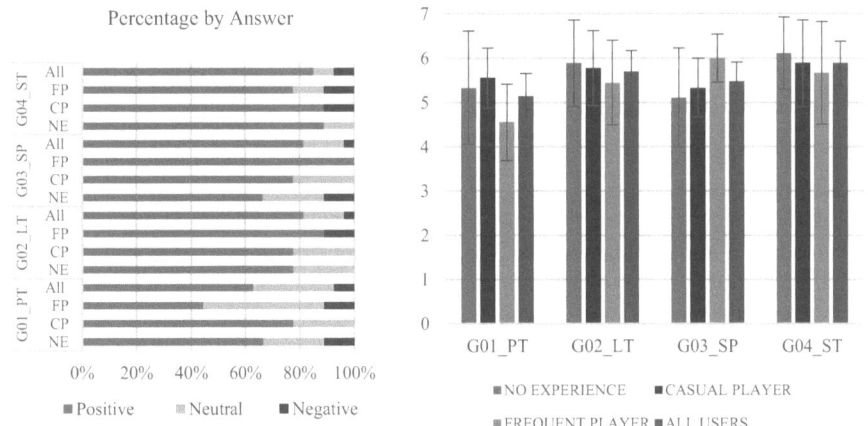

Fig. 9. Fatigue by movement scheme and user group

Arranging the results by movement scheme and user type, G04_ST stands out as less fatiguing for the *no experience* user (6.1, 95% CI 5.3,6.9), *casual player* (5.9, 95% CI 4.9, 6.9) and *all users* (5.9, 95% CI 5.4, 6.4), while G03_SP (6.0, 95% CI 5.5, 6.5) is chosen by *frequent player*. The most tiring movement schemes, by group, are

G03_SP for the *no experience* user (5.1, 95% CI 4.0, 6.2) and *casual player* (5.3, 95% CI 4.6, 6.0); and G01_PT for *frequent player* (4.6, 95% CI 3.7, 5.4) and *all users* (5.1, 95% CI 4.6, 5.6).

2- Attention (Natural interaction)

One of the goals of natural interface design is to develop systems that interfere as little as possible with the user's experience, responding to the user's desires in a fluent, comfortable and confident way. A properly designed NUI must allow the user to focus as much attention as possible on the experience instead of on the control of the device.

Figure 10 displays users' perception of their ratio of attention. It indicates the amount of attention payed to control the system versus the amount of attention attributable to the enjoyment of the experience itself. The percentages represented in the graph do not show a clear trend in one direction or another.

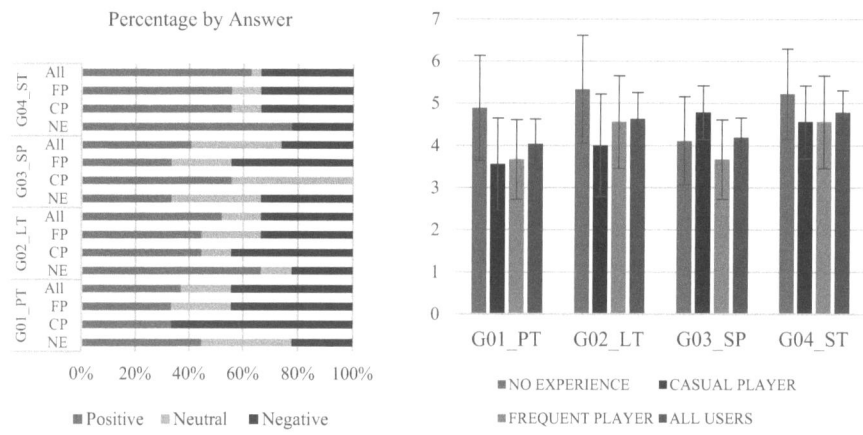

Fig. 10. Level of attention by movement scheme and user group

There are even some cases of neutral valuation. Analyzing every movement scheme individually, G04-ST obtained the highest percentage of positive answers (more attention devoted to the experience), reaching values from 63% to 77.8%, while G01-PT obtained the highest percentage of negative answers (more attention devoted to control the system), reaching values between 22.2% to 66.7%.

If we consider user groups, *no experience* users gave more attention to the experience itself when they used G02_LT (5.3, 95% CI 4.1, 6.6). G03_SP was the best for *casual player* (4.8, 95% CI 4.1, 5.4) and G04_ST for *frequent player* (4.6, 95% CI 3.5, 5.7) and *all users* (4.78, 95% CI 4.3, 5.3).

The movement schemes that required more attention devoted to system control were G01_PT for *casual player* (3.6, 95% CI 2.5, 4.7), *frequent player* (3.7, 95% CI 2.7, 4.6) and *all users* (4.0, 95% CI 3.4, 4.6), and G03_SP for *no experience* (4.1, 95% CI 3.1, 5.2). Overall, G04_ST is the movement scheme that permits players to pay more attention to the experience, although the valuations of this system do not go further than 5.3 over 7 points.

3- Comfort

Of all movement schemes, G04_SP obtained the highest percentage of positive answers (more comfortable), reaching values between 77.8% and 100%, while G01-PT obtained the highest percentage of negative answers (18.5% to 33.3%). Considering user groups, G02_LT and G03_SP reached 100% positive answers for *casual player* and *frequent player* (Fig. 11).

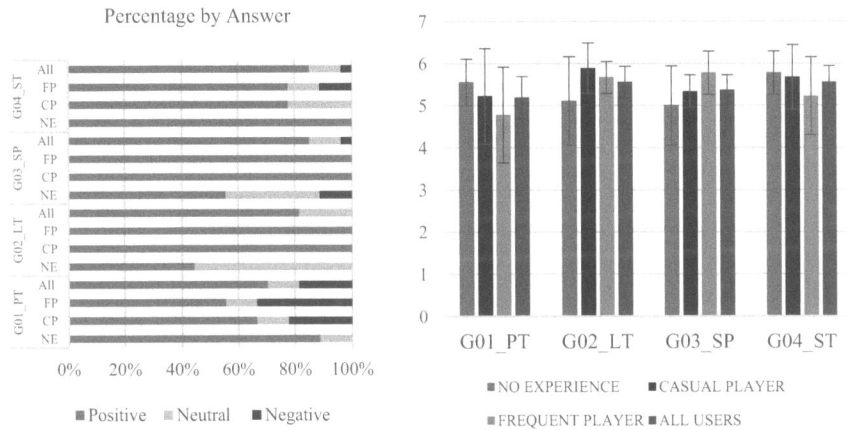

Fig. 11. Comfort by movement scheme and user group

Highest scores vary depending on the user group. G04_ST is the most comfortable scheme for *no experience* (5.8, 95% CI 5.3, 6.3) and *all users* (5.6, 95% CI 5.2, 5.9); G02_LT for *casual player* (5.9, 95% CI 5.3, 6.5) and G03_SP for *frequent player* (5.8, 95% CI 5.3, 6.3). The least comfortable scheme was G03-SP for *no experience* (5.0, 95% CI 4.1, 5.9) and G01-PT for *casual player* (5.2, 95% CI 4.1, 6.4), *frequent player* (4.8, 95% CI 3.6, 5.9) and *all users* (5.2, 95% CI 4.7, 5.7).

4- Pleasure

The percentage of positive answers with respect to user perception of pleasure is very high, surpassing 77.8%. There were no negative answers, so all movement schemes resulted in satisfactory experiences. G04_ST was the scheme best perceived as pleasing and exciting (88.9% to 100%), and was followed closely by G02_LT (77.8% to 88.9%).

Arranging the results by groups, the most pleasing schemes were G01_PT for *no experience* (6.2, 95% CI 5.8, 6.6) and G04_ST for *casual player* (5.9, 95% CI 5.2, 6.6), *frequent player* (5.8, 95% CI 5.3, 6.3) and *all users* (5.9, 95% CI 5.6, 6.2).

The less satisfying schemes, though well valuated (≥ 5.4) were G02_LT for no *experience* (5.6, 95% CI 4.8, 6.3), for *frequent player* (5.4, 95% CI 4.7, 6.1) and *all users* (5.6, 95% CI 5.2, 6.0), while G01_PT scored lower for *casual player* (5.6, 95% CI 4.8, 6.3). In short, all user groups perceived all movement schemes as pleasing and exciting, giving average values ranging between 5.4 and 6.2 (Fig. 12).

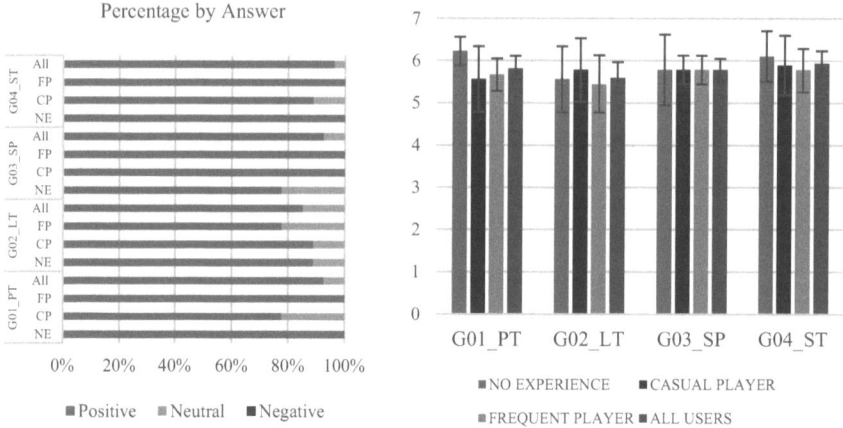

Fig. 12. Pleasing and exciting by movement scheme and user group

5 Discussion

The analysis of the previous results, supported with the users' comments and the notes taken by the authors during the experiment, provides clues to characterize the behavior and performance of the movement schemes and their suitability for their use in a museum environment for virtual walk-throughs.

From the previous analysis of the data, multiple usability metrics can be combined into a single usability metric [14] for each task, where variables correspond to each dimension analyzed for effectiveness, efficiency, and performance task and satisfaction. On the other hand, a unique value to represent general satisfaction can be obtained averaging fatigue, natural interaction (attention), comfort and pleasure.

Figure 13 synthesizes a single UX score by movement scheme and user group. This metric was obtained combining single usability metric and general satisfaction.

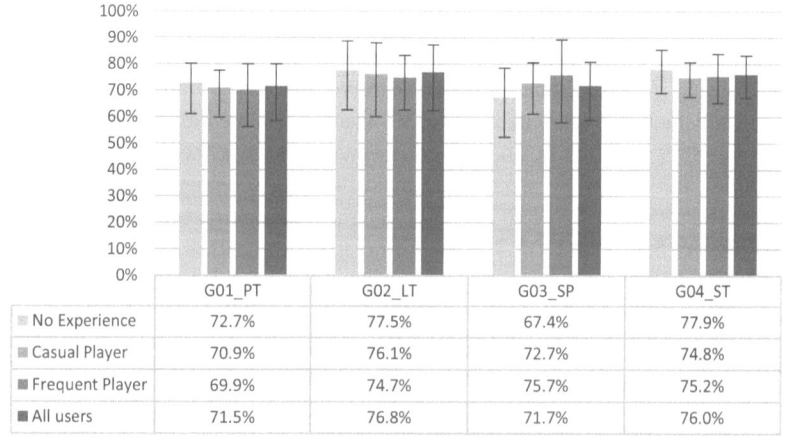

Fig. 13. UX score

As shown on the graph, all movement schemes have UX values $\geq$ 67.4%, so they all can be considered adequate for their purpose. Nevertheless, the objective of this work is to find the movement scheme that may be more suitable for a NUI museum installation, regardless of the previous skills of their users in the use of 3D virtual environments, such as videogames. Also, disaggregated results may be of interest when a museum installation is designed for specific users.

Next, we will discuss the relative results obtained by each movement scheme:

G01_Point Forward/Twist Upper Body
This movement scheme can be considered less useful for museum installations for various reasons:

- High percentage of attention devoted to control the system, less naturally interactive
- High task completion times for both tasks
- High percentage of time in collision state in relation to task time
- Several user groups considered this scheme less relaxed
- All user groups considered this scheme less comfortable, excepting for the *no experience* group, which gave a low valuation
- Users expressed doubts regarding the exact pose to hold their arm in the air. Monitors indicated that several users stretched their arm completely to point left or right, keeping it in the air during the experience, thus making the experience too fatiguing. Other users raised their forearm only, making detection of the pose by the system difficult.

The metrics for this movement put it in third place of four regarding usability, and the worst valuated in perceived satisfaction. Regarding UX metric, this scheme obtained the lowest value for casual player, frequent player and all users, and obtained a 3rd place of four for the no experience group.

G02_Lean Forward/Twist Upper Body
In general, this movement scheme obtained a middle-high valuation. It stood out in efficiency, obtaining notable records:

- Shorter average times for both tasks
- Perceived as the easiest in task accomplishment
- Considered relatively accurate
- Users commented about the precision of this scheme to accelerate, turn and slow down.

Nevertheless, this scheme had a low perception of pleasure compared to other movements, and the values regarding the ratio of attention to the experience, and attention to control the system were very heterogeneous.

This scheme obtained the best metrics in usability, and was the second best of the four in general perception of satisfaction. The UX metric for this scheme was one of the best for all groups excepting *frequent player*.

G03_Step Forward/Point with Arm
Overall, this scheme obtained a low valuation in all dimensions. It did not present any relevant aspect to stand out over the rest.

- Perceived as the most difficult for all groups
- Determined the most fatiguing for *no experience* and *casual player*
- Scored as the least comfortable for *no experience*

This scheme also obtained the worst usability score and got a low value regarding perception of satisfaction. For the UX score, this scheme obtained a middle-high value for *frequent player*, middle-low for *casual player* and *all users* and low for *no experience*.

G04_Step Forward/Twist Upper Body
This scheme constitutes a good candidate for museum installations. It obtained good scores on usability and general satisfaction for all user groups:

- This movement scheme permits users to devote the most attention to the experience instead of the control of the system
- It was the second most efficient
- It is the least fatiguing for *no experience*, *casual player* and *all users*
- Overall, it was considered the most comfortable
- It was perceived as the most pleasing and exciting for *casual player*, *frequent player* and *all users*.

Regarding metrics, this scheme obtained, just after G02_LT, the second best percentage in usability, and it was the best valued of all four in perception of satisfaction, obtaining at the same time the highest UX value for *no experience* and the second highest for *casual player*, *frequent player* and *all users*.

6 Conclusions

Virtual museums can offer to their visitors much more than the mere visual representation of things. They may be seen as sources of new experiences, hence fostering a deeper interpretation and a more persistent memory that a simple exhibit.

Natural user interfaces, such as Kinect, are extremely useful to achieve this goal, but it is important to find the movement scheme that best facilitates, in terms of HCI, visiting the virtual spaces. Of all movement schemes presented here, *Lean forward/Twist upper body* and *Step forward/Twist upper body* appear to be the most appropriate to navigate such digital environments for any kind of user, regardless of the previous expertise of the visitor in other virtual realms (i.e. video games). G02_LT proved to be the most efficient scheme, and G04_ST stood out as the most balanced in all aspects with the best valuations on natural interaction.

Although this study is centered on the evaluation and interpretation of the user experience during navigation, we should not forget that learning is one of the main goals of any museum installation. Users should be able to construct concepts through the observation and experience of the content provided. Therefore, it is necessary to find out how the UX metrics obtained relate to users' cognition, immersion and flow [28].

This could constitute a future line of research. The results obtained may also be utilized to achieve a higher level of attention to the contents inside the virtual environment as a learning tool for visitors to the museum. Hence, it is necessary to continue researching the optimization of these movement schemes and the acquisition of even more transparent movement interfaces.

The authors expect that the performance metrics and UX results presented here will be useful for designers of virtual environments to choose the natural interaction walkthrough scheme that best fits their needs based on the particular features of their installation.

References

1. Lun, R., Zhao, W.: A survey of applications and human motion recognition with Microsoft Kinect. Int. J. Pattern Recognit. Artif. Intell. **29**(05), 1555008 (2015)
2. Bowman, D.A., Johnson, D.B., Hodges, L.F.: Testbed evaluation of virtual environment interaction techniques. Presence: Teleop. Virt. Environ. **10**(1), 75–95 (2001)
3. Peterson, B., Wells, M., Furness, T., Hunt, E.: The effects of the interface on navigation in virtual environments. Hum. Factors Ergon. Soc. **42**, 1496–1505 (1998)
4. Bakker, N., Werkhoven, P., Passenier, P.: The effects of proprioceptive and visual feedback on geographical orientation in virtual environments. Presence: Teleop. Virt. Environ. **8**(1), 36–53 (1999)
5. Maier, D., Hornung, A., Bennewitz, M.: Real-time navigation in 3D environments based on depth camera data. In: 2012 12th IEEE-RAS International Conference on Humanoid Robots (Humanoids), pp. 692–697. IEEE (2012)
6. Steinicke, F., Visell, Y., Campos, J., Lécuyer, A.: Human Walking in Virtual Environments, pp. 199–219. Springer, New York (2013)
7. Riecke, B.E., LaViola Jr., J.J., Kruijff, E.: 3D user interfaces for virtual reality and games: 3D selection, manipulation, and spatial navigation. In: ACM SIGGRAPH 2018 Courses. ACM (2018)
8. Bowman, D.A., Koller, D., Hodges, L.F.: A methodology for the evaluation of travel techniques for immersive virtual environments. Virtual Reality **3**(2), 120–131 (1998)
9. Hernández-Ibáñez, L.A., Barneche-Naya, V., Mihura-López, R.: A comparative study of walkthrough paradigms for virtual environments using Kinect based natural interaction. In: 2016 22nd International Conference on Virtual System & Multimedia (VSMM), pp. 1–7. IEEE (2016)
10. Opaque Media K4U Homepage. https://www.opaque.media/kinect-4-unreal, Accessed 15 Feb 2019
11. Bowman, D., Kruijff, E., LaViola Jr., J.J., Poupyrev, I.P.: 3D User Interfaces: Theory and Practice. CourseSmart eTextbook. Addison-Wesley, Boston (2004)
12. Smith, S., Du'Mont, S.: Measuring the effect of gaming experience on virtual environment navigation tasks. In: 3D User Interfaces - 3DUI 2009, pp. 3–10. IEEE (2009)
13. Creswell, J.W.: Research Design: Qualitative, Quantitative, and Mixed Methods Approaches, 3rd edn. Sage Publications, California (2009)
14. Sauro, J., Lewis, J.R.: Quantifying the User Experience: Practical Statistics for User Research. Morgan Kaufmann, Burlington (2012)
15. Albert, W., Tullis, T.: Measuring the User Experience: Collecting, Analyzing, and Presenting Usability Metrics. Newnes, Boston (2013)
16. Petrie, H., Bevan, N.: The evaluation of accessibility, usability, and user experience. In: Stephanidis, C. (ed.) The Universal Access Handbook, pp. 299–314. CRC Press, Boca Raton (2009)

17. Lindgaard, G., Dudek, C.: What is this evasive beast we call user satisfaction? Interact. Comput. **15**(3), 429–452 (2003)
18. Hassenzahl, M.: Hedonic, emotional, and experiential perspectives on product quality. In: Encyclopaedia of Human Computer Interaction, pp. 266–272. IGI Global (2006)
19. Shackel, B.: Usability–context framework design and evaluation. In: Artikkeli teoksessa Shackel, B., Richardson, S. (eds.) Human Factors for Informatics Usability, vol. 21, p. 38. Cambridge University Press, Cambridge (1991)
20. Shneiderman, B., Plaisant, C., Cohen, M., Jacobs, S.: Designing the User Interface: Strategies for Effective Human Computer Interaction, 5th edn. Pearson Addison-Wesley, Boston (2009)
21. Seffah, A., Donyaee, M., Kline, R.B., Padda, H.K.: Usability measurement and metrics: a consolidated model. Soft. Qual. J. **14**(2), 159–178 (2006)
22. Lewis, J.R.: Usability: lessons learned… and yet to be learned. Int. J. Hum.-Comput. Interact. **30**(9), 663–684 (2014)
23. ISO 9241–11: Ergonomics of human-system interaction – Part 11: Usability: Definitions and concepts. https://www.iso.org/obp/ui/#iso:std:iso:9241:-11:ed-2:v1:en, Accessed 15 Feb 2019
24. ISO/IEC 25010: Systems, software quality requirements, and evaluation (SQuaRE) system and software quality models. https://www.iso.org/obp/ui/#iso:std:iso-iec:25010:ed-1:v1:en. Accessed 15 Feb 2019
25. Sauro, J., Dumas, J.S.: Comparison of three one-question, post-task usability questionnaires. In: Proceedings of the SIGCHI Conference on Human Factors in Computing Systems, pp. 1599–1608. ACM (2009)
26. Norman, D.: The Design of Everyday Things: Revised and Expanded. Basic Books, New York (2013)
27. Rubin, J., Chisnell, D.: Handbook of Usability Testing: How to Plan. Design and Conduct Effective Tests. Wiley, New Jersey (2008)
28. Csikszentmihalyi, M.: Flow. The Psychology of Optimal Experience. Harper & Row, New York (1990)

An Immersive Virtual Reality Experience for Learning Spanish

Sarah Garcia, Denis Laesker[(✉)], Derek Caprio, Ronald Kauer, Jason Nguyen, and Marvin Andujar

University of South Florida, Tampa, FL 33620, USA
{sarahgarcia,dlaesker,derekcl,
rkauer,jasonn1}@mail.usf.edu, andujar1@usf.edu

Abstract. While increases in the development of virtual reality (VR) have expanded the possibilities of learning foreign languages, research for computer assisted language learning in VR is lacking [1]. Virtual reality headsets continue to become more accessible to end users, and there is a current lack of educational language learning applications for such platforms. There are many tools and applications for language learning, however most lack the aspect of immersion – a proven method of learning a foreign language as seen in experiments involving overseas language experiences [2]. Therefore, this paper presents an interactive VR experience for learning Spanish through an immersive interaction and game-play, followed by the results from a focus group regarding user experience feedback. Additionally, this paper will detail the design and development of the current prototype. Results indicate that participants found this method of language learning to be more enjoyable than traditional methods because it did not feel like they were studying.

Keywords: Virtual reality · Language education · Gaming · Language learning · Game-based learning · Immersion

1 Introduction

Immersion has been shown to be a proven method for learning a foreign language, as seen in studies that involved overseas language experiences for college students, where students experienced statistically significant improvement in comprehension scores [2]. However, traveling and living overseas is costly, making it an unaffordable learning method to many. In spite of that, with the use of every day more affordable Virtual Reality technology, such as the Google Cardboard being used in education [3], one may take advantage of an immersive experience from the comfort of their own home. In this paper, we propose a VR experience that addresses the real-world cost limitation of traveling overseas to achieve immersion with another language, by providing a virtual environment where users can interact with objects and their surroundings in a different language for a lower price and at any desired time. The proposed VR language learning experience created in Unity and scripted for the Oculus Rift head-mounted display, takes advantage of the immersive capabilities offered by the Rift and extends them to the process of language learning. Also, using this application, learners can put into practice in real-time what they have learned in the 3D environment. This 3D experience allows users to explore objects and their Spanish translations in a free-roaming practice round, then apply this knowledge during game-play. Game-play involves the use of a search-and-find format, where players are given items to search for within the scene. After finding the correct item, points are awarded and a new item to search for is given. Users can view their scores to measure their success as they correctly identify objects within their environment. Currently allowing for exploration of the inside of an average home and interaction with common household items, this application can be applied to most real-world locations.

This application can be used as a supplement to Spanish classes in schools. Participants from the focus group mentioned that they felt more engaged and believed they would be able to study for longer periods of time using our application than with traditional book-learning methods. This suggests that work assigned to be completed on our application has potential to be more effective than the former. Furthermore, teachers could assign game-play for the students to complete on their own in the classroom or at home.

An important consideration to take into account for use in schools is affordability, and this language learning experience can be adapted to different affordability levels. Although this application was built and tested with the Oculus Rift, it can easily be ported to other, more affordable, VR devices such as the Oculus GO or even devices such as the Samsung Gear or Google Cardboard, that utilize smartphones for their VR display. With the ubiquity of smartphones today, this would enable those who cannot afford more expensive devices such as the Oculus Rift to still be able to improve their Spanish by using the application. Users could download our application on their smartphone and pair it with an economically priced headset such as the Google Cardboard, thus allowing them to immerse themselves into a Spanish speaking environment from anywhere in the world. Additionally, this application can be used by individuals who are interested in learning Spanish on their own or outside of a classroom.

In this paper, we discuss the user interaction involved in the language learning experience, as well as detail methods used for its creation. We then discuss the methodologies used for a focus group conducted using the proposed language learning experience. This focus group was conducted in order to gain feedback on the current working prototype, so that data collected from users can be implemented into future iterations as well as to gain interest regarding the application. Feedback from the focus group is discussed, as well as potential use cases for the VR experience in the real world. The paper ends by discussing plans for future work to be completed.

2 Related Works

Employing the use of VR technology in educational applications has gained popularity in recent years [4]. However, although of its high potential, little research can be found regarding language learning in VR [5]. VR environments provide users with an interactive and immersive experience within an artificially generated virtual world [4]. As described in [6], interactivity is achieved by designing specialized interfaces and providing users with real-time feedback. Immersion, on the other hand, is described as being divided into physical and mental immersion. The former can be accomplished by letting users navigate and control objects within the virtual environment. The latter is characterized by how engaged the user is.

2.1 Active Learning and the Search-and-Find Format

The use of the search-and-find format, where users are given prompts to search an environment for specific items, as an active learning technique has shown various benefits in the learning process. For instance, a study using this format, where undergraduates learned how to conduct research through exploring databases and reputable websites has proven to be both engaging and cognitive challenging [7]. *VEC3D* [7] is an immersive and interactive web-based online virtual environment (VEC3D website) of an English classroom that employs the use of a "Virtual Scavenger Hunt" as one of its goal-based scenarios. In this scenario, participants act as scavengers competing against a countdown timer to locate and name virtual objects scattered throughout the virtual environment. Moreover, a one-year ethnographic study with Taiwanese undergraduate students majoring in English language teaching with various levels of proficiency was conducted. Results showed that students felt motivated to use communication strategies, felt comfortable in the environment, and demonstrated positive attitudes towards the application. Differing from VEC3D, our created game employs the use of VR and the Oculus Rift head mounted display, increasing the notion of immersion.

2.2 Virtual Reality for Language Learning

Immersion plays an important role in learning a new language [4]. This immersion can be achieved by travelling to a place where the target language is predominately spoken, however, such relocation can be very costly. Therefore, the benefits of using VR to provide learners with immersive environments for a small fraction of the cost would only be beneficial. For instance, by adapting a 3D video game called *Crystallize* to work in VR, users were able to learn when to bow in Japanese greetings [9]. This was done through detecting a change in angle using an Oculus VR Headset (signifying the bowing one would do in the real world) when the user is presented with an in-game prompt from a non-playable character (NPC). Moreover, a formative study with 68 participants using both VR and non-VR versions of the game was conducted to determine whether participants would learn when and how to bow. Users were first taken through a tutorial that gradually increased the time in which the system would alert them when to bow. Learning was measured by the ability of a user to perform an unprompted bow (bowing without explicitly being told to do so). Results suggest that users were able to learn how to bow and felt more involved in Japanese culture when interacting in the VR version.

Among other language learning systems created, SeLL [10] is an English learning system aimed at improving oral skills that combines VR, speech recognition and pronunciation assessment through the use of artificial intelligence (AI) in order to provide an acoustic and visual immersive experience to its users. The system allows its users to interact with the virtual environment, which includes various activities designed for oral communication with either other learners or virtual characters equipped with intelligent dialogues. Moreover, the system provides users with feedback on their pronunciation, fluency, and expression at the end of learning.

3 User Interaction

After setting up the Oculus Rift hardware necessary, users launch the game application. Users begin their experience in a free-roaming environment, in which they interact with the environment with no defined gameplay goals to familiarize themselves with their surroundings and touch controller navigation. The left-hand controller joystick is used to walk around in the environment and the right-hand controller joystick is used to look around, moving the screen in the direction of the joystick 30°. Participants can also look around by physically turning their head. After users have familiarized themselves with the virtual environment, the gameplay section can be started. Here, users are prompted with both audible (implemented from Google Translate) and readable cues such as "dónde está la cama?" ("where is the bed?") or "dónde está la television?" ("where is the television?"), indicating which object they must search for next. The readable cue can be found near the bottom of the user's screen, and their current score is found towards the top, as seen in Fig. 1.

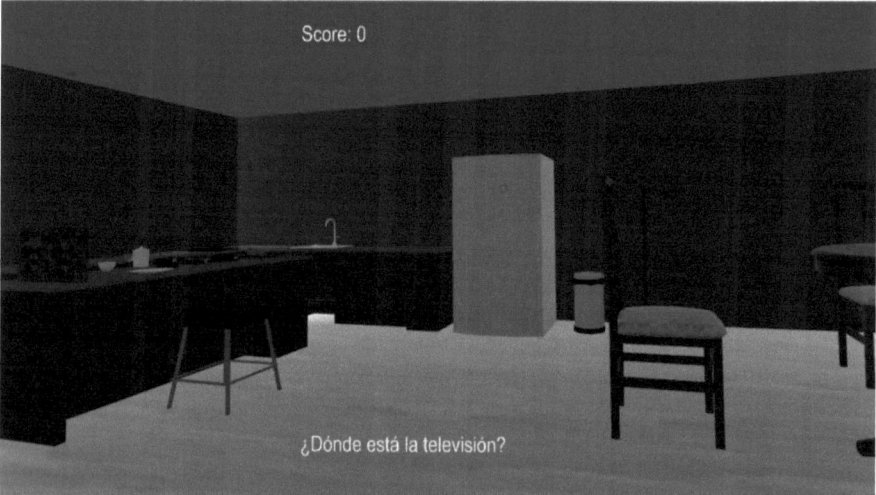

Fig. 1. Game-play depicting readable cues given to the user (bottom of image) and their current score (top of image).

After reading the cue, users would then search for the prompted item and select it by hovering over it with the gaze pointer and clicking the 'A' Button. Time taken to find all search-and find items lasts as long as needed to find all items in the scavenger hunt, usually about five to ten minutes. When searching for the needed item, users are able to see which items can be selected by hovering over them with the gaze pointer. Items that can be selected become highlighted blue, as seen in Fig. 2 on the left. If an item selected is incorrect, the item will instead highlight red, as seen in Fig. 2 on the right. After finding the correct item, its name would be audibly played back once again to the user and their score would increase by 10 points before being prompted to find the next item. This continues until all objects were found. Figure 3 shows the state diagram of the game, depicting the continuous flow of tasks given to the user until all objects in the sequence are found.

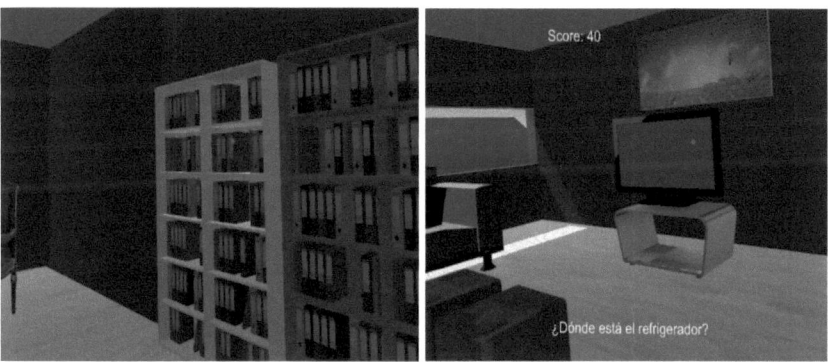

Fig. 2. Game-play depicting the changing of items when hovered over as correct (left) and incorrect (right).

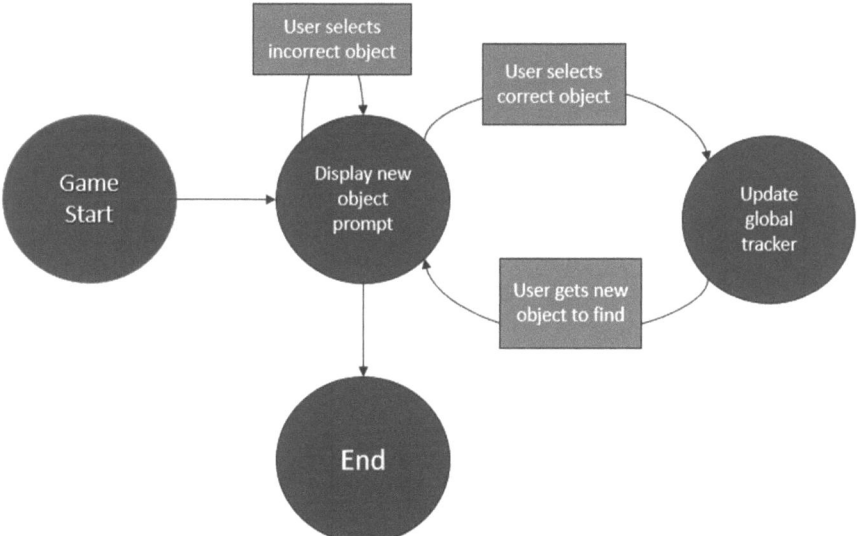

Fig. 3. Diagram of user game-play states.

4 Experience Creation

4.1 Hardware

Development of the system was performed using the Unity Video Game Engine due to its popularity and gradual learning curve. Although the created system was initially built to be used with the Oculus Rift VR headset and its complementary Oculus Touch Controllers (Fig. 4), the application is also portable to other VR headsets. The headset used is equipped with a 3.5in, OLED display, 2160×1200 resolution, and 90 Hz refresh rate.

Fig. 4. User with Oculus Rift and touch controllers.

4.2 Software Architecture

A modular and scalable software architecture was developed for this project. This allows for future developers to quickly understand the architecture and add, or remove, to and from the project as needed. All aspects of the environment and game-flow are controlled by the GameManager component, as seen in Fig. 5. This component is responsible for keeping track of the current target item, which prompt is to be displayed, and which audio files are to be played for each prompt and item. The AudioManager component allows audio files to be played and heard by the player.

Items, prompts, and audio are all objects in the game. These are stored in three global dynamic arrays that can be seen and modified through the Unity Inspector

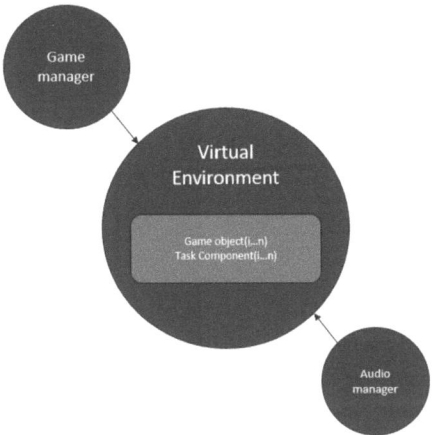

Fig. 5. Depiction of the software architecture used in creation of the game-play

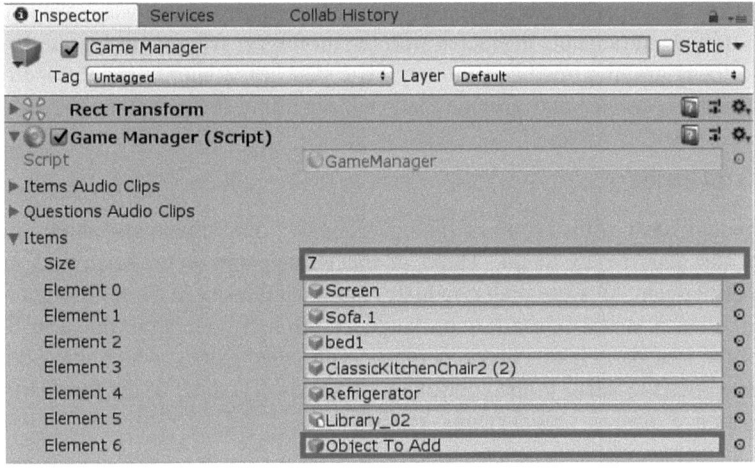

Fig. 6. Elements within the Game Manager seen in the Unity Inspector.

component. This facilitates adding more objects to be managed by the GameManager, therefore, increasing the number of items a user would need to find during gameplay. Figure 6 shows the simplicity of this process. The size of the array, or the number of objects needed, can be easily modified by setting the "Size" to the desired number. In addition, objects can be added by being dragged into an element slot. Moreover, this also makes it easier to expand the 3D environment as seen fit. Player movement and interaction with the environment was achieved by using the pre-built OVRPlayerController provided by the Oculus Software Developer Kit. The 3D environment was created using Unity primitives as well as Asset Packages obtained from the Unity Asset Store. The GameManager uses a global tracker to oversee a player's progress within the scavenger hunt. All objects that are part of the scavenger hunt contain a Task component, which determines whether a clicked object is the correct one, or not. In case the former happens, the global tracker is updated and the GameManager handles which prompts are to be displayed next. If the latter happens, the item clicked is highlighted in red denoting "wrong item".

5 Methodology

5.1 Study Design

We conducted a focus group to collect qualitative data regarding the current prototype of the immersive experience to gain insight to improve the capability to teach a foreign language. This focus group consisted of participants completing a pre-questionnaire, trying the current prototype, and finally a focus group session of a group of four. The pre-questionnaire was used to gain information regarding general demographic information, experience with learning a new language and prior usage of any virtual reality system. Participants then tested the virtual environment one at a time. A screen recording of each participant's time in the virtual environment was saved for later analysis of how participants interacted with the prototype. Afterwards, participants took part in a focus group guided by an interviewer that lasted approximately one hour, to discuss their experience and provide feedback regarding the prototype they tested.

5.2 Participants

Data was collected with a total of four participants, one female and three males, all between the ages of 18 to 24. Three of the participants were Asian and one was African-American. All were undergraduates at the University of South Florida and had some experience in learning a foreign language, though none were fluent in Spanish. Three of the four participants had experience with video games, which may show their ability and speed to adapt to the controllers. Additionally, three of the four participants had experience using a virtual reality headset.

5.3 Procedure

After being put into a group of four, participants were asked to:

1. Complete a pre-experiment survey before starting to interact with the virtual environment.
2. Participants entered the virtual environment, one at a time, for ten minutes each. Each participant was first directed to roam freely around the environment for five minutes. This was done so that participants who did not have experience with virtual reality would have the level of familiarity needed to properly interact with the application and provide valuable feedback.
3. After this, the participant was prompted in Spanish to search for specific objects in the virtual environment. This search-and-find phase lasted an additional five minutes for each participant.

After all the four participants had their chance to interact with the virtual environment and find all necessary objects, the focus group was conducted. During the focus group participants were asked questions regarding their experience with the virtual environment. These included how natural they found the interaction, what they thought of this immersive method of language learning, their likes, dislikes and suggestions to improving the prototype.

6 Results

6.1 Environment Interaction

During analysis of screen recordings taken of each participant while using the prototype, it was noticed that participants experienced confusion when trying to select certain items. This confusion occurred when there were multiple instances of that object in the room, however only one of them could be selected to complete the search-and-find task. This was seen when two participants had trouble when trying to select the couch item in the home, as two couches were present but only one could be selected (i.e. only one would highlight blue). Additionally, participants chose different methods of exploring their surroundings. Two participants primarily used the right-hand touch controller joystick to change their view of the room, while the other two instead chose to physically turn their head in order to see other areas.

6.2 Game-Play Feedback

All participants reported in the survey that they would be interested in using a virtual environment to learn a foreign language. During the focus group, participants often mentioned that they found language learning in virtual-reality to be more fun than traditional learning methods. Remarks regarding the environment included that this method of learning was "*almost like playing a game*" and that they could "*study longer without taking a break*". Participants also expressed that they believed learning while immersed in a virtual environment helped them to better remember the names of the objects since they were able to interact with them. Feedback from the focus group also suggests that the User Interface (UI) design can be improved, as participants had mixed reactions regarding the placement of the score and search-and-find task prompts displayed on the screen. Some participants viewed it as intrusive, describing them as "*on their face*", others did not notice the score display at all during gameplay, implying it was not very visible. Participants also mentioned a desire for a more complex environment, in order to learn harder words and make the environment feel more realistic by adding a backdrop around the virtual environment. In addition to more complex environments, higher level vocabulary and more objects were also commonly suggested by the focus group participants. While all participants found their movement in the virtual environment to be realistic and intuitive, three of the four were critical of the panning feature used to look around using the Oculus handheld remote, stating that it was not smooth. The panning of the character and camera 30° done by use of the joystick located on the right-hand controller was described as too sharp of a turn, causing them nausea every time the function was used. Focus group's participants also discussed that the directions for search-and-find tasks seemed to have "come out of nowhere" and did not like that the reading of the prompt came from an unseen narrator. This feedback can be remedied with the implementation of transition scenes between tasks and the potential implementation of a character in view that speaks the tasks to the user so that prompts given feel less sudden. All participants expressed enthusiasm about this method of language learning, finding it more entertaining and effective than traditional study methods.

7 Conclusion

Feedback from the focus group indicates that participants find language learning in a virtual environment using our prototype to be more enjoyable than traditional language learning methods. Positive responses imply that the use of a language learning system such as this is wanted, although studies regarding language retention and vocabulary gain are needed to investigate its success in teaching information to users. The feedback suggests improvements such as re-design of the UI, a more spacious virtual environment with a more diverse list of objects. The results from the focus group will be incorporated in future iterations of the prototype to create a more immersive environment for language learning.

8 Future Work

As this is the first iteration of the application, improvements will be made using feedback gathered from the focus group. These improvements include using changes in design choices, such as switching over to the use of touch controllers for item selection instead of using the user's line of vision, and improvements regarding character view-panning to reduce player nausea. Furthermore, participants indicated to increase the amount of scavenger hunt tasks and the environment map size. Increase in map size includes the addition of other types of locations one might encounter often or find useful vocabulary in, such as a grocery store or restaurant. Participants also expressed that the addition of differing difficulty levels would be beneficial. Implementation of elements to make the reading of new search-and-find prompts more user-friendly can be added, such as addition of transition scenes and a friendly avatar speaking so that new task announcements do not feel as sudden. Finally, the addition of a voice recording feature, where the user would be able to record and hear playback of themselves saying item names would be useful to assist users in their pronunciation skills while allowing them to compare their tries to correct pronunciations.

References

1. Lin, T.J., Lan, Y.J.: Language learning in virtual reality environments: past, present, and future. J. Educ. Technol. Soc. **18**(4), 486–497 (2015)
2. Savage, B.L., Hughes, H.Z.: How does short-term foreign language immersion stimulate language learning? Front.: Interdisc. J. Study Abroad **24**, 103–120 (2014)

3. Parmaxi, A., Stylianou, K., Zaphiris, P.: Leveraging virtual trips in Google expeditions to elevate students' social exploration. In: Bernhaupt, R., Dalvi, G., Joshi, A., Balkrishan, D.K., O'Neill, J., Winckler, M. (eds.) INTERACT 2017. LNCS, vol. 10516, pp. 368–371. Springer, Cham (2017). https://doi.org/10.1007/978-3-319-68059-0_32
4. Huang, H.M., Rauch, U., Liaw, S.S.: Investigating learners' attitudes toward virtual reality learning environments: based on a constructivist approach. Comput. Educ. **55**(3), 1171–1182 (2010)
5. Ebert, D., Gupta, S., Makedon, F.: Ogma: a virtual reality language acquisition system. In Proceedings of the 9th ACM International Conference on Pervasive Technologies Related to Assistive Environments, p. 66. ACM, June 2016
6. Huang, H.M., Liaw, S.S., Chen, W.T., Teng, Y.C.: Developing a virtual reality learning environment for medical education. In: E-Learn: World Conference on E-Learning in Corporate, Government, Healthcare, and Higher Education, pp. 1320–1329. Association for the Advancement of Computing in Education (AACE), October 2009
7. Jones, J.A., Smith, S., Royster, M.: The scavenger hunt as an active learning technique. NACTA J. **61**(1), 94 (2017)
8. Shih, Y.C., Yang, M.T.: A collaborative virtual environment for situated language learning using VEC3D. J. Educ. Technol. Soc. **11**(1), 56–68 (2008)
9. Cheng, A., Yang, L., Andersen, E.: Teaching language and culture with a virtual reality game. In: Proceedings of the CHI Conference on Human Factors in Computing Systems, pp. 541–549. ACM (2017)
10. Guo, J., et al.: SeLL: second language learning paired with VR and AI. In: SIGGRAPH Asia 2017 Symposium on Education, p. 7. ACM, November 2017

Immersive Community Analytics for Wearable Enhanced Learning

Ralf Klamma(✉), Rizwan Ali, and István Koren

Advanced Community Information Systems Group (ACIS), RWTH Aachen University, Lehrstuhl Informatik 5, Ahornstr. 55, 52074 Aachen, Germany
{klamma,ali,koren}@dbis.rwth-aachen.de

Abstract. Nowadays, we can use immersive interaction and display technologies in collaborative analytical reasoning and decision making scenarios. In order to support heterogeneous professional communities of practice in their digital transformation, it is necessary not only to provide the technologies but to understand the work practices under transformations as well as the security, privacy and other concerns of the communities. Our approach is a comprehensive and evolutionary socio-technological learning analytics and design process leading to a flexible infrastructure where professional communities can co-create their wearable enhanced learning solution. In the core, we present a multi-sensory fusion recorder and player that allows the recordings of multi-actor activity sequences by human activity recognition and the computational support of immersive learning analytics to support training scenarios. Our approach enables cross-domain collaboration by fusing, aggregating and visualizing sensor data coming from wearables and modern production systems. The software is open source and based on the outcomes of several national and international funded projects.

Keywords: Visual analytics · Communities of practice · Immersive analytics · Human activity recognition

1 Introduction

Learning analytics [1] has become a central discipline for planning, monitoring and evaluating interventions in learning processes. One of the goals of learning analytics is the use of big data for this purpose. The field has developed quite fast and applications of learning analytics cover both formal learning processes on different levels (micro, meso, macro) and informal learning processes. With respect to that, foci of analysis are learning processes on the cognitive level, e.g. learning languages and sciences. While we agree with this, we would like to suggest adding learning analytics for learning processes including manual activities quite common in assembly, production and picking workplaces to the tool set. We see here a turn from the mind to the body and with that an integration of declarative and procedural knowledge [2]. In organizational learning theories, Nonaka and Takeuchi made the first distinction between declarative and procedural knowledge [3]. In their motivating examples they came up with examples from bakers kneading bread for the design of a kneading automaton. The designers learned only by observing and practicing techniques from real bakers how to do it despite their engineering and design knowledge. We know from research on language acquisition that declarative and procedural knowledge are dependent on each other. In [4] we already wrote that learning analytics in informal learning has a social dimension. Instead of formal learning where we mostly learn from teachers, informal learning is often learning from observations of practice performed by an expert and learning with peers while sharing a practice. Communities of Practice (CoP) [5] are groups of people who interact frequently to learn from each other. CoP has been applied widely as a social learning theory, yet its relationship to learning analytics is not well understood yet. We think, that we need to incorporate practice theories and their methodologies. But we need to transform research practices as well, as work is digitally transformed.

Nowadays empirical research on practice theories at workplaces is carried out using ethnography, sometimes supported by multimedia recordings. Digital ethnography is an emerging field of research where in particular data gathering methods are supported by digital tools. We propose a digital ethnography with fine-grained descriptions of workplaces and activities, and recordings using sensor technologies. With that we can store and analyze recorded observations, share best practices and use them for training. We also propose a shift from researcher-centered data gathering methods to community-centered data gathering methods. We want to come up with a little example for data gathering in runners' communities. Wearables are becoming more social in many application domains. While their major purpose is to interact with the person wearing the device, it is commonly very attractive to users to share the data recorded by the device with a specified community. Despite common privacy concerns in the beginning and now, data sharing is quite frequently happening in communities. An example usage of shared data is keeping the long term motivation for doing sports. The company Fitbit for example is offering to share fitness data like step count with friends from its activity trackers of the same name. When we provide such information when running the feedback would be more immersive. But how to provide the motivating feedback and leave out the frustrating one?

In this little example, we can identify major challenges for **immersive community learning analytics**. Learning analytics is the use of big data for the planning and intervention of learning processes. Community learning analytics is using learning related data under the control of communities of practice [5] with respect to their learning processes in open environments like the Web. A major challenge is the privacy and security of shared data. While in many domains, users share their data voluntarily, the affordances of privacy and data security are magnitudes of order higher in domains like learning. It will not be possible to store sensitive data on repositories of companies, which cannot give guarantees for data security and protection. Privacy issues must be considered.

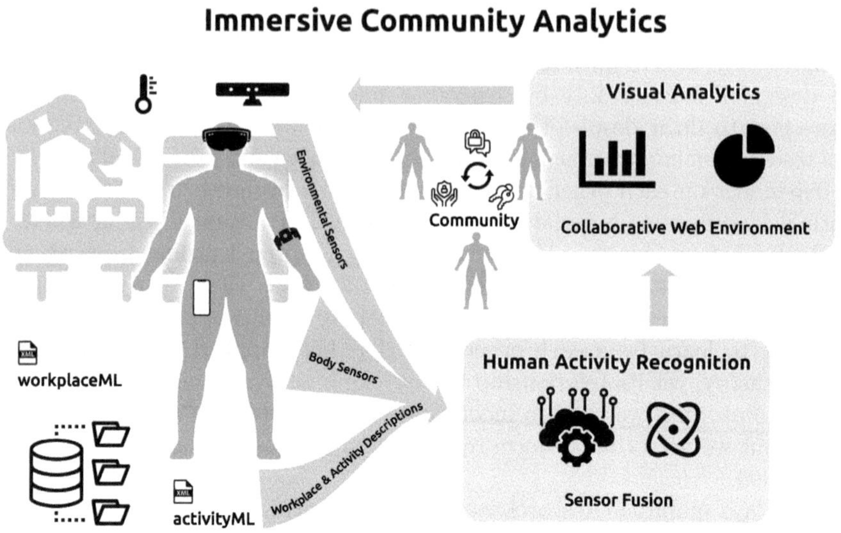

Fig. 1. Immersive community analytics scenario

Another challenge is the technological openness of the approach. In the example, data can only be shared using the same hardware and software setup, while in learning analytics, data of different devices with heterogeneous data formats should be shared in a common repository under the full control of the community sharing the data and not under the control of a company. A third challenge is that the data are visualized via Web applications and not using the wearables. So, the user cannot access the data during the learning processes but only afterwards and in a non-immersive way. Moreover, the users get a visual or non-visual presentation of the data and the analytics, which is basically generated by somebody.

Our approach is to give the community complete control over continuous visual learning analytics in an immersive way. We see the following possible contributions.

- Communities shall be able to collaboratively edit learning analytics processes.
- Communities shall be able to analyze and collaboratively visualize learning traces.
- Communities shall be able to use learning analytics in an immersive manner.
- Communities shall be able to store and retrieve their own learning traces under their own control.
- Communities shall be able to protect their data.

For covering the stated requirements, we combine our existing community analytics platform SWEVA with an immersive analytics concept based on augmented reality head mounted displays. Not only the learning process is collaborative but also the analytics process. An overview of the community learning analytics with wearables is given in Fig. 1. On the left, we see an industrial workplace equipped with sensors that are constantly measuring human movements, air temperature and other environmental factors. The human worker is wearing a number of body sensors, including a gesture-recognition device, a mobile phone in the pockets, and an augmented reality headset. Both workplace settings and necessary activities are formalized in a standardized description language. Together with the sensor data, the latter are fed into a human activity recognition machine learning algorithm. The classified output, i.e. what activity is carried out and connected qualities, are fed into a visual analytics Web cockpit. Its precise definition of how to process and visualize data are defined in a community-aware, collaborative manner. With regard to communities, there are further aspects visible, e.g. data sharing, privacy, and legislative challenges. Finally, the results are fed back to the worker in the form of immersive analytics into the augmented reality headset or other actuators at the workplace.

In this introduction we addressed our approach to collaborative immersive community analytics for wearable enhanced learning. In the next section, we will provide more background information and a state of the art. Major components of the approach are described in Sects. 3 and 4, respectively.

2 Background

In this section we discuss related work and introduce important technical concepts used in our implementation.

2.1 Related Work

Visual Analytics [6] is an emerging, interdisciplinary field of research. It "combines automatic analysis techniques with interactive visualizations for an effective understanding, reasoning and decision making on the basis of very large and complex data". Immersive Analytics is defined as "the use of engaging analysis tools to support data understanding and decision making." [7], we see it as a sub-discipline of visual analytics. What distinguishes immersive analytics from visual analytics are data physicalization, situated analytics, embodied data exploration, spatial immersion, and multi-sensory presentation. Billinghurst et al. [8] define collaborative immersive analytics as: *"The shared use of immersive interaction and display technologies by more than one person for supporting collaborative analytical reasoning and decision making."* In communities of practice [5], collaboration and mutual engagement are key features and CoPs are defined as *"groups of people who share a common concern or passion for something they do and who interact regularly to learn how to do it better"*. Practice theories [9–14] are not often connected to visual analytics since they are not yet using available digital media and tools to a full extent. However, in an organizational context, the value of practice has been considered e.g. by addressing tacit knowledge through ethnographic observations [3,15].

2.2 Technical Background

In particular in augmented reality assisted training, immersive analytics plays an important role in understanding the learning process, in providing meaningful feedback and in engaging the learner. Several approaches and prototypes have been presented and surveyed [16–22], like assembling personal computers [17], learning culturalism [18], learning history [19], learning science [21]. However, only few studies are related to learning at the workplace [17]. The European H2020 research project **WEKIT (Wearable Experience for Knowledge Intensive Training)** [23] came up with both a content authoring tool (recorder) and a training tool (player) for the Microsoft HoloLens and the Mixed Reality Toolkit. The recorder records multi-sensory input from a body-worn vest with a couple of body sensors (heart beat, temperature) and the HoloLens. The player is able to reproduce the stored training content by augmenting the HoloLens view. The software has been tested and evaluated within three main scenarios: aircraft maintenance for the support of inspections, decision making and safety, healthcare for the usage of complex ultrasound diagnostics machines and astronaut training for orbital and planetary missions. The retrieval of training scenarios is based on their description in an emerging international standard called **ARLEM (Augmented Reality Learning Experience Model)** [24] supported by the IEEE. ARLEM describes the interactions between the physical world, the virtual world and the learners. At the core of ARLEM is an activity modeling language (activityML) to describe activities of agents (human or non-human), a workplace modeling language (workplaceML) to describe the physical environment and the learning context. Concrete activities can be identified by an advanced multi-sensor fusion framework. In Listing 1.1 we can see a piece of XML for the description of an ARLEM activity.

Human Activity Recognition (HAR) tries to recognize activities of humans with the help of many sensors, using a dedicated machine learning approach. Human activities can be defined as sequences of human and object movements in a given context. The HAR task is to recognize these sequences. HAR is an active research area with many challenges coming from changing environments and light conditions (e.g. shadows), (multiple) movements of objects, sensor signal quality issues [25]. Non-visual sensors and body-worn sensors [26–28] improve the quality of HAR by improving the overall accuracy of tracking and classification tasks, but only with the help of sensor fusion approaches. The process of combining the information from different homogeneous or heterogenous sensors to provide a better description of the environment is called multi-sensor data fusion [29]. For the realization of multi-sensor data fusion, we need to process data on different levels (sensory, fusion, processing) as presented in Fig. 2. The sensor model has competitive, cooperative, and complimentary strategies, the fusion level has data, feature and decision levels and the processing level has centralized decentralized and hybrid strategies. Different combinations lead to different strategies (e.g. cooperative, decision and centralized). Machine learning techniques support the realization of such strategies.

Listing 1.1. Example of ARLEM activityML

```xml
<?xml version="1.0" encoding="UTF-8"?> <activity id="operation"
name="Operation of Ultrasonic Device" language="English"
     workplace="http://this.is.me/my-workplace.xml" start="start">
  <action id="start" viewport="actions" type="action">
    <enter removeSelf="false">
      <activate id="board1" type="tangible" predicate="point"
            poi="leftside" option="down" />
      <activate id="board1" type="tangible" predicate="label"
            poi="default" option="touch me!" />
    </enter>
    <exit>
      <deactivate id="board1" type="tangible" predicate="point" poi="leftside" />
      <deactivate id="board1" type="tangible" predicate="label" poi="default" />
      <activate type="action" viewport="actions" id="step2" />
      <deactivate type="action" viewport="actions" id="start" />
    </exit>
    <triggers>
      <trigger mode="click" type="action" viewport="actions" id="start" />
    </triggers>
    <instruction>
      <title>Operation of Ultrasonic Device</title>
      <description>
        <![CDATA[
          <p>Point to the device to start ... </p>
        ]]>
      </description>
    </instruction>
  </action>
  <action id="step2" viewport="actions" type="action">
    <enter />
    <exit removeSelf="true" />
    <triggers>
      <trigger mode="click" type="action" viewport="actions" id="step1" />
    </triggers>
    <instruction>
      <title>Welcome to step 2</title>
      <description><![CDATA[<p>Do this and that.</p>]]></description>
    </instruction>
  </action>
</activity>
```

HAR as human-object interaction is only one aspect of collaboration in wearable enhanced learning. Human-human and human-robot collaboration are scenarios with are getting more and more attention in workplace learning scenarios. Humans can collaborate with each other at the workplace, e.g. for the assembly of heavy parts or the manufacturing of complicated parts, e.g. fiber-reinforced composites in lightweight construction. Therefore, current HAR approaches need to be extended for human-human collaboration as well as for human-robot collaboration. Identified human activities can be written as Experience API (xAPI) statements, a software specification for exchanging learning data. This would fulfill three purposes. First, we can add xAPI based analytics tools from the shelf, we can share xAPI data with other researchers and practioners, even beyond the users of the ARLEM standard and we can make use of standard learning

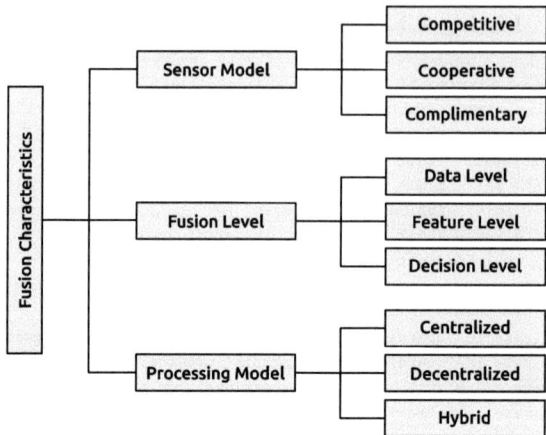

Fig. 2. Characteristics of multisensor data fusion

record stores like Learning Locker[1]. All three tasks of storing, measuring and analyzing contribute as an infrastructuring measure for CoP [30], helping them to define their own ecosystem by a wide choice of alternatives compatible to each other. For learning purposes the environment can be augmented with gamification [31,32].

3 Concept

We describe a possible learning scenario to illustrate our idea. A community of medical doctors is recording manipulative actions for diagnostics with a complicated ultrasound device using different wearable devices like an electromyographic (EMG) sensor (Myo) and a Microsoft HoloLens. The idea to record this data is that some doctors received training with this specific device while other doctors are knowing ultrasound diagnostics, but did not receive training for this specific ultrasound device. However, in a community of practice, newcomers learn from experts by observation and imitation. Consequently, recording of experts and non-experts for this specific device are made. These recordings are stored in the community specific repository of the community, e.g. the private learning record store of an ambulance center. In this sense, the data is belonging to the community of medical doctors and the data is not necessarily leaving the center. Modeling of activities and workplaces are typically activities where medical doctors do not receive much training. The idea here is to include modeling and content creation specialists from companies specialized on these tasks. They will deliver the necessary knowledge and training for the medical doctors, similar to the training with the ultrasound device. After receiving initial training, the doctors select analytic tools and visualization methods from a repository of possible templates in a collaborative online editor. Together, they can adjust the analytics

---

[1] See https://learninglocker.net.

and visualization process to their needs. They decide to use the stored learning traces as input for a privacy preserving machine learning algorithm extracting learning progress of less experienced medical doctors compared to expert users of the ultrasound device. In a training session, the medical doctors use an augmented reality head mounted device to recognize their activities and to display collaboratively selected information for additional training support in the view field of the device.

In a critical assessment of the scenario, it is fair to say, that we are not even close to its full operationalization. While training on devices through specialists for medical doctors is a profitable after-sales business and the idea that procedural medical knowledge can be shared among a community of practice is quite common in medical education, bringing together the two ideas may take some time. One challenge is the time needed for sharing practices on the job. Specialists in diagnosis with expensive devices may be very busy, too busy to spend time on sharing knowledge. More mature technical support may decrease the time needed for recording learning materials and re-purpose them for training, but still there is a lot of informal learning taking place around the recording and training sessions.

We need to implement several tools in our conceptual architecture.

- The **recorder** is consisting of the ARLEM editor, the sensor fusion framework and the activity/gesture recognition modules. The recorder processes the recorded data via the sensor fusion framework into sequences of human/robot activities and/or gestures.
- The **player** is an application that resides on the augmented reality device, in our case the MS HoloLens. The player uses the sensor fusion framework and the according modules to predict activities and gestures based on the available training data.

In Fig. 3 we can see an example for a fusion task. The abbreviations are according to Dasarathy's functional model [33].

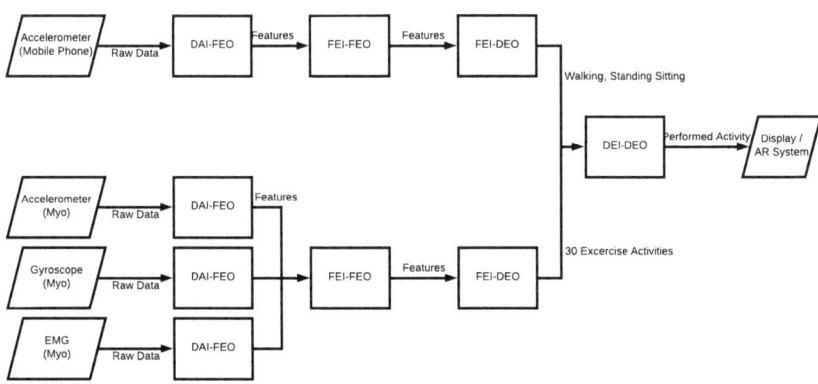

Fig. 3. Fusion task

The Social Web Environment for Visual Analytics (SWEVA) [34,35] is a collaborative environment for CoP to define tasks as described above in a collaborative and visual manner. It empowers all community members to realize their analytical requirements themselves, by using a toolset of ready-made modules for data gathering and processing. In a collaborative Web application, end users work together with developers to define data sources, aggregation and preprocessing steps, as well as to select a suitable visualization means. The resulting visualizations are highly interactive with respect to definable input parameters. They can be exported to arbitrary third-party websites running on desktop, mobile and mixed reality browsers.

4 Implementation

We implemented parts of the conceptual architecture in several EU-funded projects, also with the help of computer science students. The recorder is using an editor allowing the user to add sensors (e.g. Myo as an electromyographic (EMG) sensor, Bluetooth RFComm, Bluetooth Light Energy (BLE), Micro::bit, Microsoft Kinect, Microsoft HoloLens) as resources to a MQTT node by means of the open source library M2Mqtt. The ARLEM editor is implemented with the help of RESTful services as a node.js application with a MySQL database to store the descriptions and a single-page Web application as its frontend. The multi-sensor fusion framework is written in C#. It has many configuration parameters and is easy to extend. The player is based on the MixedRealityToolkit from Microsoft using Unity. The source code is open source and managed on GitHub[2]. At the moment, the environment is not able to describe, store or analyze human-human or human-robot collaboration use cases. A collaborative research proposal has been already submitted. In a special case, we recorded interaction between a robot and a human using a special robot model for an emergency shutdown system of the robot.

Figure 4 shows the visualization of a human-robot interaction in SWEVA. Here, we see a robot (shown in blue) working together with a human (in red) for layering textile fibre composites. The goal of this visualization is to show possibly harmful situations where a robot arm is colliding with a human. These situations are a real threat in all industries, where human-robot collaboration is happening; therefore there exists a long rat's tail of standards and other legislative regulations. The original sensor data is coming from a Microsoft Kinect device that detects human movements. We bring it together with machine data from the industrial robot. In SWEVA we designed the visualization of the process that forces the machine to stop in real-time, every time there is a risk of collision. The 3D output is accessible from every Web browser, as it is relying on state-of-the-art Web 3D technologies.

---

[2] See https://github.com/rwth-acis/kanect.

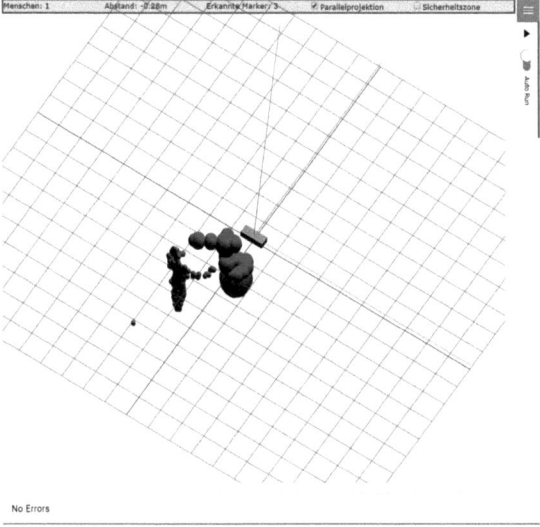

Fig. 4. SWEVA visualization of human-robot interaction at a production site (Color figure online)

5 Conclusions and Future Work

We have presented a comprehensive approach to enable collaborative immersive community analytics in wearable enhanced learning. Starting from the idea that learning analytics at the workplace is conceptually different from traditional learning analytics we incorporated practice theories under the assumption of a digital transformation of their methodological foundations, i.e. digital ethnography. As a second major point we introduced the idea that feedback is best delivered in an immersive manner while doing training and not afterwards. As a third line of argumentation, we discussed that the necessary collaborative processes are best situated in a community of practice.

Large portions of the concept have been realized in different EU projects but not yet fully integrated. A fully functional prototype will be ready soon for further testing and evaluation in realistic learning scenarios.

Acknowledgement. The authors would like to thank the German Research Foundation (DFG) for the kind support within the Cluster of Excellence "Internet of Production" (IoP) under the project id 390621612. This project has also received funding from the European Union's Horizon 2020 research and innovation programme under grant agreements No 687669 (WEKIT) and from the European Union's Erasmus Plus programme, grant agreement 2017-1-NO01-KA203-034192.

References

1. Ferguson, R.: Learning analytics: drivers, developments and challenges. Int. J. Technol. Enhanced Learn. **4**(5–6), 304–317 (2012)
2. Ullman, M.T.: Contributions of memory circuits to language: the declarative/procedural model. Cognition **92**, 231–270 (2004)
3. Nonaka, I., Takeuchi, H.: The Knowledge-Creating Company: How Japanese Companies Create the Dynamics of Innovation. Oxford University Press, New York (1995)
4. Klamma, R.: Community learning analytics – challenges and opportunities. In: Wang, J.-F., Lau, R. (eds.) ICWL 2013. LNCS, vol. 8167, pp. 284–293. Springer, Heidelberg (2013). https://doi.org/10.1007/978-3-642-41175-5_29
5. Wenger, E.: Communities of Practice: Learning, Meaning, and Identity. Learning in doing. Cambridge University Press, Cambridge (1998)
6. Keim, D., Andrienko, G., Fekete, J.-D., Görg, C., Kohlhammer, J., Melançon, G.: Visual analytics: definition, process, and challenges. In: Kerren, A., Stasko, J.T., Fekete, J.-D., North, C. (eds.) Information Visualization. LNCS, vol. 4950, pp. 154–175. Springer, Heidelberg (2008). https://doi.org/10.1007/978-3-540-70956-5_7
7. Dwyer, T., et al.: Immersive analytics: an introduction. Immersive Analytics. LNCS, vol. 11190, pp. 1–23. Springer, Cham (2018). https://doi.org/10.1007/978-3-030-01388-2_1
8. Billinghurst, M., Cordeil, M., Bezerianos, A., Margolis, T.: Collaborative immersive analytics. In: Marriott, K., et al. (eds.) Immersive Analytics. LNCS, vol. 11190, pp. 221–257. Springer, Cham (2018). https://doi.org/10.1007/978-3-030-01388-2_8
9. Bourdieu, P.: Outline of a Theory of Practice. Cambridge Studies in Social and Cultural Anthropology, vol. 16. Cambridge University Press, Cambridge (1977). English language edn
10. Giddens, A.: The Constitution of Society: Outline of the Theory of Structuration, 1st edn. University of California Press, Berkeley (1984)
11. Foucault, M.: The Archaeology of Knowledge: And the Discourse on Language. Dorset Press, New York (1987)
12. Savigny, E.V., Knorr-Cetina, K., Schatzki, T.R.: The Practice Turn in Contemporary Theory. Routledge, London (2001)
13. Schatzki, T.R.: Social Practices: A Wittgensteinian Approach to Human Activity and the Social. Digital print edn. Cambridge University Press, Cambridge (2008)
14. Butler, J.: Bodies That Matter: On the Discursive Limits of "Sex". Routledge, London (2014)
15. Polanyi, M.: The Tacit Dimension. Anchor Books, Doubleday & Co., New York (1966)
16. Santos, M.E.C., Chen, A., Taketomi, T., Yamamoto, G., Miyazaki, J., Kato, H.: Augmented reality learning experiences: survey of prototype design and evaluation. IEEE Trans. Learn. Technol. **7**(1), 38–56 (2014)
17. Chiang, H.K., Chou, Y.Y., Chang, L.C., Huang, C.Y., Kuo, F.L., Chen, H.W.: An augmented reality learning space for PC DIY. In: Proceedings of the 2nd Augmented Human International Conference, AH 2011, pp. 12:1–12:4. ACM, New York (2011)
18. Juan, M.C., Furió, D., Seguí, I., Aiju, N.R., Cano, J.: Lessons learnt from an experience with an augmented reality iphone learning game. In: Proceedings of the 8th International Conference on Advances in Computer Entertainment Technology, ACE 2011, pp. 52:1–52:8. ACM, New York (2011)

19. Tsai, C.H., Huang, J.Y.: A mobile augmented reality based scaffolding platform for outdoor fieldtrip learning. In: 2014 IIAI 3rd International Conference on Advanced Applied Informatics, pp. 307–312 (2014)
20. Oh, S., Byun, Y.C.: The design and implementation of augmented reality learning systems. In: 2012 IEEE/ACIS 11th International Conference on Computer and Information Science, pp. 651–654 (2012)
21. Ables, A.: Augmented and virtual reality: discovering their uses in natural science classrooms and beyond. In: Proceedings of the 2017 ACM Annual Conference on SIGUCCS, SIGUCCS 2017, pp. 61–65. ACM, New York (2017)
22. Dass, N., Kim, J., Ford, S., Agarwal, S., Chau, D.H.: Augmenting coding: augmented reality for learning programming. In: Proceedings of the Sixth International Symposium of Chinese CHI, Chinese CHI 2018, pp. 156–159. ACM, New York (2018)
23. Limbu, B., Fominykh, M., Klemke, R., Specht, M., Wild, F.: Supporting training of expertise with wearable technologies: the WEKIT reference framework. In: Yu, S., Ally, M., Tsinakos, A. (eds.) Mobile and Ubiquitous Learning. PRRE, pp. 157–175. Springer, Singapore (2018). https://doi.org/10.1007/978-981-10-6144-8_10
24. Wild, F.: The future of learning at the workplace is augmented reality. Computer **49**(10), 96–98 (2016)
25. Subetha, T., Chitrakala, S.: A survey on human activity recognition from videos. In: 2016 International Conference on Information Communication and Embedded Systems (ICICES), pp. 1–7 (2016)
26. Maurer, U., Smailagic, A., Siewiorek, D.P., Deisher, M.: Activity recognition and monitoring using multiple sensors on different body positions. In: 2011 Fifth FTRA International Conference on Multimedia and Ubiquitous Engineering, pp. 4–116 (2011)
27. Liu, S., Gao, R.X., John, D., Staudenmayer, J.W., Freedson, P.S.: Multisensor data fusion for physical activity assessment. IEEE Trans. Biomed. Eng. **59**(3), 687–696 (2012)
28. Lara, O.D., Labrador, M.A.: A survey on human activity recognition using wearable sensors. IEEE Commun. Surv. Tutor. **15**(3), 1192–1209 (2013)
29. Gravina, R., Alinia, P., Ghasemzadeh, H., Fortino, G.: Multi-sensor fusion in body sensor networks: state-of-the-art and research challenges. Inf. Fusion **35**, 68–80 (2017)
30. de Lange, P., Göschlberger, B., Farrell, T., Klamma, R.: A microservice infrastructure for distributed communities of practice. In: Pammer-Schindler, V., Pérez-Sanagustín, M., Drachsler, H., Elferink, R., Scheffel, M. (eds.) EC-TEL 2018. LNCS, vol. 11082, pp. 172–186. Springer, Cham (2018). https://doi.org/10.1007/978-3-319-98572-5_14
31. Klamma, R., Arifin, M.A.: Gamification of web-based learning services. In: Xie, H., Popescu, E., Hancke, G., Fernández Manjón, B. (eds.) ICWL 2017. LNCS, vol. 10473, pp. 43–48. Springer, Cham (2017). https://doi.org/10.1007/978-3-319-66733-1_5
32. Hensen, B., Koren, I., Klamma, R., Herrler, A.: An augmented reality framework for gamified learning. In: Hancke, G., Spaniol, M., Osathanunkul, K., Unankard, S., Klamma, R. (eds.) ICWL 2018. LNCS, vol. 11007, pp. 67–76. Springer, Cham (2018). https://doi.org/10.1007/978-3-319-96565-9_7
33. Dasarathy, B.V.: Sensor fusion potential exploitation-innovative architectures and illustrative applications. Proc. IEEE **85**(1), 24–38 (1997)

34. Koren, I., Klamma, R.: Community learning analytics with industry 4.0 and wearable sensor data. In: Beck, D., et al. (eds.) iLRN 2017. CCIS, vol. 725, pp. 142–151. Springer, Cham (2017). https://doi.org/10.1007/978-3-319-60633-0_12
35. Koren, I., Klamma, R.: Enabling visual community learning analytics with Internet of things devices. Comput. Hum. Behav. **89**, 385–394 (2018)

Virtual Companions and 3D Virtual Worlds: Investigating the Sense of Presence in Distance Education

Aliane Loureiro Krassmann[1(✉)], Felipe Becker Nunes[2],
Maximino Bessa[3], Liane Margarida Rockenbach Tarouco[1],
and Magda Bercht[1]

[1] Universidade Federal do Rio Grande do Sul, Porto Alegre, Brazil
`alkrassmann@gmail.com`
[2] Antonio Meneghetti Faculdade, Restinga Seca, Brazil
[3] INESC TEC and UTAD, Vila Real, Portugal

Abstract. Distance Education (DE) still have some challenges to be considered similar to the face-to-face mode of instruction regarding the quality of learning, including the lack in promoting the sense of presence. This research investigates whether a differentiated media support, complementary to the traditional Virtual Learning Environment (VLE), composed by the integration of 3D Virtual Worlds (3DVW) and Conversational Agents, in the role of a Virtual Companions, can promote the student's sense of presence in order to contribute with the learning process in DE. A quasi-experiment pilot study was conducted with 36 students enrolled in the Financial Management discipline from a DE formal course. A 3DVW was developed in the light of the pedagogical model of Experiential Learning, in the form of a role-play simulation. The results reveal that although the students positively evaluated the experience in the 3DVW, it did not stimulate the sense of presence as expected. However, better performance rates were diagnosed for students who had the help of the Virtual Companion.

Keywords: Conversational agents · Virtual worlds · Virtual companion · Sense of presence · Distance education

1 Introduction

Distance Education (DE) is increasingly being distinguished as a teaching modality capable of providing with great efficiency, effectiveness and quality of the yearnings of knowledge diffusion. By allowing access to formal education via Internet, it is possible to flexibilize the formation of individuals in time and space, learning rhythms and formative itineraries, which makes this the fastest growing instruction mode in the world [1]. It is already regulated adopted in the most varied educational levels; the number of DE students increases by about 5% each year [2].

However, in general, DE still has the challenge to move away from a widespread impression that it's quality of learning is lower than a face-to-face mode of instruction. As highlighted by De Metz and Bezuidenhout [3], DE students often experience a sense of lack of confidence in learning, which is particularly true for beginners, who are using an online platform for the first time. Among the reasons for this phenomenon, some are discussed in the next subsections.

1.1 The Lack of Individualized Monitoring

Most classrooms (in face-to-face education) contain students who, at one end of the spectrum are bored, and at the other side are overwhelmed and lost. This situation becomes more difficult to manage in the DE, since teachers do not have the face-to-face contact that allows to visually identify who these students are and take the proactive measures [4].

This happens often due to administrative and financial constraints, or even due to the inherent logistics characteristic of the DE. In this modality, the same teacher is in charge of attending, remotely and simultaneously, a massive amount of students, something around 200 [3], which is beyond reasonable for close monitoring of activities. In addition, the tutors end up spending much of their time reading posts from forums and tasks, and verifying student participation in the Virtual Learning Environment (VLE), performing informational and administrative roles, reducing the time spent engaging in actual interaction or fulfilling the important social role [5].

1.2 The Limitations of the Traditional VLE

For centuries, the text was considered the primary format for teaching scientific material, and books the main tool. Similarly, computers are often used as high-technology books that present large amounts of information in text format [6]. In this sense, it is common to observe that the web-based VLE traditionally used typically focus on providing students with information, tasks and files, making them face a mainly textual course, despite the vast technological innovation available for use. In the South Africa University, for example, the VLE still only allows asynchronous communication, which means delayed communication through discussion forums or questions and answers [3]. These environments are also known as Learning Management Systems (LMS), and a widely used example is the free open source software MOODLE (Modular Object-Oriented Dynamic Learning Environment).

1.3 The Lack of Professional Practices

Education in the 21st Century is increasingly emphasizing professional and vocational preparation, with the creation of real-world learning experiences, accompanied by greater attention to the development of the skills needed to make the individual a lifelong learner, who can effectively adapt to new situations and respond to changes in circumstances [7].

However, also exacerbated by the physical distance of the student, the professional practices are usually neglected in DE, which is also largely due to cost constraints inherent to traveling students to the practice field, in the case of public education. Dede [8] emphasizes that, this way, knowledge often becomes "insert", in which people do not know how to apply the abstract principles they have memorized to solve real-world problems. The lack of resources to carry out professional practices prevent that more practical courses be offered in DE, such as the Technical Course in Tourist Guide.

1.4 The Lack of Student's Sense of Presence

The traditional VLEs also lack the promotion of the student's sense of presence, enhanced by the physical distance from the educational environment and its infrastructure. Witmer and Singer [9] define the sense of presence as the "subjective experience of being in one place or environment, even when one is physically situated in another." The authors suggest that an increase in the feeling of "being there" (closer to the content) leads to improvements in learning, which has been validated, for example, in the studies of Mikropoulos [10] and Tüzün and Özdinç [11], although there is not a consensus in literature regarding this possibility.

Against the preceding, this research proposes to develop and investigate the use of media support, complementary to traditional VLE, involving the combination of technologies with greater potential to act in the mentioned problems. That is, it allows individualized monitoring, more interactivity, teach through practical experience and stimulate the student's sense of presence, in order to verify how this support can leverage improvements in the DE learning process. More specifically, we seek to analyze how the stimulus to the student's sense of presence when interacting with instructional content using 3D Virtual World (3DVW) and Conversational Agents can contribute to the learning process. Thus, the research question is: *is it possible to contribute to the Distance Education student's learning process by promoting the sense of presence?*

2 Theoretical Framework

2.1 3D Virtual Worlds and Conversational Agents

The dynamics of Human Computer Interaction (HCI) generally do not include immersion, i.e., the system's ability to decrease stimulation to the real world and increase the stimulation of the synthetic world [12]. Typically, the user sits on a terminal and communicates through interface devices (such as a mouse or keyboard) [9]. However, technologies that allow this kind of experience are on the rise.

3DVW are a category of Virtual Reality (VR) technology, defined by Nevelsteen [13] as time-shared, non-paused simulated environments in which many agents can virtually interact with each other, act and react to things. The difference from VR technology itself is that 3DVW does not provide a fully immersive experience, as it does not exclude external audiovisual stimuli and thus does not require additional devices as Head-Mounted Displays (HMD). For that reason, they are more accessible to large scale educational contexts as DE.

In 3DVW users are represented by avatars (personification in the environment), which allow performing actions similar to those performed by real people, such as walking, running and gesturing [14]. Real world physical characteristics such as gravity and wind, and the addition of behaviors to the 3D objects of the environment, enable the development of activities that mirror the real context.

Several platforms have been existing since late 2000's for the development of 3DVW, such as Active Worlds, Second Life (SL), OpenSimulator (OpenSim) and Open Wonderland, being the last two open source. The OpenSim platform is the one used in this research, giving its large community of developers. Linden Scripting Language (LSL) is the default scripting language in SL and OpenSim, which also uses the OpenSimulator Scripting Language (OSSL). Through these programming languages, 3D objects can acquire behavior and become sensitive to events, such as being touched. They also enable the interconnection with external systems, through Hypertext Transfer Protocol (HTTP) requests.

Because they are open and multi-directional, the experience of each individual in a 3DVW will be unique. Thus, they provide a more student-centered approach, who moves in its own rhythm (personalized learning), developing autonomy. For instance, students are free to literally "walk" and see a demonstration from different perspectives (angles), contributing to the active construction of knowledge [15].

Researches have already investigated the above assumptions to benefit learning. Ijaz et al. [16] compared instructional methods for unsupervised learning of the same content (in this case, History), and found that students who used 3DVW scored 21% better who made use of text, and 25% more than the group that used video. Nevertheless, the authors emphasize that learning in 3DVW is a less time-efficient approach compared to traditional methods. Englund [17] corroborates, saying that although it is initially time-consuming to acquire the skills and knowledge necessary to navigate and teach in 3DVW, the benefits offered, especially for DE students, may be greater than these obstacles.

Virtual Companions. Despite the mentioned advantages of 3DVW, as they become larger, with many places available to visit, guidance is needed so that students can find places, people or avatars relevant to the educational objectives [18]. According to Chen et al. [19], the navigation in open environments imposes irrelevant cognitive load. Thus, in their study, the students exposed to guided exploration significantly outperformed the ones exposed to unguided exploration. This is in accordance with Mayer's multimedia learning theory [20], which establishes that aids to stay oriented during navigation within a VLE avoid additional cognitive activities that are unnecessary.

The Non-Player Characters (NPC) feature available in 3DVW platforms, appear as a possible solution to this impasse. As highlighted by Burden [21], they are script-controlled avatars that have the same capacity for interaction as the human-controlled ones, allowing them to play a variety of roles, such as receptionists or guides. Also, they can monitor user interaction with the learning objects to ensure that it occurs accordingly [18].

As 3DVW allows the interconnection with external software, if configured, a student can send and receive instant messages to a Conversational Agent (chatbot) while inside the 3DVW, which can, upon receipt, be associated with the behavior of a NPC, so it begins to act as a Virtual Companion. This research explores this potential employing AIML (Artificial Intelligence Modelling Language) technology, interconnecting the Program-O open source software to the OpenSim 3DVW.

Kim [22] reveals that with the advances in HCI technology, the construction of anthropomorphized "looking-like" agents draws attention to the possibility of building relationships with the student. She suggests the term Pedagogical Agent as Learning Companions (PALs), defining them as those who identify with the student's actions as if they were colleagues or friends. The Virtual Companion is the terminology adopted in this research, by giving the NPC the ability of dialogue and the role of a companion. This choice is due to the less invasive character, maintaining the freedom and autonomy of the student in the 3DVW, which is especially important when it comes to the target public that is investigated, composed of adults.

2.2 Sense of Presence

According to Witmer and Singer [9], the sense of presence refers to experiencing the computer-generated environment rather than the actual physical location: the computer world becomes the user's world. For Slater and Wilbur [23], individuals with a high sense of presence will experience the virtual environment as the reality more involving than the surrounding physical world, to the point of considering it as a place visited and not as images viewed.

From this argument, it can be affirmed that the sense of presence involves the person's commitment to the "suspension of disbelief" that he is "somewhere else" [24]. Coelho et al. [12] corroborate, stating that there seems to be a compromise between man and machine in the experience of presence. Thus, Bouvier [25] suggests that it is not only with the technique that we will be successful in promoting the sense of presence, highlighting the importance of the emotional aspect.

In this context, it must be outlined the distinction between immersion and presence. Slater and Wilbur [23] suggest that immersion is an objective and quantifiable description of what any particular system provides. Already the presence is a state of consciousness, the (psychological) sense of being in the virtual environment. In other words, it is the potential psychological and behavioral response to immersion. However, the question of whether more immersion produces greater presence and when that happens is still left open [26].

Attention and involvement are responses associated with the sense of presence [27]. This is because, "to be present in an alternative world, our attention must be focused there, not in the real world" [28]. Romano and Brna [29] affirm that the sense of presence gives the virtual experience the same value as a corresponding real one, allowing to transform it into learning in the real world. Thus, they argue this is one of the key features necessary to ensure the transfer of knowledge from the virtual to the real world. Waterworth and Waterworth [26] are more reasonable, considering that it sometimes helps performance, depending on the nature of the task.

Among the methodological approaches for measuring presence, subjective, through post-tests (self-report questionnaires), and objective ones, through behavioral and physiological measurements (cerebral electrical activity, for example), are available. Subjective classifications are the most widely used, due to the less invasiveness and no use of body sensors. Considering the remote target audience of this research, this is the approach adopted, selecting the instrument proposed by Witmer and Singer [9].

As a differential of the research already done [10, 11], a comparison is made between media with different potentials of interactivity, with a target audience of formal DE students, with the use of Experiential Learning as a pedagogical model.

3 Method

A mixed methods quasi-experimental pilot study was conducted in a real educational context, with a sample of 36 students enrolled in formal courses offered in the DE. Although qualitative results were obtained, the quantitative results are the scope of this paper.

3.1 Materials

The 3DVW used in this research is part of the AVATAR Project [30], from the Universidade Federal do Rio Grande do Sul (Brazil). The service runs in a client-server mode; the client must install a viewer, which is the software that graphically renders the 3DVW. For this purpose, it was selected the Singularity viewer version 1.8.7, since it is free, robust and have Portuguese language support.

Kolb's Experiential Learning [31] is the pedagogical model chosen to guide the construction of the 3DVW, seeking to give the DE student the opportunity to apply what s/he learns in the course. Within the spectrum of Experiential Learning, role-play in VLE has been explored in recent years, which involves participants adopting a specific role, aiming to learn about it and the consequences of their actions. We assume that by identifying with a character, within a context that makes sense, students will tend to put themselves in its place and, in a sense, experience that, contributing to the sense of presence.

The 3DVW was developed towards the Financial Management discipline. It consists of a building that simulates an accounting firm, called C-Company (Fig. 1), including all the usual office furniture and divisions, as reception area, hallway, living room, small and large offices. It has a narrative that revolves around the context of this fictitious company, where the student avatar receives the role of a first-day trainee in its admission process, and is challenged to develop an understanding of the complexities of the work world, passing through its five sectors: Human Resources Board, Marketing Board, Executive Board, Administrative Board and CEO Office.

Kolb [31] suggests a non-linear cycle of experiences and reinterpretations carried out by the student, composed of four stages. The way that each of the stages was contemplated in the 3DVW is briefly presented in the sequence.

Concrete experience: students are inserted into a practical situation of their future professional life (post-training), which contextualizes the knowledge.

Reflective observation: as they experience this, students makes observations about the simulated work routine and interpret the situations.

Abstract conceptualization: students are asked to apply the theoretical knowledge acquired in the course to give continuity to the activity, responding to quizzes.

Active experimentation: at the end, students receive a different role within the simulation, being asked to respond to a slightly more complex exercise.

Seeking to provide students with the freedom to choose an appearance that best represents them. First they are instructed to walk into a corridor to pick a new avatar if desired. This moment also gives a period of recognition of the controls. Next, they are instructed to enter the C-Company building to begin the activity, being placed in the first phase of the Kolb's Cycle [31], *concrete experience*.

Fig. 1. The entrance of the 3DVW activity, C-Company building.

At this point, the Virtual Companion named Jimmy comes to meet the student avatar and presents himself as a colleague in the same role, following him/her throughout all the interaction. The chatbot knowledge base was previously created, including general social interactions and contents of Financial Management (percentage, simple interest, compound interest, amortization systems, among others). The natural language interaction occurs by typing messages in the chat bar of the viewer.

Several other NPCs with their own names are arranged throughout the simulation. They "populate" the C-Company and in some cases express themselves bodily (simulating typing on the keyboard) and textually, participating in the narrative. In this sense, the student moves on to the phase of *reflective observation*, in which s/he analyzes the scenario and begins to understand the work routine of an accounting firm.

The 3DVW has some aspects of gamification (similar to games): the practice is divided into phases. That is, the student must complete each phase before moving on to the next. However, by avoiding a lock and the use of rigid rules, the system allows them to continue even if they make mistakes.

At each room of C-Company, the avatar which represents the boss tells the student to sit in a chair to begin a quiz composed of three multiple-choice questions, adapted from an actual exercise list from the Financial Management discipline. The quiz was developed using the Heads Up Display (HUD) device available in 3DVW platforms, which temporarily attaches an object in the user's screen. By starting the quiz, the camera of the viewer is adjusted, so the user has a frontal vision of the table, that is, facing the chief, giving a more realistic view.

Students were given 10 min to answer each quiz. For each right answer a point was assigned, and at the end of each phase the score was given (from 0 to 3). Scripts capture the score of each student, recording it in an external database. At the end of the quiz, the messages pronounced by the chief indicate the next room where the student should go, and so on, in a concatenation of events.

To help with the quiz resolution, a "Help" button was placed among the answer options. When clicking it, the student's chair rotates to the front of a screen, and s/he is instructed to touch it to play a short didactic video related to the subject matter. While seeing the video, the quiz stays hidden until the student touches the button "Back to Quiz". There is also a "Calculator" button to help the student. In this context, the student is inserted in the *abstract conceptualization* stage of the Kolb's Cycle [31], in which s/he is required to apply/confront the theoretical knowledge acquired in the course to continue the activity.

When the quiz starts, the Virtual Companion automatically appears on the side of the boss's chair (in front of the student's field of view). He can perform two categories of emotional expressions, briefly described as follows.

Congratulations. When a student experiences success, admirable emotions are expressed, with the desired effect of the incentive. Thus, in case of a correctly answered question, Jimmy expresses happiness, both verbally and bodily, by clapping or jumping, presenting congratulatory messages (i.e. "Nice! Well done.") (Fig. 2).

Fig. 2. Jimmy performing the congratulations expression after a correct answer.

Support. When a student experiences failure, emotions that indicate sadness or disappointment are triggered, with the desired effect of building empathy and expressing support. Thus, in the case of a wrong answer, Jimmy expresses himself bodily by lowering his head or bringing his hands to his face (Fig. 3), in addition to verbally encouraging messages (i.e. "No problem, let's try again..."). Jimmy also suggests the use of "Help" material, pointing his arm to indicate the corresponding button.

The simulation culminates with the student reaching the goal of obtaining the internship, arriving in a large room where several "employees" (NPCs) are already actively "working" (typing on their keyboards), with a workstation reserved for the student. By touching on the computer screen of the workstation, the student receives his/her results in the activity (Fig. 4). Also, a big screen at the back shows the ranking of all participants in the activity, sorted by decreasing order.

Thus, at the end of the path the student is in the stage of *active experimentation*, in which s/he evolves to the role of a trainee hired by the company. When sitting at the

Fig. 3. Jimmy performing support expression after an incorrect answer.

Fig. 4. Student sitting at the workstation to "start the internship".

reserved workstation, s/he is also required to solve a somewhat more complex activity, on the topic "amortization systems", which consists fulfilling a spreadsheet in the screen. The whole activity has a duration estimated in 40 min.

3.2 Subjects

The research took place in the context of the Technical Course in Administration, offered in DE at a public institution in Brazil, in the context of the Financial Management discipline, which has a workload of 75 h divided in five months. The convenience sample consisted of 36 students with a mean age of 34 years (M = 34, SD = 9.2), being 14 (~39%) male and 22 (~61%) female. The type of media support was the independent variable and the sense of presence and the learning outcomes were the dependent variables. Thus, subjects were divided into the following groups/conditions of equal size.

Control Group: traditional VLE.
Experimental Group: 3DVW.
Real Experimental Group: 3DVW with the Virtual Companion.

Each group had similar distributions of gender and average grade, which was analyzed considering the mean grade in the last 10 disciplines ended by the time of the experiment (Control Group M = 7.78, Experimental Group M = 7.76, Real Experimental Group M = 7.82, p = 0.954). Therefore, the groups can be considered homogeneous or statistically equal.

3.3 Instruments

The data collection instruments are summarized in Table 1. The items that compose the Presence Questionnaire and the Agent Value Questionnaire were translated from English into Portuguese by the first author, who afterwards sent the original and translated versions to a judging panel composed of three Brazilian PhD in Informatics in Education with fluency in the English language, who agreed with the consistency of the translation and the appropriateness of the statements to the public investigated; that is, that they could be easily and autonomously interpreted by the DE students.

The questionnaires were delivered online using the free Google Drive forms service; it contained the free informed consent emphasizing that there were no right or wrong answers and that they should remember their impressions regarding the activity to respond to each question as honestly as possible.

3.4 Procedure

First, the researchers contacted the course's coordination, presenting the 3DVW, that was tested by the professor of the discipline. The institution then formally authorized the research conduction, proposing it as an extra activity in which students were given partial course credit for participation. An exploratory study previously conducted in the same context supported that decision [35].

Given that the access to the 3DVW was designed to be remote and individual to better infer the sense of presence, it was desired for the subjects to install the viewer in their own Personal Computers (PC). To do so, they should have sufficient hardware and Internet bandwidth. The Singularity viewer site contains the following system requirements: dual-core CPU, NVidia or ATI/AMD graphics chip, 2 GB RAM, Windows XP or later. As for the bandwidth, it was desired at least 2 Mbps.

Students were invited by e-mail messages, which informed the research objectives, the requirements for participation, the voluntary nature of their participation, as well as about the total confidentiality and restricted use of any information collected. As they answered it, they were randomly assigned to one of the groups.

The instructions for downloading and installing the Singularity viewer, as well as the necessary settings to access the 3DVW from their PC were delivered in step-by-step video tutorials. For the Control Group, the same didactic materials (videos) and quizzes were placed in the traditional VLE, in a space specific destined for the study. The activity had a duration of approximately 45 days, inside the time-space of the Financial Management discipline.

Table 1. Data collection instruments.

Instrument	Description
Presence questionnaire	The instrument by Witmer and Singer [9] is composed of 32 items, with a 7-point Likert scale response options. The items referring to the use of sounds and haptic sensor were withdrawn, as they were not contemplated in the 3DVW, resulting in a total of 19 items, as validated by the University of Quebec in Outaouais (UQO) Cyberpsychology Lab [32]. For the Control Group, a further six questions related to the experience with 3D environments were excluded, leaving 13 items. The instrument is composed of five constructs: realism, possibility to act, interface quality, possibility to examine, and self-evaluation of performance
Student perception of the 3DVW activity questionnaire	To capture feedback from the students about the 3DVW experienced, some questions were adapted from Rico et al. [33], which evaluated three different characteristics: (a) usability, (b) levels of the user agreement with the educational value of the tool, and (c) user satisfaction with the interface. The instrument is composed of 11 items, between open and closed questions, with 5-point Likert scale response options
Agent value questionnaire	To evaluate the Virtual Companion, it was adapted the questionnaire from Kim et al. [34], with 10 items of 5-point Likert scale response options
Institutional records	An analysis of the student's academic performance was considered (mean grade), comparing it with the final mean grade obtained in the discipline in which the approach was applied (Financial Management), verifying possible increases or decreases among groups
Performance in the 3DVW activity	The performance of the student in the 3DVW activity (average of hits in the quizzes) was also considered to allow a preliminary view of learning achievements

4 Results

Descriptive and inferential statistics techniques were performed with the data obtained using the SPSS version 18 software, considering the level of significance of 95% (p-value). Normality tests of Shapiro-Wilk, Liliefors, Anderson-Darling and Kolmogorov-Smirnov were applied to base the decision for parametric or non-parametric tests.

The presentation of the results was organized by instrument. Each subsection shows the number of students in the sample (n), as some instruments considered three, two or one group of 12 students each.

4.1 1 Presence Questionnaire (N = 36)

The Cronbach's alpha coefficient obtained for the Presence Questionnaire was 0.856, indicating good reliability. The results revealed that the Control Group (M = 5.47, SD = 0.59) scored higher than the Experimental Group (M = 4.87, SD = 1.13), which in turn scored lower than the Real Experimental Group (M = 5.07, SD = 0.78).

Analyzing the results by construct, the same pattern was observed, with an exception for the "possibility to examine", which was higher for the Experimental Group than the Real Experimental Group.

Yet, Kruskal-Wallis's test comparing the total means and medians of the three groups maintained the null hypothesis of equality (p = 0.241, p = 0.112).

The same test was applied to analyze each question individually in the cases of three groups, and the Mann-Whitney's test in the cases of two groups, considering the integral values of each item. As a result, a significant difference was observed with respect to the Question 3 *"How natural were your interactions with the virtual environment?"* (p = 0.046), indicating that the positive value obtained by Control Group was statistically superior to the other groups.

4.2 Student Perception of the 3DVW Activity Questionnaire (N = 24)

Seven questions of this instrument had 5-point Likert scale response options. Cronbach's alpha test revealed a coefficient of 0.826, demonstrating good reliability of the answers. The means obtained were very proximal in Experimental (M = 4.00, SD = 0.68), and Real Experimental groups (M = 3.99, SD = 0.57), reflecting an overall positive experience.

In order to verify a possible correlation with the Presence Questionnaire, the Spearman's test considering the total means of the experimental groups indicated a significant moderate positive correlation (r = 0.686, p = 0.000), as shown in the dispersion graphic presented in Fig. 5. The evidence suggests that the higher the average score in the Presence Questionnaire, the higher the average score in the Student Perception of the 3DVW Activity Questionnaire (and vice-versa). However, it is worth noting that this does not show a cause-effect relationship.

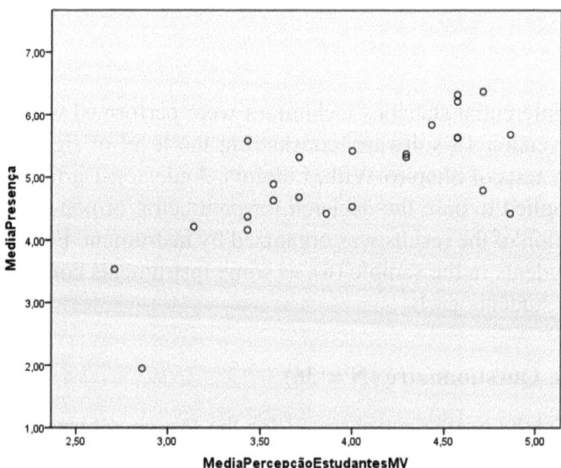

Fig. 5. Dispersion graphic from the presence questionnaire and student perception in the 3DVW activity questionnaire.

Students were also asked on how much time they considered their length of stay in the 3DVW, with objective response options ordinarily categorized. As a result, more students from the Real Experimental Group (n = 10) affirmed to remain more than 30 min, as compared to the Experimental Group (n = 7).

When considering total mean values of the Presence Questionnaire and the Student Perception of the 3DVW Activity to correlate with **time**, the Spearman's test revealed that the sample correlation, although not significant (p = 0.088, p = 0.344) is negative, allowing us to infer (with caution) that the greater the sense of presence and the more positive the perception of the 3DVW, the lower was the student's residence time in the 3DVW (r = −0.356, r = −0.202).

A question about the location of access to the 3DVW was also elaborated, trying to diagnose if the students were actually able to install and configure the viewer in their own PC, as initially conceived. Most of the students (∼58%) accessed it from the DE Center, who were equally distributed between the two experimental groups. In Brazil, a DE Center is a place where students have access to an informatics laboratory to take face-to-face tests and to perform activities, where a tutor (a professional in the course area with pedagogical experience) is available to help.

4.3 Agent Value Questionnaire (N = 12)

The Cronbach's alpha coefficient for this instrument was 0.964, which is considered highly reliable. It was obtained an overall positive mean (M = 3.8, SD = 1.1), denoting the students' general agreement with the positive characteristics provided by the Virtual Companion.

The Spearman's test maintained the null hypothesis of a correlation between this instrument and the Institutional Records (p = 0.672), but showed a moderate positive significant correlation with the Presence Questionnaire (r = 0.737, p = 0.006) and with the Student Perception of the 3DVW Activity Questionnaire (r = 0.610, p = 0.035), considering the total mean values. This probably means that the positive posture from students was consistent across instruments.

4.4 Institutional Records (N = 36)

It was observed that the student performance in the discipline where the study was applied (Financial Management) decreased for all the groups. The Wilcoxon Signed Ranks' test for paired samples rejected the null hypothesis of equality (p = 0.000), indicating that this difference is statistically significant. However, the biggest difference occurred for the Control Group (2.22 points), as shown in Table 2.

Table 2. Difference in institutional records and the discipline mean grade.

Groups	M institutional records	M discipline grade	dif
Control group	7.78	5.55	2.22
Experimental group	7.76	6.17	1.55
Real experimental group	7.82	5.97	1.84

To investigate a possible correlation of the performance in the Financial Management discipline with the Presence Questionnaire, the Pearson's test considering the total means values per group revealed the existence of a moderate negative significant correlation ($r = -0.381$, $p = 0.022$). That is, the more positive grades were obtained from those who reported lower rates of the sense of presence.

4.5 Performance in the 3DVW Activity (N = 24)

A small number of students ($n = 10$) concluded the activity in the 3DVW, responding to the 15 objective questions set in the environment. However, this number was superior in the Real Experimental Group, composed by the majority of its members ($n = 7$). In contrast, most of the Experimental Group students did not complete the activity. This result is in accordance with the time spent in the 3DVW, as more students from the Real Experimental Group stayed for more than 30 mins.

Considering the total score obtained in the 3DVW activity, in a universe of 15 possible points per user (one point per question), the average performance was also better in the Real Experimental Group, although with a higher standard deviation ($M = 9.29$, $SD = 2.60$, as compared to $M = 5.67$, $SD = 1.25$). Nevertheless, as more students from the Real Experimental Group concluded the activity, this might have contributed with this result. In addition, the Mann-Whitney's test maintained the null hypothesis of equality between groups ($p = 0.317$).

5 Discussion

The results demonstrate that the overall sense of presence was higher for the Control Group than for the experimental ones. That is, students who did the activity in the traditional VLE reported a higher sense of presence than those who used the 3DVW. This unexpected result may be associated with the higher level of complexity involving the conditions with the 3DVW, together with the novelty factor and the subjects' lack of familiarity with the new tool. The statistical test showed that in fact, students considered the interactions more natural with the VLE than with the 3DVW. It might also indicate a weakness of the instrument used to measure the sense of presence, which might not have been adequate to compare cross-media conditions, that is, different types of media support.

Considering the experimental settings, the Real Experimental Group scored slightly higher than the Experimental Group in the Presence Questionnaire, showing a positive influence of the Virtual Companion to approximate the student or get him/her more involved/engaged with the educational content, which is in agreement with the fact that they stayed longer in the 3DVW. However, the construct analysis revealed that the possibility to examine was better contemplated in the Experimental Group, indicating that the Virtual Companion possibly hindered this aspect in the sense of presence.

Conversely, time was inversely correlated (not significantly) with a higher sense of presence and with positive evaluations regarding perceptions of the 3DVW activity, meaning that the students who stayed less time gave higher scores in those instruments. This result shows that the activity time must be well weighted so students don't get bored and lose their attention, focus and interest, which can directly reflect on their overall sense of presence and satisfaction.

Also, students from the Real Experimental Group performed slightly better in the discipline where the study was conducted (Financial Management), considering the group's final mean grade. Although the activity in the 3DVW was very small when compared to the whole workload of the discipline, this result indicates some possible benefits of having the Virtual Companion in a 3DVW interaction, as the group which performed the same activity but without the Virtual Companion had a lower final mean grade. Also, more students from the Real Experimental Group finished the 3DVW activity, with higher overall performance, suggesting that maybe they were motivated by the presence of the Virtual Companion.

Correlation tests showed that students who more positively evaluated the activity in the 3DVW and the Virtual Companion had an overall higher sense of presence. That is, the more positive was the overall experience for the student, the higher was the reported sense of presence. Perhaps this shows a consistent positive attitude from students. In spite of this, the final mean grade in the discipline was inversely correlated with the sense of presence. That is, more positive grades were obtained from those inclined to report a lower sense of presence. Thus, giving that experimental groups reported a lower sense of presence, on the other hand it shows the benefits of students participating in a 3DVW activity to improve learning outcomes.

The majority of the students did not install the viewer in their PC as desired by the researchers, getting help in the DE Center. Public DE courses in Brazil are offered in municipalities with Internet beyond the ideal, with social quotas favoring the admission of the poorest. In this way, although the current great popularization of computer resources, the reality faced by the target subjects of this study does not allow to assume that they all have the minimum infrastructure conditions for 3DVW access, pointing the need to alternatives to take place.

6 Conclusion

DE grows exponentially over the years, but still have some challenges that put it into a disadvantage to face-to-face mode of instruction. More interactive media supports better approximate the advantages of face-to-face interaction while preserving the convenience of DE.

Among these new media supports, 3DVW have a significant potential for the development of the next generation of VLE, by bringing the unique characteristics of immersion and enhanced interactivity of VR technology, but without requiring the need of any additional devices as HMD, allowing to reach bigger audiences of students as in the case of DE.

This paper presented the results of a quasi-experimental pilot study conducted with 36 students enrolled in a formal course offered in DE modality, who accessed a technology different from the traditional VLE for the first time, namely a 3DVW with Conversational Agents in the role of Virtual Companions.

In conclusion, although students positively evaluated the experience in the 3DVW, it did not stimulate the sense of presence as expected. That is, we cannot say that the sense of presence, as the way it was measured, increased with the use of the mentioned tool or if in fact contributed to learning.

As the user's sense of presence is a subjective experience that relies on a number of personal aspects, which in turn may be related to individual experiences, the small sample size is the major limitation of the study, which might have opened space to personal factors of the students to influence in the results. In addition, the extra credit involved in the activity may have influenced students to give positive (biased) reports.

In this sense, future research should be conducted with larger samples and longitudinal studies to diminish the biased report and the novelty effects. Also, as the instrument used to measure the sense of presence showed some weakness in comparing cross-media conditions, a different one must be selected. Thus, in the next phase we will use the ITC Sense of Presence Inventory proposed by Lessiter et al. [27] as a Cross-Media Presence Questionnaire, in a validated Portuguese version [36]. Equally important, it seems necessary some face-to-face moments of instruction in the DE Center previous to the 3DVW activity, installing and configuring the viewers so students can access it from there.

The research brings to light the benefits in using a new media support to act in some common problems faced by the DE students, but at the same time the difficulties of integrating a technology that is not part of the daily life of individuals.

References

1. Online Learning Consortium. The Distance Education Enrollment Report (2017). https://onlinelearningconsortium.org/read/digital-learning-compass-distance-education-enrollment-report-2017/. Accessed 29 Jan 2019
2. Gregori, P., Martínez, V., Moyano-Fernández, J.J.: Basic actions to reduce dropout rates in distance learning. Eval. Prog. Plann. **66**, 48–52 (2018)
3. De Metz, N., Bezuidenhout, A.: An importance–competence analysis of the roles and competencies of e-tutors at an open distance learning. Aust. J. Educ. Technol. **34**(5), 27–43 (2018)
4. Fletcher, J.D.: Technology, the columbus effect, and the third revolution. The design of instruction and evaluation: Affordances of using media and technology, 121 (2004)
5. Alencar, M., Netto, J.F.: TUtor collaborator using multi-agent system. In: Yuizono, T., Zurita, G., Baloian, N., Inoue, T., Ogata, H. (eds.) CollabTech 2014. CCIS, vol. 460, pp. 153–159. Springer, Heidelberg (2014). https://doi.org/10.1007/978-3-662-44651-5_14
6. Moreno, R., Mayer, R.E., Spires, H.A., Lester, J.C.: The case for social agency in computer-based teaching: do students learn more deeply when they interact with animated pedagogical agents? Cogn. Instr. **19**(2), 177–213 (2001)
7. McLaughlan, R.G., Kirkpatrick, D.: Online roleplay: design for active learning. Eur. J. Eng. Educ. **29**(4), 477–490 (2004)
8. Dede, C.: The evolution of distance education: Emerging technologies and distributed learning. Am. J. Dist. Educ. **10**(2), 4–36 (1996)
9. Witmer, B.G., Singer, M.J.: Measuring presence in virtual environments: a presence questionnaire. Presence **7**(3), 225–240 (1998)
10. Mikropoulos, T.A.: Presence: a unique characteristic in educational virtual environments. Virtual Reality **10**(3–4), 197–206 (2006)

11. Tüzün, H., Özdinç, F.: The effects of 3D multi-user virtual environments on freshmen university students' conceptual and spatial learning and presence in departmental orientation. Comput. Educ. **94**, 228–240 (2016)
12. Coelho, C., Tichon, J.G., Hine, T.J., Wallis, G.M., Riva, G.: Media presence and inner presence: the sense of presence in virtual reality technologies. In: From communication to presence: Cognition emotions and culture towards the ultimate communicative experience, pp. 25–45. IOS Press, Amsterdam (2006)
13. Nevelsteen, K.J.: Virtual world, defined from a technological perspective and applied to video games, mixed reality, and the Metaverse. Comput. Animation Virtual World. **29**(1), 1752 (2018)
14. Domingo, J.R., Bradley, E.G.: Education student perceptions of virtual reality as a learning tool. J. Educ. Technol. Syst. **46**(3), 329–342 (2018)
15. Johnson, W.L., Rickel, J.W., Lester, J.C.: Animated pedagogical agents: face-to-face interaction in interactive learning environments. Int. J. Artif. Intell. Educ. **11**(1), 47–78 (2000)
16. Ijaz, K., Bogdanovych, A., Trescak, T.: Virtual worlds vs books and videos in history education. Interact. Learn. Environ. **25**(7), 904–929 (2017)
17. Englund, C.: Exploring approaches to teaching in three-dimensional virtual worlds. Int. J. Inf. Learn. Technol. **34**(2), 140–151 (2017)
18. Soliman, M., Guetl, C.: Implementing intelligent pedagogical agents in virtual worlds: tutoring natural science experiments in OpenWonderland. In: 2013 IEEE Global Engineering Education Conference (EDUCON), pp. 782–789. IEEE (2013)
19. Chen, C.J., Toh, S.C., Ismail, W.M.F.W.: Are learning styles relevant to virtual reality? J. Res. Technol. Educ. **38**(2), 123–141 (2005)
20. Mayer, R.E.: Multimedia learning. Annu. Rep. Educ. Psychol. Jpn. **41**, 27–29 (2002)
21. Burden, D.J.: Deploying embodied AI into virtual worlds. Knowl.-Based Syst. **22**(7), 540–544 (2009)
22. Kim, Y.: Desirable characteristics of learning companions. Int. J. Artif. Intell. Educ. **17**(4), 371–388 (2007)
23. Slater, M., Wilbur, S.: A framework for immersive virtual environments (FIVE): Speculations on the role of presence in virtual environments. Presence: Teleoperators Virtual Environ. **6**(6), 603–616 (1997)
24. Slater, M., Usoh, M.: Presence in immersive virtual environments. In: 1993 IEEE Virtual Reality Annual International Symposium, pp. 90–96. IEEE (1993)
25. Bouvier, P.: The five pillars of presence: guidelines to reach presence. In: Spagnolli, A. et, Gamberini, L., éditeurs: Proceedings of Presence 2008, 246–249 (2008)
26. Waterworth, E.L., Waterworth, J.A.: Focus, locus, and sensus: the three dimensions of virtual experience. CyberPsychol. Behav. **4**(2), 203–213 (2001)
27. Lessiter, J., Freeman, J., Keogh, E., Davidoff, J.: A cross-media presence questionnaire: the ITC-Sense of Presence Inventory. Presence: Teleoperators Virtual Environ. **10**(3), 282–297 (2001)
28. Darken, R.P., Bernatovich, D., Lawson, J.P., Peterson, B.: Quantitative measures of presence in virtual environments: the roles of attention and spatial comprehension. CyberPsychol. Behav. **2**(4), 337–347 (1999)
29. Romano, D.M., Brna, P.: Presence and reflection in training: Support for learning to improve quality decision-making skills under time limitations. CyberPsychol. Behav. **4**(2), 265–277 (2001)
30. Avatar Project. Official website. http://www.ufrgs.br/avatar. Accessed 29 Jan 2019
31. Kolb, D.: Experiential Learning: Experience as the Source of Learning and Development. Prentice-Hall, New Jersey (1984)

32. Presence Questionnaire of Witmer & Singer validated from the Cyberpsychology Lab da Université du Québec en Outaouais (UQO) (1998). http://w3.uqo.ca/cyberpsy/en/index_en.htm. Accessed 29 Jan 2019
33. Rico, M., Ramírez, J., Riofrío-Luzcando, D., Berrocal-Lobo, M.: A Cost-Effective Approach for Procedural Training in Virtual Worlds. J. Univ. Comput. Sci. **23**(2), 208–232 (2017)
34. Kim, Y., Baylor, A.L.: PALS Group: Pedagogical agents as learning companions: the role of agent competency and type of interaction. Educ. Technol. Res. Dev. **54**(3), 223–243 (2006)
35. Krassmann, A.L., Kuyven, N.L., Mazzuco, A.E.R., Tarouco, L.M.R., Bercht, M.: Estudo Exploratório sobre Mundos Virtuais e Agentes Conversacionais na Educação a Distância. Revista Novas Tecnologias na Educação (RENOTE) **16**(2), 1679–1916 (2018)
36. Vasconcelos-Raposo, J., et al.: Adaptation and validation of the Igroup presence questionnaire (IPQ) in a Portuguese sample. Presence: Teleoperators Virtual Environ. **25**(3), 191–203 (2016)

Pedagogical-Agent Learning Companions in a Virtual Reality Educational Experience

David Novick[✉], Mahdokht Afravi, Adriana Camacho, Aaron Rodriguez, and Laura Hinojos

The University of Texas at El Paso, El Paso, TX, USA
novick@utep.edu,
{mafravi,accamacho2,aerodriguez14,ljhinojos}@miners.utep.edu
http://www.utep.edu

Abstract. This research studies pedagogical agents as a learning companion (PALs) and aims to find which approach is more effective for learners in terms of learning, engagement and rapport: a PAL that is the same gender as the student, a PAL that is female, or a PAL that is male. We compared results in terms of learning and rapport with respect to the gender of a PAL. To this end, we implemented a multimodal interactive virtual-reality application to teach students about the 1770 Boston Massacre. Our results suggest that (1) both male and female participants will learn well with a female PAL, and (2) differences in rapport do not seem to affect learning.

Keywords: Embodied conversational agents · Human-agent dialog · Dialog system

1 Introduction

Virtual worlds are great tools for research, training, entertainment, and education. Even though virtual worlds have served well as an innovative supplementary tool for presenting educational content, students' learning is influenced by social aspects that virtual environments alone cannot accommodate. To address this problem, virtual agents can take advantage of social affordances to accomplish a learning task [9]. As a result, educational virtual environments that incorporate a virtual agent are more engaging and motivating to learners than the virtual environment alone [8].

Embodied conversational agents (ECAs) [4] are virtual characters that are placed in a virtual environment and may have different functions and different levels of interaction with a user (if any). ECAs serve in a variety of fields, such as entertainment, training, customer service, and education. In education, specifically, ECAs provide supplementary motivation and pedagogy as tutors, learning companions, mentors, tutees, and other pedagogical roles. ECAs whose role is educational are termed Embodied Pedagogical Agents (EPAs) [6]. EPAs can model different instructional roles, such as instructors, mentors, and learning companions. Their goal is, of course, to increase the student's proficiency in the material being taught by the EPA. Some EPAs have a secondary goal to engage students and in this way to increase their motivation to learn. Strategies to help EPAs achieve engagement have included changing their appearance, their teaching style, and the roles they play within the learning environment [2,5,6]. For example, children aged 7 to 11 chose an EPA learning companion over an EPA instructor to teach them multiplication, where children indicated that they could relate more to the learning companion and trusted the EPA [5].

In educational experiences conducted in virtual reality (VR), the user is typically guided by a pedagogical agent as a learning companion (PAL) [9]. While the prevailing consensus is that children tend to prefer agents that look like themselves (e.g., [2,10]), the effect of the PAL's gender on learning, rapport, and engagement is an open question. Johnson, DiDonato, and Reisslein [7] reported that children (K-12) preferred an embodied pedagogical agent that represents a young woman close to their age as a virtual learning companion. Conversely, Baylor and Kim [1] found that students showed higher interest when working with a male PAL. Other studies have looked at not only the PAL's gender but the also preference of the student based on the gender. Haake and Gulz [6], for example, found that female students tended to prefer a task- and relation-oriented communication style for their learning partner. The split in the research results makes it difficult for developers of virtual-reality educational experiences to choose the most effective PAL. Accordingly, our research aims to find which approach is more effective for learners in terms of learning, engagement, and rapport: a PAL that is the same gender as the student, a PAL that is female, or a PAL that is male.

2 The Boston History Experience

We addressed the question of students' PAL gender preference and effectiveness by comparing learning and rapport outcomes as a function of the gender of a PAL and the gender of the student. To this end, we implemented a multimodal interactive virtual-reality application to teach students about the Boston Massacre in 1770 [12]. In the application, students explore the city of Boston with an assigned PAL that plays the role of a house worker, while the user plays the role of John Adams's apprentice. In the interaction, the user walks alongside the PAL while having conversations with seven ECAs, representing characters such as Abigail Adams, a tea-shop owner, and a redcoat (see Fig. 1). The interaction between the student and the virtual agents concludes with a conversation with Abigail Adams in which the students explain what they learned and narration by John Adams about events that followed. A final non-interactive cinematic sequence presents additional facts about the events that unfolded after the Boston Massacre.

Fig. 1. Lydia, a pedagogical agent as a learning companion, and a redcoat, in the Boston Massacre history experience (Color figure online)

The application is fully functional, and the experience lasts about 20 min. The application was implemented in the Unity game engine, using the UTEP AGENT system [11] and the Microsoft speech recognizer, and was delivered via the HTC Vive VR headset. To assure accuracy, the script was developed in collaboration with a professor of history. Table 1 presents samples of the application's dialog with some of the virtual agents, with the PAL prompting the student.

For the setting, we created a virtual representation of the central section of Boston in 1770, with dozens of extra agents on the streets (see Fig. 2). The agents representing the characters, including John and Abigail Adams (see Fig. 3), Joshua, a tea-shop owner (see Fig. 4(a)), and Phoebe, a slave (see Fig. 4(b)), speak with recorded voices. Background music was composed and recorded especially for the application by a professional composer.

3 Methodology

Our study had two independent variables, the PAL's gender and the student's gender. For the first variable, the VR experience had two versions. In one version, the PAL is a female character named Lydia. In the second version, the PAL is a male character named Henry (see Fig. 5). The information material presented to the participants in both versions was the same; the only aspect that differed was the gender of the PAL. Half of the participants interacted with the female agent Lydia, and the other half interacted with the male agent Henry. We hypothesized that:

- Subjects interacting with the female PAL will perform better in recalling facts
- Subjects interacting with the female PAL will report higher rapport
- Subjects interacting with the PAL of the subject's gender will perform better in recalling facts

Fig. 2. Virtual Boston, with dozens of (non-speaking) agents on the streets, was modeled after the streets of Boston in 1770 close to the customs house.

Fig. 3. Embodied conversational agents in the roles of John Adams and Abigail Adams.

Table 1. Samples of agents' utterances, with prompts from the PAL.

	Agent utterance	PAL prompt
Joshua, tea-shop owner	You mean that ruckus? I didn't see it. I was here tending to my shop. Those redcoats will get what is coming to them, and that Townshend Revenue Act? Pff?!	Revenue Act? Ask him about that.
Phoebe, slave	Please, I'm not supposed to be here. Just leave me alone. (pause) A group of soldiers fired on a crowd. Everyone is busy choosing sides. Not that it matters anyway.	Why not? What side are you on? Why don't you care? Why wouldn't it matter
Phoebe, slave	I am still a slave. I will always have a master above me, and I will always do the same job. My voice doesn't matter.	She said she wasn't supposed to be here. Ask her what she's doing here.
Paul, Patriot	They're suffocating us! These new laws are far too harsh!	Laws? Ask him what laws he is talking about.
Hugh, Soldier	We fought the 7 years war on your behalf to keep you safe. We are just trying to recover some of what we have lost. And we are innocent for what happened last night. Did you not see the mob surround us?	N/A

Fig. 4. Embodied conversational agents in the role of (a) Joshua, the owner of tea shop, and (b) Phoebe, a slave.

- Subjects interacting with the PAL of the subject's matching gender will report higher rapport
- Subjects who report higher rapport with the PAL will perform better in recalling facts

The study used a between-subjects design with 90 participants (69 male and 21 female), all undergraduate students at a public university, who were randomly assigned to one of the four conditions.

Fig. 5. PAL companions Lydia (*left*) and Henry (*right*)

The study had two dependent variables, rapport and learning. We measured rapport with a post-interaction Likert-scale survey adapted from [3]. Table 2 presents the ten items in the survey, plus an additional open-ended question for qualitative responses. We measured learning with a post-interaction quiz, developed with the help of our consulting professor of history, presented in the appendix. The quiz had ten questions, six of which were multiple choice, two were true or false, and two were fill-in-the-blank.

4 Results

Our first hypothesis was that subjects interacting with the female PAL would perform better in recalling facts. The mean learning scores for students interacting with the male and female PALs were 53.1 and 56.0, respectively, but this difference was not significant (one-tailed t test, $p > 0.15$). If there is an effect, the effect appears to be small. Figure 6 shows the results for rapport and learning, differentiated by the two independent variables, PAL gender (L[ydia] or H[enry]), and participant gender (F or M). Table 3 reports the values across all conditions.

Table 2. Post-interaction rapport survey questions

1	The agent understood me
2	The agent seemed unengaged
3	The agent was excited
4	The agent's movements were not natural
5	The agent was not paying attention to me
6	The agent was friendly
7	The agent and I worked towards a common goal
8	The agent and I did not seem to connect
9	I feel the agent trusts me
10	I didn't understand the agent
11	The conversation would feel more real if the agent...

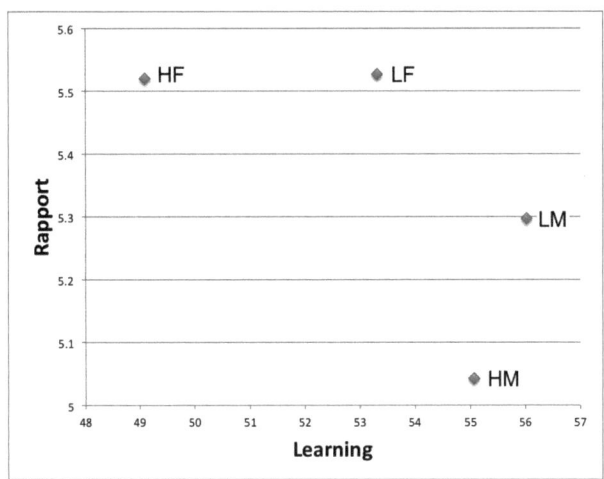

Fig. 6. Distribution of results (rapport and learning), differentiated by gender of PAL (L[ydia] or H[enry]) and gender of participant (F or M).

Our second hypothesis was that subjects interacting with the female PAL would report higher rapport. There is suggestive evidence that this is true, as can be seen in Fig. 4. The mean rapport scores for students interacting with the male and female PALs were 4.48 and 4.65, respectively. A t-test indicates that this is suggestive of a significant difference (one-tailed t-test, $p < 0.08$).

Our third hypothesis was that subjects interacting with the PAL of the subject's gender would perform better in recalling facts. Again, the evidence mildly suggests that this is true. The mean learning scores for same-gender and opposite-gender student-agents pairs were 56.8 and 52.2, respectively. A t-test indicates that this is possibly suggestive of a significant difference (one-tailed t-test, $p < 0.10$).

Table 3. Summary statistics for information recall and rapport, as a function of the gender of agent and participant.

Agent	Participant	Mean learning	Mean rapport
Henry	Male	55.07	5.04
Henry	Female	49.09	5.52
Lydia	Male	56.02	5.30
Lydia	Female	53.31	5.53

Our fourth hypothesis was that subjects interacting with the PAL of the subject's gender will report higher rapport. Our data suggest that is not true. The mean rapport scores for same-gender and opposite-gender student-agents pairs were 4.53 and 4.58, respectively. A t-test indicates that this difference is not significant (two-tailed t-test, $p > 0.67$). Indeed, the mean scores were slightly opposite of the expected effect.

Our fifth hypothesis was that subjects who report higher rapport with the PAL will perform better in recalling facts. As suggested by the scatter plot shown in Fig. 7, there appears to be no correlation between learning and rapport. The correlation is less than 0.0003, and R^2 is 6.56E-08.

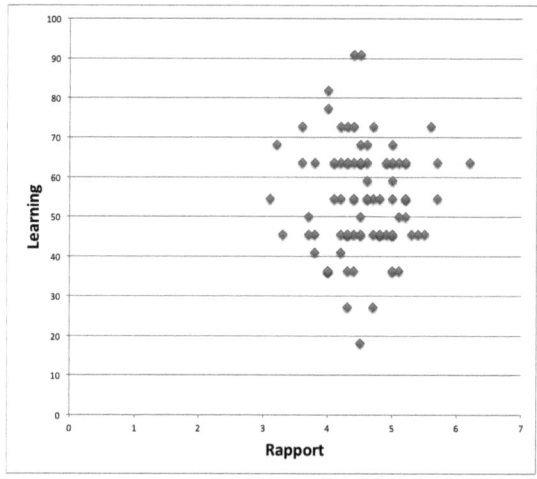

Fig. 7. Scatter plot of results (rapport and learning)

Table 4 shows the performance of all participants for each question. Multiple-choice question seven asked student which of four multiple choice responses was false. Correctly, none of the all 90 participants selected as false the response "Slavery existed in Boston at the time of the Massacre." We speculate that the reason for this being an obvious wrong choice was because the students had interacted with a slave as part of the experience.

Table 4. Percentage of people who scored the correct response for each question in the questionnaire for fact recall. Details of the questions are provided in the appendix.

	Category	Questionnaire	Correct overall	Correct Lydia	Correct Henry
1	Multiple choice (4)	What happened at the Boston Massacre?	93.3%	95.6%	91.1%
2	Multiple choice (4)	What word does not describe the Boston Massacre?	92.2%	93.3%	91.1%
3	Short answer	The Boston Massacre occurred in front of the ...	21.1%	20.0%	22.2%
4	True/False	The British imposed the Stamp Act upon the colonies several years before the Boston Massacre.	58.9%	60.0%	57.8%
5	Multiple choice (4)	Which of the following best describes the Revenue Act?	65.6%	68.9	62.2%
6	Multiple choice (4)	The Declaratory Act allowed the British the complete authority to...	74.4%	73.3%	75.6%
7	Multiple choice (4)	Which of the following is FALSE?	51.1%	55.6%	46.7%
8	True/False	John Adams defended Crispus Attucks and his fellow colonists.	54.4%	55.6%	53.3%
9	Short answer	Which TWO people were found guilty for the Boston Massacre?	12.78%	11.1%	14.4%
10	Multiple choice (4)	Which of the following is TRUE?	75.6%	75.6%	75.6%

Limitations. This study's results are subject to two possible limitations. First, the study had a gender imbalance of participants, with more males than females. By the conclusion of the experiment, 35 males and 10 females interacted with PAL companion Henry while 34 males and 11 females interacted with PAL companion Lydia. This distribution reflected the underlying student population of the college in which the participants were enrolled but made less reliable the findings with respect to female participants. Second, the Boston Massacre History Project application was designed for eighth-grade students, but despite agreement from a middle-school principal we were unable to obtain permission from the school district to conduct the study with eight-graders. Consequently, the study's participants were undergraduate students, whose learning styles and rapport preferences may differ from those of eighth-graders.

5 Conclusion

Our data suggest that female participants with the female PAL learned more than female participants with the male PAL, even though female subjects, on average, reported the same level of rapport regardless of the gender of the PAL. Our data also suggest that male participants learned marginally more with the female PAL than with the male PAL, although the male participants, on average, reported slightly higher rapport with the male PAL. These results suggest that (1) both male and female participants will learn well with a female PAL, and (2) differences in rapport do not seem to affect learning.

Appendix: Questionnaire for Boston History Fact Recall

The following is the questionnaire used after the BHE to measure the participant's fact recall

1. What Happened at the Boston Massacre?
    (a) A rowdy colonial crowd killed several British soldiers
    (b) British soldiers killed several rowdy colonists
    (c) The New York Yankees swept the Boston Red Sox in the playoffs
    (d) Wampanoag Indians attacked Boston and killed several colonists
2. What word does not describe the Boston Massacre?
    (a) Violent
    (b) Tense
    (c) Scary
    (d) Amusing
3. The Boston Massacre occurred in front of the _____
4. The British imposed the Stamp Act upon the colonies several years before the Boston Massacre
    (a) True
    (b) False
5. Which of the following best describes the Revenue Act?
    (a) a tax on documents and other printed materials
    (b) an act requiring colonists to provide housing for British soldiers
    (c) a tax on goods, such as tea
    (d) an act forbidding colonists from protesting British laws
6. The Declaratory Act allowed the British the complete authority to....
    (a) impose laws on the colonies
    (b) regulate trade in the colonies
    (c) tax printed materials in the colonies
    (d) send British troops throughout the colonies
7. Which of the following is FALSE?
    (a) The Boston Massacre was a peaceful protest turned violent
    (b) The Boston Massacre occurred in 1770
    (c) Slavery existed in Boston at the time of the Massacre
    (d) John Adams was married to Lydia Adams

8. John Adams defended Crispus Attucks and his fellow colonists
   (a) True
   (b) False
9. Which TWO people were found guilty for the Boston Massacre?
   _____   _____
10. Which of the following is TRUE?
    (a) British soldiers did not compete with colonists for jobs
    (b) British soldiers built their own homes in Boston
    (c) Colonists resented the presence of British soldiers in Boston
    (d) Colonists were required to serve British soldiers tea

References

1. Baylor, A.L., Kim, Y.: Pedagogical agent design: the impact of agent realism, gender, ethnicity, and instructional role. In: Lester, J.C., Vicari, R.M., Paraguaçu, F. (eds.) ITS 2004. LNCS, vol. 3220, pp. 592–603. Springer, Heidelberg (2004). https://doi.org/10.1007/978-3-540-30139-4_56
2. Baylor, A.L., Kim, Y.: Simulating instructional roles through pedagogical agents. Int. J. Artif. Intell. Educ. **15**(2), 95–115 (2005)
3. Brixey, J., Novick, D.: Building rapport with extraverted and introverted agents. In: Proceedings of the International Workshop on Spoken Dialogue Systems (IWSDS), IWSDS, Farmington, PA, June 2017. https://www.uni-ulm.de/fileadmin/website_uni_ulm/iui.iwsds2017/papers/IWSDS2017_paper_8.pdf
4. Cassell, J. (ed.): Embodied Conversational Agents. The MIT Press, Cambridge (2000)
5. Girard, S., Johnson, H.: What do children favor as embodied pedagogical agents? In: Aleven, V., Kay, J., Mostow, J. (eds.) ITS 2010. LNCS, vol. 6094, pp. 307–316. Springer, Heidelberg (2010). https://doi.org/10.1007/978-3-642-13388-6_35
6. Haake, M., Gulz, A.: A look at the roles of look & roles in embodied pedagogical agents-a user preference perspective. Int. J. Artif. Intell. Educ. **19**(1), 39–71 (2009)
7. Johnson, A.M., DiDonato, M.D., Reisslein, M.: Animated agents in k-12 engineering outreach: preferred agent characteristics across age levels. Comput. Hum. Behav. **29**(4), 1807–1815 (2013)
8. Johnson, W.L., Lester, J.C.: Face-to-face interaction with pedagogical agents, twenty years later. Int. J. Artif. Intell. Educ. **26**(1), 25–36 (2016)
9. Kim, Y., Baylor, A.L.: A social-cognitive framework for pedagogical agents as learning companions. Educ. Technol. Res. Dev. **54**(6), 569–596 (2006)
10. Kim, Y., Wei, Q.: The impact of learner attributes and learner choice in an agent-based environment. Comput. Educ. **56**(2), 505–514 (2011)
11. Novick, D., Gris Sepulveda, I., Rivera, D.A., Camacho, A., Rayon, A., Gutierrez, M.: The UTEP AGENT system. In: Proceedings of the 2015 ACM on International Conference on Multimodal Interaction. ACM, November 2015
12. Novick, D., et al.: The Boston massacre history experience. In: Proceedings of the 19th ACM International Conference on Multimodal Interaction, pp. 499–500. ACM (2017)

A VRLE Design Scheme for the Learning of Film Making

Xi Qiao, Zhejun Liu[✉], and Yunshui Jin

College of Arts and Media, Tongji University, Shanghai 201804, China
`719548157@qq.com`, {`wingeddreamer,
jinyunshui`}`@tongji.edu.cn`

Abstract. Education of film making has made great progress since the earliest film and television departments were established in American universities in early 1960s. Nowadays, students can learn theories and techniques of film making either online or in a classroom. But the cost of actually shooting a film for practice purposes is still too high and keeps many learners from getting enough training. In recent years, with the development of science and technology, virtual reality (VR) has been applied to various fields, including medicine, entertainment, education, military, and aerospace. The application of VR technology will promisingly become the next big leap in the future development of education. This paper focuses on how to effectively design a virtual reality learning system to help future film makers solve the problem of insufficient practice in resource-constrained situations. A prototype of the system was developed based on prior research conclusions, and 12 participants were recruited to experience the system and answer questionnaires followed by in-depth interviews. The qualitative research results shew that the practice carried out in a virtual reality environment was certainly usable and effective. In conclusion, virtual reality technology may very likely play an important role in the education of film makers.

Keywords: Virtual reality · VRLE · Film making · E-learning

1 Background

1.1 E-learning

The progress of key educational technologies in the past 30 years has transformed the prevailing teaching models from traditional in-classroom lecturing to a contemporary one in which people can learn through electronic devices at any time in any place. E-learning has become an important and ubiquitous learning and teaching mode [1], which is characterized by adopting modern scientific and technological products and centering on learners. A new teaching mode with a large number of resources for learners to share was thus created [2]. At present, e-learning mainly involves the following technologies and applications: online learning platforms based on network technology, serious gaming applications based on computer technology, simulations (e.g. virtual laboratory) based on virtual reality technology, and etc. [3–5].

Virtual reality (VR) is an integration of computer technologies, including computer graphics, simulation technologies, artificial intelligence, sensor technologies, display technologies and so forth. It is an interdisciplinary, cutting-edge and challenging research field. In a computer-generated virtual environment with multiple interactable targets, users may enjoy an immersive experience. Today, VR technology has been widely recognized and used in medicine [6], architectural [7], education and other fields. The application of VR technology will hopefully become the next great leap in the future development of education. By creating an environment suitable for self-learning, it changes the learning pattern from the traditional lecturing and listening to a new one in which learners acquire knowledge and skills proactively through the interaction with the environment. For example, in the field of medical education, VR has been used to reproduce complex human body structures to help students to study [8]. Irina Makarova et al. have discussed the application of VR technology to the automotive industry and automotive engineering education [9]. They proposed suggestions for the construction of an education system totally through VR technology. In China, VR simulations have been applied to and highly valued in the education of physics and sports [10]. Teresa Monahan et al. [11] proposed an example showing the application of VR technology in collaborative e-learning in which users were enabled to break the limitation of time and space to learn together "in a virtual classroom" with VR glasses.

In summary, VR simulations allow learners to see the result of their actions immediately, clearly and safely at a very low cost and this characteristic makes it very suitable for solving the problem of lacking practices due to limited resources.

1.2 Film Making

With the continuous development of the film industry, the requirements for a professional film maker are constantly changing, so the education should evolve and change accordingly. The traditional way of film education was like this: students listened to lectures in a classroom, watched some movies as examples, and was given chances to practice several times in one semester [12]. As a future creative worker, practice and training are essential for them to truly understand the theories and to master the skills [13]. Sufficient shooting practice can enable students to skillfully understand the use of film language and Mise-en-scène [14]. Repeated attempts to tell stories in different ways can also inspire learners. However, it is expensive and difficult for a student, or maybe even a school to build scenes and to hire actors just for learning purposes in real life. Furthermore, usually equipment and space in schools are often fully booked for specific plans [15], which also stops students from practicing freely and sufficiently. Therefore, it is worth seeking new solutions with the help of the latest technologies.

2 Aim

"Film language" refers to the language used to communicate thoughts and feelings through shots and events composed of a combination of images and sounds [16], which is basic knowledge for film makers. At the core of it is a variety of theories about the use of composition, layout, montage and etc. [17] To learn the course of film language well, one must work hard both theoretically and practically. It is a miniature of the process of learning film making.

The aim of this research was to use VR technology to create a system for learners to use easily and economically, so as to provide sufficient and effective practice they need in their education. A qualitative evaluation of the system was conducted to verify its effectiveness.

3 Experiment

3.1 Design of the "VR Film School"

The virtual training system used in this research was developed by the Non-Planar Screen Lab in the College of Arts and Media in Tongji University. It was named "VR Film School" (VRFS in short). Centering around users, VRFS aimed to allow them to explore freely and practice easily just with the help of simple guidance. Hopefully, its users could actively construct the meaning of knowledge by themselves in this process (Fig. 1).

(a) Original film

(b) Recreation in VR

Fig. 1. "Tales of Afanti" - the original film and the recreation in VR

VRFS used a segment from the famous Chinese animation "Tales of Afanti" produced in 1980s as a reference. The scenes and characters were rebuilt with 3D animation techniques. Figure 2 shows the design structure of VRFS. It was divided into three parts: *learning part*, *practice part*, and *evaluation part*.

The *learning part* included: 1. Introduction to 8 common types of shots via example movie clips; 2. Instructions on how to operate the virtual shooting and editing system.

The *practice part* included: 1. Shooting: A user was allowed to freely point and shoot in the virtual environment using the Vive controllers as a virtual camera. He or she also had the ability to lock the camera's position and/or rotation, which was similar to the use of a tripod. The virtual actors only moved when the trigger was pulled down and stopped immediately when it was released to allow changes of the location and orientation of the virtual camera so as to allow montage. 2. Simple editing: A user might also at any time go to the playback mode to review what had been recorded and perform basic non-linear editing by reshooting the unsatisfying parts.

The *evaluation part* included: 1. Watching: After the film had been fully recorded and confirmed by a user, he or she would enter a virtual cinema to appreciate his or her own work. 2. Movie export and sharing: At the end of the experience, the user's own work would be recorded as a video file so that he or she may keep it for later review or share it with instructors and friends. The procedures of using VRFS is shown in Fig. 3.

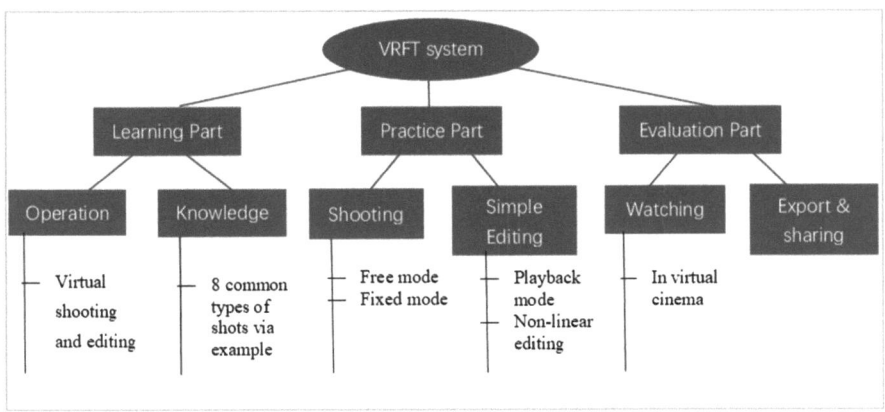

Fig. 2. Structure of VR Film School

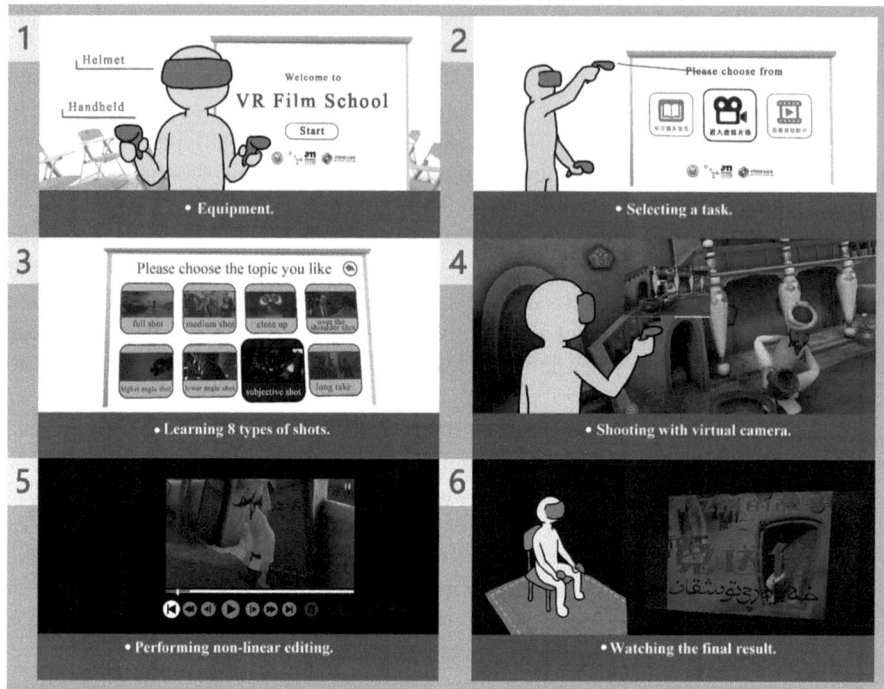

Fig. 3. Storyboard of VR Film School

3.2 Subjects

12 students from Tongji University were recruited to participate in the experiment. 8 of the participants studied in majors relevant to film making, namely "Editing and Directing of Films and TV Programs" (EDFT in short), "Animation" and "Advertising", while the other 4 participants studied in other fields. Half of the students from relevant majors were beginners (freshmen or sophomores), and the other half were more sophisticated learners with more than 2 years of experience. The participants' basic information is shown in Table 1.

Table 1. Basic Information about the Subjects = 12)

	N	%
Gender		
Female	5	42
Male	7	58
Major		
Animation	5	42
EDFT	2	17
Advertising	1	8
Other	4	33

(*continued*)

Table 1. (*continued*)

	N	%
Grade		
Freshman & Sophomore	5	42
Junior & Senior	5	42
Graduated Students	2	16
Had VR experience before		
Yes	7	58
Never before	5	42
Had film shooting experience with a real camera before		
Yes	9	75
Never before	3	25

3.3 Research Ethics

All participants were informed of the purpose of the study and agreed to have the interview recorded before the experiment began. They were also informed of the possible uncomfortableness and/or motion-sickness of the VR experience and their right to quit the experiment at any time at their free will. The experience of VRFS took about 20 min, and the subsequent in-depth interviews lasted for 20–30 min. The duration of the experiment for one participant was controlled within one hour.

3.4 Procedures

The experiment was held in the College of Arts and Media at Tongji University. After experiencing VRFS, the participants were asked to complete a short system usability questionnaire (described in Sect. 4.1) followed by an in-depth interview about his/her opinion of the system. The interviews were semi-structured and the main topics for discussion were as follow:

- What problems did you encounter when you shot a film in reality?
- How do you feel after experiencing VRFS?
- Are you willing to practice using VRFS frequently?
- In your opinion, what is the best way to practice film making?

3.5 Data Analysis

The questionnaire in this study rooted in Brooke's "System-Usability-Scale" questionnaire (SUS for short) compiled in 1986. It worked well for small sample sizes (n < 14). Aaron Bangor et al. [18] proposed an adjusted SUS questionnaire and verified the validity and reliability of it. It was further finetuned to suit the VRFS system in this study, reflecting the overall satisfaction of the respondents. Data obtained from the SUS questionnaires was then compiled and analyzed in a way proposed by Bangor et al. [19].

Records of the in-depth interviews were transcribed by software and then manually revised. The interview data was then coded and analyzed in Nvivo 11, a program for qualitative research. First, by open coding, 347 nodes were extracted and formed from the questions and answers. Participants and questions were also marked as independent nodes for the purpose of multi-angle analysis later. At this stage, reflections and inspirations were written in the memo and linked to corresponding nodes.

After the initial coding was finished, a second pass of coding, namely focus coding was performed: by classifying and merging nodes according to topic relevance, nodes were arranged into a tree structure, which made it easier to see the relationship of nodes and to rearrange, combine and delete nodes when appropriate.

Finally, theoretical coding was carried out to define the attributes of the interviewees by majors, grades and prior filming experience. The matrix query function was used to explore how users with different attributes evaluate the usability, emotional tendency and subjective effectiveness of VRFS differently.

4 Results

4.1 Data from the Questionnaires

The SUS questionnaire contained only 10 questions so as to allow quick feedback. The odd ones were positive statements and the even ones were negative. The fourth and tenth statements provided information in the learnable dimension, and the other eight, in the usability dimensions [19]. In this study, the last two statements were changed to ask about users' feeling after his/her experience, which also provided information in the usability dimension, but put more emphasis on knowing about a user's subjective feeling. Finally, because all participants were Chinese, a translated version of the SUS questionnaire was used in the study (Fig. 4).

According to the recommendations given by Bangor et al. [20], the scores of the questionnaires were calculated in the following way:

- For odd items: subtract one from the user response
- For even-numbered items: subtract the user responses from 5
- These scales all values from 0 to 4 (with 4 being the most positive response).
- Add up the converted responses for each user and multiply that total by 2.5. This converts the range of possible values from 0 to 100 instead of from 0 to 40.

The scores from the 12 questionnaires were between [52.5, 92.5] with an average of 74. Four questionnaires from participants in non-relevant majors scored 67.5, 67.5, 85, 90, with an average of 77.5, reflecting a higher level of user satisfaction. The average score of the other 8 questionnaires was 72.2. The average scores of beginners and experienced learners were 72.5 and 71.2 respectively.

The fourth statement in SUS questionnaire was "I think that I would need the support from a technical person to be able to use this system.", intending to reveal the system's learnability. The resulting average was 2.2 (total score = 4), which was not very high. Unexpectedly, VRFS was more learnable for students from non-relevant

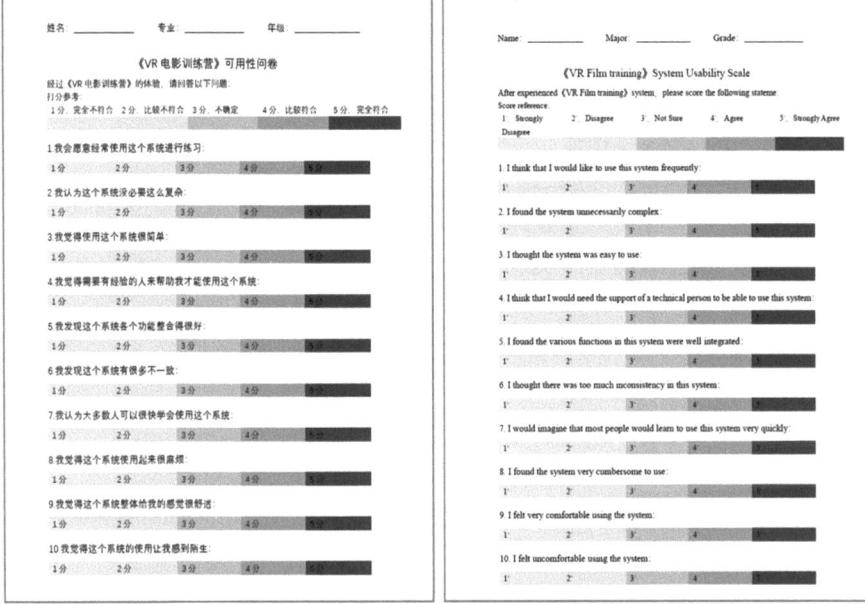

(a) the Chinese version of the SUS questionnaire in use   (b) the English version of the SUS questionnaire in use

Fig. 4. Questionnaire-SUS

majors, with an average score of 2.5. The scores of the beginners and experienced learners from relevant majors were 1.8 and 2.3.

The total average of the 9th and 10th questions was 5.8 (total score = 8) which meant that the subjective feeling of VRFS was fairly good for all the participants. The average score from participants in relevant and non-relevant majors was 5.5 and 6.3 respectively as shown in Fig. 5.

The original purpose of SUS was to measure usability quickly and dirtily [21], so this was a suitable way to recognize problems before conducting in-depth research. As Jeff Sauro [22] pointed out, the SUS score was not a percentage but rather revealed the overall satisfaction of the participants. Through many empirical tests [23], it was verified that a SUS score above 68 meant good user satisfaction. But because the questionnaire could only offer a single score, the reasons behind it and a user's true feelings must be explored using other methods, namely in-depth interviews to be discussed next.

4.2 Data from the Interviews

After sorting out the interview data from all participants, it was open-coded and formed 347 nodes according to the content analysis in Nvivo. At this stage, nodes only belonged to the specific case from which they were generated. The next stage was classifying and merging nodes according to the topics so as to generate data trees as shown in Fig. 6. Thirdly, a second pass of coding was performed through further

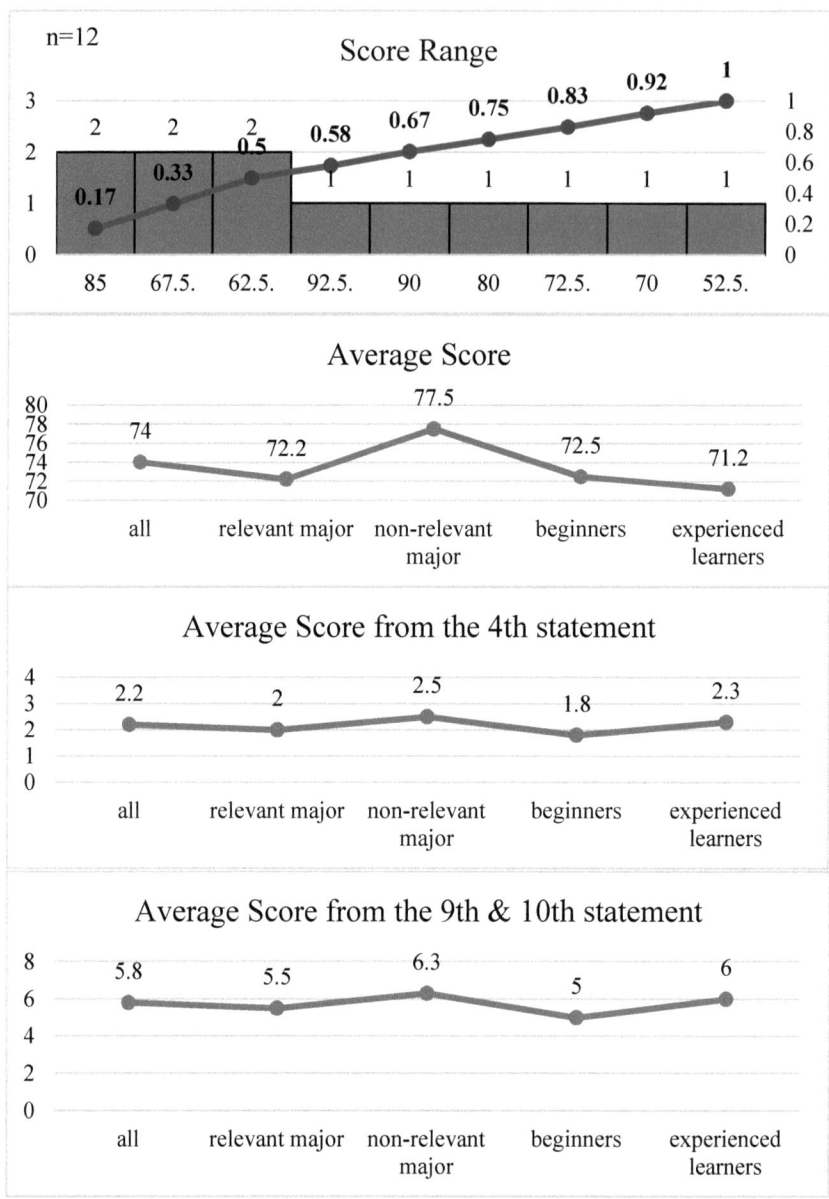

Fig. 5. SUS Score

conceptualization to summarized and to obtain the final conclusion. The conclusions shown in Fig. 7 are drawn from three perspectives: "usability and subjective effectiveness", "emotional tendency", and "target people and suggestions" (described in Sects. 4.3–4.5).

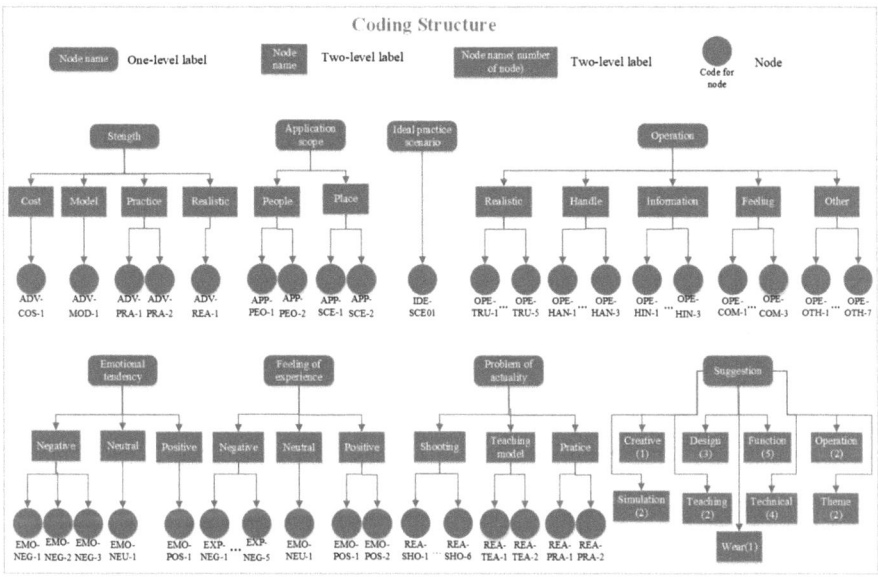

Fig. 6. Nodes Structure in second stage

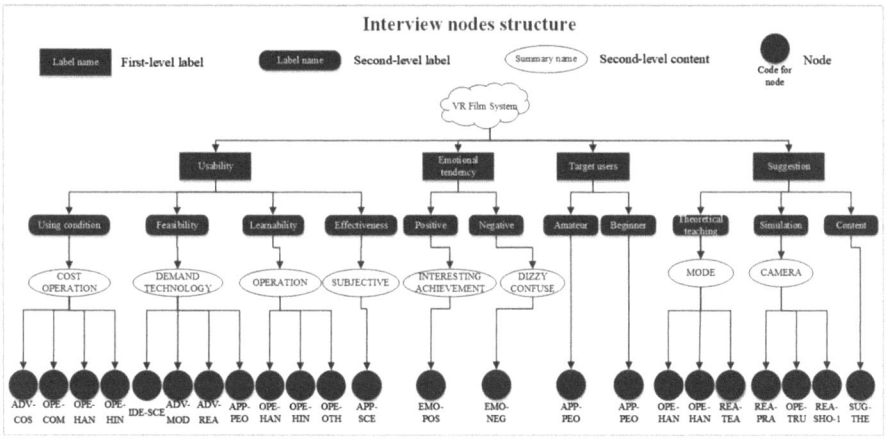

Fig. 7. Interview nodes structure in final

5 Analysis

Qualitative research was conducted to verify the participants' opinions toward VRFS. The conclusions were basically categorized into three groups: "usability and subjective effectiveness", "emotional tendency", "target people and suggestions".

5.1 Usability and Subjective Effectiveness

Usability. The usability here refers to the participants' evaluation of VRFS from various angles, including use conditions, learnability, feasibility of operation, function, and content. Most participants gave high marks to the usability of VRFS and believed that the system could be effectively mastered after simple and quick learning. This was coincident with our original intention when designing this system.

> Nan: I think this system is very comfortable to use... I think it's very enjoyable.
> Chuan: I think the usability is quite high... I think this technology, VR, is to solve the problem of time and space. So, I think this system is quite good.

Several participants expressed their views on the usability of VRFSs from the perspective of accessibility. They believed that it would be very expensive in real life to arrange a scene, to hire actors, to purchase equipment and etc. It was also restricted by time, weather and other environmental conditions. In contrast, the practice method proposed by VRFS was very convenient and accessible. One only needed a small open space, a computer and an HMD to use it. As for the space for practice, some participants suggested that it should be done in a familiar space or at home. Because when wearing a helmet, one would be isolated from the outside world. For safety reasons, it would be better to use virtual reality systems, including VRFS, in familiar environments.

> Wang: Umm...When shooting in reality, the problem is that resources are difficult to obtain, such as all equipment, manpower, and actors. In contrast, this system will be a good choice (for practice).
> Qian: Well, I feel that this idea is very good.... Well, I think there is a learning process happening with this kind of system... I think this kind of learning is more vivid. If you practice in real life, it is unlikely that you will find a suitable scene at your disposal and actors willing to cooperate with you, so this form is better.
> Pan: I used to film with my mobile phone. I needed to stand on the stool for a look down shot. I climbed up and down often and it's very tiring. But I've never encountered a similar problem in this system... It would be better if I could practice in an environment where no one is around so that I don't need to worry about whether I might seem strange in others' eyes.

Participants also discussed the feasibility of using VRFS in practical education. Participants thought that the learning mode proposed by VRFS was innovative and had great potential. Yet this system needed more content to be a complete educational platform. Some participants believed that VRFS had a good potential commercial value. With more scenes and performances added to it, VRFS might bring people, even with little knowledge of film making, a wonderful and novel experience by allowing them to merely appreciate different stories in VR. And hopefully they might also learn something about film language.

> Yu: This system will be great if you can enrich the content so that you can have different training scenarios. But I can imagine the development will need a lot of time.
> Yuan: ...if it is promoted as an entertaining device, I am actually willing to buy this. It is interesting.

The participants possessed different opinions about the learnability of the operations. Some thought VRFS was relatively complicated to use. There were too many buttons to remember and one needed to operate the camera with two controllers at the same time. It took some time to learn and to get used to. This was the reason for the low usability score from the SUS questionnaires. Some other participants, however, said that they could grasp the operations without difficulty. They could understand that in order to mimic to real camera, the operations would inevitably be complex to some extent. But they also suggested that the operations be described in more details in the tutorial session so as to make later use easier.

> Wen: *I think this system is a little bit too complicated for amateurs, but if the purpose is to serve students majoring in film making as a practice tool, of course, he can spend enough time to learn how to use this system very well... It is mainly because there are a lot of buttons on the controllers and it is complicated for me to use.*
> Li: *I think that the functions of buttons are a little bit too complicated. If there were only one button, the operations would be much easier to determine. So many buttons, separated on two controllers, are somehow confusing.*

Effectiveness (subjective). From the perspective of the effectiveness, almost all participants believed that using VRFS is helpful for learning film making. VRFS simulated the operations of a real camera, so that beginners might have a close-to-reality experience and form a basic understanding of how cameras worked. Some participants even thought that the system had certain advantages that the actual practice could not offer. For example, VRFS allowed a user to try to take the same shot from many different angles which was almost impossible in real life.

> Xin: *It is a good way of learning for students, umm, because it allows you to experience filming in a much more real way than a software running on a desktop computer.*
> Zheng: *I think it would be helpful to learn how to use different types of shots. When you experience VRFS, you need to design shots on your own by moving the virtual camera around, similar to what you do in reality. Therefore, I think it may be helpful to film language learning..*

On the other hand, some other participants thought that the current version of VRSF should further improve the simulation of reality. For example, the horizontal indicator of a camera, very important to film makers, was missing. Besides, it was also a problem mentioned by some participants that all the lights were predefined, not allowing user adjustment. Moreover, the virtual experience disturbed the judgment of some participants, which was an important thing many participants hoped to improve.

> Tang: *It will be better to allow all different kinds of shots possible in the real world.*
> Dong: *In real life, you can clearly distinguish the real world and its representation in a camera's viewfinder, but the virtual environment gives me a lot of trouble: what you see in the helmet is virtual, and what you see in the viewfinder is also virtual. This nested virtuality bewildered me sometimes.*
> Qian: *This system can be more realistic with the ability to allow light adjustment. In this way, more kinds of practices can be done and the system will be better.*

5.2 Emotional Tendency

Most of the participants showed a positive emotional tendency, and almost all participants were willing to use VRFS frequently.

The advocates in non-relevant majors agreed that they had not only a very pleasant learning experience but also an unprecedented VR enjoyment. The whole process was very interesting and they really learned something from it, making it even more rewarding and attractive. Most of the advocates from relevant majors supported VRFS because of its unique convenience, immersion and interesting interaction. Generally speaking, fun of use is the main reason for attracting them, but to be more helpful to those advanced users, VRFS needs to enhance perceivable realism.

> *Nan: I think the experience from start to the end is very interesting. Well, first of all, it is new. I have never heard about a similar system before. The fact that you can make a short film of your own is very attractive to me.*
> *Jiang: If I can use VRFS in my course for daily training, I am willing. Because it does show some benefits as a training method.*

Only three participants said they were less willing to use VRFS again. Two participants expressed their reluctance to continue because of the discomfort of wearing the VR helmet. The other one doubted that there was a large difference between the virtual and the real experience as far as operation was concerned.

> *Yang: The helmet pressed my face hard. I felt uncomfortable.*
> *Wen: I think it is not very friendly to people with glasses. It pressed my glasses hard.*
> *Jiang: I don't want it, I think it might feel better to shoot with a real camera.*

5.3 Potential Target Users

During the interview, many participants mentioned the potential target users of VRFS. After data analyzing and coding, the characteristics of them and the reasons for this conclusion are as follow.

Target Users. Most participants believed that VRFS was more suitable for two types of people: (1) junior students in majors relevant to film making and (2) amateur film makers.

For junior students just started to learn about film language, the participants agreed that they did need adequate training to understand it better. But for beginners, practice opportunities were usually scarce, and the operation of a camera was also unfamiliar. VRFS could help them in this context.

For amateurs or hobbyists of film making or maybe even VR itself, VRFS had good learnability, which meant that using it was not difficult for novices. Besides, at the same time of teaching people about film making, it also brought novel VR experience to them. Finally, the fact that a user could make a short film of his/her own and bring it back as a video file made this experience more fulfilling and appealing.

5.4 Suggestions for Future Improvement

At the end of the interviews, participants were asked to give some suggestions on how to improve VRFS in the future. Their opinions are summarized below.

Suggestion. The suggestions could be categorized into teaching, simulation, and content:

1. Teaching: The current way of introducing 8 basic types of shots was to let a user watch an example segment, which was not very interesting. Participants suggested that it would be better if the introduction were done in 3D interactively as well.

2. Simulation: The current version of the virtual camera only supported the basic functions of recording, stabilization and zooming. In the future, more important functions of a real camera (such as horizontal indicator, depth of field adjustment, etc.) should be added to offer a more realistic experience.
3. Content: VRFS had a great potential of content extension. Currently, it only had "Tales of Afanti" in it. It would become more attractive and useful if a user might choose from more stories of different genres and styles.

6 Conclusion

The influence of technological advances is gradually increasing in daily life and a lot of innovations have happened in the field of education. In recent years, the application of VR technology in education has gained much attention, but most of the applications are about medical simulation, virtual campus, virtual laboratory and so forth. Applications of VR in art education are rare. VRFS was an exceptional trial which turned out to be satisfactory in terms of usability and subjective effectiveness. The SUS questionnaires gave an average score of 74, which reveals that VR technology can provide a new way of practice. In the in-depth interviews, participants also recognized that VRFS has certain advantages for practice-intensive courses thanks to its advantages such as low cost and better accessibility. Most participants also believed it would be helpful for their practical film making in reality.

From the emotional aspect, the majority of the participants' attitudes towards VRFS were positive. It is natural because shooting in a virtual environment was a novel experience for most of them. At the end of the experience, a user could obtain a copy of his/her own film, which made it even more appealing.

The most suitable users of VRFS are likely be beginners and amateurs of film making. This conclusion is justified by the fact that interviews and SUS scores from students in non-relevant major (77.5) were higher than the counterpart (72.2). The reason may be that beginners need to practice more to master the skills of using equipment and to construct a basic understanding of film language, while sophisticated learners needed more control and close-to-reality feedback to give full play to their skills and creativity.

In general, VRFS was a novel and welcomed system. When the cost of practice was too high to afford, VRFS could be a good alternative. The effectiveness of practicing in a virtual environment was acknowledged by most participants.

7 Limitation and Future Research Proposal

In the process of seeking approaches to solve practical problems in film education with VR technologies, this research developed new learning tools and models. Though its effectiveness is verified, there are still limitations to be dealt with in future studies.

Firstly, there are some restrictions in VRFS because the virtual camera is still different from a real one and there are many functions to be added. This encourages future development of VRFS to expand the range of potential users. As a result, an upgraded system in the future need to be revisited.

Secondly, the experiments were all conducted in the College of Arts and Media in Tongji University. It's a controlled environment quite different from real-life learning scenarios. In real life, there will be no strict time limit for a user, and he/she would receive training in a cozy environment instead of an unfamiliar space. All these factors may affect the experiment result, so future researchers are encouraged to verify its effectiveness in a real educational environment.

Last but not least, the research mainly used qualitative methods, and the conclusions were derived from the subjective answers from the participants. More objective proofs are thus needed to support their validity. It is recommended that future researchers employ more objective methods, such as EEG analysis or eye tracking, to verify and extend the conclusions of this paper.

References

1. Miranda, P., Isaias, P., Costa, C.J., Pifano, S.: Validation of an e-learning 3.0 critical success factors framework: a qualitative research. J. Inf. Technol. Educ. Res. **16**, 339–363 (2017)
2. Gros, B., García-Peñalvo, F.J.: Future Trends in the Design Strategies and Techno-logical Affordances of E-Learning (2016)
3. Violante, M.G., Vezzetti, E.: Implementing a new approach for the design of an e-learning platform in engineering education. Comput. Appl. Eng. Educ. **22**(4), 708–727 (2014)
4. Connolly, T.M., Boyle, E.A., MacArthur, E., Hainey, T., Boyle, J.M.: A systematic literature review of empirical evidence on computer games and serious games. Comput. Educ. **59**(2), 661–686 (2012)
5. Dalgarno, B., Bishop, A.G., Adlong, W., Bedgood Jr., D.R.: Effectiveness of a vir-tual laboratory as a preparatory resource for distance education chemistry students. Comput. Educ. **53**(3), 853–865 (2009)
6. Cho, K.H., Kim, M.K., Lee, H.-J., Lee, W.H.: Virtual reality training with cogni-tive load improves walking function in chronic stroke patients. Tohoku J. Exp. Med. **236**(4), 273–280 (2015)
7. Bruder, G., Steinicke, F., Valkov, D., Hinrichs, K.: Immersive virtual studio for ar-chitectural exploration. In: IEEE Symposium on 3d User Interfaces, pp. 125–126 (2010)
8. Rickel, J., Johnson, W.L.: Virtual Humans for Team Training in Virtual Reality, pp. 217–238 (1999)
9. IEEE. The application of virtual reality technologies in engineering education for the automotive industry. In: Proceedings of 2015 International Conference on Interactive Collaborative Learning, pp. 536–544 (2015)
10. Zhang, K., Liu, S.-J.: The application of virtual reality technology in physi-cal education teaching and training. In: Proceedings 2016 IEEE International Conference on Service Operations and Logistics, and Informatics, pp. 245–248 (2016)
11. Monahan, T., McArdle, G., Bertolotto, M.: Virtual reality for collaborative e-learning. Comput. Educ. **50**(4), 1339–1353 (2008)
12. HE, X.: Research on teaching methods of film and television art education in colleges and universities (高等院校影视艺术教育教学方法研究). J. Art Eval. **02**, 185–186 (2016)

13. Zhou, X.: Analysis on the development of film and television education in the pat-tern of art education in the 21st century (21世纪艺术教育格局中的影视教育发展分析). J. Art Film **05**, 100–104 (2004)
14. LIU, Q.: Practice teaching of film and television education in colleges and universities (高校影视教育实践教学探析). J. Henan Inst. Educ. (Philosophy and Social Sciences Edition), **30**(06), 121–123 (2011)
15. CAI, B.: Research on the current situation of british higher film education (英国高等影视教育现状研究). J. Beijing Film Acad. **06**, 152–158 (2018)
16. MI, G.: Audio- visual language analysis of animation TV/films in contemporary context (当代语境下的影视动画视听语言研究), Shaanxi University of Science and Technology (2007). http://www.sust.edu.cn/
17. Baidu encyclopedia. (2008, 1.29). https://baike.baidu.com/item/audio-visual language/9745522?fr=aladdin
18. Bangor, A., Kortum, P.T., Miller, J.T.: An empirical evaluation of the system usa-bility scale. Int. J. Hum. Comput. Interact. **24**(6), 574–594 (2008)
19. Lewis, J.R., Sauro, J.: The factor structure of the system usability scale. In: Kurosu, M. (ed.) HCD 2009. LNCS, vol. 5619, pp. 94–103. Springer, Heidelberg (2009). https://doi.org/10.1007/978-3-642-02806-9_12
20. Bangor, A., Kortum, P., Miller, J.: Determining what individual SUS scores mean: adding an adjective rating scale, **4**(3), pp. 114–123 (2009)
21. Brooke, J.: SUS: a quick and dirty usability scale. In: Jordan, P., Thomas, B., We-erdmeester, B., McClelland, A. (eds.) Usability Evaluation in Industry, pp. 189–194 (1996)
22. Sauro, J.: Measuring Usability With The System Usability Scale (SUS), 2011.M. U. (2011, 1.29). https://www.userfocus.co.uk/articles/measuring-usability-with-the-SUS.html
23. Peres, S.C., Pham, T., Phillips, R.: Validation of the system usability scale (SUS): SUS in the wild. Proc. Hum. Factors Ergon. Soc. Annu. Meet. **57**(1), 192–196 (2013)

Application of Virtual Reality and Gamification in the Teaching of Art History

Evelyn Marilyn Riveros Huaman[✉], Roni Guillermo Apaza Aceituno, and Olha Sharhorodska

Department of Systems Engineering,
Universidad Nacional de San Agustin de Arequipa,
Santa Catalina 117, Arequipa, Peru
lynemriver@gmail.com,
roni.guillermo.apaza.aceituno@alumni.usp.br,
osharhorodska@unsa.edu.pe

Abstract. The virtual reality (VR) presents a breakthrough in the field of education and others, because it allows you to interact with a fictional world created through the technology. Users can navigate in real time with a subjective perspective of what is there and can be deployed in this three-dimensional world (3D). We use a virtual learning environment (VLE) done in the Unity3D program where you will simulate a virtual museum to enhance the teaching of history of Art. For which we use predefined stages to improve knowledge in an interactive way through gamification techniques testing was conducted on 15 students in higher education, achieving a more active learning.

Keywords: Virtual reality · Education · Virtual learning environment · History of art · Gamification

1 Introduction

In recent years the museums are being one of the areas where it has been seen more inquiries on virtual reality (VR). This technology allows to transport visitors to different parts of the world allowing recreate the spaces virtually without the need to be present in them, avoiding costs without having to travel.

Virtual reality environments offer us a great flexibility and adaptability in many training opportunities in education. For the creation of the virtual learning environment (VLE) was used Unity3D because it allows you to develop environments of virtual reality (VR), this paper proposes the implementation of a virtual reality game using gamification by elements of video games to improve the teaching of Art History; where will simulate a virtual museum, with predefined stages that expose works from different artistic currents with their respective representations all owing interact with the characters, objects, animations and sounds presented in the application.

The game will allow your users to interact with the virtual environment achieving immersion and interaction with it, allowing students to improve their learning in

History of Art through Gamification techniques used in the game. The rest of this article is organized as follows. Section 2 "Related works", they provide an overview of related jobs. Section 3 "User elicitation study", describes the methods in the proposal. Section 4 "Results", illustrates the results of the experiment. Finally, the Sect. 5 "Conclusions", concludes this article.

2 Related Works

This investigation is related to the topics: (1) Virtual Reality, (2) Gamification, (3) Virtual Museums. In the field of virtual reality and gamification we find the Gamification study [1] which proposes a game using virtual reality, where they meet the principles of gamification achieving motivate collaborative learning in students of engineering, leading them to work in a team.

In another study [2] undertaken aspects related to the development of applications of Virtual Reality (VR) and Augmented Reality (AR) such as education resources in the teaching of students.

Another form of virtual reality that we find [3] are presented in different cases: the National Archaeological Museum of Marche in Ancona and the 3D reconstruction of the Roman Forum of Fanum Fortunae that are digitized photographs with the technique-structure for the movement metrics and are integrated within the virtual surrounds pace using a PC with a HTC Live system, allowing the user to interact with the 3D models, integrating the virtual reality.

We could find applications that use virtual reality in Museums [4] Samsumg gear VR shows us a free application where recreates the city of Gyeongju in South Korea.

Another application that we find [5] shows us a virtual museum next to the co-lesson of Rijksmuseum, Amsterdam, which contains a virtual art gallery with which the user can interact.

3 User Elicitation Study

In order to find out which interactions are achieved with the application on the students; we carried out a study where a training was carried out for students in the implementation and use.

In which students were able to interact with the application deployed and interacting with objects that are in it, to finally show the scores at the end of the tour by the chambers.

The scores obtained by students will vary according as they come to finish the tour of all the chambers and the interaction achieved. The Fig. 1 shows the different rooms of Paintings presented by the application.

(a)Surrealism (b)Impressionism

(c)Symbolism (d)Abstract

Fig. 1. This figure shows the different rooms of Paintings with their artistic current. (Source: own elaboration)

3.1 Purposal and Participants

In the proposal involved 15 students between the ages of 17 to 22 years among men and women, of the top-level of the Painting are with the support of the master of specialization. All of them have had for the most part a of both gaming experience of virtual reality and other types.

Table 1. Results of the age of respondent (Source: own elaboration)

		Frequency	Percentage	Valid percentage	Percentage cumulative
Valid	17–19	11	73,3	73,3	73,3
	20–22	4	26,7	26,7	100,0
	Total	15	100,0	100,0	

It can be seen in (Table 1) that the largest number of students are among the ages of 17 and 19 years with 73.3% and the least amount between the ages of 20 and 22% in 26.67.

Table 2. Results of the sex of the respondent (Source: own elaboration)

		Frequency	Percentage	Valid percentage	Cumulative percentage
Valid	1	9	60,0	60,0	60,0
	2	6	40,0	40,0	100,0
	Total	15	100,0	100,0	

In (Table 2), we can see that the majority of the students surveyed represent 60% of "men", while 40% are women.

Our prototype was based on the virtual reality that was carried out in Unity3D to be used in the computer having as main functionality: support in learning the course on the history of art in an interactive way.

3.2 Chambers, Procedure and Interaction

We asked the students to experiment with the virtual learning environment presented in the proposal to carry out the interaction with the game. We identified 5 rooms where 4 paintings with its main representations and the fifth chamber exposes representative sculptures from different authors. The Fig. 2 shows the Room of Sculptures.

Fig. 2. This figure shows the room of sculpture where representations of several authors are exhibited. (Source: own elaboration)

Before the experiment the students had a brief description of the Characteristics of the app and its possibilities of interaction to achieve. The proposal was used in the interactive simulation because it allows you to achieve a simulation where recreates a virtual world that exists only in your computer. Noting that this simulation is interactive is what distinguishes the reality of an animation.

4 Results

4.1 Measurements and Analysis

To evaluate approaches were applied in the 2 questionnaires: The usability in virtual reality [6, 7], and the virtual learning environment [7, 8], where the following criteria were applied.

Table 3. Criteria for the evaluation of the usability of Virtual Reality (Source: own elaboration)

No	Criteria
1	Level of realism in the virtual environment
2	Level of realism to perform the tasks
3	Freedom of movement in the virtual environment
4	Response time on the screen
5	Level of perception of the virtual environment
6	Visualization and realism in the application
7	Level of navigation and guidance
8	Ease of entry and exit in the virtual environment
9	Easy use of the app
10	Organized tasks and understandable
11	Feeling of being present in the virtual world

Table 4. Criteria for the evaluation of Virtual Learning Environment (Source: own elaboration)

No	Criteria
1	Immersion in the application
2	Learningbecause of realism in the application
3	Easy manipulation of objects in the virtual environment
4	Educational Utility
5	Ease of use of the application
6	Sense of Belongingin the virtual environment
7	Motivation in learning
8	Intention to use the application
9	Cognitive Benefits
10	Effectiveness of the application in learning
11	Satisfaction when using the application

4.2 Results of the Assessment of the Instrument

For which we used the Cronbach's Alpha [9] to determine the effectiveness of the used instrument.

Table 5. Results of the Cronbach's alpha test (Source: own elaboration)

Cronbach's Alpha	Alpha coefficient based on standardized elements	Number of items
0,753	0,753	11

As can be seen in (Table 5), the Cronbach's Alpha is 0,753 (75.3%), which is located in acceptable, for good. This indicates that the internal consistency of the items analyzed is good.

4.3 Results of Statistics of the Element

The (Tables 6 and 7), shows the results for variables with their respective Arithmetic mean (average), the standard deviation.

With the data presented it is possible that you can calculate the Coefficient of Variation whose formula is: 0 do not vary, further away vary.

$$C.V. = Standard\ Deviation/Media \tag{1}$$

Value that allows us to measure the variation between the two variables is based on the average is 0 because there is no variation.

Table 6. Statistics of the element usability of virtual reality (Source: own elaboration)

Criteria	Media	Standard deviation	N	CV
Environment	3,8	0,561	15	0,148
Task	4	0,535	15	0,134
Movement	3,87	0,64	15	0,165
Time	3,87	0,743	15	0,192
Realism	4,13	0,64	15	0,155
Perception	3,67	0,488	15	0,133
Navegation	3,8	0,561	15	0,148
Ease	3,87	0,743	15	0,192
Application	4,2	0,414	15	0,099
Organization	3,47	0,64	15	0,184
Presence	3,93	0,458	15	0,117

It can be seen in (Table 6), the Coefficient of Variation (CV) measures the percentage of variation. The Level of variation between 0,099 is good approaches zero - 20% is well. As shown in Fig. 3.

It can be seen in (Table 7), the Coefficient of Variation (CV) present the Level of variation between 0, 12 is good, as shown in Fig. 4.

Table 7. Statistics element-based virtual learning environment (Source: own elaboration)

Criteria	Media	Standard Deviation	N	CV
Immersion	1,87	0,64	15	0,34
Learning	2,13	0,35	15	0,17
Easy	2,27	0,59	15	0,26
Utility	1,67	0,72	15	0,43
Ease	1,93	0,80	15	0,41
Sense	1,93	0,70	15	0,36
Motivation	1,87	0,35	15	0,19
Intention	1,93	0,46	15	0,24
Cognitive benefits	1,80	0,56	15	0,31
Effectiveness	1,93	0,59	15	0,31
Satisfaction	2,07	0,26	15	0,12

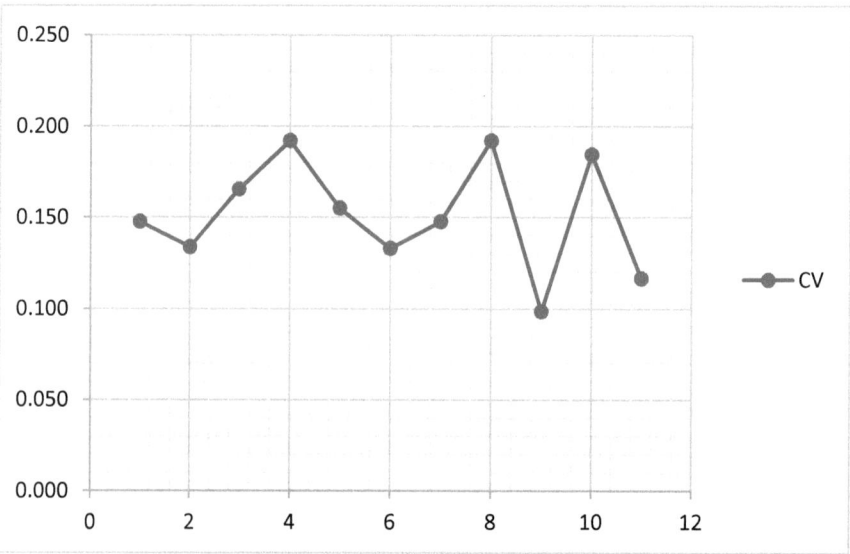

Fig. 3. Coefficient of Variation-Usability of Virtual Reality (Source: own elaboration)

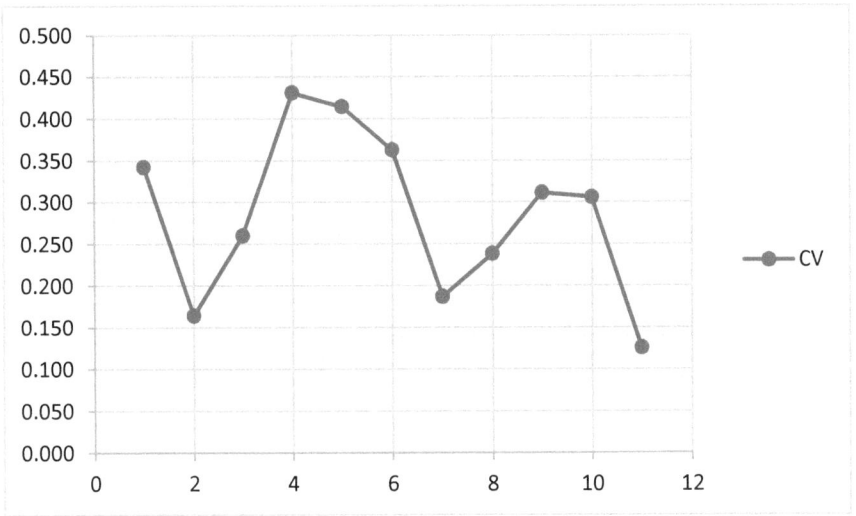

Fig. 4. Coefficient of variation- virtual learning environment (Source: own elaboration)

4.4 Results Correlation Between Elements

From the surveys carried out we determined the correlations among their elements: We find in (Table 8), of the Correlation between elements of Usability of Virtual Reality that the cells marked indicate that there is a good correlation of data between these variables in particular. With 0,715 tasks with navigation and navigation with movement with a 0,717, which are the most related.

Table 8. Correlation between elements usability of virtual reality (Source: own elaboration)

	Environment	Task	Movement	Time	Realism	Perception	Navigation	Ease	Application	Organization	Presence
Environment	1,000	0,477	0,319	0,103	0,478	0,261	0,318	0,446	0,185	0,080	-0,056
Task	0,477	1,000	0,626	0,539	0,209	0,274	0,715	0,360	0,323	0,000	0,000
Movement	0,319	0,626	1,000	0,561	0,221	-0,152	0,717	0,410	0,377	-0,360	-0,033
Time	0,103	0,539	0,561	1,000	0,491	0,066	0,446	0,224	0,325	-0,010	-0,028
Realism	0,478	0,209	0,221	0,491	1,000	0,152	0,080	0,190	-0,108	-0,163	0,033
Perception	0,261	0,274	-0,152	0,066	0,152	1,000	0,261	0,066	0,354	0,305	-0,426
Navigation	0,318	0,715	0,717	0,446	0,080	0,261	1,000	0,274	0,492	-0,119	-0,056
Ease	0,446	0,360	0,410	0,224	0,190	0,066	0,274	1,000	0,557	0,140	0,392
Application	0,185	0,323	0,377	0,325	-0,108	0,354	0,492	0,557	1,000	0,431	0,075
Organization	0,080	0,000	-0,360	-0,010	-0,163	0,305	-0,119	0,140	0,431	1,000	0,114
Presence	-0,056	0,000	-0,033	-0,028	0,033	-0,426	-0,056	0,392	0,075	0,114	1,000

It can be seen in (Table 9), of the Correlation between elements of the Virtual Learning Environment, that there is no a variable that protrudes from the other, it means, there is no significant correlation between variables, we can emphasize.

Table 9. Correlation between elements of the virtual learning environment (Source: own elaboration)

	Immersion	Realism	Manipulation	Utility	Ease	Belonging	Motivation	Intention	Benefits	Effectiveness	Satisfaction
Immersion	1,00	0,40	0,10	0,05	-0,02	0,14	-0,40	-0,28	0,12	-0,03	0,06
Realism	0,40	1,00	0,16	0,19	0,54	0,33	0,15	0,06	-0,22	0,05	-0,10
Manipulation	0,10	0,16	1,00	0,39	0,19	0,05	0,18	0,07	-0,04	-0,15	-0,12
Utility	0,05	0,19	0,39	1,00	0,70	-0,05	0,09	-0,29	-0,35	0,11	-0,25
Ease	-0,02	0,54	0,19	0,70	1,00	0,37	0,22	-0,01	-0,35	0,14	0,02
Belonging	0,14	0,33	0,05	-0,05	0,37	1,00	-0,04	-0,01	0,14	0,16	0,42
Motivation	-0,40	0,15	0,18	0,09	0,22	-0,04	1,00	0,38	-0,14	0,30	0,10
Intention	-0,28	0,06	0,07	-0,29	-0,01	-0,01	0,38	1,00	0,22	-0,02	0,04
Benefits	0,12	-0,22	-0,04	-0,35	-0,35	0,14	-0,14	0,22	1,00	-0,26	0,10
Effectiveness	-0,03	0,05	-0,15	0,11	0,14	0,16	0,30	-0,02	-0,26	1,00	0,50
Satisfaction	0,06	-0,10	-0,12	-0,25	0,02	0,42	0,10	0,04	0,10	0,50	1,00

5 Conclusions

5.1 Conclusions

- Tests conducted in the art students determined that there was good interaction with the proposed educational application although presented certain difficulties which were overcome.
- The results obtained in the correlation between elements of Usability of Virtual Reality of the cells indicate that there is a good correlation of the data highlighting the tasks with navigation with 0,715 and navigation with movement with a 0,717.
- The results obtained in the correlation between elements of evaluation of the Virtual Learning Environment indicated, that here there is no a variable that protrudes from the other, it means, there is no significant correlation between varies.
- We found several advantages in the use of this educational application that improved the learning the course of Art History motivating students although there were also some disadvantages more than everything in the application

5.2 Future Work

It is proposed to add new rooms with current artists where they can make their own virtual exhibitions, as well as integrate technology of augmented reality to improve interaction

Acknowledgement. The present investigation is part of the project "Implementacion de un Laboratorio virtual inmersivo de Astronomía usando Tecnicas de "Gamification" dirigido a Alumnos de Secundaria" BA-0026-2017-UNSA, thanks to the financiting granted by the Universidad Nacional de San Agustin de Arequipa.

References

1. Gasca-Hurtado, G.P., Peña, A., Gómez-Álvarez, M.C., Plascencia-Osuna, Ó.A., Calvo-Manzano, J.A.: Realidad virtual como buena práctica para trabajo en equipo con estudiantes de ingeniería. Revista Ibérica de Sistemas y Tecnologías de Información, No. 16, pp. 76–91 (2015)
2. Díaz, J.; Fava, L., Banchoff, C., Schiavoni, A., Martin, S.: Juegos serios y aplicaciones interactivas usando realidad aumentada y realidad virtual. In: XX Workshop de Investigadores en Ciencias de la Computación, pp. 829–834 (2018)
3. Clini, P., Ruggeri, L., Angeloni, R., Sassob, M.: Interactive immersive virtual museum: digital documentation for virtual interaction. In: ISPRS TC II Mid-term Symposium Towards Photogrammetry 2020, pp. 251–257 (2018)
4. Gyeongju vr Museum. https://www.oculus.com/experiences/gear-vr/844232452316302/. Accessed 24 Oct 2018
5. VRmuseum.nl. http://vrmuseum.nl/. Accessed 24 Oct 2018
6. Sutcliffe, A., Brian, G.: Heuristic evaluation of virtual reality applications. Interact. Comput. **16**, 831–849 (2004)
7. Aguirre, R., Nicole, S.: Experiencia de Usuario en Museos Virtuales (2015)
8. Blackledge, J., Barrett, M.: Evaluation of a prototype desktop virtual reality model developed to enhance electrical safety and design in the built. ISAST Trans. Comput. Intell. Sys. **3**(3), 1–10 (2012)
9. George, D., Mallery, P.: SPSS/PC+Step by Step: A Simple Guide and Reference. Wadsworth Publishing Co., Belmont (2003)

Indoor Navigation Through Storytelling in Virtual Reality

Philipp Ulsamer[✉], Kevin Pfeffel, and Nicholas H. Müller

Socio-Informatics and Societal Aspects of Digitalization,
Faculty of Computer Science and Business Information Systems,
Universtiy of Applied Sciences Wuerzburg-Schweinfurt,
Sanderheinrichsleitenweg 20, 97074 Wuerzburg, Germany
{philipp.ulsamer,kevin.pfeffel,nicholas.mueller}@fhws.de
https://www.fhws.de

Abstract. Storytelling is a narrative method that passes on explicit but mostly implicit knowledge. Viewers are involved in the narrated story, so that the content of the story is easier to understand and accept because you become part of it. To help guest students learn to find their way to key locations in the new environment, we've built a virtual environment so they can take a virtual tour of our university from their home. Nevertheless, it is difficult to remember a route, if all hallways look identical. With our experiment, we've examined whether users can better remember directions by watching a VR video using storytelling instead of watching a VR video of the pathway without storytelling elements. While subjects that watched the VR video without storytelling need to think about which way to go at different junctions, the other subjects could use story elements to remember elements of storytelling at certain points, which path they need to take and find their way in less time and fewer steps as the subjects without storytelling. Through storytelling, parts of the video are emotionally linked, so that the track and its elements are anchored faster in the memory. The involvement in the search process generates a higher immersion, which increases the motivation during the learning process. Increased motivation makes things more responsive and builds sustainable knowledge.

Keywords: Virtual reality · E-learning · Storytelling · Immersion · Eye tracking

1 Introduction

Virtual Reality (VR) is about to revolutionize the world of media and is considered as one of its latest developments to the most promising defining digital media [3]. VR allows the user to immerse and interact with alternative realities in a computer-generated 3D environment [1,2]. The degree of how much one immerses in the VR world can vary. Full immersion requires tools such as a head mounted display (HMD) that can generate a 3D visual and audio environment.

Also, input devices such as a data glove, which gives the user the feeling that they perceive the fictitious world as their real one [4].

The research and application of VR technology in education has enriched the way you teach and learn [5]. Today we can work in virtual environments (VE) not only in the areas of scientific visualization, monitoring of complex technical objects or entertainment, but above all in simulations and training. Computer simulations have been shown to be effective instruments for teaching. Most simulation interactions in learning environments today focus on the mouse and keyboard controls as a computer interface. However, there are other effective ways to extend learning simulations to more physical and embodied modalities, which have unique spatial characteristics that enable sophisticated knowledge representation in virtual environments [6,7].

E-learning technology improves traditional teaching techniques. Abstract concepts can be illustrated and understood better. It breaks the limitations of space and time. Lessons can be learned by students anytime, anywhere. VR supports e-learning and brings it closer to the real learning environment. In the e-learning field, practical approaches can be learned almost realistically with immediate feedback [8]. Recent research has shown that motivation to learn through virtual learning environments is increased [9].

We use storytelling to further increase that motivation and create a higher level of immersion in the VR world for the user. Storytelling is used in teaching to better communicate learning content to students. Learning content is linked to a story, making it easier for students to remember what they have learned [10]. Also, the natural interaction with virtual characters increases user immersion. An important principle in storytelling is to involve the audience in the story. They experience the story and do not just hear it. Storytelling can combine learning and emotional wellbeing to help build sustainable knowledge [11].

Guest students from other universities often find it difficult to find their way around the new environment and to find important premises. For this reason, we have built a virtual environment of our university, so that these students can do a virtual walk around from their university. This is to ensure that they can learn where at the host university certain rooms such as the deanery are located. In this paper we want to showcase that the learning process in virtual reality is much more effective when storytelling is used.

The goal of the experiment was to find a specific room in the fastest possible time. Therefore, one group had to find this way with the help of storytelling and the other group without. An important challenge which VR content creators face, is the interaction between viewer agency and narrative guidance, as viewers step into a 360° environment and have the freedom to choose where to look. We can trigger curiosity with sound, light, interaction, or movement so viewers naturally turn in a certain direction. In addition, remembering things is made easier by involving emotional experience in virtual storytelling.

First, we will summarize related work and confirm that storytelling is a missing task as a tool to guide the viewers attention in the navigation process. Afterwards, we will propose our used material and methods for this experiment. Furthermore, we will explain our results in more detail. Finally, we will give a short outlook and discuss our future work.

2 Related Works

The study of storytelling in VR involves understanding e-learning concepts, and methods of directing attention in 360° virtual environments.

2.1 Storytelling in E-Learning

The way stories are told is crucial to how much we remember details. Stories have the ability to form memories and thoughts like no other form of modern communication. To simplify remembrance of important details, abstract story skeletons are built that are central to the narrative process [12,13].

The dissertation by Oaks [14] examines the learning behavior of college students. The goal of this study was to find out what, if any, effects storytelling as a pedagogical method of information retention. Above all, it focused on whether the storytelling variant is more effective than the conventional lecture method to positively influence the recall of lesson content. It has been found that the subjects who have been instructed in the storytelling method have significantly better ability to remember learning content than the students who have been taught the same content in a more traditional lecture method.

In this paper, we want to take the approach that storytelling is more effective than traditional methods to remember learning content to the next level. Storytelling triggers emotions that make it easier to remember. Through a higher immersion which is achieved with the use of virtual reality in a 360° environment, storytelling should anchor learning content even deeper into the memory.

2.2 Directing Attention in VR

One of the main problems we have to face in the virtual world is that in a 360° canvas the viewer has the freedom to look and is not restricted to a frame view when watching a movie or playing a game. This makes it all the more difficult to direct the viewer's attention to where the action is happening. We also do not want the user to miss important story content because he is looking in the wrong direction. In addition, we want to make the experience as immersive as possible and not force it to direct in a desired direction, but the viewer should get the feeling if we direct his attention that he will do it of his free will.

Sheikh et al. [15] have tested various techniques in their work to direct the user's attention in virtual reality in a desired direction. In doing so, they analyzed qualitative and quantitative data from these tests to evaluate the effectiveness of the different attention-directing techniques. They examined in various ways how the user responds to audio or visual cues. It was found that using both cues at the same time was the most successful in the tests to direct the viewer in the desired direction. The advantage of audio is that its use, even if not fully spatialised, indicates to the viewer that something is happening and his attention is already being tempted. But with visual cues, subjects often followed the cues, but not to the very end.

They also tested subjective experience and collected data on preferences at what distance the scenes in the 360° environment happen. The results of the participants showed that the distance had no effect on following the action. The enjoyment of watching the video and the degree of immersion were adversely affected if the distance to the action was less than or more than three meters. The distance of three meters provided a good balance of being close enough to enhance immersion, but far enough that not to penetrate into the private space of the user.

In this paper, we want to use visual and acoustic cues to support them with storytelling elements. By being involved into the story, the user's attention can be more easily directed in a desired direction as our test-subjects seek the right path and immerse more and more into the VR world. By taking a role as an actor in the 360° environment, we try to direct their attention to the right path, which the viewer is supposed to remember. The fact that each junction serves as a node to reestablish the correct track, the viewer should be helped in these places by storytelling in order to trigger a recall more effectively than in the control condition without storytelling elements.

3 Method

Since we often get visited by guests from partner universities, we have provided them with a virtual environment, which allows them to conduct a virtual tour beforehand from their home in order to be able to find important rooms such as the cafeteria more quickly. The rather modern design of our faculty makes all corridors look identical, making the search for the desired location difficult. In order to make these places more easy to find, we also want to show the way from the entrance to the desired location in a video. In this paper, we want to compare two approaches. One video shows the search process using storytelling, the other video without. By this approach we want to check which method is better suited to remember a certain route in the short- and longterm.

3.1 Storytelling

Virtual characters are important components in virtual storytelling. The natural interaction with virtual people allows the user to immerse more into the virtual environment and makes the viewer feel like a part of this virtual world. We distinguish two methods of plot generation [16]:

(1) Character-driven storytelling focuses on the inner conflict of a character. The viewer is more concerned with the personal development of the characters and their attitudes and think about the reasons for making decisions and how these in turn change the form of action and the story as a whole.
(2) Plot-based storytelling places greater emphasis on the plot itself, as well as plot twists and outer conflicts. The goals of the stories focus more on the development of a situation. The user chooses between different plotlines throughout the story.

Since the goal of the video was to memorize the right path in an unknown environment, we opted for a plot-based approach that traditionally presents the storyline in a predefined way. However, this process lacks the refinement of character behavior. Since we only see the 360° movie and do not interact with the characters it contains, this is not relevant to us.

3.2 Storyboard

For our experiment, we shot the 360° video as a single take. We wanted to avoid that the user is torn by scene change from the VR world. We have used narrative anchors in certain places with the help of storytelling in order to let the user look in the desired direction and memorize junctions. As a pretest, we have provided the viewer with a simple and essential task for a student, which the user has to fulfill in the context of a story. They are supposed to find the machine with which you can charge the chip card from the canteen for the cafeteria. The starting point is the entrance to the university. In order to guide the viewer to the right room or giving important hints, people in the video interact with the viewer. The path to the cards charger has six junctions where we want to direct the attention through storytelling as seen in Fig. 1. In the first scene, the viewer sees two students talking about wanting to eat in the canteen. One student remembers that he/she has no more money left on the card and says he's/she's going to the charger. This person speaks to the viewer and asks if he or she wants to do the same and takes him/her over the stairs to the next floor (Scene 1). This is the point where the viewer gets involved in the story.

On the next floor, the student talks to the spectator and tells the subject that they are going to race down the long hallway and meet up on the next floor, showing the viewer the way to run (Scene 2). In order to optically control the viewer with the help of light, the viewer sees light sources on the stairs at the end of the hallway, which implies to take this way up (Scene 3).

Arrived on the next floor, the student comes to meet the test subject. The actor admits that the spectator won the race, which gives the audience a sense of achievement and captivates the viewer more in the story (Scene 4). In addition, the actor tells the viewer that he/she should go on, because the actor is too exhausted from the race. In the next scene, the viewer meets a game master congratulating the viewer on his/her victory. The game master shows three possible ways that the viewer can follow (Scene 5). On the basis of cards the spectator pulls the number for the next way. By picking number three, the viewer continues on the path on a long hallway again. Attention can be directed acousitcally, as sounds come out of a room as you approach an important door. That is why acoustic elements are only executed when the viewer enters a certain area in our video (Scene 6). The test-subject hears a conversation between two people discussing how much money they should load onto their chip card. Once the viewer enters the door, he/she sees the cards charger at the end of the room and the video is finished.

Indoor Navigation Through Storytelling in Virtual Reality 235

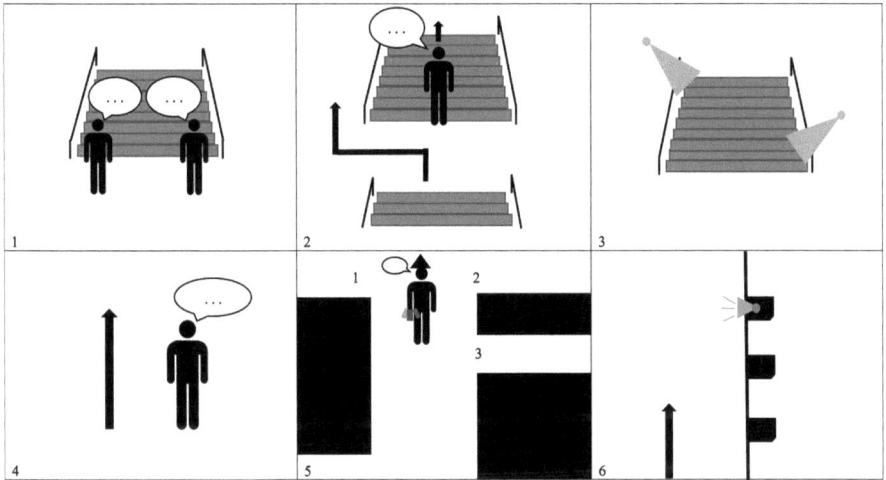

Fig. 1. Storyboard of the video with storytelling.

3.3 Participants

Subjects were recruited from students from various faculties of the University of Wuerzburg. All data used was collected at the University of Applied Sciences Wuerzburg-Schweinfurt. 30 people participated in the study. 15 people were shown the video with storytelling and the other 15 a video with the same process only without the storytelling elements such as light, acoustics or the participation of actors. Both groups then had to find their way from the university entrance to the cards charger.

3.4 Materials

The video was shot with the GoPro Fusion Black 360. It takes a video of 180° via two internal cameras and then stitches them into a 360° film. To this view, this camera also takes on spatial audio. So that subjects can watch the video, the HTC Vive Pro is used as a virtual reality glasses. Also, the subjects wear the Tobii Pro Glasses 2 eye tracking glasses for the second part of the test. This high definition camera captures a full HD video of what is happening in front of the participant, as well as its eye movements and orientation.

3.5 Process

First, the subjects got the HTC Vive Pro glasses and watched two initial videos for acclimatisation purposes. After that, both the storytelling group and the group without it got notified about the task of watching the following video and memorizing the way to the card charger. After watching the video, they answered the immersion questionnaire by Jennet et al. [17] and then set off to find their destination again. The test persons were given the eye-tracking glasses, with which we tracked their gaze behavior during the search. In addition, metrics such as the number of steps and duration for the entire search process were also collected. Finally, a concluding interview was conducted on the experiences of the entire experiment.

4 Results

The descriptive results of the experiment are shown in Table 1 and Figs. 2 and 3. The variant with storytelling was far more effective than the variant without. 93% of the subjects with storytelling have found their way back. In the conventional one, the success rate was only 66%. Even the average time and number of steps in finding the way was less in the group with storytelling than in the group without. The difference between the average of the steps is not so great because the subjects lingered on the site for a long time thinking about the way without storytelling.

It was interesting to observe that of the presented storytelling elements the junction with the game master was the most effective. From the personal interviews it has become apparent that this part was best remembered, because to the subjects this was very surprising and unexpected. By using visual and audio cues at the same time, it was easier for the viewer to take the path to the left of the stairs the actor had shown before the race started. The fact that the viewer has been told by the actor that the way is at the end of the corridor, the subjects were more easily guided by the light cues. By using spatial audio, all subjects were able to find their orientation to the right door, which made the subsequent search process easier, because they could remember which direction they were turning when hearing the sound. Participants were prompted for their thoughts and emotions on the videos by being asked to rate their experience using the immersion questionnaire [17] and rate between 1 represents 'not at all' and 5 'a lot'. When comparing the ratings, the variant with storytelling always performed better than the variant without. Many factors have contributed to better memorizing the path through storytelling. Subjects who answered the Immersion questionnaire have been given more attention by the task. The personal appeal of the actor to the user increased the involvement. The urge to win was therefore also higher and the fun factor through the various elements was also raised. Ultimately, the increased immersion and the other mentioned emotional stimuli leads to an increased motivation to find the way and remember this better than without storytelling.

Table 1. Average time and steps as well as the success rate at completion of the search process with and without storytelling.

Method	⌀ Time	⌀ Steps	Success rate
Storytelling	1:51 min	162	93%
No storytelling	2:18 min	175	66%

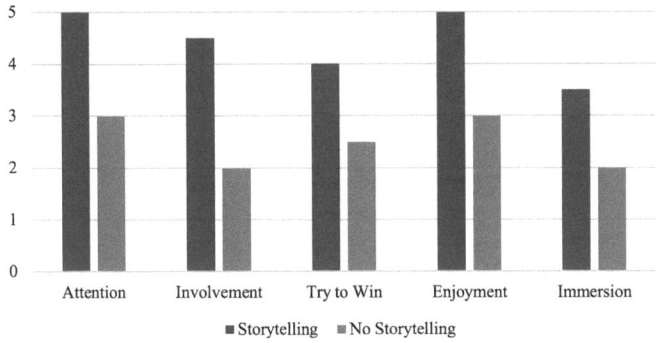

Fig. 2. Evaluation of the immersion questionnaire of the subjects with and without storytelling.

Heat maps and gaze plots are data visualizations that can reveal important data about gaze movements and their behavior. Heat charts show how the gaze spreads across the stimulus and can simultaneously represent the gaze movements of several people. Gaze plots on the other hand can represent gaze fixations and the order of gaze movements. Through data visualizations and personal interviews, we found out that, at the recollection of the path, 73% of the subjects in their head went through the video sequence. This gaze plot depicts a looking pattern for this reason.

The subjects generally viewed the game master as he spoke to them where also in both visualizations increased residence time can be determined. Afterwards, their gaze mostly went through the path ways, which are responsible for the outer viewpoints.

(a) Heat map. (b) Gaze plot.

Fig. 3. Heat map and gaze plot of the gaze samples from the scene with the game master.

5 Future Work

There are many approaches to explore. After this pretest, we will examine how sustainable the learning success of indoor navigation through storytelling is.

This means that the same subjects should each repeat the search process after longer intervals in order to test the mentioned metrics. Furthermore, we want to test the cognitive load in the learning process to find out how high the load is when remembering the way or how the interaction is when you have to remember the way and must follow a story at the same time.

In addition, one could test how effective different types of directing attention methods are in a 360° environment at each junction. A reaction test could then be used to check how quickly the attention is directed in the desired direction in order to stay on the right path.

To give the viewer more freedom to find a path, one could support the search process with interactive storytelling. The search process would no longer be limited to a single path, but would give the viewer several options for targeting. Interacting with virtual people would totally immerse a user into what might impact the learning process. The story would be co-created by the user because each action section depends on his decision and is not fixed [18].

References

1. Van Dam, A., Forsberg, A.S., Laidlaw, D.H., La Viola, J.J., Simpson, R.M.: Immersive VR for scientific visualization: a progress report. IEEE Comput. Graphics Appl. **20**(6), 26–52 (2000). https://doi.org/10.1109/38.888006
2. Sherman, W., Craig, A.: Understanding Virtual Reality: Interface Applications and Design. Morgan Kaufmann Publishers, San Francisco (2003)
3. Bucher, J.: Storytelling for Virtual Reality: Methods and Principles for Crafting Immersive Narratives. Taylor & Francis Group, New York (2017)
4. Giraldi, G., Silva, R., de Oliviera, J. C.: Introduction to Virtual Reality. LNCC Research Report (2003)
5. Pan, Z., Cheok, A.D., Yang, H., Zhu, J., Shi, J.: Virtual reality and mixed reality for virtual learning environments. Comput. Graph. **30**(1), 20–28 (2006). https://doi.org/10.1016/j.cag.2005.10.004, http://www.sciencedirect.com/science/article/pii/S0097849305002025
6. Dalgarno, B., Lee, M.J.: What are the learning affordances of 3-D virtual environments? Br. J. Educ. Technol. **41**(1), 10e32 (2010)
7. Falloon, G.: Using avatars and virtual environments in learning: what do they have to offer? Br. J. Educ. Technol. **41**(1), 108–122 (2010)
8. Yang, F., Wu, W.: The application of virtual reality in E-Learning. In: 2010 International Conference on E-Business and E-Government (2010)
9. Christopoulos, D., Mavridis, P., Andreadis, A., Karigiannis, J. N.: Using virtual environments to tell the story. In: 2011 Third International Conference on Games and Virtual Worlds for Serious Applications (2011)
10. Barret, H.: Researching and evaluating digital storytelling as a deep learning tool. In: Proceedings of SITE 2006, pp. 647–654 (2006)
11. Danilicheva, P., Klimenko, S., Baturin, Y., Serebrov, A.: Education in virtual worlds: virtual storytelling. In: 2009 International Conference on CyberWorlds (2009)
12. McGregor, I., Holmes, J.G.: How storytelling shapes memory and impressions of relationship events over time. J. Pers. Soc. Psychol. **76**(3), 403–419 (1999)

13. Schank, R.C., Abelson, R.P.: Knowledge and memory: The real story. In: Wyer Jr., R.J., (ed.) Advances in Social Cognition, vol. 8, pp. 1–86 (1995)
14. Oaks, T.: Storytelling: a natural mnemonic: a study of a storytelling method to positively influence student recall of instruction. Doctoral Dissertation, University of Tennessee, Knoxville (1995)
15. Sheikh, A., Brown, A., Watson, Z., Evans, M.: Directing attention in 360-degree Video. In: IBC 2016 Conference (2016)
16. Cai, Y., Miao, C., Tan, A.-H., Shen, Z.: A hybrid of plot-based and character-based interactive storytelling. In: Hui, K., Pan, Z., Chung, R.C., Wang, C.C.L., Jin, X., Göbel, S., Li, E.C.-L. (eds.) Edutainment 2007. LNCS, vol. 4469, pp. 260–273. Springer, Heidelberg (2007). https://doi.org/10.1007/978-3-540-73011-8_27
17. Jennett, C., et al.: Measuring and defining the experience of immersion in games. Int. J. Hum.-Comput. Stud. **66**, 641–661 (2008)
18. Handler Miller, C.: Digital Storytelling: A Creator's Guide to Interactive Entertainment. Taylor & Francis Ltd., Abingdon-on-Thames (2014)

Collaboration Technology

Accessibility in Mobile Applications of Portuguese Public Administration

Marcos Carneiro[1], Frederico Branco[2], Ramiro Gonçalves[2], Manuel Au-Yong-Oliveira[4], Fernando Moreira[5], and José Martins[2,3(✉)]

[1] University of Trás-os-Montes e Alto Douro, Vila Real, Portugal
al51388@utad.eu
[2] INESC TEC and UTAD, Vila Real, Portugal
{fbranco,ramiro,jmartins}@utad.pt
[3] Polytechnique Institute of Bragança - EsACT, Mirandela, Portugal
[4] GOVCOPP, Department of Economics, Management, Industrial Engineering and Tourism, University of Aveiro, 3810-193 Aveiro, Portugal
mao@ua.pt
[5] Research on Economics, Management and Information Technologies – REMIT, Univ Portucalense, Portucalense Institute for Legal Research – IJP, Porto, Portugal
fmoreira@upt.pt

Abstract. Today's society presents a fast development marked by the digital era, where the sharing, disclosure and access to information is made through information and communication technologies.

The use of mobile applications is growing exponentially, spreading to the most varied social classes and everyday activity areas. Worldwide, its use in the most variety of services, has been increasing significantly. Given that, it is essential that mobile applications are accessible in a way that allows access conditions and equal opportunities to all the users.

With this study we present indicators regarding the state of accessibility in mobile applications through the evaluation of five Portuguese public administration applications. The methodology used was a fully manual evaluation through a proposal of a model of evaluation divided by quantitative and qualitative requirements created by us, as well as the use of functionalities such as VoiceOver and TalkBack.

Taking into account that the study initially proposed on accessibility in mobile applications is the first to be carried out in Portugal and one of the few currently worldwide, it is believed that its content may help, in some way, to raise awareness of the state of accessibility in the Portuguese mobile applications, to create measures that make these applications more accessible to all and that this work could be taken into account in future studies of the topic.

Keywords: Accessibility · Mobile apps · Accessibility mobile apps · WCAG 2.0 · W3C · Public administration

1 Introduction

The existing literature about accessibility in the mobile apps don't show enough studies that aim the comprehension and evaluation of accessibility of the mobile apps. The fact that there aren't enough studies and knowledge about this topic, were the main factors that motivated the present article. Also, there were some other facts like the growth of the global use of these mobile devices and consequently the use of mobile apps for all kind of day-a-day activities.

According to (WHO 2018), there are more than a million people that have some sort of disabilities, what translates to 15% of the world population. In Europe, according to the data that was collected by the European Union, there are more than 80 million people in the same situation (EU-FRA 2017). In Portugal, there are more than a million people that which have some sort of disabilities, more specifically 980 thousand that can't walk or climb stairs, 27 thousand that can't see and 26 thousand that can't hear (GEP 2016).

In the current society of information its common the preoccupation of universal access to the various services through the digital environments, having as objective to improve the quality of life of the users. Although, this access may end up be conditioned because specific groups of our society may face problems of accessibility, eventually being excluded from the advantages that this new society brings. The first time that Web Accessibility was taken into consideration at European level it was in September 25 of 2001, where the theme of action plan was the "eEurope 2002" (Comissão Europeia 2014). Although, at World level, the Web Accessibility was already being referenced when W3C created in 1997 the Web Accessibility Initiative program (W3C 2009).

Relatively to the accessibility on mobile apps, this is a new topic and something where there aren't many studies to take conclusions. Also, there aren't many guidelines or requirements to be followed in order to make them accessible to everyone.

Considering the things previously said, what we pretend with this paper is to present and discuss the results of the evaluations made to the apps with an adapted approach of the WCAG 2.0 Guidelines of Web Accessibility to the mobile apps context and some good practices, contributing to the increase of knowledge of this topic.

2 Mobile Accessibility - Current State of Things

2.1 Conceptualizing Accessibility

Accessibility can be defined by the possibility of people that have some sort of disabilities, incapacities or limitations use one specific resource or product in the same way as a person without these particularities (Henry 2007).

The World Wide Web provide an abundance of services and information's to a large group of users. Her fast growth contributed to the formation for actual formation of the society highly focused on information. In the specific context of Web, Accessibility can be related to the application of concepts of the general accessibility in the digital environment, making the web and the devices useful to every user, providing maximum flexibility in order to adapt to the user's needs (Clark 2003).

To (Henry 2007), "an accessible Web means that the people with some sort of disabilities can use the Web". It is intended that people can understand, navigate and interact with the web and even contribute to the Web. Beyond this, the Web accessibility can benefit the others with some limitations like older people that with the advance of the tears they lose some of their capabilities due to aging (Thatcher et al. 2006).

2.2 Mobile Apps Accessibility

Being that the smartphones market is growing fast, there is the necessity of exploring and develop this kind of devices to meet the demand (Lecheta 2010). With that being said, we can define a smartphone as a mobile that it has evolved capabilities and characteristics of a personal computer (Santhipriya et al. 2011).

According to W3C (W3C 2017a), the mobile accessibility aims to make the websites and the apps more accessible to people with some sort of disabilities either these are using their mobile phone or other devices like tablets, digital televisions, smartwatches, among others.

To develop an application, its necessary to think how the users with disabilities or special necessities will use that application with assistive technologies. Some of other concerns are questions like the contrast and the size of the clickable zones that are very important, and their implementation and respect should be followed on the development of the apps so, it is necessary to define requirements that are fundamental to create accessible content.

2.3 Legal Rules and Regulations

World Wide Accessibility Norms and Regulation
As we previously said, to make the world more accessible to everyone it's necessary to define requirements and guidelines that must be followed. So, to achieve this, were implemented norms and regulations by various internationals organizations and countries like United Nations, EUA, European Union and Portugal.
United Nations approved on 13 of December of 2006 a convention that gives instructions to 160 countries to take measures that guarantees the access to people with disabilities on an equal basis with the others, to the information and services provided to public (Nações Unidas 2006).

EUA have some laws for accessibility like Rehabilitation law of 1973, Americans with Disabilities Act (ADA) (ADA n.d.) and the Individual with Disabilities Education Act (IDEA) (IDEA n.d.).

In European Union there are national legislations that coexists with several European legislation for accessibility like, for example, countries like France, England or Ireland have their own laws for this subject. So, the European council in 2010 propose actions like a systematic evaluation to Web services so the laws could be updated more frequently, and public services would be more accessible in 2015 for every country in Europe (Comissão Europeia 2010). In December of 2010, the ratification of the convention of the rights of people with disabilities and the adoption of WCAG 2.0 were announced (Comissão Europeia 2014). In 13 of December of 2012 the European Commission, through the proposal for a directive about accessibility on the websites of organism of the public sector, wrote in the digital agenda a set of mandatory directives, to websites of public organisms (Comissão Europeia 2012). These new rules represent a try to improve the accessibility web in the organism of the state. At 2 of December of 2016 the European Parliament and the European council published a directive called 2016/2102 related to the accessibility on the websites and the mobile apps of the organism of public sector (Parlamento Europeu and Conselho Europeu 2016).

In Portugal it was created in 1999, through the RCM 96/99 the national initiative to the citizens with special needs in the information society (DRE 1999). In June of 2000, the European council endorsed the "e-Europe 2002" action plan, covering the Portuguese initiative for the 15 European countries (Comissão Europeia 2000). In 2007 through the RCM 155/2007, it was defined that the level of conformity A of WCAG 1.0 was required for most web sites, and the AA level for thores that entail the provision of transactional services (DRE 2007). In 2012 through RCM 91/2012 and it was determined that all websites that provide only information are obligated to comply with level A of WCAG 2.0 and that all websites that provide online services are obligated to comply with AA level of WCAG 2.0 (DRE 2012). More recently, it was published a new law n°83/2018 relatively to a definition of requirements of accessibility to Websites and mobile applications of the public sector, although this law only applies in 2019 (DRE 2018).

WCAG Norms

The World Wide Web Consortium (W3C) is an non-profit organization funded in 1994 by Tim Berners-Lee having as objective "develop standards and directives that ensure the growth in a long term of the Web". (W3C 2017b). So, in 1997, this organization propose the WAI (Web Accessibility Initiative) where their main objective was to allow the access to the various websites, independently of their users needs (W3C 2009). In 1999 it was launched the first version of WCAG which contained 14 directives and several checkpoints that could be used to determine the accessibility of a web page (W3C 1999). Over the years, were emerging new Web technologies, whereby the WCAG 1.0 started to present difficulties. In order to overcome these difficulties, in 2008 was published the second version of WCAG, in which came establish the international standard introducing a change to the rules in order to make them neutral and always updated, so they created 4 basic principles (W3C 2008). The first principle is perceptible, the second one is operable, the third one is understandable, the last one is robust. In order to say that something is considered accessible, these principals must be verified, necessarily. Recently the W3C published the WCAG 2.1 which has 17 new success criteria (W3C 2018). These changes are mainly in the accessibility of Web content so there have not yet been major changes in the Accessibility of mobile applications. However, the W3C provides a section recently created for the mobile accessibility (W3C 2015). This section is still quite limited because it is an adaptation of the Web Accessibility model, and only provides informative guidelines and not necessarily requirements. As in Web Accessibility, there are 4 basic principles: perceivability, operability, comprehension, and robustness of content.

We can verify that there is work being done in this type of accessibility. However, this work ends up being reduced because great part of these criteria and guidelines are adapted from the Web Accessibility. Furthermore, Google and iOS published a set of good practices to the developers, in order to make the apps more accessible.

Android and iOS Good Practices

In addition to the previously W3C guidelines, the Google and the Apple provide a list of good practices of Accessibility on the development of the applications. In the case of Google, they present a list with some good practices that should be followed by the developers to make the applications accessible. The first one is that all applications must show some descriptive text of the user interface controls. The second one is that audio solicitation must be followed by visual solicitations. The third one says that the clickable area of elements must be bigger than 9 × 9 mm. The forth is about the contrast between background and foreground, and it should be at least 4:5:1. And the last one is for test the accessibility using the "TalkBack" (Google n.d.-a).

In the case of the Apple and the operating system they present some good practices that should be followed. The first one says to give some descriptive text to the elements of interface in order to support screen read. The second one says that is a need to notify every time that is a change in the elements of interface. And the last one is for test the accessibility using "VoiceOver" (Apple 2012).

2.4 Portuguese Perspective on Accessibility

The first studies founded about this topic are evaluations carried out by Accenture (1st Edition) and 2003 (2nd Edition) to the sites of Public Administration entities (Accenture 2003). Another study was "Relatório Vector21 sobre Acessibilidade Web em Portugal", translated "Report Vector21 about Web Accessibility in Portugal", having as objective testing web accessibility in Portugal through the analyses to a group of 200 websites of Public Administration (Vector 21 2008).

There are also several research projects that have been devoted to this subject, like for example "Avaliação da Acessibilidade dos Sítios Web das Empresas Portuguesa" (Martins 2008), "Acessibilidade dos Conteúdos Web dos Municípios Portugueses" (Fernandes 2009), "Acessibilidade Web: Ponto de situação das Maiores Empresas Portuguesas" (Gonçalves et al. 2009), "Estudo sobre o estado da Acessibilidade dos sítios Web dos estabelecimentos de Ensino superior" (Fernandes and Cardoso 2013), "A Acessibilidade das Plataformas de e-learning em Instituições de Ensino Superior Público em Portugal: Contributos Iniciais" (Tomás 2014), "Acessibilidade dos Conteúdos Web no Setor da Saúde" (Moreira 2014), "A review on the Portuguese Enterprises Web Accessibility Levels – A website accessibility high level improvement proposal" (Goncalves et al. 2014) and "AccessWeb- Uma perspective sobre a Acessibilidade Web em Portugal" (Ramiro et al. 2015).

3 Accessibility Evaluation of Mobile Applications

The guidelines for this section aren't enough and are very ambiguous so it was necessary to create a model of evaluation, presented in (Table 1), with an adaptation of the WCAG 2.0 mobile recommendations section, as well as some good practices of both operating systems and a checklist from a study (Apple n.d.-b; Google n.d.-b; W3C 2015; White 2015).

Table 1. Adaptation of WCAG 2.0 mobile guidelines, iOS and Google good practices and thesis model (Apple n.d.-b; Google n.d.-b; W3C 2015; White 2015).

Requirements	Context	Reference
Quantitative requirement/Guidelines		
REQ01	Size of the buttons of action < 9 × 9 mm	W3C Mobile and Google/iOS
REQ02	Size of selected text < 9 × 9 mm	W3C Mobile and Google/iOS
REQ03	Spacing < 2 mm	W3C Mobile and Google/iOS
REQ04	Contrast Errors AA (ratio 4.5:1)	W3C Mobile
REQ05	Contrast Errors AAA (ratio 7:1)	W3C Mobile
Qualitative requirements/Guidelines		
REQ06	Increase the size of the text	W3C Mobile
REQ07	Do zoom	W3C Mobile
REQ08	Color to grayscale	Thesis Model
REQ09	Invert the colors	Thesis Model
REQ10	Remove the color of emphasized information	Thesis Model
REQ11	Compatibility with the TalkBack	Google
REQ11A	Compatibility with the VoiceOver	Thesis Model and iOS
REQ12	Supports both orientations	W3C Mobile
REQ13	Non-textual content also available in a text form	Thesis Model
REQ14	Clear indication that the elements are actionable	W3C Mobile
REQ15	Use of simple and direct language	Thesis Model and iOS/Google

3.1 Evaluation Procedure

There are in the market a wide variety of Android devices either in terms of sizes, of display, thickness, among others. Unlike Android smartphones, iPhones exist in limited models and are controlled by the same provider which in some way limits the differences in terms of characteristics between these devices. The tests on the two devices were made according to the following circumstances: same level of intensity and environment brightness and operating system not too outdated. In terms of requirements for the selection of the devices, there weren't any because the main objective with this study was to obtain results and an idea of the state of this kind of accessibility and not making a comparison between both operating systems. In the table Table 2 are the characteristics of both devices used in this study:

Table 2. Mobile devices characteristics

Device	OS	Display	CPU	Weight	Year
Vodafone Smart Prime 7	Android 6.0.1	720 × 1280p and 5'	1.8 Ghz	120 g	2016
iPhone 4S	iOS 9.3.5	960 × 640p and 3,5'	1 Ghz	140 g	2011

Relatively to the evaluation method used in the present work, it was done through a manual evaluation with the help of two functionalities each one present in the respective device and one application to make the contrast evaluation.

We used the model previously mentioned, as well as a Likert scale from 1 to 7 for the quantitative evaluation where the classification 1 corresponds to the minimum of the evaluation and the 7 to the maximum (Harry et al. 2012). In addition, it was necessary to use a qualitative evaluation to some requirements that couldn't be quantified (Wainer 2018). We used a verification of these requirements in both systems and posteriorly presented some consequences of the disrespect of these requirements. device.

3.2 Tools/Functionalities for Evaluating Accessibility of Mobile Apps

The tools of automatic evaluation of accessibility were created to assist the developers of websites and mobile applications to apply simplicity the directives of accessibility (Ivory et al. 2003). Although there are many tools to do an automatic evaluation of web accessibility, there aren't any capable of doing a complete evaluation of the mobile applications accessibility. However there is a tool called Accessibility Scanner developed by Google that only evaluates some requirements of the different parts of an application through screenshots (Google n.d.-d).

Since there aren't any tools capable of doing an automatic and complete evaluation of the accessibility in the mobile applications, we used the functionalities presented on both systems (TalkBack and VoiceOver). The TalkBack was developed by Google and is a screen reader that allows the user to handle the device without being able to see the display (Google n.d.-c). The VoiceOver was developed by Apple and communicates with the user giving information about what his touching or pressing (Apple n.d.-a).

For the contrast evaluation we used the color contrast application developed by UserLight and uses the WCAG 2.0 directives with regard to contrast of level AA and level AAA (UserLight n.d.).

3.3 Target Group

To these evaluations, there were considered 5 applications of the Portuguese public administration. The first one was the MySNS from National Health Service and has as main objective to allow the users to consult health information and news (SNS n.d.). The second one was IRS 2017 from Tax Authority and has as main objective to allow the users to do and give the tax documents through the mobile device (Autoridade Tributária n.d.). The third one was MyAdse from ADSE and has as main objective to simplify all the available services through a digital card (ADSE n.d.). The fourth was the iMetro of Porto from metro of Porto and has as main objective to provide real time schedules, frequencies and state of the lines (Metro do Porto n.d.). The last one was the município of Vila Real developed by the municipality and has as main objective to provide information regarding future events, contacts and points of interest of the city (CMVilaReal n.d.).

4 Mobile Apps Accessibility Evaluation Results

As mentioned before, these evaluations were divided by quantitative and qualitative requirements. Firstly, we evaluated all the quantitative requirements in the iOS operating system through the VoiceOver functionality. All the classifications can be observed on the Table 3.

Table 3. Classification of the quantitative requirements on the iOS system

Requirements	MySNS	Municipio of Vila Real	MyADSE	iMetro of Porto	IRS 2017
Size of clickable areas < 9 mm	1	5	1	5	6
Size of action buttons < 9 mm	2	6	4	6	6
Spacing	1	2	1	1	3
Contrast AA	1	1	2	2	3
Contrast AAA	1	1	1	1	1
Total	1	3	2	3	4

We can verify that in the evaluation of the quantitative requirements on the iOS system, the app IRS 2017 obtained the best classification and the app MySNS obtained the worst classification.

Relatively to the evaluation of the quantitative requirements on the Android system, we can observe the results on the Table 4.

Table 4. Classification of the quantitative requirements on the Android system

Requirements	MySNS	Municipio of Vila Real	MyADSE	iMetro of Porto	IRS 2017
Size of clickable areas < 9 mm	1	3	1	6	4
Size of action buttons < 9 mm	3	6	6	6	7
Spacing	1	4	1	5	5
Contrast AA	1	1	2	5	3
Contrast AAA	1	1	1	1	1
Total	1	3	2	5	4

We can verify that in the Android system the application iMetro of Porto obtained the best classification and the application MySNS obtained the worst classification.

After all the quantitative questions were evaluated, we proceed to the qualitative ones. In the Table 5, are the results of the evaluation on iOS system

Table 5. Classification of the qualitative requirements on the iOS system

Requirements	Verification	
	Yes	No
REQ06	1	4
REQ07	0	5
REQ08	0	5
REQ09	0	5
REQ10	0	5
REQ11A	1	4
REQ12	0	5
REQ13	2	3
REQ14	5	0
REQ15	3	2

Analyzing the results on the iOS system, we can verify that there aren't any extra functionalities that allows the user to increase the size of the text, making zoom, convert to grayscale, invert the colors or take the colors of emphasized text with the exception of Municipio of Vila Real that allows the user to increase the size of the text. Relatively to the compatibility with the VoiceOver functionality, we can verify that only one app is totally compatible with this functionality. Regarding the support of both orientations, we can verify that none of the apps support both orientations. We can also notice that all the applications provide information on the most relevant elements like buttons and links. Lastly, we can verify that the apps that presented more errors on the quantitative requirements are the ones that have more pages and information on their applications.

Then we have on Table 6 the results of the qualitative evaluation on the Android system.

Table 6. Classification of the qualitative requirements on the android system

Requirements	Verification	
	Yes	No
REQ06	1	4
REQ07	0	5
REQ08	0	5
REQ09	0	5
REQ10	0	5
REQ11	1	4
REQ12	0	5
REQ13	1	4
REQ14	5	0
REQ15	3	2

In a first look we can verify that the results are very similar to the iOS ones. This is justified by the fact that the interfaces of the applications on both systems are the same, with the exception of the iMetro of Porto.

For the functionalities issues, we can verify that all the apps don't provide any of them with exception of the Municipio of Vila Real that gives us a functionality that allow us to increase the size of the text. Relatively to the compatibility with the TalkBack functionality, we can verify that only one application is completely compatible with this functionality. In the requirement of the support of the app on both orientations (landscape and portrait) we can verify that none of them supports both orientations. The only orientation of this applications is the portrait one what may difficult the handling of these apps. Relatively to the text availability for non-text content, only one application fully covers them. The other apps have issues on the buttons and menus. Regarding if the app provides clear information that the elements are clickable, we can notice that all the apps provide this information on the most relevant elements like buttons and links. Lastly, and like we previously said, we can verify that the apps that presented more errors on the quantitative requirements are the ones that have more pages and information on their applications.

5 Results Discussion

In a deep analysis, we can say that the results that we collected from all applications are a reflection of the state of the public administration mobile apps in Portugal. In general, we can affirm that the results obtained are unsatisfactory, observing low classifications and disrespect of most of qualitative requirements. With this, we can say that there is still a lot of work to do in order to make the applications accessible to all. In a particular way, we can say that, in the quantitative questions, the requirements with the worsts classifications were the contrast ones followed by the spacing errors. The ones that presented the best results were the clickable areas and buttons size errors. Relatively to the qualitative questions, we can verify that there isn't in any application (with exception of Municipio of Vila Real) that has implemented the several functionalities like zoom, increase the size of the text, greyscale. Also, all the apps in both systems, don't support both orientations.

Between both Android and iOS systems, we can conclude that in a global way the results are very similar. This can be justified by the simple reason that all the interfaces and information of the applications are the same in both systems as well as the detection of the areas of these and the menus, with the exception of iMetro of Porto.

Also, it should be noted that the applications that obtained the worsts classifications in the different requirements are the ones that have a huge number of pages and information.

6 Conclusions

Although we had some limitations, the main objective was achieved, and got a view of the actual state of the accessibility in the applications of Portuguese Public Administration. Relatively to the limitations, these were related to the fact that there aren't legal requirements to be followed, as well as there aren't any tools or applications that can do a fully automatic evaluation of accessibility of mobile applications on both systems. It was necessary to make a fully manual evaluation through an adapted model evaluation model. Also, it was necessary to define a new evaluation system since we couldn't evaluate the quantitative requirements with the WCAG methods. It was also necessary to make manual evaluations of all apps with the help of the functionalities presented in both systems (Voice Over and Talkback). For the qualitative requirements we did a verification, on both systems, to know that they had or not a certain requirement.

Since there are many organizations and causes to help and improve life of people with disabilities and with the technological improvement, it was expected better results in terms of accessibility on these applications.

With this being said and looking to the results that we obtained, we can conclude that there is much work to be done in order to make the mobile applications accessible to all. The good practices announced by the Android and Apple as well as the recommendations presented by W3C to the accessibility on mobile apps are still very limited and there's still a lot of room to improve.

6.1 Theoretical Implications

In Portugal the accessibility in mobile applications is, until now, a topic where aren't many studies so, the results and conclusions about the actual state of accessibility is something new. Even if we search about this topic all over the world, there aren't enough studies to take the proper conclusions and compare results. So, with this being said, we couldn't compare these results with any study as well as use some eventual methodology to evaluate these apps.

6.2 Practical Implications

So, with the collected results, we can conclude that the mobile applications of the Portuguese public administration have an unsatisfactory level of accessibility. This has consequences, like for instance people with some sort of difficulties can have problems when trying to handle these applications or can't even handle it at all. That is, these people are being somewhat excluded from these technological worlds.

6.3 Final Considerations

The principal objective of this work was, although with some limitations, achieved, where five applications of the Portuguese Public Administration were evaluated. Two of the main reasons for these limitations were the fact that there aren't any legal requirements to be followed in this particularity, as well as the fact that there aren't any applications or tools that make a fully automatic evaluation of the accessibility in the mobile apps. In terms of recommendations, and addition to those presented on the proposal model of evaluation, it is necessary to do a larger study about this topic, is also needed to extend the actual monitorization of accessibility to the mobile applications and also an adoption of some legislations that promotes this accessibility on the applications.

References

Accenture: Relatório final: Avaliação externa de web sites dos organismos da administração directa e indirecta do estado (segunda ed.). Unidade de Missão Inovação e Conhecimento da Presidência do Conselho de Ministros, Lisboa (2003)

ADA: The Americans with Disabilities Act of 1990 and Revised ADA Regulations Implementing Title II and Title III (n.d.)

ADSE: Já conhece a app MyADSE? (n.d.). https://www2.adse.pt/myadse/

Apple: Accessibility Programming Guide for iOS (2012). https://developer.apple.com/library/archive/documentation/UserExperience/Conceptual/iPhoneAccessibility/Making_Application_Accessible/Making_Application_Accessible.html#//apple_ref/doc/uid/TP40008785-CH102-SW5

Apple: Accessibility: VoiceOver (n.d.-a). https://www.apple.com/accessibility/iphone/vision/

Apple: Testing for Accessibility on OS X: Using the Accessibility Inspector (n.d.-b). https://developer.apple.com/library/archive/documentation/Accessibility/Conceptual/AccessibilityMacOSX/OSXAXTestingApps.html

Autoridade Tributária: IRS 2017 (n.d.). https://play.google.com/store/apps/details?id=pt.gov.portaldasfinancas.irs&hl=pt_PT

Clark, J.: Understanding Web accessibility (2003). https://joeclark.org/access/webaccess/JVoluntAdmin.html

CMVilaReal: Município de Vila Real (n.d.). https://play.google.com/store/apps/details?id=com.goodbarber.agendacmvr

Comissão Europeia: eEurope 2002: Projecto de Plano de Acção (2000). https://eur-lex.europa.eu/legal-content/pt/TXT/PDF/?uri=CELEX:52000DC0330&rid=13

Comissão Europeia: COMUNICAÇÃO DA COMISSÃO AO PARLAMENTO EUROPEU, AO CONSELHO, AO COMITÉ ECONÓMICO E SOCIAL EUROPEU E AO COMITÉ DAS REGIÕES: Uma Agenda Digital para a Europa (2010). https://eur-lex.europa.eu/LexUriServ/LexUriServ.do?uri=COM:2010:0245:FIN:PT:HTML

Comissão Europeia: Comunicado de Imprensa IP/12/1305 (2012). www.europa.eu/rapid/press-release_IP-12-1305_pt.pdf

Comissão Europeia: EU Policy (2014). https://ec.europa.eu/ipg/standards/accessibility/eu_policy/index_en.htm

DRE: PRESIDÊNCIA DO CONSELHO DE MINISTROS: Resolução do Conselho de Ministros n.º 96/99 (1999). https://arquivo.pt/wayback/20170823011153/https://www.umic.pt/images/stories/publicacoes/RCM%2096%2099.pdf

DRE: Resolução do Conselho de Ministros n.º 155/2007 (2007). https://dre.pt/pesquisa-avancada/-/asearch/642547/details/maximized?perPage=100&anoDR=2007&types=SERIEI&search=Pesquisar

DRE: Resolução do Conselho de Ministros n.º 91/2012 (2012). https://dre.pt/web/guest/pesquisa/-/search/191863/details/normal?l=1

DRE: Decreto-Lei n.º 83/2018 (2018). https://dre.pt/web/guest/pesquisa/-/search/116734769/details/normal?l=1&fbclid=IwAR0h2e9QPRkVVm-cDoFWuCv46sJfq6l1pGQ79xuB0nOtO3HF8PhxRZanM_M

EU-FRA: People with disabilities (2017). https://fra.europa.eu/en/theme/people-disabilities

Fernandes, J.: Acessibilidade dos conteúdos web dos municípios portugueses (2009)

Fernandes, J., Cardoso, C.: Estudo sobre o estado da acessibilidade dos sítios web dos estabelecimentos de ensino superior (2013)

GEP: Estatísticas sobre Deficiências ou Incapacidades (2016). https://oddh.iscsp.ulisboa.pt/index.php/pt/2013-04-24-18-50-23/outras-publicacoes/item/281-estat%C3%ADsticas-sobre-defici%C3%AAncias-ou-incapacidades

Goncalves, R., Martins, J., Branco, F.: A review on the Portuguese enterprises web accessibility levels - a website accessibility high level improvement proposal. In: 5th International Conference on Software Development and Technologies for Enhancing Accessibility and Fighting Info-Exclusion, Dsai 2013, 27, pp. 176–185 (2014). https://doi.org/10.1016/j.procs.2014.02.021

Gonçalves, R., Pereira, J., Martins, J., Martins, J., Branco, F.: Acessibilidade web: Ponto de situação das maiores empresas portuguesas. Paper presented at the APDSI (2009)

Google: Accessibility (n.d.-a). https://google-developer-training.gitbooks.io/android-developer-advanced-course-concepts/content/unit-3-make-your-apps-accessible/lesson-6-accessibility/6-1-c-accessibility/6-1-c-accessibility.html

Google: Accessibility: Material Design (n.d.-b). https://material.io/design/usability/accessibility.html

Google: Get started on Android with TalkBack (n.d.-c). https://support.google.com/accessibility/android/answer/6283677?hl=pt

Google: Primeiros passos com o Scanner de acessibilidade (n.d.-d). https://support.google.com/accessibility/android/answer/6376570?hl=pt-BR

Harry, N., Boone, J., Boone, D.A.: Analyzing likert data. J. Extension **50**, 1–3 (2012)

Henry, S.L.: Accessibility in User-Centered Design: What is Accessibility? (2007). https://www.uiaccess.com/accessucd/background.html

IDEA: Statute and Regulations (n.d.). https://sites.ed.gov/idea/statuteregulations/

Ivory, M.Y., Mankoff, J., Le, A.: Using automated tools to improve web site usage by users with diverse abilities. Hum.-Comput. Interact. Inst. **1**(3), 117 (2003)

Lecheta, R.R.: Google Android: aprebda a criar aplicações para dispositivos móveis com o Android SDK. Novatec, São Paulo (2010)

Martins, J.L.B.: Avaliação de acessibilidade dos sítios web das empresas portuguesas. UTAD (2008)

Metro do Porto: iMetro do Porto: a nova aplicação mobile grátis (n.d.). https://www.metrodoporto.pt/frontoffice/pages/513?news_id=237

Moreira, P.: Acessibilidade dos contéudos web no setor da saúde (2014)

Nações Unidas: Convention on the Rights of Persons with Disabilities and Optional Protocol (2006). https://www.un.org/disabilities/documents/convention/convoptprot-e.pdf

Parlamento Europeu and Conselho Europeu: Directive (EU) 2016/2102 of the European Parliament and of the Council of 26 October 2016 on the accessibility of the websites and mobile applications of public sector bodies (2016). https://eur-lex.europa.eu/legal-content/EN/TXT/?qid=1481550842681&uri=CELEX:32016L2102

Ramiro, G., Jorge, P., José, M., Frederico, B., Carlos, P.: Acessweb–uma perspetiva sobre a acessibilidade web em portugal (2015)

Santhipriya, S., Sastry, B., Akshitha, K.: Securing smartphone apps in online environment. Int. J. Math. Arch. (IJMA) **2**, 2462–2469 (2011)

SNS: MySNS – SNS (n.d.). https://www.sns.gov.pt/apps/mysns/

Thatcher, J., Henry, S., et al.: Web Accessibility: Web Standards and Regulatory Compliance. friends of ED (2006)

Tomás, C.: A acessibilidade das plataformas de e-learning em instituições de ensino público em portugal: contributos iniciais (2014). https://www.panoramaelearning.pt/wp-content/uploads/2014/04/AcessibilidadeElearningESPP.pdf

UserLight: Color Contrast (n.d.). https://itunes.apple.com/na/app/color-contrast/id1095478187

Vector 21: Relatório vector21 sobre acessibilidade web em portugal (2008). https://www.vector21.com/?idc=27&idi=4953

W3C: Web Content Accessibility Guidelines 1.0 (1999). https://www.w3.org/TR/WAI-WEBCONTENT/

W3C: Web Content Accessibility Guidelines (WCAG) 2.0 (2008). https://www.w3.org/TR/WCAG20/

W3C: WAI early days (2009). https://www.w3.org/WAI/history

W3C: Mobile Accessibility: How WCAG 2.0 and Other W3C/WAI Guidelines Apply to Mobile (2015). https://www.w3.org/TR/mobile-accessibility-mapping/

W3C: Mobile Accessibility at W3C (2017a). https://www.w3.org/WAI/standards-guidelines/mobile/

W3C: W3C Mission (2017b). https://www.w3.org/Consortium/mission

W3C: Web Content Accessibility Guidelines (WCAG) 2.1 (2018). https://www.w3.org/TR/WCAG21/

Wainer, J.: Métodos de pesquisa quantitativa e qualitativa para a Ciência da Computação (2018)

White, K.: Determining Accessibility for iOS Applications: Piloting a Checklist for Practitioners. University of Wisconsin-Milwaukee (2015). https://dc.uwm.edu/cgi/viewcontent.cgi?article=2096&context=etd

WHO: Disability and health (2018). https://www.who.int/mediacentre/factsheets/fs352/en/

Toward Improving Situation Awareness and Team Coordination in Emergency Response with Sensor and Video Data Streams

Samantha Dubrow[✉] and Brenda Bannan

George Mason University, Fairfax, VA 22030, USA
{sdubrow, bbannan}@gmu.edu

Abstract. Emergency response teams must coordinate their actions and goals in dynamic and demanding situations to ensure patient health and safety. It is a major challenge to measure and model such dynamic phenomenon under real world conditions. However, measuring coordination in real world conditions is necessary to better understand how teams function and to enhance their individual situation awareness, coordination, and learning. The use of sensor-based and video-based behavioral measurement of coordination within and between teams has been a suggested method for continuously recording dynamic, physical behavioral data streams related to proximity, movement or positioning to inform the team. However, very few studies have attempted to implement unobtrusive sensor-based data collection, especially in messy and challenging conditions. If we are to truly embrace the dynamic and complex nature of team-based behaviors and learning with new forms of data collection such as unobtrusive sensors, digital video and audio, we need to better understand the reality of the difficulties of collecting, processing and integrating these multiple digital data streams in real time to generate meaning in demanding, continually evolving, real world contexts such as emergency response. In the current paper, we strive to advance our understanding of the ground truth of leveraging sensor-based and other digital data streams to identify valid constructs, uncover meaningful indicators, and target relevant combinations of digital data streams to visualize and improve understanding of how teams coordinate and learn in team environments.

Keywords: Learning · Situation awareness · Unobtrusive measures · Sensors · Training · Emergency response

1 Introduction

Emergency response teams need to coordinate their actions and goals in dynamic and demanding situations to ensure patient health and safety. Unfortunately, Measuring and modeling the dynamic phenomenon of coordination in large groups under real world conditions is a major challenge. Modeling coordination is critical to develop a better understand how teams work together and function, enhancing situation awareness, learning, and performance. A progressive step toward examining the processes and performance of emergency response teams is to gather information during in-situ simulations, or, ideally, during live events.

If we are to truly embrace the dynamic and complex nature of team-based behaviors and learning, new forms of data collection such as unobtrusive sensors, digital video and audio should be utilized. We need to understand the reality of the difficulties of collecting, processing and integrating these multiple digital data streams in real-time to generate meaning in demanding, continually evolving contexts such as emergency response. Challenges faced in complex environments such as those with emergency response teams are exacerbated when multiple teams across multiple agencies must come together for a unified response. Interdependent networks of teams that work together toward a common goal are referred to as *multiteam systems (MTSs*; Mathieu et al. 2001; Zaccaro et al. 2012).

MTSs, particularly those that are comprised of teams from multiple agencies (i.e., *external MTSs*; Zaccaro et al. 2012), will benefit from continuous learning both during simulations and during live events. MTS learning is expected to promote situation awareness and a shared understanding across component teams. While learning and training have been studied briefly in empirical studies of MTSs (e.g., Anania et al. 2017; Firth et al. 2015; McGuire 2016), research is limited and deserves further attention. To date, there are no studies of MTSs that utilize truly unobtrusive measures to collect and share critical information about between-team coordination or situation awareness, both of which are critical for performance (Davison et al. 2012; DeChurch and Marks 2006; Flestea et al. 2017). MTS learning and situation awareness are dependent on collecting relevant information and getting the right people the right information at the right time.

The primary purpose of this paper is to consider best practices and next steps for utilizing unobtrusive sensor-based and video data streams to promote processes and outcomes of interest in emergency response MTSs (Feese et al. 2013; Kranzfelder et al. 2011; Olguin et al. 2009). We strive to advance our understanding of the ground truth of leveraging sensor-based and other digital data streams to measure variables with high content validity (i.e., data that represent what we intend for them to represent; Haynes et al. 1995). Uncovering meaningful indicators and targeting relevant combinations of digital data streams, and subsequently visualizing the data collected, could result in a vastly improved understanding of how teams coordinate and learn in MTSs, and hence suggest how to maximize emergency response performance. To truly improve the effectiveness and learning of MTSs in emergency response providers such as fire-and-rescue, police, and emergency medical personnel in real world conditions with multiple sensor-based digital data streams, we need to better understand how to meaningfully and reliably collect, integrate and visualize this data in real-time in demanding real world contexts.

In this paper, we begin by elaborating on the complexity of emergency response contexts, and the challenges faced by external (i.e., interagency) MTSs attempting to coordinate under strict time constraints. Then, we introduce the concepts of MTS learning and MTS situation awareness, focusing on how these constructs relate to performance in emergency response MTSs performed in a live simulation exercise. The limited existing literature on the use of unobtrusive sensor data and video data to study team-based behaviors is reviewed, and key considerations for future use of such measures are explained. Finally, notable challenges and recommendations for researchers, technologists, and public safety personnel are offered.

2 Emergency Response Multiteam System Contexts

Large emergency situations that require teams from multiple agencies (e.g., fire, police, and EMS) to work together range from multi-vehicle accidents to active shooter events. Typically, there are protocols for how the teams should interact with one another and for how command and control is structured (e.g., InterAgency Board 2015). For example, when there is a large multi-vehicle car accident, teams from fire, police, and EMS agencies come together to respond (see Fig. 1). Figure 1 illustrates four fire teams with four members each, three police cars with two members each, and three ambulances with two members each, who are all dispatched to the scene. The number of response teams is dependent on the severity of the accident. Additionally, a battalion chief, a police chief, and an EMS captain all arrive and act as a unified operational leadership team. The fire teams each report to the battalion chief, the police teams report to the police chief, and the ambulance teams report to the EMS captain.

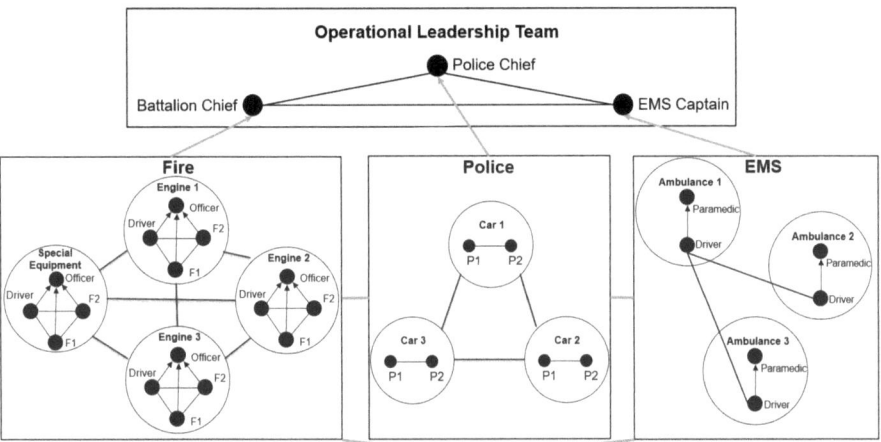

Fig. 1. Multi-vehicle car accident emergency response MTS example. Adapted from Dubrow, S., Shulman, M., Torres, E., Dobbins, C, Zaccaro, S, and Bannan, B. (2018). Leader roles and shifts in crisis management multiteam systems. Symposium presented at the 33rd Annual Conference of the Society for Industrial and Organizational Psychology, Chicago, IL.

While interdependencies and leadership structures across emergency response systems may seem standardized and relatively simple, coordination between teams can still be a challenge in every event. First responders work in situations that are complex, physically and cognitively demanding, time urgent, mission critical, and change quickly over time. Additionally, even external MTSs with only a few teams face coordination challenges beyond those faced by teams that are all from the same agency, due to differences in working norms, communication techniques, culture, competencies, and training. These differences can create boundaries between the teams that keep them from coordinating and performing optimally (Luciano et al. 2018; Mathieu et al. 2018). Each agency also uses different technology and radio channels to communicate. While differences in technology systems may seem like an easy problem to solve, first responders often report that they are often hampered by use of the same communication technology or radio channels because at times, hearing each other's communication lines can be more distracting than helpful.

Before we can begin resolving the technological challenges faced by emergency response MTSs, we need to dedicate our efforts to learning more about the specific processes of coordination, learning, and situation awareness they experience. Only then can we consider the use of unobtrusive sensor-based measures and video data that will allow us to collect granular information without disrupting the teams while they work. Significant observation and study through a sustained contextual analysis efforts are needed to deeply understand the context of the work of these teams, can thorough and accurate suggestions be made to enhance future performance. Despite this call for the use of unobtrusive measures of team behavior, very few studies that exist have attempted to implement this form of data collection, especially in messy and challenging real-world conditions such as emergency response live simulations. Thus, we need to understand the reality of the difficulties of identifying relevant constructs as well as collecting, processing and integrating these valid multiple digital data streams in real-time to generate meaning in demanding, continually evolving, real world contexts such as emergency response.

3 MTS Learning and Situation Awareness

MTS learning and situation awareness are two critical factors affecting MTS performance (Firth et al. 2015; Flestea et al. 2017). Thus, we should carefully consider unobtrusive measures that will capture these phenomena. In Mathieu et al. 2001, Marks, Mathieu, and Zaccaro suggested that team performance is influence by both team processes (e.g., team behaviors including learning, information sharing, and coordinating) and emergent states (e.g., shared conditions including situation awareness, cohesion, and collective cognition). Both processes and emergent states can develop and change over time to influence performance. In this paper, we consider learning and situation awareness as the process and emergent state, respectively, that should be measured through the use of unobtrusive sensors and video to provide MTSs with the information they need to increase future performance.

3.1 MTS Learning

Team learning behaviors include processing new information, generating knowledge, decision-making based on experience, problem solving, and adjusting behavior to improve performance (Edmondson et al. 2001; Hirst et al. 2009). In MTSs, learning includes engaging in these behaviors both within and between teams. Typically, MTS learning behaviors in emergency response contexts will occur through collaboration between agency leaders (e.g., the battalion chief, police chief, and EMS captain). Thus, unobtrusive measures of learning should likely focus on the interactions between component team leaders and their agency-level leaders, as well as the interactions between the agency leaders. Learning is highly contextualized, and before unobtrusive measures can be used for data collection, the first step for ensuring content validity is to operationalize what the construct of interest (in this case, MTS learning) will occur in the specific situation being studied.

MTS learning likely results in MTS situation awareness. As teams and their leaders encode and share new information about the environment and how to interact with the other teams in the situation, a stronger collective understanding of the MTS environment and how to act within it should emerge (Edmondson 1999; Fischer et al. 2018; Waring et al. 2018).

3.2 MTS Situation Awareness

At the individual level, situation awareness has been defined as a strong understanding of the task environment, current level of goal accomplishment, and strong predictions of future performance on the task (Endsley 1995). In MTSs, situation awareness is a "compilational emergent state that describes the task-related knowledge that becomes activated within the MTS at a particular time, and is necessary for performing the goal directed" (Flestea et al. 2017, p. 46). The strength and accuracy of MTS-level situation awareness is dependent on both individual and team situation awareness.

Teams that do not maintain an accurate understanding of their MTS environment are unlikely to have strong situation awareness (Flestea et al. 2017). As emergencies grow larger in size, severity, and urgency, MTS shared situation awareness becomes increasingly important for coordination and performance. MTS processes such as learning and information sharing can improve situation awareness in many cases, but it is important to understand the conditions under which those processes are able to occur. There are still many questions around how situation awareness is built and maintained in MTSs, with only one empirical paper to date (i.e., Flestea et al. 2017). Fleastea and colleagues (Flestea et al. 2017) found that MTSs with leaders who do not provide clear direction and with poor coordination processes have trouble developing strong shared situation awareness. Unobtrusive sensor and video data are ideal for collecting information seamlessly during an in-situ simulation or during a live event to identify the within - and between-team behaviors that can potentially provide evidence of MTS learning and situation awareness to improve future training, protocols, and ultimately, performance.

4 Unobtrusive Sensor-Based and Video Data Streams

Ensuring content validity of new measures of MTS behaviors and states requires several steps. Additionally, as we collect more data from a greater number of streams with a greater number of data points per minute, researchers and technologists should consider how to ensure the data is digestible, interpretable, and usable. In a recent interview conducted in 2018, a retired Commanding Officer in the Navy stated that in his 26 years in the Navy he never once wished to have *less* information about the situation he was in. Therefore, the question is, how can we collect as much useful information as possible while ensuring data quality and interpretability without creating information overload for users.

The first step is to operationalize what the constructs of interest (e.g., MTS learning and situation awareness) may look like in emergency response MTS settings. Second, researchers and technologists should decide what sensors they are going to use to make inferences about those constructs, and what information they intend to collect from each sensor. After data is collected, it needs to be processed in near real-time and meaningfully integrated quickly and effectively. Finally, data should be visualized and presented in a way that is easily interpretable and relevant to users during live events and/or during after-action reviews.

The goal is to employ the data collected to better understand observable behaviors that represent MTS learning and MTS situation awareness during an in-situ simulation or live event. Not all technologies currently available can be seamlessly integrated and interpreted quickly and seamlessly as imagined in near real-time given latency and delay of some sensor information processing at the time this paper is being written, so a more tangible goal might be for research teams to strive for optimal capture, process and integrate data possible for use during an after-action review.

4.1 Step 1: Operationalize Constructs of Interest

The first step for leveraging unobtrusive measures of behavior is to operationalize how those behaviors are expressed. For example, team learning has been associated with distinctive behaviors such as communicating knowledge with teammates, encoding new information, problem solving and decision making, seeking alternatives to current routines, and adjusting actions based on new information (Edmondson 1999; Edmondson et al. 2001; Fischer et al. 2018; Hirst et al. 2009; Van den Bossche et al. 2006). These behaviors are typically studied using self-report surveys of learning and human observation, but real-time unobtrusive sensors and video capture far more detailed information that may not be within team members' conscious awareness.

Similarly, situation awareness has been described as a shared perception and understanding of the current situation, shared predictions and expectations of the future of the team and its performance, (Endsley 1995; Shrestha et al. 1995 Kranzfelder et al. 2011) were the first to utilize radiofrequency identification (RFID) measures to capture situation awareness. As with emergency response situations, one might expect that surgical teams should be highly standardized, and therefore measuring situation awareness should be a relatively simple task. However, Kranzfelder et al. (2011) found that modeling situation awareness is still "extremely challenging" (p. 697).

There are many benefits to utilizing unobtrusive measures of MTS behavior. However, this is not to say that traditional measures such as self-report are still not important (Chan 2009). Every measure, whether it be collected via a retroactive self-report survey or an unobtrusive sensor, constitutes only a proxy for the construct of interest (Dubrow et al. 2017). In other words, the researchers are attempting to capture how and when MTS learning and situation awareness occur, however, there will never be a perfect measure of cognitive processes or states. Therefore, triangulation of multiple data streams, including both prior and new measures of the same construct, should help to enhance content validity to ensure that what is being measured is what is intended to be measured.

The example of MTS learning and situation awareness is an important one, as their definitions and operationalizations can seem fairly similar. They are differentiated by the fact that learning is a process through which individuals and teams are encoding new information and changing their actions accordingly, whereas situation awareness is the state in which teams share an understanding of the status of the MTS and the likelihood of its future performance. The theoretical distinction between MTS learning and situation awareness is important, and thus high-quality measures of the constructs should also be able to differentiate between them. Therefore, identified patterns or a change in activity related to provided information, action or state of teams detected through continuous streams of data might be important information to capture and distinguish related to these constructs of interest.

4.2 Step 2: Choose Data Collection Streams

Once constructs of interest are operationalized, the second step is to align data collection streams. Researchers and technologists should consider what other researchers have done in the past (e.g., RFID and barcode registration for automatic detection of situation awareness; Kranzfelder et al. 2011) and determine what new forms of data collection or combination of data streams could provide additional information for a particular construct and still be viable. There are only a few sensor-based measures of team behaviors that have been studied by previous researchers to date. Such data streams have mostly focused on generating spatial or temporal information, and have been used to inform both behaviors and outcomes. Measures of effort, coordination, and communication include the amount, intensity, and variability of physical activity captured by seamlessly by proximity sensors and other devices (Feese et al. 2013; Olguín et al. 2009). Outcomes including effectiveness and performance depend heavily on the context of interest (e.g., emergency response, patient safety) and have included calculating the length of a patient's stay in a hospital and number of delays in their care, which were tracked by GPS, video, proximity between care providers and the patient, and proximity between care providers and their teammates (Dubrow et al. 2017; Feese et al. 2013; Olguín et al., 2009). Sociometric badges have also been used to track team member interactions including speech, tone, and direction of communications (e.g., Rosen et al. 2014). Existing measures can be considered as a base from which to build new and improved sensor-based measures that can withstand the complexities and challenges of emergency situations and detect behaviors with high reliability and validity.

Orvis et al. (2013) introduced *The Rational Approach to Developing Systems-based Measures (RADSM)*, which consists of six steps for developing measures of individual and team behaviors that utilize scientific theory, the availability of data, and how data collected will be analyzed. In addition to creating unobtrusive sensor-based measures, the RADSM approach ensures that data collected will be useful for measuring specific constructs of interest and will be analyzable and interpretable. The six steps include (1) choosing a construct of interest, (2) identifying indicators of the construct,

(3) choosing existing measures that could detect potentially detect the construct, (4) creating new measures, (5) representing measures, and (6) validating measures (see Orvis et al. 2013, Fig. 1). Orvis and colleagues (2013) use situation awareness as an example for how to use the RADSM approach, and ultimately suggest using sociometric badges and network and text analysis of messages between teammates (i.e., email, text chat, meeting transcripts, call logs, filing systems, and radio). Sociometric badges and other communication tracking mechanisms can help indicate whether there is a shared understanding of a team by processes coordination, communication, and rapport between teammates. These measures may also be helpful for understanding the process of team learning by using text analysis to indicate when new information is being shared and actions are being altered to improve performance (Edmondson 1999; Edmondson et al. 2001). Measures suggested for situation awareness are excellent for retrospective measurement and reporting. However, there is ample opportunity for researchers to leverage emerging and future technologies to capture and deliver information in real-time and near real-time during an event.

Finally, maximizing the benefit of data collection from unobtrusive streams depends on getting the right information to the right people at the right time. In addition to collecting beneficial and valuable information, the selection of data collection mechanisms should consider when and to whom the information will be delivered. In emergency response training scenarios, individuals who are leading the training exercise will likely benefit the most from real-time and near real-time information. Additionally, data that can be presented to all participants during after-action reviews or debriefing sessions have the potential to enhance learning and situation awareness across an entire MTS. During live events, the MTS leadership team (e.g., Unified Command) will likely benefit from knowing where teams are located and who is interacting with whom, so information and direction can be passed to team leaders to alter decision-making and behaviors if the situation changes. Delivering data quickly and effectively depends heavily on the data processing and integration of data and data collection methods used.

4.3 Step 3: Data Processing and Integration

Data processing and integration is the important step that can make the difference between real-time and retrospective data presentation. Faster data processing prevents lag-time and leads to more immediate data analysis and visualization, allowing data to become actionable either during or immediately after an event. Wallach and Scholz (2012) suggest a *user-centered design approach* to data processing and integration, such that the users of data and their work practices are considered before a system is designed. Information from wearable sensors, video, and other unobtrusive streams should be integrated in a way that can be easily presented to users. Purohit et al. (2019) propose a multimodal streaming analytics system that unifies these heterogeneous streams into a single visual visualization to be utilized by first responders. Purohit and colleagues (2019) also suggest that data streams should be triangulated trough redundancy, providing multiple measures informing the same construct. When redundant data streams are easily and meaningfully integrated, they can quickly become useful to emergency response providers. In sum, when researchers and technologists choose and design potential heterogeneous data collection streams, the selectivity of the data to be processed, integrated, and ultimately presented to users is equally important as the reliability and validity of the data collected.

4.4 Step 4: Data Presentation

The important considerations that go into designing measures, collecting data, and integrating redundant information streams all come to fruition when the data is finally presented to users. In emergency situations, the ability of training coordinators and MTS members and leaders to make use of the information provided should be considered regarding where, when, and how they will be able to access information. Measures of MTS behavior, specifically those that infer MTS learning and situation awareness in emergency situations, can be presented in several ways. Depending on the speed of data integration, information can be presented in real-time (e.g., via dashboards and video available to trainers and leaders during an incident) or near real-time during after-action reviews.

Current data collection methods, such as GPS, RFID, proximity sensors, sociometric badges, video, and audio, are not available in real-time during an event. However, technology integration and information processing is becoming faster with systems such as the multimodal streaming analytics system presented by Purohit and colleagues harnessing near real-time data (2019). Some information may be readily available during an event, such as GPS and video, but many data streams will need time to be interpreted after the conclusion of an event or post-event for more detailed analysis until technology advances further. Thus, we should consider how to best visualize captured data for retrospective interpretation of MTS learning and situation awareness. In the near future, technologists and researchers should approach data presentation with a user-centered design focus, likely to provide emergency response trainers and leaders with more meaningful statistics and images that consider the users' point of view to represent MTS learning and situation awareness that can be shared with and across teams during future trainings. Data can also be collected continuously across several simulations and training exercises to see whether there is a change in behavior or pattern of information potentially indicating that learning and situation awareness are improved when new training methods are implemented. The goal for the distant future is to provide actionable information during actual events that can enhance learning and situation awareness as these changes occur and adaptation of the team and multiteam system that is necessary for success. In the following section, we offer challenges and recommendations for the development of future technology and analytics to be implemented in emergency response contexts.

5 What the Future Holds

5.1 Challenges

Technologists and researchers are likely to face several challenges when designing unobtrusive sensor-based and video measures of team and MTS behavior in emergency response contexts. First, emergency situations are often loud, visibility is limited, Wi-Fi and Cellular connections are often unavailable, and responders typically wear heavy gear, helmets, and masks. Without visibility or the ability to block out noise, video and audio data lose much of their usefulness, and sensor-based measures currently on the market almost all rely of Wi-Fi or Cellular connections to transfer data from the sensor back to a receiver and to cloud-based storage and computational processing. Fortunately, in interagency emergency response scenarios, observations reveal that police, fire, and EMS dress differently from one another providing a simple way of distinguishing teams and roles. While it may be more challenging to differentiate between teams from the same organization, sensor-based data identifiers could potentially be collected and interpretable when examining and reporting who comes together at what point in time evidencing interagency coordination and communication efforts.

Another challenge is creating truly unobtrusive sensors that do not disrupt the individuals trying to do their jobs (Orvis et al. 2013). For example, a sensor that someone can fit in their pocket would be considered unobtrusive, but a ten-pound helmet attachment would not be unobtrusive given the demands of this work. Many wearable sensors utilize wristbands to collect movement (e.g., proximity, acceleration) and biometric data (e.g., heartrate, blood pressure; Dubrow et al. 2017). Ideally, wearable sensors will be able to collect multiple data streams at once in alignment. One wristband may be unobtrusive, but our contextual analysis reveals that first responders will not be able to wear five separate wristbands in hopes of collecting five different streams of data nor is it convenient. Firefighters for example, have significant gear and equipment that may compromise receptivity of Bluetooth signals reaching the designated receiver. Utilizing a reliable, single sensor for multiple measures tested under severe real-world conditions in emergency response will also help mitigate challenges with time synchronization across data streams.

Finally, human processing and analysis of video and audio streams can be too slow to be meaningful, and automatic processing and analysis tools are not yet intelligent enough yet to be immediately meaningful to first responders without some human processing. Despite the advances in facial recognition and other video processing innovations, the majority of research involving video analysis still includes the human observer or coder. This laborious work can take several hours to analyze a few minutes of video, depending on what information analysts are attempting to uncover. While technology continues to develop, unobtrusive sensors can be used to capture, integrate, and present information quickly, and for now, video and audio analysis can be used later to triangulate and validate new measures. As more unobtrusive measures are developed and validated, researchers, technologists, and first responders will need to rely less on measures with significant lag time and benefit from the incorporation of artificial intelligence to quickly and effectively analyze rich sources of information from the field, such as video and audio data.

5.2 Recommendations

The most important recommendation we can provide at this point is for technologists, researchers, and first responders to work together to come up with ideas for new technologies, protype, test, validate, prototype, and test again (Orvis et al. 2013;

Purohit et al. 2019). The human-centered design or user experience design process focused on the end user is especially important in emergency response contexts, where it is critical to uncover through in-depth contextual analysis constructs and technological mechanisms for the right people to get easily interpretable, meaningful, and actionable information as quickly as possible. Data redundancy can help to ensure that information is accurate and reliable, but if it is not well integrated then too many data streams can also create information overload and no longer be useful to first responders.

As technologies are being developed and prototyped, they should be carefully validated against existing measures including other unobtrusive measures, self-report surveys, observational techniques and subject matter expert review of videos at the point of data collection. Subject matter experts, including MTS leadership and emergency response trainers, can identify strong and weak coordination behaviors by comparing unobtrusive measures to timestamps and task completion shown in videos. Additionally, they can review physical techniques, such as tourniquet application to patients, and report the behaviors as correct or incorrect. Expert observer ratings should then be compared to the sensor-based measures intended to capture the same information, in hopes of validating the use of chosen sensors.

Unobtrusive measures have benefits beyond self-report, such as capturing more granular information and not relying on human cognitive biases, but humans are still needed to confirm data streams are picking up the information they are expected to collect. The most perfect unobtrusive measure of a behavior will still be a *proxy* for the actual behavior (Dubrow et al. 2017). For example, RFID, GPS, proximity, and sociometric measures of interaction will always be *representations* of coordination, and do not equal acts of coordination themselves. Triangulation and redundancy of multiple measures of the same construct will help increase content validity of future technologies.

6 Conclusion

In sum, existing research creates a strong frame for building future unobtrusive sensor-based measures to be utilized in emergency response scenarios (e.g., Feese et al. 2013; Kranzfelder et al. 2011; Olguín et al. 2009), and data integration systems are being developed to integrate new streams of information (Purohit et al. 2019). The primary goal of future technologies is to build on existing measures and put new measures to the test in complex, dynamic environments such as emergency response. All four steps of technology development and use suggested in this paper (i.e., operationalizing constructs of interest, choosing data collection mechanisms, processing and integrating data, and visualizing and reporting data) should be considered *before* technology development begins. Multidisciplinary teams of researchers, technologists, and first responders who partner to create new technologies through a human-centered design approach are expected to achieve far greater success in measure development and validation compared to teams that build new measures from a single disciplinary perspective.

References

Anania, E.C., et al.: Communication in the spaceflight multi-team system: training and technology recommendations to support boundary spanners. In: Human Factors and Ergonomics Society Annual Meeting Proceedings, vol. 61. no. 1, pp. 150–154. SAGE Publications, Los Angeles (2017)

Davison, R.B., Hollenbeck, J.R., Barnes, C.M., Sleesman, D.J., Ilgen, D.R.: Coordinated action in multiteam systems. J. Appl. Psychol. **97**(4), 808–824 (2012)

DeChurch, L.A., Marks, M.A.: Leadership in multiteam systems. J. Appl. Psychol. **91**(2), 311–329 (2006)

Dubrow, S.: Using IoT sensors to enhance simulation and training in multiteam systems. In: The Interservice/Industry Training, Simulation and Education Conference (I/ITSEC) Published Proceedings, pp. 1–10 (2017)

Edmondson, A.: Psychological safety and learning behavior in work teams. Adm. Sci. Q. **44**(2), 350–383 (1999)

Edmondson, A.C., Bohmer, R.M., Pisano, G.P.: Disrupted routines: team learning and new technology implementation in hospitals. Adm. Sci. Q. **46**(4), 685–716 (2001)

Endsley, M.R.: Toward a theory of situation awareness in dynamic systems. Hum. Factors **37**(1), 32–64 (1995)

Feese, S., Arnrich, B., Troster, G., Burtscher, M., Meyer, B., Jonas, K.: CoenoFire: monitoring performance indicators of firefighters in real-world missions using smartphones. In: Proceedings of the 2013 ACM International Joint Conference on Pervasive and Ubiquitous Computing, pp. 83–92 (2013)

Firth, B.M., Hollenbeck, J.R., Miles, J.E., Ilgen, D.R., Barnes, C.M.: Same page, different books: extending representational gaps theory to enhance performance in multiteam systems. Acad. Manag. J. **58**(3), 813–835 (2015)

Fischer, F., Hmelo-Silver, C.E., Goldman, S.R., Reimann, P.: International Handbook of the Learning Sciences. Routledge, London (2018)

Fleştea, A.M., Fodor, O.C., Curşeu, P.L., Miclea, M.: 'We didn't know anything, it was a mess!' Emergent structures and the effectiveness of a rescue operation multi-team system. Ergonomics **60**(1), 44–58 (2017)

Haynes, S.N., Richard, D., Kubany, E.S.: Content validity in psychological assessment: a functional approach to concepts and methods. Psychol. Assess. **7**(3), 238–247 (1995)

Hirst, G., Van Knippenberg, D., Zhou, J.: A cross-level perspective on employee creativity: goal orientation, team learning behavior, and individual creativity. Acad. Manag. J. **52**(2), 280–293 (2009)

InterAgency Board: Improving active shooter/hostile event response. Best practices and recommendations for integrating law enforcement, fire, and EMS. pp. 1–24 (2015)

Kranzfelder, M., Schneider, A., Gillen, S., Feussner, H.: New technologies for information retrieval to achieve situational awareness and higher patient safety in the surgical operating room: the MRI institutional approach and review of the literature. Surg. Endosc. **25**(3), 696–705 (2011)

Luciano, M.M., DeChurch, L.A., Mathieu, J.E.: Multiteam systems: a structural framework and meso-theory of system functioning. J. Manag. **44**(3), 1065–1096 (2018)

Mathieu, J., Luciano, M.M., DeChurch, L.: Multiteam systems: the next chapter. The SAGE Handbook of Industrial, Work and Organizational Psychology, Organizational Psychology, pp. 333–362 (2018)

Mathieu, J.E., Marks, M.A., Zaccaro, S.J.: Multi-team systems. Int. Handb. Work Organ. Psychol. **2**, 289–313 (2001)

McGuire, F.R.D.S.: Cohesion in multiteam systems: effects of type of training and adaptation triggers on levels of social and task cohesion-an experimental study. Doctoral dissertation, pp. 1–43 (2016)

Olguín, D.O., Waber, B.N., Kim, T., Mohan, A., Ara, K., Pentland, A.: Sensible organizations: technology and methodology for automatically measuring organizational behavior. IEEE Trans. Syst. Man Cybern. Part B (Cybern.) Proc. **39**(1), 43–55 (2009)

Orvis, K.L., Dechon, A., DeCostanza, A.: Developing system-based performance measures: a rational approach. In: The Interservice/Industry Training, Simulation and Education Conference (I/ITSEC) Published Proceedings, pp. 1–12 (2013)

Purohit, H., Dubrow, S., Bannan, B.: Designing a multimodal analytics system to improve emergency service training. To be Presented at the 5th Annual International Conference on Learning and Collaboration Technology (2019)

Rosen, M.A., Dietz, A.S., Yang, T., Priebe, C.E., Pronovost, P.J.: An integrative framework for sensor-based measurement of teamwork in healthcare. J. Am. Med. Inform. Assoc. **22**(1), 11–18 (2014)

Shrestha, L.B., Prince, C., Baker, D.P., Salas, E.: Understanding situation awareness: concepts, methods, and training. Hum./Technol. Inter. Complex Syst. **7**, 45–83 (1995)

Van den Bossche, P., Gijselaers, W.H., Segers, M., Kirschner, P.A.: Social and cognitive factors driving teamwork in collaborative learning environments: team learning beliefs and behaviors. Small Group Res. **37**(5), 490–521 (2006)

Wallach, D., Scholz, S.C.: User-centered design: why and how to put users first in software development. In: Maedche, A., Botzenhardt, A., Neer, L. (eds.) Software for People. Management for Professionals. Springer, Heidelberg (2012). https://doi.org/10.1007/978-3-642-31371-4_2

Waring, S., et al.: Information sharing in interteam responses to disaster. J. Occup. Organ. Psychol **91**(3), 591–619 (2018)

DeChurch, L.A., Marks, M.A., Zaccaro, S.J.: Multiteam Systems: An Organization Form for Dynamic and Complex Environments, vol. 1. Routledge, London (2012)

Zaccaro, S.J., Marks, M.A., DeChurch, L.A.: Multiteam systems: an introduction. In: Multiteam Systems. 1st edn. Routledge (2012)

Parent and Child Voice Activity Detection in Pivotal Response Treatment Video Probes

Corey D. C. Heath[✉], Troy McDaniel, Hemanth Venkateswara, and Sethuraman Panchanathan

Arizona State University, Tempe, AZ, USA
{corey.heath,troy.mcdaniel,hemanthv,panch}@asu.edu

Abstract. Training parents, and other primary caregivers, in pivotal response treatment (PRT) has been shown to help children with autism increase their communication skills. This is most effective when the parent maintains a high degree of fidelity to the PRT methodology. Evaluation of a parent's implementation is currently limited to manual review of PRT sessions by a trained clinician. This process is time consuming and limited in the amount of feedback that can be provided. It also makes long term support for parents who have undergone training difficult. Providing automated data extraction and analysis would alleviate the costs of providing feedback to parents.

Since vocal communication is of the most common target skills for PRT implementation, audio analysis is critical to a successful feedback system. Speech patterns in PRT sessions are atypical to common speech that provide a change for audio analysis systems. Adults involved in the treatment often use child-directed language and over exaggerated exclamations as a means of engaging the child. Child speech recognition is a difficult problem that is compounded when children have limited vocal expression. Additionally, PRT sessions depict joint play activities, often producing loud, sustained noise. To address these challenges, audio classification techniques were explored to determine a methodology for labeling audio segments in videos of PRT sessions. By implementing separate support vector machine (SVM) implementations for speech activity, and speaker separation, an average accuracy of 79% was achieved.

Keywords: Pivotal response treatment · Vocal activity detection · Speaker separation · Child speech detection · Autism spectrum disorder · Dyadic audio analysis

1 Introduction

Applied behavioral analysis (ABA) techniques have been proven to be an effective methodology for helping to improve social and communication skills in children with autism spectrum disorder (ASD). Pivotal response treatment (PRT) is a naturalistic ABA approach that focuses on incorporating learning objectives into the context of various situations, such as play activities or daily routine tasks. Fundamentally, PRT focuses on dyadic interaction between an interventionist and a treatment recipient. The interventionist engages with the recipient in an activity to present in-context learning opportunities. The choice of the activity is dependent on the recipient, requiring the interventionist to follow the recipient's lead, interject themselves into the activity, and adapt target learning objectives accordingly. Allowing the recipient to choose the activity affords the interventionist the opportunity to capitalize on the recipient's natural motivation at the given moment to help ensure compliance [1].

Research studies show that parents, and other primary caregivers, are effective interventionists after receiving PRT training [2, 3]. In addition to demonstrated communication skill improvement from the child, parents participating in PRT research have also reported reduced stress levels as well as improved affective states for their children [4]. Although the benefits of teaching parents to implement PRT are clear, there are several obstacles to ensuring proper treatment, including access to resources, the amount of time required, and the cost of training programs. Current training programs consist of in-person groups or individual classes taught by trained clinicians, which can be difficult for parents to accommodate. Even after training, support for parents is limited and parents often show a decline in implementation fidelity [5]. This could be due to lack of practice or inability to adapt training methodology as the child progresses.

Measurements of parent fidelity to PRT are often conducted using video probes. These probes typically consist of 10 mins of video of the parent utilizing PRT techniques with their child. Each one minute section of the video is scored based on 12 categories using a binary scale. Additionally, child responses to the parent's instructions are tallied in 15 s increments. The data from the video probes is extracted by trained clinicians. Due to the time required to process the videos, the amount of feedback the parent receives is limited. Implementing automated data collection procedures on the video probes could allow for greater amounts of data that could be used for both automated feedback and clinician feedback. Extracting the parent speech and child vocalizations from the PRT video probes is an important step toward providing automated data collection.

Detecting vocal activity in PRT video probes is difficult. Often, the audio tracks contain background noise from the environment, along with sounds from the activity the child and parent are participating in. This could include sounds from play activities, toys that emit songs, chimes, or speech recordings, or dialog from electronic media. These noises can obscure the parent or child vocalizations or create opportunities for misidentifying a speech event. The recording quality of the child and parent can also be problematic, as the videos are often recorded using handheld phones or cameras with built-in microphones. This leads the quality to be dependent on proximity to the camera's microphone. This is particularly limiting for children with low energy vocalizations.

An additional challenge, and what distinguishes this research from other works on voice activity detection (VAD), is that the parent and child exhibit atypical speech patterns. To engage the child, the parent often utilizes child-directed speech patterns, or baby-talk, drawing out syllables and using a higher pitched voice, in a way that is not common in adult speech. Child speech is already a difficult problem for automatic speech detection [6], as children speak more slowly than adults and make more phonetic or grammatical errors. This could be more prevalent in children with ASD who have limited communication skills. Additionally, in PRT, a valid vocalization from a child is determined by their communication ability. This means that a child who is non-verbal or whose speech is limited to single words may only be able to respond with a phoneme in response to a learning objective. Because of this, it is important to detect all the child's vocalizations, not just articulated speech.

The research presented below evaluates methods for detecting parent and child vocalizations in PRT video probes. Several detection methods were examined including filter-based implementation, clustering algorithms, and machine learning approaches. These results are compared to the open source VAD system, WebRTC VAD [7].

1.1 Related Work

VAD encompasses the preprocessing techniques for discriminating speech signals from other noises in an audio file. Generally, approaches to classifying speech versus non-speech signals involves using discriminatory feature sets, statistical approaches, or machine learning techniques [8]. A common feature-based technique is the use of frequency ranges as a filter for selecting speech signals [9, 10]. Statistical approaches focus on modeling the noise spectra using a defined distribution to extract impertinent signals.

Both unsupervised and supervised machine learning methods have been explored for VAD. In unsupervised methods, k-means [11] and Gaussian mixture models (GMM) [12] have been explored. Unsupervised methods benefit from the ability to use large amounts of data, however, the algorithms falter in difficult separation tasks, such as when a noise signal has a steady repetition [8].

Support vector machines (SVM) have been a commonly utilized algorithm for VAD [13–15]. These approaches focus on utilizing the SVM for a binary classification problem, requiring labeled corpora of noise and speech data. The requirement for label data is the primary drawback for these approaches, particularly due to the variety in noise and speech signals. This means that the model may not be able to generalize to compensate for different types of noise.

Deep learning approaches for VAD seek to address generalization by utilizing the network layers to capture more information about the data's feature set. The use of a feedforward recurrent neural network (RNN) model for VAD was explored by [16]. A single hidden layer neural network implemented by [17] was applied to test VAD application in real world environments. Also exploring application to real world scenarios, [18] utilized multiple layers of encoder and decoder to networks to create a classification model.

Performing speech recognition on children presents additional challenges. At an auditory level, children's voices tend to be higher frequency and display more rational and spectral variability [6]. Regarding language modeling, children are more prone to mispronouncing words than adults, have a restricted vocabulary, and tend to speak at a lower rate [19]. These challenges are more apparent the younger the child is. Research into child speech classification has been undertaken using SVM models [20], DNN models [21, 22], and hybrid DNN-hidden Markov model (HMM) classifiers [23]. Discerning adult from child speech was explored in [24]. Adding adult speech samples when training child speech recognition models has been shown to improve classification accuracy [22, 23].

For dyadic speech classification, domain adaptation and the utilization of contextual information was implemented to increase recognition accuracy by [25]. Their system examined speech from child-adult interactions in child mistreatment interviews using separate networks for the adult and child speech recognition.

Domain adaptation on the children's speech network consisted of incorporating transcripts in training to aid in structuring the data. Additionally, the researchers sought to use the recognized adult speech as context to infer more accurate transcription of the speech from the child in the interaction. Using this approach, they showed that substantial improvements in word recognition accuracies were made in comparison to a baseline measure measurement.

Much of the research regarding the implementation of ASR systems for individuals with Autism has focused on diagnosis and emotion detection. Exploration of the application of ASRs for emotion detection in children with Autism was undertaken by [26]. The dataset consisted of both children with autism and children without acting out emotions based on story prompts. Classification of emotion class was undertaken using an SVM. Their findings indicate that larger feature sets equated to better performance. They found that system had a higher detection recall rate for the children without an ASD diagnosis.

Researching Autism detection, [27] used the Language Environment Analysis (LENA) audio recording system to record children with autism in a home environment. Their goal was to alleviate the human processing time for evaluating language skills for people with autism. After recording the audio, the system sought to classify the vocal data into classes, including the target child, the adult's other children, and the voices from electronic media with a GMM-HMM model [28] using a high dimensional set of features. They concluded that their work illustrates a high degree of difference in speech between children with autism and children without a diagnosis of ASD that can be suitably differentiated using machine learning techniques.

The LENA recording system was also used by [29] to analyze vocalizations of children with autism and their interaction with adults. Their approach utilized a SVM classifier to distinguish between adult and child utterances as well as detect laughing. Their results were comparable with [27, 28].

This project differs from much of the work on VAD and speaker separation because of its implementation in handling adult and child vocalizations, along with unpredictable noise. Additionally, the project needs to account for children with limited verbal skills that may not be able to formulate complete words and adequately recognize all vocal utterances.

The LENA system provides a similar function to the research presented in this paper. This paper focuses on classifying audio from untrimmed videos of PRT sessions. This is intended to work within the current structure of PRT implementation and research practices. The videos can be unpredictable in the interactions depicted, along with the quality of the recording. The LENA system benefits from using hardware attached to the child's clothing. This likely provides higher quality recordings, particularly in the child's vocal utterances; however, it is dependent on a specific device.

2 Corpus Description

Fourteen videos were randomly selected from a PRT study [30]. Each video contains a parent-child dyad. There are seven parent-child dyads in total, with each pair appearing in two videos. The videos consist of a pretraining baseline and a post-video after the parent has received five days of PRT training with a behavioral analyst. Each video is approximately 10 mins long, however, due to a recording malfunction only the first four minutes and two seconds of audio is available from the Dyad1_Post video. During the recorded sessions, the parent is instructed to compel the child to vocalize as much as possible.

Each of the parent-child dyads consisted of an adult female and a male child. The children ranged in age from 24 to 60 months. The communication skills exhibited varies depending on the child. Table 1 provides an observation of the vocal abilities that the child shows in each of the videos. Most of the child vocalizations expressed do not consist of fully articulated words. The data from five of the seven children contained few single word utterances, but many primarily consist of sounds unrelated to speech or attempts to pronounce the first phoneme of a prompted word. The child from the Dyad4 videos spoken in single words, or two-word phrases, with some additional non-speech vocalizations related to play activities. The child in Dyad7 spoken in multi-word phrases with few non-speech utterances.

Table 1. Speech level exhibited in the video probes by the child in each dyad.

Child	Exhibited vocal skill
Dyad1	Vocal attempts, single words
Dyad2	Vocal attempts, no fully articulated speech
Dyad3	Vocal attempts, single words
Dyad4	Single words, two-word phrases
Dyad5	Vocal attempts, single words, two-word phrases
Dyad6	Vocal attempts, single words
Dyad7	Multi-word phrases, full sentences

The parent speech consists of individual words, sentences, and exclamations. Much of the parent's speech follows child-directed speech patterns. This consists of using a higher pitch than is used in normal conversational speech, along with extending syllables and exaggerated excitement or surprise. Only the parent's vocal utterances were attributed to the adult in the labeled audio segments. Sounds made by the parent that were not verbalization, such as clapping, sneezing, or coughing, were labeled as noise.

In the video, various play scenarios are participated in, creating different types of noises including shuffling toy pieces and objects banging together. Additionally, the toys themselves often emitted noise, such as a dinosaur roar, music, or audible speech. In one video, Dyad2_Post, the parent and child are watching a popular children's movie on a mobile phone. Speech from the toys or movies were omitted from the dataset. Sounds from the movie that were not recognizable speech were labeled as noise.

In addition to the parent talking in the video, there are some instances of an additional adult in the room speaking. For this publication, only audio from the parent is used in the dataset. Audio segments were labeled at 250 ms increments as either parent speech, child vocalization, or non-speech sounds. Segments with an energy level below $1e^{-6}$ were excluded. The number of labeled segments for each video are posted in Table 2.

Table 2. Number of labeled samples for each of the three classes for each video probe.

Video	Parent vocalization	Child vocalization	Non-speech audio
Dyad1_Base	797	591	1049
Dyad1_Post	156	162	622
Dyad2_Base	763	120	1533
Dyad2_Post	365	64	700
Dyad3_Base	1017	124	1208
Dyad3_Post	477	247	1645
Dyad4_Base	1358	375	702
Dyad4_Post	967	429	1009
Dyad5_Base	705	97	1538
Dyad5_Post	509	248	1686
Dyad6_Base	574	108	1778
Dyad6_Post	295	132	1996
Dyad7_Base	923	785	708
Dyad7_Post	797	591	1049

3 Experiments and Results

The objective of the experiments is to find an algorithm that can detect vocalizations in the video, determine if they are from a child or an adult, and to identify noise segments. To achieve this, methods incorporating WebRTC VAD, pitch-based filtering, clustering algorithms, and machine learning techniques were explored.

The first experiment was conducted to determine how well a state-of-the-art VAD system performed on the video probe data. Google's WebRTC VAD [7] is an open-source tool for extracting speech segments from audio files. Each of the video probe files was processed using WebRTC VAD independently. The VAD can be configured to integer-based levels of aggression that influence the threshold for determining noise from valid speech. The two lowest levels of aggression, one and two, were tested. The results are presented in Table 3.

The results show that WebRTC cannot accurately filter the video probes. On the lowest setting, most vocal samples were correctly captured by the VAD; however, noise was not sufficiently filtered. On this setting, 73% of the noise samples were included in the processed audio segments. Conversely, on aggression setting two, 91% of the noise was correctly removed, but most of speech samples were not captured, particularly for the child utterances. This performance is likely due to several factors.

Table 3. The percent of label segments that were correctly included in an audio segment if a vocalization or excluded if noise after processing each video with WebRTC VAD.

Aggression level	Ave. correct noise	Ave. correct adult speech	Ave. correct child vocalization
One	0.27	0.98	0.97
Two	0.91	0.12	0.06

The VAD may be designed to filter environmental noises which may be periodic or droning and is thus looking for anomalous signal magnitudes to detect speech events. The noise in the video probes does not fit this pattern and is usually the result of the child or parent playing with a toy or participating in an activity. Detecting noise may also be based on energy levels. The noises in the video probes are often high energy events whereas the vocalizations, particularly from the child, may be low energy.

The second experiment sought to distinguish between noise, child vocalization, and adult speech using a filter on the estimated signal pitch for each 250 ms segment. The estimated pitch was extracted using PRAAT [31] within a range of 75–600 Hz. The average estimated pitch for the segment was calculated and used for classification. The classification model used a rule based on the expected average range for female adults and male children. The range for adults was 165–255 Hz [32]. The child range was 260–440 Hz, based on information from [33]. The results are illustrated in Fig. 2. This method had marginal success in determining noise segments, with an average F1 score of 80%. Adult and child segments were less successful, with average F1 scores of 52% and 39% respectively. This shows that much of the noise in the segments falls outside of the pitch range of 165–440 Hz. It is also notable that the method had the best success in classifying child vocalization in Dyads 4, 6 and 7. These children exhibited more complete word usage.

Recorded pitch frequencies for children in research studies is varied [33]. In the corpus presented in this study, both the child vocalizations and the adult speech registers at a higher estimated pitch than other publications. Figure 1 presents a box plot for the average estimated pitch frequencies for adult, child, and noise segments for each video. The range of all three classes extends from 75–600 Hz based on the parameters provided to PRAAT. This indicates that samples in the adult and child classes contain samples outside the expected vocal range. The means of both are higher than reported in other publications. For child samples, the mean is 343 Hz and for adult samples it is 279 Hz. The means of each class are distinct; however, the interquartile range shows a large degree of overlap.

The estimated pitch-based classifier described above was rerun using ranges from the dataset distribution. The adult and child ranges were based on the 1st and 3rd quartiles. The region of overlap between the parent and child data was handled by dividing the region and ascribing samples in the higher frequencies to the child. This gave an adult range of 202–308 Hz and a child range of 308–396 Hz. The results are compared to the previous implementation in Fig. 2. This method gives a narrower range of values for the adult and child classes and exhibits a lower accuracy than the previous method based on published frequencies. This discrepancy likely shows that

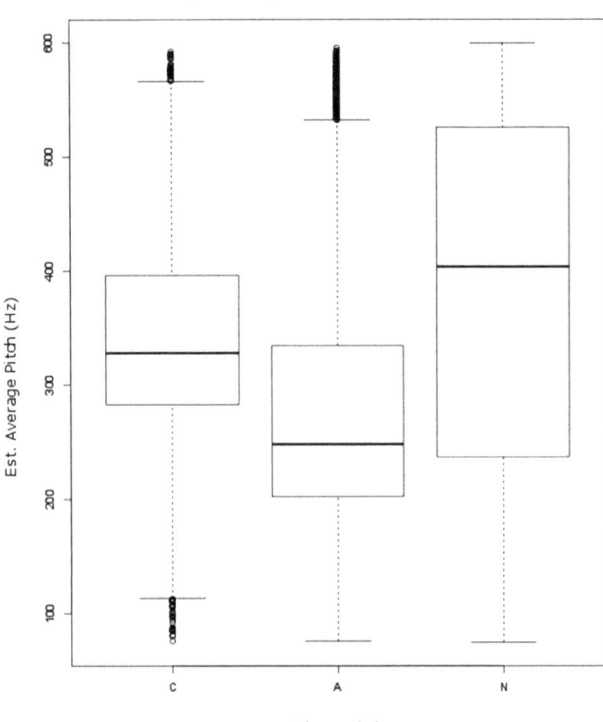

Fig. 1. Box plot showing the average estimated pitch for segments in the video probes. The plot shows the distribution for class labels C, A, N, or child, adult, and noise respectively.

outliers in the data are skewing the frequencies. This could be due to variance in the energy of samples causing less accurate estimates of the pitch quality. It could also be the case that exclamations and exaggerated excitement could cause the adult pitch estimations to be higher than spoken language.

The third set of experiments utilized the open-source library PyAudioAnalysis [34] for feature extraction and running machine learning algorithms. This experiment compared five classifiers that are available in PyAudioAnalysis: support vector machines (SVM), k-nearest neighbors (KNN), random forests, extra trees, and gradient boosting. Each of these classifiers is implemented with the Scikit-Learn python library [35].

For processing, each labeled 250 ms segments was saved to a wav file. The wav files were converted into 68 element vectors consisting of the midterm features extracted by PyAudioAnalysis. The feature vectors consist of values for zero cross rate (ZCR), energy, energy atrophy, spectral spread, spectral flux, spectral runoff, mel-frequency cepstrum coefficients (MFCC), chroma, and chroma standard deviation. The feature set is then standardized prior to training the classifier.

Twelve of the 14 videos were used for training each classifier. The remaining 2 videos, the base and post video for a single dyad, were used as a validation set. The

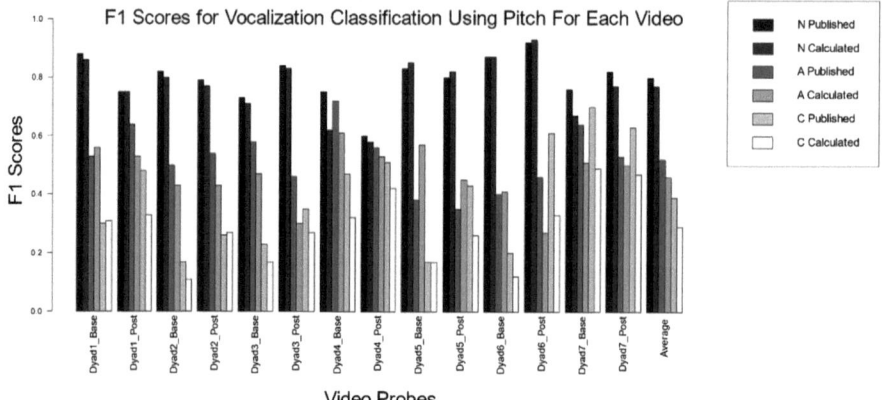

Fig. 2. F1 scores based on classifiers using published pitch values and pitch values calculated from the dataset.

average results across all validation sets for each model are displayed in Fig. 3. These results are similar across each of the classifiers, with gradient boosting and SVM providing the best F1 scores for each class. These results also mirror the filter-based results. This shows that the noise segments are easily distinguishable from the other classes, but the human vocalizations are more difficult to classify.

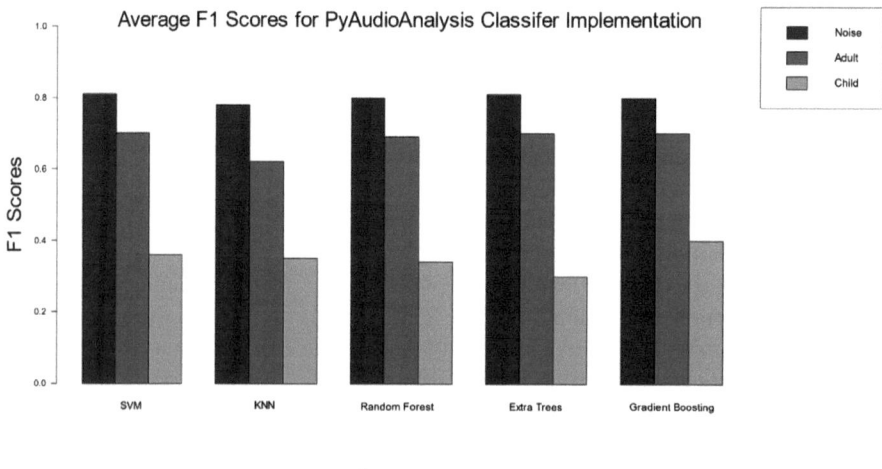

Fig. 3. Average F1 scores from five classification algorithms in the PyAudioAnalysis library.

The results from the PyAudioAnalysis algorithms illustrate that there is a high degree of variability amongst the data samples that is preventing adequate classification. This is particularly clear with the voice sample classes.

To address the between-video variability in the data, k-means clustering was explored. Using an unsupervised method would allow each individual video to be assessed without incorporating samples from other videos. Each 250 ms sample was converted to vector representation of the midterm features extracted by PyAudioAnalysis and standardized. Additionally, to aid classification, the samples were divided into 25 ms subsamples with 5 ms of overlap between each sample. The 25 ms samples consisted of short-term features extracted from PyAudioAnaylsis. Subsamples with an energy value less than $1e^{-6}$ were discarded. Each video was clustered independently without regard to the sampling labeling. The sample labels were then used to assess the clustering accuracy based on the assignments for each class. The k-means algorithm was implemented using the Scikit-Learn python library [35] with 10 maximum iterations.

The F1 scores from implementing k-means clustering are presented in Fig. 4. These results varied between videos, however, performance was poorer than previous methods. Often, one cluster would dominate the data, accounting for the majority of the samples. This was particularly true for the child and adult speech samples. A predominate issue with using clustering algorithms on this data set is the level of data imbalance. The majority of the samples from each video are classified as noise, with a small minority of the samples coming from child utterances. In the cluster algorithm, this means that noise samples that have similar feature vectors to the speech samples will skew cluster centers, preventing the speech samples from creating distinguishable groupings.

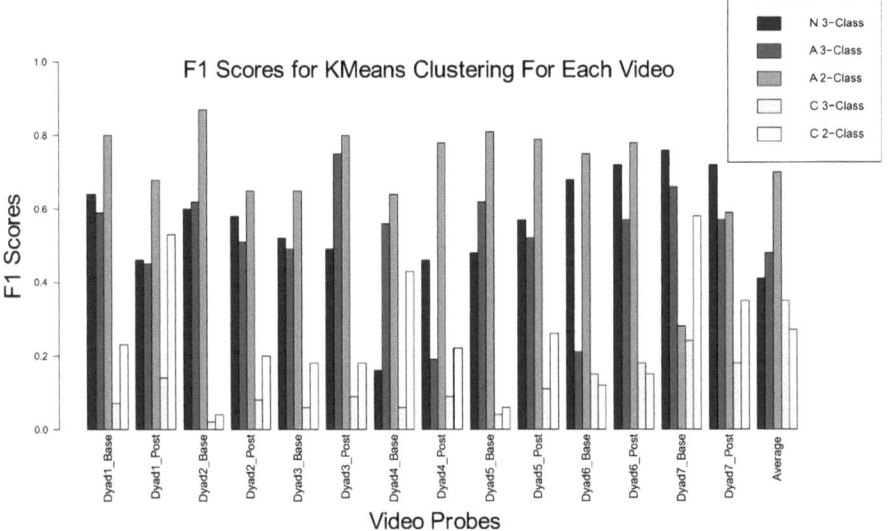

Fig. 4. Child (C), adult (A), and noise (N) F1 scores from k-means clustering.

To account for the imbalance with noise samples, just the adult and child utterance samples were used in a two-cluster implementation. This shows improvement over the three-class classification, however, classification on child segments was still poor.

This also could be due to data imbalance, as parent samples were more plentiful in the data set. Child directed speech patterns could also cause the adult speech samples to be similar to child samples, preventing effective cluster differentiation.

The final set of experiments revisited SVM implementation to explore approaching the VAD and speaker separation problems separately. To account for VAD, an SVM was trained using the noise samples as one class and the combined adult and child speech samples as a second class. Similarly, speaker separation was accomplished by using child speech samples as a class, with the noise and adult samples as the second class. Both SVM implementations used a C value of 1 and a RBF kernel. As with the PyAudioAnalysis experiments, the SVMs were trained using 12 of the 14 videos, using the remaining videos for validation, and the feature set consisted of the PyAudioAnalysis midterm extracted features. Data imbalance in the training set was addressed by under-sampling the overrepresented class. The results are presented in Fig. 5.

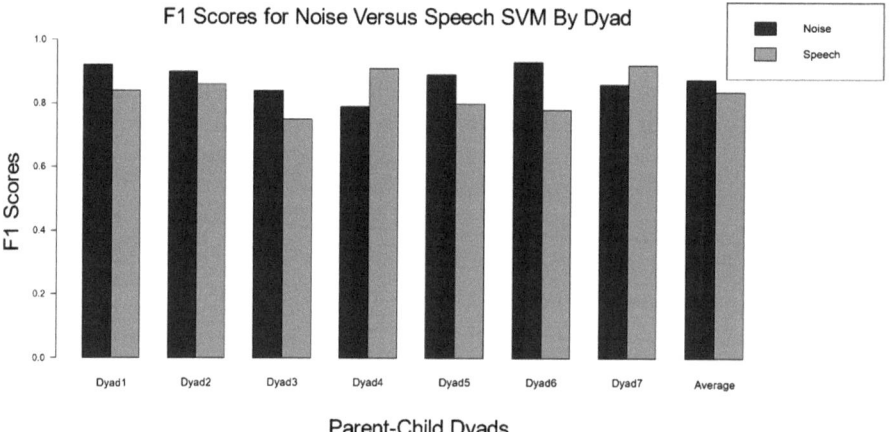

Fig. 5. F1 scores for speech detection using a 2-class SVM model.

The separate VAD and speaker separation SVM implementations had a greater performance than the three-class classification techniques, particularly in distinguishing speech and noise samples. Classifying 250 ms segments on noise versus speech had an average F1 score of .85 over both classes across all seven validation sets in Fig. 5.

The average F1 score for speaker separation is lower than the VAD implementation, at .69, however, this is still higher than previous methods (Fig. 6). In addition to testing 250 ms samples, the samples were divided into 100 ms subsamples with 25 ms overlap and used to train a separate SVM. Each 100 ms sample was processed through PyAudioAnalysis to obtain the same feature set as previously noted. The goal of this was to determine if the subsamples were more diagnostic than the full sample. The F1 scores for the 100 ms samples were nearly identical to the 250 ms samples.

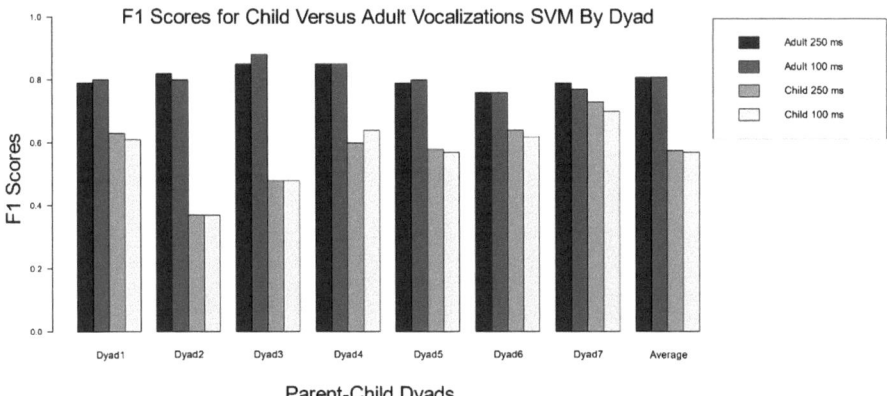

Fig. 6. F1 scores for speaker classification using a two-class SVM model. Results for 250 ms and 100 ms samples are shown.

The VAD and speaker separation SVM models were used to classify the audio in each of the 14 videos mimicking the intended implementation. The overall accuracy was 78%, with a range of 70 to 91% (Fig. 7). Similar to results presented in Fig. 5, classifying noise samples had the highest accuracy at 87%. Noise samples are the highest represented class in the videos, leading this score to largely influence the overall accuracy. The speech accuracy was lower, averaging 65% for both classes. The Dyad3_Post had the lowest accuracy for both the parent and the child at 42% and 46% respectively. This video had relatively low instances of vocalization for both individuals. The highest degree of error occurred by misclassifying speech as noise. Most of the utterances made by the child in the video are attempts at the first phoneme of the prompted word. These attempts are generally short and clipped. This contrasts to the other children in the corpus that had longer vocalizations, even when they were only able to attempt a word. The parent in the video is drawing out words, pronouncing each syllable distinctly as an example for the child.

Each video was also evaluated for accuracy using the 100 ms speech classification model (Fig. 8). The 100 ms samples were classified, then a label for the 250 ms segment was determined based on a voting scheme. This implementation had a similar overall accuracy of 79% compared to the 250 ms implementation. The average for both speech classes was slightly lower at 64%. The adult recognition improved over the 250 ms implementation, however, the child accuracy decreased. The increase in overall accuracy is due to the adult samples being more numerous than child samples in each video.

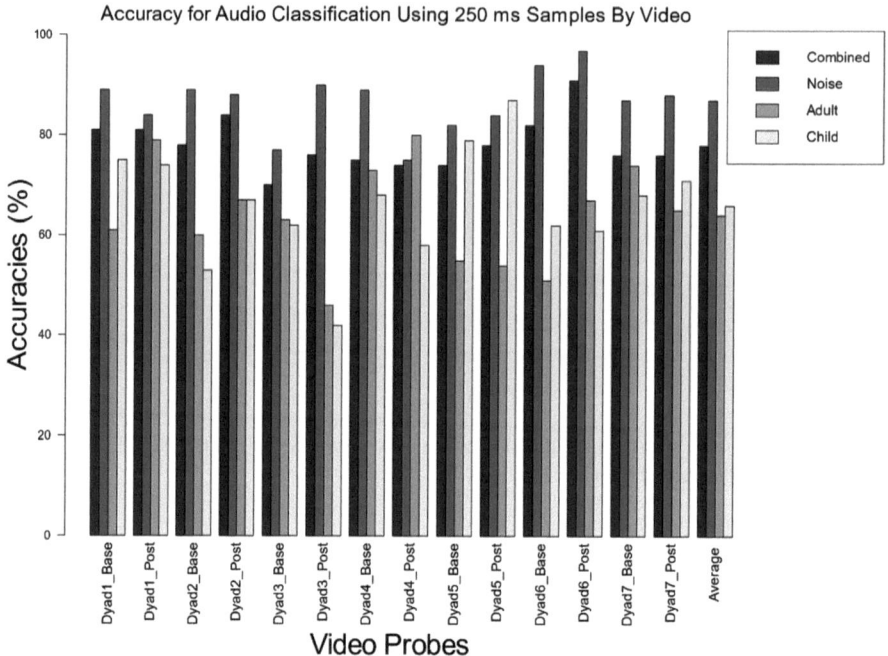

Fig. 7. Accuracy for 250 ms noise and speech segments per video after SVM classification.

4 Discussion

When considering obvious differences between adult and child speech, pitch becomes one of the key components. As was shown in the pitch estimation analysis (Fig. 1) and the results from the rule-based classifier, differentiation of pitch can be seen between sample classes. However, pitch alone could not be fully utilized to discern the vocal samples. As seen in the corpus and in other research studies, the most common composition for the parent-child dyad is an adult female with a child male, which have more similar vocal frequency than may be present with other compositions. In addition to this, the adults in the videos have been shown to utilize child-directed speech, raising the intonation of their speech. This further limits the differences in frequency between the child and the adult and necessitates exploring more features for speaker separation and the creation of classification models.

Evaluating the PRT audio corpus illustrates that a large degree of variability can be expected. Examining the participants' age range and communication skills accounts for much of the difficulty in creating a generalized solution with limited data. Child development rate is an important factor, with large differences between children at 24 months and 60 months. This is elevated when differences of development rates are factored in. These factors complicate the training of adequate models to encompass the dataset, making overfitting a large problem. This can particularly be a problem with deep learning algorithms using a small dataset. This lead to the decision to focus on traditional machine learning implementations.

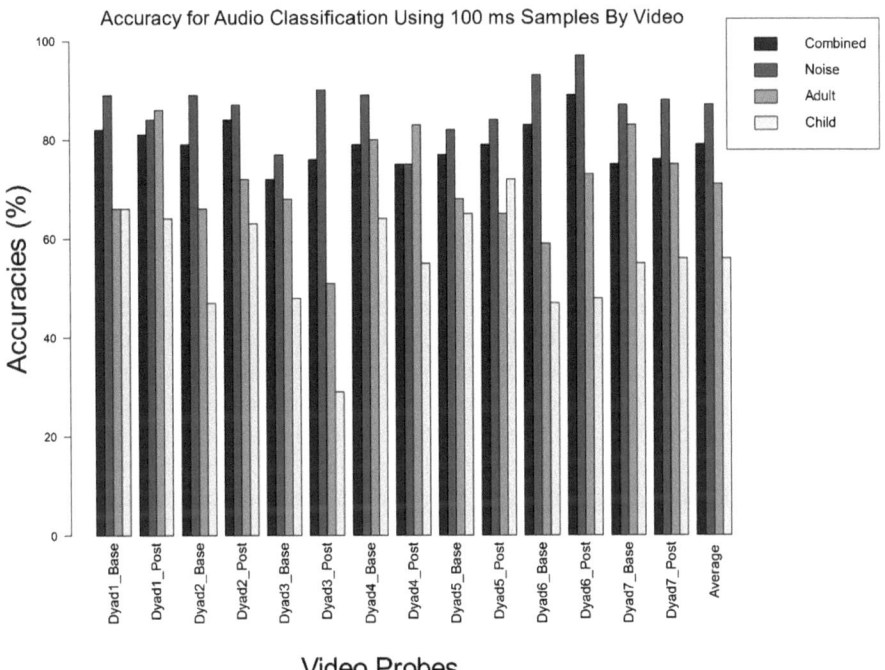

Fig. 8. Accuracy for 250 ms noise and 100 ms speech samples per video after SVM classification.

As PRT is implemented on a wide range of individuals of all ages and communication abilities, it is necessary to look for ways of addressing these large variations. This is illustrated by the three-class classification results presented in Fig. 3. These results show moderate performance on distinguishing noise and adult samples, but a low performance on child sample classification. This is likely due to the underrepresentation of similar child data samples across the videos. The lowest average child F1 scores were seen in Dyad2 and Dyad3. The children in these videos exhibited few fully formed words, but with very different patterns. The child in Dyad2 is the youngest amongst the dataset. His vocalizations are largely akin to babble. The child in Dyad3 communicated in short attempts at a specific word.

In this study, we examined unsupervised clustering to address variability between videos. The clustering algorithm allowed each video to be classified only on samples from the same video. This eliminates model confusion based on sample variation in the same class. In terms of the PRT corpus, this means that the model was not trying to associate the limited vocal attempts from the child with less developed communication skills with the more articulated speech from other videos. This approach proved to be impractical for the PRT videos, largely due to data imbalance, along with between class similarity. The results in Fig. 4 shows that the child samples, which are underrepresented in each video, are poorly differentiated from the noise or adult classes. This is still an issue when performing clustering on the child and adult speech samples without incorporating the noise segments. The larger number of adult samples causes the adult class to have a greater influence on the clusters in the algorithm. This, along with the prevalence of outliers that are similar to child samples, could prevent the clusters from adequately distinguishing between samples.

Ultimately, the best results on the dataset were achieved by training separate classifiers for differentiating between noise and speech, and child vocalizations from adult speech. The VAD classification performed adequately across the dataset. This is congruent with the results from the three-class classifier results. This shows that much of the ambiguity in the data is in the speech samples.

Spot checking the full video classifications showed several trends in misidentified segments. For speech segments, adult samples labeled as child speech often contained low energy speech or have limited amounts of speech in the segment. This was most commonly seen at the end of a multi-segment vocal event where the trailing speech was presenting in a portion of the last labeled segment. The misclassification was also more prevalent if the trailing syllables of the word were elongated. When full vocal events spanning multiple labeled segments were misclassified, the adult speech often had more inflection and a higher tone, typical of child-directed speech.

Child speech segments that were classified as adult vocalization often didn't consist of speech or attempted speech sounds. Most commonly the misclassified segments were excited babbling or higher pitched vocal sounds. This is likely due to examples of exaggerated excitement present in the adult training set.

Misclassifying either adult or child vocal segments as noise was most commonly due to segment containing sounds other than the vocalizations. This could also occur in segments where the vocalization was low energy. In noise segments misclassified as adults, sounds from the adult not associated with speech, such as coughing, were classified as adult speech. Interestingly, a toy's tinkling chime was consistently classified as adult speech in the Dyad1_Base video. Noises that were misclassified as child speech were either low energy or consisting of a brief sharp sound.

In the Dyad1_Base video, the parent and child are playing with a toy that emits intelligible speech when being played with. These sounds were classified as noise. The toy's speech sounds are noticeably lower tone, resembling an adult male's speaking voice, than the child and parent vocalizations. Audible speech from a movie the parent and child are viewing in the Dyad2_Post was classified in part as noise, as well as adult and child speech.

Future work regarding VAD and speaker separation in PRT videos should continue to focus on sample variability. This work utilized a feature set consisting of midterm or short term features extracted using PyAudioAnalysis. Additional work could be undertaken to explore which features most adequately capture the differences between adult speech and child vocalizations. Increasing the number of samples could also help account for the variability seen between participating dyads. Including more samples representative of each child's age and communication ability could aid classification. It may also be beneficial to use separate models or classes for different child ability or age groups. Adding more data by using models pretrained on other speech corporation could aid classification. Including more samples would also allow utilization of more data intensive algorithms, such as deep learning networks.

5 Conclusion

Classifying audio segments in PRT videos is a challenging problem due to the video capture techniques, atypical adult vocal patterns, and limited child vocal activity. Using a limited data corpus, adequate results were achieved by separating the VAD and speaker separation tasks between two SVM models. Incorporating more data samples and pretrained models will likely produce greater accuracies by addressing the variability across sample videos due to the child's age and vocal acuity.

Acknowledgements. The authors thank Arizona State University and the National Science Foundation for their funding support. This material is partially based upon work supported by the National Science Foundation under Grant No. 1069125 and 1828010.

References

1. Koegel, R.L.: How To Teach Pivotal Behaviors to Children with Autism: A Training Manual (1988)
2. Hardan, A.Y., et al.: A randomized controlled trial of pivotal response treatment group for parents of children with autism. J. Child Psychol. Psychiatry **56**(8), 884–892 (2015)
3. Smith, I.M., Flanagan, H.E., Garon, N., Bryson, S.E.: Effectiveness of community based early intervention based on pivotal response treatment. J. Child Dev. Disord. **45**(6), 1858–1872 (2015)
4. Lecavalier, L., et al.: Moderators of parent training for disruptive behaviors in young children with autism spectrum disorder. J. Abnormal Child Psych. **45**(6), 1235–1245 (2017)
5. Gengoux, G.W., et al.: Pivotal response treatment parent training for autism: findings from a 3-month follow-up evaluation. J. Autism Dev. Disord. **45**(9), 2889–2898 (2015)
6. Lee, S., Potamianos, A., Narayanan, S.: Acoustics of children's speech: developmental changes of temporal and spectral parameters. J. Acoust. Soc. Am. **105**(3), 1455–1468 (1999)
7. WebRTC. https://webrtc.org
8. Zhang, X.L., Wang, D.: Boosting contextual information for deep neural network based voice activity detection. IEEE TALSP **24**(2), 252–264 (2016)
9. McLoughlin, I.V.: The use of low-frequency ultrasound for voice activity detection. In: International Speech Communication Association (2014)
10. Aneeja, G., Yegnanarayana, B.: Single frequency filtering approach for discriminating speech and nonspeech. IEEE TASLP **23**(4), 705–717 (2015)
11. Gorriz, J.M., Ramrez, J., Lang, E.W., Puntonet, C.G.: Hard c-means clustering for voice activity detection. Speech Commun. **48**(12), 1638–1649 (2006)
12. Sadjadi, S.O., Hansen, J.H.: Unsupervised speech activity detection using voicing measures and perceptual spectral flux. IEEE SPL **20**(3), 197–200 (2013)
13. Enqing, D., Guizhong, L., Yatong, Z., Xiaodi, Z.: Applying support vector machines to voice activity detection. IEEE SP **2**, 1124–1127 (2002)
14. Jo, Q.H., Chang, J.H., Shin, J., Kim, N.: Statistical model-based voice activity detection using support vector machine. IET SP **3**(3), 205–210 (2009)
15. Shin, J.W., Chang, J.H., Kim, N.S.: Voice activity detection based on statistical models and machine learning approaches. Comput. Speech Lang. **24**(3), 515–530 (2010)
16. Hughes, T., Mierle, K.: Recurrent neural networks for voice activity detection. In: ICASSP, pp. 7378–7382 (2013)

17. Drugman, T., Stylianou, Y., Kida, Y., Akamine, M.: Voice activity detection: merging source and filter-based information. IEEE SPL **23**(2), 252–256 (2016)
18. Kim, J., Hahn, M.: Voice activity detection using an adaptive context attention model. Interspeech **25**(8), 1181 (2017)
19. Potamianos, A., Narayanan, S.: Spoken dialog systems for children. In: IEEE SPL, pp. 197–200 (1998)
20. Boril, H., et al.: Automatic assessment of language background in toddlers through phonotactic and pitch pattern modeling of short vocalizations. In: WOCCI, pp. 39–43 (2014)
21. Liao, H., et al.: Large vocabulary automatic speech recognition for children. In: International Speech Communication Association, pp. 1611–1615 (2015)
22. Ward, L., et al.: Automated screening of speech development issues in children by identifying phonological error patterns. In: Interspeech, pp. 2661–2665 (2016)
23. Smith, D., et al.: Improving child speech disorder assessment by incorporating out of-domain adult speech. In: Interspeech, pp. 2690–2694 (2017)
24. Aggarwal, G., Singh, L.: Characterization between child and adult voice using machine learning algorithm. In: IEEE ICCCA, pp. 246–250 (2015)
25. Kumar, M., et al.: Multi-scale context adaptation for improving child automatic speech recognition in child-adult spoken interactions. In: Interspeech, pp. 2730–2734 (2017)
26. Marchi, E., et al.: Typicality and emotion in the voice of children with autism spectrum condition: evidence across three languages. In: International Speech Communication Association, pp. 115–119 (2018)
27. Xu, D., et al.: Child vocalization composition as discriminant information for automatic autism detection. In: IEEE EMBS, pp. 2518–2522 (2009)
28. Xu, D., et al.: Signal processing for young child speech language development. In: First Workshop on Child, Computer and Interaction (2008)
29. Pawar, R.: Automatic analysis of LENA recordings for language assessment in children aged five to fourteen years with application to individuals with autism. In: IEEE EMBS, pp. 245–248 (2017)
30. Signh, N.: The effects of parent training in pivotal response treatment (PRT) and continued support through telemedicine on gains in communication in children with autism spectrum disorder. University of Arizona (2014)
31. Boersma, P., Weenink, D.: PRAAT: doing phonetics by computer (2018). http://www.fon.hum.uva.nl/praat/
32. Titze, I.R., Martin, D.W.: Principles of Voice Production. ASA, Marylebone (1998)
33. Hunter, E.J.: A comparison of a child's fundamental frequencies in structured elicited vocalizations versus unstructured natural vocalizations: a case study. J. Ped. Otorhinolaryngol. **73**(4), 561–571 (2009)
34. Giannakopoulos, T.: pyAudioAnalysis: an open-source python library for audio signal analysis. PLoS ONE **10**(12), e0144610 (2018)
35. Pedregosa, F., et al.: Scikit-learn: machine learning in python. J. Mach. Learn. Res. **12**, 2825–2830 (2011)

Geolocation Search with SharePoint Fast Search Feature and A (star) Search Algorithm

H. Chathushka Dilhan Hettipathirana[1(✉)]
and Thameera Viraj Ariyapala[2]

[1] University of Moratuwa,
Bandaranayake Mawatha, Moratuwa 10400, Sri Lanka
chathuskadilhan@gmail.com
[2] Teesside University,
Campus Heart, Southfield Rd, Middlesbrough TS1 3BX, UK
thameeraviraj@gmail.com

Abstract. This paper represents a review on geolocation finding mechanism through SharePoint fast search and A* search algorithm. As a part of the SharePoint Fast search authors will compare two algorithms; Euclidean distance and Taxicab geometry distance in order to find a geolocation based on the shortest path. Throughout the paper, authors have highlighted the use of each individual algorithm (Euclidean distance, Taxicab geometry distance, and A* search algorithm) in terms finding the shortest path.

Keywords: SharePoint fast search · A* algorithm · Heuristic function · Euclidean distance · Taxicab geometry

1 Introduction

The search functionality of SharePoint is very robust and brings a Google or Bing-type experience to the corporate documents, and other contents. It is a combination of many components and complex search algorithms and path finding algorithms to ultimately produce quality search result sets.

SharePoint's Search algorithm takes into account many factors when ranking search results and finding content for display. Some of these are inherent in the content being searched or determined by the way users select and reference contents. Where developer can't control those factors. Other SharePoint search ranking elements can be influenced by the user, though.

Whereas, A* algorithm is a computer algorithm that is widely used in path finding and graph traversal, the process of plotting an efficiently traversable path between points, called nodes. A* uses a best-first search and finds the least cost path from a given initial node to one goal node (out of one or more possible goals). It uses a distance-plus-cost heuristic function f(x) to determine the order in which the search visits nodes in the tree.

It's possible to get the shortest path of one location to another and compute distances between them in a lot of different ways. For example, address can be queried against SQL Server (if the correct data is available), or those addresses can be used in conjunction with the Bing Geocode services. A custom webpart[1] with logic to query one of those services with the users/objects current location and all list items with location information takes little time, but performance issues can pop up in no time.

How is the performance when there are 200 items in a list? And 2000? 20000? Maybe 200000? Surely, it is possible to imagine that there are some smart solutions to send 200000 locations to the geocode service and receive them back, yet it is not an easy task to extract that information from a SharePoint list. That takes quite some time. It is even getting harder when data comes from several lists[2], not even thought about data from several site collections[3], external data or, location information that resides inside document. This is where the use of efficient path finding algorithms are required.

Throughout this paper authors will discuss how to use SharePoint fast search and A* to find Geolocation, and most suitable out of both.

2 Scenario - SharePoint Fast Search to Find Geolocation

SharePoint Fast Search is a very powerful search engine that can be customized in various ways. First of all, Fast search can index all of the information that lives inside SharePoint, or outside of SharePoint (using, for example, the Business Connectivity Service or a custom connector). No matter what (besides security), but whenever a query is executed on a certain keyword, all indexed data can be checked against that keyword.

At second comes the ability to enrich the index with extra information. The source for this information can be existing metadata from site columns (address, city), data from inside the document, or data that is already extracted using the entity extractor. These sources can be used to query the geocode service to retrieve the spatial data for that source and can be added to the fast index. This metadata can be used to query the index, determine distances to items within the index.

2.1 Indexing the Data

Fast web crawls data and puts this data into the index. Web crawlers, also known as spiders are used to crawl through hundreds of millions of Web pages that exist, in order to grasp the information (Fig. 1).

According to [6, 8] one of the processes that happens during the indexation process, is processing the content. During this process, this data is traversed through a "pipeline", which consists of several stages:

---

[1] In SharePoint, a Web Part is a component on a web page. It can act like a window to a component that may be displayed on another SharePoint page.

[2] A list in SharePoint is used to store data across columns in separate rows. For example, a list as a table in a database that will have columns and rows.

[3] Site collection is a hierarchical site structure that is made up of one top-level site and sites below it. This top-level website can have multiple sub sites, and each sub site can have multiple sub sites, for as many levels as required.

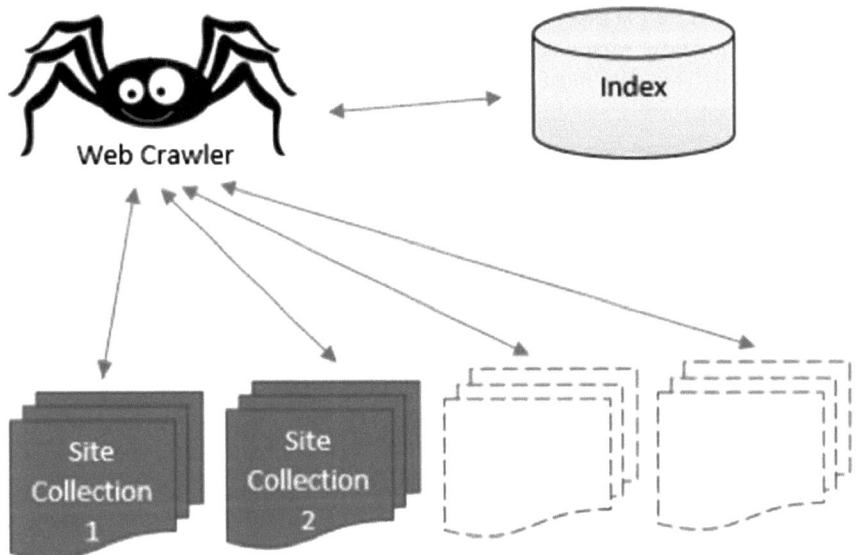

Fig. 1. Crawling site collections

Format Conversion → Language Detection → Lemmatize → Tokenizer → Entity Extraction → Vectorizer → Web Analyzer → Properties Mapper

The stages as shown above is just a small subset of the entire process, but basically, it does the following:

1. **Normalize the document** - the data of each input is normalized, so that every stage doesn't have problems processing this content.
2. **Language detection** - determine the language of the document. This metadata is used in other pipelines to, for example, determine what dictionary should be used.
3. **Lemmatizer** - based on the language that is detected, lemma and stemma are determined of words[4].
4. **Entity Extraction** - extracts entities, based on a dictionary, from the data that is processed. Out of the box Locations, Persons are extracted.

However, this pipeline can be extended based on the requirements. As pre-this scenario it can be extended to identify the latitude and longitude.

2.2 Extending the Pipeline

As author want to work with spatial data, a custom pipeline needs to be created, which has any location data as input, and which can output spatial data: latitude and longitude. All these properties need to be crawled properties:

---

[4] The definition on Wikipedia: canonical form, dictionary form, or citation form of a set of words (headword). Think about the following: bank – banks or good – better – best.

In order to create the pipeline, it's a must to know what kind of data is available. It's important to know what data is available, where it resides, and how it can be used to be processed. This data must be available through crawled properties (Fig. 2).

Fig. 2. Extend pipeline

2.3 SharePoint Fast Search Query to Find Location

After implementing the custom pipeline extension and all the data has been re-indexed, the index is enriched with the latitude and longitude information. This information can be used for some interesting queries and some interesting sorting algorithms.

When working with spatial data, there are some different approaches that can be used to retrieve the nearest locations and sort them. There is however one caveat to take care of, when a custom sorting formula is used. For the current scenario, author is querying directly against the Fast query service application using the code below. And, also return a set of 3 managed properties: title, latitude and longitude.

```
var proxy = (SearchServiceApplicationProxy) SearchSer-
viceApplicationProxy.GetProxy(SPServiceContext.Current);
var keywordQuery = new KeywordQuery(proxy)
    {
        EnableFQL = true,
        RowLimit = 20,
        ResultProvider = SearchProvider.FASTSearch,
        ResultTypes = ResultType.RelevantResults
    };
//define the managed properties that are returned
keywordQuery.SelectProperties.Add("title");
keywordQuery.SelectProperties.Add("latitude");
keywordQuery.SelectProperties.Add("longitude");
```

The above code gets the proxy that will be used and instantiates a new keyword Query object.

2.4 Retrieve All Results and Sort Them by Distance to a Certain Point

This query is easy to execute, as the query "#" will retrieve all items. But when the managed properties are used in a sorting formula, things change. As the managed properties are of type decimal, these properties are handled differently, as described in this paper. For the search formula, different algorithms can be used. Two popular algorithms are the following:

1. **Euclidean distance:** the shortest, unique distance between two points.
2. **Taxicab distance:** the distance between two points is the absolute difference of their coordinates. The path between the two points doesn't have to be unique.

3 Euclidean Distance

Joo Ghee Lim and S V Rao described a grid-based location estimation scheme. The scheme is to use hop counts between the nodes and the markers to determine location in square monitoring region. The scheme has several features like locating quickly, saving energy and strong robustness [3]. However, the location accuracy of the scheme above is stable in simulation due to multi-solution and no-solution. The details are as follows: [1, 7].

The grid-based location estimation scheme is improved by distributed grid location estimation scheme based on Euclidean distance, but its location accuracy is higher than Taxicab distance, and it is able to solve the shortest path problem (Fig. 3).

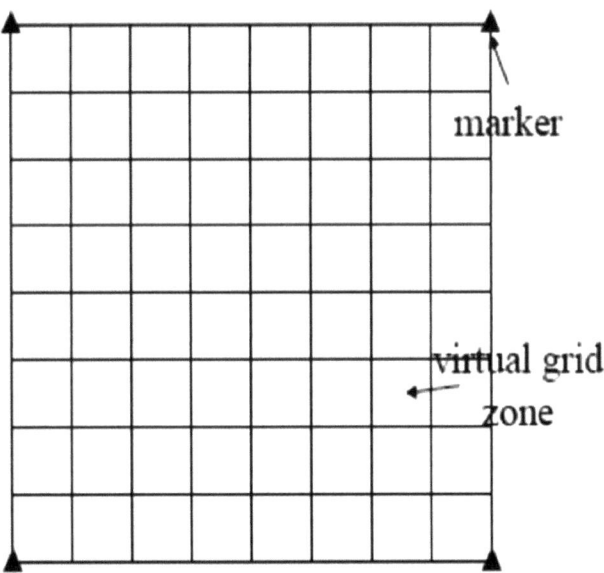

Fig. 3. Location based on grid extraction

Euclidean Distance: [2] it is generally a measure function, of which the computational complexity is O(d). It can be described as follow:

$$D(x,y) = \sqrt{\sum_{i=1}^{d}(x_i - y_i)^2}$$

Where x_i and y_i are vectors, and $D(x, y)$ is the distance between them. Considering the balance between the accuracy and the computational complexity, author contend that Euclidean distance is better than any other measure function in this scheme (this will be proven later part of this paper).

4 Taxicab Geometry

Taxicab Geometry is a form of geometry in which the usual distance function or metric of Euclidean geometry is replaced by a new metric in which the distance between two points is the sum of the absolute differences of their Cartesian coordinates.

The taxicab distance, d_1, between two vectors p, q in an n-dimensional real vector space with fixed Cartesian coordinate system, is the sum of the lengths of the projections of the line segment between the points onto the coordinate axes. More formally,

$$d_1(p,q) = ||p - q||_1 = \sum_{i=1}^{n}|p_i - q_i|$$

Where (p, q) are vectors.

The next image shows the difference between the two different algorithms (Euclidean distance and Taxicab distance). The green line represents the Euclidean algorithm and is the unique, shortest path between two points. The red, blue and yellow paths represent variations on the taxicab geometry and are indeed, not unique (Fig. 4).

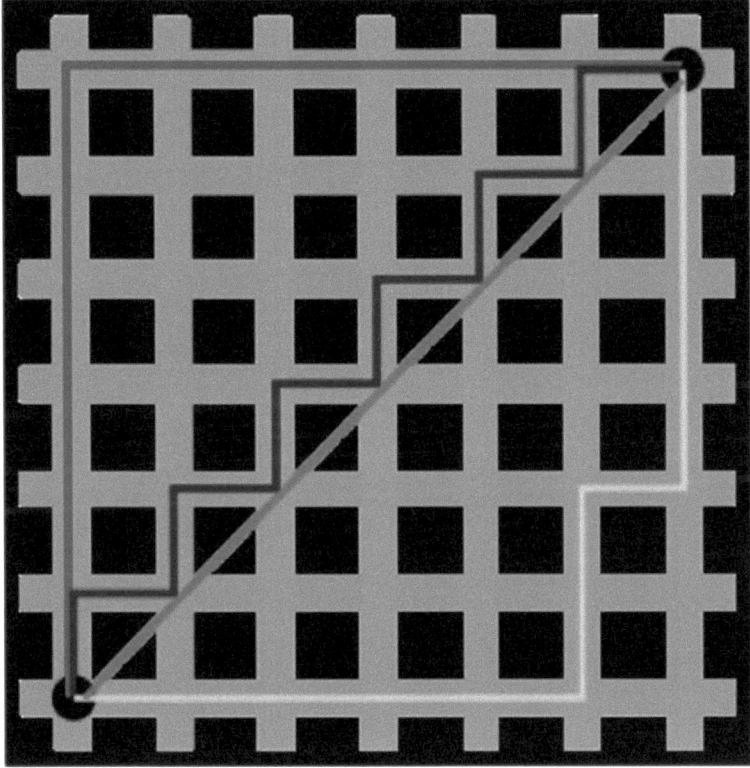

Fig. 4. Euclidean distance vs Taxicab distance (Color figure online)

5 A* Search Algorithm

In the field of heuristic searching algorithm, A* algorithm which is widely applied is a graph searching algorithm applying evaluation function to sort the nodes [9]. The basic idea of this algorithm is to avoid expanding paths that are already expensive. This algorithm uses mainly an evaluation function [4].

The distance-plus-cost heuristic is a sum of two functions:

$$f(x) = g(x) + h(x)$$

- The path-cost function, which is the cost from the starting node to the current node $g(x)$.
- And an admissible "heuristic estimate" of the distance to the goal $h(x)$.

The $h(x)$ part of the $f(x)$ function must be an admissible heuristic; that is, it must not overestimate the distance to the goal. Thus, for an application like routing, $h(x)$ might represent the straight-line distance to the goal, since that is physically the smallest possible distance between any two points or nodes.

Basically, A* search is considering the path costs in order to calculate the shortest path, which is $g(x)$ path cost from initial node to node x, and $h(x)$ estimated cost from x to goal (Fig. 5).

```
function (start, goal)
    closedset:= the empty set //The set of nodes already evaluated
    openset:= {start} //The set of tentative nodes to be evaluated, initially containing the start node
    came_from:= the empty map //The map of navigated nodes

    g_score[start]:= 0 //Cost from start along best known path
    //Estimated total cost from start to goal through y
    f_score[start]:= g_score[start] + heuristic_cost_estimate(start, goal)

    while openset is not empty
        current:= the node in openset having the lowest f_score[] value
        if current=goal
            return reconstruct_path(came_from, goal)

        remove current from openset
        add current to closedset
        for each neighbor in neighbor_nodes(current)
            if neighbor in closedset
                continue

            tentative_g_score:= g_score[current] + dist_between(current, neighbor)

            if neighbor not in openset or tentative_g_score < g_score[neighbor]
                came_from[neighbor]:= current
                g_score[neighbor]:= tentative_g_score
                f_score[neighbor]:= g_score[neighbor] + heuristic_cost_estimate(neighbor, goal)
                if neighbor not in openset
                    add neighbor to openset

    return failure


function reconstruct_path(came_from, current_node)
    if current_node in came_from
        p:= reconstruct_path(came_from, came_from[current_node])
        return (p + current_node)
    else
        return current_node
```

Fig. 5. Pseudocode for the A* algorithm

6 Conclusion

As authors have explained throughout the paper, it is noticeable that both Euclidean Distance and A* search algorithm are much optimal and efficient when comparing with Taxicab distance calculation in terms of finding the shortest path. Yet, the implementation of the Euclidean distance is bit of hard with its complexity. However, author propose to use hybrid approach as combining the both algorithm's novel features as it will enable much more accurate, optimal and cost-effective mechanism to calculate the shortest path.

References

1. Chen, H., Wu, H., Tzeng, N.F.: Grid-based approach for working node selection in wireless sensor networks. IEEE Commun. Soc. **6**, 3673–3678 (2004)
2. Jia, Z.-X., et al.: Distributed grid location estimation scheme based on Euclidean distance. In: IEEE Industrial Electronics and Applications, Singapore, pp. 1128–1132 (2008)

3. Lim, J.G., Rao, S.V.: A grid-based location estimation scheme using hop counts for multi-hop wireless sensor networks. In: International Workshop on Wireless Ad-Hoc Networks, pp. 330–334 (2004)
4. Yao, J., et al.: Path planning for virtual human motion using improved A* algorithm. In: Seventh International Conference on Information Technology, pp. 1154–1158. IEEE (2010)
5. Lemmatization - Wikipedia, the free encyclopedia. Wikipedia (2018). http://en.wikipedia.org/wiki/Lemmatisation. Accessed 10 Sept 2018
6. MSDN Blogs (2018). http://blogs.msdn.com/b/sharepointdev/archive/2010/12/09/tokenization-in-the-sharepoint-2010-server-ribbon.aspx. Accessed 9 Sept 2018
7. Patwari, N., Hero, A.O., et al.: Relative location estimation in wireless sensor networks, signal processing. IEEE Trans. Signal Process. **51**(8), 2137–2148 (2003)
8. SharePoint for Squirrels - by Natalya Voskresenskaya [MVP]: SharePoint Search 101: How does an indexer work? What is Lemmatization? What is Tokenization? http://spforsquirrels.blogspot.com/2011/01/sharepoint-search-101how-does-indexer.html. Accessed 9 Sept 2018
9. Sun, S., Lin, M.: The coordination path planning of multiple moving robots based on GA. Autom. J. **26**(5), 672–676 (2000)

A Study of Internship Satisfaction and Future Job Intention of Taiwanese Young Generation Z Students with Different Levels of Technology

Yi-an Hou[✉]

St. Mary's Junior College of Medicine,
Nursing, and Management, Yilan County, Taiwan
hyn@smc.edu.tw

Abstract. The study aimed to investigate Taiwanese young Generation Z students' internship satisfaction and future job intention from an aspect of gender and major. A quantitative method was adapted and a total of 270 junior college students in Taiwan served as subjects to fill out the 26-item questionnaire dealing with their demographic profiles, part-time job experience, internship satisfaction, and future job intention. All available data were computed by SPSS for descriptive analysis, t-test, ANOVA, Pearson correlation, and Regression analysis. Findings revealed that gender difference and majors with different technology levels did make a difference in student intern's satisfaction and future job intention. Recommendations were provided for the three main stakeholders for a more successful "win-win-win" triangular internship program to help the young digital generation students get ready for the job market.

Keywords: Generation Z · Internship · Satisfaction · Gender · Major · Technology

1 Introduction

1.1 Background of the Study

To bridge the gap of theory and practice and to cultivate both "hard-skills" and "soft-skills", many schools have been providing students with some kind of internship for "hands-on" experiences. In fact, internship plays an important role in the triangle partnership, and a successful internship can benefit the three main stakeholders of the school's curricular assessment, the student's preparing better for the future endeavors, and the industry's hiring potential talented individuals. However, internship experience may also bring about some frustration or dissatisfaction for students and discourages them to stay in the field. In Taiwan, there are three major sources of the higher education providing basic workforce, high school, junior college, and college/university. Many of them are the so-called "Generation Z", the first all-digital generation, being technology savvy, very entrepreneurial, emphasizing on work-life balance, and searching how to take advantage of relevant professional opportunities for providing them experience for the future. Specifically, males are often found to be stronger with mathematical/logical intelligence (Hou 2015, 2016), which is expected to have higher connection with technology, hence the above mentioned characteristics of Generation Z tend to be more obvious for those majors with more male students.

As the coming young workforce will be the new Generation Z, the "digital natives", and more and more females have been entering into the job market, some relative issues dealing with gender difference and majors with different levels of technology related to internship satisfaction should be paid more attention. Hence, the study intends to investigate the young workforce's internship satisfaction to provide some hints for the stakeholders to get ready for the new coming generation.

1.2 Purpose of the Study

The study aims to investigate Taiwanese young Generation Z students' internship satisfaction and future job intention from an aspect of gender and major with different levels of technology, expecting to find out the answers to the following research questions: What is Taiwanese Generation Z workforce's internship satisfaction and future job intention? Is there any difference on their internship satisfaction and future job intention between genders and among different majors? and What factors relate to their internship satisfaction and future job intention?

2 Related Literature

Most courses taken in schools are helpful for a future career in a specific field, yet, students still need some practical skills, hands-on experiences, and marketability provided by the industry to enter the field successfully, and internship is the time to help students well equip themselves with soft skills complementing their hard skills. Hence, internship can be regarded as the last mile of students' education journey.

Internship is a triangular partnership among the school, the students, and the industry. When it runs well, all the three main stakeholders benefit, including first, the school's being able to receiving feedback from the industry and students as input for curriculum improvement and build up closer ties with local relevant business community; second, the student's availing a practical learning environment to understand the reality of professional commitment and develop people skills (soft skills) (Schulz 2008) for future foundation of career development; and the third, the industry's providing workplace training for recruiting potential talented individuals and also strengthening bonds with academic institutions and incorporating new ideas (Swanson and Tomkovick 2012). However, as Hou (2018) pointed out that some students may not be fully aware of the workload, job demands, and requirements in advance, and are not ready to work in the real world situations, together with some other personal reasons, all cause their being dissatisfied about the internship, pessimistic about their career development, and even decide to turn away from the field. Hence, it has been supported that students' satisfaction about the internship plays a very important role in their future job intention. Normally, factors relative to students' internship satisfaction are divided into five factors, namely, about job itself, about superior, about training and development, about pay and welfare, as well as about peer relationship (Bao and Fang 2014).

In addition, as more and more females have been entering into the work force, some issues relevant to gender differences have been generated considerable interest in the job, such as salary, position, performance, satisfaction, etc. Generally speaking, in many cases of the society, many females are not expected to take more responsibilities to support a family like males, hence, as Clark (1997) mentioned that more women are happy at work, because they tend to be less likely to identify earning as the most important aspect of a job. Instead, for many females, to identify social relations at work is one of the benefits. Hence, a significant gender difference exists in expectation about jobs which correlates with levels of job satisfaction, and many findings indicated that females have higher satisfaction about jobs (Bender et al. 2005; Okpara et al. 2005).

Generation Z is the name used for the group of people born after the Generation Y, the Millennial. There are no precise dates for when to start or end of Generation Z. According to Sunburn (2015), Generation Z were those born after December 2000; next to Generation Y (born from 1981 to 2000), Generation X (born from 1965 to 1980), Baby Boomers (born between 1946 and 1964), and the Sages (born between 1925 and 1945). In fact, Generation Z is the first cohort to have Internet technology readily available at a young age (Prensky 2001). They use the Internet as a way to gain access to information and to interact with others. In addition, the use of social media has become integrated into the daily lives of most of the Generation Z'ers who have access to mobile technology, earning them the nickname "digital natives" (Dill 2015). On the other hand, they are faced with a growing income gap and a shrinking middle-class, which all have led to increasing stress levels in families (Turner 2015), and some of their competencies, for example, reading competence, are being transformed because of their familiarity with digital device, platforms, and texts (Amiama-Espaillat and Mayor-Ruiz 2017). Furthermore, Generation Z students are found to be loyal, compassionate, thoughtful, open-minded, responsible, and determined (Seemiller 2016). With the technological proficiency they possess, Generation Z'ers have the advantage to be helpful to the typical company, but they no longer just want a job, instead, they want a feeling of fulfillment and excitement in their job (Williams 2015). In fact, they are ready to make the best use of relevant professional chances for providing them experience for the future (Levit 2015). Consequently, to attract the new incoming Generation Z workforce, Dill (2015) pointed out seven things that employers should know, including (1) their parents have the greatest influence on their educational and professional decision- making, but the perspectives of friends and teachers are important too; (2) curiosity is the strongest motivator for choosing a course of study; (3) they are interested in entering the workforce without higher education, but fear actually doing so; (4) they are very entrepreneurial; (5) despite their entrepreneurial nature, work-life balance and job security are the two career goals most important to this generation; (6) they want lots of information; and (7) they may be less optimistic than Millennials about their work opportunities. Specifically, males are found to be stronger with mathematical/logical intelligence (Hou 2015, 2016), which is expected to have higher connection with technology, hence the above mentioned characteristics of Generation Z for those majors with more male students tend to be more obvious.

As the coming young workforce will be the new Generation Z, the "digital natives" (Dill 2015), and more and more females have been entering into the job market, some relative issues dealing with gender difference and majors with different levels of technology related to internship satisfaction should be paid more attention.

3 Methodology

3.1 Research Design

The study employed a quantitative approach with data gathered through a 26-item questionnaire to get necessary information from the target participants. They helped to fill out the questionnaire and provided valuable reflections about their internship experience and satisfaction toward the internship.

3.2 Subjects of the Study

A total of 270 seniors of a private five-year junior college in North-East Taiwan served as subjects of the study, including 65 males (24.1%) and 205 females (75.9%). They were from the five departments of the college. They just completed their two consecutive semesters internship off campus and came back to school for their last semester, including 54 from Nursing Department, 60 from Hospitality Management Department, 67 from Cosmetic Application and Management Department, 55 from Information Management Department, and 34 from Child Education Department. Subjects of the study by gender and major were displayed in Table 1.

3.3 Research Instrument

The research instrument was a 26-item questionnaire based on an extensive review of related literature, which consisted two sections. The first section collected students' demographic data (4 items), including gender, major, intern-related part-time job experience and duration, as well as intern with pay or not. The other section included 22 items of students' opinions about internship satisfaction, composing of 2 items relating to the school (items 5, 7), 3 items relating to the teacher (items 6, 8, 9), 7 items relating to the company (items 10–16), and 8 items relating to students themselves (items 17–24), as well as 2 items relating to their future job intention (items 25, 26). Students were requested to give a score to each of the 22 items using a 5-point Likert-type scale ranging from very dissatisfied (1) to very satisfied (5), and the mean score of 1.0–2.4, 2.5–3.4, and 3.5–5.0 was regarded as Low, Medium, and High (Oxford 1990).

3.4 Procedure and Data Analysis

The study was conducted in the second semester of the academic year of 2017 in a private five-year junior college in North-East Taiwan. The data were collected from the seniors of the five departments of the college. They just completed their two consecutive semesters' internship out of campus and came back to school for their last semester in the college. All available data were computed by the Statistical Package of

Social Science (SPSS) for windows. Along with descriptive analysis of mean and standard deviation to display the distributions of students' demographic profiles, the data were analyzed by t-test and ANOVA to find out if there was any difference on internship experience/satisfaction between males and females, as well as among the five major students. In addition, Pearson correlation analysis and Liner Regression analysis were adopted to investigate the correlation among the factors of internship experience, and the factors relative to students' internship satisfaction and future job intention, respectively.

4 Findings

Results and discussions included (1) reliability of the research instrument, (2) students' demographic profiles and ratings of internship satisfaction and future job intention, (3) gender difference, (4) major difference of internship satisfaction and future job intention, (5) correlation among internship variables, and (6) factors relative to internship satisfaction and future job intention. They were described below:

4.1 Reliability of the Research Instrument

The reliability of the research instrument was Cronbach's Alpha .920 (n = 22). According to Gay and Airasian (2003), 'If a test were perfectly reliable, the reliability coefficient would be 1.00. However, no test is perfect reliable" (p. 141), hence, the research instrument of the study with an Alpha value of .920 was quite reliable.

4.2 Students' Ratings of Demographic Profiles, Internship Satisfaction, and Future Job Intention

Findings showed that among the 270 participants, more than three fourths (75.9%) were females, while slightly less than one-fourth of the students were from Department of Cosmetic Application Management (24.8%), followed by Hospitality Management (22.2%), Information Management (20.4%), Nursing (20.0%), and Child Education Management (12.6%). Based on their self-reports, more than half (54.9%) of the students had some intern-related part-time job experiences, including less than 1 year (18.5%), 1–3 years (21.2%), and more than 3 years (15.2%). As for the required two consecutive semesters' internship, slightly more than two-fifths (41.9%) of the students were unpaid, while the remaining, nearly three-fifths (58.1%), were paid.

The findings also presented students' rating of their internship satisfaction and future job intention. First, findings showed that students had good satisfaction about the school (items 5, 7) (M = 3.49, rank 2nd in total), including the school helped them know more and get ready for the intern in advance by holding meetings (item 5, rank 9th), as well as the school's curriculum matched the need in their intern practice (item 7, rank 18th). Second, for their satisfaction about the teachers (items 6, 8, 9) (M = 3.45, rank 3rd in total), students expressed that teachers helped them feel to be cared by visiting them (item 8, rank 11th), solve the problems encountered in intern (item 9, rank 12th), and choose appropriate intern units (item 6, rank15th). Third, among the four factors of students' internship experience, students' expressed the lowest satisfaction about the company (items 10–16) (M = 3.29, rank 4th in total). In general, students seemed to be satisfied about the company's "working environment" (item 12, rank 10th), "providing pre-job or in-job training" (item 10, rank 13th), "working time arrangement" (item 16, rank 14th), and "the convenience of transportation" (item 11, rank 16th); while they tended to be less satisfied about the company about "salary" (item 13, rank 22nd), "system" (item 14, rank 21st), and "welfare" (item 15, ranked 20th). Fourth, for students themselves, they felt most satisfied with what they learned from the valuable intern experience. In particular, the top eight were that the intern could "expand social experience" (item 21, 1st), "strengthen practical skills" (item 20, 2nd), "increase the ability to resist pressure" (item 18, 3rd), "increase professional knowledge" (item19, 4th), "peer relationship" (item 17, 5th), "be challenging" (item 23, 6th), "help with career planning" (item 22, 7th), and "create more chances for work" (item 24, 8th), respectively. Lastly, for students' future job intention, findings revealed that the mean score of students' stay in the intern-related field (M = 3.34, SD = .95) was lower than that of considering to change to other fields (M = 3.39, SD = .94). In other words, more students would consider to change the field than those who intended to stay in their present field.

To summarize, in the study, majority of the participants were females (75.9%), more than half (54.9%) had some intern-related part-time jobs, and nearly three-fifths (58.1%) of their internship were paid. As a whole, students' satisfaction mean score on their overall internship was high (3.54 out of 5.00), ranging from 2.98 to 3.98. In general, students had rated their internship satisfaction about themselves first, followed by the school, the teachers, and the company; in particular, the top three variables were students' satisfaction about their increasing "social experience", "practical skills" and "pressure resistance", while the bottom three were the company's "salary", "systems", and "welfare".

4.3 Gender Difference of Students' Intern Experience, Satisfaction, and Future Job Intentions

The findings consisted of two parts. The first part explored the general gender difference of students' intern experiences, including their intern-related part-time job experiences, intern with/without pay, as well as their satisfaction (about the school, the teachers, the company, students themselves), and future job intention. As for the second part, it focused on descriptions of individual items with significant gender difference on the variables mentioned above. The findings were displayed in Tables 2 and 3.

Gender Difference of Students' Intern Experience, Satisfaction, and Future Job Intention

The study found that males had significant higher means in "intern with pay" ($p < .01$) and "satisfaction about the company" ($p < .01$) than females. Though males also had higher means in "part-time job experience" and "considering to change the field", while females had higher means in satisfaction about "the school", "the teacher", "students themselves", "overall satisfaction", and "intention to stay in the field", yet the differences didn't reach significant levels. As for rankings of the four variables of intern satisfaction, both males and females ranked satisfaction about students themselves the first (1st), but ranked the school and the company the last (4th), respectively. In other words, males significantly had more intern experiences with pay and were more satisfied with the company than females ($p < .01$), and satisfaction rankings differed in males' ranking the school the last, while the company was females' last ranking. The findings were presented in Table 2.

Variables of Gender Difference of Students' Internship Experience, Satisfaction, and Future Job Intentions

The findings included items of gender difference of students' internship experience, satisfaction (about the school, the teachers, the company, students), and future job intention. First, males had higher mean in intern with pay (item 4) ($p < .01$) and in satisfaction about the company ($p < .01$), but females had higher mean in the company's "convenient transportation" (item 11) ($p < .01$). Second, among the four factors of satisfaction of internship, students had the highest mean about students themselves, especially females. In particular, females had higher means in feeling that the intern could "increase professional knowledge" (item 19) ($p < .05$), "strengthen practical skills" (item 20) ($p < .01$), "help with career planning" (item 22) ($p < .05$), "be challenging" (item 23) ($p < .01$), and "help to create more chances for work" (item 24) ($p < .01$). Third, as for future job intention, males had higher mean in "considering change the field" (item 26), while females were higher in "staying in the field" (item 25), however, the differences didn't reach significant levels. The findings were presented in Table 3.

4.4 Major Difference of Students' Internship Experience, Satisfaction, and Future Job Intention

The same as that of gender difference, the findings of major difference also consisted of two parts. The first part explored the general major difference of students' intern experience (such as intern-related part-time job experience and intern with/without pay), satisfaction (about the school, the teachers, the company, and students themselves), as well as future job intention (to stay in the field or change to other fields). As for the second part, it focused on descriptions of individual variables of the major difference mentioned above. They were described below:

General Major Difference of Students' Internship Experience, Satisfaction, and Future Job Intention

Among the five majors, first, Nursing students ranked 3, 4, 3, 3, 3, 4, 4, 2, 5 for intern-related part-time job experience, intern with pay, satisfaction about the school, the teachers, the company, the students, overall satisfaction, to stay in the field, and to change to other fields. As for Hospitality Management students, Cosmetic Management students, Information Management students, and Child Education students, the rankings were 1, 2, 5, 5, 5, 5, 5, 5, 4; 2, 1, 4, 4, 2, 2, 3, 3, 3; 4, 3, 2, 2, 1, 3, 2, 4, 1; and 5, 5, 1, 1, 4, 1, 1, 1, 2, respectively.

Second, in general, for overall intern satisfaction, Child Education students had the highest mean, followed by Nursing students, Cosmetic Management students, Information Management students, and Hospitality Management students. In particular,

Nursing students had more intention to stay in the field (rank 2nd), while Hospitality Management students had most intern-related part-time job experience (rank 1st) and intern with pay (rank 2nd), but had lowest intern satisfaction (about the school, the teachers, the company, the students themselves) and future job intention to stay in the field (all rank 5th). In addition, Cosmetic Management students had highest mean of intern with pay (rank 1st) followed by inter-related part-time experience, satisfaction about the company and students themselves (all rank 2nd).

Third, Information Management students had highest satisfaction about the company (1st), followed by the school, the teacher, and overall intern satisfaction (all rank 2nd), but surprisingly, they also had the highest intention to change the field after the intern (1st). Furthermore, Child Education students had least intern-related part-time job experience and intern with pay opportunity (both rank 5th), but they had highest intern satisfaction about the school, the teachers, students themselves, overall satisfaction, and future job intention to stay in the field (all rank 1st), however, they had lower satisfaction about the company next to the last (4th) and higher future job intention to change the field (2nd) next to the first.

In short, among the five department students, some results need to be paid more attention. One is the result of students of Hospitality Management Department, who had the most part-time job experience (1st) and more internship with pay (2nd), but they had the lowest internship satisfaction (5th) and future job intention to stay in the field (5th), though they also had the next to the lowest desire to change the field (4th). The results typically supported that the Generation Z might be "less optimistic about their work opportunities" (Dill 2015), consequently, though they were not satisfied about the internship, yet they were less confident to find a better job in other field, so they hesitated to turn away. Another example was that, with more male students, who were believed to be stronger with Mathematical/Logical intelligence and higher levels of technology as expected, Information Management majors were more "digital natives" together with their "entrepreneurial nature", and were more interested in changing the field (1st), though they had favorable overall internship satisfaction (2nd). And the other was the result of students of Child Education Department, who had the strongest allover internship satisfaction, including satisfaction about the school, the teachers, and the company, but excluded the company; and though they had the strongest intention to stay in the field (1st), yet they also had strong desire to change to other fields (2nd). It seems that many of the three department students were at the crossroads in their career decision. The findings were presented in Table 4.

Variables of Major Difference of Students' Internship Experience, Satisfaction, and Future Job Intention

First, in light of intern experience, students of Hospitality Management Department (H) had higher mean of intern-related part-time job experience (item 3), mostly with pay (item 4), than other department students ($p < .01$).

Second, among the five department students, significant differences existed in their overall satisfaction about the school ($p < .01$), including school's holding meetings with students prior to the intern to help them know more and get ready for it (item 5) ($p < .05$), as well as providing curriculum matched the need in intern practice (item 7)

($p < .01$), in which students of Nursing Department and Child Education Department had higher satisfaction than students of Hospitality Management Department ($p < .05$).

Third, as for their satisfaction about the teachers, in a whole, students of Nursing Department, Information Management Department, and Child Education Management Department tended to have higher satisfaction than students of Hospitality Management Department and Cosmetic Application and Management Department ($p < .05$).

Fourth, students' satisfaction about the company was the least among the four factors, and there was a significant difference among the five department students ($p < .05$). The differences included the company's "working environment" (item 12), in which students of Hospitality Management Department was less satisfied than students of Information Management Department ($p < .05$) and Child Education Department ($p < .05$); and "salary" (item 13), in which students of Child Education Department seemed to be the least satisfied than their counterparts ($p < .05$); as well as "working-time arrangement" (item 16), in which students of Information Management Department were more satisfied than students of Hospitality Management Department and Cosmetic Application and Management Department ($p < .01$).

Fifth, among the four factors of intern satisfaction, students had the most satisfaction about the benefits they gained from the intern experience. In lights of major difference, the students of Child Education Department seemed to be more satisfied than the other four, including about "professional knowledge" (item 19), in which they were more satisfied than other three (except Cosmetic Application and Management Department) ($p < .05$), about "practical skills" (item 20) and "career planning" (item 22), ($p < .05$), in which they were more satisfied than students of Hospitality Management ($p < .05$); about "social experience" (item 21), in which they were the most satisfied ($p < .05$); as well as about "more chances for work" (item 24), in which they were more satisfied than students of Hospitality Management Department and Information Management Department ($p < .05$).

Last, regarding to students' future job intention, students of Child Education Department and Nursing Department had higher intention to stay in the field, while students of Hospitality Management Department and Information Management Department had the lower intention (item 25). Consequently, it was reasonable to find that students of Nursing Department (with higher intention to stay, rank 2nd) had the lowest intention to change the field (item 26) (rank 5th), and students of Information Department (with lower intention to stay in the field, rank 4th) had the highest intention to change the field (item 26) (rank 1st). However, it was surprising to find that students of Hospitality Department (with the lowest intention to stay in the field, rank 5th) also had the lower intention to change the field (4th); and students of Child Education Department (with the highest intention to stay in the field, 1st) also had higher intention to change the field (rank 2nd), just next to students of Information Management Department. Furthermore, for the overall internship satisfaction, students of Child Education Department had the highest (1st), followed by Information Management Department (2nd), Cosmetic Application Management Department (3rd), Nursing Department (4th), and Hospitality Management Department (5th), respectively.

4.5 Correlation Among Variables of Intern Satisfaction and Future Job Intention

Findings showed that except for future job intention to change the field, strong correlations existed among variables of intern satisfaction about the school, the teachers, the company, the students, and future job intention to stay in the field ($p < .01$) positively.

4.6 Regression Analysis of Factors Relative to Internship Satisfaction and Future Job Intention

Regression Analysis of Factors Relative to Overall Internship Satisfaction

By Regression analysis, it was found that among the variables of students' demographic profiles of gender, major, intern-related part-time job experience, and intern with pay, major was the only factor relative to students' overall internship satisfaction ($t = 2.287$, Sig = .023).

In fact, based on what Table 4 presented, students of Child Education Management had the highest overall internship satisfaction (1st), especially higher than students of Hospitality Management Department (5th) significantly ($p < .05$).

Regression Analysis of Factors Relative to Future Job Intention

Findings revealed that factors relative to students' future job intention to stay in the filed were gender ($t = 2.774$, Sig = .006), part-time job experience ($t = 2.624$, Sig = .009), intern with pay ($t = 3.977$, Sig = .000), satisfaction about the company ($t = 5.744$, Sig = .000), and about students themselves ($t = 4.894$, Sig = .000). That is to say, students, especially females, who had more intern-related part-time job experiences, intern with pay, had more intern satisfaction about the company and about students themselves tended to have more future job intention to stay in the field.

On the other hand, findings presented that major was the only factor to be relative to students' future job intention to change the field ($t = 3.557$, Sig = .000). As stated in Table 4, it can be seen that students of Information Management (I) had highest intention to change the field (1st), while students of Nursing had the least intention to change the field (5th).

5 Conclusions

Majority of the students of Departments of Nursing, Cosmetic Application Management, and Child Education Management were females (94.1%–98.1%), while Department of Information Management had more males (61.8%) and 40% of the students of Department of Hospitality Management were males (Table 1). It's supported that more and more females have been entering into the work force and which brings about some issues relevant to gender differences in the job market, including satisfaction (Clark 1997, Bender et al. 2005, Okpara et al. 2005).

In a whole, students' mean score of internship satisfaction was 3.54 (Table 2). According to Oxford (1990) (p. 300), the average was high (High = 3.5 to 5.0, Medium = 2.5 to 3.4, Low = 1.0 to 2.4). In particular, they were more satisfied with themselves for their "social experience", "practical skills", and "pressure assistance" being strengthened. On the contrary, they were less satisfied with the company's "salary", "systems", and "welfare", as well as the school's "curriculum" and the teachers' help to "choose appropriate intern units". Additionally, their future job intention to stay in the field was lower than to consider changing the field (Table 2). The finding of high internship satisfaction and lower intention to stay in the field was not commensurate with general phenomenon that high internship satisfaction led to high intention to stay in the field (Chen et al. 2011, Cook et al. 2004).

As for gender differences, overall, males had more intern-with-pay experiences ($p < .01$) and were more satisfied about overall of the company ($p < .01$) (Table 2). In particular, females were more satisfied with the company's "convenient transportation" ($p < .01$) and what they gained from the internship experience, including "professional knowledge" ($p < .05$), "practical skills" ($p < .01$), "career planning" ($p < .05$), "challenging" ($p < .01$), and "more work chances" ($p < .01$) (Table 3).

For major differences, among students of the five majors, comparatively, Nursing students had medium levels of internship satisfaction and had the weakest intention to change the field after graduation; while Hospitality students had more intern-related part-time jobs, and with pay, but they were least satisfied with internship, and had the weakest desire to stay in the field (Table 4). That Hospitality students had low internship satisfaction was consistent with Bao and Fang (2014)'s finding. As for Cosmetic Application students, everyone was paid (100%) during their internship, and their satisfaction and future job intention were between medium to high (M = 3.32–3.83). In addition, Child Education students were most satisfied about the school, the teachers, the students, overall internship satisfaction, and had the strongest intention to stay in the field; while Information students had the highest satisfaction about the company, but had the strongest intention to change to other field after graduation. In a whole, the results indicated that Hospitality students had the weakest intention to stay in the field, but they also had the weaker desire to turn away from the industry; similarly, Child Education students had higher internship satisfaction and strongest intention to stay in the field, yet on the other hand, they also had strong desire to change to other fields. Both the two phenomena should be noticed with care (Table 4).

By regression analysis, apparently, majors were found to be relative to students' overall internship satisfaction ($p < .05$) and intention to change the field after graduation, hence, students of Hospitality, Nursing, and Cosmetic Application with low overall internship satisfaction, as well as students of Hospitality, Information, and Cosmetic Application with low future job intention to stay, all need to be paid more attention trying to find out the possible reasons.

The most important is students' internship satisfaction plays an important role in their future job intention, and factors of internship satisfaction (the school, the teachers, and company, and the students) and future job intention to stay in the field were found to be strongly correlated with one another ($p < .01$), as a result, it's suggested that for a more successful and more satisfied internship program, the triangular partnership among the school/teachers, the company, and the students work together to evaluate the school's curriculum and internship policy, the company's system and program, as well as students' individual differences and expectation so as to run the "win-win-win" triangular network well and benefit the three stakeholders, especially the students.

Last, some individual suggestions are provided for the five majors:

Nursing Department: Overall, nursing students had high level of internship satisfaction (M = 3.59) about the school (M = 3.72) and the teachers (M = 3.56), especially they had stronger intention to stay in the field (M = 3.59) (Table 3). However, comparatively, nursing students seemed to be less confident about themselves in the internship performance of "professional knowledge" (item 19) and "social experience" (item 21) (Table 4). In addition, the majority of the nursing students are females (98.1%), who are less satisfied about the company/hospital ($p < .01$) (Table 2). Hence, it is suggested that the school teachers and the hospital nurses provide more assistance and encouragement to help the student interns build up self-confidence to overcome the "Reality Shock" in the internship.

Hospitality Management Department: Hospitality students had more intern-related part-time jobs, and with pay, but among the five majors, they were the least satisfied with the internship (Table 4), which was commensurate with Bao and Fang' s (2014) finding that hospitality students' internship satisfaction was low. In particular, next to information Management major, male students occupied high percentage (40%) (Table 1); comparing with females, they were less satisfied about the school and had lower satisfaction about the company's transportation, as well as what they gained from the internship, including "professional knowledge", "practical skills", "career planning", "challenging", and "more work chances" (Table 3). However, an example of Generation Z's characteristics of being "less optimistic about their opportunities" (Dill 2015), though they had the lowest future job intention to stay in the field, they also had lower desire to turn away from the hospitality industry (Table 4). It seems that they are at the crossroads in their career decision. So, it's time that the school and the company work together to bring the education-service split to keep more potential talents in the industry.

Cosmetic Application Management Department: Students had more intern-related part-time job experiences and everyone was paid (100%). Among the five majors, they belonged to be "medium" of internship satisfaction (rank 3rd) and future job intention (rank 3rd) (Table 4). The same as that of Nursing students, the majority of Cosmetic Application Management students were females (94%), and seemed to be less satisfied with teachers' visit for feeling "care and concern" (item 8) than Child Education majors, as well as less satisfied with the company's "working time arrangement" (item 16) than Information Management majors. Consequently, it's suggested that the school teacher, if possible, a full-time specialist staff, preferably with industrial experience, can arrange more time to visit the student interns and the company can notice the arrangement of working time.

Information Management Department: In the study, it is the only department in the college with more male students (61.8%) than females (38.2%). Consequently, it had more gender differences in males' favorable intern-related part-time job experiences, interns with pay, and higher overall internship satisfaction (2nd), especially about the company (1st). In addition, males are found to be stronger with Mathematical/Logical intelligence (Hou 2015), and their better technology skills of "digital natives" are expected, together with another characteristics of Generation Z's "entrepreneurial nature" (Dill 2015), not surprisingly, they had weaker future job intention to stay in the field (4th) but had the strongest desire to turn away from the industry (1st) (Table 4).

Hence, it's suggested that the school and the department need to pay attention to the phenomena and to help students to ease the school-to-work transition.

Child Education Management Department: Similar to Nursing majors and Cosmetic Application management majors, the Child Education Management majors had more female students (94.1%). They had least intern-related part-time job experiences, and unlike Cosmetic Application Management students all with pay (100%), they all were unpaid (100%) in their internship. Nevertheless, they had highest overall internship satisfaction, including about the school, the teachers, and their own performance from the internship, but they had lower satisfaction about the company, in fact, next to the last (4th). In addition, they had strongest future job intention to stay in the field, but, surprisingly, they also had stronger desire to turn away from the field, in fact, next to the first (2nd). Hence, it's suggested that the school and the company work together to help the students bridge the gap of education-service and the Role Transition and consider to stay in the field.

All in all, gender difference and majors with different technology levels were found to make a difference in the young Generation Z students' internship satisfaction and future job intention, and factors of internship dealing with the school, the teacher, the company, the students, and the future job intention to stay in the field were found to be strongly correlated with one another. Hence, all the three main stakeholders of the school/department, the company/industry, and the students themselves should work together to take students' individual differences into consideration for a more successful "win-win-win" triangular internship program to avoid the possible gap of "Reality Shock", "Role Transition", "Education-Service Split", and "School-to-Work Transition" to help the students, especially the young Generation Z, to get ready for the job market. More importantly, some characteristics of the young generation had been supported to be relevant to their internship satisfaction and future job intention, such as their "digital natives", "being very entrepreneurial", "less optimistic about work opportunities", and the like. Consequently, the young Generation Z students' individual differences need to be paid much more attention.

Appendix

See Tables 1, 2, 3 and 4.

Table 1. Subjects of the study

Majors	Male (n/%)	Female (n/%)	All
Nursing (N)	1 (1.9%)	53 (98.1%)	54
Hospitality management (H)	24 (40%)	36 (60.0%)	60
Cosmetic application (C)	4 (6.0%)	63 (94.0%)	67
Information management (I)	34 (61.8%)	21 (38.2%)	55
Child education management (CE)	2 (5.9%)	32 (94.1%)	34
All	65 (24.1%)	205 (75.9%)	270

Table 2. Gender difference of students' internship experience, satisfaction, and future job intention (n = 270)

Gender	Part-time M	Pay M	School M (rank)	Teacher M (rank)	Company M (rank)	Student M (rank)	Satisfaction M (rank)	Stay M	Change M
Male	2.66	1.66	3.32 (4)	3.40 (2)	3.37 (3)	3.71 (1)	3.53	3.10	3.60
Female	2.14	1.55	3.55 (2)	3.46 (3)	3.26 (4)	3.83 (1)	3.55	3.42	3.33
All (M)	2.27	1.58	3.49 (2)	3.45 (3)	3.29 (4)	3.80 (1)	3.54	3.34	3.39
Sig	.091	.000	.171	.605	.006	.076	.053	.354	.802

**$p < .01$ * $p < .05$

Table 3. Variables of gender difference of students' internship experience, satisfaction, and future job intentions

I. Students' demographic profiles	Gender	1%	2%	3%	4%	5%	M	SD	Sig
4. Nature of internship 1. Unpaid 2. Paid	male	33.9	66.1				**1.66**	.47	**.000**
	female	44.4	55.6				1.55	.49	
	all	41.9	58.1				1.58	.49	
II. Variables of internship satisfaction	Gender	1%	2%	3%	4%	5%	M	SD	Sig
11. Convenient transportation (company)	male	66.7	31.3	17.5	23.8	25.7	3.20	1.23	**.001**
	female	33.3	68.7	82.5	76.2	74.3	**3.46**	.87	
	all	5.6	5.9	44.4	31.1	13.0	3.40	.97	
19. Professional knowledge (students)	male	71.4	0	22.0	23.1	24.1	3.70	1.05	**.023**
	female	28.6	100	78.0	76.9	75.9	**3.84**	.80	
	all	2.6	1.1	30.0	44.8	21.5	3.81	.87	
20. Practical skills (students)	male	83.3	0	23.1	23.3	21.5	3.70	1.05	**.006**
	female	16.7	100	76.9	76.7	78.5	**3.93**	.77	
	all	2.2	0.4	28.9	44.4	24.1	3.87	.85	
22. Career planning (students)	male	80.0	20.0	25.2	20.0	25.5	3.53	1.03	**.027**
	female	20.0	80.0	74.8	80.0	74.5	**3.70**	.81	
	all	1.9	3.7	38.1	38.9	17.4	3.66	.87	
23. Challenging (students)	male	80.0	33.3	25.6	18.3	26.7	3.64	1.08	**.001**
	female	20.0	66.7	74.4	81.7	73.3	**3.83**	.79	
	all	1.9	2.2	33.3	40.4	22.2	3.78	.87	
24. More work chances (students)	male	75.0	22.2	23.0	20.8	25.5	3.49	1.11	**.004**
	female	25.0	77.8	77.0	79.2	74.5	**3.69**	.82	
	all	3.0	3.3	37.0	39.3	17.4	3.64	.90	
About the company	male						**3.37**	.90	**.006**
	female						3.26	.68	
	all						3.29	.74	

Table 4. General majors difference of students' Intern experience

Majors	Part-time M (rank)	Pay M (rank)	School M (rank)	Teacher M (rank)	Company M (rank)	Students M (rank)	Satisfaction M (rank)	Stay M (rank)	Change M (rank)
1. N	2.01 (3)	1.03 (4)	3.72 (3)	3.56 (3)	3.27 (3)	3.68 (4)	3.52 (4)	3.59 (2)	3.05 (5)
2. H	3.16 (1)	1.96 (2)	3.24 (5)	3.07 (5)	3.07 (5)	3.65 (5)	3.34 (5)	3.11 (5)	3.20 (4)
3. C	2.38 (2)	2.00 (1)	3.36 (4)	3.32 (4)	3.41 (2)	3.83 (2)	3.56 (3)	3.34 (3)	3.31 (3)
4. I	1.80 (4)	1.54 (3)	3.49 (2)	3.63 (2)	3.47 (1)	3.79 (3)	3.63 (2)	3.12 (4)	3.90 (1)
5. CE	1.61 (5)	1.00 (5)	3.86 (1)	3.86 (1)	3.16 (4)	4.22 (1)	3.76 (1)	3.73 (1)	3.61 (2)
All (M)	2.27/5	1.58/2	3.49/5	3.45/5	3.29/5	3.80/5	3.54/5	3.34/5	3.39/5
Sig	.000 2 > 1, 3, 4, 5*	.000 2 > 1, 4, 5*	.001 1 > 2* 5 > 2* 3 > 1, 4, 5* 4 > 1, 5*	.000 2 > 1, 4, 5* 3 > 1, 4, 5* 4 > 1, 5*	.010	.306 5 > 1, 2*	.177 5 > 2*	.002	.009 4 > 1, 2, 3*

Note. Majors: 1. Nursing (N) 2. Hospitality Management (H) 3. Cosmetic Application and Management (C) 4. Information Management (I) 5. Child Education (CE)

References

Amiama-Espaillat, C., Mayor-Ruiz, C.: Digital reading and reading competence –the influence in the Z generation from the dominican republic. Comunicar (in Spanish). **25**(52), 105–114 (2017). https://doi.org/10.3916/c52-2017-10. ISSN1134-3478

Bao, Y., Fang, G.: A study on hospitality students' satisfaction towards their internship: a case from Hang Zhou, China. Int. J. Contemp. Hosp. Manag. **12**, 1069–1076 (2014)

Bender, K.A., Donohue, S.M., Heywood, J.S.: Job satisfaction and gender segregation. Oxford Econ. Pap. **57**, 479–496 (2005)

Chen, C.T., Tu, J.L., Wang, C.C., Chen, C.F.: A study of the effects of internship experiences on the behavioral intentions of college students majoring in leisure management in Taiwan. J. Hosp. Leisure Sport Tourism Educ. **10**, 61–73 (2011)

Clark, A.: Why are women so happy at work? Labour Econ. **4**, 341–372 (1997)

Cook, S.J., Parker, R.S., Pettijohn, C.E.: The perceptions of interns: a longitudinal case study. J. Educ. Bus. **79**, 179–185 (2004)

Dill, K.: 7 Things employers should know about the gen Z workforce (2015). https://www.forbes.com/sites/kathryndill//11/06/7-things-employers-should-know-about-the-gen-z-workforce/#2f744db3fad7. Accessed 15 Sep 2018

Gay, L.R., Airasian, P.: Educational Research: Competencies for Analysis and Applications, 7th edn. Merrill Prentice Hall, New Jersey (2003)

Hou, Y.-A.: The relationship of multiple intelligences, foreign language learning anxiety and English proficiency-a case study of Taiwanese EFL college students. Int. J. Commun. Linguist. Stud. **12**(2), 15–29 (2015). ISSN: 1447-9508

Hou, Y.-A.: The impacts of multiple intelligences on tolerance of ambiguity and english proficiency-a case study of Taiwanese EFL college students. Open J. Mod. Linguist. **6**, 255–275 (2016)

Hou, Y.-A.: Avoiding the gap of college students' internship expectations and perceptions – a case study in Taiwan. Open J. Nurs. **8**(8), 531–551 (2018)

Levit, A.: Make Way for Generation Z. The New York Times (2015). Accessed 20 Sep 2018

Okpara, J.O., Squillace, M., Erondu, E.A.: Gender difference and job satisfaction: a study of university teachers in the United States. Women Manag. Rev. **20**(3), 177–190 (2005)

Oxford, R.: Language Learning Strategies: What Every Teacher Should Know, p. 02116. Heinle and Heinle Publishers, Boston (1990)

Prensky, M.: Digital natives, digital immigrants part 1. Horizon **9**(5), 1–6 (2001)

Schulz, B.: The importance of soft skills: education beyond academic knowledge. J. Lang. Commun. 146–154 (2008)

Seemiller, C.: Generation Z Goes to College. Jossey-Bass, Hoboken (2016). ISBN 978-1-119-143451

Sunburn, J.: Here's What MTV Is Calling the Generation After Millennials. Time, 1 December 2015. Accessed 18 Sep 2018

Swanson, S., Tomkovick, C.: Marketing internships: how values and search strategies differ across the student-employer dyad. Mark. Educ. Rev. **22**, 251–262 (2012)

Turner, A.: Generation Z: technology and social interest. J. Individ. Psychol. **71**(2), 103–113 (2015). https://doi.org/10.1353/jip.2015.0021

Williams, A.: How to Spot a Member of Generation Z. New York Times, 18 September 2015. Accessed 10 Sep 2018

Requirements for Wearable Technologies to Promote Adherence to Physical Activity Programs for Older Adults

Robert Klebbe[1(✉)], Anika Steinert[1], Ilona Buchem[2], and Ursula Müller-Werdan[1]

[1] Geriatrics Research Group, Charité Universitaetsmedizin Berlin,
Reinickendorfer Str. 61, 13347 Berlin, Germany
robert.klebbe@charite.de
[2] Department I Economics and Social Sciences, Beuth University of Applied Sciences, Luxemburger Str. 10, 13353 Berlin, Germany

Abstract. Regarding healthy ageing, physical activity (PA) is one of the most important prerequisites as it improves several health outcomes as well as reduces the risk of various chronic diseases. Despite these positive effects, the participation and adherence of older people to PA programs is often low as there are several barriers that prevent older people engaging in PA on a regular basis. Great expectations are placed on technology-based exercise programs that use wearable and mobile technologies to promote PA. Since these technologies are primarily adapted to the needs and abilities of young target groups, however, there is a great need for empirical insights into their use by older adults. Within the publicly funded R&D-project fMOOC, a wearable-enhanced training system was developed to increase the PA of older people. Based on the user-centered design approach, four studies were conducted to investigate the requirements of older adults in wearable-enhanced training. Results showed that the majority of subjects (55%) engaged in the PA program on a regular basis. Furthermore, the most important motivation factors for use were the evidence-based training program, the fitness tracking device and the visualization of training results. In summary, it can be stated that wearable-enhanced training programs can support older people to increase their PA in everyday life. At the same time, however, various requirements must be considered to ensure continued, long-term use. In addition to technical design and robustness, there is a need for a stronger theoretical as well as empirical foundation.

Keywords: Older adults · Wearable-enhanced learning · Physical activity

1 Introduction

For many older adults, maintaining their health is a complex and long-term life task. In addition to impairments in the areas of physical and cognitive abilities caused by age-related and chronic degenerative diseases, lifestyle and social factors also influence the health and risk behavior of older people [1]. In this context, regular physical activity (PA) is seen as a prerequisite for healthy ageing, as it can contribute to improving physical, psychological, cognitive and functional health outcomes [2, 3]. At the same time, it reduces the risk of several health problems such as hypertension, hyperlipidemia, type 2 diabetes and obesity or constitutes an essential part of their treatment [4, 5]. Because of the health-promoting effects of PA, the WHO recommends that older adults should perform at least 150 min of moderate intensity, aerobic PA per week and engage in mobility and strength training at least twice weekly [6]. However, several studies show that the majority of older people in many countries do not achieve these goals [3, 7]. One third of older adults aged 70 to 79 and about half of those aged 80 and older do not meet WHO recommendations [8]. Furthermore, with regard to available best-practice guidelines, studies show, that exercise participation and adherence is often low in older adults [9, 10].

The main obstacles to regular participation and adherence are lack of time, motivation or knowledge or low self-efficacy and self-esteem, as well as cognitive or physical coupled with a fear of injury. In addition, there is also a lack of age-appropriate PA programs and information on how to access them [11, 12].

As a consequence, there is a need for strategies which take into account the individual barriers and activity goals of older adults as well as the socio-spatial context and the associated time resources and opportunities for PA (e.g., in the domestic and communal environment as well as in health care institutions). Furthermore, strategies should also promote and enhance adherence to the regular practice of exercises, since the positive effects of PA disappear quickly if training terminates.

In this context, technology-based interventions have shown promising results in terms of the increase of as well as adherence to PA exercise programs. In a systematic review, Valenzuela et al. found that adherence to technology-based intervention was higher than it was to traditional intervention "[…] independent of study site, level of supervision, and delivery mode" [12]. Furthermore, in a meta-analysis on the effect of PA interventions based on wearable and smartphone applications, Gal et al. discovered a small to moderate increase in PA [13]. In the field of technology-based intervention, mobile technologies such as wearables and smartphones are considered to be potentially useful in increasing PA. On the one hand, this is due to their enormous socio-economic potential[1] and their already extensive user penetration; for example, according to the Pew Research Center, 77% of Americans owned a smartphone in 2018. In the group of older adults between 50 and 64 years, this figure was 73% and in over 65s, 46% [15]. In contrast, the user penetration of wearables in 2017 averaged 17.6%. In the group of older people between 55 and 64 years it was 6.3% and in the group of over 65s, 4.6% [16].

On the other hand, these technologies offer great potential to assist people of all ages in the process of habit formation to increase PA. Key characteristics of these technologies include their high degree of miniaturization (making them easy to integrate into everyday life). The automatic gathering and analysis of a wide range of activity data, such as steps taken, altimetry, calories, sleep, distance. Moreover, the visualization of these data within web services, mobile apps or on the wearable itself

---

[1] Forecasts for 2019 predict that sales of wearables will reach 225 million devices, totaling 42 billion USD [14].

[17, 18]. These opportunities for self-monitoring should help users gain self-awareness regarding different entities of health-related behavior, thus empowering them to achieve specific health and activity related goals. In addition to self-monitoring capabilities, accompanying mobile apps and websites of wearable devices promote further behavior change techniques (BCT's) such as goal setting, tailored feedback and instruction as well as and social support to enhance acceptance and performance towards changed-based interventions [17]. Finally, motivational elements taking a gamification approach - such as badges and trophies, leader boards and progress bars - were used to increase long-term exercise compliance by increasing enjoyment and stimulation levels in the exercising experience [17, 18].

However, most of these devices are predominantly adapted to the needs of younger target groups, already familiar with intelligent technologies. Older adults, on the other hand, often have poor access to technology, deriving from a low belief in their technology competence as well as sensory, physical and cognitive impairments. This specific target group thus has special needs concerning the design and usability of wearable technologies.

The objective of the present research was to advance knowledge about the specific needs, preferences and requirements of older adults regarding the development of a wearable-enhanced training program that would increase their PA in everyday life.

1.1 Project Approach

As part of the publicly funded R&D project fMOOC (Fitness MOOC - interaction of older adults with wearable fitness trackers in a Massive Open Online Course), a wearable-enhanced training system was developed to increase the PA of older people. The system comprised social exchange and information possibilities in a MOOC platform, motivational elements according to the gamification approach and data analyses with learning analytics as well as senior-friendly control elements. The developed smartphone app also included evidence-based fitness exercises especially for older adults that enhanced basic motor skills such as endurance, strength and balance. Twelve training plans were developed for a four-week training program. Furthermore, a wearable activity tracker was integrated to track and monitor PA. For an appropriate degree of individual load intensity, the exercises could be adapted to three levels of difficulty (easy, medium and difficult). Motivational elements were implemented to stimulate fitness and learning-related activities and to acknowledge achievements. In this context, the participants had the opportunity to receive badges for taking a specific number of steps, for completing an entire week's training program (three training and four regeneration days) and for socially exchanging activities with other users on the fMOOC platform via comments and likes. In addition, a group competition between men and women was set up in which the number of steps taken was compared. The fMOOC project was a cooperation between the Beuth University of Applied Sciences and the Geriatrics Research Group, Charité, one of the largest medical universities in Europe.

2 Methods

2.1 Approach

The fMOOC project was based on the User-Centred Design approach, in which the needs, abilities and expectations of future end users are placed at the center of the development process. For this purpose, the User Centered Design approach is iterative and goes through several phases. Classically, this involves the analysis of the usage context, the definition of specific (system) requirements, the creation of initial (design) concepts and mockups as well as evaluation.

Four studies were carried out in the one-year fMOOC project.

2.2 Procedure

Requriement analysis. In order to investigate the specific requirements of older adults regarding the fMOOC system, six semi-structured interviews with the target group were conducted. The investigation focused on the needs and expectations of older adults regarding the design of the training concepts, the platform and user interface, the motivation and evaluation system as well as ethical and data security requirements. Furthermore, specific usability requirements of a fitness tracker and a health application on a smartphone were determined based on demonstrators. In addition to the interviews, questionnaires were completed on the subject of current technology usage and commitment.

Interim stage examination. The concept- and design phase of the training programs and the fMOOC user interface was followed by an interim test with six seniors. The aim was to investigate the feasibility and comprehensibility of the training plans as well as the graphical design of the user interface. The test persons were recruited from the contact data pool of the Geriatrics Research Group and the study took place in the research facility of the Geriatrics Research Group within one study visit. As a first step, the individual level of difficulty was determined, at which the study subject performed the exercises. Based on a standardized test protocol, a total of 33 exercises were evaluated. Furthermore, the participants were asked to give their opinion on the level of difficulty of each exercise and the entire training as well as on the implementation of the video and image instructions. The graphical user-interface was examined based on different mock-ups which were rated by the subjects in terms of comprehensibility, preferred graphical illustration and the description of different functionalities such as training-programs, commentary, the badge system and activity progress.

PrefMOOC Study. As part of a comparative, crossover-designed, monocentric pilot study, 20 older adults were invited to test five fitness-tracking devices available on the market, including their associated firm apps (Nike FuelBand, Sony SmartBand, Garmin Vivofit, Jawbone UP24, Fitbit Flex). The aim of this study was to investigate the requirements for a fitness tracker suitable for seniors and to identify problems in the usability of existing systems. The participants were recruited from different senior facilitations and the contact data pool of the Geriatrics Research Group. The inclusion criteria for the study were for participation to be of an age of ≥ 60 years and to have no previous experience with activity trackers.

The study included two study visits of approx. 1.5 h each in the research facility of the Geriatrics Research Group. In a first of these, the participants were introduced to the aim and subject of the study. After giving their formal consent, the attitudes of the participants towards the importance of different usage criteria of fitness-tracking devices without any previous experience were analyzed. The participants then tested five different systems (fitness trackers and their associated applications) by executing three specific tasks (the putting on and taking off, the opening of the associated firm's app of the tested fitness-tracking device and the synchronizing of the wristband data with the associated firm's app). After this, they were asked to rate the systems in terms of comfort, design, product quality, presentation, the comprehensibility of data and the ease of use. Following a randomized procedure, each participant was assigned one of the five systems to take one week for independent testing. In the final examination after one week, the respondents were asked about their attitudes towards the importance of several usage criteria again. Furthermore, acceptance and usability were recorded based on a self-developed questionnaire.

fMOOC@Home. The focus of the end-evaluation of the entire system was the investigation of the influence of a digital training platform on the user behavior and physical fitness of older adults as well as the special importance of motivational elements concerning use.

Participants numbering 20 were included in the study and they were recruited from the contact data pool of the Geriatric Research Group. During a telephone screening, participants were tested for inclusion and exclusion criteria. Inclusion criteria were having an age of ≥ 60 years; exclusion criteria were defined as doing sport on a regular basis, having previous experience with the use of fitness-tracking devices, having a high risk of falling (≤ 14 points on the short-fall efficacy scale [19]) and having an implanted defibrillator (due to bioelectrical impedance analysis). The study included two study visits of approximately 1.5 to 2 h each in the research facility of the Geriatrics Research Group and an intervention phase of four weeks.

During the first study visit, sociodemographic data as well as the current use and technology commitment of the participants were surveyed. In order to investigate the influence of the training system on the physical fitness of the participants, the following basic measurements were recorded: self-assessment of health behavior, fitness status and knowledge, balance ability (Fullerton Advanced Balance Scale [20]), hand and leg strength (strength dynamometer), endurance (six-minute walk test [21]), body composition using bioelectric impedance analysis (BIA Mbca 515), self-assessment of motor skills (FFB Mot [22]), and current PA (German Physical Activity Questionnaire 50+ [23]).

Following these extensive tests, participants were introduced to the entire system. Simultaneously, individual levels of difficulty for training were determined and the entire system was handed out to the participants for a four-week independent test (smartphone with pre-installed application and a connected fitness-tracking device). In the final examination after four weeks, the assessments of the basic measurement were repeated. Furthermore, self-developed questionnaires for usability and acceptance as well as for the evaluation of the subjective performance increase were issued. The evaluation of the general usability of the fMOOC system was based on the SUS-Questionnaire [24].

Analysis. Qualitative Data within the requirements analysis were analyzed based on the qualitative summarizing content analysis by Mayring. Quantitative data were analyzed using IBM SPSS Statistics 21.0. Categorical variables were analyzed using frequency of responses and percentages. Depending on the results of the normal distribution and variance homogeneity of the data, both t-tests and non-parametric tests such as the Mann-Whitney U test, the Kruskal-Wallis test or the Wilcoxon signed rank test were conducted.

3 Results

3.1 Overview of Study Participants

Overall, the study population in all studies can be described as urban, well-educated and technology oriented; more than three-quarters of the participants stated that they used a computer and the Internet. In addition, more than two thirds used a mobile phone (Table 1).

Table 1. Overview of the different study-populations within the fMOOC project

		Requirements analysis	Interims study	PrefMOOC – study	fMOOC@Home - study
N		6	6	20	20
Age	mean	70	–	72	69
	min–max	(64–78)	–	(64–87)	(62–75)
Sex	female	3	3	11	10
	male	3	3	9	10

3.2 Requirements Analysis

The results of the interviews with the older adults showed that a scientifically sound training concept is expected to be important, wherein the benefits are clear. On the one hand, training plans should be suggested and on the other, it should be possible to individually compile training units. Furthermore, training programs should include different degrees of intensity and it should be possible to decide for oneself when the training will take place. The execution of the exercises should be illustrated by video instructions and the actor should also be a senior to increase acceptance. Each training activity should also include an achievable and motivating goal and a control of success. In addition, safety instructions and additional information regarding the exercises should be provided. The visualization of the training program should be in the format of a to-do list in which the completed exercises can be marked off. There should also be an opportunity to evaluate the exercise units. As preferred measurement data, the study participants named step number, distance, pulse and sleep rhythm and felt that these data should be able to be viewed over time. Furthermore, the study participants wanted training parameters to be visible immediately after training. In general, participants wanted a simple and clear presentation of the contents on the training platform as well as a small range of functions. The exchange with other participants should not be obligatory and it should be possible to register using a pseudonym.

During testing of a fitness tracker to demonstrate the planned hardware, it became evident that the manner of fastening the fitness-tracking device can create problems under certain circumstances due to the decreasing fine motor skills of old age. This result was even more evident when putting on and taking off the device as well as adjusting the size of the chest strap.

3.3 Interims Stage Examination

The interim testing of the conceptualized training plans (including N = 33 exercises) showed that most of the exercises (n = 26) were understood by the study participants. In the case of n = 9 exercises, assistance was needed from study staff. The external evaluation of the degree of intensity in the execution of the exercises showed that 22 exercises were appropriate in the chosen intensity, three exercises were too easy and eight too intensive. In contrast, the self-assessment by the test persons showed a more differentiated pattern; 15 exercises were assessed as appropriate, 13 as too easy and five as too intensive. In total, four test persons found the training to be not to less intensive at all, while two found it rather intensive. Against the background of these results, the training plans and exercise instructions were adapted again. After the removal of exercises, which were too intensive or too difficult, to understand, 29 exercises were available to create the training plans.

Regarding the graphic implementation of the training plans, all participants rated the instructions in the form of video sequences and pictures as good. In addition, the most of the study participants found these to be quite helpful or very helpful for the execution of the exercises.

The mock-up testing of the platform's graphic design showed that less information was preferred in cases where the test persons had the choice between more or less information. Furthermore, regarding badges for successes, icons representing classic competition awards such as medals or trophies were preferred. Furthermore, high contrasts in the presentation were preferred as well as short names for functions. Regarding the design notes, the app design was adapted.

3.4 PrefMOOC – Study

A comparison of the expectations regarding the importance of usage criteria at the beginning of the study (without any previous experience of fitness-tracking devices) as well as after one week of use (see Fig. 1) showed that the ease of use of the app and the wristband, the comprehensibility of the contents (app/wristband) the presentation of the data (app/wristband), and the measurement accuracy were of great importance for the participants. Less important were the brand and price. Furthermore, the design aspect differed significantly between the first and last study visit ($z = -3,67$; $p < .001$).

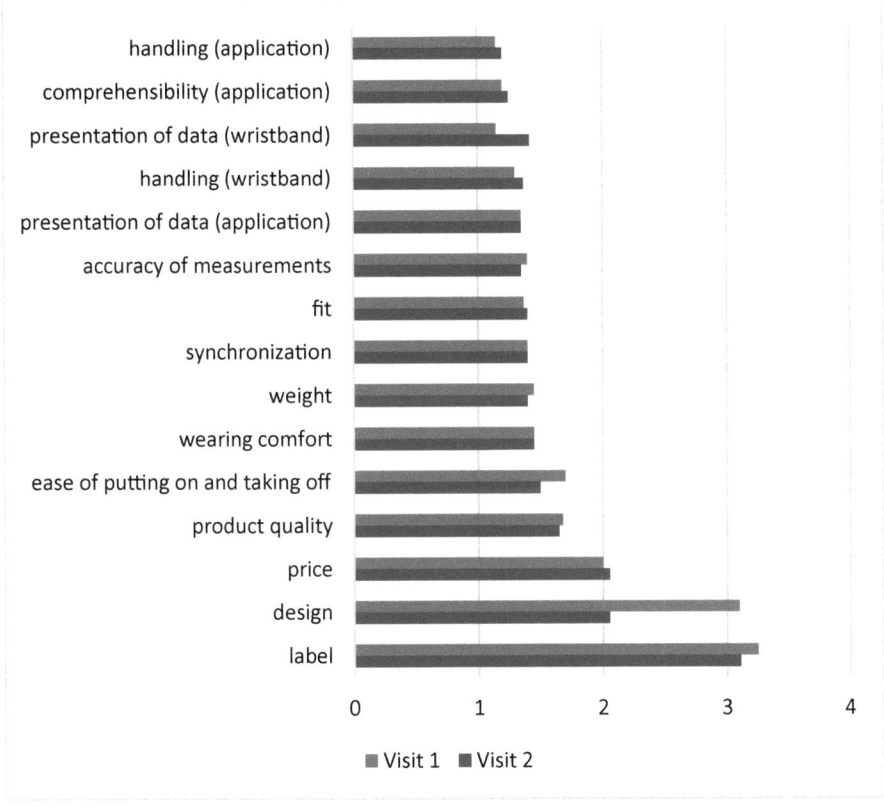

Fig. 1. Importance of different aspect before and after testing the devices, n = 20 (1 = very important, 2 = rather important, 3 = rather unimportant, 4 = very unimportant)

During the task of putting on and taking off the wristband, difficulties were observed, particularly regarding to the type of fastening. Greater difficulties were encountered with the insertion of pins into the wristband (Garmin Vivofit, Fibit Flex and Sony SmartBand) due to the higher demands made on fine motor skills. As a result, wristbands that had a simple clasp (Nike FuelBand) or no clasp at all (Jawbone UP24) were rated higher. At the same time, however, participants expressed concern that they may lose a wristband that did not have a clasp. In addition to how adjustments were made, the flexibility of the wristband was also a relevant factor for the ease with which it could be put on or taken off. Finally, the test persons critically emphasized that the material of the bracelet caused sweating and skin redness.

The testing of the firmware app related to each tracker showed that those GUIs that had a clearly structured interface and contained few playful elements were rated higher. A special critique of the participants was the insufficient description of the presented data. Comprehension problems existed in particular regarding to the method of measuring the data as well as its graphical representation (e.g. as point metrics) or in the case where several parameters were presented together.

Furthermore, various difficulties could be observed in the context of data synchronization. Although in most cases synchronization was automatic and wireless, in some the participants did not see the notification because the message was too small and disappeared too quickly. In most cases, the application also had to be closed before the data presentation was updated – an aspect that often could not be understood. In addition, some test persons did not know how to close the application. Moreover, one of the devices required pressing a button for a certain time to trigger the data transmission (Garmin Vivofit). Difficulties existed in this case in pressing the relatively small button as well as in the fact that if the button was pressed for too long, further functions were opened and the users did not know what to do. In addition, it was rated negative that in one case the synchronization did not operate in real time and the test persons had to wait for up to five minutes before the data appeared in the app (Sony SmartBand).

After completing the three tasks the participants were asked to rate each system regarding to its comfort, design, product quality, presentation and comprehensibility of data, and ease of use. The best-rated activity tracker became part of the fMOOC system developed in this project (Garmin Vivofit).[2]

3.5 fMOOC@HOME-Study

Adherence to the physical training program. Out of the 20 participants in the study, four completed the training program at a simple level, 12 at a moderate level and a further four at a difficult level. To objectively quantify the performed exercises, computer-generated logging data were used. During the intervention period 55% of the subjects completed all exercises, 50% performed 10 out of 12 and only 10% less than a quarter. Although more than half of the participants rated the exercises as less challenging, 80% found the individually adjusted intensity appropriate. In addition, the participants were asked how they liked the individual exercises. The average score was 2.9 on a scale from 1 (poor) to 4 (very good), which can be rated as good. The participants were also asked whether they would continue to use the fMOOC system or its subsystems (training platform/fitness tracker). In this context, 55% of the respondents stated that they would continue to use the entire system, 10% only the training platform and 15% only the fitness tracker. A further 15%, on the other hand, would not be interested in continuing to use the system. In two cases, the reasons for this were in first a lack of interest in gymnastics and the second a lack of interest in sports at all.

Changes after Intervention. At both the beginning and the end of the study, participants were asked to rate their state of health, current fitness level, knowledge of how to improve their fitness, strength, balance and endurance workout, building a well-structured training plan as well as their knowledge of how to use a fitness tracker.

A comparison of the respective self-assessments showed no significant changes with regard to their current state of health ($z = -.378$; $p = .273$), knowledge about how to increase one's own fitness, strength, balance and endurance workout as well as the development of a well-structured training plan. In contrast, however, the subjects rated

---
[2] For further information on the results of the PrefMOOC project see [11].

their current state of fitness ($z = -2.828$; $p < .01$), in particular their endurance ($z = 2.081$; $p < .05$) better than in visit 1. Moreover, their knowledge of fitness trackers ($z = -3,741$; $p < .001$) as well as their knowledge of how to execute a training plan ($z = -2.179$; $p < .05$) were rated significantly better at the end of the study, too.

More than half (55%) of the respondents felt motivated to do more physical activities in the post-intervention period as part of everyday life and to take better care of their own health. In addition, 40% of the participants stated that after the intervention they could move more safely.[3]

Usage of the fMOOC System. Regarding the use of the fMOOC platform, 45% of participants stated that they used it daily. Another 45% used the platform more than twice a week. Only 10% mentioned using the training platform less than once a week. Reasons for irregular use were technical problems (n = 4), a lack of time (n = 2), health problems (n = 2) and a lack of motivation (n = 1). Analysis of the logging data showed that the usage of the platform differed a lot (on average 44 times within the four weeks of intervention (14–90 times)).

Moreover, the logging data showed that participants synchronized their data 128 times on average within the four weeks of usage. On the one hand, this can be viewed as evidence of the difficulties already observed in previous studies regarding data synchronization. A further indication of this might be the fact that within the final evaluation of different usage criteria of the fitness tracker, synchronization was rated worst (3.65 on average (1 = very good to 7 = very poor)). On the other hand, this could also be evidence for the great importance of actual measurement data in the respective overviews. However, the frequency of synchronizations decreased during the intervention phase, so that by the end, only half as many synchronizations were undertaken by the participants as at the beginning of the independent testing of the system.

Regarding the motivational elements to encourage PA among older adults, the logging data showed that the participants most often visited the results of the competition of the total number of steps completed between the two sexes. Secondly, the results of the individual number of steps were viewed most frequently. Least frequently, the participants looked at the results of the badges[4] received. Furthermore, 95% of participants rated the trainings program, 85% the fitness tracker and 75% the visualization of the trainings results as very or rather motivating to use the training platform. Badges were rated lowest again with 60% being very or rather motivating for system usage. At the same time, however, a statistically significant correlation between the number of badges achieved and their rating as motivating was found ($r_s = -.468$, $p = .037$, n = 20).

---

[3] For further information, in particular regarding the results of balance ability (Fullerton Advanced Balance Scale), hand and leg strength (strength dynamometer), endurance (six-minutes' walk test), body composition using bioelectric impedance analysis (BIA Mbca 515), self-assessment of fitness status and fitness knowledge, self-assessment of motor skills (FFB Mot), current PA (German Physical Activity Questionnaire 50+) and the User Experience Questionnaire (UEQ), see [25].

[4] Badges could be received for a certain number of steps, for completed training weeks (three days of training and four days of regeneration), for the number of written comments and for 'likes' of these comments.

The overall usability of the fMOOC training system was rated by the System Usability Scale (SUS) and the average score was 71 out of 100 possible points, which can be interpreted as a C grade (65–71 = C) [24].

In addition, 65% of the participants rated the system as very or rather user or senior-friendly.

4 Discussion

Although the intervention period within the presented study for the evaluation of a wearable-enhanced training platform was relatively short, the results show that most participants engaged in the training on a regular basis and reported positive effects on well-being and physical fitness.

For regular use of a PA training program based on wearable and mobile technologies, however, the presented results also show that various prerequisites are required.

Appropriate PA-programs and Comprehensibility
On the level of a training program suitable for seniors to engage in PA on a regular basis, the studies showed that evidence-based training plans are of great importance. Moreover, the health-promoting benefits must be clearly comprehensible for older people. In this context, the results of the interim study as well as the final evaluation of the fMOOC system showed that the visualization of the exercises in the form of videos and images was considered relevant for their correct execution. Such an adaptation of the intervention materials and instructions to the characteristics of the target group has also been identified as a necessary condition for promoting the commitment to the long-term achievement of PA goals [26].

Additionally, the results showed that the variation within the training programs regarding the addressed PA goals such as strength, endurance and balance exercises as well as the possibility for adopting the training program to the individual's capabilities seem to be further relevant factors to motivate older people to long-term engagement. Thereby, the orientation towards individual barriers and activity goals as well as the consideration of the social context with regard to time resources and possibilities of realizing PA exercises are further requirements for an appropriate PA program [27].

Furthermore, besides different exercise modalities a wide variety of exercises as well as physically and cognitively challenging exercises was stated to increase the enjoyment and stimulation of exercise experience and thus increase motivation for engagement [12].

Finally, wearable-enhanced training programs offer older people the opportunity to do exercises at home without supervision, which can reduce some of the adherence barriers [12]. At the same time, however, it must be noted that their use should be accompanied by trained experts to help older people utilize the results for a healthy lifestyle [18, 28, 29].

User Interface and Data Visualization
There was a distinct preference for a clearly structured GUI regarding its functionality and data visualization. In this context, a simple menu structure with fewer levels and

changing sequences can reduce navigation difficulties. In addition, the number of parameters presented should be kept low to avoid confusion among participants. We also observed that the comprehensibility of the relationship between one's own activities and the results achieved within the framework of the PA program is of great importance.

Meng et al. also recommend that the functions and services provided by wearable systems should, on the one hand, include only low but consistent user involvement and, on the other hand, correspond to their expectations and needs [30]. Further recommendations include detailed and easily comprehensible instructions of data collection, measurement methods and basic functions, as well as notifications according to the specific target group [31].

In addition to easy-to-understand visualization and analysis when using mobile applications, participants in the PrefMOOC study rated the ability to display instant data on the wrist and interoperability with additional sensors for health-specific conditions highly.

Generally however, applications have to be designed in such a way that they avoid mental overload, making it necessary to increase user involvement in stages of development, especially when it concerns older users [18].

Technological Robustness

As the PrefMOOC and fMOOC@Home studies showed, difficulties in synchronizing the collected data had an impact on the perceived usability of a system. In particular, there were difficulties in triggering data transmission, the perceptibility of confirmation of successful transmission, and irritation when synchronization was not performed in real time. These findings are consistent with recommendations made by Meng et al. when they highlighted the importance of the systems capability to transmit and process data in real-time to gain the users' acceptance [30]. Similarly, Maher et al., in their cross-sectional study on the user experience of activity trackers amongst Australian adults, reported that technical problems with the device or accompanying software, along with breakage and loss, were the most important barriers to continuous use [32].

Furthermore, different studies emphasize the importance of advanced measurement accuracy as well as the need for the standardization of data collection, processing and analytical procedures [18, 30–32]. In this context Modave et al. [33] found that accuracy in step counting has been an issue with some of the tested commercial wearable devices, as they undercount steps especially with in the older age test groups. The reasons for this include the tendencies for reduced walking speed and varying gait patterns among older adults [29]. Therefore, to achieve the validity of the measurement results, it is necessary to refine existing algorithms in such a way that they can also reliably trace the specific movement patterns of older users. On the one hand, this is necessary, since users often express concerns about the accuracy of the data collected and the promotion of health advice [34]. On the other hand, it also plays an important role if the results of wearable technologies are be used in medical treatment processes [18].

Finally, in an online survey involving 237 participants, Maher et al. identified further issues especially with regard to "[…] low battery life (19%), difficulties with the support software, (17%) and perceived inaccuracy of data collected (17%) […]" [32].

Engagement and Motivation for Long-term use

As discussed, one of the main prerequisites for a sustainable promotion of PA is following an appropriate training program. This can have an important influence on the enjoyment and motivation of the participants to engage with it on a regular basis. Regarding gamification elements used in the fMOOC-Systems, the group comparison between men and women and the possibility of monitoring one's own activity was rated as motivating by most participants. A reason for this could be the interest of users in comparing their own activities with a baseline which is formed by other users with similar characteristics to themselves [32]. Badges, on the other hand, seemed to be less important in terms of motivation for regular training. Furthermore, the result of a significant correlation between the number of badges and their evaluation as motivating could be viewed critically.

To explain, different studies have stated that especially for extrinsic rewards there is a danger that they themselves become the object of an action and thus counteract the development of a desired behavior [35, 36]. At the same time, there is the question of whether the badges chosen were meaningful enough for the participants to support the goal of long-term, regular training.

With regard to the support of habit formation Stawarz et al. stated that several functionalities such as reminders, tracking capabilities, self-monitoring as well as positive reinforcement can be useful at an early stage of a behavior change process by helping people "[…] to understand their behavior, set realistic goals, monitor progress and maintain motivation[…]" [1]. In addition, however, there is a danger that users will be tempted to rely too much on technology, counteracting this process in the longer term. Through the repeated use of these functionalities, it can be the case that habit formation can become less associated with the desired behavior, than with the objective of their use [35, 36].

As a conclusion, it can be stated that external motivating elements in particular counteract the process of habit formation. When designing technology-based exercise programs, the focus should therefore be on feedback elements that support intrinsic motivation, self-determination and autonomy [36]. Stawarz et al. make a number of recommendations as design principles for habit-forming apps as follows. First, the formation of implementation intentions through the selection of individual trigger events. Second, reminders to strengthen the connection between a task and its triggering event, though these should be decreased in the course of habit formation. Thirdly, they recommend that users do not use functions, which would result in them relying too heavily on technology [35].

Ergonomic

In particular, the result of the PrefMOOC study showed, that there were further requirements regarding how to fasten the wristband onto the wrist. On the one hand, it was felt that this should be flexible so that it could easily be adjusted. Yet on the other, it was felt that the locking mechanism should ensure a simple but secure fastening. In any case, the comfort of the clasp was rated higher than the insertion of pins into the watchband. Moreover, it was felt that buttons on the wearables should be large enough to be easily used yet that there should be only a few functions assigned to them to avoid improper use and uncertainty. In addition, materials used were expected to be skin-compatible even for older adults. These findings are consistent with further studies on the requirements for wearable technologies to promote assistance in the improvement of health- and fitness-related behavior. The importance for the user experience and acceptance especially with regard to real-life situations and long-term usage is also emphasized [18, 30, 32]. Moreover, features such as a small size and a low weight as well as a discreet design (to suit users' images) create additional requirements in terms of ergonomics [18, 30, 32].

5 Conclusion

This study explored users' experiences and requirements regarding a wearable-enhanced training platform to promote PA in older people. Within a user centered design approach four studies were conducted. In summary, it can be concluded that wearable-enhanced training programs have the potential to help older people to increase their daily PA. At the same time, however, various requirements must be considered to promote long-term adherence to health-promoting exercise goals. Conclusions to be drawn from the study are as follows:

- To ensure long-term adherence to PA programs, evidence-based exercises with clear health benefits and the correct performance of them being clearly demonstrated, should be included. At the same time, appropriate programs must be variable in terms of PA goals (e.g., combining strength, endurance and balance exercises) and consider the specific capabilities of and barriers facing older adults.
- The graphical user interface should be clearly and intuitively structured and include easy-to-understand instructions on data-presentation and the programs functionalities. Deficiencies in these areas significantly reduce users' motivation.
- A further key prerequisite involves technological robustness. The systems' functionalities must be robust, reliable and easy to use. Particular attention should be paid to real-time data transmission, the accuracy of measurements and a long battery life.
- The use of behavioral change technologies (BCT's) needs to be more grounded in habit formation theory. More specifically, externally motivating elements should only be used at an early stage of the habit-forming process and should be rapidly replaced by feedback elements that support intrinsic motivation, self-determination and autonomy.
- To ensure a high level of usability, ergonomic requirements should also be considered. These consist of easy and safe fastening techniques as well as a simple size adjustment processes. In addition, materials' skin compatibility needs to be ensured.

Finally, it should be stated that research on the effects of technology-based promotion of PA among older adults is still in an early stage. Three interrelated research desiderates appear to be of importance:

First, the empirical investigation of the requirements for and the long-term effectiveness of technology-based interventions within the framework of sophisticated RCT studies. Second, the development and empirical evaluation of differentiated exercise programs for older people. Third, the empirical investigation of the requirements for BCTs to promote the intrinsic motivation of older people in the context of a specific behavioral change.

References

1. Saß, A.-C., Lampert, T., Ziese, T., Kurth, B.-M.: Robert-Koch-Institut hrsg: Gesundheit in Deutschland: Gesundheitsberichterstattung des Bundes: gemeinsam getragen von RKI und DESTATIS. Robert Koch-Institut, Berlin (2015)
2. Krug, S., Jordan, S., Mensink, G.B.M., Müters, S., Finger, J., Lampert, T.: Körperliche Aktivität: Ergebnisse der Studie zur Gesundheit Erwachsener in Deutschland (DEGS1). Bundesgesundheitsblatt - Gesundheitsforschung - Gesundheitsschutz. **56**, 765–771 (2013). https://doi.org/10.1007/s00103-012-1661-6
3. Muellmann, S., Forberger, S., Möllers, T., Zeeb, H., Pischke, C.R.: Effectiveness of eHealth interventions for the promotion of physical activity in older adults: a systematic review protocol. Syst. Rev. **5**, 47 (2016). https://doi.org/10.1186/s13643-016-0223-7
4. Physical Activity Guidelines Advisory Committee Scientific Report. 779 (2018)
5. Manz, K., Mensink, G.B.M., Jordan, S., Schienkiewitz, A., Krug, S., Finger, J.D.: Predictors of physical activity among older adults in Germany: a nationwide cohort study. BMJ Open **8**, e021940 (2018). https://doi.org/10.1136/bmjopen-2018-021940
6. Global recommendations on physical activity for health. WHO, Genève (2010)
7. Smith, G.L., Banting, L., Eime, R., O'Sullivan, G., van Uffelen, J.G.Z.: The association between social support and physical activity in older adults: a systematic review. Int. J. Behav. Nutr. Phys. Act. **14**, 56 (2017). https://doi.org/10.1186/s12966-017-0509-8
8. World Health Organization (ed.): World report on ageing and health. World Health Organization, Geneva, Switzerland (2015)
9. Nyman, S.R., Victor, C.R.: Older people's participation in and engagement with falls prevention interventions in community settings: an augment to the cochrane systematic review. Age Ageing **41**, 16–23 (2012). https://doi.org/10.1093/ageing/afr103
10. Sun, F., Norman, I.J., While, A.E.: Physical activity in older people: a systematic review. BMC Public Health. **13**, 449 (2013). https://doi.org/10.1186/1471-2458-13-449
11. Steinert, A., Haesner, M., Steinhagen-Thiessen, E.: Activity-tracking devices for older adults: comparison and preferences. Univ. Access Inf. Soc. **17**, 411–419 (2018). https://doi.org/10.1007/s10209-017-0539-7
12. Valenzuela, T., Okubo, Y., Woodbury, A., Lord, S.R., Delbaere, K.: Adherence to technology-based exercise programs in older adults: a systematic review. J. Geriatr. Phys. Ther. **41**, 49–61 (2018). https://doi.org/10.1519/JPT.0000000000000095
13. Gal, R., May, A.M., van Overmeeren, E.J., Simons, M., Monninkhof, E.M.: The effect of physical activity interventions comprising wearables and smartphone applications on physical activity a systematic review and meta-analysis. Sports Medicine - Open **4**, 42 (2018). https://doi.org/10.1186/s40798-018-0157-9
14. Gartner, Inc.: Gartner Says Worldwide Wearable Device Sales to Grow 26 Percent in 2019. https://www.gartner.com/en/newsroom/press-releases/2018-11-29-gartner-says-worldwide-wearable-device-sales-to-grow-
15. Pew Research Center: Demographics of Mobile Device Ownership and Adoption in the United States (2019). http://www.pewinternet.org/fact-sheet/mobile/

16. eMarketer: Wearable user penetration rate in the United States, in 2017, by age. https://www.statista.com/statistics/739398/us-wearable-penetration-by-age/
17. Mercer, K., Giangregorio, L., Schneider, E., Chilana, P., Li, M., Grindrod, K.: Acceptance of commercially available wearable activity trackers among adults aged over 50 and with chronic illness: a mixed-methods evaluation. JMIR mHealth uHealth **4**, e7 (2016). https://doi.org/10.2196/mhealth.4225
18. Schwartz, B., Baca, A.: Wearables and apps – modern diagnostic frameworks for health promotion through sport. Deutsche Zeitschrift für Sportmedizin. **2016**, 131–136 (2016). https://doi.org/10.5960/dzsm.2016.237
19. Kempen, G.I.J.M., et al.: The Short FES-I: a shortened version of the falls efficacy scale-international to assess fear of falling. Age Ageing **37**, 45–50 (2007). https://doi.org/10.1093/ageing/afm157
20. Schott, N.: Erfassung der Gleichgewichtsfähigkeit bei selbstständig lebenden Erwachsenen: Reliabilität und Validität der deutschsprachigen Version der Fullerton Advanced Balance Scale. Zeitschrift für Gerontologie und Geriatrie. **44**, 417–428 (2011). https://doi.org/10.1007/s00391-011-0236-8
21. Enright, P.L.: The six-minute walk test. Respir. Care. **48**, 783–785 (2003)
22. Bös, K., Abel, T., Woll, A., Niemann, S., Tittlbach, S., Schott, N.: Der Fragebogen zur Erfassung des motorischen Funktionsstatus (FFB-Mot). Diagnostica. **48**, 101–111 (2002). https://doi.org/10.1026//0012-1924.48.2.101
23. Huy, C.: Körperliche Aktivität erfassen und operationalisieren: Instrumente, Methoden und epidemiologische Praxis für die Altersgruppe 50+. VDM Verlag Dr. Müller, Saarbrücken (2007)
24. Lewis, J.R., Sauro, J.: Item benchmarks for the system usability scale. J. Usability Stud. **13**, 10 (2018)
25. Steinert, A., Buchem, I., Merceron, A., Kreutel, J., Haesner, M.: A wearable-enhanced fitness program for older adults, combining fitness trackers and gamification elements: the pilot study fMOOC@Home. Sport Sci. Health. **14**(2), 275–282 (2018). https://doi.org/10.1007/s11332-017-0424-z
26. Muellmann, S., et al.: Development and evaluation of two web-based interventions for the promotion of physical activity in older adults: study protocol for a community-based controlled intervention trial. BMC Public Health. **17**, 512 (2017). https://doi.org/10.1186/s12889-017-4446-x
27. Rütten, A., Pfeifer, K.: hrsg: Nationale Empfehlungen für Bewegung und Bewegungsförderung. Bundeszentrale für gesundheitliche Aufklärung (BZgA), Köln (2017)
28. Genaro Motti, V., Caine, K.: An overview of wearable applications for healthcare: requirements and challenges. Gehalten auf der (2015)
29. Ehn, M., Eriksson, L.C., Åkerberg, N., Johansson, A.-C.: Activity monitors as support for older persons' physical activity in daily life: qualitative study of the users' experiences. JMIR mHealth and uHealth **6**, e34 (2018). https://doi.org/10.2196/mhealth.8345
30. Meng, Y., Choi, H.-K., Kim, H.C.: Exploring the user requirements for wearable healthcare systems. Gehalten auf der Juni (2011)
31. AARP: Building a better tracker: older consumers weigh in on activity and sleep monitoring devices (2015)
32. Maher, C., Ryan, J., Ambrosi, C., Edney, S.: Users' experiences of wearable activity trackers: a cross-sectional study. BMC Public Health. **17**, 880 (2017). https://doi.org/10.1186/s12889-017-4888-1
33. Modave, F., et al.: Mobile device accuracy for step counting across age groups. JMIR mHealth and uHealth **5**, e88 (2017). https://doi.org/10.2196/mhealth.7870

34. Bitkom e.V.: Fast ein Drittel nutzt Fitness-Tracker. https://www.bitkom.org/Presse/Presseinformation/Gemeinsame-Presseinfo-von-Bitkom-und-BMJV-Fast-ein-Drittel-nutzt-Fitness-Tracker.html
35. Stawarz, K., Cox, A.L., Blandford, A.: Beyond self-tracking and reminders: designing smartphone apps that support habit formation. In: Proceedings of the 33rd Annual ACM Conference on Human Factors in Computing Systems - CHI 2015, pp. 2653–2662. ACM Press, Seoul (2015)
36. Attig, C., Franke, T.: I track, therefore I walk – Exploring the motivational costs of wearing activity trackers in actual users. Int. J. Hum.-Comput. Stud. (2018). https://doi.org/10.1016/j.ijhcs.2018.04.007

Facilitating Access to Cross-Border Learning Services and Environments with eIDAS

Tomaž Klobučar[✉]

Jozef Stefan Institute, Jamova 39, 1000 Ljubljana, Slovenia
klobucar@e5.ijs.si

Abstract. Learners face various challenges when accessing cross-border learning services or collaborating with learners from other countries in shared learning environments. This paper shows how the eIDAS Regulation can be used for enabling seamless registration to learning services and access to the learning content, as well as facilitating transmission of the personal academic information in an electronic form from reliable sources. Several eID4U improvements to existing procedures and learning services are proposed, including three upgraded cross-border e-services based on electronic identities and trusted sources of academic information. The improvements help learning service providers improving the reliability of the identification of foreign learners, while at the same time reducing the administrative burden in dealing with such learners.

Keywords: Electronic identification · Cross-border learning service · Shared learning environment · Identity provider · Attribute provider · E-learning

1 Introduction

In learning systems and shared learning environments identity is the key concept around which other services revolve. Even when learning services are provided to anyone with no costs or other constraints, such as in the case of MOOCs, learners still need to be reliably identified and authenticated, and some of their attributes validated, e.g. names or e-mail addresses. In learning environments, the learners often face different authentication and authorisation systems that require the use of several means for electronic identification, and thus creating difficulties in maintaining the large number of credentials for a single user [1]. The current approach to dealing with these issues is the so called 'federated identity model' with 'single sign-on', which enables secure and uninterrupted services provision by employing a single credential. Security Assertion Markup Language (SAML)-based solutions, Open Authentication (OAuth) and OpenID [2, 3] enable the single sign-on process by allowing the identity provider to share the authentication and authorization information with the service providers. PKI-based models for identification of the learners are also used, for example in the MOOC environment [4].

When accessing cross-border learning services or collaborating with learners from other countries in shared learning environments other requirements need to be met, e.g.

recognizing learners' national identification means/credentials as valid abroad and making available the learner data in an electronic form from trusted sources. To solve these issues, at least on a continental level, European Union has been working for many years on an interoperability framework for electronic identity management [5] and aiming at improving the quality of student mobility. The efforts of several large-scale EU projects, such as STORK and STORK 2.0 [6–8], resulted in an infrastructure that is currently being put into production in the EU Member States.

Digital technology is crucial in further improvement of the learner mobility [9]. The majority of student exchanges between European higher education organizations take place under the Erasmus program (or now the Erasmus+ program), which began in 1987 [10]. It involves more than 4,000 universities, and every year, few hundred thousand students are allowed to study abroad (303,880 in 2015). Slovene higher education institutions participating in the program, for example, take slightly over 2,000 new students from abroad (2,248 in 2014 and 2,465 in 2015), while about 2,000 Slovenian students are given the opportunity to visit foreign universities (1,987 in 2014 and 2,084 in 2015) [11, 12]. European Commission set a goal in the Digital education action plans that by 2025, all students in Erasmus+ mobility should be able to have their national identity and student status recognised automatically across the EU Member States, including access to university services when arriving abroad (e.g., study materials, subscription services, libraries) [9]. The learners should also be enabled to identify themselves in "line with the once-only principle" and secure exchange and verification of learner data should be allowed [9].

To meet these objectives, the European Commission implements or co-finances various measures. One of them is the eID4U (eID for University) project from the Connecting Europe Facility (CEF) programme [13]. The goal of the project, which began on February 1, 2018 and is expected to be completed in autumn 2019, is to include higher educational institutions and trusted learner data sources in the eIDAS pan-European infrastructure and enable the infrastructure for learner cross-border electronic identification. The Slovenian part of this eIDAS infrastructure has been established in the second CEF project SI-PASS (Slovenian eIDAS node and integrated services) [14], which was coordinated by the Laboratory for Open Systems and Networks of the Jožef Stefan Institute and was completed in April 2019. The goal of the SI-PASS project (https://cef.si-pass.si) was to establish the central eIDAS node in Slovenia and to connect with the node various cross-border e-services of Slovenian public and private organisations. In the eID4U project, secure cross-border services (e-registration, e-login and e-access) will be further established, which will enable foreign users, for example exchange students, to easily use services (enrolment, learning environment) and wireless networks with national means of electronic identification. The project involves five EU institutions: Politecnico di Torino (Italy), Jozef Stefan Institute (Slovenia), Graz University of Technology (Austria), Universidad Politecnica de Madrid (Spain) and Universidade de Lisboa (Portugal). The solutions developed will also be suitable for other educational e-services accessed by the users from different EU countries.

This paper describes the eIDAS-enabled learning services and the benefits they bring to the learners and learning service providers, especially higher education organisations. The second section first briefly presents the legal basis for the identification of foreign users in EU and the technical infrastructure that enables such identification. An example of the use of infrastructure in education clearly shows its usefulness for the establishment of secure cross-border learning services. Section 3 deals with the challenges related to the availability and reliability of learner data, for example the students under the Erasmus+ exchange programme, and the use of cross-border learning services, while Sect. 4 proposes several solutions to improve those e-services. Finally, related work and other European Commission measures are presented.

2 EU eIDAS Regulation

In 2014, a new legal basis for the provision of secure cross-border electronic transactions was adopted in the EU Member States. It aims to ensure the proper functioning of the EU's internal market and to achieve an adequate level of security for electronic identification and trust services [15]. The EU Regulation on electronic identification and trust services for electronic transactions in the internal market (eIDAS), which entered into force on 1 July 2016, eliminates the existing obstacles to the electronic identification of users from abroad. Defined conditions for mutual recognition of electronic identification means also provide the basis for safer electronic commerce within the EU.

The regulation allows natural and legal persons to use certain national electronic identification means for access to public e-services, for example learning services, in other EU Member States. Examples of the means are national ID cards with digital certificates, digital mobile keys, and one-time password-based means.

2.1 Technical eIDAS Infrastructure

Technical infrastructure eIDAS provides a technical basis for the implementation of the eIDAS regulation. The infrastructure combines identity, service and attribute providers, and national eIDAS nodes from the EU Member States.

Identity Providers
Identity providers issue electronic identification means and authenticate users. They provide users with a secure electronic identity within the framework of the notified electronic identification schemes. Electronic identification means are more or less resistant to misuse and alteration of identities, so the level of trust in the identified e-identity of a service user largely depends on the type of electronic identification used [16]. Also, the consequences of potential abuses and irregularities in the identification and verification of identities can be less or more serious for different services. The assurance level (low, substantial or high) indicates the level of reliability that the electronic identification mean determines the person's identity. It depends on the method of proving and verifying the identity of a legal or natural person at the time of registration (e.g., with an identification document without an image or with an image), the type of connection between the electronic identification means of natural and legal persons, the procedure of issuing, delivery and activation of electronic identification

means, management of the means, resilience to security threats in authentication, management and organization procedures at the identity providers and technical supervision of the identity providers [16]. For example, a qualified electronic certificate issued on a smart card has a higher assurance level than a qualified certificate stored in a web browser, and the level of this certificate is higher than the password or Facebook and Google accounts.

Service Providers
Service providers are institutions, e.g. higher education organizations, that provide citizens with online services. Based on a verified user identity the service providers decide whether to grant access to the services or not and to what extent. The required assurance level of the identification means, selected by the service provider, depends on the consequences that could arise if the identity of the user was not correct. Those public service providers, e.g. learning service providers, requesting a substantial or high assurance level of the users' identification means must from 29 September 2018 recognize the means issued as part of the notified schemes of other EU Member States [15]. For now, this is only a German national identity card, and in the last quarter of 2019, it will be necessary to recognize the identification means from Belgium, Estonia, Croatia, Italy, Luxembourg, and Spain. Other EU countries will soon follow.

Attribute Providers
Attribute providers are entities that manage electronic identity data (specific data describing this identity) that go beyond the minimum identification data set as specified in the eIDAS Regulation and presented in Sect. 3. Additional information (e.g., specific to the sectors such as e-learning, e-banking, or e-health) may be necessary to verify authenticity in certain circumstances or grant access to a service for a particular type of user (e.g., learners with valid student status).

Attribute providers should also be connected to the national eIDAS node, so that their data is available in the eIDAS network. Higher educational institutions are just one example of trusted attribute providers. Learning attributes include information on previous education (e.g., title obtained, information on the study program, length of study) for all who have already completed studies, information on the current study, information on the role of an individual, and other information.

eIDAS Node
The last infrastructure element is an eIDAS node that acts as the central point of trust in a country. On the one hand, it connects national infrastructure with foreign service providers, and on the other hand, national identity, attribute and service providers with the infrastructures of other EU countries. Since all national nodes form a circle of trust, it is sufficient that each service or attribute provider establishes trust only with a node in its own country. Educational service providers will thus not have to deal with the verification of identification means from abroad, but will leave this to the identity providers and national eIDAS nodes. Another authentication model, so called middleware model, is also being used in the infrastructure. As only one country is using it, it will not be further discussed in the paper.

The central node in Slovenia was established at the Ministry of Public Administration within the SI-PASS project. The Ministry also provides access to the Central Population Register, which serves as a trusted source of basic identification data such as name, surname, gender, date of birth, etc.

2.2 Use of the eIDAS Infrastructure in Higher Education

Figure 1 shows an example of the use of the eIDAS technical infrastructure in higher education. A learner from Slovenia wants to access a learning service in Italy, e.g. apply for a student Erasmus+ exchange. When registering for the exchange, she will use her Slovenian identification means, and at the same time provide the necessary evidence of the current and previous studies in an electronic way. The learner first tells the service provider her origin country. She is then being redirected by the Italian national eIDAS node to a similar node in Slovenia, and then to a Slovenian identity provider that verifies her identity on the basis of the provided identification means. Certified electronic evidence of academic qualifications is obtained from a home academic registry (attribute provider). The Slovenian national eIDAS node sends the collected identity and academic data to the Italian national node, and the data is then forwarded to the service provider. It should be emphasized that for the protection of personal data, the initiator of all actions is the learner alone. Likewise, the learner selects which personal information (qualifications) should be disclosed to the service provider and explicitly gives consent for their disclosure. In the next section, an example of learner data required for the student exchange service is analysed.

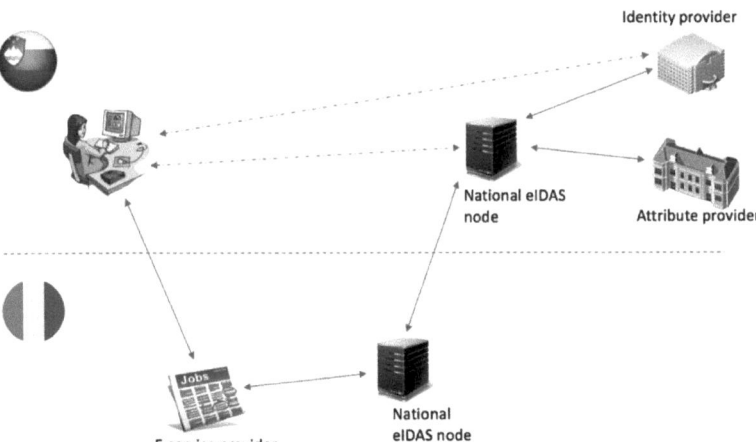

Fig. 1. Example of the use of the eIDAS infrastructure in education

3 Learner Data in the Case of Students Exchange

3.1 Students Exchange

The Erasmus+ programme allows a student to perform part of the regular study obligations in the partner institution (host) abroad instead of at the home institution. Partner institutions are those institutions with which a home institution has signed a bilateral agreement on the exchange of students in a given academic year.

The exchange is a two-step process:

- Student submits the application to the home institution
- Student is registered at the host institution

For the registration of foreign students at the host institution in Slovenia, for example, the University of Ljubljana (https://studij.uni-lj.si/studexchange/tujci_prva.asp) and the University of Maribor have uniform registration pages for all their faculties. The student first enters the personal data, the name of the exchange program and the year of the foreseen exchange to obtain a unique code. Then, with the help of the birth date and the acquired code, she enters information about current and past studies and information about the exchange.

The expected advantage of using the eIDAS infrastructure in this process is for learners to use their national identification means for registration, and to obtain and provide the required data from trusted sources in electronic form instead of typing them into the form. This could reduce the time of entering the data in the registration forms and verifying their validity.

3.2 Sources of Learner Data

The data that learners must submit at registration for the Erasmus+ exchange can be divided into four groups: identification data, current study data, past performance data, and information on the proposed exchange.

Part of the identification data can be provided by the user's origin country through the notified schemes, while the remaining data will have to be obtained from other sources. Data sources may vary, for example, a central population register for identification data, a higher education institution or other registers, such as the Slovenian Central Evidence System for Higher Education (eVŠ), for information on the current and past studies. The data may also be provided by students, for example preferences about the envisaged Erasmus+ exchange.

The following are briefly presented learner data needed at the time of registration, and the proposed sources of this information. Among the data sources in Tables 1, 2, 3 and 4, *AP* indicates an attribute provider, *eIDAS* the notified scheme of the EU Member State, and the *student* a student herself.

Table 1 lists the identification data required by the higher education institution at the time of application. Some of them are already available in the eIDAS infrastructure itself. The European Union defines a minimum set of identification data that uniformly represent the natural and legal person [17]. Mandatory data for a physical person includes current name, current surname, date of birth, and unique identifier, while optional data are name and surname at birth, place of birth, current address, and gender. EU Member States are obliged to provide mandatory information on users of services, while it is their choice to provide the optional data or not. Thus, learning service providers can only expect mandatory data from other countries, even though some countries have announced that they will also include various optional data in their identification schemes. Croatia and Portugal, for example, will include all the optional data in their scheme, while Austria none of them.

Table 1. List of identification attributes

Attribute	Source
Name	eIDAS
Surname	eIDAS
Date of birth	eIDAS
Place of birth	eIDAS, AP
Country of birth	AP, student
Gender	eIDAS, AP
Personal document	student
Personal document number	student
Country of citizenship	AP, student
Permanent address	eIDAS, AP
Temporary address	student
Phone number	student, AP
E-mail address	student, AP

The second set of data is related to the current study (Table 2) and the student's home institution. The most reliable source of this data is the higher education institution or the central higher education register, such as eVŠ in Slovenia. To make this information available, the institution or central register must be included in the eIDAS infrastructure. Otherwise, the user must still enter the information in the application form by herself.

Table 2. List of the current study related attributes

Attribute	Source
Home institution	AP, student
Address and country of home institution	AP, student
Level of study	AP, student
Field of study	AP, student
Name of study	AP, student
Transcript of records	AP, student

For student exchange, information on current degree, successfully finished studies and acquired competencies, such as foreign language skills, are also important (Table 3). Again, the most reliable data sources are the educational institutions the student attended or central registries.

Table 3. List of the past study related attributes

Attribute	Source
Degree	AP, student
Name of the educational institution	AP, student
Date of graduation	AP, student
Country of study	AP, student
Level of language knowledge	AP, student
Language knowledge certificate	AP, student

The last set includes information on the proposed student exchange at the host institution (Table 4). In this case, data is not yet available in any of the information systems or registers, so they must be provided by each student.

Table 4. List of the exchange related attributes

Attribute	Source
Exchange programme	student
Learning agreement	student
Study period	student
Semester	student
Name of the faculty at the receiving institution	student
Field of study	student
Envisaged number of credit points	student
Language of instruction	student
Contact person or coordinator at home institution	AP, student

4 Improvements

The proposed eID4U improvements aim at more reliable and simpler user identification through the eIDAS infrastructure and the acquisition of the highest possible volume of data electronically from reliable sources that are part of the infrastructure.

4.1 Upgrade of the eIDAS Node for the Needs of Education

The eIDAS infrastructure currently supports only a limited number of identification data to be exchanged through the eIDAS nodes. The current EU DIGIT reference implementations of an eIDAS node (latest versions 1.4.3 and 2.2, both released in

September 2018) do not yet allow the identification and treatment of other (sector-specific) attributes except those from the eIDAS minimum data set.

The first eID4U improvement was therefore an upgrade of the eIDAS node (*eIDAS-proxy* and *eIDAS-connector* in Fig. 2). Support (marshaller and changed configuration) for additional academic attributes related to the current study, the learner's home institution, information on current degree, successfully finished studies, and acquired competencies has been included in eID4U in the reference implementation version 1.4.3. The project has also defined an XML scheme and the XML definitions of the attributes, reusing some of the existing learning data schemes [18]. Examples of the defined academic attributes include *HomeInstitutionName*, *HomeInstitutionIdentifier*, *CurentLevelOfStudy*, *FieldOfStudy*, *CurrentDegree* or *LanguageProficiency*. The eID4U project partners have already set up modified eIDAS nodes, connected them into a test network, and tested their interoperability, i.e. that the academic attributes are successfully transferred through the network. An example of a modified eIDAS node is provided at https://eidas.e5.ijs.si/SP/.

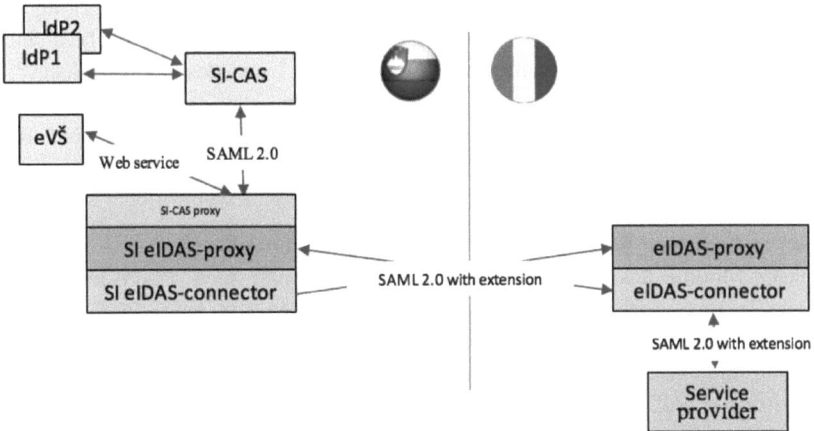

Fig. 2. Schematic representation of the infrastructure

4.2 Integration of Academic Attribute Providers

The second step was integration of the national academic attribute providers into the eIDAS technical infrastructure. AP Connectors have been developed to integrate higher education institutions and central education registries to the national eIDAS nodes. This connection can be achieved either through national eID proxies, such as SPID in Italy [19], or directly with the educational institutions and other trusted sources of academic attributes. In the case of Slovenia, the connector (*SI-CAS proxy* in Fig. 2), which has been integrated into the eIDAS node, connects directly to the national Evidence and Analytical Information System for Higher Education (eVŠ) and uses the eVŠ web services for accessing the academic attributes. The eVŠ system contains information on all study programs and enrolled students in Slovenian higher education organizations.

The information includes, for example, the year of study, the field of study, the name and status of the higher education institution, the study program, the length of the program, the method of study, the date of the first enrolment, etc. Slovenian central authentication system (SI-CAS) plays role of an eID proxy that provides basic identification attributes, such as name, surname and eid.

4.3 Upgrade of the Learning E-Services

The last step was upgrade of existing learning e-services and procedures for registering and identifying learners from abroad. In Slovenia, for example, learning service providers can connect to the Slovenian eIDAS node in two ways: directly to the node or through the Slovenian central authentication system SI-CAS.

Learner Registration

The registration service is one of the most widely used services in educational institutions. The eID4U project results extend the systems and websites for registering learners with an additional login method called "eIDAS Login". The foreign learner can use this method to register to learning services with her national identity. By clicking on the eIDAS Login button, the user is redirected to the eIDAS infrastructure where she uses her national means of identification as shown in Fig. 1 and described in Sect. 2.2. In addition, the required identification and academic data (data that have *eIDAS* or *AP* identified as source in Sect. 3.2) are automatically obtained from the academic attribute providers. The rest of the data, not available at the identity and attribute providers, still need to be entered manually into the registration system or web form.

Access to Learning Services and Learning Environments

For years Moodle has been one of the most widespread open source learning management systems with almost 100.000 registered sites and more than 147 million users.[1] The system supports different learning and administration services, such as learner administration, virtual learning rooms (courses) or learning content creation and administration, and different actors. Within eID4U, an open source plug-in for Moodle v3.6 has been developed that enables direct connection to the eIDAS node and identity verification using the eIDAS infrastructure. The user is given the appropriate role in the system and access to learning material is provided on the basis of national identification means and provided verified academic attributes. An example of the eIDAS-enabled Moodle installation (Fig. 3) can be seen at https://e-learn.e5.ijs.si.

Wireless Network Access

The last e-service, which is still being upgraded, is access to a wireless network at a foreign institution. Similar to the Eduroam network, the service will allow users to access the wireless network by electronic identification means issued under the notified eIDAS schemes. In contrast with Eduroam that serves academic users (students, professors) only, other users with valid national means of identification who are authorized to access the network, for example participants at the project meetings, conferences and other events, will also be able to seamlessly connect to the internet.

---

[1] Source: https://moodle.net/stats/, obtained on 25 January 2019.

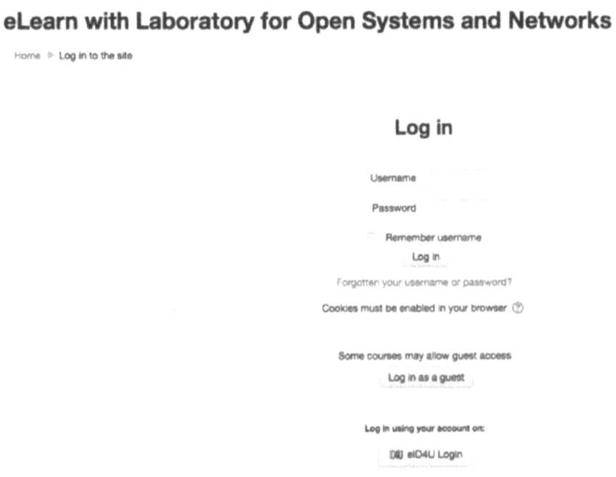

Fig. 3. Example Moodle login page with the eID4U Login button

5 Related Work

In this section, we briefly present some other approaches that aim at facilitating learner identification and learner mobility in the future and reducing the burden of learning service providers. Most of the approaches are part of the actions implemented under the Erasmus+ and Connecting Europe Facility programmes.

Gerakos et al. describe the connection of the Erasmus exchange student identification service to the eIDAS node, however only with the use of a minimum set of identification data [20]. The Erasmus Without Paper project (EWP) [21] is preparing solutions for the safe exchange of student data. The EWP will link university student information systems into a single network facilitating the preparation of mutual cooperation agreements between institutions, informing selected students for exchange, and transfer of certificates of achievements in the ELMO format [21]. EMREX [22] is building a decentralized system designed to facilitate the transfer of achievements or learning outcomes from students who were abroad on exchange. A student in the information system of a home institution can choose a country and a foreign institution from which she wishes to transfer her achievements and identifies himself or herself with an identification institution for the institution or state at a foreign institution or national contact point covering several institutions at the same time. The selected achievements, written in the ELMO format and electronically signed, are then passed on to them and included in the home information system. Unlike eIDAS, the user needs more means of identification (one for each foreign institution or country). The aim of the European Student Card [23] project is to create a single student card in the form of a smart card for all European students. A student could have several student cards, one for each higher education institution to which she is enrolled. The card can only be used at those universities that recognize it. The ESMO project [24], co-financed by the Connecting Europe Facility, started on April 1, 2018. Its goal is to establish a central hub in each EU country, linking all higher education organizations in that country. The nodes will share data that are not already provided on the eIDAS network. The StudIES+ project [25] is implemented in the same program as the eID4U and ESMO projects. Its purpose is to facilitate the mobility of students in the European Union through a platform that will include digital services for students of higher education institutions accessed by electronic identity and provide an electronic signature, electronic seal and timestamp.

The largest identity inter-federation system in the area of educational institutions so far has been the eduGAIN service with 59 identity federations, 2986 identity providers and 2344 service providers[2]. The service is worldwide and not restricted only to Europe. Two of the main differences with the described eIDAS infrastructure are lower levels of assurance of the identification means and an attribute scheme that is not suitable for some of the learning services presented in this paper. Nevertheless, there have already been attempts in the past to match the eduGAIN identities with the identities of the eIDAS infrastructure predecessors [6].

6 Conclusion

This paper presents the eID4U approach on improving the cross-border learning services and environments with eIDAS. The main eID4U contributions are integration of the sector specific attributes (academic attributes) into the EU reference implementation of the eIDAS node, integration of the trusted sources of academic attributes in the eIDAS infrastructure, and upgrade of the learning e-services with the mechanisms for easier registration and authentication of foreign users. Learning service providers, higher education organizations and learners will benefit from the established infrastructure and upgraded e-services.

Learning service providers can increase the level of reliability of user identity verification and increase the number of potential service users with learners from other EU countries. Identity checks are delegated to the identity provider, and the infrastructure itself allows the introduction of new services based on strong authentication and verified electronic evidence of academic qualifications. As national identification schemes usually cover the whole population in a country (e.g. with national id cards), the eIDAS-based approaches also significantly increase the number of users.

Accessing verified academic information in an electronic form simplifies certain administrative tasks, such as checking learner paper documents from abroad, and eliminates the possibility of errors in entering data in online forms. Higher education organizations that are included in the infrastructure as trusted sources of academic data on students and graduates enable them to access new cross-border services in other EU Member States. The infrastructure ensures that personal data is adequately protected and the learner decides which information she is willing to disclose.

The presented approach is currently limited to the European Union Member States. For wider coverage, an interoperable framework and federation with other infrastructures is needed, such as an attempt to match identities from eduGAIN and the large-scale pilot STORK project [6].

---

[2] eduGAIN technical site: https://technical.edugain.org/.

Acknowledgments. The presented work is result of the eID4U (eID for University, code 2017-EU-IA-0051) and SI-PASS (Slovenian eIDAS node and integrated services, code 2017-SI-IA-0037) projects, co-financed by the European Union from the Connecting Europe Facility instrument.

References

1. Indu, I., Rubesh Anand, P.M., Bhaskar, V.: Identity and access management in cloud environment: mechanisms and challenges. Eng. Sci. Tech. Int. J. **21**, 574–588 (2018)
2. Naik, N., Jenkins, P.: Securing digital identities in the cloud by selecting an apposite federated identity management from SAML, OAuth and OpenID connect. In: 11th International Conference on Research Challenges in Information Science (RCIS) (2017)
3. Kunz, M., Puchta, A., Groll, S., Fuchs, L., Pernul, G.: Attribute quality management for dynamic identity and access management. J. Inf. Secur. Appl. **44**, 64–79 (2019)
4. Miguel, J., Caballé, S., Prieto, J.: Providing information security to MOOC: towards effective student authentication. In: Proceedings - 5th International Conference on Intelligent Networking and Collaborative Systems, INCoS, pp. 289–292 (2013)
5. García, S.S., Gómez Oliva, A., Pérez-Belleboni, E.: Is Europe ready for a pan-European identity management system? IEEE Secur. Priv. **10**(4), 44–49 (2012)
6. Torroglosa, E., Ortiz, J., Skarmeta, A.: Matching federation identities, the eduGAIN and STORK approach. Future Gener. Comput. Syst. **80**, 126–138 (2018)
7. Stepančič, Ž., Jerman Blažič, B.: Exploring European digital single market: user adoption and preferences for eID services. Int. J. Electron. Gov. **10**(4), 382–422 (2018)
8. Priesnitz Filho, W., Ribeiro, C., Zefferer, T.: Privacy-preserving attribute aggregation in eID federations. Future Gener. Comput. Syst. **92**, 1–16 (2019)
9. Commission Staff Working Document Accompanying the document Communication from the Commission to the European Parliament, the Council, the European Economic and Social Committee and the Committee of the Regions on the Digital Education Action Plan (SWD (2018) 12 final) (2018)
10. 87/327/EEC: Council Decision of 15 June 1987 adopting the European Community Action Scheme for the Mobility of University Students (Erasmus), Official Journal L 166, 25/06/1987 pp. 0020–0024 (1987)
11. Erasmus+ Annual Report 2016, ISBN 978-92-79-73890-6
12. Erasmus+ Programme Annual Report 2015, ISBN 978-92-79-63820-6
13. eID4U (eID for University) project. https://ec.europa.eu/inea/en/connecting-europe-facility/cef-telecom/2017-eu-ia-0051
14. SI-PASS (Slovenian eIDAS node and integrated services) project. https://ec.europa.eu/inea/en/connecting-europe-facility/cef-telecom/2017-si-ia-0037
15. Regulation (EU) No 910/2014 of the European Parliament and of the Council of 23 July 2014 on electronic identification and trust services for electronic transactions in the internal market and repealing Directive 1999/93/EC
16. Commission Implementing Regulation (EU) 2015/1502 of 8 September 2015 on setting out minimum technical specifications and procedures for assurance levels for electronic identification means pursuant to Article 8(3) of Regulation (EU) No 910/2014 of the European Parliament and of the Council on electronic identification and trust services for electronic transactions in the internal market

17. Commission implementing Regulation (EU) 2015/1501 of 8 September 2015 on the interoperability framework pursuant to Article 12(8) of Regulation (EU) No 910/2014 of the European Parliament and of the Council on electronic identification and trust services for electronic transactions in the internal market
18. Berbecaru, D., et al.: eID4U – Definition of academic attributes. eID4U Technical report (2018)
19. Berbecaru, D., Lioy, A.: On integration of academic attributes in the eIDAS infrastructure to support cross-border services. In: 22nd International Conference on System Theory, Control and Computing (ICSTCC), pp. 691–696 (2018)
20. Gerakos, K., Maliappis, M., Costopoulou, C., Ntaliani, M.: Electronic authentication for university transactions using eIDAS. In: Katsikas, S., Zorkadis, V. (eds.) e-Democracy 2017. CCIS, vol. 792, pp. 187–195. Springer, Cham (2017). https://doi.org/10.1007/978-3-319-71117-1_13
21. Mincer-Daszkiewicz, J.: Mobility scenarios supported by the Erasmus without paper network. In: EUNIS 2018, pp. 189–190 (2018)
22. Mincer-Daszkiewicz, J.: EMREX and EWP offering complementary digital services in the higher education area. In: EUNIS 2017, pp. 354–357 (2017)
23. European Student Card project. http://europeanstudentcard.eu/
24. Gumbau, J.P., Arago Monzonis, F.J.: ESMO project: towards European identity federation convergence for a simpler and trusted student mobility. In: EUNIS 2018, pp. 206–208 (2018)
25. Strack, H., Schmidt, A., Schmidsberger, F., Wefel, S.: eIDAS based applications at University Management. In: EUNIS 2018, pp. 11–13 (2018)

Barriers to Success in a Collaborative Technological Ecosystem: A Study on the Perception of the Interoperability Problem in Civil Engineering Education

Jeffrey Otey[1(✉)], Jorge D. Camba[2], José Ángel Aranda Domingo[3], and Manuel Contero[4]

[1] Zachry Department of Civil Engineering, Texas A&M University,
199 Spence Street, College Station TX 77840, USA
j-otey@tamu.edu
[2] Department of Computer Graphics Technology, Purdue University,
401 N. Grant Street, West Lafayette IN 47907, USA
jdorribo@purdue.edu
[3] Departamento de Ingeniería Gráfica,
Escuela Técnica Superior de Ingenieros de Caminos,
Universitat Politècnica de València, Camino de Vera s/n, 46022 Valencia, Spain
jaranda@dig.upv.es
[4] Instituto de Investigación e Innovación en Bioingeniería (I3B),
Universitat Politècnica de València, Camino de Vera s/n, 46022 Valencia, Spain
mcontero@upv.es

Abstract. In this paper, we report some issues in the learning ecosystem at Zachry Department of Civil Engineering at Texas A&M University related to software interoperability problems that can be considered a limiting factor in the efficiency of the CAD workflow in Civil Engineering education. We describe the structure of an undergraduate course where various CAD packages are used where data must be shared and exchanged among them. We provide a discussion about participant responses and perception toward interoperability, instructor observations, and suggest solutions to common interoperability problems, along with concrete plans to improve the course. The interoperability issues associated with designing in multi-CAD environments may have significant impact on productivity, the level of user-engagement, and the student learning experience.

Keywords: Interoperability · BIM · Curriculum development

1 Introduction

In the Zachry Department of Civil Engineering at Texas A&M University, Building Information Modeling (BIM) software has recently been incorporated as one of the technological tools to support the civil engineering learning ecosystem. Related topics to BIM are first introduced in a compulsory sophomore-level course focusing on Computer-Aided Design (CAD) and visualization skills, with the expectation that students will apply these new tools in future courses. The course has undergone continuous modification, with new material initiated based on industry and capstone design class professor feedback. Previously, students have received instruction in a variety of CAD software commonly used in the civil engineering profession (AutoCAD, AutoCAD Civil 3D, and Revit), but each of these programs was used independently of each other, exclusively employing the design aspects for which they were designed. In application, specific projects were assigned considering the capabilities of each program, covering both land development and structural engineering disciplines. Specifically, AutoCAD Civil 3D was previously used for land development projects (rural runway redesign, shopping center construction, and improvements for a city park) and Revit was used to either design a freestanding structure or to provide a structural skeleton for an existing architectural project. The purpose of this course, as well as for the continuous improvements, is to provide for increased competitiveness for student internships and proficiency with industry-standard BIM software so that new graduates can quickly implement their skills.

A new ambit for the class was removing the structural engineering component and instead concentrating on land development projects. This decision was made to better reflect the enrollment numbers between the areas of emphasis offered in the department (General Civil Engineering, Structures, and Transportation). Moreover, another class was developed entirely focusing on BIM and Revit, so these topics were not entirely removed from the curriculum. In order to accomplish this task, two commercial BIM programs (AutoCAD Civil 3D and Autodesk InfraWorks) were used, which generate data and files, which are then shared between them. More specifically, InfraWorks was used to collect and create 3D surface data (terrain and existing roads) in a format that could be exported to AutoCAD Civil 3D for further design modifications. An example is shown in Fig. 1. This process also supplied exact geolocation and aerial imagery to place the surfaces in context (see Figs. 2, 3 and 4). InfraWorks is a cloud-based software, requiring an Autodesk account to access stored design files.

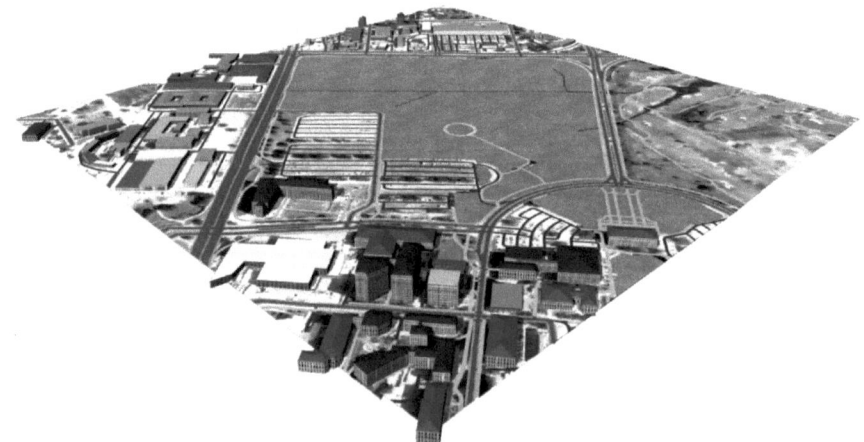

Fig. 1. InfraWorks model of polo field at Texas A&M University

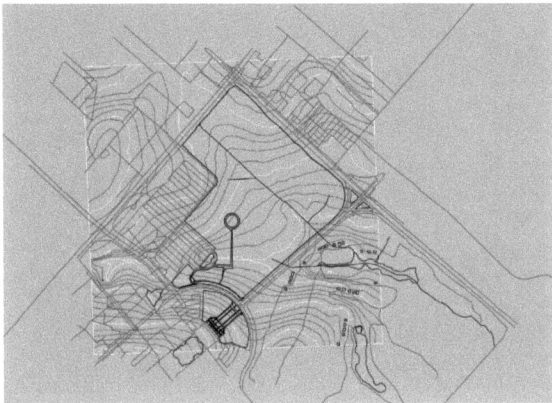

Fig. 2. Civil 3D drawing with imported InfraWorks model.

Fig. 3. Civil 3D drawing with imported InfraWorks model with road map and existing transportation surface.

The College of Engineering has instituted a "Bring Your Own Device" program that requires students to purchase a laptop computer that meets stringent specifications. Furthermore, Autodesk provides a useful scholastic community that allows the students to download and access educational versions of professional software. These educational versions have all functionality of the corresponding professional software, but the licenses expire after three years. Certain problems develop because general College of Engineering laptop specifications are not in alignment with specific CAD software system requirements. As an example, college requirements specify 8 GB RAM machines, while AutoCAD Civil 3D can marginally perform on an 8 GB RAM computer (minimum requirements), Autodesk recommends 16 GB RAM.

Ideally, data sharing among these applications and integration within the overall course workflow should be seamless; especially since the same software company developed all CAD packages used in the course. However, various problems were

Fig. 4. Civil 3D drawing with imported InfraWorks model with aerial map and existing transportation surface.

observed and reported which can have a negative impact on the dynamics of the course as well as on the overall student learning experience. In this paper, we discuss the students' view on CAD interoperability in the context of this course and explore the effects on a collaborative CAD environment and civil engineering education.

2 Interoperability

Many definitions of interoperability have been proposed in the technical and academic literature. For example, IEEE defines interoperability as "the ability of two or more systems or elements to exchange information and to use the information that has been exchanged" [1]. According to authors Levine et al. [2], interoperability can be understood as "the degree to which a set of communicating systems are (i) able to exchange specified state data, and (ii) operate on that state data according to specified, agreed to, operational semantics." Carney et al. [3] introduced the ideas of purpose (or goal) and context (or environment), and added them to the definition provided by Levine et al. [2]: "the ability of a collection of communicating entities to (i) share specified information and (ii) operate on that information according to a shared operational semantics (iii) in order to achieve a specified purpose in a given context." Compatibility was described by Panetto as a prerequisite for interoperability [4]. Regarding technological ecosystems, researchers García-Holgado and García-Peñalvo [5] stated that "the information flow between two software components implies there is an integration between those components."

For the purposes of this paper, interoperability is defined as the ability of a system to provide services to and accept services from other systems, which involves communication, with the purpose of operating together in a more effective manner [4, 6]. Researchers generally agree on the barriers that hinder interoperability [6–8]. Although barriers may exist at technical, operational, and organizational levels, this paper focuses exclusively on technical barriers, specifically software interoperability and how users in the context of civil engineering education perceive these barriers.

The problem of interoperability has a long history in the field of CAD and Computer-Aided Engineering (CAE). In the Architecture, Engineering, and Construction (AEC) industries, problems continue to exist concerning a lack of interoperability of software in reference to exchanging design information in electronic format [9]. Historically, interoperability problems have resulted in geometric errors, inconsistencies, broken geometry, and loss of design intent. These problems may result in longer product development cycles due to rework, inefficient reuse of designs, translation costs, and wasted opportunities for innovation, which often translate to significant losses for the company, both in terms of time and money [10].

Over time, CAD systems have evolved considerably to include more than just the geometric representation of a product. Today's CAD systems are capable of conveying material information, design intent, annotations, product structure and manufacturing process data, to name a few, within the 3D model. Furthermore, many modern CAD packages also include collaborative tools across the enterprise and/or cloud-based services. Although some efforts have been made to facilitate information exchange (such as the development of neutral translation formats and the implementation of modules and pre-processing interfaces for these formats), the increase in complexity along with the understandable reluctance of vendors to share their intellectual property, have naturally contributed to this problem.

From a technical standpoint, basic interoperability aspects and data exchange issues in CAD were originally discussed by Gerbino and colleagues [11]. These aspects include the accuracy of the mathematical descriptions of the model in the different CAD systems, the types of geometry representations, and the different internal description and interpretation of the model by the kernel of each CAD system. Interoperability problems can also originate from poor modeling practices. Substandard geometry often results in poor data exchange. As a result, software vendors have not yet been able to fully solve the problem of interoperability and users are still far from working on a completely interoperable multi-CAD environment.

Realizing interoperability as being an important problem, several Architecture, Engineering and Construction groups have taken steps toward the development of standards to facilitate data exchange between software platforms [12]. Examples include the Open Geospatial Consortium [13] and ifcXML model and implementation support groups [14]. In the context of civil engineering CAD education, the integration of CAD product data among the various systems is a fundamental aspect to ensure efficiency of the learning process and facilitate course dynamics. By focusing on design and modeling tasks rather than data translation and migration issues, students will be able to collaborate more effectively, shorten the time to complete assignments, reduce frustration, and improve the overall quality of the deliverables. This paper primarily examines CAD interoperability from a student's perspective, the goal of which is to understand how interoperability is perceived in the overall CAD workflow, and identify problems that may hinder student learning. In the next section, we discuss the results of a user study conducted as part of a civil engineering course.

3 User Study

In the context of the course previously described in the introductory section of this paper, a commonly reported and important student problem involved creation of large surface files on the computer lab workstations, which were split into several temporary files (or may have existed as one file) stored on the local machine, which was/were externally referenced in the surface files exported to AutoCAD Civil 3D and were therefore inaccessible on student laptops. Recognizing this and other problems concerned with the interoperability between these CAD programs, a user study was conducted to investigate user perception and the extent to which interoperability can be considered a limiting factor in the efficiency of the CAD workflow in civil engineering education.

A survey was constructed to investigate problems encountered with software interoperability and completed by fifty-one students. The survey utilized a 5-point Likert Scale (questionnaire designating gradations of approval) [15]: 1 = Strongly Disagree; 2 = Disagree; 3 = Neutral; 4 = Agree; and 5 = Strongly Agree.

The results of this survey reveal that eighty-six percent of the respondents downloaded the free education software from Autodesk, with ninety-one percent of those students using this software to complete assignments, in addition to using university-provided workstations. As the College of Engineering requires all students to purchase a computer that meets required specifications, student unwillingness to access the free software is not related to lack of computer ownership. The survey asked the respondents to respond the following seven statements:

1. Using each individual software package and managing files within that package was easy and straightforward (Ex. External References and Blocks).
2. From a user interaction standpoint, sharing files between programs was easy, intuitive, and straightforward (Ex. Civil 3D and InfraWorks).
3. Sharing files between programs is a reliable and seamless process.
4. I trust the accuracy of my imported files.
5. In terms of interface design and overall user interaction, it was easy for me to work and switch from one software package to another.
6. When sharing files between applications, it was easy for me to keep track of all my files and the overall workflow.
7. It was easy to share files and work on different computers (e.g. lab workstation, personal laptop, etc.).

Students were also afforded an opportunity to provide detailed responses to the following questions:

1. What problems did you encounter using an individual software package?
2. What problems did you encounter when sharing files between programs?
3. What problems did you encounter when sharing files between computers (e.g. personal device vs. lab workstation)?

4 Results and Discussion

The student responses are shown in Table 1.

Table 1. Student response to interoperability questionnaire.

Question	Student response	Std. dev.
Using each individual software package and managing files within that package was easy and straightforward (e.g. external references and blocks)	3.94	0.68
From a user interaction standpoint, sharing files between programs was easy, intuitive and straightforward (e.g. Revit, Civil 3D and InfraWorks)	3.90	0.76
Sharing files between programs is a reliable and seamless process	3.65	0.93
I trust the accuracy of my imported files	4.00	0.89
In terms of interface design and overall user interaction, it was easy for me to work and switch from one software package to another	3.69	0.95
When sharing files between applications, it was easy for me to keep track of all my files and the overall workflow	3.94	0.76
It was easy to share files and work on different computers (e.g. lab workstation, personal laptop, etc.)	3.27	1.15

For Question 1, the students agreed with the statement, "Using each individual software package and managing files was easy and straightforward," responding with a value of 3.94. The respondents almost replied with an identical score (3.90) to the second question, "From a user interaction standpoint, sharing files between programs was easy, intuitive, and straightforward." In regard to the third question, students largely agreed (3.65) with the statement, "Sharing files between programs is a reliable and seamless process." For the fourth question, students agreed (4.00) with the statement, "I trust the accuracy of my files." For the fifth question, student respondents mostly agreed (3.69) with the statement, "In terms of interface design and overall user interaction, it was easy for me to work and switch from one software package to another." For the sixth question, students agreed (3.94) with the statement, "When sharing files between applications, it was easy for me to keep track of all my files and the overall workflow." For the final question, students were generally neutral (3.27) in their response to the question, "It was easy to share files and work on different computers."

When examining the standard deviation of the responses, all values were moderately large, considering the 5-point possible scale. They ranged from a low value of 0.68 (for Question 1) to a high value of 1.15 (for Question 7). That these values were so wide-ranging leads one to surmise that there is a definite vagueness to the responses, with the highest standard deviation value corresponding to the question with the least amount of agreement. Anecdotally, it appears that most students were unsure of their replies, but the general pattern appears to be in agreement with all queried statements.

The responses to the open-ended questions were examined and placed in comparable sub-categories in order to compile the information in a useable format. All fifty-one students answered these questions, providing additional, unprompted specific feedback facilitating course improvement.

The first question queried problems encountered using an individual software package. Ten students reported that their own personal device was slower than the departmental-provided computer, which is an unexpected response, since the lab computers are relatively dated, leading one to question if the students purchased a machine that satisfied college required specifications. Ten students reported issues with corrupted files and frequent program crashes. Other reported problems included issues with a smaller screen with their own laptops and the inability of InfraWorks to create a model (encountered by the instructor also). Moreover, and mentioned in one student comment, is that some students opted not to purchase an external wireless mouse, even though the cost is minimal. CAD design using the track pad is considerably more arduous.

The second open-ended question ascertained student problems sharing files between AutoCAD Civil 3D and InfraWorks. The students overwhelmingly responded (thirty-five responses) that no problems were encountered when sharing files between these programs. The student response to this question is not in alignment with their answer to Question 2 using the Likert Scale (3.94), however. This lack of congruence could be reinforced by the wide-ranging standard deviation values reported for the seven questions.

The third open-ended question addressed sharing files between computers. Twelve students reported experiencing no problems sharing files, but six students admitted that they only used one device for all assignments (either laptop-only or lab computer-only). The other response of particular interest was that temporary files were either missing or difficult to locate when using different machines. These responses seem to mimic what was illustrated in Question 7 using the Likert Scale (3.27). For this case, the InfraWorks models are by default located in the "Documents" folder, and it is not readily apparent (or possible?) to browse for another location when creating them.

5 Instructor Observations

The instructor also encountered various file sharing issues when deploying the class during the semester, as he primarily used his office computer for lecture development and the instructor machine in the classroom. Since all curriculum preparation was accomplished on his office workstation, he failed to foresee these file sharing issues.

Student refusal to download the free educational CAD software was based on either absence of scholastic engagement, lack of hard drive space, or reluctance to install *Boot Camp Assistant* on their personal device. In addressing the latter issue, a technology help desk, funded by the college, is staffed to assist students with this task. Some students may have chosen not to run the programs on Mac OS because of a reluctance to decrease available hard drive space or a perceived reduced battery life in labs without adequate electric outlets, but this issue was not queried on the questionnaire. Since utilizing one machine for all design steps helps to reduce interoperability issues (at least between devices), future versions of this course will require students to download the free educational software, even if their personal laptop only meets minimum specifications. Proof of successful software installation will also be required.

The issue of whether the college required device specifications are adequate is a thornier issue. The requirements are college-wide, with many majors not requiring the high-end computer speed or graphic cards of computers performing CAD design. To further complicate the issue, students are not enrolled in a major until their sophomore year, before the specifications of the computer they need is known. It is unrealistic to expect the college to upgrade their computer specifications for the small number of departments that need a more robust machine. So, in the end, there may not exist a practical solution.

6 Conclusions

This paper examined the issue of CAD interoperability from a student perspective in the context of Civil Engineering education. Our results shed light on the impact of interoperability on course dynamics and the overall learning experience. The problem becomes more relevant as more institutions embrace "Bring Your Own Device" type of policies.

While interoperability issues continue to cause complications with using CAD software in the classroom, the advantages dwarf these problems. As the software continues to become more complex, useful, and powerful, it is vital that the newest technologies are discussed and utilized in an educational setting so that the next generation of engineers has state-of-the-art tools in which to be successful.

The proposed solutions, (1) requiring one computer to be used for all design work (either student device or lab workstation), (2) encouraging students to purchase (or upgrade to) a CAD-ready machine, and (3) compelling students with Mac OS systems to have their hard drive partitioned and having *Boot Camp Assistant* installed, are only quick fixes, so that the learning process is not disrupted. Hopefully the technological irregularities will be ironed out in future versions of the software as their adoption becomes more commonplace.

References

1. IEEE, Standard Computer Dictionary – A Compilation of IEEE Standard Computer Glossaries (1990)
2. Levine, L., Meyers, B.C., Morris, E., Place, P.R., Plakosh, D.: In: Proceedings of the System of Systems Interoperability Workshop (No. CMU/SEI-2003-TN-016), Carnegie-Mellon Univ Pittsburgh Pa Software Engineering Institue, February 2003
3. Carney, D., Fisher, D., Place, P.: Topics in Interoperability: System-of-Systems Evolution, University of Pittsburgh, Software Engineering Institute, Technical Note CMU/SEI-2005-TN-002 (2005)
4. Panetto, H.: Towards a classification framework for interoperability of enterprise applications. Int. J. Comput. Integr. Manuf. **20**, 727–740 (2007)

5. García-Holgado, A., García-Peñalvo, F.J.: The evolution of the technological ecosystems: an architectural proposal to enhancing learning processes. In: García-Peñalvo, F.J. (ed.) Proceedings of the First International Conference on Technological Ecosystems for Enhancing Multiculturality (TEEM 2013), pp. 565–571, Salamanca, Spain, New York, NY, USA. ACM, 14–15 November 2013
6. Yahia, E., Aubry, A., Panetto, H.: Formal measures for semantic interoperability assessment in cooperative enterprise information systems. Comput. Ind. **63**(5), 443–457 (2012)
7. Chen, D., et al.: Enterprise Interoperability-Framework and Knowledge corpus, INTEROP-NOE FP6 IST-2003-508011, Deliverable DI.2 (2006). http://www.interop-vlab.eu
8. Chituc, C.M., Toscano, C., Azevedo, A.: Interoperability in collaborative networks: independent and industry-specific initiatives – the case of the footwear industry. Comput. Ind. **59**(7), 741–757 (2008)
9. Grilo, A., Jardim-Goncalves, R.: Value proposition on interoperability of BIM and collaborative working environments. Autom. Constr. **19**, 522–530 (2010)
10. Markson, H.: Achieving CAD interoperability in global product design environments. White Paper, SpaceClaim Corporation (2007)
11. Gerbino, S., Crocetta, S., di Martino, C.: Data exchange in CAD systems: limits, solutions, perspectives. In: Proceedings of X ADM International Conference, pp. 423–434, Florence, Italy, 17–19 September 1997
12. Akin, O.: CAD and GIS Interoperability Through Semantic Web Services. CAD and GIS Integration, pp. 202–225. Auerbach Publications, Boca Raton (2009)
13. OGC: Open Geospatial Consortium, Inc. (2007). http://www.opengeospatial.org/. Accessed 10 Jan 2019
14. IAI: IFC/ifcXML Specifications (2007). http://www.buildingsmart-tech.org/specifications/ifcxml-releases. Accessed 10 Jan 2019
15. Likert, R.: A technique for the measurement of attitudes. Arch. Psychol. **140**, 1–55 (1932)

Towards Supportive Mechanisms for Crowd Collaboration – Design Guidelines for Platform Developers

Navid Tavanapour[(✉)] and Eva A. C. Bittner

University of Hamburg, Hamburg, Germany
{Tavanapour,Bittner}@informatik.uni-hamburg.de

Abstract. Crowd work can be distinguished from crowdsourcing mainly with regard to the monetary remuneration of crowd workers for tasks similar to an employment. The crowd work platform delivers the environment and tool to connect crowdsourcer and crowd worker in order to orchestrate the collaboration between them as well as generally among individuals of the crowd. Increasing collaboration on platforms presupposes a design that involves actors and functionalities that support the collaboration beyond the individual. We conduct a systematic literature review with the main focus on incentive systems, management approaches for collaborative crowd work process and control as well as guidance of the crowd activities towards specific directions. We consolidate recommendations from prior studies for designers and providers of crowd work platforms by introducing design principles, to be considered for informed design decisions. We contribute an integrated overview of functionalities and mechanisms explored in crowd work literature so far to advance the understanding and design of crowd work processes.

Keywords: Crowd work · Crowdsourcing · Mass collaboration · Open Innovation · Platform · Literature review · Design principles

1 Introduction

Crowd work is based on crowdsourcing and describes a digital kind of employment where crowd workers - individuals of the crowd [1] - are rewarded monetarily [1]. "Crowd work offers remarkable opportunities for improving productivity, social mobility, and the global economy by engaging a geographically distributed workforce to complete complex tasks on demand and at scale" [2]. Therefore, crowd work platforms have evolved and are used as intermediaries between worker and employer. In addition, they are the essential connecting work environment and tool to orchestrate collaboration between crowdsourcer and crowd worker and generally among individuals of the crowd. Platforms make it possible to efficiently assign individual stand-alone tasks to dispersed workers. However, also larger projects can be managed through a platform by splitting more complex tasks and assigning subtasks to workers or by assigning larger tasks to a crowd for collaborative solving. As collaboration between heterogeneous participants can lead to better results in solving complex tasks [3–6], crowd work platforms may benefit from explicitly fostering and facilitating collaboration processes. However, collaboration requires a closely coordinated joint work of several workers on the same artefact [7], e.g. a design draft or a software component, which poses advanced requirements on the platform's functionalities. For example, (a) functionalities for attracting skilled workers willing to collaboratively participate in the crowd work process include various possibilities for targeted **incentives**, which are not limited to a monetary reward. A distinction for incentives can be made between extrinsic and intrinsic motivation [8–12]. Furthermore, (b) functionalities for the **management** of the joint work process must be implemented. In the whole crowd work process, especially if not only individual jobs are assigned, but many workers shall work together on a project, coordination and communication are substantial and need to be supported by a set of suitable functionalities. In addition, (c) the crowd needs to be guided well in order to **control** for high quality reliable work results. Crowd work platform designers and providers thus face a multitude of design challenges and no common standard has evolved in this dynamic domain yet on how to design effective crowd work platforms, especially when it comes to more complex tasks that require collaboration of crowd workers. These challenges appear from a platform designers point of view.

To address (a), (b) and (c), design principles could guide platform designers towards suitable solutions for supportive functionalities for digital crowd collaboration. As a structured collaboration process has already been in the scope of research (see [13, 14]), we extend this stream of research by deriving design principles to implement collaborative crowd work platforms. Previous reviews on crowdsourcing literature have made contributions to shed light on this rising domain, in particular with respect to the general crowdsourcing field, but without addressing the specifics of collaborative work in detail and only cover the literature until January 2012 [15]. These efforts have a focused scope on collaboration between crowd workers, however they do not consider literature from relevant related fields, e.g. open innovation and social computing [13] and lack an operationalization of findings towards design principles. Therefore, we address this knowledge gap by building on and extending this stream of work with respect to design knowledge for collaboration support from a broad and up-to-date literature basis. Additionally, we derive helpful design principles that should be utilized when designing the functionalities for collaboration support on crowd work platforms. With respect to a, b, and c, we guide our research by the following research questions: Q1: What kind of **incentive** mechanisms can be used to promote collaboration on crowd work platforms? Q2: How can the collaborative work process between different actors on the platform be **managed** via functionalities? Q3: What kind of guidance or scripts can crowd work platforms implement to **control** the activities of the crowd or guide them to a specific direction?

To answer these research questions, we conduct a systematic literature review by following the guidelines of vom Brocke et al. [16]. The aim is to consolidate the literature to set up a basis in order to derive suitable design principles from the literature to answer Q1, Q2, and Q3.

The structure of this paper is as follows: First, we present the methodology for the systematic literature review. Second, we consolidate the findings to present the status quo of research and categorize them in implications for platform functionalities for incentive structures, the management of the work process and for crowd control. Third, we derive meta-requirements, formulate corresponding design principles, discuss and consolidate the current literature to answer Q1, Q2 and Q3. We close this paper with a conclusion.

2 Methodology and Scoping of the Literature

This paper presents the state of research on crowd work platforms with respect to the challenge of designing effective platform functionalities for complex, collaborative tasks. More specifically, we analyze incentive structures, the management of the work process, and crowd control. Therefore, we follow the guidelines of vom Brocke et al. [16] for a comprehensive search process to ensure the completeness and thoroughness. First, the scope of the review is defined. The analysis covers publications from different areas: crowdsourcing, crowd work, mass collaboration and open innovation. In our study, we refer to the following conceptualizations of the terms:

"In **crowdsourcing**, a Crowdsourcer (e.g., a company, an institution, a group, or an individual) proposes a task via an open call to an undefined amount of potential contributors (crowd workers)" [1, 17]. **Crowd work** is based on the concept of crowdsourcing with the difference that the potential contributors/crowd workers are in a gainful employment [1]. **Mass collaboration** is characterized by the involvement of a large group of people (as a mass) e.g. the crowd, the usage of digital tools e.g. crowd work platform and the digital outcome they produce together [18]. Chesbrough and Bogers [19], define "**open innovation** as a distributed innovation process based on purposively managed knowledge flows across organizational boundaries, using pecuniary and non-pecuniary mechanisms in line with the organization's business model" [19]. By considering these domains, we are open to concepts for platform solutions from different fields potentially dealing with distributed collaboration via platforms to inform our analysis.

We used the search string: (("crowd work*" OR "crowdso*" OR "mass collaborati*" OR "open innovation") AND ("platform*")). This search string includes the logical OR operator, the logical AND operator and the free variable parameter*. The logical operators provide the correct relation among the substrings and the free variable parameter considers the string to be a substring of any other string, e.g. crowdso* considers crowdsourcing as well as crowdsource. With the logical AND operator, the first part of the term will only be a match in combination with platform*. The decision to specify the search towards papers containing the term "platform*" was made to exclude the vast number of crowd work publications outside the scope of design research for crowd platforms, e.g. concerning crowd work business models. With this focus, we aimed to identify papers that have platform design or functionalities within the core of their contribution. Consequently, a wide range of literature is considered and literature with different focus than crowd work platforms is excluded.

We considered the six databases listed in Table 1 due to their relevance for high-quality peer-reviewed information systems research and searched in each database in title, keywords and abstract. Table 1 also shows the number of results found in each database in October 2018 when we conducted the search (S1).

Table 1. Considered databases and search results

Database	S1	S2	S3
IEEE Xplore Digital Library	716	29	
Ebscohost research database	1268	46	
ACM Digital Library	51	5	
Emerald insight	518	16	
Sciencedirecct	337	19	
Academic OneFile	265	12	
+Backward/Forward Search			11
Total number of results after each step	3155	127	**137**

In step 2 (S2), by reviewing title, keywords and abstract of these 3155 publications, we could reduce the amount to 127 papers for in depth analysis. Most of the excluded papers had been selected by the search string, because the term "platform" was used in another context unrelated to crowd work. Reasons for exclusion covered paper foci other than supporting crowd worker collaboration or platform functionalities unrelated to influencing crowd worker behavior and interaction. Excluded were articles with the main goal to define phenomena in the crowdsourcing domain or to technically deploy platforms and features. We also excluded publications that targeted optimization of platform functionalities such as task breakdowns or task integration that happen without any direct crowd worker involvement. Task breakdown is a highly relevant topic in the crowdsourcing field, but it mostly focuses on how to break down tasks so that crowd worker can accomplish them, not on crowd collaboration. Considering the fact that crowd workers are in the center of each of our research questions, we excluded those articles. Eleven additional articles were added while conducting a backward and a forward search (S3) in these 127 publications. After a thorough analysis of the 137 full texts, **27 publications were considered for the study** at hand. In this step, papers were excluded because the articles did not include any information that could contribute to answering our research questions. In particular, publications are not reported within the scope of this paper, that do not discuss aspects related to the three categories outlined in the introduction (incentive structures, management of the work process, crowd control) or do not report insights that can be used to derive design implications for platform functionalities.

Only the selected 27 publications are included in the following analysis and are reflected in our findings. Table 2 summarizes the considered literature and the results of the review. We identified, which of the three specified topics (Management of work process (WP), incentive system (IS), crowd control (CC)) were addressed by each publication. Some of the publications addressed two of the topics and are listed twice in Table 2.

Table 2. Examined articles categorized by management of work process (WP), incentive system (IS), crowd control (CC)

Topic	Literature
IS	[8–12, 20–29]
WP	[30–35]
CC	[20, 26, 31, 36–40]

3 Consolidation of the Literature: Status Quo of Research on Platform Functionalities

In this section, we consolidate the literature in light of the three guiding research questions (Q1, Q2 and Q3) and discuss their impact on platform design in relation to incentive structures, management of the crowd work process and crowd control. Furthermore, in this section we derive meta-requirements (MR) and corresponding design principles (DP) by referring to the literature.

3.1 Platform Functionalities for Incentive Systems

More and more crowdsourcing and crowd work platforms are being created, which are used in different domains to get work done by the crowd. However, to motivate the crowd in the long term, incentive structures that meet the requirements of all actors involved must be created. This section shows, which platform functionalities the literature suggests for this purpose.

In order to determine, which incentive structures should be implemented, it is necessary to understand the effect of different structures and how to motivate the crowd first. After all, one's motivation has an impact on the quality of the contributions [41] (**MR1**). Thus, performance is often described as a function with the factors motivation and ability [9]: *Performance = f (Motivation x Ability)*.

In the case of motivation, a distinction can be made between extrinsic and intrinsic motivation [8–12]. Hobbies, pleasure, and interests are intrinsic motivators, while extrinsic motivation delivers some compensation for work [11]. This can, e.g. be remuneration [9] or fulfilling the desire to learn and improve one's own abilities [12]. Extrinsic motivation can be further divided into financial (e.g. money or job opportunities), social (e.g. knowledge or experience) and organizational (e.g. career prospects or responsibilities) motivators [11]. These types of motivation can have an impact on the submitted contributions. According to Frey et al. [9], intrinsic motivation may significantly increase the number of substantial contributions. A contribution is classified as substantial when it is both new and relevant. In contrast, extrinsic motivation may increase the number of non-substantial contributions [9].

It is also important to consider that there are different platform users who can have different motivations (**MR2**). For example, Schultheiss et al. [10] identified four different types of crowdsourcing users: the female creatives, the male technicians, the academics and the alternative all-rounders [10]. The exact differences in the motivation of the user groups are not exactly investigated, but such differences in the user groups have to be taken into account when implementing incentive systems. In addition, there may also be differences between different population groups and regions [24] (**MR3**). For example, in a survey, Americans viewed the earned money generated as additional extra income, while Indians (depending on the region in which they live) viewed the rewards as a primary source of income, with which they could buy basic supplies to survive [24].

For the platform providers, it is obviously ideal, if exclusively intrinsic motivation and non-monetary extrinsic motivation were sufficient for the crowd, so there would be no expenses for remuneration. Prior work within the analysis provides indication that crowd workers can be driven by both intrinsic and extrinsic motivation [12]. However, the motivation may change over time (**MR4**), if the platform is used for a long time. According to Soliman and Tuunainen [12] motivation factors such as monetary rewards or curiosity are of great importance when using a platform for the first time. Over time, these factors are losing importance and are getting replaced by social motivation factors such as enjoyment, altruism, non-monetary rewards, and publicity [12]. After all, the main reason to participate in online platforms is to help the community [42].

Incentives and motivators are strongly linked [11]. Incentives ensure sufficient motivation and thus represent an important factor for the cooperation in crowd work. An incentive does not always have to be monetary. Chittilappilly et al. [8] generally, distinguishes between two types of incentives: monetary incentives and non-monetary incentives. In this respect, non-monetary incentives mainly address the non-monetary types of motivation: fun and entertainment, personal development, competition as well as moral, purposive and material incentives in the form of points or credits [8] (Fig. 1).

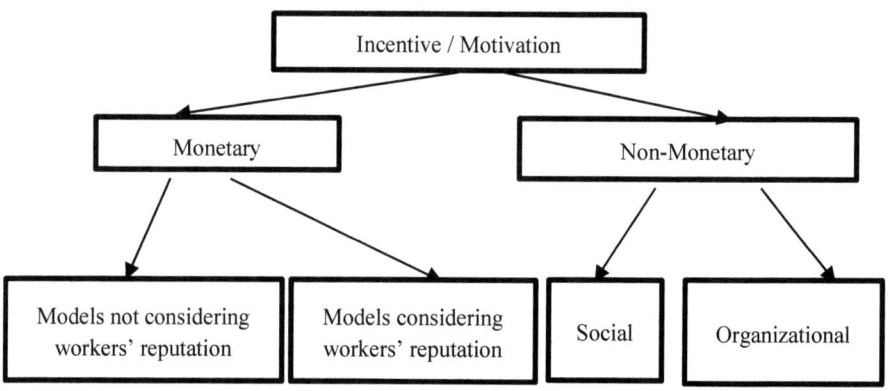

Fig. 1. Categorization of incentives (based on [11] and [8])

In particular, the last point is important for crowd work platforms. For completed tasks, crowd workers earn points that enhance their reputation and help with other job applications on the platform [8]. With a point system, a monetary reward can also be gained, for example, by exchanging points against awards [20]. However, monetary incentives are usually preferred by workers [8, 24]. The reward is generally paid only, if the work is accepted by the client, which can lead to a high rejection rate and anger among the workers. It is important to set the rewards correctly, as too much reward will lead to unnecessarily high costs and too little reward may result in crowd workers neglecting the task.

Chittilappilly et al. [8] distinguishes between two different types of monetary incentive systems, systems that do not consider the reputation of the worker and systems that consider the worker's reputation, each of which is subdivided. Table 3 gives an overview of the categorizations with advantages and disadvantages of each method. **The relevance-based model** uses an incentive system based on the relevance of the task. In Harris [23] the task was to review resumes for a company. Four different variations of rewards were compared: (1) fixed reward for each review; (2) increased remuneration, if the review is identical to that of an expert (positive incentive); (3) reduced remuneration, if the review differs from that of an expert (negative incentive); (4) combination of the previous methods (payment + deduction). In this study, the positive incentive and the combined approach provide the best results [8] **(MR5)**. **The survival analysis method** is used to determine the time t until a certain event occurs [22]. With the aid of this analysis, a recursive algorithm could be developed that returns the price, which is the least necessary wage to complete the task in desired time [8]. The desired time must therefore be set before each task. In **the reputation-based method** [29], crowd workers were considered who received the payment before completing the task. The free-riding problem was prevented by assigning orders based on the previous interaction with the crowdsourcing platform. In addition, there was a punishment system for low quality work. In order to improve quality, the upcoming tasks were assigned to the workers who had a better reputation.

Table 3. Pros and cons of monetary incentive models [8]

Category	Technique	Pros	Cons
Not considering workers' reputation	Relevance-Based Model	• Easy to implement • Easy to keep track of payment	• Does not consider workers' rating or expertise level
	Survival Analysis Method	• Given the time t, algorithm generates minimum wage for the task.	• Does not consider workers' level of expertise • High computation cost
Considering workers' reputation	Reputation-Based Method	• Addresses free-riding problem • Integrates payment and reputation elements • Maximizes website's revenue	• Assuming tasks are homogenous and workers have equal expertise
	Rating and Reward Dividing Model	• Considers heterogeneous skill sets of workers • An administrator in the system makes sure that the requester is not taking advantage	• Depending on the expertise of workers, there is a possibility that the requester might get only low-quality answers

In **the rating and reward dividing model** [28] workers are heterogeneous. In the system, there is a rating scheme, a reward dividing system and other important crowdsourcing elements. New workers can only participate until a limit is reached, and since their work may be of low quality, there is a "reputation protocol". To ensure that the employer does not benefit from the rejection of all submitted results (**MR6**), an administrator distributes the reward to all participating workers in case that all results are rejected.

A challenge is to find the right incentive type and a suitable amount of remuneration (**MR7**). With an increase in remuneration, the number of results submitted may increase significantly [25, 27] (**MR8**) and the quality of the best result also increases [27]. However, the quality of the average results does not necessarily increase [25, 27]. It is also possible that the workers are not paid per job, but in bulk for many tasks.

Ikeda and Bernstein [43] show that a bulk-payment after ten tasks under the conditions within their study increased the rate of the tasks completed while the quality was not significantly different [43].

Once different incentives have been identified, they must be implemented in the platform. Various algorithms are therefore presented in the literature for different purposes. In Tian et al. [26], for example, an algorithm is presented that encourages the crowd to do tasks in less popular areas (**MR9**) in mobile crowdsourcing. Another article deals with incentive mechanisms for crowd workers who perform binary tasks [44]. Incentive models for a single-requester single-bid model, a single-requester multiple-bid model, and a multiple-requester multiple-bid model are presented in Zhang et al. [45]. Xie et al. [28] propose an incentive system that is robust against human factors [28] (**MR10**).

Three more articles deal with the topic of mobile crowdsensing: Dai et al. [21] provide an incentive framework for this domain, where the employer performs a gambling process for checking the negative feedback in case of a poor assessment (**MR11**). A certain number of "players" are recruited who receive a small reward. Players then give feedback on data quality. If it turns out that the data quality of the submitted work is insufficient, the employer will be refunded. If this is not the case, the employer pays the wage, the platform fees, the gamification costs as well as a penalty for the wrong feedback. This framework can help motivate participants to contribute high-quality work, lead employers to truthful feedback, and can make the platform more profitable [21]. Zhang et al. [46] also provide three incentive mechanisms for mobile crowdsensing, one of which is to maximize the platform utilization and make recruitment decisions based on a control group. The other two aim to fulfil the criteria of truthfulness. Wen et al. [47] present a quality-oriented incentive mechanism for mobile crowdsensing. The algorithm can maximize the social welfare of all participants and lead to more submissions of high-quality data with less required computing power.

One potential conclusion we draw from the analysis concerning incentive systems is, that social motivation factors deserve special attention when designing collaborative crowd work, as crowd workers may need to interact more intensively and for a longer duration with other users on the platform. Monetary rewards, which are common in small individual task crowd work and in the studies we found, may fail to work in complex, collaborative settings, especially if goal achievement can hardly be attributed to individual workers. This assumption should be investigated in future research.

Furthermore, it would be interesting to examine, whether collaborative crowd work platforms attract workers with different types of motivation than do platforms focused on individual contributions.

3.2 Platform Functionalities for the Management of the Work Process

For the crowd work process to run without major complications, a crowd work platform must be implemented with functions for the management of the work process. They should ensure good communication and interaction between the employer and the workers, but also promote collaboration between them. The claims of both sides must be considered to allow a fair exchange of the different actors. It is not trivial to identify, which specific functions should be implemented for this purpose and demands can vary from platform to platform. This section shows which platform functionality literature suggests for the management of the work process.

In software engineering, one major domain for crowd work, communication, coordination and collaboration in many different facets are key factors that connect successful teams. For example, requirements for the tasks, assessment criteria or the progress of the task are exchanged among actors (**MR12**) [33]. In terms of communication, the exchange of messages and information on the platform is inevitable so the employer can communicate requirements and conditions, and the worker may communicate technical and organizational problems. With respect to collaboration, the platform should, for example, synchronize the work progress of other users, if several people work on on the same task (**MR13**). In terms of coordination, the platform must support management at both technical and business level. Furthermore, intellectual property should be protected [33]. The comparison of different types of crowdsourcing platforms by Peng et al. [33] discloses several weaknesses of some of these systems, especially with respect to collaboration support, awareness and value transfer (see Table 4).

Table 4. Crowdsourcing support from various software development platforms [33]

Platform type	Communication	Collaboration	Coordination	Awareness	Value transfer
Crowdsourcing-platform	Fair	Poor	Fair	Fair	Good
Platform as a service (PaaS)	Poor	Fair	Fair	Poor	Poor
Open source platform	Good	Good	Fair	Fair	Poor
Collaborative testing platform	Good	Poor	Fair	Poor	Good
Enterprise collaboration platform	Good	Good	Good	Good	Poor

In crowd work management, socio-technical dependencies must also be considered. According to Conway's law, social structures, e.g. the team composition, have a great influence on the later technical structure of the product [34] (**MR14**).

Andersen and Mørch [30] investigated interaction patterns between end-users and developers in mass collaboration. Four different interaction patterns were identified (**MR15**). In the case of "gatekeeping", an actor determines, which information is passed on in order to protect other stakeholders from unnecessary information. The "bridge builder" instead distributes the information to other stakeholders, whereby they receive the information very early and to a sufficient extent. "General development" is when a local solution of an end user is taken over by a developer and the solution becomes part of the product. If users need to make adjustments to fit the software to a particular situation, they speak of "user-user collaboration" as they make these adjustments supported by interaction with other end users [30].

The management of the work process also includes giving feedback (**MR16**). According to Dow et al. [31] the important decisions are, when feedback should be given and who should give this feedback. The feedback can be given directly during work execution or after completed work. Very early feedback means that there is very little time for the customer to provide feedback, which requires tools and algorithms for fast feedback generation. Feedback at a later stage gives the client more time to provide feedback, but a worker will not improve the work anymore subsequently. Even simple binary feedback may improve the results. The more detailed and personal the feedback, the more the workers can learn, but this costs time and money. As long as a worker does not complain, there is often no additional feedback, which goes beyond "accepted" or "rejected". In the case of feedback generation, it is a good idea to select the customer to provide feedback. However, they cannot always get involved in the problems of the workers. Alternatively, workers can be paid to evaluate other workers (peer feedback). According to Yang et al. [35] identifying valuable workers (**MR16**) based on the existing data and recruiting them for the feedback would be one solution. To this end, Dow et al. [31] have designed a system that supports peer feedback. The feedback is sent to the worker as soon as he begins a new task of the same kind. The quality of the following results is increased by the feedback [31].

3.3 Platform Functionalities for Crowd Control

For crowd work platforms to be effective, mechanisms are necessary to control the crowd. This includes both the review of completed work and steering the crowd consciously. Efficient verification mechanisms such as quality control and methods for controlling the crowd activities are required. For example, can users be guided in a direction that is of advantage for the task completion? This section discusses, which platform features are suggested in literature for controlling the crowd.

Crowd sensing often involves the problem of an unequal distribution of workers. To counteract this problem, Tian et al. [26] describe a mechanism that encourages the crowd through intelligent task assignment to take over tasks in less popular areas. It is represented in pseudo code and can be implemented in platforms. All parties can benefit from this opportunity to control the crowd, as more tasks may be completed, the workers earn more money and the platforms get more advertising revenues, mediation fees or at least publicity due to the higher number of completed tasks [26].

Ankolekar et al. [20] describe the crowdsourcing platform MET (Market for Enterprise Tasks). By completing tasks, the workers receive so-called MET coins, a virtual currency that can be exchanged for real dollars or other goods. The employer can place a maximum reward for a specific task on the platform. The workers can then indicate and bid how much the task is worth. Afterwards, the employer chooses the winner of the bid who will perform the task. Due to the possibility of changing the exchange rate from MET coins to real world dollars, there are possibilities to motivate workers differently in various situations. The platform therefore offers an incentive system linked to real money with very precise market regulation possibilities [20]. These are very helpful for platforms, but they can be non-transparent and arbitrary for the workers. However, MET uses concrete elements for controlling the market and thus controlling the crowd. In order to control the market, a maximum reward can be defined for each task. In addition, a maximum reward per worker can be set for a specific period. Since the rewards of the completed tasks are paid out in so-called MET coins, the exchange rate of the MET coins to dollars or other goods obtainable for the MET coins can be determined and changed for further market control (**MR18**). This results in a number of ways to closely monitor and control the market.

In order to control the crowd, it is helpful to predict how well the quality of a solution will be. To make such a prediction, the required knowledge, skills and other characteristics, such as motivation or personal attitude, to solve the task must be known. Given that, as described in Hassan and Curry [36], task performance can be relatively accurately predicted [36] (**MR19**). Workers can be clustered based on the probability to submit good results. A worker can also be assigned a confidence interval, for example the worker X1 can have a confidence interval of [0.4, 0.8] for successful task completion. The ability to estimate performance offers different advantages. Tasks can only be assigned to workers with specific traits. If active feedback is given to the workers, the overall quality of the performance can be increased by such predictions, and the feedback can even serve as a motivation factor [36].

Mok et al. [32] describe how workers delivering poor quality work can be identified in the field of crowd testing. Most of them would like to get paid for minimal effort. By identifying these people, the reliability of crowd testing can be significantly increased. Various factors such as start times, breaks, or the number of clicks are used to identify work behaviours. However, since mouse movements and mouse clicks are analysed, this method cannot be transferred without problems to all types of crowdsourcing or crowd work. Therefore, other methods, e.g. identifying fraud by analysing the order of answers to specific questions [48] or analysing user behaviour to predict the quality of work [49] (**MR20**), are possible concepts platform designers could adopt. Furthermore, the framework of Gomez and Laidlaw [50] proposes an approach to collect user interaction data from which an estimated completion time for results can be used. In addition, factors such as completion time, working time in the individual phases (such as "read" or "answer questions") and the time of observation can be analysed, for a prediction of the quality of the work results [37]. All of these works aim at assessing the quality and are thus important for controlling the crowd.

Another way of recognizing workers who deliver low quality work is a qualification test. In addition, there are methods to recognize bad or careless workers, so-called spammer, based on the results submitted. Workers with low quality values or spammers can be excluded from the platform, which is already a common method for quality improvement [38].

Naderi et al. [39] investigate the reliability of responses in the field of crowdsourcing. In one study, a method was used that is non-noticeable to the worker, while in another study both noticeable and non-noticable methods were used. In the study with the obvious method, workers gave more consistent answers. When users know that their work is being reviewed, they respond more reliably [39]. This can be exploited for crowd work platforms by making quality checks transparent to their users and use them both as selection mechanisms as well as steering tools to enforce reliable behaviour (**MR21**).

The work of Abhinav et al. [40] presents an intelligent assistant for besides the crowd worker to support them with recommendation and guidance. Platforms could use artificial intelligence in form of virtual intelligent assistants to shape crowd workers' behaviour in a direction that is beneficial for the platform (**MR22**). This approach could be used to influence workers' behaviour and would be one way to control the crowd.

3.4 Design Principles

By consolidating the current literature, we derived 22 meta-requirements. Based on the scoping of the literature, MR1-11 refer to the design of incentive systems, MR12-16 to work process and MR17-22 refer to crowd control. With reference to MR1-MR22, we formulated eight action oriented design principles (Table 5) according to Chandra et al. [51]. Some of the MRs were considered more than once to formulate the design principles. Even though, we assigned the DPs to one of the scopes IS, WP or CC (Table 5), the DPs are not exclusively limited to our assignment. Therefore, the DPs can have effects and overlap with more than one of them.

The design principles serve as a basis to consider collaborative task accomplishment by platform designers and developers.

Table 5. Meta-requirements (MR) and the derived design principles (DP) for collaboration on crowd work platforms.

MR	Description of MR	Design principle	
MR1	There are different structures to motivate the crowd, which can have an impact on the quality of the contributions	**DP1:** Provide the crowd work platform with diverse positive non-monetary incentive structures and monetary remuneration to address the workers' motivation in any state of time on the platform and to increase the probability to get the most submissions with better quality	**Incentive system**
MR4	The motivation may change over time. Therefore, different approaches are needed to keep the crowd motivated over time		
MR5	Positive incentives provide the best results for the motivation and outcome		
MR8	By increasing remuneration, the number of results submitted and the quality of the best result elevate		
MR2	There are different types of platform users (e.g. female creatives, male technicians, the academics and the alternative all-rounders) who can have different motivations	**DP2:** Provide the crowd work platform with non-monetary and monetary incentive structures by considering the type of workers, the background of the workers such as population group and geographical region, the social structures and norms that the workers value and the possible influence of human factors, when designing incentive structures for the platform to ensure a positive effect on the workers' motivation	
MR3	Different population groups and geographical regions can have different motivation on crowd work platforms		
MR5	Positive incentives provide the best results for the motivation and outcome		
MR10	Human factors can have an influence on the impact of incentive systems		
MR14	Social structures, (e.g. social norms in specific groups) and the team composition can have an influence on the outcome of collaborative tasks		
MR7	Each task or type of task should have the right incentive type and a suitable amount of remuneration	**DP3:** Provide the crowd work platform with a unique monetary incentive system based on a virtual platform currency with an adjustable rate to exchange to real currency and consider it for remuneration of tasks to ensure regulation of the crowd market with the right amount of payment that suits the task	
MR8	By increasing remuneration, the number of results submitted and the quality of the best result elevate		
MR18	Unique virtual currency with the option to exchange to real currency can add more control of the crowd by having the options to regulation		

(*continued*)

Table 5. (*continued*)

MR	Description of MR	Design principle	
MR6	The employer should not benefit from unfair rejection of submitted results, if worker's payment depends on employer's acceptance	**DP4:** Provide the crowd work platform with functionalities, methods and processes to enable exchange among actors and also identifying unfairly given feedback, unfairly rejected submissions with compensation as well as transparency through the state of processes among actors to prevent negative effects on the collaboration by designing a fair environment for crowd workers and not only for crowdsourcer	**Work process**
MR11	In the event of unfair negative feedback, the worker should not suffer any disadvantages		
MR12	Exchange among actors on the platform (e.g. regarding the task progress) can have an impact on the collaboration		
MR12	Exchange among actors on the platform (e.g. regarding the task progress) can have an impact on the collaboration	**DP5:** Provide the crowd work platform with functionalities, and processes to identify different type of workers to enable optimum team composition and enable (a) synchronous communication through different integrated media channels among team members, synchronize any work progress and set up social rules, norms and behavioral boundaries to achieve better productivity of teams on the crowd work platform	
MR13	Synchronize the work progress of different workers on the same task		
MR14	Social structures, (e.g. social norms in specific groups) and the team composition can have an influence on the outcome of collaborative tasks		
MR17	Automatic identification of valuable workers on the platform can lead to better task assignment, team composition and outcome regulation		
MR20	Identification of minimal effort worker, who submit low quality contributions can lead to approaches to handle those workers		
MR9	The crowd should be encouraged to do tasks even in less popular areas	**DP6:** Provide the crowd work platform with capabilities to identify valuable crowd workers to recruit them with suitable remuneration for the task of giving feedback to others state of work in early stages for higher probability to get better submissions on the platform	**Crowd control**
MR16	Feedback can result in better outcome		
MR17	Automatic identification of valuable workers on the platform can lead to better task assignment, team composition and outcome regulation		

(*continued*)

Table 5. (*continued*)

MR	Description of MR	Design principle
MR16	Feedback can result in better outcome	**DP7:** Provide the crowd work platform with capabilities to identify crowd workers with minimal effort or low quality submissions and guide them with recommendation and training via capable virtual intelligent assistants and inform them about the conduction of random quality checks of their work to reach higher effort or/and better quality in the submission of those workers
MR20	Identification of minimal effort worker, who submit low quality contributions can lead to approaches to handle those workers	
MR21	Quality checks, which workers know of, can lead to better outcomes and more control of the crowd	
MR22	Virtual intelligent assistants can support workers on the platform	
MR15	Different interaction patterns provide insights about the suitability of tasks for worker with different strengths.	**DP8:** Provide the crowd work platform with functionalities to identify valuable worker, minimal effort or worker with low quality submissions and capabilities to analyze the interaction pattern of the worker to identify the strengths of workers to consider them for optimum team composition and task assignment as well as methods to consider the existing data to predict the quality of their work and gather data for better regulation purposes e.g. with incentive systems, different team composition or assigning other task
MR17	Automatic identification of valuable workers on the platform can lead to better task assignment, team composition and outcome regulation	
MR19	Workers' existing data can be utilized to predict the quality of submissions when assigning tasks	
MR20	Identification of minimal effort worker, who submit low quality contributions can lead to approaches to handle those workers	

4 Discussion and Conclusion

Based on the analysis of the reviewed literature and the derivation of meta-requirements, we formulated design principles for designers and providers of crowd working platforms that may improve the incentive mechanisms, management of the work process, and crowd control for collaborative crowd work.

Concerning incentive structures (as in Q1), it turned out to be important to understand how people are motivated and how incentives may trigger the motivation of crowd workers. For crowd work platforms this knowledge can be used to motivate workers, depending on the specific field of activity and crowd worker characteristics. In this paper, the various aspects of labour motivation are consolidated and suggestions are derived for design. For example, if workers are mainly working out of intrinsic motivation, this motivation can be further promoted, e.g. by making the work more entertaining and pleasurable for e.g. with gamification, learning and social factors. As a result, a remuneration may be less important to motivate workers, since individuals have fun with the task.

The reviewed studies also suggest that all presented incentive systems have advantages and disadvantages and must be cautiously adopted to different conditions. Using the incentive options presented in this paper (also in scope of DP1, DP2, DP3) and combining it with their domain knowledge, the best individual solution can be identified for a platform.

Regarding the second topic under study, management of the work process (as in Q2), this work identifies interaction patterns, and describes the process of generating feedback in a consolidated way based on different views in literature. Crowd work platforms, which depend on the collaboration between individual crowd workers or aim to extend collaboration functionality towards more complex tasks, can check whether their platform meets the requirements and possibly adapt functionalities (DP4 and DP5) presented here.

With respect to Q3, control mechanisms for the crowd workers and the market are explained and methods for predicting the worker quality are described. In particular, we found transparent quality tests to be promising means to improve quality, e.g. by considering different human factors such as skills, motivation and attitude to profile and predict the crowd workers qualitative level of work or by considering other factors such as start times, breaks and number of clicks to identify poor quality. Also in the aim for crowd control, mechanisms building on user collaboration, such as user evaluation of contributions, are strikingly prevalent. Through this knowledge, platforms can more accurately and with limited resource commitment anticipate worker quality and adapt their algorithms accordingly (DP6, DP7 and DP8).

In sum, we were able to answer Q1, Q2 and Q3. This paper consolidates the current state of research on platform functionalities in the field of collaborative crowd work for the three key areas described. The review excluded other aspects of crowd work platforms beyond the three guiding research questions. For example, many articles in the literature deal with task matching, which has not been considered in our analysis with a focus on collaboration. Nevertheless, task matching is a topic which is of course relevant for crowd work platforms. Through efficient task matching, competitive advantages can be increased. How the crowd work platforms can use task-matching in collaborative tasks and how well implemented algorithms are in practice have to be examined more closely in future work. In addition, there are other challenges and problems in crowd work that deserve to be addressed, but are outside the scope of this work. For example, there is a research gap concerning working conditions [52].

The question of how crowd workers should be best supported to work together most effectively within a project that requires collaboration is not answered by the current state of the literature in detail. While we found insights on each of the three fields of interest, the approaches until now are still in an explorative state or have been applied in very specific domains. Additionally, while we only used publications that explicitly address collaboration in crowdsourcing, most of the work does not specifically distinguish the unique demands that result from collaborative tasks. To address this issue, further research needs to be done. Moreover, we could not identify decision criteria for choosing suitable functionalities to promote the collaboration on crowd work platforms in the current state of research. We propose the following avenues for future research: How does combining different functionalities on crowd work platforms affect the collaboration process on platforms? What kind of behaviour is fostered by adopting different functionalities on the platform? How should functionalities effectively be implemented on the platform? Do the functionalities show impact distinction in different domains or target groups with respect to the interaction beyond the individual?

This paper aims to contribute with prescriptive knowledge according to Gregor and Hevner [53] towards a "theory of design and action" [54] with a set of derived meta-requirements and corresponding design principles to guide platform designers/developers to consider for collaboration on crowd work platforms.

References

1. Durward, D., Blohm, I., Leimeister, J.M.: Crowd work. Bus. Inf. Syst. Eng. **58**, 281–286 (2016)
2. Kittur, A., et al.: The future of crowd work. In: Proceedings of the 2013 Conference on Computer supported Cooperative Work (CSCW 2013), pp. 1301–1318. ACM, New York (2013)
3. Bowers, C.A., Pharmer, J.A., Salas, E.: When member homogeneity is needed in work teams a meta-analysis. Small Group Res. **31**, 305–327 (2000)
4. Bittner, E.A.C., Leimeister, J.M.: Creating shared understanding in heterogeneous work groups: why it matters and how to achieve it. J. Manag. Inf. Syst. **31**, 111–144 (2014)
5. Langan-Fox, J., Anglim, J., Wilson, J.R.: Mental models, team mental models, and performance: process, development, and future directions. Hum. Factors Ergon. Manuf. **14**, 331–352 (2004)
6. Wegge, J., Roth, C., Neubach, B., Schmidt, K.-H., Kanfer, R.: Age and gender diversity as determinants of performance and health in a public organization: the role of task complexity and group size. J. Appl. Psychol. **93**, 1301–1313 (2008)
7. Roschelle, J., Teasley, S.D.: The construction of shared knowledge in collaborative problem solving. In: O'Malley, C. (ed.) Computer Supported Collaborative Learning, pp. 69–97. Springer, Heidelberg (1995). https://doi.org/10.1007/978-3-642-85098-1_5
8. Chittilappilly, A.I., Chen, L., Amer-Yahia, S.: A survey of general-purpose crowdsourcing techniques. IEEE Trans. Knowl. Data Eng. **28**, 2246–2266 (2016)
9. Frey, K., Lüthje, C., Haag, S.: Whom should firms attract to open innovation platforms? The role of knowledge diversity and motivation. Long Range Plan. **44**, 397–420 (2011)
10. Schultheiss, D., Blieske, A., Solf, A., Staeudtner, S.: How to encourage the crowd? A study about user typologies and motivations on crowdsourcing platforms. In: 2013 IEEE/ACM 6th International Conference on Utility and Cloud Computing (UCC), Dresden, Saxony, Germany (2013)
11. Hossain, M.: Users' motivation to participate in online crowdsourcing platforms. In: Proceedings of the International Conference on Innovation, Management and Technology Research (ICIMTR), Malacca (2012)
12. Soliman, W., Tuunainen, V.K.: Understanding continued use of crowdsourcing systems: an interpretive study. J. Theor. Appl. Electron. Commer. Res. **10**, 1–18 (2015)
13. Tavanapour, N., Bittner, E.A.C.: Collaboration among crowdsourcees. towards a design theory for collaboration process design. In: Proceedings of the 50th Hawaii International Conference on System Sciences, Hawaii (2017)

14. Tavanapour, N., Bittner, E.A.C.: The collaboration of crowd workers. In: Proceedings of the 26th European Conference on Information Systems, Portsmouth, UK (2018)
15. Pedersen, J., et al.: Conceptual foundations of crowdsourcing. A review of IS research. In: 2013 46th Hawaii International Conference on System Sciences (HICSS), pp. 579–588 (2013)
16. Vom Brocke, J., Simons, A., Niehaves, B., Riemer, K., Plattfaut, R., Cleven, A.: Reconstructing the giant: on the importance of rigour in documenting the literature search process. In: 17th European Conference on Information Systems (2009)
17. Howe, J.: The rise of crowdsourcing. Wired Mag. **14**(6), 1–4 (2006)
18. Cress, U., Jeong, H., Moskaliuk, J.: Mass collaboration as an emerging paradigm for education? Theories, cases, and research methods. In: Cress, U., Moskaliuk, J., Jeong, H. (eds.) Mass Collaboration and Education. CCLS, vol. 16, pp. 3–27. Springer, Cham (2016). https://doi.org/10.1007/978-3-319-13536-6_1
19. Chesbrough, H., Bogers, M.: Explicating open innovation: clarifying an emerging paradigm for understanding innovation. In: Chesbrough, H., Vanhaverbeke, W., West, J. (eds.) New Frontiers in Open Innovation, pp. 3–28. Oxford University Press, Oxford (2014)
20. Ankolekar, A., Balestrieri, F.E., Asur, S.: MET: an enterprise market for tasks. In: Gergle, D., Morris, M.R., Bjørn, P., Konstan, J. (eds.) CSCW 2016. Proceedings & Companion of the ACM Conference on Computer-Supported Cooperative Work and Social Computing: 27 February–2 March 2016, San Francisco, CA, USA, pp. 225–228. Association for Computing Machinery, New York (2016)
21. Dai, W., Wang, Y., Jin, Q., Ma, J.: An integrated incentive framework for mobile crowdsourced sensing. Tinshhua Sci. Technol. **21**, 146–156 (2016)
22. Faradani, S., Hartmann, B., Ipeirotis, P.G.: What's the right price? Pricing tasks for finishing on time. Hum. Comput. **11**, 11 (2011)
23. Harris, C.G.: You're hired! An examination of crowdsourcing incentive models in human resource tasks. In: WSDM Proceedings of the Workshop on Crowdsourcing for Search and Data Mining (CSDM 2011) (2011)
24. Jiang, L., Wagner, C., Nardi, B.: Not just in it for the money: a qualitative investigation of workers perceived benefits of micro-task crowdsourcing. In: Bui, T.X., Sprague, R.H. (eds.) 48th Hawaii International Conference on System Sciences (HICSS), Kauai, Hawaii, 5–8 January 2015, pp. 773–782. IEEE, Piscataway (2015)
25. Mason, W., Watts, D.J.: Financial incentives and the "performance of crowds". SIGKDD Explor. Newsl. **11**, 100 (2010)
26. Tian, F., Liu, B., Sun, X., Zhang, X., Cao, G., Lin, G.: Movement-based incentive for crowdsourcing. IEEE Trans. Veh. Technol. **66**(8), 7223–7233 (2017)
27. Wu, H., Corney, J., Grant, M.: Relationship between quality and payment in crowdsourced design. In: Hou, J.-L. (ed.) Proceedings of the 2014 IEEE 18th International Conference on Computer Supported Cooperative Work in Design (CSCWD), Hsinchu, Taiwan, 21–23 May 2014, pp. 499–504. IEEE, Piscataway (2014)
28. Xie, H., Lui, J.C.S., Jiang, J.W., Chen, W.: Incentive mechanism and protocol design for crowdsourcing systems. In: 52nd Annual Allerton Conference on Communication, Control, and Computing (Allerton), 30 September–3 October 2014, Monticello, IL, pp. 140–147. IEEE, Piscataway (2014)
29. Zhang, Y., van der Schaar, M.: Reputation-based incentive protocols in crowdsourcing applications. In: Proceedings/IEEE INFOCOM, 2012, Orlando, Florida, USA, 25–30 March 2012, pp. 2140–2148. IEEE, Piscataway (2012)
30. Andersen, R., Mørch, A.I.: Mutual development in mass collaboration: identifying interaction patterns in customer-initiated software product development. Comput. Hum. Behav. **65**, 77–91 (2016)

31. Dow, S., Kulkarni, A., Bunge, B., Nguyen, T., Klemmer, S., Hartmann, B.: Shepherding the crowd. In: Tan, D. (ed.) Proceedings of the 2011 Annual Conference Extended Abstracts on Human Factors in Computing Systems, p. 1669. ACM, New York (2011)
32. Mok, R.K.P., Li, W., Chang, R.K.C.: Detecting low-quality crowdtesting workers. In: 2015 IEEE 23rd International Symposium on Quality of Service (IWQoS), 15–16 June 2015 in Portland, OR, USA, pp. 201–206. IEEE, Piscataway (2015)
33. Peng, X., Ali Babar, M., Ebert, C.: Collaborative software development platforms for crowdsourcing. IEEE Softw. **31**, 30–36 (2014)
34. Skopik, F., Schall, D., Dustdar, S.: Discovering and managing social compositions in collaborative enterprise crowdsourcing systems. Int. J. Coop. Info. Syst. **21**, 297–341 (2012)
35. Yang, P., Zhang, N., Zhang, S., Yang, K., Yu, L., Shen, X.: Identifying the most valuable workers in fog-assisted spatial crowdsourcing. IEEE Internet Things J. **4**, 1193–1203 (2017)
36. Hassan, U., Curry, E.: A capability requirements approach for predicting worker performance in crowdsourcing. In: Bertino, E., Georgakopoulos, D., Srivatsa, M., Nepal, S., Vinciarelli, A. (eds.) 2013 9th International Conference on Collaborative Computing: Networking, Applications and Worksharing (Collaboratecom), 20–23 October 2013, Austin, Texas, United States, [including workshop papers]. IEEE, Piscataway (2013)
37. Hirth, M., Scheuring, S., Hossfeld, T., Schwartz, C., Tran-Gia, P.: Predicting result quality in crowdsourcing using application layer monitoring. In: 2014 IEEE Fifth International Conference on Communications and Electronics (ICCE), pp. 510–515 (2014)
38. Li, G., Wang, J., Zheng, Y., Franklin, M.J.: Crowdsourced data management: a survey. IEEE Trans. Knowl. Data Eng. **28**, 2296–2319 (2016)
39. Naderi, B., Wechsung, I., Moller, S.: Effect of being observed on the reliability of responses in crowdsourcing micro-task platforms. In: 2015 Seventh International Workshop on Quality of Multimedia Experience (QoMEX), 26–29 May 2015, Costa Navarino, Pylos-Nestoras, Messinia, Greece, pp. 1–2. IEEE, Piscataway (2015)
40. Abhinav, K., Dubey, A., Jain, S., Bhatia, G.K., McCartin, B., Bhardwaj, N.: Crowdassistant: a virtual buddy for crowd worker. In: Sartor, J.B., et al. (ed.) CSI-SE 2018: IEEE/ACM 5th International Workshop on Crowd Sourcing in Software Engineering (CSI-SE 2018), Crowdassistant, pp. 17–20. Association for Computing Machinery, New York (2018)
41. Janzik, L.: Contribution and participation in innovation communities: a classification of incentives and motives. Int. J. Innov. Technol. Manage. **07**, 247–262 (2010)
42. Wasko, M., Faraj, S.: "It is what one does": why people participate and help others in electronic communities of practice. J. Strateg. Inf. Syst. **9**, 155–173 (2000)
43. Ikeda, K., Bernstein, M.S.: Pay it backward. In: Kaye, J., Druin, A., Lampe, C., Morris, D., Hourcade, J.P. (eds.) CHI 2016. #chi4good Proceedings the 34rd Annual CHI Conference on Human Factors in Computing Systems, San Jose, CA, USA, 07–12 May 2016, pp. 4111–4121. ACM, New York (2016)
44. Zhang, Q., Wen, Y., Tian, X., Gan, X., Wang, X.: Incentivize crowd labeling under budget constraint. In: IEEE Conference on Computer Communications (INFOCOM), Hong Kong, P.R. China, 26 April 2015–1 May 2015, pp. 2812–2820. IEEE, Piscataway (2015)
45. Zhang, X., Xue, G., Yu, R., Yang, D., Tang, J.: Truthful incentive mechanisms for crowdsourcing. In: IEEE Conference on Computer Communications (INFOCOM), 26 April 2015–1 May 2015, Hong Kong, P.R. China, pp. 2830–2838. IEEE, Piscataway (2015)
46. Zhang, X., Yang, Z., Zhou, Z., Cai, H., Chen, L., Li, X.: Free market of crowdsourcing: incentive mechanism design for mobile sensing. IEEE Trans. Parallel Distrib. Syst. **25**, 3190–3200 (2014)
47. Wen, Y., et al.: Quality-driven auction-based incentive mechanism for mobile crowd sensing. IEEE Trans. Veh. Technol. **64**, 4203–4214 (2015)

48. Costagliola, G., Fuccella, V., Giordano, M., Polese, G.: Logging and visualization of learner behaviour in web-based e-testing. In: Leung, H., Li, F., Lau, R., Li, Q. (eds.) ICWL 2007. LNCS, vol. 4823, pp. 452–463. Springer, Heidelberg (2008). https://doi.org/10.1007/978-3-540-78139-4_40
49. Rzeszotarski, J.M., Kittur, A.: Instrumenting the crowd. In: Pierce, J. (ed.) Proceedings of the 24th Annual ACM Symposium on User Interface Software and Technology, p. 13. ACM, New York (2011)
50. Gomez, S., Laidlaw, D.: Modeling task performance for a crowd of users from interaction histories. In: Konstan, J.A., Chi, E.H., Höök, K. (eds.) CHI 2012, It's the experience. The 30th ACM Conference on Human Factors in Computing Systems; Austin, Texas, USA, 5 May–10 May, 2012, p. 2465. ACM, New York (2012)
51. Chandra, L., Seidel, S., Gregor, S.: Prescriptive knowledge in IS research: conceptualizing design principles in terms of materiality, action, and boundary conditions. In: 2015 48th Hawaii International Conference on System Sciences, pp. 4039–4048. IEEE (2015)
52. Leimeister, J.M., Zogaj, S., Blohm, I.: Crowdwork-digitale Wertschöpfung in der Wolke. Grundlagen, Formen und aktueller Forschungsstand. In: Benner, C. (ed.) Crowdwork - zurück in die Zukunft? Perspektiven digitaler Arbeit, pp. 9–41. Bund-Verlag, Frankfurt am Main (2014). (in German)
53. Gregor, S., Hevner, A.R.: Positioning and presenting design science research for maximum impact. MIS Q. **37**, 337–355 (2013)
54. Gregor, S.: The nature of theory in information systems. MIS Q. **30**, 611–642 (2006)

Interactive System for Collaborative Historical Analogy

Ryo Yoshikawa[1(✉)], Ryohei Ikejiri[2], and Yasunobu Sumikawa[3]

[1] Faculty of Information and Media Studies,
Nagoya Bunri University, Inazawa, Japan
`yoshikawa.ryo@nagoya-bunri.ac.jp`
[2] Interfaculty Initiative in Information Studies,
The University of Tokyo, Tokyo, Japan
`ikejiri@iii.u-tokyo.ac.jp`
[3] University Education Center, Tokyo Metropolitan University, Hachioji, Japan
`sumikawa-yasunobu@tmu.ac.jp`

Abstract. Supporting learning history has become an important topic in education research. To discuss social issues using historical analogy, group learning composed of two pairs is effective. In this paper, we propose a novel interactive system for collaborative historical analogy. This system first provides news articles to users from our database. Then, it uses a clustering algorithm that makes groups from what the users assign event categories for news articles. After assessing the result of the clustering algorithm, our system provides two functions for promoting collaborative learning: discussion spaces and archiving the discussions. The results of quantitative and qualitative evaluation show that our system have the potential to enhance group discussion and collaborative historical analogy in class.

Keywords: Collaborative learning · History education · Analogy · Grouping

1 Introduction

One of the goals of teaching history is to find meaningful connections or analogies over time, and supporting learning historical analogy has become an important topic in education research. Historical analogy allows learners to study how people in the past tried to solve issues, and then apply the acquired knowledge in order to propose alternative solutions to similar issues in other periods. Indeed, Staley claims that history provides not only information on the past but also alternative solutions to similar modern issues [1]. Teaching guidelines for high school education published by the Japanese government include the ability to apply historical knowledge and concepts to modern issues using collaborative learning [2]. Furthermore, to support collaborative historical analogy, researchers have developed effective learning methods [3,4], algorithms mining past events similar to a given present event [5], and an interactive system that is useful in class [6].

Finding similar past and present events plays a key role in promoting historical analogy. However, how people believe that a past and present event is similar is up to them [7]. Furthermore, Fischer found that historical analogies are often misused, and it is necessary to be cautious when using historical analogy [8]. According to [4], group learning composed of two-pair discussions in history has been found to be effective for collaborative learning, checking the validity of each historical analogy, and for improving each historical analogy with various points of view. Although the present study's findings also showed the positive potential for group learning, the gap that needs to be addressed is that no interactive system that makes groups for studying collaborative historical analogy currently exists.

In this paper, a novel interactive system for collaborative historical analogy is thus proposed. The proposed system first shows news articles describing present social issues to users. It then considers users' interests in specific issues and the particular aspects they focus on. From this information, the system groups users by combining similar users as pairs, and not similar pairs as groups. After this step, users can have a discussion within their own groups, and an online text editor and chat plugins to facilitate the discussions are provided. Finally, the system archives the results of the users' discussions and chat logs to use them for reflection in post-learning.

Contributions. The core contribution of the system proposed by the present paper is that it is *interactive*. There are several grouping systems that function as learning environments [9,10]; however, these require pre-testing to analyze what the users are interested in. The present system obtains the information by having users assign one or more event categories that are originally defined as connecting past and present events.

2 Related Works

This section compares the proposed system with two research fields: clustering algorithms and Computer-Supported Collaborative Learning (CSCL).

2.1 Clustering Algorithm

Clustering is an algorithm to make groups. This algorithm is an important and fundamental technique in NLP, ML, and other computer science related research fields.

One of the most popular algorithms is K-means [11], which divides data into groups satisfying the following two conditions: (1) each group must contain at least one object, and (2) each object must belong to exactly one group. K-means updates the centers of clusters by iteratively computing the averages of all points and coordinates representing the arithmetic mean until the specific criteria are satisfied.

Gaussian mixture model (GMM) [12] is another popular algorithm, which takes the assumption that each object in the same cluster is generated from several Gaussian distributions.

The main difference between our system and these past works is *objective*. Our system focuses on how to collect data for clustering and to output the results of the discussions, whereas the clustering algorithms focus on how to make groups. Thus, our framework is orthogonal compared to past clustering work.

2.2 Computer-Supported Collaborative Learning

Computer-supported Collaborative Learning (CSCL) is a major research topic in educational technology and learning sciences with recent findings showing that well-designed technologies can have positive effects on collaborative learning, as well as describing the contexts where students' collaboration and interaction were promoted through some technologies [13].

In CSCL, visualization and awareness are key point to promote collaborative learning. For example, it has been reported that the visualization of participation contributed more to performance with the designed tool that can visualize how much each group member contributes to his/her communication in online groups than without such tool [14]. Other research has shown that a designed online collaborative writing tool with a group awareness functionality, which can analyze and visualize their engagement, increased students' behavioral engagement conpared with students not using the tool [15].

How to form an effect group has been getting more attention in CSCL research lately [16]. According to research reviewing Argumentation-Based CSCL (ABCSCL), many studies have focused on group composition and students' traits [17]. For this paper, the quality of performance in heterogeneous groups is better in homogeneous ones and there are important traits of students in ABCSCL: Gender, learning styles, willingness to argue, openness to argue, internal argumentative script. Moreover, new methods of forming groups automatically in CSCL have been proposed based on two criteria: the complementary skills on concepts and the learning styles obtained according to the Felder-Silverman model to make heterogeneous groups [18]. This research, however, did not evaluate the learning effect but showed its usefulness compared with random grouping. Similar research has provided other systems for clustering heterogeneous groups automatically [19]. This system used the students' grades and showed that this system could determine heterogeneous groups as good as groups created by a teacher.

To sum up, former CSCL research points out that the visualization of interaction that corresponds to the effect grouping with some students' important traits is essential for enhancing collaborative learning. However, there is no research to date about interactive system to visualize collaborative writing by using historical analogy.

Compared with these past works, our system can easily performs group learning in history. If group learning is required with changing news articles and/or users several times, it is possible to change the selections of the new data, and because the system does not require data to make groups, it is easy to set up classes.

3 Design of System

3.1 System Overview

Figure 1 shows an overview of process in our system. First, our system gets news articles from a database. We can dynamically determine which and how many news articles we will use. Note that we assume that teachers or lecturers prepare this database before using our system. After collecting the texts, this system

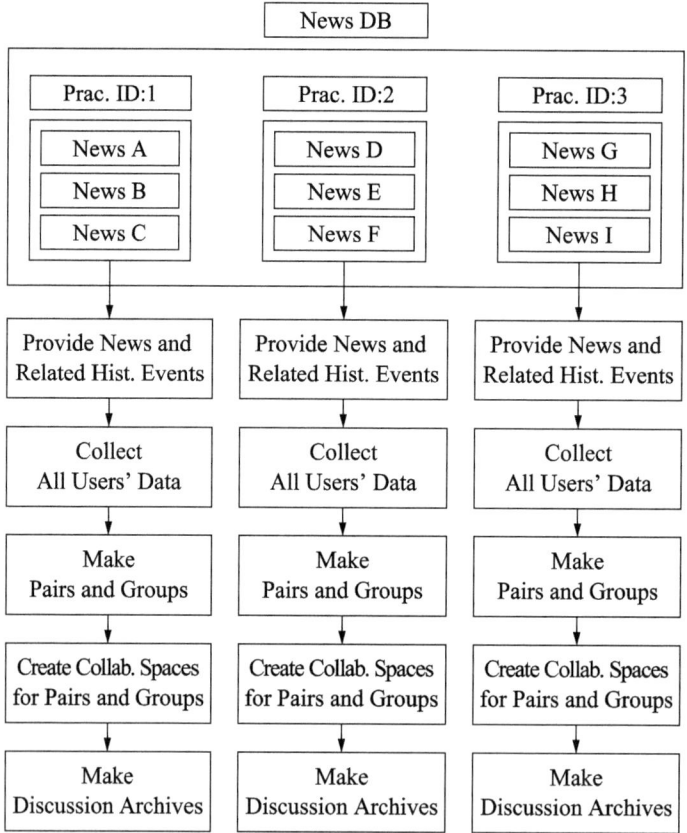

Fig. 1. System overview. Each practice has some news articles about modern social issues. According to selected news, historical events user selected, this system can make pairs and groups interactively.

performs five steps: providing news and related historical events, making feature vectors, making pairs and groups, making collaborative spaces for pairs and groups, and archiving results of the discussion. In the remainder of this section, we detail each step. If the database is available, we can quickly use this system by changing news articles and users.

3.2 Provision of News and Related Historical Events

The objective of this step is to provide historical events to users. This system performs this using a search engine [5]. As this search engine takes event categories that connect past and present events, our system must show news articles to users before using the search engine. From these, the users select news in which they have an interest, and then assign one or more suitable event categories to the news. After obtaining historical events from the search engine, this system records the two kinds of information (the assigned event categories and histori-

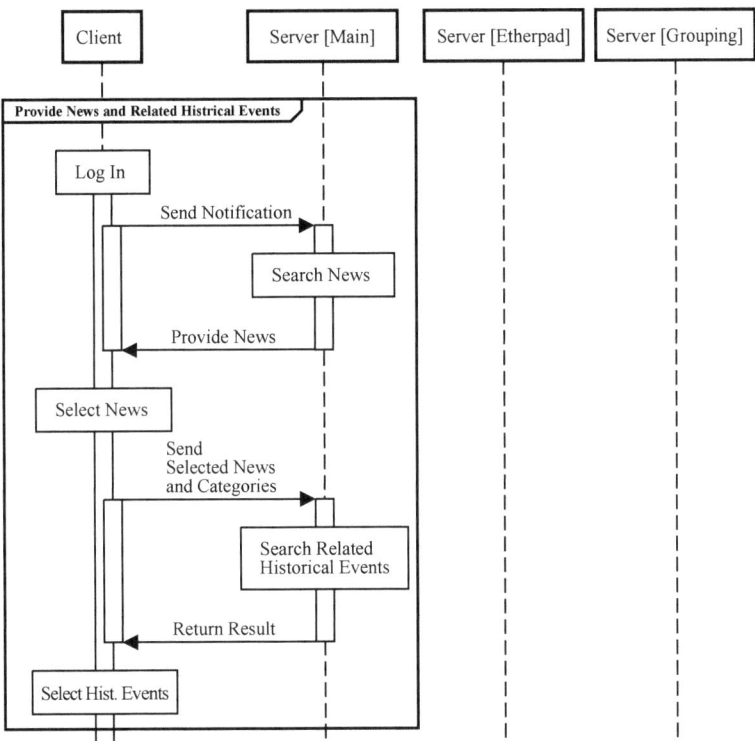

Fig. 2. Sequence diagram of providing news and related historical events. When a user logs into the system, the system server get news linked to user's practice ID from DB. After users selecting news and categories, the server searches historical events related to user interests. Users can choose one of historical events as a source of historical analogy.

cal events that are results of the search engine) for each user in order to make groups that are performed in the following steps. To make association between IDs of the users and the two kinds of information, our system first requires a log-in process. Figure 2 details the process between a server and clients.

3.3 Feature Vectors Creation

In this step, our system takes recorded results of the previous step, and then translates them into feature vectors to make pairs and groups for the next step. Given the complete event category list E, this step creates a feature vector for each user. If an event category $e_i \in E$ is stored in the results of the previous step, we use 1 as the ith element of the feature vector; otherwise, we use 0.

3.4 Make Pairs and Groups

This step inputs the feature vectors created in the previous step into clustering algorithms [20]. This algorithm outputs groups taking care to maximize improvements in discussions. This algorithm first solves maximizing problem to combine two users who focus on similar aspects for the same news. It then makes groups by solving minimizing problem to combine two pairs that focus on different aspects for the same news. Figure 3 shows processes for using the clustering algorithm. The main server sends users' future vectors to grouping program. Once the program receiving them, the program starts to make pairs and groups. Each pair contains two students who have the same concerns. In contrast to pair creation, each group consists of two pairs with different concerns. This pairs and groups creation method is designed to enhance discussion from various perspectives. When all pairs and groups are made, the grouping program sends the result of the creation to the main server. After the server receives data, the server collates the received result and user ID, and sends the number of their pair ID and group ID to clients.

3.5 Creation of Collaborative Editor Spaces for Pairs and Groups

After taking groups of users, our system prepares their discussions. The system creates collaboration editor spaces for both pairs and groups. The trigger for this creation is a log-in notification from the client who is the first to log into the pair discussion page. Clients send the number of clients in a practice. Once the main server acquires this number, the main server calls API to create a designated number of collaborative editor spaces and set instructional text into them. To create spaces, the system uses Etherpad-lite plugin. This plugin provides function such as coloring text and user chatting space to make collaborative editor environment. After these processes, the server sends a pair and group ID to each client. Once clients receive these IDs, clients use these IDs as a part of the URL of the collaboration editor embedded in discussion pages, then clients can access designated discussion pages.

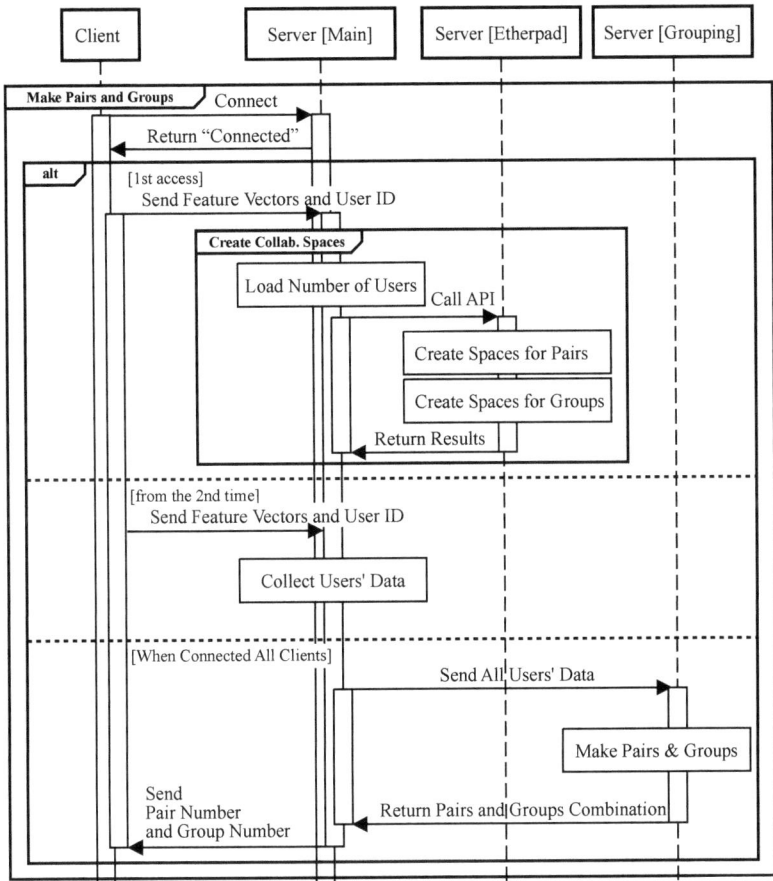

Fig. 3. Sequence diagram of making pairs and groups. In a practice, when a user reaches this phase first, the server get the number of users in this client sent from this user. The server calls API to Etherpad (collaborative editor plugin) server to make half number of users edit spaces for pairs, quarter number of users spaces for groups. After collected all users' data, the server sends this data to grouping program. The detail of this grouping algorithm, refer Ikejiri et al. [20].

3.6 Archiving Results of the Discussion

Figure 4 shows how our system archives the results of all discussions. This is performed if a member of a group decides to store their discussions. When the server receive the request of archiving from the clients, the main server calls API to the Etherpad server to make an copy of discussion. If the copying is successful, the server sends an URL of archive discussion and strings of discussion. Once clients receive the notification and data, they embed the data into the archive phase pages to ease the viewing of the results. We believe that this is useful when the users engage in post-study of the lecture.

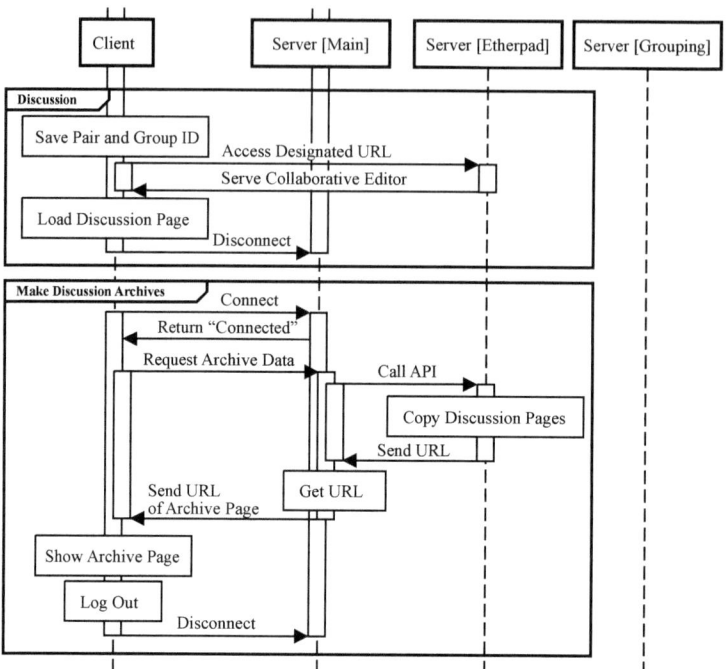

Fig. 4. Sequence diagram of discussion phase and making archives. In discussion phase, clients save received pair and group IDs. To access collaborative editor spaces, clients use these IDs as a part of URL.

4 Evaluation

In this section, we evaluate the usability of our system. We first evaluate *how fast our system outputs results*. From this quantitative analysis, we show that our system can be a useful learning system without making students frustrations in practice. We then perform qualitative analysis to understand *how well our system can enhance collaborative historical analogy in class*. This analysis investigates by asking teachers after using this system in practice.

4.1 Quantitative Analysis

Data Preparation. We evaluate our system by changing the numbers of clients from 4 to 40. As our system makes groups, we use the five different multiples of four: 4, 8, 16, 32, and 40. Note that each class usually has 40 students in Japanese high schools. As we focus on process times in this analysis, we created artificial data to perform our system. In other words, we randomly assign the event categories for the data by assuming that the data selected the categories to a present news. Then, we apply the clustering algorithm [20] described in Sect. 3.4. Analyzing qualities of the results obtained by the algorithm is reported in the paper, we skip taking care of the qualities.

Table 1. Average duration on server [ms].

| | Number of clients | | | | | | |
Process	4	8	16	32	40	Ave.	S.D.
Create collab. spaces	1.878	4.093	7.718	12.362	16.009	8.412	5.199
Make pairs & groups	136.922	115.857	128.041	136.637	113.893	126.270	9.856
Discussion	0.552	1.095	1.976	3.329	3.729	2.136	1.231
Make discussion archives	3.154	1.826	2.579	4.082	5.117	3.352	1.150
TOTAL	142.505	122.872	140.314	156.410	138.748	140.170	10.681

Table 2. Average duration on clients [ms].

| | Number of clients | | | | | | |
Process	4	8	16	32	40	Ave.	S.D.
Make pairs & groups	193.800	191.037	163.669	172.378	167.948	177.766	12.308
Discussions	297.775	387.762	289.906	361.322	384.235	344.200	42.182
Make discussion archives	389.300	377.538	366.062	375.691	348.444	371.407	13.653
TOTAL	880.875	956.337	819.637	851.206	894.202	880.452	45.829

Measurements. For each the number of clients, we prepare desktop computers whose OS is Windows 10. To measure process times, we use log files stored in the server or clients. Tables 1 and 2 show results of average of process time of server and clients, respectively. We can see that each process in the server outputs results within 140 ms and each process in clients outputs results within 400 ms.

Process Times on the Server. We show that each process in our system outputs results of making pairs and groups within 140 ms in the case where there are 40 users in Table 1. Results also show total process time the on server side is within 160 ms in the same case. This result indicates that we can use our system in practical situations because each class has on average 40 students in Japanese high school. The process times of Create Collab. Spaces and Discussion are linear orders with the number of users. This may be caused by the amount of clients.

Process Times on Clients. Table 2 shows that the average duration of each phase is within 150 ms, and the average of total process time is 880 ms. Even the case when 40 clients connect to the server, an average of total process time is within 900 ms. It means this framework has a stability and a scalability for various cases.

4.2 Qualitative Analysis

Procedure. We hold an interview for a high school history teacher. The purpose of this evaluation is to verify whether this system is useful for collaborative historical analogy. For the evaluation, we set an online environment in which the teacher can experience each phase we presented above. To let the teacher experience a pair discussion and a group discussion, we let researchers who have an ability of historical analogy. This evaluation held the following steps: Description of this evaluation, the purpose, and the usage of this system (10 min.), Using this system actually (50 min.), Interview to the teacher about this system (30 min.). We asked to the teacher from two perspectives:

- Which part of this system can be effective positively for collaborative historical analogy?
- Which part of this system should be modified for enhancing collaborative historical analogy?

After the interview, we collect comments about features that may enhance collaborative historical analogy and improvements for enhancing collaborative historical analogy.

Results. The teacher referred to two features for enhancing collaborative historical analogy.

The first was *collaborative editing and diversified perspectives*. The teacher said that each student would be thinking about how their opinion could be connected to historical events.

> *Writing sentences with others was interesting for me. Students will demonstrate their thinking ability to edit sentences in his/her own way taking other members' feelings and what other members intend to write down into consideration. So, I guess that students will be thinking about how their opinion can be connected with historical events and to each other, although I don't know if they can achieve this type of thinking level. I feel it's very interesting that students can connect historical events with their opinions together with everyone in a group instantly and simultaneously, while I'm not sure if their final opinions can include other viewpoints of world history.*

- Did you feel that students think differently between pair discussion and group discussion?

> *I think that working in pairs makes it easier to think, but more diversified perspectives are added into sentences when working in groups. In fact, because viewpoints in our opinion were increased after Y joined in our discussion, I think there is a merit to adding diversified perspectives in working in groups. I feel this is a good point.*

The second is *coloring the authorship text*. The teacher also pointed out that the authorship color function on texts is needed for collaborative editing and could be helpful for facilitating an activity.

I think it's an essential function. [...] It's better to write sentences about their opinion by coloring text in which writers can be distinguished. If there is no feature for coloring sentences by each student, this activity would be difficult, I think. I guess students will fail to recognize the sentence he/she wrote.

On the other hand, the teacher commented about two improvements for enhancing collaborative historical analogy. The first is *decreasing consciousness to apply historical events while working in groups*. She said that when the teacher worked in pairs and groups, she tried to apply the historical events she selected to solve the modern issues but that could not be accomplished completely due to the amount of thought required.

Each pair would try to tell their intention to the other when working in pairs. However, they have to make a conclusion together based on the pairs' opinion when working in a group. Because of this, it was difficult for me to apply my intention from applying the historical event I selected, although a situation would be different if we chose a different historical event from this one. Asserting my opinion was difficult because working with four people required to think more diversely than in pairs. On the other hand, I also felt something new will be created from discussions in a group since various opinions in a group can be told.

The second is *spreading gazing while editing sentences and chatting in pairs or groups*. The teacher pointed out that some of students would not be able to both edit sentences in a collaborative editor window and participate in discussions in the chat window.

Let me see... comments... some impressions came up, but I worked on this activity desperately. Users have to watch both the edit window and chat window, right? While they are concluding their discussion about what should be in the future, the discussion is also proceeding in chat window. I felt it is more or less tough for unskillful high school students to work on editing sentences and applying the ideas in the chat window simultaneously.

4.3 Discussion

The result of measuring duration of process time proved that the system will not prevent working on a collaborative historical analogy even if the number of students increases up to 40. This proves the scalability of this system for enhancing collaborative historical analogy.

According to the interview for the teacher, we found that this system has the possibility of enhancing collaborative historical analogy in the part of providing collaborative editor spaces and coloring authorship text. These functions of the system can be effect positively on collaborative historical analogy.

From these evaluations both from quantitative and qualitative, we proved that this system has an eligibility for enhancing collaborative historical analogy held in high school history lessons.

We also found two improvements, (1) scattering gazing while editing sentences in editor window and discussing in chat window while working in pairs and a group, (2) decreasing consciousness of applying historical events. To improve (1), we may need to embed additional instruction in a lecture or in the system. To improve (2), showing text of selected historical events and future prediction user wrote in even if working in pairs and a group can be a solution.

5 Conclusion

Supporting collaborative historical analogy is becoming popular studies to enhance the historical analogy with checking the validity of its usage. In this paper, a novel interactive system for collaborative historical analogy was proposed. The proposed system creates groups from users' interests in specific issues and the particular aspects they focus on to the same news article. After the grouping users, they can have a discussion within their own groups. The results can be archived for reflection in post-learning.

Future work will identify (a) *how the system is useful for collaborative historical analogy with several users*. As it was confirmed that it is possible to provide a practical learning environment by checking whether the system can output results within a second, the authors will, in the future, investigate how this system can enhance collaborative historical analogy; and, (b) *how stable the system works in the case of simultaneous use in several classes*. By studying this, the system will be able to provide a collaborative historical analogy environment, not only in one high school, but with remote high schools also.

Acknowledgments. This work was supported by JSPS KAKENHI Grant Number 16K16314.

References

1. Staley, D.J.: A history of the future. Hist. Theor. **41**(4), 72–89 (2002)
2. Ministry of Education, Culture, S.S., Technology: The course of study for senior high school (2018)
3. Boix-Mansilla, V.: Historical understanding: beyond the past and into the present. In: Stearns, P.N., Seixas, P., Wineburg, S. (eds.) Knowing, Teaching, and Learning History: National and International Perspectives, pp. 390–418. New York University Press, New York (2000)
4. Ikejiri, R., Fujimoto, T., Tsubakimoto, M., Yamauchi, Y.: Designing and evaluating a card game to support high school students in applying their knowledge of world history to solve modern political issues. In: International Conference of Media Education, Beijing Normal University (2012)
5. Sumikawa, Y., Ikejiri, R.: Mining historical social issues. In: Neves-Silva, R., Jain, L.C., Howlett, R.J. (eds.) Intelligent Decision Technologies. SIST, vol. 39, pp. 587–597. Springer, Cham (2015). https://doi.org/10.1007/978-3-319-19857-6_50
6. Ikejiri, R., Sumikawa, Y.: Developing world history lessons to foster authentic social participation by searching for historical causation in relation to current issues dominating the news. J. Educ. Res. Soc. Stud. **84**, 37–48 (2016). (in Japanese)

7. Holyoak, K.J., Thagard, P.: Mental Leaps: Analogy in Creative Thought. MIT Press, Cambridge (1980)
8. Fischer, D.H.: Historians' Fallacies: Toward a Logic of Historical Thought. Harper & Row Publishers, New York (1970)
9. Pratiwi, O.N., Rahardjo, B., Supangkat, S.H.: Clustering multiple mix data type for automatic grouping of student system. In: 2017 International Conference on Information Technology Systems and Innovation (ICITSI), pp. 172–176, October 2017
10. Mehennaoui, Z., Lafifi, Y., Seridi, H., Boudria, A.: A new approach for grouping learners in CSCL systems. In: 2014 International Conference on Multimedia Computing and Systems (ICMCS), pp. 628–632, April 2014
11. Macqueen, J.: Some methods for classification and analysis of multivariate observations. In: 5-th Berkeley Symposium on Mathematical Statistics and Probability, pp. 281–297 (1967)
12. Rasmussen, C.E.: The infinite gaussian mixture model. In: Proceedings of the 12th International Conference on Neural Information Processing Systems. NIPS 1999, pp. 554–560, Cambridge, MA, USA, MIT Press (1999)
13. Kollar, I., Fischer, F., Slotta, J.D.: Internal and external scripts in computer-supported collaborative inquiry learning. Learn. Instr. **17**(6), 708–721 (2007)
14. Janssen, J., Erkens, G., Kanselaar, G., Jaspers, J.: Visualization of participation: does it contribute to successful computer-supported collaborative learning? Comput. Educ. **49**, 1037–1065 (2007)
15. Liu, M., Liu, L., Liu, L.: Group awareness increases student engagement in online collaborative writing. Internet High. Educ. **38**, 1–8 (2018)
16. Reis, R.C.D., Isotani, S., Rodriguez, C.L., Lyra, K.T., Jaques, P.A., Bittencourt, I.I.: Affective states in computer-supported collaborative learning: studying the past to drive the future. Comput. Educ. **120**, 29–50 (2018)
17. Noroozi, O., Weinberger, A., Biemans, H., Mulder, M., Chizari, M.: Argumentation-based computer supported collaborative learning (ABCSCL). A synthesis of fifteen years of research. Educ. Res. Rev. **7**(2), 79–106 (2012)
18. Mehennaoui, Z., Lafifi, Y., Seridi, H., Boudria, A.: A new approach for grouping learners in CSCL systems. In: 2014 International Conference on Multimedia Computing and Systems (ICMCS), pp. 628–632. IEEE (2014)
19. Pratiwi, O.N., Rahardjo, B., Supangkat, S.H.: Clustering multiple mix data type for automatic grouping of student system. In: 2017 International Conference on Information Technology Systems and Innovation (ICITSI), pp. 172–176. IEEE (2017)
20. Ikejiri, R., Yoshikawa, R., Sumikawa, Y.: Towards enhancing historical analogy: clustering users having different aspects of events. In: Arai, K., Bhatia, R. (eds.) FICC 2019. LNNS, vol. 69, pp. 756–772. Springer, Cham (2020). https://doi.org/10.1007/978-3-030-12388-8_52

Author Index

Aceituno, Roni Guillermo Apaza II-220
Adiani, Deeksha II-3
Afravi, Mahdokht II-193
Aikawa, Daigo I-227
Ali, Rizwan II-162
Alier, Marc I-3
Alsina, María I-3
Alves Moreira, Eliana I-237, I-315
Amado-Salvatierra, Héctor R. I-64
Amo, Daniel I-3
Andujar, Marvin II-151
Aranda Domingo, José Ángel II-343
Ariyapala, Thameera Viraj II-287
Arques-Corrales, Pilar I-171
Arya, Ali I-402
Asai, Yasutaka I-227
Ault, Bryce II-122
Au-Yong-Oliveira, Manuel II-243
Avellar, Gustavo Martins Nunes II-37

Babić, Snježana II-110
Bannan, Brenda I-89, II-257
Baranauskas, Maria Cecília Calani I-237, I-315
Barbosa, Ellen Francine II-37
Barneche-Naya, Viviana II-133
Barrett, Kevin II-3
Benitti, Fabiane Barreto Vavassori I-155
Bennett, Amelia II-3
Bercht, Magda II-175
Bessa, Maximino II-175
Biala, Toheeb II-3
Biddle, Robert I-402
Bittner, Eva A. C. II-353
Bonacin, Rodrigo I-237
Botega Tavares, Deisymar I-380
Branco, Frederico II-243
Brennand, Camilla V. L. T. I-237
Buchem, Ilona II-13, II-312

Caceffo, Ricardo I-237
Caires Carvalho, Jordana I-380
Camacho, Adriana II-193
Camba, Jorge D. II-343

Caprio, Derek II-151
Carneiro, Marcos II-243
Casañ, María José I-3
Champalle, Olivier I-142
Charraire, Sarah I-142
Clarke, Patrick II-122
Çollaku (Xhaja), Denada I-370
Compañ-Rosique, Patricia I-332
Conde, Miguel Á. II-26
Contero, Manuel II-343
Coulter, Garrett II-3
Cruz-Benito, Juan I-15
Çuka, Verina I-370
Cummings, Robert II-80

D'Abreu, João Vilhete V. I-237
de Oliveira, Camila Dias II-37
de Souza Lima, Adriano Luiz I-155
dos Reis, Julio Cesar I-237
Dubrow, Samantha I-89, II-257

Egi, Hironori I-227
Ehlenz, Matthias I-423

Faheem, Muhammad II-99
Fernández-Guinea, Sara I-115
Ferrándiz, Jose I-346
Fertig, Tobias I-26, I-390
Fidalgo-Blanco, Ángel I-127
Fioravanti, Maria Lydia II-37
Fiorentino, Michele Giuliano I-191
Fonseca, David I-3, I-115, I-346
Fraoua, Karim Elia I-142

Garcia, Sarah II-151
García-Holgado, Alicia I-38, I-50
García-Peñalvo, Francisco José I-3, I-15, I-38, I-50, I-127
Gilbert, Juan E. II-80
Gonçalves, Ramiro II-243
Gosha, Kinnis II-80
Guerrero-Higueras, Ángel M. II-26
Gutiérrez-Fernández, Alexis II-26

Hambly, Derick II-3
Han, Ting I-101
Hayashi, Rina I-357
Heath, Corey D. C. II-270
Heljakka, Katriina II-68
Hernández-Ibáñez, Luis A. II-133
Hettipathirana, H. Chathushka Dilhan II-287
Hinojos, Laura II-193
Hiramatsu, Yuko I-357
Hou, Yen-ju I-256
Hou, Yi-an II-296
Huaman, Evelyn Marilyn Riveros II-220
Huff Jr., Earl W. II-80
Hussain, Zahid II-99

Ihamäki, Pirita II-68
Ikejiri, Ryohei II-373
Ito, Atsushi I-357

Jin, Yunshui II-204
Jones, Stone II-122

Kakui, Miki I-357
Kakui, Yasuo I-357
Kauer, Ronald II-151
Kearney, Nick I-38
Kika, Alda I-370
Klamma, Ralf II-162
Klebbe, Robert II-312
Klobučar, Tomaž II-329
Koren, István II-162
Koroveshi, Jezuina I-370
Krassmann, Aliane Loureiro II-175
Ktona, Ana I-370

Labrador, Emiliano I-115
Laesker, Denis II-151
Leblanc, Jean-Marc I-142
Leonhardt, Thiemo I-423
Lewis, Daniel II-3
Liu, Zhejun II-204
Llorens-Largo, Faraón I-171
Lombello, Luma I-237
Lu, Meiyu II-99
Luque Carbajal, Marleny I-237, I-315

Mack, Naja A. II-80
Makram, Rober II-122
Marchetti, Emanuela I-206

Mariotti, Maria Alessandra I-191
Martins, José II-243
Martinus, Charlotta I-38
McDaniel, Troy II-270
Meagher, Sam II-122
Miranda Júnior, Aléssio I-380
Mischke, Adam II-122
Molina-Carmona, Rafael I-171, I-332
Montone, Antonella I-191
Moreira, Fernando I-115, II-243
Motti, Vivian Genaro II-55
Müller, Nicholas H. I-26, I-266, I-277, I-390, II-230
Müller-Werdan, Ursula II-312
Müller-Wuttke, Madlen I-266

Nguyen, Jason II-151
Novick, David II-193
Nunes, Felipe Becker II-175

Oliva Córdova, Luis Magdiel I-64
Oliveira, Raul Donaire Gonçalves II-37
Orehovački, Tihomir II-110
Otey, Jeffrey II-343

Palilonis, Jennifer I-77
Panchanathan, Sethuraman II-270
Paparisto, Anila I-370
Pfeffel, Kevin I-277, II-230
Poudel, Khem II-122
Purohit, Hemant I-89

Qiao, Xi II-204
Qin, Xiangang II-99

Reiris, Iñaki Tajes I-38
Rodriguez, Aaron II-193
Rodríguez-Lera, Francisco J. II-26
Rodríguez-Sedano, Francisco J. II-26

Sánchez-Prieto, José Carlos I-15
Sarkar, Medha II-3, II-122
Sarkar, Nilanjan II-3, II-122
Satorre-Cuerda, Rosana I-332
Schmidt, Michael II-122
Schütz, Andreas E. I-26, I-390
Sein-Echaluce, María Luisa I-127
Serao, Vanessa II-3
Shagal, Sultan II-3

Sharhorodska, Olha II-220
Shen, Tianjia I-101
Shenoda, Martina II-3
Sockhecke, Austin II-122
Spears, Marcus II-122
Spero, Eric I-402
Steinert, Anika II-312
Stojmenović, Milica I-402
Sumikawa, Yasunobu II-373

Tang, Tiffany Y. I-288
Tarouco, Liane Margarida
  Rockenbach II-175
Tavanapour, Navid II-353
Therón, Roberto I-15

Ueda, Kazutaka I-357
Ulsamer, Philipp I-277, II-230

Valente, Andrea I-206
Valente, José Armando I-237
van der Haar, Dustin Terence I-301
Vázquez-Ingelmo, Andrea I-50
Venkateswara, Hemanth II-270
Villalba Condori, Klinge Orlando I-64
Villegas, Eva I-115

Wade, Joshua II-3, II-122
Walters, Robert II-122
Weber, Kristin I-26, I-390
West, Samuel II-3
Wilkowska, Wiktoria I-423
Winoto, Pinata I-288
Womack, Kevin II-80

Yoshikawa, Ryo II-373

Ziefle, Martina I-423

MIX
Papier aus verantwortungsvollen Quellen
Paper from responsible sources
FSC® C105338

If you have any concerns about our products,
you can contact us on
ProductSafety@springernature.com

In case Publisher is established outside the EU,
the EU authorized representative is:
**Springer Nature Customer Service Center GmbH
Europaplatz 3, 69115 Heidelberg, Germany**

Printed by Libri Plureos GmbH
in Hamburg, Germany